Technology *in* Action

Companion Website Premium Content
Access Number

Improve your grade with hands-on tools and resources!

- Master key terms and vocabulary
- Assess your knowledge with fun Crossword Puzzles and Jeopardy games
- Prepare for exams by taking practice quizzes
- *Check Your Understanding* section

And for even more tools, you can access the following Premium Resources using your Access Code.
Register now to get the most out of *Technology in Action!*

- Practice what you learn with interactive Active Helpdesk Calls*
- Use the Sound Byte lessons to practice your skills*
- Use the Audio PPTs for a personal lecture
- Explore the Try This Videos to see how the book projects work
- Experience real-world computer situations with Simulations*
- *Replay* videos from the authors provide a video review of each chapter Part
  in an easy-to-use format you can use on your phones, tablets, or computers!*

*Access code required for these premium resources

Companion Website Premium Content Access Number:

Note: If there is no silver foil covering the access code, it may already have been redeemed,
and therefore may no longer be valid. In that case, you can purchase online access using a
major credit card or PayPal account. To do so, go to **www.pearsonhighered.com/techinaction**,
select your book cover, click on "Buy Access" and follow the on-screen instructions.

To Register:

- To Start you will need a valid email address and this access code.
- Go to **www.pearsonhighered.com/techinaction** and scroll to find your text book.
- Once you've selected your text, on the Home Page, click the link to access the Student Premium Content.
- Click the Register button and follow the on-screen instructions.
- After you register, you can sign in any time via the log-in area on the same screen.

System Requirements

Windows 8 Ultimate Edition; IE 10   Full Pass
Windows 7 Ultimate Edition SP1; Chrome (latest version) Spot Check
Mac OS 10.8; Firefox 21   Spot Check
Mac OS 10.7; Safari 6   Spot Check

Technical Support

http://247pearsoned.custhelp.com

Photo credits: Goodluz/wrangler/Elena Elisseeva/Shutterstock

Technology in Action

INTRODUCTORY

12TH EDITION

Technology in Action

INTRODUCTORY

12TH EDITION

Alan Evans | Kendall Martin | Mary Anne Poatsy

PEARSON

Boston   Columbus   Indianapolis   New York   San Francisco   Upper Saddle River
Amsterdam   Cape Town   Dubai   London   Madrid   Milan   Munich   Paris   Montréal   Toronto
Delhi   Mexico City   São Paulo   Sydney   Hong Kong   Seoul   Singapore   Taipei   Tokyo

VP, Editorial Director: Andrew Gilfillan
Executive Acquisitions Editor: Jenifer Niles
Production and Program Team Lead: Laura Burgess
Program Team Lead: Laura Burgess
Project Manager: Rhonda Aversa
Program Manager: Emily Biberger
Editorial Assistant: Victoria Lasavath
Development Editor: Shannon LeMay-Finn
Director of Marketing: Maggie Waples
Marketing Coordinator: Susan Osterlitz
Marketing Assistant: Jeremiah Drozd
Operations Specialist: Diane Peirano

Director of Digital Studio Worforce Readiness: Taylor Ragan
Digital Strategy: Eric Hakanson
Media Project Manager, Production: John Cassar and Jose Carchi
Art Director: Diane Ernsberger
Cover Design: Studio Montage
Cover Art: © Mahout/Shutterstock
Full-Service Project Management: Lumina Datamatics, Inc.
Composition: Lumina Datamatics, Inc.
Printer/Binder: Courier/Kendallville
Cover Printer: Courier/Kendallville
Text Font: 9/11 Helvetica Neue LT Std

Credits and acknowledgments borrowed from other sources and reproduced, with permission, in this textbook appear on the appropriate page within the text.

Microsoft and/or its respective suppliers make no representations about the suitability of the information contained in the documents and related graphics published as part of the services for any purpose. All such documents and related graphics are provided "as is" without warranty of any kind. Microsoft and/or its respective suppliers hereby disclaim all warranties and conditions with regard to this information, including all warranties and conditions of merchantability, whether express, implied or statutory, fitness for a particular purpose, title and non-infringement. In no event shall Microsoft and/or its respective suppliers be liable for any special, indirect or consequential damages or any damages whatsoever resulting from loss of use, data or profits, whether in an action of contract, negligence or other tortious action, arising out of or in connection with the use or performance of information available from the services.

The documents and related graphics contained herein could include technical inaccuracies or typographical errors. Changes are periodically added to the information herein. Microsoft and/or its respective suppliers may make improvements and/or changes in the product(s) and/or the program(s) described herein at any time.

Microsoft® and Windows® are registered trademarks of the Microsoft Corporation in the U.S.A. and other countries. This book is not sponsored or endorsed by or affiliated with the Microsoft Corporation.

Library of Congress Control Number: 2014958206

10 9 8 7 6 5 4 3 2 1

ISBN 10: 0-13-407947-7
ISBN 13: 978-0-13-407947-9

Contents at a Glance

Contents

Chapter 3

Using the Internet: Making the Most of the Web's Resources

Chapter 4

Chapter 5

System Software: The Operating System, Utility Programs, and File Management............................ 158

TECHNOLOGY IN FOCUS

Chapter 6

Understanding and Assessing Hardware: Evaluating Your System

Chapter 7

Chapter 8

Chapter 9

TECHNOLOGY IN FOCUS

Dedication

For my wife, Patricia, whose patience, understanding, and support continue to make this work possible . . . especially when I stay up past midnight writing! And to my parents, Jackie and Dean, who taught me the best way to achieve your goals is to constantly strive to improve yourself through education.

Alan Evans

For all the teachers, mentors, and gurus who have popped in and out of my life.

Kendall Martin

For my husband, Ted, who unselfishly continues to take on more than his fair share to support me throughout this process, and for my children, Laura, Carolyn, and Teddy, whose encouragement and love have been inspiring.

Mary Anne Poatsy

What's New
Technology in Action, 12th Edition

We are delighted for you to explore the Twelfth Edition of *Technology in Action*!

Explore, discover, and experience technology with the immersive and adaptive **Technology in Action**—*the book that uses technology to teach technology!*

Technology in Action is a learning system that pushes the envelope of what is possible in technology, and what is helpful in teaching. It is a system that fits the way students are learning today and uses rich companion media to engage students in and out of the classroom while providing essential training on computer concepts.

What's New?

- All content has been updated as needed to ensure coverage of the most current technology, and updated end-of-chapter exercises are included throughout the book, including a NEW end-of-chapter quiz and updated versions of the Check Your Understanding reviews.

- **NEW Make This** projects address the hot area of mobile app creation! Mobile app creation skills are already highly valued in the workplace. The Make This projects are a fun way to engage your students while helping them develop cutting-edge skills. Each chapter includes a *Make This* mobile app project, most of which use App Inventor. By the end of the course, students will have completed 13 small app projects that provide them with new skills they can use to create their own apps. And if they don't have an Android device, they can use the emulator and still learn the skills.

- **NEW Solve This** projects put the concepts students are learning into action through real-world problem solving using a Microsoft Office application or other technology tool! For Word and Excel projects, there is also a grader version in MyITLab.

UPDATED AND ENHANCED media offerings including:

- **Sound Bytes:** These multimedia lessons help demystify computer concepts with audio and video presentations. All Sound Bytes have been reviewed and updated as needed to provide timely and accurate information. This edition also includes two NEW Sound Bytes: "Using the Arduino Microcontroller" and "Programming with the Processing Language."

- **Active Helpdesk:** These highly interactive, engaging activities provide students with a realistic experience of how help is delivered via live chat, FAQ searches, etc. at a helpdesk. Students play the role of a helpdesk staffer answering technology questions using these various approaches. All Helpdesks have been reviewed and updated as needed.

- A virtual supervisor provides support to the student throughout the activity.

- Assessment questions after each Helpdesk provide instructors with a tool to gauge and track students' progress. This edition includes three NEW or completely revised Helpdesks: "Evaluating Websites," "Working with Smartphones," and "Keeping Your Data on Hand."

MyITLab • **Enhanced eBook:** The Enhanced eBook in MyITLab provides continuous digital learning in a completely interactive environment that allows students to use technology as they learn. They don't have to stop reading to go find the activities such as Helpdesks, Sound Bytes, and Replay Videos—they just click on them and immediately experience the activity.

MyITLab • **TechTown:** This fully interactive scenario-based simulation game lets students create their own avatar and interact in a series of knowledge and puzzle-based scenarios. As they work and play, they explore the core topics of computer concepts—from what a computer is to software, hardware, networking, the Internet, social media, and more.

MyITLab • **UPDATED Adaptive Dynamic Study Modules:** Updated specifically for *Technology in Action,* 12th Edition, these study modules provide students with personalized review based on their strengths and weaknesses.

- **UPDATED** *Replay* **Videos:** The *Replay* Videos provide an author-narrated video review of each chapter part in an easy-to-use format students can view on their phones, tablets, or computers.

- **With Tech Bytes Weekly, every week is new!** This weekly newsfeed provides two timely articles to save instructors the prep time required for adding interesting and relevant news items to their weekly lectures. Tech Bytes Weekly also features valuable links and other resources, including discussion questions and course activities.

- **Jeopardy! Game and Crossword Puzzles:** These engaging games give students a fun way to challenge their knowledge.

In addition to these changes, all chapters have been updated with new images, current topics, and state-of-the art technology coverage. Some of the chapter changes are listed here:

Chapter 1: Using Technology to Change the World

- Throughout the chapter, text, figures, and photos have been updated.

- A new example of social networking tools used in political context has been added.

- The Ethics in IT, "The Digital Divide and the Mobile Bridge" has been updated.

- The Try This has been updated to reflect Skype site content changes.

- The concept of Big Data has been introduced in the section on data mining.

- The end-of-chapter Ethics Project has been replaced with a new project on big data, "Can Big Data Predict Your Grade?"

- NEW Bits & Bytes "Compute Me a Picture" on generative design using the free tool Processing has been added, replacing the previous edition Bits & Bytes, "NASA Wants You to Learn."

Chapter 2: Looking at Computers: Understanding the Parts

- Throughout the chapter, text, figures, and photos have been updated.

- Next generation gesture technology is now covered in the "How Cool Is This?" feature.

- NEW Bits & Bytes "Forget HDTV...Here Comes Ultra HD!" has been added, replacing the previous edition Bits & Bytes "Testing and Calibrating Your PC Monitor."

- NEW Bits & Bytes "Green Computing" has been added, replacing the previous edition Bits & Bytes "Taking Care of Flash Drives."

- Throughout the chapter, text and figures have been updated to reflect Windows 8.1 changes.

- The end-of-chapter Team Time project has been replaced with a new project, "Data Storage Options."

Chapter 3: Using the Internet: Making the Most of the Web's Resources

- Throughout the chapter, text, figures, and photos have been updated.

- Updated Bits & Bytes on HTML5 versus Flash.

- Revised Bits & Bytes "Making Safe Online Payments" to include Apple Pay.

- Try This has been updated to reflect Microsoft Office Online changes.

- NEW "Evaluating Websites" Helpdesk has been added, replacing the "Using Subject Directories and Search Engines" Helpdesk.

Technology in Focus: The History of the PC

- This Tech in Focus has been updated as needed.

Chapter 4: Application Software: Programs That Let You Work and Play

- Throughout the chapter, text, figures, and photos have been updated.

- "How Cool Is This?" feature on eye-tracking software has been updated.

- "Trends in IT: Mobile Commerce: What Have You Bought with Your Phone Lately?" has been updated.

- New Alternative Note-Taking Applications have been added to Figure 4.12.

Chapter 5: System Software: The Operating System, Utility Programs, and File Management

- Throughout the chapter, text, figures, and photos have been updated.

- Content throughout has been updated to include coverage of Windows 8.1 update and OS X Yosemite.

- NEW "How Cool Is This?" feature has been added on smartwatches.

- "The Windows Interface" section has been revised and updated to reflect changes in Windows 8.1 update.

- UPDATED Sound Byte, "File Management," to reflect Windows updates.

- UPDATED Sound Byte, "Customizing Windows," to reflect Windows updates.

Technology in Focus: Information Technology Ethics

- This Tech in Focus has been updated throughout.

- A new section "Who Sets the Ethics for Robots?" has been added, replacing the "Brain Technology: Creating Cyborgs" section.

Chapter 6: Understanding and Assessing Hardware: Evaluating Your System

- Throughout the chapter, text has been updated to match current hardware standards, and figures and photos have been updated.

- All references to operating system utilities have been updated to reflect changes in Windows 8.1.

- UPDATED Sound Byte, "Installing RAM," to show RAM being added to a laptop computer.

- NEW Sound Byte, "Installing an SSD Drive," has been added, replacing the Sound Byte "Installing a Blu-Ray Drive."

Chapter 7: Networking: Connecting Computing Devices

- Throughout the chapter, text, figures, and photos have been updated.

- NEW Bits & Bytes "The Internet of Things" has been added, replacing "How Do You Find Your WiFi?"

- NEW Bits & Bytes "Analyzing Network Problems" has been added, replacing "Want to Use Your Phone as a Remote Control?"

- The content on Network-Attached Storage Devices has been updated to include Apple AirPort Time Capsule.

- The Trends in IT: "Where Should You Store Your Files: The Cloud Is Calling" has been updated.

Technology in Focus: Under the Hood

- This Tech in Focus has been updated throughout, with several new photos.

- Bits & Bytes "Forget CPUs: SoC Is the Future for Mobile Devices!" has been updated to reflect current trends in SoC.

Chapter 8: Digital Devices and Media: Managing a Digital Lifestyle

- Throughout the chapter, text, figures, and photos have been updated.

- NEW Bits & Bytes "Bluetooth and LE Beacons" has been added, replacing Bits & Bytes on mobile speech recognition.

- NEW "Working with Smartphones" Helpdesk has been added, replacing the "Using Portable Media Players" Helpdesk. This new Helpdesk uses much of the information previously found in the "Keeping Data on Hand" Helpdesk.

- REVISED "Keeping Your Data on Hand" Helpdesk to include coverage of cloud computing.

- UPDATED Sound Byte, "Smartphones Are Really Smart" for currency.

- UPDATED Sound Byte, "Connecting with Bluetooth," to include other uses of Bluetooth.

Chapter 9: Securing Your System: Protecting Your Digital Data and Devices

- Throughout the chapter, text, figures, and photos have been updated.

- Screenshots throughout have been updated to reflect changes in the Windows 8.1 update.

- NEW "How Cool is This?" on biometric authentication using vein scanning technology has been added.

- NEW Bits & Bytes "Multifactor Authentication: Don't Rely Solely on Passwords" has been added, replacing "Can't Remember Passwords? Try a Passphrase Instead!"

- UPDATED Sound Byte, "Installing a Personal Firewall," to cover wireless connections and Windows updates.

Technology in Focus: Careers in IT

- This Tech in Focus has been updated throughout.

- NEW Bits & Bytes "Cool New Jobs on the Horizon" has been added, replacing Bits & Bytes "Matching a Career to Your Skills."

About the Authors

Alan Evans, MS, CPA
aevans@mc3.edu

Alan is currently a faculty member at Moore College of Art and Design and Montgomery County Community College, teaching a variety of computer science and business courses. He holds a BS in accounting from Rider University and an MS in information systems from Drexel University, and he is a certified public accountant. After a successful career in business, Alan finally realized that his true calling is education. He has been teaching at the college level since 2000. Alan enjoys attending technical conferences and meets regularly with faculty and administrators from other colleges to discuss curriculum development and new methods of engaging students.

Kendall Martin, PhD
kmartin@mc3.edu

Kendall is a professor of Computer Science at Montgomery County Community College with teaching experience at both the undergraduate and graduate levels at a number of institutions, including Villanova University, DeSales University, Ursinus College, and Arcadia University.

Kendall's education includes a BS in electrical engineering from the University of Rochester and an MS and a PhD in engineering from the University of Pennsylvania. She has industrial experience in research and development environments (AT&T Bell Laboratories), as well as experience with several start-up technology firms.

Mary Anne Poatsy, MBA
mpoatsy@mc3.edu

Mary Anne is a senior faculty member at Montgomery County Community College, teaching various computer application and concepts courses in face-to-face and online environments. She enjoys speaking at various professional conferences about innovative classroom strategies. She holds a BA in psychology and education from Mount Holyoke College and an MBA in finance from Northwestern University's Kellogg Graduate School of Management.

Mary Anne has been in teaching since 1997, ranging from elementary and secondary education to Montgomery County Community College, Gwynedd-Mercy College, Muhlenberg College, and Bucks County Community College, as well as training in the professional environment. Before teaching, she was a vice president at Shearson Lehman Hutton in the Municipal Bond Investment Banking Department.

Acknowledgments

First, we would like to thank our students. We constantly learn from them while teaching, and they are a continual source of inspiration and new ideas.

We could not have written this book without the loving support of our families. Our spouses and children made sacrifices (mostly in time not spent with us) to permit us to make this dream into a reality.

Although working with the entire team at Pearson has been a truly enjoyable experience, a few individuals deserve special mention. The constant support and encouragement we receive from Jenifer Niles, Executive Acquisitions Editor, and Andrew Gilfillan, VP, Editorial Director, continually make this book grow and change. Our heartfelt thanks go to Shannon LeMay-Finn, our Developmental Editor. Her creativity, drive, and management skills helped make this book a reality. We also would like to extend our appreciation to Rhonda Aversa, our Editorial and Production Project Manager, who works tirelessly to ensure that our book is published on time and looks fabulous. The timelines are always short, the art is complex, and there are many people with whom she has to coordinate tasks. But she makes it look easy! We'd like to extend our thanks to the media and MyITlab team: Eric Hakanson, Taylor Ragan, Jaimie Noy, and Jessica Brandi for all of their hard work and dedication.

There are many people whom we do not meet in person at Pearson and elsewhere who make significant contributions by designing the book, illustrating, composing the pages, producing multimedia, and securing permissions. We thank them all. We would also like to thank the supplement authors for this edition: Wanda Gibson, Doug Courter, Lori Damanti, Linda Pogue, Elizabeth Lockley, and Stacy Everly.

And finally, we would like to thank the reviewers and the many others who contribute their time, ideas, and talents to this project. We appreciate their time and energy, as their comments help us turn out a better product each edition.

12th Edition Reviewers

Pearson and the authors would like to thank the following people for their help and time in making this book what it is. We couldn't publish this book without their contributions.

Neale Adams	Iowa Central Community College
Paul Addison	Ivy Tech
Afrand Agah	West Chester
Jack Alanen	CSU–Northridge
Karen Allen	Community College of Rhode Island
Ted Allen Reasoner	IUPUI
Peggy Anderson	SUNY at Cortland
Barry Andrews	Mt. SAC
Lou Ann Stroup	Ivy Tech
Mary Ann Zlotow	College of DuPage
Sabum Anyangwe	Harford Community College
Linda Arnold	HACC
Adnan Atshan	Passaic County Community College
Adeleye Bamkole	Passaic County Community College
Guarav Bansal	Wisconsin–Green Bay
Susan Barkalow	St. Cloud State
Bill Barnes	Catawba Valley Community College
Ricky Barnes	Catawba Valley Community College
Carolyn Barren	Macomb Community College
Tony Basilico	Community College of Rhode Island
Steven Battilana	West Chester
Michelle Beets	Iowa Central Community College
Kourosh Behzadnoori	Tarrant SE
Chris Belcher	CCAC–South
Elise Bell	CCSF
Julie Bell	Delgado Cmty Clg
Robert Benavides	Collin Cty
Garland Berry	Columbia College
Diane Bittle	HACC
Burton Borlongan	Mesa Community College
Carolyn Borne	Louisiana State University
Gina Bowers-Miller	HACC–Wildwood
Jeff Bowker	Montco
Vicki Brooks	Columbia College
Gerald Burgess	Western New Mexico University
Dave Burgett	McLennan
Ed Bushman	Yavapai College
Marcus Butler	West LA
Eric Cameron	Passaic County Community College
Jill Canine	Ivy Tech
Gene Carbonara	Long Beach Community College
Gene Carbonaro	Long Beach City College
John Carlisle	Nashua Community College
Glenn Carter	Sonoma State
Steve Carver	Ivy Tech
Patricia Casey	Trident Tech
Joni Catanzaro	Louisiana State University
Afi Chamlou	NOVA Alexandria
Robert Chirwa	KCTCS–Bluegrass–Cooper–CIT 105
Debbie Christenberry	Randolph Community College
Desmond Chun	Chabot College
Sherri Clark	Ivy Tech
Kevin Cleary	SUNY at Buffalo
Cynthia Collings	Central AZ
Mark Connell	SUNY at Cortland
Kae Cooper	BCTC/KCTCS
Dale Craig	Fullerton College
Becky Curtain	William Rainer Harper College
Juliana Cypert	Tarrant County College
Paul Dadosky	Ivy Tech
Enoch Damson	Akron
James Dang	Tarrant SE
Marvin Daugherty	Ivy Tech
John Dawson	IUPUI
Robert Deadman	IUPUI
Ed Delean	NOVA Alexandria
Mary Dermody	Chabot College
Don Dershem	Mt View
Charles Dessasure	Tarrant SE
Jeanette Dix	Ivy Tech
Sally Dixon	Skagit Valley Community College
Gretchen Douglas	SUNY at Cortland
Judy Duff	Louisiana Delta College
Stacia Dutton	SUNY Canton
Donna Earhart	Genesee Community College
Ed Eill	Delaware City Community College
Pam Ellis	PA College of Technology
Sylvia Emerson	Rock Valley College
John Enomoto	East LA
Ron Enz	Chattahoochee Tech
Nancy Evans	Indiana University–Purdue University Indianapolis
James Fabrey	West Chester
Deb Fells	Mesa Community College
Pat Fenton	West Valley
Marjorie Feroe	Delaware City Community College
Beverly Fite	Amarillo
Carol Fletcher	Louisiana Delta College
Barbara Fogle, Stuhr	Trident Tech
Ann Ford Tyson coordinator)	Florida State University
Tom Foster	Chandler Gilbert Community College
Susan Fry	Boise State University
Barb Garrell	Delaware City Community College
Barbara Garrell	Delaware County Community College
Rich Geglein	Ivy Tech
Janet Gelb	Grossmont Community College
Kevin Gentry	Ivy Tech
Ian Gibbons	Hillsborough Community

College–Ybor	
Randy Gibson	Indian River State College
Ernie Gines	Tarrant SE
Rebecca Giorcelli	Fairmont State University
Anita Girton	PA College of Technology
Ellen Glazer	Broward Community College, South
Cathy Glod	Mohawk Valley Cmty College
Valerie Golay	Ivy Tech
Jerry Gonnella	Northern KY
Holly Gould	Ivy Tech
Deidre Grafel	Chandler-Gilbert Community College
Diedre Grafel	Chandler Gilbert Community College
Kemit Grafton	Oklahoma State University– Oklahoma City
Debra Grande	Community College of Rhode Island
Nancy Grant	CCAC–South
Wade Graves	Grayson
Natalia Grigoriants	Pierce College
Glen Grimes	Collin Cty
Toby Gustafson	UCR
Greg Hanson	Ivy Tech
A.C. Chapin	Harford Community College
Marie Hartlein	Montco
Meng Has	Burlington County College
Lisa Hawkins	Frederick Community College
Joan Heise	Ivy Tech
Sue Heistand	Iowa Central Community College
Jessica Helberg	Northern Virginia Community College
Terri Helfand	Chaffey Community College
Jaime Hicks	Ivy Tech
Fred Hills	McLennan
Timothy Hinz	Genesee Community College
Andrew Hobbs	Delaware State University
Kristen Hockman	Univ of Missouri–Columbia
Susan Hoggard	Tulsa Community College
Don Holcomb	KCTCS–Bluegrass–Cooper–CIT 105
Terry Holleman	Catawba Valley Community College
Debbie Holt	KCTCS–Bluegrass–Cooper–CIT 105
Barbara Hotta	Leeward Community College
Bunny Howard	SJRCC (St. John's River)
Virginia Huegel	Western New Mexico University
Jim Hughes	Northern KY
Donald Humphrey	Columbia Basin College
Laura Hunt	Tulsa Community College
Brent Hussin	Wisconsin–Green Bay
Steve Hustedde	South Mountain
Laurene Hutchinson	Louisiana State University
Bobbie Hyndman	Amarillo
Rosie Inwang	Olive Harvey
Hal Broxmeyer	IUPUI
Jennifer Ivey	Central Carolina Community College
Lisa Jackson	Phoenix College
Christie Jahn Hovey	Lincoln Land Community College
Betsy Jenaway	Macomb Community College
Gina Jerry	Santa Monica College
Duane Johnson	Ivy Tech
Kay Johnson	Community College of Rhode Island
Mary Johnson	Kingwood
Stacy Johnson	Iowa Central Community College
Tiffany Johnson	Tulsa Community College
Tammy Jolley	University of AR Community College –Batesville
Sharon Karonias	Northampton Cmty Coll
Kathy Kelly	Montco
Mike Kelly	Community College of Rhode Island
Clarence Kennedy	Louisiana Delta College
David Kerven	Georgia Gwinnett College
Annette Kerwin	College of DuPage
Ellen Kessler	HACC–Wildwood
Allyson Kinney	Gateway Community College
REBECCA KIRK	Augusta State University
Ronald Kizior	Loyola University Chicago
Meg Kletke	Oklahoma State University
Paul Koester	Tarrant County College, Northwest
Kam Kong	Delaware State University
Hon-Chung Kwok	CCSF
Susan LaBrie	Northampton Community College
Don Lafond	SJRCC (St. John's River)
Rose LaMuraglia	San Diego City
David Lange	Grand Valley
Earl Latiolas	Delgado Cmty Clg
Janet Laubenstein	Northampton Cmty Coll
Lori Laudenbach	St. Cloud State
Krista Lawrence	Delgado Cmty Clg
Dr. Kate LeGrand	Broward College
Kate LeGrand	Broward Community College, South
Yi Li Zhuang	Macomb Community College
Darrell Lindsey	SJRCC (St. John's River)
Bob Lingvall	Southwestern
Duane Lintner	Amarillo
Thomas Liu	New Jersey City Univ.
Wei Liu	Georgia Gwinnett College
Lynne Lyon	Durham College
Lydia Macaulay	Tarrant SE
Norma Marler	Catawba Valley Community College
Benjamin Marrero	Ivy Tech
Ben Martz	Northern KY
Lydia Mata	Eastern AZ
Jenny Maurer	PA College of Technology
John Mayhorne	Harford Community College
Glendora Mays	SJRCC (St. John's River)
James McBride	Eastern AZ
Kari Meck	HACC
Doug Medin	Western New Mexico University
John Messer	PA College of Technology
Hillary Miller	Kingwood
Saeed Molki	South TX College
Phil Moorhead	Ivy Tech
Linda Moulton	Montco
Rob Murray	Ivy Tech
Blankenstein	Nashua Community College
Denise Nearing	Indian River State College
Jean-Claude Ngatchou	New Jersey City Univ.

Name	School
Doreen Nicholls	Mohawk Valley Cmty College
Brenda Nielsen	Mesa Community College
Keith Noe	Ivy Tech
Kathy Olson	Ivy Tech
Helen Ortmann	CCAC–South
Meshack Osiro	Ivy Tech
Shelly Ota	Leeward Community College
ChongWoo Park	Georgia Gwinnett College
Lucy Parker	CSU–Northridge
Rachel Pena	South TX College
Wayne Phillips	Chabot College
Jennifer Pickle	Amarillo
Blanca Polo	Leeward Community College
Jim Poole	Honolulu Community College
Brian Powell	West Virginia University
Ernest Proctor	LA Trade
Diane Puopolo	Bunker Hill Community College
Mike Puopolo	Bunker Hill Community College
James R. Anthos	South University–Columbia
David R. Surma	Indiana University South Bend
Charles R. Whealton	Delaware Technical and Community College
Pat Rahmlow	Montco
Michelle Reznick	Oakton Community College
Leasa Richards	Columbia College
Kathie Richer	Edmonds Community College
Darrell Riddell	Ivy Tech
Donald Riggs	Schenectady County Community College
Don Riggs	Schenectady County Community College
Terry Rigsby	Hill College
Amy Roche	Northampton Community College
Scott Rosen	Santa Rosa Junior College
Peter Ross	Univ. of Albany
Scott Russell	Eastern AZ
Amy Rutledge	Oakland University
Tom Ryan	SJRCC (St. John's River)
Jessie Saldana	Cypress
Lorraine Sauchin	Duquesne
Judy Scheeren	Duquesne
Lois Scheidt	Ivy Tech
Marcia Schlafmitz	New Jersey City Univ.
NAME	SCHOOL
Ken Schroeder	Ivy Tech
Todd Schultz	Augusta State University
Dick Schwartz	Macomb Community College
Francis Seidel	Frederick Cmty College
Lili Shashaani	Duquesne
Emily Shepard	Central Carolina Community College
Helen Sheran	East LA
Cliff Sherrill	Yavapai College
Lisa Simpson-Kyle	Yavapai College
Noah Singer	Tulsa Community College
Steve Singer	Kapiolani Community College
Ann-Marie Smith	Delaware City Community College
Will Smith	Tulsa Community College
Michele Smolnik	Columbia College
Ali Soleymani	NOVA Alexandria
Steve St. John	Tulsa Community College
Neal Stenlund	Northern Virginia Community College
Steve Stepanek	CSU–Northridge
Jo Stephens	University of AR Community College –Batesville
Dennis Stewart	NOVA Alexandria
Ben Stonebraker	Ivy Tech
Lynne Stuhr	Trident Tech
Alexis Stull	Fairmont State University
Denise Sullivan	Westchester Community College
Dottie Sunio	Leeward Community College
Dave Surma	IU South Bend
Michael Swafford	Tulsa Community College
Cheryl Sypniewski	Macomb Community College
Ann Taff	Tulsa Community College
James Taggart	Atlantic Cape Community College
Mel Tarnowski	Macomb Community College
Juliana.P. Cypert	Tarrant County College–NE
Joyce Thompson	Lehigh Carbon Community College
Janine Tiffany	Reading Area Comm College
Faye Tippey	Ivy Tech
Matthew Trotter	South TX College
Pam Uhlenkamp	Iowa Central Community College
Pat Vacca	El Camino College
Nelmy Vasquez	Broward Community College, South
Pete Vetere	Montco
Susie Viars-Thomas	Grayson
Gabriel Viera	South TX College
Cynthia Wagner	McLennan
Rod Waller	Indian River State College
Laurie Wallmark	Raritan Valley Community College
Kari Walters	Louisiana State University
Stacy Ward	Grafton High School
Karen Weil	McLennan
Charles Whealton	Del Tech & Community College–Dover
Deena White	Grayson
Phil Whitney	Bakersfield College
Casey Wilhelm	North Idaho College
Billie Williams	San Diego City
Melanie Williamson	KCTCS–Bluegrass–Cooper–CIT 105
Xin Xu	Georgia Gwinnett College
Thomas Yip	Passaic County Community College
Roger Young	Ivy Tech
Mary Zegarski	Northampton Community College

Letter from the Authors
Our 12th Edition—A Letter from the Authors

Why We Wrote This Book

The pace of technological change is ever increasing. In education, we have seen this impact us more than ever in the past year—MOOCs, touch-screen mobile delivery, and Hangouts are now fixed parts of our environment.

Even the most agile of learners and educators need support in keeping up with this pace of change. We have responded by integrating material to help students develop skills for web application and mobile programming. We see the incredible value of these skills, and their popularity with students, and have introduced Make This exercises for each chapter. These exercises gently bring the concepts behind mobile app development to life. In addition, we have added a Solve This exercise in each chapter that reinforces chapter content while also reinforcing Microsoft Office skills. These projects help to promote students' critical thinking and problem-solving skills, which employers highly value.

Our combined almost 50 years of teaching computer concepts have coincided with sweeping innovations in computing technology that have affected every facet of society. From iPads to Web 2.0, computers are more than ever a fixture of our daily lives—and the lives of our students. But although today's students have a much greater comfort level with their digital environment than previous generations, their knowledge of the machines they use every day is still limited.

Part of the student-centered focus of our book has to do with making the material truly engaging to students. From the beginning, we have written *Technology in Action* to focus on what matters most to today's student. Instead of a history lesson on the microchip, we focus on tasks students can accomplish with their computing devices and skills they can apply immediately in the workplace, the classroom, and at home.

We strive to keep the text as current as publishing timelines allow, and we are constantly looking for the next technology trend or gadget. We have augmented the text with weekly technology updates to help you keep your classroom on top of the latest breaking developments and continue to include a number of multimedia components to enrich the classroom and student learning experience. The result is a learning system that sparks student interest by focusing on the material they want to learn (such as how to integrate computing devices into a home network) while teaching the material they need to learn (such as how networks work). The sequence of topics is carefully set up to mirror the typical student learning experience.

As they read through this text, your students will progress through stages of increasing difficulty:

1. Thinking about how technology offers them the power to change their society and their world
2. Examining why it's important to be computer fluent
3. Understanding the basic components of computing devices

4. Connecting to and exploring the Internet
5. Exploring software
6. Learning the operating system and personalizing their computer
7. Evaluating and upgrading computing devices
8. Understanding home networking options and keeping computing devices safe from hackers
9. Going mobile with smartphones, netbooks, tablets, and laptops
10. Going behind the scenes, looking at technology in greater detail

We continue to structure the book in a "spiraling" manner, intentionally introducing on a basic level in the earlier chapters concepts that students traditionally have trouble with and then later expanding on those concepts in more detail when students have become more comfortable with them. Thus, the focus of the early chapters is on practical uses for the computer, with real-world examples to help the students place computing in a familiar context.

For example, we introduce basic hardware components in Chapter 2, and then we go into increasingly greater detail on some hardware components in Chapter 6 and in the "Under the Hood" Technology in Focus feature. The Behind the Scenes chapters venture deeper into the realm of computing through in-depth explanations of how programming, networks, the Internet, and databases work. They are specifically designed to keep more experienced students engaged and to challenge them with interesting research assignments.

In addition to extensive review, practice, and assessment content, each chapter contains several problem-solving, hands-on activities that can carried out in the classroom or as homework:

- The Try This exercises lead students to explore a particular computing feature related to the chapter.

- The Make This exercises are hands-on activities that lead students to explore mobile app development.

- The Solve This exercises integrate and reinforce chapter concepts with Microsoft Office skills.

Throughout the years we have also developed a comprehensive multimedia program to reinforce the material taught in the text and to support both classroom lectures and distance learning:

- The **Helpdesk training content**, created specifically for *Technology in Action*, enables students to take on the role of a helpdesk staffer fielding questions posed by computer users. These have been updated to reflect the way in which users access help today.

- Exciting **Sound Byte multimedia**—fully updated and integrated with the text—expand student mastery of complex topics.

- The **Tech Bytes Weekly updates** deliver the latest technology news stories to you for use in your classroom. Each is accompanied by specific discussion topics and activities to expand on what is within the textbook materials.

This book is designed to reach the students of the twenty-first century and prepare them for the role they can take in their own community and the world. It has been an honor to work with you over the past 12 years to present and explain new technologies to students, and to show them the rapidly growing importance of technology in our world.

Visual Walk-Through

Topic Sequence

Concepts are covered in a progressive manner between chapters to mirror the typical student learning experience.

Hardware First Introduced
Chapter 2 is the first time students read about introductory hardware. It's covered at the beginning level because this is students' experience level at this point of the book.

Hardware Taught in More Depth in Additional Chapters
In later chapters, students read about hardware in greater depth because they're more experienced and comfortable working with their computers.

Technology in Focus
Four special features that teach key uses of technology today.

Multimedia Cues
Visual integration of multimedia.

How Cool Is This?
Highlights the latest and greatest websites, gadgets, and multimedia.

Student Textbook

Bits & Bytes
Help make the topics immediately relevant to students' lives.

Ethics in IT
Boxes examine the ethical dilemmas involved with technology.

Trends in IT
Boxes explore hot topics in computing.

Dig Deeper
Boxes cover technical topics in depth to challenge advanced students.

Try This and Make This
Hands-on activities found between Parts 1 and 2 of each chapter.

End of Chapter Quiz
Multiple Choice, True/False, and Critical Thinking questions at the end of each chapter help students assess their comprehension of chapter material.

Solve This
Exercises that put the concepts students are learning into action using a Microsoft Office application

MyITLab and Companion Media

MyITLab for *Technology in Action* with the Enhanced eBook personalizes learning to help your students better prepare and learn—resulting in more dynamic experiences in the classroom and improved performance in the course. Specific features include:

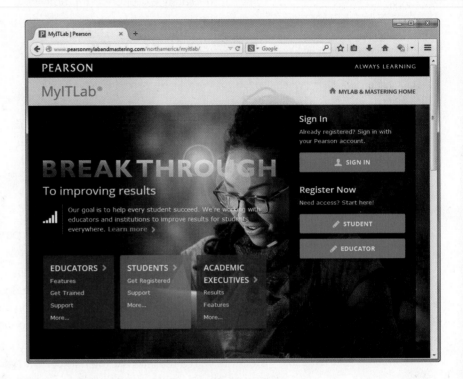

- **Adaptive Learning:** *A way to enable personalized learning at scale.* Not every student learns the same way and at the same rate. MyITLab with Adaptive Learning continuously assesses student performance and activity in real time, and, using data and analytics, personalizes content to reinforce concepts that target each student's strengths and weaknesses.

    - **NEW! Adaptive Dynamic Study Modules**, created specifically for *Technology in Action,* 12th Edition, provide students with personalized review based on their strengths and weaknesses.

- **A powerful homework and test manager:** MyITLab lets you create, import, and manage online homework assignments, quizzes, and tests that are automatically graded. The bottom line: MyITLab means less time grading and more time teaching.

- **Comprehensive online course content:** Filled with a wealth of content that is tightly integrated with your textbook, MyITLab lets you easily add, remove, or modify existing instructional material. You can also add your own course materials to suit the needs of your students or department. In short, MyITLab lets you teach exactly as you'd like.

- **Robust Gradebook tracking:** The online Gradebook automatically tracks your students' results on tests, homework, and practice exercises and gives you control over managing results and calculating grades. And, it lets you measure and document your students' learning outcomes.

- **Easily scalable and shareable content:** MyITLab enables you to manage multiple class sections, and lets other instructors copy your settings so a standardized syllabus can be maintained across your department.

The following media is available in MyITLab, and selected items are also on the companion website.

Note: To access the premium content, including Helpdesks, Sound Bytes, and Replay Videos from the companion site, students need to use the access code printed on the card in the front of the book.

Companion Website
Includes an interactive study guide, online end-of-chapter material, additional Internet exercises, and much more.

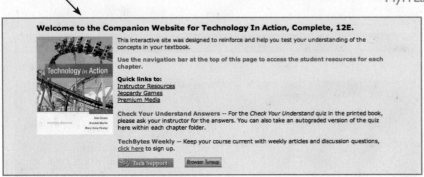

Welcome to the Companion Website for Technology In Action, Complete, 12E.

This interactive site was designed to reinforce and help you test your understanding of the concepts in your textbook.

Use the navigation bar at the top of this page to access the student resources for each chapter.

Quick links to:
Instructor Resources
Jeopardy Games
Premium Media

Check Your Understand Answers -- For the *Check Your Understand* quiz in the printed book, please ask your instructor for the answers. You can also take an autograded version of the quiz here within each chapter folder.

TechBytes Weekly -- Keep your course current with weekly articles and discussion questions, click here to sign up.

Tech Support   Browser Tuneup

pearsonhighered.com/techinaction

MyITLab • **Enhanced eBook:** The Enhanced eBook in MyITLab provides a continuous digital learning in a completely interactive environment that allows students to use technology as they learn. They don't have to sto p reading to go find the activities such as Helpdesks, Sound Bytes, and Replay Videos—they just click on them and immediately experience the activity.

MyITLab • **TechTown**: This fully interactive scenario-based, simulation game lets students create their own avatar and interact in a series of knowledge and puzzle-based scenarios. As they work and play, they explore the core topics of computer concepts—from what a computer is to software, hardware, networking, the Internet, social media, and more!

• **Adaptive Dynamic Study Modules**, created specifically for *Technology in Action,* 12th Edition, provide students with personalized review based on their strengths and weaknesses.

• **UPDATED Sound Bytes:** These multimedia lessons help demystify computer concepts with audio and video presentations. Select Sound Bytes have been updated to provide timely and accurate information. This edition includes two NEW Sound Bytes: "Using the Arduino Microcontroller" and "Programming with the Processing Language."

• **UPDATED Active Helpdesk:** These highly interactive, engaging activities provide students with a realistic experience of how help is delivered via live chat, FAQ searches, and so on. Students play the role of a helpdesk staffer answering technology questions using these various approaches**.**
  • A virtual supervisor provides support to the student throughout the activity.
  • Assessment questions after each Helpdesk provide instructors with a tool to gauge and track students' progress. This edition includes three NEW or completely revised Helpdesks: "Evaluating Websites," "Working with Smartphones," and "Keeping Your Data on Hand."

• **NEW Make This** projects address the hot area of mobile app creation! Each chapter includes a Make This mobile app creation project, most of which use App Inventor. By the end of the course, students will have completed 13 small app projects that provide them with new skills they can use to create their own apps. And if they don't have an Android phone, they can use the emulator and still get creating.

• **NEW! Solve This** projects put the concepts students are learning into action through real-world problem solving using a Microsoft Office application or other technology tool! For projects, there is also a grader version in MyITLab.

• **UPDATED!** *Replay* **videos:** The *Replay* videos provide an author-narrated video review of each *Chapter Part* in an easy-to-use format students can view on their phones, tablets, or computers!

• ***With Tech Bytes Weekly, every week is new!*** This weekly newsfeed provides two timely articles to save instructors the prep time required for adding interesting and relevant news items to their weekly lectures. Tech Bytes Weekly also features valuable links and other resources, including discussion questions and course activities.

• **Jeopardy! Game and Crossword Puzzles:** These engaging games give students a fun way to challenge their knowledge.

Transcript button
Used to turn transcript on or off

Sound Bytes
Multimedia lessons with video, audio, or animation and corresponding labs featuring multiple-choice quizzing.

Navigational tool

Audio lead students through

Video or animation teaches key concepts

Technology in Action
Welcome to the Web

1	Introduction
2	What We Will Cover
3	The New York Times Learning Network
4	Microsoft at Home
5	How Stuff Works
6	Webopedia
7	Wrapping Up
8	Web Links

Transcription ON

WELCOME TO THE WEB

Active Helpdesk
Interactive training that puts the student in the role of a helpdesk staffer fielding questions about technology.

Supervisor available to assist students.

Features textbook references within each Helpdesk and assessment at the end.

Choosing Software

MENU

Learning Objectives

At the end of this exercise, you should be able to answer the following questions:

- What kinds of applications are included in productivity software I might use at home?

- What are the different types of multimedia software?

- What are the different types of entertainment software?

- What are the different types of drawing software?

*Click **Next** to continue.*

HIDE

PEARSON   Sound Bytes   Replay   Pause   Mute

NEXT

Related Sound Bytes are referenced.

Audio on or off.

Annotated Instructor Edition

Provided with each chapter are two divider pages like the ones outlined below.

FRONT OF CHAPTER TAB

On the front side of each chapter tab, you'll find the following categories:

IN THE CLASSROOM: Activities you can use in a classroom or in online classes, including:

- PowerPoint Presentations
- Discussion Exercises
- Active Helpdesk
- Sound Bytes

HOMEWORK: Activities used out of class for assessment or preparation for the next chapter, including:

- Web Resource Projects
- Active Helpdesk
- Sound Byte Labs

ASSESSMENT:

- Blackboard
- WebCT
- TestGen
- myitlab
- Student Text Test Bank
- Sound Byte Test Bank
- Helpdesk Test Bank

The back side of each chapter tab includes notes about that chapter's Try This, Make This, and Solve This exercise.

ETHICS TAB

On the Ethics tab, you will find the following:

OPPOSING VIEWPOINTS TABLE: Outlines ethics topics that you can use to debate in the classroom.

KEYWORDS: Provides you with additional words with which to search the Internet for more information related to the ethics topic.

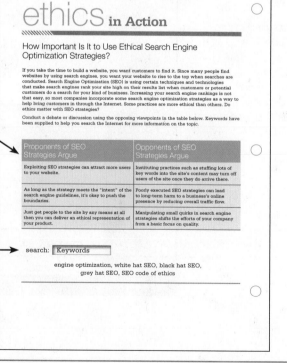

Chapter 3

Using the Internet:
Making the Most of the Web's Resources

In the Classroom

	PowerPoint Presentation (located on the IRC)	*Chapter 3* Consider using the PowerPoint presentation as a lecture guide, weaving it throughout the entire class. You can also customize it with additional art images from the IRC.
	Audio PowerPoint Presentation (located on the IRC)	Can be used for online courses. Audio content expands on topics covered in the presentation.
	Clicker PowerPoint Presentations (located on the IRC)	Ready interactive PowerPoint presentations
	Discussion Exercise	*Evaluating Websites* After reviewing the online tutorial at www.widener.edu/about/campus_resources /wolfgram_library/evaluate or library.acadiau.ca/tutorials/webevaluation, show students three examples of good websites and three examples of bad websites. Ask them to explain what makes the sites good or bad based on the material in the tutorial.
	Active Helpdesk (located on the Companion Website)	*Evaluating Websites* This Helpdesk presents a topic that students need to master: how to evaluate websites as appropriate to use for research. As you run the Helpdesk, have a browser open so that you can expand on what's discussed.

Homework

3	Chapter Assessment	*Chapter Assessment* Check Your Understanding with Multiple Choice Questions, Chapter Summary and Key Terms, Chapter Quiz, Team Time Project, Ethics Project, Solve This Project
	Writing Exercise (located on the Companion Website)	*Making the Transition to ... the Workplace Exercise 1: Online Resume Resources* Have your students work through this exercise and discuss their results in class.
	Preparing for the Next Technology in Focus	*Writing Exercise: Computer Survey* Have students conduct a survey of their parents or other family members as to the first computer each person remembers using. Have them ask such questions as, What were the features they most remember, and why? How much did the system cost? How big was the monitor? How much memory did it include? Which of these technologies are now considered to be legacy technologies?

Assessment

	Test Bank (located on the IRC)	To test student comprehension, use the Test Bank questions for Chapter 3 general content. You can include questions from the Helpdesk and Sound Byte Test Banks, as well. This week, design the quiz as a timed, one-attempt quiz with some essay questions included.

ethics in Action

How Important Is It to Use Ethical Search Engine Optimization Strategies?

If you take the time to build a website, you want customers to find it. Since many people find websites by using search engines, you want your website to rise to the top when searches are conducted. Search Engine Optimization (SEO) is using certain techniques and technologies that make search engines rank your site high on their results list when customers or potential customers do a search for your kind of business. Increasing your search engine rankings is not that easy, so most companies incorporate some search engine optimization strategies as a way to help bring customers in through the Internet. Some practices are more ethical than others. Do ethics matter with SEO strategies?

Conduct a debate or discussion using the opposing viewpoints in the table below. Keywords have been supplied to help you search the Internet for more information on the topic.

Proponents of SEO Strategies Argue	Opponents of SEO Strategies Argue
Exploiting SEO strategies can attract more users to your website.	Instituting practices such as stuffing lots of key words into the site's content may turn off users of the site once they do arrive there.
As long as the strategy meets the "intent" of the search engine guidelines, it's okay to push the boundaries.	Poorly executed SEO strategies can lead to long-term harm to a business's online presence by reducing overall traffic flow.
Just get people to the site by any means at all then you can deliver an ethical representation of your product.	Manipulating small quirks in search engine strategies shifts the efforts of your company from a basic focus on quality.

search: Keywords

engine optimization, white hat SEO, black hat SEO, grey hat SEO, SEO code of ethics

Instructor Resources

Online Instructor Resources Include:

- PowerPoint Presentations
- Student Text Test Bank
- Sound Byte Test Bank
- Help Desk Test Bank
- End of Chapter Answer Keys
- Rubrics
- Web Resources

- Image Library
- Sample Syllabi
- Additional Web Projects
- What's New in 12e
- Transition Guide
- TestGen

Technology In Action Complete, 12/E
Alan Evans
Kendall Martin
Mary Anne Poatsy

ISBN-10: 0133949567
ISBN-13: 9780133949568

Contact your local Pearson sales rep to learn more about the *Technology in Action* instructional system.

Technology
in Action

1

Using Technology to Change the World

How Will You Put Technology in Action?

Technology on the World Stage

OBJECTIVE

1. How can becoming proficient with technology help you understand and participate in important issues in the world at large? **(pp. 4–6)**

Technology and Our Society

OBJECTIVE

2. How can knowledge of technology help you influence the direction our society takes? **(pp. 8–10)**

How Will Technology Improve Your Life?

Technology at Home

OBJECTIVES

3. What does it mean to be computer literate? **(pp. 14–15)**

4. How does being computer literate make you a savvy computer user and consumer? **(pp. 14–15)**

🔊 **Sound Byte:** Questions to Ask Before You Buy a Computer

Technology and Your Career

OBJECTIVE

5. How can becoming computer literate help you in a career? **(pp. 16–22)**

Make This: Explore an App Builder Skill on **page 13**

For all media in this chapter go to **pearsonhighered.com /techinaction** or **MyITLab**.

HOW COOL IS THIS?

Scan here for more info

Want to **make a difference with technology**? The good news is that it has never been easier. Technology is allowing more and more of us to become agents of change in our communities and in the world. For example, in London, over 20,000 school-age children are joining **Apps for Good**, a program that links students, educators, and local experts to guide students in designing and building apps to help solve problems they see around them. In the United States, the **Verizon Innovative App Challenge** offered schools across the United States prize money for student teams to design apps to address the needs of their communities. In Philadelphia, people met for a weekend-long civic hacking event called **Random Hacks of Kindness**. They created apps to keep track of lobbyists in city government, to map the location of murals in the city, and to help organize people to dig out fire hydrants after snowstorms. What kind of good

How Will You Put Technology in Action?

Ask yourself: Why are you in this class? Maybe it's a requirement for your degree, or maybe you want to improve your computer skills. But let's step back and look at the bigger picture.

Technology today is not just a means for career advancement or merely a skill set needed to survive in society. It's a tool that enables us all to make an impact beyond our own lives. We've all seen the movies that dangle the dream in front of us of being the girl or guy who saves the world—and gets to drive a nice car while doing it! Whether it's *Transformers* or *Spider-Man,* we are drawn to heroes because we want our work and our lives to mean something and to benefit others.

Technology can be your ticket to doing just that, to influencing and participating in projects that will change the world. We'd like to ask you to think about how your talents and skills in technology will let you contribute on a larger scale, beyond the benefits they will bring to you personally.

 technology on the
WORLD STAGE

Recent political and global issues are showing that technology is accelerating change around the world and galvanizing groups of people in new ways. Let's look at a few examples.

Political Issues

Social Networking Tools. Social networking tools enable the gathering of groups of people to connect and exchange ideas, and they have brought together people facing repression and censorship in many countries. In fact, in 2014, uprisings in the Ukraine were organized using Facebook pages. Managing control of the media is no longer simple for regimes.

Politicians worldwide have also begun to incorporate social networking as part of their political strategy (see Figure 1.1). In the United States, politicians like Barack Obama have Twitter and Facebook accounts that they use to communicate with their constituents. In Italy, Beppe Grillo drew the largest vote in a recent election for a single party using mainly Facebook and Twitter in place of television and newspaper ads. In India, the finance minister took his public discussion about budget not to the airwaves but to a Google+ Hangout session. Yatterbox, a British social media website, follows the social media activities of members of the House of Commons, the Scottish Parliament, and the Northern Ireland Assembly. UK politicians post over two million social media updates a year.

An advantage of social media is that others can immediately connect and engage in a two-way conversation. During the debate in the British Parliament on the legalization of gay marriage, for example, lawmakers were leaving chambers to tweet updates. The public had a chance to try to influence how the vote went through real-time feedback using social media. Social networking tools are therefore providing a level of instant connection and information distribution that is reshaping the world. What can you do with social networking tools that will change the future of your community?

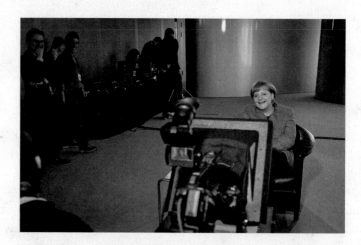

FIGURE 1.1 German Chancellor Angela Merkel is one of many politicians using a Google+ Hangout to reach out to her constituents. Has technology ushered in a new, more participatory style of democracy? *(Steffen Kugler/picture-alliance/dpa/AP Images)*

Crisis-Mapping Tool. Another example of the interaction of technology and society is the software tool Ushahidi. Following a disputed election in Kenya, violence broke out all over the country. Nairobi lawyer Ory Okolloh tried to get word of the violence out to the world through her blog, but she couldn't keep up with the volume of reports. But two programmers saw her request for help and in a few days created Ushahidi (Swahili for "testimony"). It is a **crisis-mapping tool** that collects information from e-mails, text messages, blog posts, and Twitter tweets and then maps them, instantly making the information publicly available. The developers then made Ushahidi a free platform anyone in the world can use (see Figure 1.2). So when earthquakes rocked Haiti, Ushahidi instantly told rescuers where injured people were located. When a tsunami brought Japan to the brink of a nuclear catastrophe, Ushahidi let anyone with a mobile phone find locations with clean water and food.

FIGURE 1.2 During a natural disaster in Haiti, Ushahidi crisis-mapping software helped identify areas of violence, helped people locate food and water, and directed rescuers to those in need. *(Courtesy of Ushahidi)*

Chile, Palestine, Somalia, and the Democratic Republic of Congo have all used this crisis-mapping software to save lives in times of political upheaval. In what other ways could technology help us face times of crisis?

Other Global Issues

Political crises are not the only arena in which technology is enabling global change.

Health Care. Infectious diseases account for about one-fifth of all deaths worldwide. Researchers say the odds of a flu pandemic occurring in the next century are nearly 100%. Could technology help us develop and deliver vaccines in a way that saves lives? With newer scientific visualization tools, scientists are developing antibodies for flu viruses and even HIV, viruses that are difficult to target because they continually change shape. Computationally intense modeling software is helping researchers increase the pace of vaccine production, saving lives.

Retinal prosthetics are another example of global health concerns being addressed with technology. Macular degeneration and retinitis pigmentosa are two diseases that destroy the retina; they account for the majority of blindness in developing nations. Sheila Nirenberg of Cornell University is working on a microchip that can replace the function of the retina, translating incoming light into the electrical pulses the brain needs for vision. These biomedical chips could restore quality vision to the blind.

The Environment. What if every cell phone in the world had built-in atmospheric sensors? Then millions of points of air and water quality data from around the world could be constantly acquired. Tagged with geographical information, the data could alert scientists to new trends in our environment. And what if phone sensors could monitor for flu viruses? We could protect ourselves from pandemics by identifying outbreaks very early. Ideas like these are being explored by University of California—Los Angeles researcher Dr. Deborah Estrin, the director at the Center for Embedded Networked Sensing. Can you think of other ways you could use your cell phone to improve society?

The Digital Divide. There is a great gap in the levels of Internet access and the availability of technical tools in different regions of the world. The term coined for this difference in ease of access to technology is the **digital divide**. One danger of a digital divide is that it prevents us from using all the minds on the planet to solve the planet's problems. But this challenge created by technology is also being answered by technology.

The Next Einstein Initiative (NEI) is a plan to focus resources on the talented mathematical minds of Africa (see Figure 1.3). By expanding the African Institute for Mathematical Sciences (AIMS) across the continent, the future of Africa can be

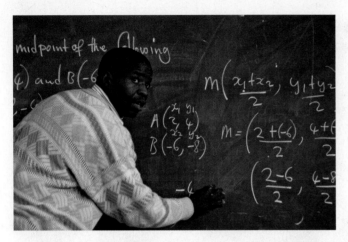

FIGURE 1.3 The Next Einstein Initiative is supporting the development of mathematical talent in Africa. Students from 38 African countries have studied with the program and then moved into graduate school in the mathematical sciences. (*Andrew Aitchison/Alamy*)

profoundly changed. Cambridge professor Neil Turok founded AIMS to bring together the brightest young minds across Africa with the best lecturers in the world. The NEI has won funding from Google's Project 10^{100}, an initiative to award $10 million to a set of five projects selected by open public voting. By capturing the enthusiasm of the world with presentations distributed through TED (**ted.com**) and Project 10^{100}, there is now a push to create 15 additional AIMS centers across Africa.

Figure 1.4 shows additional examples of people putting technology into action to impact the world. How will you join them? ■

FIGURE 1.4

Technology in Action: Taking on Global Problems

PERSON/ ORGANIZATION	GLOBAL PROBLEM	TECHNOLOGY USED	ACTION	FIND OUT MORE . . .
Peter Gabriel/ The Witness Project	Human rights abuses	Video cameras	Provides video documentation of human rights abuses; the project contributed to the arrest of warlords in the Democratic Republic of Congo for the recruitment of child soldiers	The Witness Project: **witness.org**
Johnny Lee/Google	The digital divide prevents many from taking advantage of modern learning devices like smartboards	Nintendo Wii remote and open source software	Enables users to create a smartboard for $50; the smartboard can record and store lecture content and is touch sensitive	Johnny Lee's blog: **procrastineering .blogspot.com**
United Nations World Food Programme (WFP)	One in seven people in the world do not get enough food to eat	GIS (geographical information systems) and mobile devices	The WFP can analyze the location and need for food, positioning food where it will help the most	World Food Programme: **wfp.org**
Hod Lipson and Evan Malone/The Fab@Home Project	Cost and access barriers prevent people from having basic devices, gears, and parts	3-D printers and open source software	Printers enable users to fabricate 3-D objects such as electrical parts	Fab@Home: **fabathome.org**
Massachusetts Institute of Technology (MIT) Center for Future Civic Media	Disposal of so many display devices into landfills	Software that allows multiple displays to connect and be reused	The software enables users to create one huge display device from a set of smaller units, thereby keeping monitors out of landfills	Junkyard Jumbotron: **jumbotron.media .mit.edu**

(*Charles Sykes/AP Images; Fab@Home*)

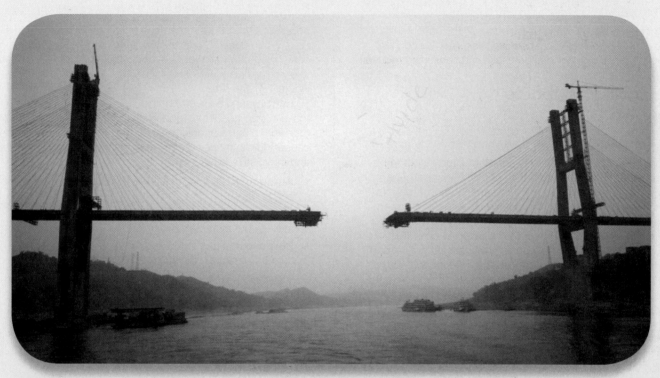

FIGURE 1.5 Can we bridge the digital divide through mobile devices? Should we? *(xPacifica/Alamy)*

The digital divide, the gap between those with easy access to technology and those with little to no access (see Figure 1.5), is a problem that leads to complex social issues. For those who lack access to the Internet and computers, it is difficult to develop computer skills, which are very often critical to future success. Less familiarity with the Internet can also lead to a lower level of active, engaged citizenship. How should we attack the problem of the digital divide in the United States?

Recent studies from the University of Michigan show that without Internet access at home, teens from low-income households (family income under $30,000 a year) are more likely to use their cell phones to go online. So the widening penetration of cell phones might be the answer to ending the digital divide. Or is it?

Going online using a cell phone plan is the most expensive of all options, and data transfer speeds are often slow. So teens with the least money are likely paying the most to get the slowest online experience.

In addition, teen cell phone usage is often focused on managing social networks, playing games, or listening to music. Computer tasks and skills that could lead to economic advancement, like creating formulas in spreadsheets or editing video are not as easy to do on mobile devices. So by not having free Internet access available, is our society placing those groups least able to afford access at an unfair disadvantage?

Will the increasing penetration of smartphones and faster cellular Internet access eliminate the digital divide in the United States? Should our government intervene and make sure there is sufficient free Internet access for all? Would it be an acceptable solution to have Internet service providers increase the price of high-speed connectivity to allow them to drop the price of slower connections? Is it ethical to deprive the poorer segment of our society of a needed commodity? Answering challenging questions like these is part of being an informed citizen.

technology and
OUR SOCIETY

Technology is also allowing us to redefine very fundamental parts of our social makeup—how we think, how we connect with each other, and how we purchase and consume products.

Technology Impacts How We Think

What We Think About. What do you think about in your free time? In the late twentieth century, a common trend was to think about what to buy next—or perhaps what to watch or listen to next. Information and products were being served up at an amazing rate, and the pattern of consumption became a habit. As more and more web applications began to appear that allowed each individual to become a "creator" of the web, a new kind of Internet came into being. It was nicknamed **Web 2.0**, and it had a set of new features and functionality that allowed users to contribute content easily and to be easily connected to each other. Now everyone could collaborate internationally at the click of a mouse.

Web 2.0 has fostered a dramatic shift across the world from simply consuming to having the ability to volunteer and collaborate on projects. In his book *Cognitive Surplus: Creativity and Generosity in a Connected Age*, author Clay Shirky created the term **cognitive surplus** to mean the combination of leisure time and the tools to be creative. The world's population has an estimated one trillion hours a year of free time. When coupled with the available media tools and the easy connectivity of Web 2.0, and with generosity and a need to share, projects like Ushahidi and the Witness Project (see Figure 1.4) emerge.

But why would anyone bother to work on projects like these in their free time? Modern theories of motivation show that what pushes people to apply their free time in altruistic causes, for no money, is the excitement of autonomy, mastery, and purpose (see Figure 1.6):

- **Autonomy:** the freedom to work without constant direction and control.
- **Mastery:** the feeling of confidence and excitement from seeing your own skills progress.
- **Purpose:** the understanding that you are working for something larger than yourself.

Together, these three factors play into how we are fundamentally wired and can produce incredibly motivated behavior. The combination of motivation, technology, and a cognitive surplus is leading to powerful projects that are changing the world.

Technology Impacts How We Connect

Connecting Through Music. In many societies, people connect intimately in gatherings and local celebrations through shared experiences. Technology like classical composer and conductor Eric Whitacre's Virtual Choir has added breadth to this aspect of our lives. Whitacre began the idea of a virtual choir by posting to YouTube a video of himself conducting one of his works, "Lux Aurumque." The idea was that listeners would follow his lead and, as they heard the piano track, each would record their part of the piece as either a soprano, an alto, a tenor, or a bass. The submitted videos were edited together, the audio was aligned, and the first piece from the Virtual Choir was released, with 50 recorded voices. By the fourth Virtual Choir performance piece, almost 6,000 singers were participating. A blog connects the members of the choir and builds a real sense of community between members. A glance at the Virtual Choir Map (**ericwhitacre.com/the-virtual-choir/map**) shows the physical location of each voice (see Figure 1.7).

Connecting Through Business. One of the most profound ways we can connect with each other is to support other people's dreams.

```
        Mastery
Autonomy        Purpose
        Better
      Performance
      & Personal
      Satisfaction
```

FIGURE 1.6 Our understanding of human motivation can play a role in our use of technology to impact society.

FIGURE 1.7 The Virtual Choir 4 performance of "Fly to Paradise" included over 5,900 singers from 101 countries. *(Eric Whitcare's Virtual Choir 4 - Fly to Paradise. Courtesy of Music Productions, Ltd.)*

Kickstarter (**kickstarter.com**) helps us connect in this way by allowing people to post their ideas for community projects, games, and inventions and to ask for funding directly. Donors are given rewards for different levels of pledges, such as a signed edition of a book or a special color of a product. This style of generating capital to start a business is known as **crowdfunding**, asking for small donations from a large number of people, often using the Internet.

Technology Impacts How We Consume

Technology is changing all aspects of how we decide what we'll purchase and how we actually buy goods and services— from strategies for convincing you to purchase a certain product to the mechanics of how you buy and own things.

Marketing. New strategies in marketing are counting on the fact that most people have a cell phone with a camera and Internet access. **QR (quick response) codes** let any piece of print host a link to online information and video content. From your smartphone, simply run your QR app and hold the phone near the QR image anywhere you see it—like the ones you see in this chapter. Your phone scans the QR image and then takes you to a website, video, or Facebook page for more information about the product.

Studies show 82% of shoppers go to the Internet on their cell phone before they make a purchase. They are often using so-called location-aware price comparison tools. Apps like ShopSavvy and RedLaser scan the bar code of the item and then compare prices with those of nearby stores and with the best prices available online. Techy shoppers can then

get "mobile coupons" (or *mobicoupons*) delivered to their cell phones thanks to sites like SnipSnap and Coupon Sherpa. The future promises specialized coupons created just for you based on your location and past buying preferences.

Marketers also have to be aware of the phenomenon of **crowdsourcing**—checking in with the voice of the crowd. Consumers are using apps like MobileVoice to check people's verdicts on the quality of items. Forward-thinking companies are using this input to improve their products and services. AT&T, for example, has an app that lets customers report locations of coverage gaps.

Access Versus Ownership. Even the idea of ownership is evolving thanks to new technologies. Items like cars and bikes can become "subscriptions" instead of large one-time purchases. For example, Zipcar allows hundreds of thousands of people to use shared cars. With Zipcar, a phone call or online reservation activates your personal Zipcard. This card allows you to automatically open the door of the car you have reserved, and away you drive. GPS technology is used to track where the car is, whether it has been dropped off at the right location, and how far it has been driven. Call a Bike is a bike-sharing program in Germany. Racks of Call a Bikes are located at major street corners in large cities in the country. Simply call the phone number printed on the bike and it texts you a code to unlock the bike. When you're done riding the bike, simply relock it and you're billed automatically. The New York City version of this program, Citi Bike, has already seen riders take over 7 million trips (see Figure 1.8).

These subscription-style business models are spreading now to smaller goods. Swap.com helps people trade books, clothes, and video games with one another using the power of peer-to-peer connections—for example, to find the best set of matches for used roller blades in exchange for a baby crib.

Rachel Botsman and Roo Rogers make the case in their book *What's Mine Is Yours: The Rise of Collaborative Consumption* that the real fuel beneath these services is a shift in our acceptance of sharing. **Collaborative consumption** implies that we are joining together as a group to use a specific product more efficiently. We are so constantly connected with each other that we have again found the power of community. There are increasing opportunities to redistribute the things we have purchased and to share the services a product provides instead of owning it outright. Add in the pressure of mounting environmental concerns and global financial pressures, and we are migrating toward collaborative consumption. ■

> **Before moving on to Part 2:**
> • **Watch Replay Video 1.1** ⏵.
> • **Then check your understanding of what you've learned so far.**

FIGURE 1.8 New York City's Citi Bike program uses digital technology to change our lifestyle from one of ownership to one of subscription. Riders have already taken over 7 million trips.
(Tim Clayton/TIM CLAYTON/Corbis)

check your understanding// review & practice

For a quick review to see what you've learned so far, answer the following questions. Visit **pearsonhighered.com/techinaction** to check your answers.

multiple choice

1. Which is NOT a technology that has been used to deliver assistance during times of crisis?

   a. Ushahidi   **c.** social networking

   b. QR codes   **d.** e-mail

2. Cognitive surplus means that we now find many people with

   a. more money than free time.

   b. limited access to the Internet.

   c. excess time and free tools for collaboration.

   d. mobile devices.

3. Collaborative consumption is when people get together to

   a. find the best prices on products.

   b. exchange reviews on services and goods they have purchased.

   c. fight diseases of the respiratory tract.

   d. increase the use of a single product by sharing access to it.

4. Crowdfunding helps startup businesses by

   a. selling stock more easily.

   b. gathering financial contributions from supporters.

   c. using QR codes to advertise and market products.

   d. replacing Web 2.0 technology.

5. The crisis of a growing digital divide is being addressed by

   a. Ushahidi.

   b. the Next Einstein Initiative project.

   c. the Freecycle program.

   d. building faster computers.

To take an autograded version of this review, please go to the companion website at **pearsonhighered.com/techinaction,** or go your MyITLab course.

Continue

Understanding what your computer can do to improve your life is one of the benefits of being computer literate. In this exercise, we'll show you how to make a free phone call over the Internet using Skype, a popular Voice over Internet Protocol (VoIP) service.

What You Need

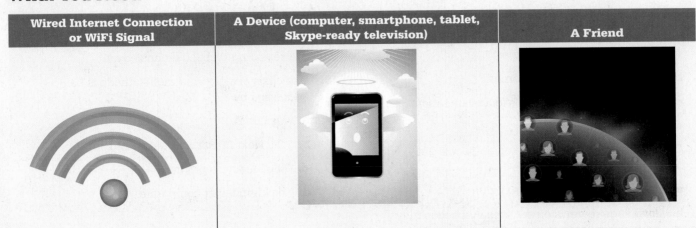

Wired Internet Connection or WiFi Signal	A Device (computer, smartphone, tablet, Skype-ready television)	A Friend

(Gst/Shutterstock; Dvougao/Getty Images; Filo/Getty Images)

Step 1   Set Up an Account. Go to Skype (**skype.com**), click on the **Join Us** tab, and create an account. Download the proper version for your device and install. You'll be able to call anyone with Skype and talk with just audio, with audio and video, or with free instant messaging.

Step 2   Build Your Contact List. To build your list of contacts, you can add friends one at a time by clicking **Contacts**, **Add Contact**, then **Search Skype Directory** (as shown here). You can search for people using their name, their Skype name, or their e-mail address.

(You only need to add a phone number if you plan on using Skype to call people on their *phone*, which, unlike computer-to-computer calls, is not a free service.)

For people you call frequently, drag their name up into the Favorites section.

incamerastock/Alamy

Step 3 **Make a Call.** Now we're ready to call someone! Let's start by calling the people at Skype and making sure everything is hooked up properly. Under your Contacts list, click the **Echo/Sound Test Service**. Then call in by clicking the green **Call** button. The Skype service will answer your call, record a short message from you, and play it back to you. You'll know everything is set to go, and you can begin calling the world for free!

Make This

TOOL: IFTTT.com (If This Then That)

MAKE: A Virtual Assistant

If This Then That is an Internet-based tool that helps you get things done automatically. By using "recipes" within this web-based tool, you can automate tasks you do during the day, for example:

- automatically silencing your phone when you go into class,
- automatically texting your manager when you're on your way to work, or
- notifying you when the president signs a new law.

In this exercise, you'll explore using IFTTT to create recipes like these.

Make the Internet work for you by knowing this one programming statement: IF THIS, THEN THAT.

For the instructions for this exercise, please go to pearsonhighered.com/techinaction or MyITLab.

How Will Technology Improve Your Life?

Technology is creating huge changes in the world as well as in how we behave socially, but it is also important to you on a more personal level. Being **computer literate** means being familiar enough with computers that you understand their capabilities and limitations and that you know how to use them safely and efficiently. As we discuss here, the more you understand technology, the more productive and protected you'll be at home, and the better prepared you'll be for any career.

 technology at
HOME

Everywhere you go, you see ads like the one in Figure 1.9 for computers and other devices. Do you know what all the words in the ad mean? What is RAM? What is a GPU? What are MB, GB, GHz, and cache? How fast do you need your computer to be, and how much memory should it have? If you're computer literate, you'll be a more informed consumer when it comes time to buy computers, peripherals, and technology services. Understanding computer terminology and keeping current with technology will help you better determine which computers and devices you need.

Let's look at a few more examples of what else it means to be a savvy computer user and consumer—in other words, computer literate (see Figure 1.10). If you're not a savvy user now, don't worry—the following topics and more are covered in detail in the remaining chapters.

- **Avoiding hackers and viruses.** Do you know what hackers and viruses are? Both can threaten a computer's security. Being aware of how hackers and viruses operate and knowing the damage they can do to your computer can help you avoid falling prey to them.

- **Protecting your privacy.** You've probably heard of identity theft—you see and hear news stories all the time about people whose "identities" are stolen and whose credit ratings are ruined by "identity thieves." But do you know how to protect yourself from identity theft when you're online?

- **Understanding the real risks.** Part of being computer literate means being able to separate the real privacy and security risks from things you don't have to worry about. For example, do you know what a *cookie* is? Do you know whether it poses a privacy risk for you when you're on the Internet? What about a *firewall*? Do you know what one is? Do you really need a firewall to protect your computer?

- **Using the web wisely.** Anyone who has ever searched the web can attest that finding information and finding *good* information are two different things. People who are

Processor:	Intel i7-4960X, Factory O'Cd to 3.6 GHz
RAM:	16 GB *Tri Channel* Corsair DDR3 (1866 MHz)
Video:	AMD Radeon R9 295X2 with 8 GB GDDR5 and dual GPUs
Audio:	Creative Labs X-Fi Elite Pro; HDA 7.1 surround channel sound
Network:	Native *Gigabit* Ethernet
Storage Drive:	256 GB SSD boot drive 2 TB SATA-III with support for up to 5 additional drives with *RAID* options
Ports:	8 USB and 2 USB 3.0 2 DVI and 1 S-Video 2 IEEE 1394 1 *S/PDIF* out
Cooling:	Two-stage *liquid cooling* system
Portable Storage:	Bluetooth wireless 19-in-1 media hub with *VoIP* stereo headset

FIGURE 1.9 Do you know what all the words in a computer ad mean? Can you tell whether the ad includes all the information necessary to make a purchasing decision?

computer literate know how to find the information they want effectively. How effective are your searches?

- **Avoiding online annoyances.** If you have an e-mail account, chances are you've received electronic junk mail, or **spam**. How can you avoid spam? What about adware and spyware—do you know what they are? Do you know the difference between those and viruses, worms, and Trojan horses? Do you know which **software** programs— the instructions that tell the computer what to do—you should install on your computer to avoid online annoyances?

- **Being able to maintain, upgrade, and troubleshoot your computer.** Learning how to care for and maintain your computer and knowing how to diagnose and fix certain problems can save you a lot of time and hassle. Do you know how to upgrade your computer if you want more memory, for example? Do you know which software and computer settings can keep your computer in top shape?

Finally, becoming computer literate means knowing which technologies are on the horizon and how to integrate them into your own life. Can you connect your television to your wireless network? What is Bluetooth, and does your computer need it?

Can a USB 3.0 flash drive be plugged into a USB 2.0 port? Knowing the answers to these and other questions will help you make better purchasing decisions.

This book and course will help you become computer literate. In Chapter 3, you'll find out how to get the most from the web while staying free from the spam and clutter Internet surfing can leave behind on your computer. Chapter 6 shows you how to determine if your hardware is limiting your computer's performance and how to upgrade or shop for a new system. Chapter 9 covers how to keep your computer and your digital life secure. You'll be able to save money, time, and endless frustration by understanding the basics of how computers and computer systems operate. ∎

SOUND BYTE
Questions to Ask Before You Buy a Computer

This Sound Byte will help you consider important questions to ask before you buy a computer.

FIGURE 1.10

What Does It Mean to Be Computer Literate?

You can **avoid falling prey to hackers and viruses** because you are aware of how they operate.

You know how to **protect yourself from identity theft**.

You can **separate the real privacy and security risks from things you don't have to worry about**.

You know how to find information and **use the web effectively**.

You can **avoid being overwhelmed by spam, adware, and spyware**.

You know how to **diagnose and fix problems** with your hardware and software.

technology and
YOUR CAREER

Information technology (IT) is a field of study focused on the management and processing of information and the automatic retrieval of information. IT careers include working with computers, telecommunications, and software deployment. Career opportunities in IT are on the rise, but no matter what career you choose, new technology in the workplace is creating a demand for new skill levels in technology from employees. A study from the National Research Council concludes that by the year 2030, computers will displace humans in 60% of current occupations. Having advanced skills is becoming more critical every year.

One of the benefits of being computer literate is that you will undoubtedly be able to perform your job more effectively. It also will make you more desirable as an employee and more likely to earn more and to advance in your career. In fact, your understanding of key concepts in technology can "future-proof" you, letting you easily and quickly react to the next round of new technologies.

Before we begin looking at a computer's parts and how a computer operates in Chapter 2, let's look at a whole range of industries and examine how computers are a part of getting work done.

Retail: Working in a Data Mine

The amount of data generated each minute of the day is staggering. Big Data is the term for this new easy accessibility to large data sets. But how do businesses make sense of it? They use a technique known as **data mining**, the process of searching huge amounts of data with the hope of finding a pattern (see Figure 1.11). For example, retailers often study the data gathered from register terminals to determine which products are selling on a given day and in a specific location. In addition to inventory control systems, which help managers figure out how much merchandise they need to order to replace stock that is sold, managers can use mined data to determine that if they want a certain product to sell well, they must lower its price—especially if they cut the price at one store and see sales increase, for example. Data mining thus allows retailers to respond to consumer buying patterns.

Have you ever wondered how Amazon or Netflix suggest items that fit your taste? Data mining can keep track of the purchases customers make, along with their geographic data, past buying history, and lists of items they looked at but did not purchase. This data can be translated into marketing that is customized to your shopping. This is the motivation behind the discount cards grocery stores and drugstores offer. In exchange for tracking your buying habits, they offer you special pricing. In the age of Big Data, you may be using data mining in a number of careers.

Arts: Ink, Paints, and a Laptop?

Some design students think that because they're studying art, there's no reason for them to study computers. Of course, not all artwork is created using traditional materials such as paint and canvas. Many artists today work exclusively with computers. Mastery of software such as Adobe Illustrator, Adobe Photoshop, and Corel Painter is

FIGURE 1.11 Data mining is the art of translating huge volumes of raw data into presentations like charts and graphs that provide managers with information, such as buying trends, that enable them to make better decisions. *(a McIek/Shutterstock; Richard Peterson/Shutterstock; Pressmaster/Shutterstock)*

essential to creating digital art. Eventually you'll want to sell your work, and you'll need to showcase your designs and artistic creations to employers and customers. Wouldn't it be helpful if you knew how to create and manage a website?

Using computers in the arts and entertainment fields goes far beyond just producing web pages, though. Dance and music programs like the ones at the Atlanta Ballet and the Juilliard School use computers to create new performances for audiences. A live dancer can be wired with sensors connected to a computer that captures the dancer's movements. Based on the data it collects, the computer generates a virtual dancer on a screen. The computer operator can easily manipulate this virtual dancer, as well as change the dancer's costume and other aspects of the dancer's appearance, with the click of a mouse. This allows artists to create new experiences for the audience.

And what if you see yourself working in an art museum? Today, museums are using technology to enhance visitors' experiences (see Figure 1.12). New York's Museum of Modern Art (MoMA), for example, offers a full range of options for tech-savvy visitors: old-fashioned museum audio guides, podcasts that visitors can listen to with their smartphones, and multimedia tours that visitors download through MoMA WiFi (**moma.org**) to their own mobile device. These multimedia guides even enable visitors to listen to music the artist listened to when he or she was creating a particular work or to look at other works that reflect similar techniques or themes as those

FIGURE 1.12 Multimedia tours using mobile devices and wireless technology are commonplace in museums and galleries. *(ZUMA Press, Inc. / Alamy)*

BITS&BYTES

Compute Me a Picture

Generative design is a revolutionary new method of creating artwork, models, and animations from sets of rules, or algorithms. Artists use simple programming languages, like the free product Processing, to produce designs and animations. Try this new-age tool for self-expression! Download Processing and generate your own artistic works like the one shown here.

they're viewing. Developing these solutions for museums is a great career for someone with an artistic education and knowledge of technology.

Education: Teaching and Learning

The education industry uses computer technology in numerous ways. Courses are designed around course management software such as Blackboard or Moodle so that students can communicate outside of class, take quizzes online, and find their class materials easily. The Internet has obvious advantages in the classroom as a research tool for students, and effective use of the Internet allows teachers to expose students to places students otherwise couldn't access. There are simulations and instructional software programs on the web that are incredible learning tools. For example, teachers can employ these products to give students a taste of running a global business (see Figure 1.13) or the experience of the Interactive Body (**bbc.co.uk/science/humanbody**).

Want to take your students to a museum in another state or country? There's no need to board a plane—many museums offer virtual tours on their websites that allow students to examine the museum collections. Another resource, the Art Project, is a collaboration of several museums that allows online visitors to explore over a thousand pieces of art using the same technology employed in Google Street View (see Figure 1.14). A custom viewer allows visitors to zoom in on the

FIGURE 1.13 Internet applications have become sophisticated learning resources. For example, SimVenture (**simventure.co.uk**) allows students to compete online for domination of a global market while giving instructors the chance to introduce many business concepts. *(Reprinted by permission of Venture Simulations, Ltd.)*

artwork itself at incredibly high resolution. The information panel takes you to related videos and other related websites. So, even if you teach in Topeka, Kansas, you can take your students on a virtual tour of the Tate Britain in London.

Computerized education in the classroom may prove to be the tool that helps teachers reach greater success, despite increasing class sizes and tightening financial constraints. The Khan Academy (**khanacademy.org**) is a terrific example of a technological tool for education. Salman Khan was an investment analyst in Boston in 2006 when he began to post videos to YouTube so that he could teach algebra to his young cousins in New Orleans. Today, his nonprofit Khan Academy contains over 3,000 videos, and several million students a month use the site.

A classroom teacher can also follow what is happening in the classroom by using the *dashboard*, a screen that shows which topics each student has mastered, which they are making progress with, and which have them spinning their wheels. Now a teacher can approach a student already knowing exactly what is frustrating them and can avoid the dreaded question, "Oh, what don't you understand?"

FIGURE 1.14 The Google Art Project (**googleartproject.com**) uses a custom camera on a moving trolley to generate a high-resolution experience of art museums located in more than 40 different countries. *(Richard Bord/Getty Images)*

FIGURE 1.15 Tissue-rendering programs add layers of muscles, fat, and skin to recovered skulls to create faces that can be used to identify victims. *(Plxologicstudio/Science Photo Library/Glow Images)*

As an educator, being computer literate will help you constructively integrate computer technologies like those discussed here into lesson plans and interactions for your students.

Law Enforcement: Put Down That Mouse— You're Under Arrest!

Today, wearing out shoe leather to solve crimes is far from the only method available to you if you want to pursue a career in law enforcement. Computers are being used in police cars and crime labs to solve an increasing number of crimes. For example, facial reconstruction systems like the one shown in Figure 1.15 can turn a skull into a finished digital image of a face, allowing investigators to proceed far more quickly with identification than before.

One technique used by modern detectives to solve crimes uses the vast number of databases on the Internet. Proprietary law enforcement databases such as the National Center for the Analysis of Violent Crime database enable detectives to analyze a wealth of information for similarities between crimes in an attempt to detect patterns that may reveal serial crimes. In fact, a law enforcement specialty called computer forensics is growing in importance in order to fight modern crime. **Computer forensics** analyzes computer systems with specific techniques to gather potential legal evidence. For example, Steven Zirko was convicted for two Chicago-area murders based on computer forensics work. Computer forensics examiners trained by the FBI scoured Zirko's computer and located searches for terms like *hire a hitman* and *GHB*, the date-rape drug. Zirko had also used his computer to find the daily schedule for one of his victim's two school-aged children and to get directions

to her home. In many cases, files, videos, and conversations conducted using a computer can be recovered by forensics specialists and can be used as evidence of criminal activity.

Medicine: The Chip Within

A career in medicine will connect you to new ways of using technology to better people's lives. Earlier we mentioned how biomedical chips may one day restore sight to the blind. Indeed, the goals of modern biomedical chip research are to provide technological solutions to physical problems and a means for identifying individuals.

There has already been experimentation on implanting chips in humans as a means of verifying a person's identity. Called VeriMed, this personal identification chip is about the size of a grain of rice and is implanted under the skin. When exposed to radio waves from a scanning device, the chip transmits its serial number to the scanner. The scanner then connects to a database that contains the name, address, and medical conditions of the person in whom the chip has been implanted. In the course of a nursing career, you may be using a device like VeriMed to help keep Alzheimer's patients safe, for example.

Currently, nonimplant versions of identity chips are used in hospitals. When chips are attached with bands to newborn infants, the hospital staff can instantly monitor the location of any baby. Elevators and doors are designed to allow only certain people to enter with a specific baby, even if hospital power is interrupted. Although the use of implantable tags is becoming more commonplace, it remains to be seen whether people will decide that the advantages of having their medical data quickly available justifies having chips implanted in their bodies. As a doctor, would you advise your patients to use an implantable chip?

We're comfortable with carrying around digital data in our pockets. But the advent of wearable computing is now allowing us to integrate digital information directly into our reality, both to add more detail and at times to remove unwanted visual effects. How does this happen?

Augmented reality combines our normal sense of the world around us with an additional layer of digital information. The extra information can be displayed on a separate device, such as in augmented reality apps for smartphones. Displays in stores can even augment your image with the clothing you're interested in, creating a virtual fitting room (see Figure 1.16).

But having to carry and position a separate device is clunky. Google Glass is a project that augments reality using a "third eye," a separate camera mounted to the side of a lightweight headset (see Figure 1.17). You can record images and videos by simply saying, "Take a picture." When you say "Glass, how long is the Brooklyn Bridge?," Glass communicates wirelessly with your phone and issues a request to the Internet. The returned information is formatted and then sent to a projector. Instead of the projector you're used to seeing in your classroom, this projector is so small it fits into the armband of the glasses. The output beam from the projector bounces off a glass prism that

FIGURE 1.17 Google Glass is a tool that adds digital information directly into your view of the world. *(Sean Gallup/Getty Images)*

is aligned so that the beam is sent directly to the retina of your eye, as shown in Figure 1.18. (This is why Google Glass is not available for those who wear glasses now. To adjust the prism so that the projector's beam goes through the person's

FIGURE 1.16 This high-tech fitting room uses augmented reality technology to allow shoppers to try on clothes virtually. *(Yoshikazu Tsuno/AFP/Getty Images)*

Prism

Projector

2.4 cm

Retina

Fovea (sharpest image)

FIGURE 1.18 Google Glass eliminates the need for a separate hand-held device by projecting an image directly on the retina of your eye. *(Upper Saddle River, New Jersey)*

FIGURE 1.19 Google Glass displays additional information so that it hovers in front of your eyes. *(Google/AP Images)*

eyeglasses and then hits the retina would require individual adjustment to the prism.) When you're wearing Google Glass, the additional information hovers in space in front of you (Figure 1.19).

Meanwhile, researchers like Stephen Mann at the University of Toronto are working with wearable computers that use "point of eye" (PoE) cameras. A PoE camera is designed so that the camera is positioned directly in front of the eye itself. The ultimate PoE camera would be one that is implanted within the eye or eye socket. Mann's research group is exploring this as a way to assist partially sighted or blind people.

Digital medication has arrived with the FDA approval of digestible microchips (see Figure 1.20). Looking like regular pills, these medications have embedded sensors that transmit information to the doctor. The sensor itself is the size of a grain of sand. As it is digested, a small voltage is generated and detected by a patch worn on the patient's skin. The patch then transmits to the physician that the pill was taken; it also monitors the patient's heart rate, respiration, and temperature.

Science: Simulating Reality

Thanks to a partnership between the National Severe Storms Lab and the National Center for Supercomputing Applications, tornado forecasting is becoming increasingly accurate.

FIGURE 1.20 Digital medications are able to report back to physicians information about how the patient is responding to the medicine. *(ImageBROKER/SuperStock)*

Scientists have been able to create a model so detailed that it takes nine days for a supercomputer to generate it, even though the computer is executing four trillion operations a second. Simulations also can model the structure of solar magnetic flares, which can interfere with broadcasts on Earth. With a career in meteorology, you will be studying the data produced by these simulations, hoping to improve predictions about weather phenomena.

Other technological applications in the sciences are being used on some of the oldest sites on Earth. For example, the Galassi Tomb, located in the ancient Italian city of Caere, was originally designed in 650 B.C. and was rich with ornamentation and jewelry. These treasures were taken to the Vatican State collection in the 1800s when the tomb was discovered. Today, scientists are using 3-D scanners and imaging software to re-create the experience of seeing the tomb and the artifacts together as they once were (see Figure 1.21). This virtual re-creation is so lifelike that archaeologists can study the ruins on-screen instead of at the actual site. Will you be using these tools someday to make records of other decaying sites?

Psychology: Computerized Coach

Fear of speaking in public is common, but for people with autism spectrum disorders, making proper eye contact and reacting to social cues is so difficult it can severely limit their opportunities for jobs and relationships. Researchers at the MIT Media Lab have developed a system to help improve interpersonal skills for people who have autism.

MACH (My Automated Conversation Coach) is a computer system that generates an on-screen person that can, for example, conduct a job interview or appear ready for a first date.

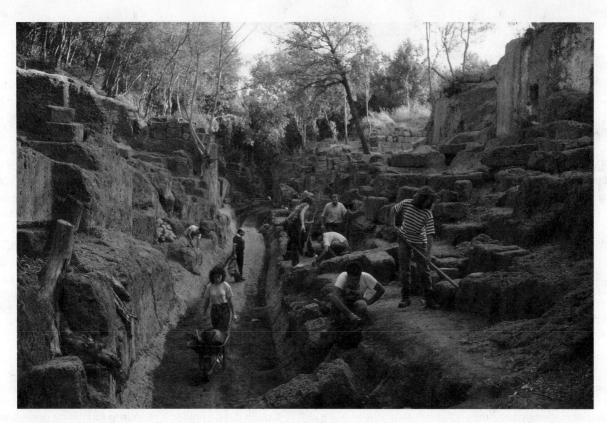

FIGURE 1.21 Archeologists use computer-aided design (CAD) systems to build virtual reconstructions of ancient sites like this one. *(O. Louis Mazzatenta/Getty Images)*

The computerized person (see Figure 1.22) nods and smiles in response to the user's speech and movement. This is an example of **affective computing**, developing systems that can recognize and simulate human emotions. MACH users can practice as many times as they wish in a safe environment. They receive an analysis that shows how well they modulated their voices, maintained eye contact, smiled, and how often they lapsed into "umms" and "uhhhs." The software runs on an ordinary laptop, using a webcam and microphone.

While engineers work to create computers that can process data faster and faster, psychologists and computer scientists are also working to evolve systems toward a more complete understanding of human behavior. With a career that blends computer science and psychology, you could find yourself at the heart of developing a new kind of relationship between man and machine. ■

FIGURE 1.22 My Automated Conversation Coach (MACH) generates an on-screen interviewer you can practice with over and over. *(Cultura Limited/Superstock)*

Before moving on to the Chapter Review:
- **Watch Replay Video 1.2** ↻ .
- **Then check your understanding of what you've learned so far.**

check your understanding// review & practice

For a quick review to see what you've learned so far, answer the following questions. Visit **pearsonhighered.com/techinaction** to check your answers.

multiple choice

1. Medication delivered through pills with embedded sensors

    a. is dangerous to humans.

    b. will be available in the next decade.

    c. allows the physician to track the patient's heart rate.

    d. requires hospitalization.

2. The MACH project shows that

    a. there is a digital divide limiting access to computer systems.

    b. sports performance can be recorded and analyzed by software.

    c. there are some things computers cannot teach.

    d. computers can help people with interpersonal skills development.

3. Which of the following allows retailers to respond to consumer buying patterns?

    a. outsourcing   **c.** smart labels

    b. data mining   **d.** Bluetooth technology

4. Computer forensics uses computer systems and technology to

    a. simulate a person's anatomical system.

    b. train law enforcement officers to be more effective.

    c. create a crisis map.

    d. gather potential legal evidence.

5. IT is the abbreviation for

    a. information training.

    b. Internet training.

    c. Internet technology.

    d. information technology.

To take an autograded version of this review, please go to the companion website at **pearsonhighered.com/techinaction,** or go your MyITLab course.

Continue

1 Chapter Review

summary//

Technology on the World Stage

1. How can becoming proficient with technology help you understand and participate in important issues in the world at large?

- Whether it's political issues, environmental issues, or questions addressing the global digital divide, it's important that you become proficient with technology to be able to participate.
- Technology can be the means by which you find your voice in the world and impact others in meaningful ways.

Technology and Our Society

2. How can knowledge of technology help you influence the direction our society takes?

- Technology is changing how we think, how we connect with each other, and how we purchase and consume products and services.
- By using current technology, you can become a creator of new pieces of music, connect with people from around the world, and collaborate to create or consume.

Technology at Home

3. What does it mean to be computer literate?

- Computer literacy goes beyond knowing how to use a mouse and send e-mail. If you're computer literate, you understand the capabilities and limitations of computers and know how to use them wisely.

- Being computer literate also enables you to make informed purchasing decisions, use computers in your career, and understand the many ethical, legal, and societal implications of technology today. Anyone can become computer literate.

4. How does being computer literate make you a savvy computer user and consumer?

- By understanding how a computer is constructed and how its various parts function, you'll be able to get the most out of your computer.
- Among other things, you'll be able to avoid hackers, viruses, and Internet headaches; protect your privacy; and separate the real risks of privacy and security from things you don't have to worry about.
- You'll also be better able to maintain, upgrade, and troubleshoot your computer; make good purchasing decisions; and incorporate the latest technologies into your existing equipment.

Technology and Your Career

5. How can becoming computer literate help you in a career?

- As computers increasingly become part of our daily lives, it is difficult to imagine any career that does not use computers in some fashion.
- Understanding how to use computers effectively will help you be a more productive and valuable employee, no matter which profession you choose.

> Be sure to check out the companion website or MyITLab for additional materials to help you review and learn—**pearsonhighered.com/techinaction**. And don't forget the Replay Videos ▶ .

key terms//

chapter quiz // assessment

For a quick review to see what you've learned, answer the following questions. Submit the quiz as requested by your instructor. If you are using MyITLab, the quiz is also available there.

multiple choice

1. Social networking
   a. prevents two-way dialog between people.
   b. is incorporated as part of political strategy by many politicians.
   c. cannot be immediate enough to react to quickly developing issues.
   d. only is useful for personal friendships.

2. Web 2.0 has led to a shift from just consuming content toward
   a. spending all our time on leisure activities.
   b. less sharing of the work we produce.
   c. new standards for HTML.
   d. producing content.

3. Examples of crowdfunding and crowdsourcing include
   a. KIckstarter and MobileVoice.
   b. Bing and Google.
   c. Call A Bike and ZipCar.
   d. Ushahidi and Kiva.

4. Being computer literate includes being able to
   a. avoid spam, adware, and spyware.
   b. use the web effectively.
   c. diagnose and fix hardware and software problems.
   d. all of the above.

5. Computer forensics
   a. tests computers for hardware malfunction.
   b. analyzes computer systems to gather potential legal evidence.
   c. analyzes the design of a computer system.
   d. is used to create three-dimensional art.

6. The Khan Academy is
   a. a free technology tool used for education.
   b. a program in Africa to encourage study of mathematics.
   c. of use to students but not useful for instructors.
   d. a simulation package to teach users how to run a business.

true/false

_____ **1.** The move toward access instead of ownership is a sign of collaborative consumption.

_____ **2.** The Next Einstein Initiative uses the power of supercomputing to enhance mathematical education.

_____ **3.** QR codes conduct a "quick release" of information from your phone to a website.

_____ **4.** Criminal investigators may find evidence on a computer, but that evidence cannot be used in court.

critical thinking

1. **What Occupies Your Mind?**

   What we think about is influenced by the information fed to our mind all day long. Web 2.0 has created numerous channels for people to offer their own work for free—open-source software, free music, books, and artworks. How has this affected your thinking? Have you created things to share freely with the online world? Has it changed the value you put on music, books, and art?

2. **Working 9 to 5**

   This chapter lists many ways in which becoming computer literate is beneficial. Think about what your life will be like once you're started in your career. What areas of computing will be most important for you to understand? How would an understanding of computer hardware and software help you in working from home, working with groups in other countries, and contributing your talents?

team time//

A Culture of Sharing

Problem

As more and more peer-to-peer music-sharing services appeared, like BitTorrent and LimeWire, many felt a culture of theft was developing. Some argued there was a mindset that property rights for intellectual works need not be respected and that people should be able to download, for free, any music, movies, or other digital content they wanted.

But there is another view of the phenomenon. Some are suggesting that the amount of constant access to other people—through texting, e-mail, blogging, and the easy exchange of digital content—has created a culture of trust and sharing. This Team Time will explore both sides of this debate as it affects three different parts of our lives—finance, travel, and consumerism.

Task

Each of three groups will select a different area to examine—finance, travel, or consumerism. The groups will find evidence to support or refute the idea that a culture of sharing is developing. The finance group will want to explore projects like Kickstarter (**kickstarter.com**) and Kiva (**kiva.org**). The travel group should examine what is happening with Couchsurfing (**couchsurfing.org**) to start their research. The team investigating consumerism will want to look at goods-exchange programs like Freecycle (**freecycle.org**).

Process

1. Divide the class into three teams.
2. Discuss the different views of a "culture of sharing." With the other members of your team, use the Internet to research up-and-coming technologies and projects that would support your position. People use social media tools to connect into groups to exchange ideas. Does that promote trust? Does easy access to digital content promote theft, or has the value of content changed? Are there other forces like the economy and the environmental state of the world that play a role in promoting a culture of sharing? What evidence can you find to support your ideas?
3. Present your group's findings to the class for debate and discussion.
4. Write a strategy paper that summarizes your position and outlines your predictions for the future. Will the pace of technology promote a change in the future from the position you are describing?

Conclusion

The future of technology is unknown, but we do know that it will impact the way our society progresses. To be part of the developments that technology will bring will take good planning and attention, no matter what area of the culture you're examining. Begin now—learn how to stay on top of technology.

ethics project//

Can Big Data Predict Your Grade?

Problem

As you move through your academic career, you leave an enormous swath of data: which courses you chose to register for, which ones you looked at but didn't pick, and how you did on each homework assignment, test, and project. Could this massive amount of data be analyzed to predict your grade in a course? To suggest which courses you should take next? Should those predictions be public to your instructor? To you? To financial aid officers?

Research Topics to Consider

- Course Signals
- Degree Compass

Process

1. Divide the class into teams. Each team will select a web-based tool that allows access to information.

2. Team members should each think of a situation where a person would benefit from the type of results data mining of Big Data can bring to campus and a situation where it might be undesirable.

3. Team members should select the most powerful and best-constructed arguments and develop a summary conclusion.

4. Team members should present their findings to the class or submit a PowerPoint presentation for review by the rest of the class, along with the summary conclusion they developed.

Conclusion

As technology becomes ever more prevalent and integrated into our lives, ethical dilemmas will present themselves to an increasing extent. Being able to understand and evaluate both sides of the argument, while responding in a personally or socially ethical manner, will be an important skill.

How Technology Is Used on the World Stage and in My Personal Life

In this activity, you'll use Microsoft Word to reflect on how technology is affecting the world as well as you, personally and professionally. Reflect on the content in Chapter 1 as you work through this exercise.

You will use the following skills as you complete this activity:	
• Open and Modify a Document Template	• Insert Text
• Apply Styles and Advanced Font Formats	• Apply Themes
• Use Format Painter	• Create a Header and Footer

Instructions

1. Start Microsoft Word 2013 and open the Facet design (Blank) template. Save the document as **TIA_Ch1_LastFirst**, using your own Last and First names.

2. Double-click the Title placeholder and type **Technology**, then double-click the Heading placeholder and type **Introduction**. Replace the remainder placeholder text with the following: **Political and global issues are showing that technology is accelerating change around the world and galvanizing groups of people in new ways. Technology allows us to refine how we connect with each other, and it also impacts our daily personal and professional experiences.** Press Enter.

3. Type **How Technology Impacts Society** and type a few sentences that describe how technology is impacting global events such as political revolutions, health care, the environment, and the digital divide. In addition, address how businesses are using social media. Press Enter.

4. Type **How Technology Impacts Me Personally and Professionally** and type a few sentences that describe how technology is impacting your personal life. You should address the importance of being computer literate. You should also address the kinds of technology being used in the industry of your current or desired career.

5. Click anywhere in the title *Technology*, then using **Format Painter**, apply the **Heading 1** format to the paragraph headers: *Select How Technology Impacts Society* and *How Technology Impacts Me Personally and Professionally.*

    a. Hint: Format Painter is in the Clipboard group on the HOME tab.

6. Change the Document Theme style to the **Slice Theme**.

    a. Hint: Document Themes are found on the DESIGN tab, in the Document Formatting group.

7. Select the title *Technology*, then format the font as **Small Caps. Center align** the title.

    a. Hint: Click the dialog box launcher in the Font group on the HOME tab to access the Small Caps font style.

8. Apply the **Whisp** header style to the document. Click to add Today's date in the Date header, and delete the Document Title header. Add a **File Path** to the document footer. Select the footer text, and change the font size to 8. Close the Header and Footer.

    a. Hint: Headers are found on the INSERT tab in the Header & Footer group. File Path is found in Document Info in the Insert group on the HEADER & FOOTER tab.

9. **Save** the document and submit based on your instructor's directions.

2 Looking at Computers: Understanding the Parts

Understanding Digital Components

Understanding Your Computer

OBJECTIVES

1. What exactly is a computer, and what are its four main functions? **(p. 30)**

2. What is the difference between data and information? **(p. 30)**

3. What are bits and bytes, and how are they measured? **(pp. 30–34)**

🔊 **Sound Byte:** Binary Numbers Interactive

👤 **Active Helpdesk:** Understanding Bits and Bytes

Input Devices and Output Devices

OBJECTIVES

4. What devices can I use to get data into the computer? **(pp. 35–41)**

5. What devices can I use to get information out of the computer? **(pp. 42–49)**

👤 **Active Helpdesk:** Using Output Devices

Processing, Storage, and Connectivity

Processing, Memory, and Storage

OBJECTIVES

6. What's on the motherboard? **(pp. 52–53)**

7. Where are information and programs stored? **(pp. 54–56)**

🔊 **Sound Byte:** Virtual Computer Tour

Ports and Power Controls

OBJECTIVES

8. How are devices connected to the computer? **(pp. 57–58)**

9. What's the best way to turn my computer on and off, and when should it be done? **(pp. 59–60)**

👤 **Active Helpdesk:** Exploring Storage Devices and Ports

🔊 **Sound Byte:** Port Tour: How Do I Hook It Up?

Setting It All Up

OBJECTIVE

10. How do I set up my computer to avoid strain and injury? **(pp. 61–63)**

🔊 **Sound Byte:** Healthy Computing

Make This: Explore an App Builder Skill on **page 51**

The information in this text is written for Windows 8.1, update 2. If you are running a different version of Windows 8, your screens and task instructions may vary slightly.

For all media in this chapter go to **pearsonhighered.com /techinaction** or **MyITLab**.

HOW COOL IS THIS?

Now that we are used to the **touch experience** with our devices, where do we go next? How about **no touch**! The Ring from Logbar, Inc. is a wearable device that **senses the movements of the finger** on which it is worn and transmits those gestures to compatible devices (iOS and Android). You can type text, control home appliances, or make payments all by **making gestures with one finger**. The device has preprogrammed gestures, but you can also customize them (or create your own) with the **companion app**. So controlling your devices may soon only require a small wave of your finger! *(© 2014 Logbar Inc. All rights reserved)*

Scan here for more info

Understanding Digital Components

After reading Chapter 1, you can see why becoming computer literate is important. But where do you start? You've no doubt gleaned some knowledge about computers just from being a member of society. However, even if you have used a computer before, do you really understand how it works, what all its parts are, and what those parts do?

understanding your
COMPUTER

Let's start our look at computers by discussing what a computer does and how its functions make it such a useful machine.

Computers Are Data Processing Devices

Strictly defined, a **computer** is a data processing device that performs four major functions:

1. **Input:** It gathers data, or allows users to enter data.
2. **Process:** It manipulates, calculates, or organizes that data into information.
3. **Output:** It displays data and information in a form suitable for the user.
4. **Storage:** It saves data and information for later use.

What's the difference between data and information? People often use the terms *data* and *information* interchangeably. Although they may mean the same thing in a simple conversation, the distinction between data and information is an important one.

In computer terms, **data** is a representation of a fact, a figure, or an idea. Data can be a number, a word, a picture, or even a recording of sound. For example, the number 7135553297 and the names Zoe and Richardson are pieces of data. Alone, these pieces of data probably mean little to you. **Information** is data that has been organized or presented in a meaningful fashion. When your computer provides you with a contact listing that indicates that Zoe Richardson can be reached at (713) 555-3297, the data becomes useful—that is, it becomes information.

How do computers interact with data and information? Computers are excellent at **processing** (manipulating, calculating, or organizing) data into information. When you first arrived on campus, you probably were directed to a place where you could get an ID card. You most likely provided a clerk with personal data that was entered into a computer. The clerk then took your picture with a digital camera (collecting more data). All of the data was then processed appropriately so that it could be printed on your ID card (see Figure 2.1). This organized output of data on your ID card is useful information.

FIGURE 2.1 Computers process data into information.

Bits and Bytes: The Language of Computers

How do computers process data into information? Unlike humans, computers work exclusively with numbers (not words). To process data into information, computers need to work in a language they understand. This language, called **binary language**, consists of just two digits: 0 and 1. Everything a computer does, such as processing data, printing a report, or editing a photo, is broken down into a series of 0s and 1s. Each 0 and 1 is a **binary digit**, or **bit** for short. Eight binary digits (or bits) combine to create one **byte**. In computers, each letter of the alphabet, each number, and each special character (such as @, pronounced "at") consists of a unique combination of eight bits, or a string of eight 0s and 1s. So, for example, in binary language, the letter *K* is represented as 01001011. This is eight bits, or one byte.

What else can bits and bytes be used for? Bits and bytes not only are used as the language that tells the computer what to do, they are also used to represent the *quantity* of data and information that the computer inputs and outputs. Word processing files, digital pictures, and even software are represented inside computing devices as a series of bits and bytes. These files and applications can be quite large, containing thousands or millions of bytes.

To make it easier to measure the size of such files, we need units of measure larger than a byte. Kilobytes, megabytes, and gigabytes are therefore simply larger amounts of bytes. As shown in Figure 2.2, a **kilobyte (KB)** is approximately 1,000 bytes, a **megabyte (MB)** is about 1 million bytes, and a **gigabyte (GB)** is around 1 billion bytes. Today, personal computers are capable of storing **terabytes (TB)** of data (around 1 trillion bytes), and many business computers can store up to a **petabyte (PB)** (1,000 terabytes) of data. The Google search engine processes more than 1 PB of user-generated data per *hour*!

How does your computer process bits and bytes? Your computer uses hardware and software to process data into information that lets you complete tasks such as writing a letter or playing a game. **Hardware** is any part of the computer you can physically touch. However, a computer needs more than just hardware to work. **Software** is the set of computer programs that enables the hardware to perform different tasks.

There are two broad categories of software: *application software* and *system software*. **Application software** is the set of programs you use on a computer to help you carry out tasks such as writing a research paper. If you've ever typed a document, created a spreadsheet, or edited a digital photo, for example, you've used application software.

System software is the set of programs that enables your computer's hardware devices and application software to work together. The most common type of system software is the **operating system (OS)**—the program that controls how your computer system functions. It manages the hardware, such as the monitor and printer, and provides a means by which users can interact with the computer. Most likely, the computer you own or use at school runs a version of Windows as the system software. However, if you're working on an Apple computer, you're probably running OS X.

Types of Computers

What types of computers are popular for personal use? There are two basic designs of computers: portable and stationary. For portable computers, a number of options exist:

- In 2010, Apple introduced the iPad, which created a new class of portable computers. A **tablet computer**, such as the iPad or Samsung Galaxy Tab, is a portable computer integrated into a flat multitouch-sensitive screen. It uses an onscreen virtual keyboard, but you can connect separate keyboards to it via Bluetooth or wires.
- A **laptop** or **notebook computer** is a portable computer that has a keyboard, monitor, and other devices integrated into a single compact case.
- A **netbook** is a small, lightweight laptop computer that is generally 7 to 10 inches wide and has a longer battery life than a laptop. They usually sacrifice performance for portability.
- An **ultrabook** is a full-featured but lightweight laptop computer designed to compete with the MacBook Air. Ultrabooks feature low-power processors and solid-state drives and try to reduce their size and weight to extend battery life without sacrificing performance.
- A **tablet** (or **convertible**) **PC** is similar to a laptop computer, but the monitor swivels and folds flat (see Figure 2.3a). This allows it to function both as a conventional laptop and as a tablet computer using its touchscreen.

A **desktop computer** is intended for use at a single location, so it's stationary. Most desktop computers consist of a separate case or tower (called the **system unit**) that

FIGURE 2.2

How Much Is a Byte?

NAME	NUMBER OF BYTES	RELATIVE SIZE
Byte (B)	1 byte	One character of data (8 bits, or binary digits)
Kilobyte (KB)	1,024 bytes (2^{10} bytes)	1,024 characters, or about 1 page of plain text
Megabyte (MB)	1,048,576 bytes (2^{20} bytes)	About 4 books (200 pages, 240,000 characters)
Gigabyte (GB)	1,073,741,824 bytes (2^{30} bytes)	About 4,500 books, or over twice the size of Sir Isaac Newton's library (considered very large for the time)
Terabyte (TB)	1,099,511,627,776 bytes (2^{40} bytes)	About 4.6 million books, or about the number of volumes in the Rutgers University Library
Petabyte (PB)	1,125,899,906,842,624 bytes (2^{50} bytes)	About 4.7 billion books, which would fill the Library of Congress (the United States' largest library) 140 times!
Exabyte (EB)	1,152,921,504,606,846,976 bytes (2^{60} bytes)	About 4.8 trillion books, which, if stored as they are in the Library of Congress, would occupy about 11,000 square miles, or an area almost the size of the state of Maryland
Zettabyte (ZB)	1,180,591,620,717,411,303,424 bytes (2^{70} bytes)	The library required to house the 4.9 quadrillion books equal to a ZB of data would occupy about 11.3 million square miles, or an area about 1 million square miles larger than all of North America

Ninice64/Fotolia; Georgios Kollidas/Fotolia; D.Aniel/Fotolia; Flavijus Piliponis/Fotolia

FIGURE 2.3 (a) A convertible PC has a monitor that swivels to become a touch-sensitive input device; (*Dell Computer Corporation*) (b) an all-in-one computer does not need a separate tower. (*Anonymous/PRNewsFoto/Apple/AP Image*)

houses the main components of the computer plus peripheral devices. A **peripheral device** is a component, such as a monitor or keyboard, that connects to the computer. An **all-in-one computer**, such as the Apple iMac (Figure 2.3b) or HP TouchSmart, eliminates the need for a separate tower because these computers house the computer's processor and memory in the monitor. Many all-in-one models, such as the TouchSmart, also incorporate touch-screen technology.

Are there other types of computers? Although you may never come into direct contact with the following types of computers, they are still very important and do a lot of work behind the scenes of daily life:

- A **mainframe** is a large, expensive computer that supports many users simultaneously. Mainframes are often used in businesses that manage large amounts of data, such as insurance companies, where many people are working at the same time on similar operations, such as claims processing. Mainframes excel at executing many computer programs at the same time.

- A **supercomputer** is a specially designed computer that can perform complex calculations extremely rapidly. Supercomputers are used when complex models requiring intensive mathematical calculations are needed (such as weather forecasting or atomic energy research). Supercomputers are designed to execute a few programs as quickly as possible, whereas mainframes are designed to handle many programs running at the same time but at a slower pace.

- An **embedded computer** is a specially designed computer chip that resides in another device, such as your car or the electronic thermostat in your home. Embedded computers are self-contained computer devices that have their own programming and that typically don't receive input from you or interact with other systems (see Figure 2.4).

FIGURE 2.4 This robot vacuum includes an embedded computer. (*Jirsak/Shutterstock*)

Even your smartphone is a computer. Today's **smartphones** offer many features you probably use day to day, including a wide assortment of apps, media players, high-quality cameras, and web connectivity. And just like your laptop computer, your smartphone has a CPU, memory, and storage. Examples of smartphones include the iPhone and the Galaxy S5.

Each part of your computer has a specific purpose that coordinates with one of the functions of the computer—input, processing, output, or storage (see Figure 2.5). Additional devices, such as modems and routers, help a computer communicate with the Internet and other computers to facilitate the sharing of documents and other resources. Let's begin our exploration of hardware by looking at your computer's input devices. ◼

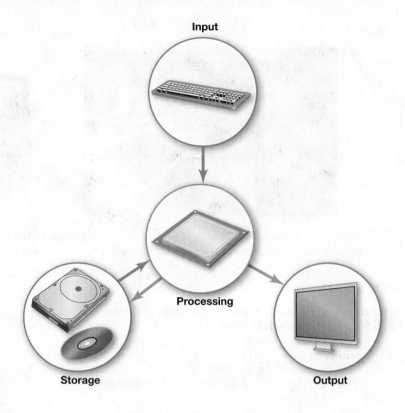

Input

Processing

Storage

Output

FIGURE 2.5 Each part of the computer serves a special function.

BITS&BYTES

Putting Your Computer to Work . . . While You Sleep

Complex scientific research, such as human genome exploration, requires vast computing power. Software has been developed to tie individual computing devices (including tablets and smartphones) in a grid to enable them to work together. This effectively creates a cheap supercomputer that many not-for-profit research organizations use to research problems that will benefit the greater good...and your computer can help. Visit the World Community Grid (**worldcommunitygrid.org**) and download its software. Once installed on your device, it allows your computer to work on research during the many times when your CPU is idle (or at least not working to its full potential). Your computing device can participate in exciting research projects on new drugs, sustainable water, and cancer. So tell your computer to get to work!

FIGURE 2.6 Help solve complex problems by adding your computer to the World Community Grid. *(Adimas/Fotolia)*

input
DEVICES

An **input device** lets you enter data (text, images, and sounds) and instructions (user responses and commands) into your computer. A **keyboard** is an input device you use to enter typed data and commands, and a **mouse** is used to enter user responses and commands.

There are other input devices as well. Microphones input sounds, scanners input nondigital data (such as magazine articles and old photographs) by turning it into a digital form, and digital cameras input digital images. A **stylus** is an input device that looks like a pen, which you use to tap commands or draw on a screen. We'll explore these and other input devices next.

Keyboards

What is the most common way to input data and commands? Most computing devices, such as smartphones and tablets, now respond to touch. **Touch screens** are display screens that respond to commands initiated by touching them with your finger or a stylus. Touch-screen devices use a virtual keyboard (see Figure 2.7) that displays on screen when text input is required. These keyboards show basic keyboard configurations and use special keys to switch to numeric, punctuation, and other special keys.

Are all keyboards the same? Whether onscreen touch keyboards or physical keyboards, the most common keyboard layout is a standard **QWERTY keyboard**. This keyboard layout gets its name from the first six letters in the top-left row of alphabetic keys and is the standard English-language keyboard layout. The QWERTY layout was originally designed for typewriters and was meant to slow typists down and prevent typewriter keys from jamming. Although the QWERTY layout is considered inefficient because it slows typing speeds, efforts to change to more efficient layouts, such as that of the Dvorak keyboard (see the Bits and Bytes on the next page), have not been met with much public interest.

What alternatives are there to an onscreen touch keyboard? Touchscreen keyboards are not always convenient when a great deal of typing is required. Most computing devices can accept physical keyboards as an add-on accessory. Wired keyboards plug into a data port on the computing device. Wireless keyboards send data to the computer using a form of wireless technology that uses *radio frequency (RF)*. A radio transmitter in the keyboard sends out signals that are received either

FIGURE 2.7 Virtual keyboards are found on tablets and other touch-screen devices. *(Nathan Alliard/Photononstop/Glow Images)*

by a receiving device plugged into a port on the device or by a Bluetooth receiving device located in the device. You've probably heard of **Bluetooth technology** if you use a headset or earpiece with your cell phone. Bluetooth is a wireless transmission standard that lets you connect devices such as smartphones, tablets, and laptops to peripheral devices such as keyboards and headsets. Often, wireless keyboards for tablets are integrated with a case to protect your tablet (see Figure 2.8a).

FIGURE 2.8 (a) Cases with integrated physical keyboards make tablets more typing-friendly. (b) Virtual keyboard devices project the image of a QWERTY keyboard on any surface. Sensors detect typing motions, and data is transmitted to a computing device via Bluetooth technology. *(Courtesy of Logitech, Inc.; Hammacher Schlemmer/Splash News/Newscom)*

BITS&BYTES

Switching Your Keyboard Layout

The Dvorak keyboard is an alternative keyboard layout that puts the most commonly used letters in the English language on "home keys"—the keys in the middle row of the keyboard. The Dvorak keyboard's design reduces the distance your fingers travel for most keystrokes, increasing typing speed.

But did you know that you can change your keyboard from the QWERTY layout to the Dvorak layout without buying a new keyboard? You can use the Windows operating system to customize the keyboard by changing the keyboard layout. The keyboard layout then controls which characters appear on the screen when you press the keys on your keyboard. If you suffer from a repetitive strain injury such as carpal tunnel syndrome, you may find it useful to switch to the Dvorak keyboard layout. You can also switch layouts to conform to different foreign languages. Instructions for changing keyboard layouts are shown in Figure 2.9.

You might also find it useful to cover the keys on the keyboard with stickers of the corresponding characters of the newly configured layout so that the characters on your keyboard match up to the new layout.

FIGURE 2.9 You can customize the layout of your keyboard using the Windows operating system.

>*To change the keyboard layout in Windows 8.1, open Control Panel, click* **Change input methods** *in the Clock, Language, and Region section. Click the* **Options link**. *Click the* **Add an input method** *link. Scroll to find the appropriate keyboard and click the* **Preview link** *to view it. Then left-click the keyboard, and click* **Add**. *(Windows 8.1.)*

Flexible keyboards are a terrific alternative if you want a full-sized keyboard for your laptop, netbook, or tablet. You can roll one up, fit it in your backpack, and plug it into a USB port when you need it. Another compact keyboard alternative is the VK200 KEYFOB® Virtual Keyboard (see Figure 2.8b) from CTX, which is about the size of a matchbox. It projects an image of a keyboard onto any flat surface, and sensors detect the motion of your fingers as you "type." Data is transmitted to the device via Bluetooth. The keyboard works with the latest iPhones, iPads, and Android devices.

How can I use my keyboard most efficiently?
All keyboards have the standard set of alphabetic and numeric keys that you regularly use when typing. As shown in Figure 2.10, many keyboards for laptop and desktop computers have additional keys that perform special functions. Knowing how to use the special keys shown in Figure 2.10 will help you improve your efficiency.

Mice and Other Pointing Devices

What kinds of mice are there?
The mouse type you're probably most familiar with is the **optical mouse**. An optical mouse uses an internal sensor or laser to detect the mouse's movement. The sensor sends signals to the computer, telling it where to move the pointer on the screen. Optical mice don't

require a mouse pad, though you can use one to enhance the movement of the mouse on an uneven surface or to protect your work surface from being scratched.

If you have special ergonomic needs or want to customize the functionality of your mouse, there are plenty of options (see Figure 2.11). Most mice have two or three buttons that let you execute commands and open shortcut menus. (Mice for Macs sometimes have only one button.) Many mice, such as the Cyborg R.A.T. 9 Gaming Mouse, have additional programmable buttons and wheels that let you quickly maneuver through web pages or games. In addition, the R.A.T. 9 is customizable to fit any size hand and grip style by allowing for length and width adjustments. Aside from gamers, many people use customizable mice to reduce susceptibility to repetitive strain injuries.

How do wireless mice work?
Wireless mice usually connect the same way that wireless keyboards do—either through Bluetooth or a receiver that plugs into a USB port. Wireless mice have receivers that often clip into the bottom of the mouse for easy storage when not in use.

Why would I want to use a mouse with a touch-screen device?
If you're using a conventional keyboard with your touch-screen device, it's often easier to perform actions with a mouse rather than taking your hands off the keyboard and reaching to touch the screen. In addition, there are new kinds of mice that are designed with touch-screen computers

FIGURE 2.10 Keyboards have a variety of keys that help you work more efficiently. (Note that on Macs, function keys are slightly different: The Control function is the Apple key or Command key, and the Alt function is the Option key.)
(Artur Synenko/Shutterstock)

Toggle keys: keys whose function changes between two options. (Example: Caps Lock key)

Internet controls

Multimedia controls

Numeric keypad: lets you enter numbers quickly.

Function keys (F keys): shortcut keys you press to perform special tasks in software programs.

Cursor control keys

Alt key: works with other keys to execute shortcuts and special tasks.

Control (Ctrl) key: used with other keys to perform shortcuts. (Example: Ctrl + B makes text bold)

Windows key: used alone, it toggles between the Start screen and the foremost running app. Used with other keys, it performs shortcuts. (Example: Windows key + C displays charms)

BITS&BYTES

Keystroke Shortcuts

Did you know that you can combine certain keystrokes to take shortcuts within an application, such as Microsoft Word, or within the operating system itself? The following are a few of the most helpful Windows-based shortcuts. For more, visit **support.microsoft.com**. For a list of shortcuts for Macs, see **apple.com/support**.

TEXT FORMATTING	FILE MANAGEMENT	CUT/COPY/PASTE	WINDOWS CONTROLS
Ctrl+B applies (or removes) **bold** formatting to/from selected text.	**Ctrl+O** opens the Open dialog box.	**Ctrl+X** cuts (removes) selected text and stores it in the Clipboard.	**Alt+F4** closes the current window.
Ctrl+I applies (or removes) *italic* formatting to/from selected text.	**Ctrl+N** opens a new document.	**Ctrl+C** copies selected text to the Clipboard.	**Windows Key+Tab** displays open Windows 8 apps.
Ctrl+U applies (or removes) underlining to/from selected text.	**Ctrl+S** saves a document.	**Ctrl+V** pastes selected text (previously cut or copied) from the Clipboard.	**Windows Key+L** locks the computer.
	Ctrl+P opens the Print page (backstage view) in Office 2013.		**Windows Key+F** opens the Search bar in Files mode.

FIGURE 2.11 Customizable mice offer programmable buttons and adjustable fittings to meet most any need. *(Kirill87/Fotolia)*

in mind. For example, the Logitech Touch Mouse is a multitouch wireless mouse that allows you to perform a variety of touch-screen tasks (see Figure 2.12). Unlike older mice, there are no specifically defined buttons. The top surface of this mouse is the button. You use one, two, or three fingers to perform touch-screen tasks such as scrolling, switching through open apps, and zooming. The mouse also allows you to perform traditional mouse tasks, such as moving the cursor when you move the mouse.

FIGURE 2.12 The Logitech Touch Mouse features multitouch technology that lets you perform a variety of touch-screen tasks using the surface of the mouse by tapping, clicking, and using various finger movements. *(Hugh Threlfall/Alamy)*

What input devices do laptops use? Most laptops have an integrated pointing device, such as a **touch pad (**or **trackpad)**, a small, touch-sensitive area at the base of the keyboard. Mac laptops include multitouch trackpads, which don't have buttons but are controlled by various one-, two-, three-, and four-finger actions. For example, scrolling is controlled by brushing two fingers along the trackpad in any direction. Most touch pads are sensitive to taps, interpreting them as mouse clicks. Most laptops also have buttons under or near the pad to record mouse clicks.

What input devices are used with games? Game controllers such as joysticks, game pads, and steering wheels are also considered input devices because they send data to the computer. Game controllers, which are similar to the devices used on gaming consoles such as the Xbox One and the PlayStation, are also available for use with computers. They have buttons and miniature pointing devices that provide input to the computer. Most game controllers, such as those for Rock Band and the Wii system, are wireless to provide extra mobility.

Image Input

What are popular input devices for images? Digital cameras, camcorders, and cell phones are common devices for capturing pictures and video and are all considered input devices. These devices can connect to your computer with a cable, transmit data wirelessly, or transfer data automatically through the Internet. **Scanners** can also input images. They work similarly to a photocopy machine; however, instead of generating the image on paper, they create a digital image, which you can then print, save, or e-mail.

How do I capture live video from my computing device? A **webcam** is a small camera that sits on top of your computer monitor (connected to your computer by a cable) or is built into a laptop, tablet, or smartphone. Although webcams are able to capture still images, they're used mostly for capturing and transmitting live video. Videoconferencing technology lets a person using a device equipped with a webcam and a microphone transmit video and audio across the Internet. Video call sites such as Skype (see the Try This in Chapter 1, pages 12–13) and ooVoo (see Figure 2.13) make it easy to videoconference with as many as 12 people. You can also exchange files, swap control of computers, and text message during the call. There is also a mobile application to make it easy to conference on the go.

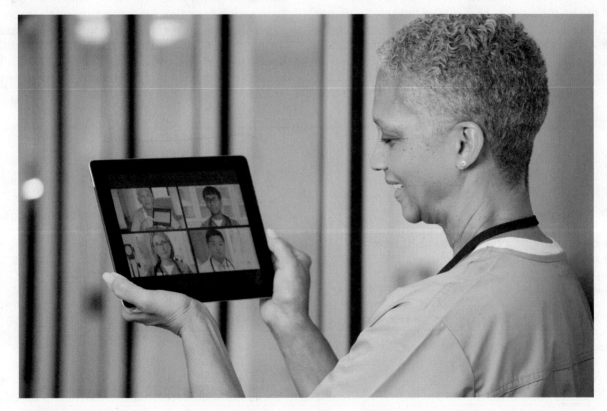

FIGURE 2.13 Videoconferencing is simplified with software from **ooVoo.com**. *(Ariel Skelley/Getty Images.209209)*

Touch-screen technology was developed in 1971 and used primarily with ATMs and fast-food order displays. The technology for monitors and other displays was made popular by the iPod Touch in 2007 and is now in many smartphones, tablets, and laptop and desktop monitors. Windows 8 finally brought the touch-screen interface to Windows users. But how do touch-screen monitors know where you're touching? How do they know what you want them to do?

The basic idea behind touch screens is pretty straightforward—when you place your finger or stylus on a screen, it changes the physical state of the screen and registers your touch. The location of your touch is then translated into a command. Three basic systems are used to recognize a person's touch: *resistive, capacitive,* and *surface acoustic wave.* All of these systems require the basic components of a touch-responsive glass panel, controller, and software driver, combined with a display and computer processor.

The *resistive system* maps the exact location of the pressure point created when a user touches the screen. The *capacitive system* (see Figure 2.14) uses the change in the electrical charge on the glass panel of the monitor, which is created by the user's touch, to generate a location. The third technology, *surface acoustic wave system,* uses two transducers (electrical devices that convert energy from one form to another) that are placed along the *x* and *y* axes of the monitor's glass plate. Reflectors, which

FIGURE 2.14 Some basic touch screens use a capacitive system to detect touches and translate them into meaningful commands that are understood by the computer's operating system.

are also placed on the glass, are used to reflect an electric signal sent from the sending transducer to the receiving transducer. The receiving transducer determines whether the signal has been disturbed by a touch event and locates the touch instantly. With all three systems, the display's software driver then translates the touch into something the operating system can understand, similar to how a mouse driver translates a mouse's movements into a click or drag.

Sound Input

How do my computing devices benefit from accepting sound input? In addition to letting others hear you in a videoconference, equipping your device to accept sound input opens up a variety of possibilities. You can conduct audio conferences with work colleagues, chat with friends or family over the Internet, record podcasts, and more. Inputting sound to your computer requires using a **microphone (or mic),** a device that lets you capture sound waves (such as your voice) and transfer them to digital format on your computer. Most laptop and tablet computers come with built-in microphones.

What types of add-on microphones are available? For specialized situations, built-in microphones don't always provide the best performance. You may want to consider adding other types of microphones, such as those shown in Figure 2.16, to your system for the best results. ■

Because the resistive system uses pressure to register a touch, it doesn't matter if the touch is created by a finger or another device. On the other hand, a capacitive system must have conductive input, so generally a finger is required. The surface acoustic wave system allows touches by any object.

The iPhone introduced another complexity to the touch-screen system—a multitouch user interface. In addition to just pressing the screen in one location, multitouch technology can process multiple simultaneous touches on the screen. For example, pinching or spreading out your thumb and finger together makes the display zoom out and in, respectively. The features of each touch, such as size, shape, and location, are also determined.

A touch-sensitive screen, like the one used with the iPhone and iPad and with many other smartphones and tablets, arranges the capacitors in a coordinate system so the circuitry can sense changes at each point along the grid (see Figure 2.15). Consequently, every point on the grid generates its own signal when touched, and can do so even as another signal is being generated simultaneously. The signals are then relayed to the device's processor. This allows the device to determine the location and movement of simultaneous touches in multiple locations.

After detecting the position and type of touch occurring on the display, the device's processor combines this information with the information it has about the application in use and what was being done in the application when the touch occurred. The processor relays that information to the program in use, and the command is executed. All this happens seemingly instantaneously.

FIGURE 2.15 Multitouch screens use a coordinate-based grid to arrange the capacitors so the circuitry can detect and respond to multiple touches occurring at the same time.

FIGURE 2.16

Types of Microphones

MICROPHONE TYPE	ATTRIBUTES	BEST USED FOR	MICROPHONE TYPE	ATTRIBUTES	BEST USED FOR
Close Talk	• Attached to a headset (allows for listening) • Leaves hands free	• Video conferencing • Phone calls • Speech recognition software	**Unidirectional**	• Picks up sounds from only one direction	• Recordings with one voice (podcasts)
Omnidirectional	• Picks up sounds equally well from all directions	• Conference calls in meeting rooms	**Clip-on (Lavalier)**	• Clips to clothing • Available as wireless	• Presentations requiring freedom of movement • Leaves hands free for writing on whiteboards

You've probably heard news stories about people using computers to unleash viruses or commit identity theft. You may also have read about students who were prosecuted for illegally sharing copyrighted material, such as songs and videos. These are both examples of *unethical* behavior while using a computer. However, what constitutes *ethical* behavior while using a computer?

Loosely defined, *ethics* is a system of moral principles, rules, and accepted standards of conduct (see Figure 2.17). So what are the accepted standards of conduct when using computers? The Computer Ethics Institute has developed the Ten Commandments of Computer Ethics, which is widely cited as a benchmark for companies developing computer usage and compliance policies for employees. These guidelines are applicable for schools and students, as well. The ethical computing guidelines listed below are based on the Computer Ethics Institute's work:

FIGURE 2.17 Strive to take the "high road" and behave ethically by not claiming others' work as your own intellectual output. *(Andy Dean Photography/Shutterstock)*

Ethical Computing Guidelines

1. Avoid causing harm to others when using computers.
2. Do not interfere with other people's efforts at accomplishing work with computers.
3. Resist the temptation to snoop in other people's computer files.
4. Do not use computers to commit theft.
5. Agree not to use computers to promote lies.
6. Do not use software (or make illegal copies for others) without paying the creator for it.
7. Avoid using other people's computer resources without appropriate authorization or proper compensation.
8. Do not claim other people's intellectual output as your own.
9. Consider the social consequences of the products of your computer labor.
10. Only use computers in ways that show consideration and respect for others.

The United States has enacted laws that support some of these guidelines, such as Guideline 6, the breaking of which would violate copyright laws, and Guideline 4, which is enforceable under numerous federal and state larceny laws. Other guidelines, however, require more subtle interpretation as to what behavior is unethical because there are no laws designed to enforce them.

Consider Guideline 7, which covers unauthorized use of resources. The school you attend probably provides computer resources for you to use for coursework. But if your school gives you access to computers and the Internet, is it ethical for you to use those resources to run an online business on the weekends? Although it might not be technically illegal, you're tying up computer resources that other students could use for their intended purpose: learning and completing coursework. (This behavior also violates Guidelines 2 and 10.)

Throughout the chapters in this book, we touch on many topics related to these guidelines. So keep them in mind as you study, and think about how they relate to the actions you take as you use computers in your life.

output DEVICES

An **output device** lets you send processed data out of your computer in the form of text, pictures (graphics), sounds (audio), or video. The most common output device is a **monitor** (sometimes referred to as a **display screen**), which displays text, graphics, and video as soft copies (copies you can see only on screen). Another common output device is the **printer**, which creates hard copies (copies you can touch) of text and graphics. Speakers and earphones (or earbuds) are the output devices for sound.

Monitors

What are the different types of monitors? The most common type of monitor is a **liquid crystal display (LCD)**. An LCD monitor, also called a flat-panel monitor, is light and energy efficient. Some newer monitors use **light-emitting diode (LED)** technology, which is more energy efficient and may have better color accuracy and thinner panels than LCD monitors. LCD flat-panel monitors have replaced cathode ray tube (CRT) monitors. CRT monitors are considered **legacy technology**, or computing devices that use techniques, parts, and methods that are no longer popular. Although legacy technology may still be functional, it has been replaced by newer technological advances.

Organic light-emitting diode (OLED) displays use organic compounds that produce light when exposed to an electric current. Unlike LCDs and LEDs, OLEDs do not require a backlight to function and therefore draw less power and have a much thinner display, sometimes as thin as 3 mm. They are also brighter and more environmentally friendly than LCDs. Because of their lower power needs, OLED displays run longer on a single battery charge than do LEDs, which is why OLED technology is probably the technology used in your cell phone, iPod, and digital camera.

Companies like LG are now working on transparent and flexible OLED display screens (see Figure 2.18). These screens allow you to see what is behind the screen while still being able to display information on the screen. These types of screens present interesting possibilities for augmented reality. *Augmented reality (AR)* is a view of a real-world environment whose elements are *augmented* (or supplemented) by some type of computer-generated sensory input such as video, graphics, or GPS data (see Chapter 1, pages 20–21). For instance, if you had a transparent screen on your smartphone and held it up to view street signs that were in English, you could possibly have your phone display the signs in another language. Currently, applications like this exist but require the use of a camera as well as your screen. But transparent screens will eliminate the need for the camera.

How do LCD monitors work? Monitor screens are grids made up of millions of tiny dots, called **pixels**. When these

FIGURE 2.18 Because they don't need a backlight, OLED displays can be made transparent and flexible!. *Yonhap/EPA/Newscom*

pixels are illuminated by the light waves generated by a fluorescent panel at the back of your screen, they create the images you see on the screen or monitor. Each pixel is actually made up of four yellow, red, blue, and green subpixels; some newer TVs further split the subpixels into upper and lower, which can brighten and darken independently. LCD monitors are made of two or more sheets of material filled with a liquid crystal solution (see Figure 2.19). A fluorescent panel at the back of the LCD monitor generates light waves. When electric current passes through the liquid crystal solution, the crystals move around and either block the fluorescent light or let the light shine through. This blocking or passing of light by the crystals causes images to form on the screen. The various combinations of yellow, red, blue, and green make up the components of color we see on our monitors.

What factors affect the quality of an LCD monitor? When choosing an LCD monitor, the most important factors to consider are aspect ratio and resolution. The **aspect ratio** is the width-to-height proportion of a monitor. Traditionally, aspect ratios have been 4:3, but newer monitors are available with an aspect ratio of 16:9 to accommodate HD format video. The screen **resolution**, or the clearness or sharpness of the image, reflects the number of pixels on the screen. An LCD monitor may have a native (or maximum) resolution of 1600 × 1200, meaning it contains 1,600 vertical columns with 1,200 pixels

FIGURE 2.19 A magnification of a single pixel in a conventional LCD monitor. (The newest 4K resolution TVs and monitors also have a yellow subpixel.)

in each column. The higher the resolution, the sharper and clearer the image will be, but generally, the resolution of an LCD monitor is dictated by the screen size and aspect ratio. Although you can change the resolution of an LCD monitor beyond its native resolution, the images will become

distorted. Generally, you should buy a monitor with the highest resolution available for the screen size (measured in inches). Figure 2.20 lists these and other factors to consider when judging the quality of an LCD monitor.

Is a bigger screen size always better? The bigger the monitor, the more you can display, and depending on what you want to display, size may matter. In general, the larger the panel, the larger number of pixels it can display. For example, a 27-inch monitor can display 2560 × 1440 pixels, whereas a 21.5-inch monitor may only be able to display 1680 × 1050 pixels. However, most new monitors have at least the 1920 × 1080 resolution required to display Blu-ray movies.

Larger screens can also allow you to view multiple documents or web pages at the same time, creating the effect of using two separate monitors side by side. However, buying two smaller monitors might be cheaper than buying one large monitor. For either option—a big screen or two separate screens—check that your computer has the appropriate video hardware to support these display devices.

What other features should I look for in an LCD monitor? Some monitors, especially those on laptop

FIGURE 2.20

Factors to Consider When Shopping for a Monitor

FACTOR	POSSIBLE PROBLEMS	LOOK FOR
Aspect ratio: Width-to-height proportion of a screen	• An odd aspect ratio may make images look distorted	• Ratios of 4:3 or 16:9 (HDTV)
Screen resolution: Number of pixels displayed on the screen	• Low screen resolution = unclear image • High resolution on a small size monitor results in image being too small	• Highest resolution monitor is capable of displaying (make sure you are comfortable viewing that size image)
Contrast ratio: Difference in light intensity between brightest white and darkest black a monitor can produce	• Ratio too low results in colors fading when adjusting brightness	• Ratios between 400:1 and 1,000:1
Viewing angle: Distance in degrees from which you can move to the side of (or above or below) a monitor before the image degrades	• Angle too low means people not sitting directly in front of the monitor will see a poor image	• 150 degrees or more is preferable
Brightness: Greatest amount of light showing when the monitor is displaying pure white (measured in candelas per square meter [cd/m^2] or *nits*)	• Image will be hard to see in bright rooms if brightness level is too low	• $300 \ cd/m^2$ or greater
Response time: Time it takes for a pixel to change color (in milliseconds)	• High response time results in images appearing jerky	• Seek lowest possible response time if viewing live action sports

BITS&BYTES

Forget HDTV...Here Comes Ultra HD!

Now that everyone loves their HDTVs, what can manufacturers do next? Ultra HD (otherwise known as 4K) TV is the emerging standard. HDTVs feature a resolution of 1920 × 1080 pixels (height and width, respectively). Ultra HD TVs, on the other hand, boast 3840 × 2160 resolution, which provides screens with four times as many pixels as HDTV devices. More pixels generally provides a sharper picture on a large screen, so screen sizes of 50 inches and up should have a noticeable difference in picture quality.

So should you throw away your HDTV and replace it with an Ultra HD TV? Probably not yet. Ultra HD TVs are expensive, and there is not much programming available yet in the Ultra HD format. But as more programming becomes available and prices of Ultra HD TVs fall, it may soon make sense to consider a higher resolution TV.

Or, you may just hang on and wait for 8K TVs (7680 × 4320 resolution), which may be available on the consumer market within three years. The technology to record 8K already exists—in fact, the BBC recorded much of the 2012 Summer Olympics in 8K format. Whatever happens, expect your TV picture to just keep getting better!

computers, come with built-in features such as speakers, webcams, and microphones. A built-in multiformat memory card reader is convenient for displaying images directly on the monitor or for downloading pictures quickly from a camera memory card to your PC. Another nice feature to look for in a desktop LCD monitor is a built-in USB port. This feature lets you connect extra peripherals easily without reaching around the back of the PC.

How do I show output to a large group of people? A **projector** lets you project images from your computing device onto a wall or viewing screen. Projectors are commonly used in business and education settings such as conference rooms and classrooms. Many projectors are small and lightweight (see Figure 2.21), and some, such as the AAXA P3X Pico, are small enough to fit in the palm of your hand. These portable projectors are ideal for businesspeople who have to make presentations at client locations. *Entertainment projectors,* such as the Epson Home Cinema 5030UB, include stereo speakers and an array of multimedia connectors, making them a good option for use in the home to display TV programs, DVDs, digital images, or video games in a large format. If your computing device is equipped with an HDMI port, you can also choose to connect your computer directly to an HDTV.

FIGURE 2.21 Small projectors provide portability as well as connectivity to your devices. *(Wenn Ltd/Alamy)*

Printers

What are the different types of printers?
There are two primary categories of printers: inkjet and laser, both of which are considered nonimpact printers. A **nonimpact printer** such as an inkjet printer sprays ink or uses laser beams to transfer marks onto the paper. An **impact printer** has tiny hammer-like keys that strike the paper through an inked ribbon to make marks on the paper. For most users, impact printers are legacy technology.

What are the advantages of inkjet printers?
An **inkjet printer** (see Figure 2.22) is the type of printer found in many homes. These printers are popular because they're affordable and produce high-quality printouts quickly and quietly. Inkjet printers work by spraying tiny drops of ink onto paper and are great for printing black-and-white text as well as color images. In fact, when loaded with the right paper, higher-end inkjet printers can print images that look like professional-quality photos. One thing to consider when buying an inkjet printer is the type and cost of the ink cartridges the printer needs. Some printers use two cartridges: black and color. Others use four or more cartridges: typically, black, magenta, cyan, and yellow.

Why would I want a laser printer?
A **laser printer** uses laser beams and static electricity to deliver toner (similar to ink) onto the correct areas of the page (see Figure 2.23). Heat is used to fuse the toner to the page, making the image permanent. Laser printers are often used in office or classroom settings because they print faster than inkjet printers

FIGURE 2.23 Laser printers print quickly and offer high-quality printouts. *(Xerox Corporation)*

and produce higher-quality printouts. Black-and-white laser printers have also been common in homes for a decade. Over the past few years, the price of color laser printers has fallen dramatically, making them price competitive with high-end inkjet printers. Thus, color laser printers are a viable option for the home. If you print a high volume of pages, consider a laser printer. When you include the price of ink or toner in the overall cost, color laser printers can be more economical than inkjets.

What's the best way to print from portable devices such as tablets and smartphones?
Wireless printers are a good option for home networks as they let several people print to the same printer from different devices and any location in the home. There are two types of wireless printers: WiFi and Bluetooth. Both WiFi and Bluetooth printers have a range of up to approximately 300 feet. WiFi, however, sends data more quickly than Bluetooth.

Wireless printers are also great for printing from portable devices. If you're using a device running Apple's iOS (such as an iPhone), AirPrint makes printing easy. AirPrint is a feature of iOS that facilitates printing to AirPrint-compatible wireless printers, and many printers produced today are AirPrint compatible.

For non-Apple mobile devices (or if your printer isn't compatible with AirPrint), you should try other solutions, such as Presto by Collobos Software and ThinPrint Cloud Printer by Cortado. Once you install one of these apps on your portable device, you can send documents to printers that are connected to PCs and Macs on your home network. It makes printing from mobile devices as simple as hitting print on your laptop.

FIGURE 2.22 Inkjet printers are popular among home users, especially with the rise of digital photography. Many inkjet printers are optimized for printing photos from digital cameras. *(The Vectorminator/Shutterstock)*

FIGURE 2.24 Specialty printers: (a) all-in-one printer, (b) plotter, (c) thermal printer. *(Adisa/Fotolai; Xerox corportation; Velkit/Fotolia)*

Can I carry my printer with me? Although some inkjet printers are small enough to be considered portable, you may want to consider a printer designed for portability. These compact printers can connect to your computer, tablet, or smartphone via Bluetooth technology or through a USB port. Portable printers are often compact enough to fit in a briefcase or backpack, are lightweight, and can run on batteries as well as AC power.

Are there any other types of specialty printers? Although you'll probably use laser or inkjet printers most often, you might also encounter several other types of printers (shown in Figure 2.24):

- An **all-in-one printer** combines the functions of a printer, scanner, copier, and fax into one machine. Popular for their space-saving convenience, all-in-one printers may use either inkjet or laser technology.
- A **plotter** prints oversize pictures that require the drawing of precise and continuous lines, such as maps and architectural plans. Plotters use a computer-controlled pen that provides a greater level of precision than the series of dots that laser or inkjet printers make.

 ACTIVE HELPDESK
Using Output Devices

In this Active Helpdesk, you'll play the role of a helpdesk staffer, fielding questions about different output devices.

- A **thermal printer** works either by melting wax-based ink onto ordinary paper (a process called *thermal wax transfer printing*) or by burning dots onto specially coated paper (a process called *direct thermal printing*). Thermal printers are used in stores to print receipts and in airports for electronic ticketing, and many models feature wireless technology. Thermal printers are also popular for mobile printing in conjunction with smartphones and tablets.

How do I choose the best printer? Your first step is to decide what your primary printing need is. If you're planning to print color photos and graphics, an inkjet printer or color laser printer is a must, even though the cost per page will be higher. If you'll be printing mostly black-and-white, text-based documents or will be sharing your printer with others, a black-and-white laser printer is best because of its speed and overall economy for volume printing. It's also important to determine whether you want just a printer or a device that prints and scans, copies, or faxes (an all-in-one). In addition, you should decide whether you need to print from mobile devices.

Once you have narrowed down the *type* of printer you want, you can use the criteria listed in Figure 2.25 to help you determine the best model to meet your needs.

Sound Output

What are the output devices for sound? Most computers include inexpensive **speakers**, which are the output devices for sound. These speakers are sufficient to play the standard audio clips you find on the web and usually for letting you participate in videoconferencing or phone

BITS&BYTES

Does It Matter What Paper I Print On?

The quality of your printer is only part of what controls the quality of a printed image. The paper you use and the printer settings that control the amount of ink used are equally important.

- If you're printing text-only documents for personal use, using low-cost paper is fine. You also may want to consider selecting draft mode in your printer settings to conserve ink. However, if you're printing more formal documents, such as business correspondence, you may want to choose a higher-quality paper (determined by the paper's weight, whiteness, and brightness) and adjust your print setting to "normal" or "best."
- The weight of paper is measured in pounds, with 20 pounds being standard. A heavier paper may be best for projects such as brochures, but be sure to check that your printer can handle the added thickness of the paper.
- The degree of paper whiteness is a matter of personal preference. Generally, the whiter the paper, the brighter the printed color. However, for documents that are more formal, you may want to use a creamier color.
- The brightness of paper usually varies from 85 to 94. The higher the number, the brighter the paper, and the easier it is to read printed text.
- Opacity, or the "show through" of ink from one side of the paper to the other, is especially important if you're printing on both sides of the paper.

If you're printing photos, paper quality can have a big impact on your results. Photo paper is more expensive than regular paper and comes in a variety of textures ranging from matte to high gloss. For a photo-lab look, high-gloss paper is the best choice. Semigloss (often referred to as satin) is good for formal portraits, while a matte surface is often used for black-and-white photo printing.

calls over the Internet. However, if you plan to digitally edit audio files or are particular about how your music sounds, you may want a more sophisticated speaker system, such as one that includes subwoofers (special speakers that produce only low bass sounds) and surround-sound speakers. A **surround-sound speaker** is a system of speakers and audio processing that envelops the listener in a 360-degree field of sound. In addition, wireless speaker systems are available to help you avoid cluttering up your rooms with speaker wires.

FIGURE 2.25

Major Printer Attributes

ATTRIBUTE	CONSIDERATIONS
Speed	• Print speed is measured in *pages per minute (PPM)*. • Black-and-white documents print faster than color documents. • Laser printers often print faster than inkjets.

Resolution	• Resolution refers to a printer's image clarity.
	• Resolution is measured in *dots per inch (dpi)*.
	• Higher dpi = greater level of detail and clarity.
	• Recommended dpi:
	  • Black-and-white text: 300
	  • General purpose images: 1200
	  • Photos: 4800

Color Output	• Printers with separate cartridges for each color produce the best quality output. • Inkjet and laser color printers generally have four cartridges (black, cyan, magenta, and yellow). • Higher-quality printers have six cartridges (the four above plus light cyan and light magenta). • With separate cartridges, you only need to replace the empty one.
Cost of Consumables	• Consumables are printer cartridges and paper. • Printer cartridges can exceed the cost of some printers. • Consumer magazines such as *Consumer Reports* can help you research costs.

If you work in close proximity to other employees or travel with a laptop, you may need to use headphones or earbuds to avoid distracting other people. Both devices plug into the same jack on the computing device to which speakers connect. Studies of users of portable media players have shown that hearing might be damaged by excessive volume, especially when using earbuds because they fit into the ear canals. Exercise caution when using these devices. ■

Before moving on to Part 2:
- **Watch Replay Video 2.1** ↻.
- **Then check your understanding of what you've learned so far.**

check your understanding // review & practice

For a quick review to see what you've learned so far, answer the following questions. Visit **pearsonhighered.com/techinaction** to check your answers.

multiple choice

1. Which of the four major functions of a computer is responsible for manipulating, calculating, and organizing data into information?
   a. input
   b. processing
   c. storage
   d. output

2. The system unit is a component of which type of computer?
   a. a tablet computer
   b. an ultrabook
   c. an embedded computer
   d. a desktop computer

3. Which of the following display screens does not require a backlight to function?
   a. an organic light-emitting diode (OLED) display
   b. a liquid crystal display (LCD)
   c. a light-emitting diode (LED) display
   d. a cathode ray tube (CRT)

4. What type of printer uses wax-based ink?
   a. inkjet
   b. plotter
   c. thermal
   d. laser

5. When buying a monitor, which factor determines the difference in light intensity?
   a. screen resolution
   b. contrast ratio
   c. color depth
   d. aspect ratio

To take an autograded version of this review, please go to the companion website at **pearsonhighered.com/techinaction,** or go your MyITLab course.

Continue »

TRY THIS

What's Inside My Computer?

Understanding what capabilities your current computer has is one of the first steps toward computer literacy. In this exercise, you'll learn how to explore the components of your Windows computer.

Step 1 To gather information about the storage devices on your computer, on the Start screen, click **File Explorer** (previously called Windows Explorer) to switch to the Desktop and display File Explorer. In the navigation pane, click **This PC** to display information about your computer's drives.

Start Screen

File Explorer

Step 2 The File Explorer This PC screen displays information about internal storage devices (such as internal hard drives), optical storage devices (such as DVD drives), and portable storage devices (such as flash drives and external hard drives). The total amount of usable storage space, as well as the amount of space actually free (unused), on the devices is shown. To display the System screen, click the Computer tab on the File Explorer ribbon, and then the System properties button.

Ribbon

Total device storage space

Space available (unused or free)

Step 3 You can gather quite a bit of information from the System screen, such as:

- Version of Windows
- Type of processor
- Speed of the processor
- Amount of RAM installed
- System type (32-bit or 64-bit)

Make This

TOOL: App Inventor 2

MAKE: A Mobile App

Want to build your own Android app from scratch? You can, with a simple tool called **App Inventor**. To get started, have ready:

1. A computer connected to a WiFi network
2. The Chrome browser
3. A Google account
4. The MIT AI2 Companion app
5. [optional] An Android device connected to the same WiFI network

In this exercise, you'll explore the **App Inventor** tool and begin working with your first simple app. As you'll see, making your device work for you is as easy as drag and drop with **App Inventor**.

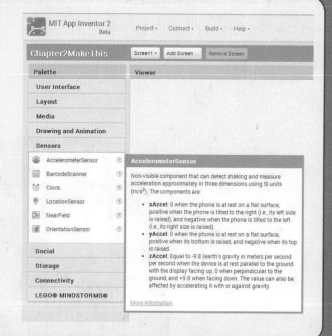

App Inventor is a programming platform used to create apps for Android devices. Using App Inventor, you can easily drag and drop components to design your App's interface...and its behavior.

For the instructions for this exercise, please go to pearsonhighered.com/techinaction or MyITLab.

Processing, Storage, and Connectivity

So far, we have explored the components of your computer that you use to input and output data. But where does the processing take place, and where is the data stored? And how does your computer connect with peripherals and other computers?

 processing and memory on the
MOTHERBOARD

The **motherboard** is the main circuit board that contains the central electronic components of the computer, including the computer's processor (CPU), its memory, and the many circuit boards that help the computer function (see Figure 2.26). On a desktop, the motherboard is located inside the system unit, the metal or plastic case that also houses the power source and all the storage devices (CD/DVD drive and hard drive). In a laptop or all-in-one computer, the system unit is combined with the monitor and the keyboard into a single package.

What's on the motherboard besides the CPU and memory? The motherboard also includes slots for **expansion cards (or adapter cards)**, which are circuit boards that provide additional functionality. Typical expansion cards found in the system unit are sound and video cards. A **sound card** provides a connection for the speakers and microphone, whereas a **video card** provides a connection for the monitor. Laptops and tablets have video and sound capabilities integrated into their motherboards. High-end desktops use expansion cards to provide video and sound capabilities.

Other expansion cards provide a means for network and Internet connections. A **network interface card (NIC)**, which enables your computer to connect with other computers or to a cable modem to facilitate a high-speed Internet connection, is often integrated into the motherboard. Lastly, some expansion cards provide additional USB and FireWire ports.

Expansion slots

Memory (RAM) slots

CPU socket

Ports

FIGURE 2.26 A motherboard contains the socket for the computer's processor (CPU), the memory (RAM) modules, ports, and slots for expansion cards. (S.Dashkevych/Shutterstock)

Memory

What exactly is RAM? Random access memory (RAM) is the place in a computer where the programs and data the computer is currently using are stored. RAM is much faster to read from and write to than the hard drive and other forms of storage. The processor can request the RAM's contents, which can be located, opened, and delivered to the CPU for processing in a few nanoseconds (billionths of a second). If you look at a motherboard, you'll see RAM as a series of small cards (called *memory cards* or *memory modules*) plugged into slots on the motherboard (see Figure 2.26).

Because the entire contents of RAM are erased when you turn off the computer, RAM is a temporary or **volatile storage** location. To save data permanently, you need to save it to your hard drive or to another permanent storage device such as a CD or flash drive.

Does the motherboard contain any other kinds of memory besides RAM? In addition to RAM, the motherboard contains a form of memory called **read-only memory (ROM)**. ROM holds all the instructions the computer needs to start up when it's powered on. Unlike data stored in RAM, which is volatile storage, the instructions stored in ROM are permanent, making ROM a **nonvolatile storage** location, which means the data isn't erased when the power is turned off.

Processing

What is the CPU? The **central processing unit (CPU, or processor)** is sometimes referred to as the "brains" of the computer because it controls all the functions performed by the computer's other components and processes all the commands issued to it by software instructions. Modern CPUs can perform as many as tens of billions of tasks per second without error, making them extremely powerful components.

How is processor speed measured? Processor speed is measured in units of hertz (Hz). Hertz is a measurement of machine cycles per second. A machine cycle is the process of the CPU getting the data or instructions from RAM and decoding the instructions into something the computer can understand. Once the CPU has decoded the instructions, it executes them and stores the result back in system memory. Current systems run at speeds measured in **gigahertz (GHz)**, or billions of machine cycles per second. Therefore, a 3.8 GHz processor performs work at a rate of 3.8 billion machine cycles per second. It's important to realize, however, that CPU processor speed alone doesn't determine the performance of the CPU.

What else determines processor performance? Although speed is an important consideration when determining processor

performance, CPU performance is also affected by other factors. One factor is the number of *cores,* or processing paths, a processor has. Initially, processors could handle only one instruction at a time. Now, processors have been designed so that they can have two, four, or even ten different paths, allowing them to process more than one instruction at a time (see Figure 2.27). Applications such as virus protection software and the operating system, which are always running behind the scenes, can have their own processor paths, freeing up the other paths to run other applications such as a web browser, Word, or iTunes more efficiently.

Besides the number of cores, what other factors determine processing power? The "best" processor will depend on your particular needs and is not always the processor with the highest processor speed and the greatest number of cores. Intel, one of the leading manufacturers of computer processor chips, has created a pictorial rating system for CPU chips. Intel provides a website (**ark.intel.com**) that assists in comparing the performance of different models of CPUs. ∎

FIGURE 2.27 With multi-core processors, CPUs can work in parallel, processing two or more separate programs at the same time instead of switching back and forth between them.

storing data and
INFORMATION

Because RAM is volatile storage, it can't be used to store information indefinitely. To save your data and information permanently, you need to save it to a nonvolatile storage device, such as a hard drive, cloud storage location, DVD, or flash drive.

Hard Drives

Are there different kinds of hard drives? The **hard disk drive (HDD,** or **hard drive)** is your computer's primary device for permanent storage of software and documents. The hard drive is a nonvolatile storage device. An **internal hard drive** resides within the system unit and usually holds all permanently stored programs and data. Today's internal hard drives (see Figure 2.28) have capacities of as much as 8 TB or more. **External hard drives** offer similar storage capacities but reside outside the system unit and connect to the computer via a port.

The most common type of hard drive has moveable parts—spinning platters and a moving arm with a read/write head—that can fail and lead to devastating disk failure. However, the **solid-state drive (SSD)** has recently become a popular option for ultrabooks and laptop storage. SSDs have no moving parts, so they're more efficient, run with no noise, emit little heat, and require little power. In addition, they're less likely to fail after being bumped or dropped.

Permanent storage devices are located in your desktop or laptop computer in a space called a **drive bay**. There are two kinds of drive bays:

1. *Internal drive bays* cannot be seen or accessed from outside the system unit. Generally, internal drive bays are reserved for internal hard drives.
2. *External drive bays* can be seen and accessed from outside the system unit. External drive bays house CD and DVD drives, for example. On desktop computers, sometimes there are empty external drive bays that can be used to install additional drives. These extra spaces are covered by a faceplate on the front panel. Laptop computers generally do not give you the ability to add additional drives. Such expansion is done by attaching an external drive to the computer through a USB port.

FIGURE 2.28 Internal hard drives are a computer's primary nonvolatile storage. *(Ragnarock/Shutterstock)*

Cloud Storage

How can I easily access my files if I constantly switch between devices? You may find yourself using multiple devices, such as a smartphone, laptop, and a tablet, at different times during the day. Invariably, you'll find you need access to a current version of a file that is stored on a device other than the one you're using. If your devices are connected to the Internet, cloud storage provides a convenient option.

Cloud storage refers to using a service that keeps your files on the Internet (in the "cloud") rather than storing your files solely on a local device. Using a cloud storage service requires that you install software/an app on your device. A popular web-based application for storing files on the cloud is Dropbox. Dropbox supports computers running Windows, OS X, and Linux as well as many smartphones and tablets. After installing the Dropbox software on your devices, any files you save in the Dropbox folder are accessible by all your other devices via the Internet. You can also share folders in Dropbox with other Dropbox users, making it ideal for group projects.

For example, when you save a history term paper to Dropbox on your laptop, the Dropbox software also copies the paper onto a computer attached to the web. Now when you grab your smartphone and head off to class, you can access the paper created on your laptop through the Internet connection on your smartphone and make changes to it if necessary.

Dropbox storage capacity is limited to between 2 GB and 18 GB for free accounts. Other cloud storage alternatives include Microsoft OneDrive and Google Drive, each of which provide 15 GB of free space, and Apple iCloud, which offers 5 GB of free storage.

Portable Storage Options

How can I take my files with me without relying on cloud storage? For large portable storage needs, there are portable external hard drives, which are small enough to fit into your pocket and have storage capacities of 4 TB (or larger). These devices are lightweight and enclosed in a protective case. They attach to your computer via a USB port (see Figure 2.29).

FIGURE 2.29 Smaller, portable external hard drives enable you to take a significant amount of data and programs on the road with you. *(Inga Nielsen/Shutterstock)*

BITS&BYTES

Green Computing

"Going green" is a goal for many modern businesses. The computing industry is no exception. **Green computing** is a movement to encourage environmentally sustainable computing (or IT).

The goals of green computing are:

1. Reducing the use of hazardous processes or materials in the production of computing equipment
2. Producing products that use energy efficiently
3. Promoting the use of recyclable or biodegradable materials to facilitate safe disposal of products

However, it's not all up to the manufacturers. Here are a few ways you can practice green computing:

1. Turn off your computing devices when they are not in use.
2. Enable power-management features on your computing devices to reduce power consumption while they are in use.
3. Buy energy-efficient computing devices.
4. Dispose of old computing devices only at certified e-waste disposal facilities (or better yet, donate them).

A **flash drive** (sometimes referred to as a **jump drive**, **USB drive**, or **thumb drive**) uses solid-state flash memory, storing information on an internal memory chip (see Figure 2.30). When you plug a flash drive into your computer's USB port, it appears in the operating system as another disk drive. You can write data to it or read data from it as you would a hard drive. Because a flash drive contains no moving parts, it's quite durable. It's also tiny enough to fit in your pocket. Despite their size, flash drives can have significant storage capacity—currently as much as 1 TB. Often, flash drives are combined with other devices such as pens or pocketknives for added convenience.

New wireless flash drives, like the SanDisk Connect, are also appearing on the market to make transferring files from portable devices easier. Although they look like normal flash drives, these wireless drives can connect to your portable devices via WiFi after installing the appropriate app. Up to eight devices can be connected to the flash drive at once, and the drive can even stream media to three devices simultaneously. So your friend could be watching a movie stored on the flash drive while you're uploading pictures from your phone.

Another convenient means of portable storage is a **flash memory card**, such as an SD card. Like the flash drive, memory cards use solid-state flash memory. Most desktops and laptops include slots for flash memory cards, but if your computer is not equipped, there are memory card readers that you can plug into a USB port. Flash memory cards let you transfer digital data between your computer and devices such as digital cameras, smartphones, tablets, video cameras, and printers. Although incredibly small—some are even smaller than the size of a postage stamp—these memory

cards have capacities that exceed the capacity of a DVD. Figure 2.31 compares the storage capacities of hard drives and flash drives.

FIGURE 2.30 Flash drives are a convenient means of portable storage and come in many different shapes and sizes. *(ekler/Shutterstock)*

FIGURE 2.31

Hard Drive and Flash Drive Storage Capacity

DRIVE TYPE	IMAGE	TYPICAL CAPACITY	DRIVE TYPE	IMAGE	TYPICAL CAPACITY
Solid-state drive (SSD)		1 TB or more	Flash drive		256 GB or more
External portable hard drive		4 TB or more	Flash memory card		128 GB
Mechanical internal hard drive		As much as 8 TB or more			

Oleksiy Mark/Shutterstock; Julia Ivantsova/Shutterstock; D. Hurst/ Alamy; Cphoto/fotolia; ZUMA Press, Inc/Alamy

Optical Storage

What other kinds of storage devices are available?
Most desktop and laptop computers come with at least one **optical drive** that can read from and maybe even write to CDs, DVDs, or Blu-ray discs. Data is saved to such discs as tiny pits that are burned into the disc by a high-speed laser. **Compact discs (CDs)** were initially created to store audio files. **Digital video (or versatile) discs (DVDs)** are the same size and shape as CDs but can store up to 14 times more data than CDs.

What if you want even more storage capacity? Blu-ray is the latest incarnation of optical storage to hit the market. **Blu-ray discs (BDs)**, which are similar in size and shape to CDs and DVDs, can hold as much as 50 GB of data—enough to hold approximately 4.5 hours of movies in high-definition (HD) digital format. Many systems are now available with BD-ROM drives and even Blu-ray burners. External BD drives are

another inexpensive way to add HD storage capacity to your system. Figure 2.32 shows the storage capacities of the various optical storage media. ■

FIGURE 2.32

Optical Storage Media Capacities

MEDIUM TYPE	TYPICAL CAPACITY
Blu-ray (dual layer)	50 GB
Blu-ray	25 GB
DVD DL (dual layer)	8.5 GB
DVD	4.7 GB
CD	700 MB

connecting peripherals to the COMPUTER

Throughout this chapter, we have discussed peripheral devices that input, store, and output data and information. A **port** is a place through which a peripheral device attaches to the computer so that data can be exchanged between it and the operating system. Although peripherals may connect to devices wirelessly, ports are still often used for connections.

High-Speed and Data Transfer Ports

What is the fastest data transfer port available on today's computing devices? Thunderbolt is the newest input/output technology on the market. It was developed by Intel using fiber optic technology and can achieve blazingly fast transfer speeds of up to 20 Gb/s. **Thunderbolt ports** (see Figure 2.33) are very useful for laptops and ultrabooks because one Thunderbolt port can allow you to connect up to six different peripherals to your computer. Apple was the first computer maker to integrate the ports into their hardware although other manufacturers are now following suit.

What is the most common port on digital devices? A **universal serial bus (USB) port** is the port type most commonly used to connect input and output devices to the computer. This is mainly because of the ready availability of USB-compatible peripherals. USB ports can connect a wide variety of peripherals to computing devices, including keyboards, printers, mice, smartphones, external hard drives, flash drives, and digital cameras. The new USB 3.1 standard provides transfer speeds of 10 Gbps and charges devices faster than previous USB ports. USB ports come in three standard configurations (see Figure 2.34), plus the new Type-C connector (and port), which is expected to supplant older connections as USB 3.1 rolls out.

What other types of data transfer ports are there? You may also see other ports, especially on Apple computers. The current standard, **FireWire 800**, provides a fast transfer rate of 800 Mbps. Devices such as external hard drives and digital video cameras benefit from the speedy data transfer capabilities of FireWire. However, as more peripherals

FIGURE 2.33 Thunderbolt ports are slim and speedy, making them popular on today's ultrabooks and laptops. *(Paul Morris/Bloomberg/Getty Images)*

FIGURE 2.34 USB connector types (from left to right): standard, micro, and mini. *(Nikita Buida/Fotolia)*

are released with Thunderbolt capabilities, we should see FireWire declining in popularity.

Connectivity and Multimedia Ports

Which ports help me connect with other computers and the Internet? Another set of ports on your computer helps you communicate with other computers. A **connectivity port** can give you access to networks and the Internet. To find a connectivity port, look for a port that resembles a standard phone jack but is slightly larger. This port is called an **Ethernet port**. Ethernet ports transfer data at speeds up to 10,000 Mbps. You can use an Ethernet port to connect your computer to either a cable modem or a network.

How do I connect monitors and multimedia devices? Other ports on the back and sides of the computer include audio and video ports. Audio ports are where you connect headphones, microphones, and speakers to the computer. Whether you're attaching a monitor to a desktop computer, or adding a second, larger display to a laptop computer, you'll use a video port. HDMI ports are now the most common video port on computing devices.

A **high-definition multimedia interface (HDMI) port** is a compact audio–video interface that allows both HD video and uncompressed digital audio to be carried on one cable. Because HDMI can transmit uncompressed audio and video, there's no need to convert the signal, which could ultimately reduce the quality of the sound or picture. All currently available monitors, DVD players, televisions, and game consoles have at least one HDMI port (see Figure 2.35).

 ACTIVE HELPDESK
Exploring Storage Devices and Ports

In this Active Helpdesk, you'll play the role of a helpdesk staffer, fielding questions about the computer's main storage devices and how to connect various peripheral devices to the computer.

FIGURE 2.35 HDMI is the latest digital connector type for HD monitors, televisions, and home theater equipment. *(Feng Yu/Shutterstock)*

What ports might I encounter on older computers and peripherals? The **video graphics array (VGA) port** and the **digital video interface (DVI) port** are two ports to which older LCD monitors and televisions connect (see Figure 2.36). Some Apple computers still feature a Mini DisplayPort for connection of video peripherals. Adapters are available for the Mini DisplayPort that allow the connection of older DVI and VGA devices.

Adding Ports: Expansion Cards and Hubs

What if I don't have all the ports I need? If you're looking to add the newest ports to an older desktop computer or to expand the number of ports on it, you can install special expansion cards (Figure 2.37) into an open expansion slot on the motherboard to provide additional ports.

Another alternative is adding an expansion hub (shown in Figure 2.38). An expansion hub is a device that connects to one port, such as a USB port, to provide additional ports. It works like the multiplug extension cords used with electrical appliances. ∎

FIGURE 2.36 DVI (left) and VGA (right) cables are used to connect older LCD monitors and televisions to computing devices. *(Marek Kosmal/Fotolia)*

FIGURE 2.37 Expansion cards fit into slots on the motherboard in a desktop computer. *(Andrew Kitching/Alamy)*

FIGURE 2.38 If you don't have enough USB ports to support your USB devices, consider getting an expansion hub, which can add four or more USB ports to your system. *(Norman Chan/Fotolia)*

 SOUND BYTE
Port Tour: How Do I Hook It Up?

In this Sound Byte, you'll take a tour of both a desktop system and a laptop system to compare the number and variety of available ports. You'll also learn about the different types of ports and compare their speed and expandability.

power CONTROLS

What's the best way to turn my computer on and off? The **power supply**, which is housed inside the system unit, transforms the wall voltage to the voltages required by computer chips. Powering on your computer from a completely turned off state, such as when you start your computer in the morning, is called a **cold boot**. In Windows 8.1, you can turn your computer off by pressing the computer's power button or by using the Shut down option from the power icon found in the upper right-hand corner of the Start screen.

Should I turn off my computer every time I'm done using it? Some people say you should leave your computer on at all times. They argue that turning your computer on and off throughout the day subjects its components to stress because the heating and cooling process forces the components to expand and contract repeatedly. Other people say you should shut down your computer when you're not using it. They claim that it's not as environmentally friendly and that you'll end up wasting money on electricity from the computer running all the time.

Modern operating systems include power-management settings that allow the most power-hungry components of the system (the hard drive and monitor) to shut down after a short idle period. With the power-management options of Windows 8, for example, you only need to shut down your computer

completely when you need to repair or install hardware in the system unit or move it to another location. However, if you use your computer only for a little while each day, it would be best to power it off completely after each daily use.

Can I "rest" my computer without turning it off completely? In Windows 8.1, the main method of power management is Sleep. When your computer enters **Sleep mode**, all of the documents, applications, and data you were using remain in RAM (memory), where they're quickly accessible when you restart your computer.

In Sleep mode, the computer enters a state of greatly reduced power consumption, which saves energy. To put your computer into Sleep mode in Windows 8.1, click (or touch) the Power button on the Start screen, then select the Sleep option. To wake up your computer, press a key or the physical power button. In a few seconds, the computer will resume with exactly the same programs running and documents displayed as when you put it to sleep.

If you don't ever want to completely turn off your computer, you can change what happens when you press the power button or close the lid on your laptop. By accessing the Power Options System Settings window (see Figure 2.39), you can decide if you want your computer to Sleep, Hibernate, or Shut down when you press the power button. The **Hibernate**

FIGURE 2.39 You can determine what happens when you click the power button on your computer or close the lid through the Power Options System Settings screen.

>*To access Power Options System Settings, display the Control Panel, click* **Hardware and Sound,** *and then select* **Change what the power buttons do** *under Power Options.*

Define power buttons and turn on password protection

Choose the power settings that you want for your computer. The changes you make to the settings on this page apply to all of your power plans.

🛡️ Change settings that are currently unavailable

Power button and lid settings

	🔋 On battery	🔌 Plugged in
When I press the power button:	Hibernate ▾	Sleep ▾
When I close the lid:	Sleep ▾	Sleep ▾

Do nothing
Sleep
Hibernate
Shut down

Password protection on wakeup

⊙ Require a password (recommended)
When your computer wakes from sleep, no one can access your data without entering the correct password to unlock the computer. <u>Create or change your user account password</u>

○ Don't require a password
When your computer wakes from sleep, anyone can access your data because the computer isn't locked.

option is similar to Sleep except that your data is stored on your hard drive instead of in RAM and your computer is powered off. This uses much less battery power than Sleep and is a good choice if you won't be using your laptop for a long time and won't have the opportunity to charge it. However, Sleep is still a good option to choose if you just won't be using your computer for a short time. You may want to set your computer so it sleeps when you close the lid but hibernates when you press the power button, giving you quick access to either option.

What's the Restart option in Windows for? If you're using Windows 8.1, you have the option to restart the computer when you click (or touch) the Power button (see Figure 2.40). Restarting the system while it's powered on is called a **warm boot**. You might need to perform a warm boot if the operating system or other software application stops responding or if you've installed new programs. It takes less time to perform a warm boot than to power down completely and then restart all your hardware. ■

FIGURE 2.40 The Power button in Windows 8.1 presents several power options. For a warm boot, choose **Restart**. To power down the computer completely, choose **Shut down**. To put your computer into a lower power mode, select **Sleep**. *(Windows 8.1,)*

setting it
ALL UP

It's important that you understand not only your computer's components and how they work together but also how to set up these components safely. **Ergonomics** is the science that deals with the design and location of machines and furniture so that the people using them aren't subjected to an uncomfortable or unsafe experience. In terms of computing, ergonomics refers to how you set up your computer and other equipment to minimize your risk of injury or discomfort.

Why is ergonomics important? Studies suggest that teenagers, on average, spend 7.5 hours per day using computing devices. When you factor in other computer uses such as playing video games, there is great potential for injury. The repetitive nature of long-term computing activities can place too much stress on joints and pull at the tendons and muscles, causing repetitive stress injuries such as carpal tunnel syndrome and tendonitis. These injuries can take months or years to develop to a point where they become painful, and

by the time you notice the symptoms, the damage has already taken place. If you take precautionary measures now, you may prevent years of unnecessary pain later.

How can I avoid injuries when I'm working at my computer? As Figure 2.41 illustrates, it's important to arrange your monitor, chair, body, and keyboard in ways that will help you avoid injury, discomfort, and eyestrain. The following additional guidelines can help keep you comfortable and productive:

- **Position your monitor correctly.** Studies suggest it's best to place your monitor at least 25 inches from your eyes. Experts recommend that you position your monitor either at eye level or at an angle 15 to 20 degrees below your line of sight.

- **Purchase an adjustable chair.** Adjust the height of your chair so that your feet touch the floor (or use a footrest to get the right position). The back support needs to be adjustable

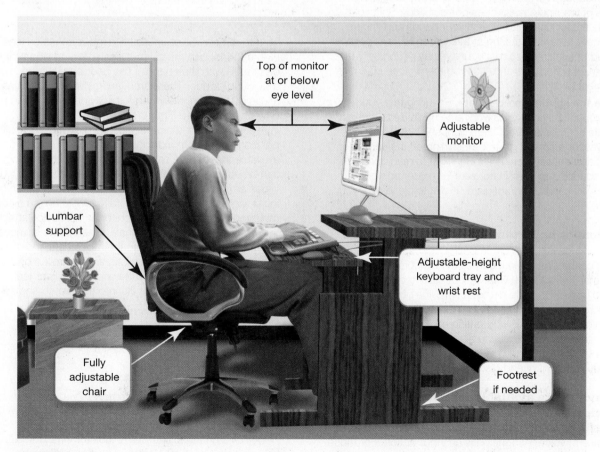

FIGURE 2.41 Using proper equipment that is adjusted correctly helps prevent repetitive strain injuries while working at a computer.

so that you can position it to support your lumbar (lower back) region. You should also be able to move the seat or adjust the back so that you can sit without exerting pressure on your knees. If your chair doesn't adjust, place a pillow behind your back to provide support.

- **Assume a proper position while typing.** Improperly positioned keyboards are one of the leading causes of repetitive stress injuries in computer users. Your wrists should be flat (not bent) with respect to the keyboard, and your forearms should be parallel to the floor. Additionally, your wrists should not be resting on the keyboard while typing. You can adjust the height of your chair or install a height-adjustable keyboard tray to ensure a proper position. Specially designed ergonomic keyboards such as the one shown in Figure 2.42 can help you achieve the proper wrist position.

- **Take breaks.** Remaining in the same position for long periods of time increases stress on your body. Shift your position in your chair and stretch your hands and fingers periodically. Likewise, staring at the screen for long periods can lead to eyestrain, so rest your eyes by periodically taking them off the screen and focusing them on an object at least 8 feet away.

- **Ensure the lighting is adequate.** Ensuring that you have proper lighting in your work area minimizes eyestrain. Eliminate sources of direct glare (light shining directly into your eyes) or reflected glare (light shining off the computer screen) and ensure there is enough light to read comfortably. If you still can't eliminate glare from your computer screen, you can buy an antiglare screen to place over your monitor.

Is ergonomics important when using mobile devices? Working with mobile computing devices presents interesting challenges when it comes to injury prevention. For example, many users work with laptops resting on their laps, placing the monitor outside of the optimal line of sight and thereby increasing neck strain. Figure 2.43 provides guidelines on preventing injuries when computing on the go.

So, whether you're computing at your desk or on the road, consider the ergonomics of your work environment. Doing so will help you avoid injury and discomfort.

What devices are available for people with disabilities? People who have physical challenges sometimes need special devices to access computers. For visually impaired users, voice recognition is an input option. For those users whose visual limitations are less severe, keyboards with larger keys are available. Keyboards that display

FIGURE 2.42 Ergonomic keyboards, like the Truly Ergonomic Mechanical Keyboard shown here, which help users type with straight wrists and contain built-in wrist rests, facilitate proper hand position and minimize wrist strain. *(Truly Ergonomic)*

on a touch screen or specialized input consoles (see Figure 2.44a) can make input easier for individuals who can't type with their hands: The user presses the keys with a pointing device. There are also keyboards, such as those made by Maltron, designed for individuals who can use only one hand (see Figure 2.44b).

People with motor control issues may have difficulty with pointing devices. To aid such users, special trackballs are available that can be easily manipulated with one finger and can be attached to almost any surface, including a wheelchair. When arm motion is severely restrained, head-mounted pointing devices can be used. Generally, these involve a camera mounted on the computer monitor and a device attached to the head (often installed in a hat). When the user moves his or her head, the camera detects the movement and moves the cursor. In this case, mouse clicks are controlled by a switch that can be manipulated by the user's hands or feet or even by using an instrument that fits into the mouth and senses the user blowing into it. ∎

 SOUND BYTE
Healthy Computing

In this Sound Byte, you'll see how to set up your workspace in an ergonomically correct way. You'll learn the proper location of the monitor, keyboard, and mouse, as well as ergonomic features to look for when choosing the most appropriate chair.

FIGURE 2.43

Preventing Injuries While on the Go

	SMARTPHONE REPETITIVE STRAIN INJURIES	PORTABLE MEDIA PLAYER HEARING DAMAGE	SMALL-SCREEN VISION ISSUES	LAP INJURIES	TABLET REPETITIVE STRAIN INJURIES
Malady	Repetitive strain injuries (such as DeQuervain's tendonitis) from constant typing of instant messages	Hearing loss from high-decibel sound levels in earbuds	Blurriness and dryness caused by squinting to view tiny screens on mobile devices	Burns on legs from heat generated by laptop	Pain caused from using tablets for prolonged periods in uncomfortable positions
Preventative measures	Restrict length and frequency of messages, take breaks, and perform other motions with your thumbs and fingers during breaks to relieve tension.	Turn down volume (you should be able to hear external noises, such as people talking), use software that limits sound levels (not to exceed 60 decibels), and use external, over-ear style headphones instead of earbuds.	Blink frequently or use eye drops to maintain moisture in eyes, after 10 minutes take a break and focus on something at least 8 feet away for 5 minutes, use adequate amount of light, and increase the size of fonts.	Place a book, magazine, or laptop cooling pad between your legs and laptop.	Restrict the length of time you work at a tablet, especially typing or gaming. Use the same ergonomic position you would use for a laptop when using a tablet.

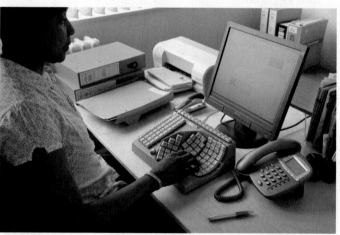

FIGURE 2.44 (a) Input consoles for people who can't type with their hands and (b) keyboards designed for one-handed use make computer interaction easier for individuals with disabilities. *(Maltron Ltd; Maltron Ltd)*

With the advent of the computer, many speculated that ours would become a paperless society. Instead of saving printed documents and other output as was done prior to the PC, information would be saved in a digital state: hard drives replacing filing cabinets, online photo buckets replacing photo albums and scrapbooks, and e-books replacing our favorite texts. Hard drive capacities do enable us to save more content, and online storage systems enable us to save pictures and other files to the "cloud." Additionally, e-book readers have increased in popularity. But has this push toward digital content begun to make the printer obsolete? Surprisingly, no. People still have a deep-rooted need to see, feel, mark, share, or use their digital images or information in a physical form. New technologies that push the boundaries of printing, such as printing from the cloud and 3-D printing, are being developed and refined.

Cloud Printing

To print a document from a desktop or laptop computer, you must have a printer associated with your computer. Usually this is not a problem because at home, at school, or in the office, there is generally one printer, and all the PCs connected to it have the software and cables or wireless capabilities needed to use it. But what happens if you want to print something from your smartphone or tablet? Common solutions have been to e-mail the document to yourself or transfer the document to a web-based storage service such as Dropbox so that a printer-connected computer could access it. Another solution is Google Cloud Print, a service that lets you configure your printers so you can access them from mobile devices.

Google Cloud Print uses cloud-ready printers (see Figure 2.45) that are now available from manufacturers such as HP, Kodak, and Epson. These printers connect directly to the Internet and register themselves with Google Cloud Print without needing to be connected to a computer. Once a printer is registered with Cloud Print, printing jobs can be sent to it from mobile devices (such as tablets and smartphones) using the Internet. Conventional printers that you already own can

FIGURE 2.45 Cloud-ready printers only need an Internet connection to be accessed from any mobile device.

also be registered with Cloud Print, although they require connection to the Internet through a computer.

3-D Printing

Printing a 3-D model of a proposed building or new prototype is common for architects and engineers. The process builds a model one layer at a time from the bottom up. The procedure begins by spreading a layer of powder on a platform. Then, depending on the technology, the printer uses nozzles similar to those in an inkjet printer to spray tiny drops of glue at specific places to solidify the powder, or the powder is solidified through a melting process. The printer repeats solidifying layers of powder until the model is built to specifications. This technology has spurred the manufacturing of a variety of consumer goods, from toys to clothing (see Figure 2.46). Shapeways (**shapeways.com**) uses 3-D printing to enable anyone to turn his or her 3-D designs into real physical models. Then, those models can be personalized, bought, or sold through Shapeways's online community.

3-D printing is being used in the medical community as well. Bespoke Innovations (**bespokeinnovations.com**) is using 3-D printing to create prosthetic limbs with more lifelike form and textures as well as to give the recipient the ability to further personalize the prosthetic to include tattoos! And researchers at Wake Forest Institute for Regenerative Medicine have developed a way to use similar inkjet technologies to build heart, bone, and blood vessel tissues in the lab. They have also developed a way to "print" restorative cells directly into a soldier's wound at the site where the injury occurred, thus significantly improving the soldier's chances of survival.

Taking traditional technologies, such as inkjet printing, and applying them to solve current human struggles is a long and tedious process, but without these pioneers experimenting with different applications, society would advance a lot more slowly.

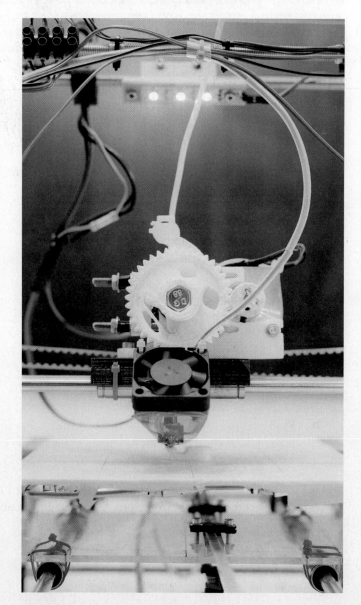

FIGURE 2.46 3-D printing is being used to fabricate parts for machines on demand. *(Tomas Mikula/Shutterstock)*

Before moving on to the Chapter Review:
- Watch Replay Video 2.2 .
- Then check your understanding of what you've learned so far.

check your understanding// review & practice

For a quick review to see what you've learned so far, answer the following questions. Visit **pearsonhighered.com/techinaction** to check your answers.

multiple choice

1. Which of the following is NOT found on a motherboard?

   a. network interface card

   b. CPU

   c. SSD

   d. sound card

2. Which of these is an example of optical storage media?

   a. DVD

   b. SSD

   c. thumb drive

   d. a flash memory card

3. Which of the following is NOT a video port?

   a. HDMI   c. DVI

   b. VGA   d. Thunderbolt

4. Which of these is considered nonvolatile storage?

   a. CPU

   b. ROM

   c. FireWire 800

   d. expansion card

5. Which power control option stores data on the hard drive?

   a. Hibernate

   b. Sleep

   c. Log off

   d. Shut down

To take an autograded version of this review, please go to the companion website at **pearsonhighered.com/techinaction,** or go your MyITLab course.

Continue

2 Chapter Review

summary //

Understanding Your Computer

1. What exactly is a computer, and what are its four main functions?

- Computers are devices that process data. They help organize, sort, and categorize data to turn it into information.
- The computer's four major functions are: (1) input: gather data, or allow users to enter data; (2) process: manipulate, calculate, or organize that data; (3) output: display data and information in a form suitable for the user; and (4) storage: save data and information for later use.

2. What is the difference between data and information?

- Data is a representation of a fact or idea. The number 3 and the words *televisions* and *Sony* are pieces of data.
- Information is data that has been organized or presented in a meaningful fashion. An inventory list that indicates that "three Sony televisions" are in stock is processed information. It allows a retail clerk to answer a customer query about the availability of merchandise. Information is more powerful than raw data.

3. What are bits and bytes, and how are they measured?

- To process data into information, computers need to work in a language they understand. This language, called *binary language*, consists of two numbers: 0 and 1.
- Each 0 and each 1 is a binary digit, or bit. Eight bits create one byte.
- In computers, each letter of the alphabet, each number, and each special character consists of a unique combination of eight bits (one byte)—a string of eight 0s and 1s.
- For describing large amounts of storage capacity, the terms *megabyte* (approximately 1 million bytes), *gigabyte* (approximately 1 billion bytes), *terabyte* (approximately 1 trillion bytes), and *petabyte* (1,000 terabytes) are used.

Input Devices and Output Devices

4. What devices can I use to get data into the computer?

- An input device enables you to enter data (text, images, and sounds) and instructions (user responses and commands) into a computer.
- You use keyboards to enter typed data and commands, whereas you use the mouse to enter user responses and commands.
- Touch screens are display screens that respond to commands initiated by a touch with a finger or a stylus.
- Images are input into the computer with scanners, digital cameras, camcorders, and smartphones.
- Live video is captured with webcams and digital video recorders.
- Microphones capture sounds. There are many different types of microphones, including desktop, headset, and clip-on models.

5. What devices can I use to get information out of the computer?

- Output devices enable you to send processed data out of your computer. It can take the form of text, pictures, sounds, or video.
- Monitors display soft copies of text, graphics, and video, whereas printers create hard copies of text and graphics.
- There are two primary categories of printers: inkjet and laser. Specialty printers are also available. These include all-in-one printers, plotters, and thermal printers. When choosing a printer, you should be aware of factors such as speed, resolution, color output, and cost.
- Speakers are the output devices for sound. Most computers include speakers; more-sophisticated systems include subwoofers and surround sound.

Processing, Memory, and Storage

6. What's on the motherboard?

- The motherboard, the main circuit board of the system, contains a computer's CPU, which coordinates the functions of all other devices on the computer. The performance of a CPU is affected by the speed of the processor (measured in GHz), the amount of cache memory, and the number of processing cores.

- RAM, the computer's volatile memory, is also located on the motherboard. RAM is where all the data and instructions are held while the computer is running.
- ROM, a permanent type of memory, is responsible for housing instructions to help start up a computer.
- The motherboard also houses slots for expansion cards, which have specific functions that augment the computer's basic functions. Typical expansion cards are sound and video cards.

7. Where are information and programs stored?

- To save programs and information permanently, you need to save them to the hard drive or to another permanent storage device such as a DVD or flash drive, or to the cloud.
- The hard drive is your computer's primary device for permanent storage of software and files. The hard drive is a nonvolatile storage device, meaning it holds the data and instructions your computer needs permanently, even after the computer is turned off.
- Mechanical hard drives have spinning platters on which data is saved, whereas newer solid-state drives (SSDs) use solid-state memory, similar to that used with flash drives.
- External hard drives are essentially internal hard drives that have been made portable by enclosing them in a protective case and making them small and lightweight.
- Cloud storage refers to nonvolatile storage locations that are maintained on the Internet (in the "cloud") by companies such as Dropbox. Storing your data in the cloud allows you to access it from almost any computing device that is connected to the Internet.
- Optical drives that can read from and write to CD, DVD, or Blu-ray discs are another means of permanent, portable storage. Data is saved to CDs, DVDs, and Blu-ray discs as pits that are burned into the disc by a laser.
- Flash drives are another portable means of storing data. Flash drives plug into USB ports.
- Flash memory cards let you transfer digital data between your computer and devices such as digital cameras, smartphones, video cameras, and printers.

Ports and Power Controls

8. How are devices connected to the computer?

- There is a wide variety of ports that allow you to hook up peripheral devices (such as your monitor and keyboard) to your system.

- The fastest type of port used to connect devices to a computer is the Thunderbolt port.
- The most common type of port used to connect devices to a computer is the USB port.
- FireWire ports provide additional options for data transfer.
- Connectivity ports, such as Ethernet ports, give you access to networks and the Internet.
- HDMI ports are the most common multimedia port. They are used to connect monitors, TVs, and gaming consoles to computing devices and handle both audio and video data.
- Audio ports are used to connect headphones, microphones, and speakers to computing devices.

9. What's the best way to turn my computer on and off, and when should it be done?

- Power on your computer from a completely turned-off state. In Windows 8.1, you can turn your computer off by pressing the computer's power button or by using the Shut down option from the power icon found on the Start screen.
- With the power-management options of Windows 8.1, for example, you only need to shut down your computer completely when you need to repair or install hardware in the system unit or move it to another location. However, if you use your computer only for a little while each day, it would be best to power it off completely after each daily use.

Setting It All Up

10. How do I set up my computer to avoid strain and injury?

- *Ergonomics* refers to how you arrange your computer and equipment to minimize your risk of injury or discomfort.
- Ergonomics includes positioning your monitor correctly, buying an adjustable chair, assuming a proper position while typing, making sure the lighting is adequate, and not looking at the screen for long periods. Other good practices include taking frequent breaks and using specially designed equipment such as ergonomic keyboards.
- Ergonomics is also important to consider when using mobile devices.

Be sure to check out the companion website for additional materials to help you review and learn, including a Tech Bytes Weekly newsletter—
pearsonhighered.com/techinaction.
And don't forget the Replay Videos .

key terms //

all-in-one computer **33**

all-in-one printer **47**

application software **31**

aspect ratio **43**

binary digit (bit) **31**

binary language **31**

Bluetooth technology **35**

Blu-ray disc (BD) **56**

byte **31**

central processing unit (CPU, or processor) **53**

cloud storage **54**

cold boot **59**

compact disc (CD) **56**

computer **30**

connectivity port **57**

data **30**

desktop computer **31**

digital video (or versatile) disc (DVD) **56**

digital video interface (DVI) port **58**

drive bay **54**

embedded computer **33**

ergonomics **61**

Ethernet port **57**

expansion cards (or adapter cards) **52**

external hard drive **54**

FireWire 800 **57**

flash drive (jump drive, USB drive, or thumb drive) **55**

flash memory card **55**

gigabyte (GB) **31**

gigahertz (GHz) **53**

green computing **55**

hard disk drive (HDD, or hard drive) **54**

hardware **31**

Hibernate **59**

high-definition multimedia interface (HDMI) port **57**

impact printer **46**

information **30**

inkjet printer **46**

input device **35**

internal hard drive **54**

keyboard **35**

kilobyte (KB) **31**

laptop (or notebook) computer **31**

laser printer **46**

legacy technology **43**

light-emitting diode (LED) **43**

liquid crystal display (LCD) **43**

mainframe **33**

megabyte (MB) **31**

microphone (mic) **40**

monitor (display screen) **43**

motherboard **52**

mouse **35**

netbook **31**

network interface card (NIC) **52**

nonimpact printer **46**

nonvolatile storage **53**

operating system (OS) **31**

optical drive **56**

optical mouse **37**

organic light-emitting diode (OLED) displays **43**

output device **43**

petabyte **31**

peripheral device **33**

pixel **43**

plotter **47**

port **57**

power supply **59**

printer **43**

processing **30**

projector **45**

QWERTY keyboard **35**

random access memory (RAM) **53**

read-only memory (ROM) **53**

resolution **43**

scanner **39**

Sleep mode **59**

smartphone **34**

software **31**

solid-state drive (SSD) **54**

sound card **52**

speakers **47**

stylus **35**

supercomputer **33**

surround-sound speaker **48**

system software **31**

system unit **31**

tablet computer **31**

tablet (or convertible) PC **31**

terabyte (TB) **31**

thermal printer **47**

Thunderbolt port **57**

touch pad (trackpad) **39**

touch screen **35**

ultrabook **31**

universal serial bus (USB) port **57**

video card **52**

video graphics array (VGA) port **58**

volatile storage **53**

warm boot **60**

webcam **39**

chapter quiz // assessment

For a quick review to see what you've learned, answer the following questions. Submit the quiz as requested by your instructor. If you are using MyITLab, the quiz is also available there.

multiple choice

1. What is a terabyte?
   a. one million bytes
   b. one trillion bytes
   c. one billion bits
   d. one trillion bits

2. Which of the following is NOT an input device?
   a. a touch-screen monitor
   b. an optical mouse
   c. a keyboard
   d. a laser printer

3. Monitor screens are made up of millions of tiny dots known as
   a. bytes.
   b. resolution points.
   c. pixels.
   d. bits.

4. Which of these is NOT located on the motherboard?
   a. CPU
   b. ROM
   c. RAM
   d. DVD drive

5. Which of these is NOT an optical storage device?
   a. flash drive
   b. CD drive
   c. DVD drive
   d. Blu-ray drive

6. Ergonomics is an important consideration
   a. only for desktop computers.
   b. only for laptop computers.
   c. only for laptop and desktop computers, but never for mobile devices.
   d. for all computing devices.

true/false

_____ 1. Data and information are NOT interchangeable terms.

_____ 2. The operating system is a type of application software.

_____ 3. The Ethernet port is an example of a connectivity port.

_____ 4. A typical CPU can complete billions of machine cycles in one second.

critical thinking

1. **Computers of the Future**

   Embedded computers keep turning up in new places. They can be found in cars, household appliances, smoke detectors, and thermostats too, enabling us to interact with even more of these "smart" devices every day. What common objects do you think might benefit from an embedded computer? What capabilities can you envision?

2. **New Display Features**

   The display screen of the future may be paper-thin, flexible, and transparent. Companies like Samsung and LG are already working on it. What uses can you envision for this new technology? What advantages and disadvantages do you foresee? Do you have any suggestions for the manufacturers to help make this successful?

team time//

Data Storage Options

Problem

You've joined a small business that's beginning to evaluate its technology setup. Because of the addition of several new sales representatives and other administrative employees, the company needs to reconsider the various ways its data is stored. You've been asked to evaluate options for on-site and off-site data storage.

Task

Split your class into teams of three and assign the following tasks:

- Member A explores the benefits and downfalls of cloud storage.
- Member B explores the benefits and downfalls of external hard drives.
- Member C explores the benefits and downfalls of portable storage devices.

Process

1. Think about what the storage needs are for the company and what information and resources you will need to tackle this project.

2. Research and then discuss the components of each method you're recommending. Are any of these options better suited for the particular needs of certain types of employees (sales representatives versus administrative staff)? Consider the types of data to be stored. Is some data confidential? How long should it be retained?

3. Consider the different types of employees in the company. Would a combination of methods be better than a single solution? If so, what kinds of employees would use which type of storage?

4. As a team, write a summary position paper. Support your recommendation for the company. Each team member should include why his or her data storage option will or will not be part of the solution.

Conclusion

There are advantages and disadvantages to any data storage option. Being aware of the pros and cons and knowing which method is best for a particular scenario or employee will help you to become a better consumer as well as a better computer user.

Green Computing

Ethical conduct is a stream of decisions you make all day long. In this exercise, you'll research and then role-play a complicated ethical situation. The role you play may or may not match your own personal beliefs, but your research and use of logic will enable you to represent whichever view is assigned. An arbitrator will watch and comment on both sides of the arguments, and together, the team will agree on an ethical solution.

Background

Green computing—conducting computing needs with the least possible amount of power and impact on the environment—is on everyone's minds. Although it's hard to argue with an environmentally conscious agenda, the pinch to our pocketbooks and the loss of some comforts sometimes make green computing difficult. Businesses, including colleges, need to consider a variety of issues and concerns before jumping into a complete green overhaul.

Research Areas to Consider

End-of-life management: e-waste and recycling

- Energy-efficient devices
- Renewable resources used in computer manufacturing
- Costs of green computing
- Government funding and incentives

Process

1. Divide the class into teams.
2. Research the areas cited above and devise a scenario in which your college is considering modifying its current technology setup to a more green information technology (IT) strategy.
3. Team members should write a summary that provides background information for their character—for example, environmentalist, college IT administrator, or arbitrator—and that details their character's behaviors to set the stage for the role-playing event. Then, team members should create an outline to use during the role-playing event.
4. Team members should arrange a mutually convenient time to meet, using a virtual meeting tool or by meeting in person.
5. Team members should present their case to the class or submit a PowerPoint presentation for review by the rest of the class, along with the summary and resolution they developed.

Conclusion

As technology becomes ever more prevalent and integrated into our lives, more and more ethical dilemmas will present themselves. Being able to understand and evaluate both sides of the argument, while responding in a personally or socially ethical manner, will be an important skill.

Technology Wish List

You are in need of a significant technology upgrade, and your parents have told you they will help you finance your purchases by loaning you the money. You will need to repay them with a modest 2.5% interest rate over two years. The only catch is that they want you to create a list of all the new devices that you need, note the cost, and provide a website for each device where they can find more information. Then, they want you to calculate how much you will need to give them each month to pay them back.

You will use the following skills as you complete this activity:	
• Merge and Center	• Modify Column Widths
• Modify Workbook Themes	• Insert a Hyperlink
• Apply Number Formats	• Create a Formula
• Use the SUM, PMT, and COUNTA Functions	• Wrap Text

Instructions:

1. Open TIA_Ch2_Start and save the workbook as TIA_Ch2_LastName. Format the title *Technology Wish List* with the **Title Cell Style**, and format the column headers in cells A3:F3 with the **Heading3 Cell Style**.

   a. Hint: To format cell styles, on the HOME tab, in the Styles group, click Cell Styles.

2. **Merge and Center** A1 across columns A through F, and **Center align** the column headers in Cells A3:F3.

   a. Hint: To Merge and Center text, on the HOME tab, in the Alignment group, click Merge & Center

3. Modify column widths so that Column A is 25 and Column D is 45.

   a. Hint: To modify column widths, on the HOME tab, in the Cells group click Format, and then select Column Width.

4. Starting in cell A4, fill in the table with the Brand and Model of the six devices that you would like to purchase. The device type is filled out for you. In the *Reason* column, write a brief note as to why this device will help you. (You'll format the text so it all displays later.) Enter the cost of the device in the Cost column. Don't include tax and/or shipping.

5. Change the Workbook Theme to **Integral**.

   a. Hint: To apply the Theme, on the Page Layout tab, in the Theme group, click Themes.

6. In cells F4 through F9 create a Hyperlink to a webpage that features each respective product so your grandparents can have access to more information if they need it.

   a. Hint: To insert a hyperlink, on the INSERT tab, in the Links group, click Hyperlink.

7. Wrap the text in cells C4:C9, D4:D9, and F4:F9 so all text displays.

   a. Hint: To wrap text, on the HOME tab, in the Alignment group, click Wrap Text. .

8. Format the values in cells E4:E7 with the Accounting Number format with two decimals.

   a. Hint: To apply number and decimal formats, look on the HOME tab, in the Number group.

9. In cell A10, type Subtotal, then in cell E10 use a SUM function to calculate the total cost of all devices. Format the results in the Accounting Number format with two decimals.

10. In cell A11, type Estimated Tax, then in cell E11 create a formula that references the subtotal in cell E10 and multiplies it by a tax of 6%. Format the results in the Accounting Number format with two decimals.

    a. Hint: The formula will be =E10*0.06

11. In cell A12, type Estimated Shipping, then in cell E12 create a formula to calculate the shipping charge by using the COUNTA function to determine the number of devices being purchased and then multiplying that by a $10 shipping charge. Format the results in Accounting Number Format with two decimals.

    a. Hint: The formula will be =COUNTA(B4:B9)*10.

12. In cell A13, type Total Cost, then in cell E13 use the SUM function to create a formula that adds up the *Subtotal, Estimated Tax,* and *Estimated Shipping costs*. Format the results in Accounting Number Format with two decimals. Format the cells A13:E13 with the **Total Cell Style**.

13. **Right align** cells A10:A13.

14. In Cell D14, type Estimated Monthly Payment, and then in cell E14, use the PMT function to calculate the monthly payment owed to your parents to pay back the total purchase amount in two years at a 2.5% annual interest rate.

    Hint: The formula will need to adjust the annual interest rate to a monthly rate, and adjust the annual term of the loan to monthly payments.

15. **Save** the workbook and submit based on your instructor's directions.

3

Using the Internet: Making the Most of the Web's Resources

Working and Playing on the Web

The Internet and How It Works

OBJECTIVES

1. What is the origin of the Internet? **(pp. 76–77)**
2. How does data travel on the Internet? **(pp. 77–78)**

Communicating and Collaborating on the Web

OBJECTIVES

3. How can I communicate and collaborate using Web 2.0 technologies? **(pp. 79–84)**
4. How can I communicate using e-mail and instant messaging? **(pp. 79–81)**

🔊 **Sound Byte:** Blogging

Web Entertainment

OBJECTIVE

5. What multimedia files are found on the web, and what software is needed to access those files? **(pp. 85–86)**

Conducting Business over the Internet: E-Commerce

OBJECTIVE

6. What is e-commerce, and what online safeguards are available? **(pp. 87–89)**

🧑 **Active Helpdesk:** Doing Business Online

Using the Web Effectively

Accessing and Moving Around the Web

OBJECTIVES

7. What is a web browser, and what are a URL and its parts? **(pp. 93–96)**
8. How can I use hyperlinks and other tools to get around the web? **(pp. 96–97)**

🔊 **Sound Byte:** Welcome to the Web

Searching the Web Effectively

OBJECTIVE

9. How do I search the Internet effectively, and how can I evaluate websites? **(pp. 100–103)**

🧑 **Active Helpdesk:** Getting Around the Web

🧑 **Active Helpdesk:** Evaluating Websites

🔊 **Sound Byte:** Finding Information on the Web

Make This: Explore an App Builder Skill on **page 93**

For all media in this chapter go to **pearsonhighered.com/techinaction** or **MyITLab**.

HOW COOL IS THIS?

Have you ever wanted to **share your computer screen** with someone but couldn't because you didn't know how or didn't have the right software? Now you can share your computer screen with anyone on **any device via the web** with one click, hassle-free, with **Screenleap (screenleap.com)**.

All you need to do is **click a link that generates a code**, then send the code to whomever you want to share your screen with; they will be able to view your screen immediately from their web browser on their smartphone, tablet, or PC. You can share your screen publicly, or privately to only a select few. There is also an extension to initiate sharing directly from your Gmail account. Using this technology may help you to **better communicate** with classmates or your professors when seeking or offering help. A **free account** will give you two hours of sharing time per day. So, share your

Working and Playing on the Web

You most likely know at least a little bit about how to use the web's resources to communicate and collaborate with others, how to work with multimedia files, and how business is conducted over the web. In this section, we'll explore these and other topics. But first, let's start with a brief lesson on the history of the Internet.

the internet and how
IT WORKS

It's hard to imagine life without the **Internet**, the largest computer network in the world. The Internet is actually a network of networks that connects billions of computer users globally, but its beginnings were much more modest.

The Origin of the Internet

Why was the Internet created? The concept of the Internet was developed in the late 1950s while the United States was in the midst of the Cold War with the Soviet Union (see Figure 3.1). At that time, the U.S. Department of Defense needed a computer network that wouldn't be disrupted easily in the event of an attack.

At the same time, researchers for the Department of Defense were trying to get different computers to work with each other using a common communications method that all computers could use. The Internet was created to respond to these two concerns: establishing a *secure* form of

FIGURE 3.1 How the Internet Began.

1958 The **Advanced Research Projects Agency (ARPA)** is established for the U.S. Department of Defense. This agency creates the ARPANET—the beginnings of the Internet.

1963 **ASCII code** is developed as the standard for computers from different manufacturers to exchange data.

1969 Researchers at UCLA **send the first message via a networked computer system** to researchers at Stanford University.

1964 A **new network scheme** is developed with multiple paths so if one communication path was destroyed (from a potential Soviet Union attack), the rest of the network would still be able to communicate.

ASCII Code - Character to Binary

0	0011 0000	I	0100 1001	b	0110 0010	v	0111 0110
1	0011 0001	J	0100 1010	c	0110 0011	w	0111 0111
2	0011 0010	K	0100 1011	d	0110 0100	x	0111 1000
3	0011 0011	L	0100 1100	e	0110 0101	y	0111 1001
4	0011 0100	M	0100 1101	f	0110 0110	z	0111 1010
				g	0110 0110		

communications and creating a means by which *all* computers could communicate.

Who invented the Internet? The modern Internet evolved from an early U.S. government-funded "internetworking" project called the Advanced Research Projects Agency Network (ARPANET). ARPANET began as a four-node network involving UCLA, Stanford Research Institute, the University of California at Santa Barbara, and the University of Utah in Salt Lake City. The first real communication occurred in 1969 between the computer at Stanford and the computer at UCLA. Although the system crashed after the third letter of "Login" was transmitted, it was the beginning of a revolution. Many people participated in the creation of the ARPANET, but two men, Vinton Cerf and Robert Kahn, are generally acknowledged as the "fathers" of the Internet. These men earned this honor because in the 1970s they were primarily responsible for developing the communications protocols (standards) still in use on the Internet today.

So are the web and the Internet the same thing? Because the **World Wide Web** (**WWW** or the **web**) is what we use the most, we sometimes think of the Internet and the web as being interchangeable. However, the web is only a subset of the Internet, dedicated to broadcasting HTML pages; it is the means by which we access information over the Internet. The web is based on the Hypertext Transfer Protocol (HTTP), which is why you see an *http://* at the beginning of web addresses. What distinguishes the web from the rest of the Internet is its use of the following:

- Common communications protocols that enable computers to talk to each other and display information in compatible formats
- Special links that enable users to navigate from one place to another on the web

Who created the web? The web began in 1991. It was based on a protocol developed by Tim Berners-Lee, a physicist at the European Organization for Nuclear Research (CERN), who wanted a method for linking his research documents so that other researchers could access them. In conjunction with Robert Cailliau, Berners-Lee developed the basic architecture of the web and created the first **web browser**, software that lets you display and interact with text and other media on the web. The original browser could handle only text. Then, in 1993, the Mosaic browser, which could display graphics as well as text, was released. The once-popular Netscape Navigator browser evolved from Mosaic and heralded the beginning of the web's monumental growth.

How the Internet Works

How does the Internet work? All computers and other devices such as tablets and smartphones that are connected to the Internet create a network of networks. These

Vincent Cerf and Bob Kahn develop a set of communication rules—the **TCP/IP protocol**—that allow different types of computers to communicate.

1973

Tim Berners-Lee developed and made public **HTTP protocol and the World Wide Web**. WWW is a subset of the Internet that is connected via hypertext (text containing hyperlinks to other documents and media).

1991

Ray Tomlinson writes a program to send **e-mail** over the ARPANET and develops the "user@host" convention.

1972

By 1978, there were 111 Internet domains on ARPANET.

1978

By 1997, there were over 1 million Internet domains on ARPANET.

1997

Internet Domains (1989–1997)

Domains

1,600,000
1,400,000
1,200,000
1,000,000
800,000
600,000
400,000
200,000
0

Jul-89 Dec-89 May-90 Oct-90 Mar-91 Aug-91 Jan-92 Jun-92 Nov-92 Apr-93 Sep-93 Feb-94 Jul-94 Dec-94 May-95 Oct-95 Mar-96 Aug-96 Jan-97 Jun-97

BITS&BYTES

Ever Heard of Internet2?

Although Internet2 may sound like a new and separate network meant to replace the Internet, this is not the case. Internet2 is actually a consortium of U.S. leaders in education, research, industry, and government that seeks to expand the possibilities of the existing Internet by developing new technologies and applications and then deploying them to the public. These experimental technologies require a faster and more efficient Internet, so the researchers use separate data lines that support extremely high-speed communications—up to 8.8 terabits per second (Tbps). In fact, many of the Internet's current technologies are possible because of the research done by the Internet2 consortium.

Internet-connected devices communicate with each other in turns, just as we do when we ask a question or reply with an answer. Thus, a computer (or other device) connected to the Internet acts in one of two ways: Either it's a **client**, a computer that asks for data, or it's a **server**, a computer that receives the request and returns the data to the client. Because the Internet uses clients and servers, it's referred to as a **client/server network**.

When a client computer puts out a request for information from the server computer, the request travels along transmission lines. These transmission lines are similar to our highway system of roads, with some roads having different speed limits. The transmission lines with the fastest speeds are referred to as **Internet backbones**.

How do computers talk to each other? Suppose you want to order something from Amazon.com. Figure 3.2 illustrates what happens when you type **www.amazon.com** into your web browser and when Amazon's home page displays on your computer monitor. As you can see, the data request from your computer (the client computer) is sent via Internet communication pathways to a server computer. The server computer (in this case, Amazon's server) processes the request and returns the requested data to your client computer via Internet communication pathways. The data reply most likely takes a different route than did the data request. The web browser on your client computer interprets the data and displays it on its monitor.

How does the data get sent to the correct computer? Each time you connect to the Internet, your computer is assigned a unique identification number. This number, called an **Internet Protocol (IP) address**, is a set of four groups of numbers separated by periods, such as 123.45.245.91, and is commonly referred to as a *dotted quad* or *dotted decimal*. IP addresses are the means by which computers connected to the Internet identify each other. Similarly, each website is assigned a unique IP address. However, because the numbers that make up IP addresses are difficult for people to remember, websites are given text versions of their IP addresses. So, Amazon's website has an IP address of 72.21.211.176 and a name of **www.amazon.com**. When you type "www.amazon.com" into your browser, your computer (with its unique IP address) looks for Amazon's IP address (72.21.211.176). Data is exchanged between Amazon's server computer and your computer using these unique IP addresses. ∎

STEP 4: The server returns the requested data to your computer using the fastest pathway, which may be different from the one the request took.

Amazon.com's server

STEP 3: Your data flows along the backbone and on to smaller pathways until it reaches its destination, which is the server computer for Amazon's website.

STEP 5: The web browser interprets the data and displays it on your monitor.

HTML

URL

Client

STEP 1: You enter www.amazon.com in your web browser. Your computer is the client requesting information from Amazon.com's website.

STEP 2: The request is sent to the server via a system of data pathways, similar to a roadway system.

FIGURE 3.2 How the Internet's Client/Server Model Works.

communicating and collaborating
ON THE WEB

Over time, our use of the web has evolved from passively browsing web pages that were created for us to actively creating our own web content and sharing and collaborating on it with others. This new collaborative, user-created web content has been dubbed **Web 2.0**. Web 2.0 can be classified as the *social web,* in which the user is also a participant. Before Web 2.0 technologies were in place, we were unable to collaborate with others through web applications such as Google Drive, to rate and recommend products or services with Yelp, to tag a friend on social networks such as Facebook, or to share a video on YouTube or a favorite image on Pinterest. These new means of Web 2.0 communication are collectively called *social media* and include social networking, blogs, wikis, podcasts, and webcasts. Although **e-mail** (short for **electronic mail**) still remains the most widely used form of communication on the Internet, social media has truly changed how we communicate.

Social Networking

Who hasn't heard of Facebook or social networking? As you probably know, **social networking** refers to using the web to communicate and share information among your friends and others. Social networking services such as Facebook and Twitter have become widely popular because they provide fun ways for users to communicate with their friends through wall posts, chats, tagged images, and tweets. Other social networking sites, such as YouTube, Instagram, and Pinterest, provide ways for users to show friends their favorite videos or images that they have taken themselves or have found on the web.

How is social networking used in business? In the business community, professionals often engage in in-person networking to locate and fill open job positions as well as to find clients. Today, networking also happens online. Professional, business-oriented online networks such as LinkedIn are helpful for members seeking potential clients, business opportunities, jobs, or job candidates. Like a true business network, these sites can help you meet other professionals through the people you already know. In addition, businesses use social networking for marketing and communicating directly with their customers. For example, companies may post special deals and offers on their Facebook page or solicit responses from followers that may help with product development or future marketing campaigns.

Figure 3.3 shows various sites that are considered Web 2.0 social networking sites. As you can see, there is more to social networking than just Facebook and Twitter.

What are some dos and don'ts of social networking? When social networking sites first became popular, there was concern over privacy issues, especially for school-aged children who put personal information on their pages without considering the possibility of that information being misused by a stalker or identity thief. Although those concerns still exist, many of the most popular social networking sites have improved their privacy policies, thereby reducing, but not eliminating, such concerns. Still, users must be cautious about the type of content they post on these sites. Consider these precautions as you use social networking sites:

- Keep your personal information personal. The year you were born, your physical address, and the routines of your life (sports games, practices, work schedules) should not be broadcast to the general public.
- Know who your friends are, and know who can see the information you post. Review your privacy settings periodically, as sites change and update their privacy practices frequently.
- Do not post information such as your favorite teacher or your first pet's name because these are often used as security questions to verify your identity.
- Use caution when posting images, and know what images others are posting of you. Although privacy settings may offer some comfort, some images may be available for viewing through search engines and may not require site registration to be seen. Online images may become public property and subject to reproduction, and you might not want some—or any—of those images to be distributed.

Many employers and colleges use social networks as a means of gaining information about potential applicants before granting an interview or extending admission or a job offer. In fact, there have been instances of people being fired from their jobs and being expelled from school for using social media, such as Facebook, Twitter, and blogs, in a questionable way. Generally, questionable content on social media includes negative discussion about the poster's job, employer, or colleagues or inappropriate content about the poster. The responsibility for your content rests with you. Even though you may have strong privacy settings, you can't control what those who you allow to see your content do with it. Therefore, treat all information posted on the web as public, and avoid posting damaging words and pictures. Bottom line: Make sure your profile, images, and site content project an image that positively and accurately represents you.

E-Mail

Why do I need e-mail? Despite the increasing popularity of social networking, e-mail is still the primary means of communication over the Internet. E-mail is a written message sent or received over the Internet. E-mail is the primary method of electronic communication worldwide because it's fast and convenient. And because it's *asynchronous,* users do not need to be communicating at the same time. They can send and

(Kevin Britland/Alamy; M4OS Photos/Alamy; Anil Kumar/Alamy; Kristoffer Tripplaar/Alamy; PhotoEdit/Alamy; PhotoEdit/Alamy Web Pix/Alamy; PhotoEdit/Alamy; Gil C/Shutterstock; M4OS Photos/Alamy; NetPics/Alamy)

FIGURE 3.3

Types of Social Networking Sites

	DESCRIPTION	SUGGESTED URLS
Social Exchange Networks	Allow users to connect with others, provide status updates	facebook.com facebook twitter.com twitter
Create Your Own Social Networks	Allow users to create their own social network around a common topic; groups can be public or private	ning.com NING
Business-Related Social Networks	Allow users to seek potential clients, business opportunities, jobs, or job candidates	linkedin.com Linked in
Media Sharing Networks	Allow users to share pictures and videos	youtube.com YouTube instagram.com pinterest.com
Information Sharing Networks	Allow users to share information	delicious.com delicious wikipedia.org WIKIPEDIA The Free Encyclopedia slideshare.net
Information Recommendations and Filtering (Bookmarking) Networks	Allow users to post their opinion of a product, service, news, or web item for others to see and use	reddit.com reddit digg.com digg

respond to messages at their own convenience. E-mail is also convenient for exchanging and collaborating on documents via attachments.

How private is e-mail? Although e-mail is a more private exchange of information than public social networking sites, e-mails are not really private. Consider the following:

- Because e-mails can be printed or forwarded to others, you never know who may read your e-mail.
- Most e-mail content is not protected, so you should never use e-mail to send personal or sensitive information such as bank account or Social Security numbers. Doing so could lead to identity theft.
- Employers have access to e-mail sent from the workplace, so use caution when putting negative or controversial content in e-mail.
- Even after you've deleted a message, it doesn't really vanish. Many Internet service providers and companies archive e-mail, which can be accessed or subpoenaed in the event of a lawsuit or investigation.

What are some tips on e-mail etiquette? When you write a casual e-mail to friends, you obviously don't need to follow any specific e-mail guidelines (except to remember that your e-mail may be forwarded). But when you send e-mail for professional reasons, you should use proper e-mail etiquette. The following are a few guidelines (also see Figure 3.4):

- Be concise and to the point.
- Use the spell-checker and proofread your e-mail before sending it.
- Avoid using abbreviations such as *u*, *r*, *LOL*, and *BTW*.
- Include a meaningful subject line to help recipients prioritize and organize e-mails.
- Add a signature line that includes your contact information.
- Include only those people on the e-mail who truly need to receive it.

Following such guidelines maintains professionalism, increases efficiency, and might even help protect a company from lawsuits.

Are there different types of e-mail systems? There are two different types of e-mail systems:

1. **Web-based e-mail**, such as Yahoo! mail or Gmail, is managed with your web browser and allows you to access your e-mail from the web.
2. An **e-mail client** requires a program, such as Microsoft Outlook, to be installed on your computer. When you open the program, your e-mail is downloaded to your computer.

The primary difference between the two is access. Web-based e-mail allows you to access e-mail from any Internet-connected device, but you can't use your e-mail when you're offline. With an e-mail client, you view your e-mail on the computer on which the e-mail client software has been installed, but you can then view and manage your e-mail while you're offline. Both systems can be used together for the "best of both worlds." You can have a Gmail account, for example, so that you can read your e-mail from any computer connected to the

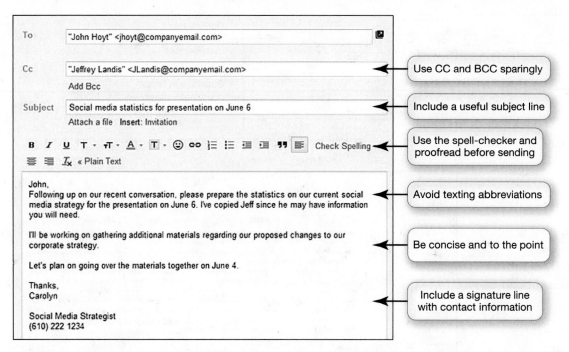

To   "John Hoyt" <jhoyt@companyemail.com>

Cc   "Jeffrey Landis" <JLandis@companyemail.com> ◄——— Use CC and BCC sparingly
     Add Bcc

Subject   Social media statistics for presentation on June 6 ◄——— Include a useful subject line
     Attach a file   Insert: Invitation

B *I* U   T ⋅ ₸ ⋅ **A** ⋅ T ⋅ ☺ ∞ ⋮≡ ⋮≡ ⇥ ⇤ " ▤   Check Spelling ◄——— Use the spell-checker and proofread before sending
≡ ≡ *I*ₓ « Plain Text

John,
Following up on our recent conversation, please prepare the statistics on our current social ◄——— Avoid texting abbreviations
media strategy for the presentation on June 6. I've copied Jeff since he may have information
you will need.

I'll be working on gathering additional materials regarding our proposed changes to our ◄——— Be concise and to the point
corporate strategy.

Let's plan on going over the materials together on June 4.

Thanks,
Carolyn

Social Media Strategist ◄——— Include a signature line with contact information
(610) 222 1234

FIGURE 3.4 Using simple guidelines of e-mail etiquette can promote a professional image and make your message more effective.

Internet, and you can also have Outlook installed on your primary computer and set up the program to display your Gmail account (see Figure 3.5).

Instant Messaging

Is instant messaging just for friends? You've most likely used **instant messaging (IM)** services—programs that let you communicate in real time over the Internet. Although IM is most often used for conversations between friends, many businesses use IM as a means of instant communication between co-workers. Some IM systems provide mechanisms to hold conversations with more than one person, either through simultaneous individual conversations or with group chats. And some programs even let you conduct video chats using a webcam.

AIM, Google Chat, Windows Messenger, and Yahoo! Messenger are proprietary IM services, meaning you can IM or chat only with those who share the same IM service and are on your contact or buddy list. Another option is to chat with those you've "friended" on Facebook through Facebook's chat option. There are also universal chat services such as Trillian and Digsby that you install on your computer and that allow you to chat with users of all popular IMs, regardless of the service they use.

Wikis

What are wikis? You've no doubt heard of Wikipedia (**wikipedia.org**), the popular collaborative online encyclopedia. Wikipedia is one example of a **wiki**, a web application that allows users to add, remove, or edit its content. Wiki content

BITS&BYTES

Outlook.com

With the release of Office 2013, Microsoft introduced Outlook.com, a free web-based e-mail service that is linked to your desktop Outlook data and can pull additional contact information from Facebook, Twitter, and LinkedIn as well as your calendar. Outlook.com is a combination of Hotmail and Windows Live (which no longer exist). All you need in order to access the web-based e-mail is a Windows account—which you already may have if you have access to OneDrive, Xbox Live, or have a current Hotmail or Windows Live account. Outlook.com offers a clean, ad-free inbox, with additional features borrowed from the installed version of Outlook that can simplify using e-mail. If you already have another web-based e-mail account (such as Gmail) and you don't want to switch your e-mail address, you can still enjoy the features of Outlook.com; just plug in your Gmail e-mail address, and it syncs automatically.

such as that found on Wikipedia is created collaboratively by multiple users, resulting in an emergent "common" opinion rather than the opinion of an individual writer. Because of wiki technology, Wikipedia's content can be updated continually.

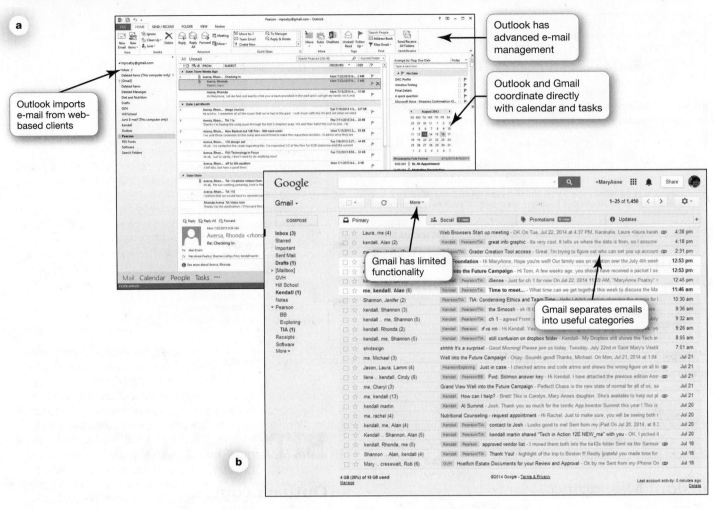

FIGURE 3.5 (a) Client-Based and (b) Web-Based E-mail Systems *(Courtesy of Google, Inc.)*

Annotations on figure:
- Outlook imports e-mail from web-based clients
- Outlook has advanced e-mail management
- Outlook and Gmail coordinate directly with calendar and tasks
- Gmail has limited functionality
- Gmail separates emails into useful categories

What else are wikis used for? Wikis are not just used to create Wikipedia; they're also useful tools for business collaboration. Rather than needing to pass documents back and forth via e-mail and possibly losing track of which version is the most recent, wikis allow all who have access to the wiki page to post their ideas and modify the content of the current version of a single document (see Figure 3.6). Wikis provide the extra benefit of users being able to access, review, and even revert back to past versions at any time.

Some web-based document products, such as Google Drive (**drive.google.com**), have wiki-like features to promote similar online collaboration, and specific wiki software, such as Wikispaces (**wikispaces.com**) and MediaWiki (**mediawiki.org**), is available that you can download for free. The Wikimedia Foundation, which hosts Wikipedia, also hosts other collaborative projects, such as Wikibooks (textbooks), Wikiversity (learning tools),

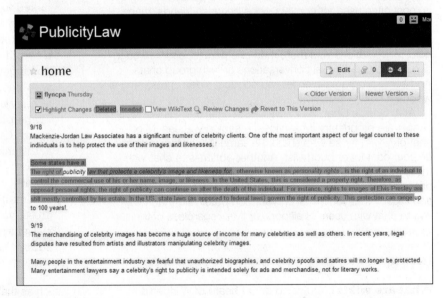

FIGURE 3.6 Different users can collaborate on a wiki page. A member of this wiki's group has modified the original text. Text that the person deleted appears in red, while inserted text appears in green. *(Wikimedia Foundation)*

and Wikisource (a document library). These wiki-type collaborative efforts apply to a variety of other useful applications. For example, wikiHow (**wikihow.org**) is an online project that uses both wikis and the collaborative process to build a large, online how-to manual.

Why isn't Wikipedia good to use as a source for a research paper? The idea behind content that is managed and edited by many users, such as that found on Wikipedia and other large public wikis, is that the group will keep the content current and valid. However, because wikis are publicly editable, they can't be trusted completely. If a user adds erroneous content, the community of users can quickly catch and correct it, but if you used Wikipedia as a source, you may have referenced erroneous content before it was corrected. To help address these concerns, Wikipedia has implemented tighter access controls, requiring users who want editing privileges to register with the site, but the risks still remain. Citizendium (**citizendium.org**), another open wiki encyclopedia, requires contributors to provide real names and sign an ethics pledge, and all postings are monitored.

Blogs

Why do people write blogs? A **blog** (short for **weblog**) is a personal log or journal posted on the web. Anyone can create a blog, and there are millions of blogs available to read, follow, and comment on. Blogs are generally written by a single author and are arranged as a listing of entries on a single page, with the most recent blog entry appearing at the top of the list. In addition, blogs are public. Blogs have searchable and organized content, making them user friendly. They're accessible from anywhere using a web browser.

Many people use blogs as a sort of personal scrapbook. Whenever the urge strikes, they report on their daily activities. Many other blogs focus on a particular topic. For example, the Movie Blog (**themovieblog.com**) contains reviews and opinions about movies, and engadget (**engadget.com**) is a blog devoted to discussing technogadgets. Many corporations, such as Walmart and Best Buy, have blogs written by employees. Blogcatalog (**blogcatalog.com**) is a blog directory that can help you find blogs that fit your interests.

Are all blogs text-based? The traditional form of a blog is primarily text-based but may also include images and audio. A **video log** (**vlog** or **video blog**) is a blog that uses video as the primary content (although it can also contain text, images, and audio). Vlogs are quickly becoming a popular means of personal expression, and many can be found by searching YouTube (**youtube.com**) and Tout (**tout.com**).

How do I create a blog? Many websites provide the tools you need to create your own blog. Two sites that offer free blog hosting are Blogger (**blogger.com**) and WordPress (**wordpress.com**). Such tools also let you add features like pictures or subpages to your blog. You can also choose to host your blog yourself so that the URL reflects your name or the name of your business. If you choose this option, you'll need your own website and a URL so people can access it.

 SOUND BYTE

Blogging

In this Sound Byte, you'll see why blogs are one of today's most popular publishing mediums. You'll also learn how to create and publish your own blog.

Are there any problems with blogs? The popularity of blogs has brought about a new problem: *spam blogs* (*splogs*), which are artificially created blog sites filled with fake articles or stolen text (a tactic known as *blog scraping*). Splogs, which contain links to other sites associated with the splog's creator, have the intention of either increasing traffic to, or increasing search engine rankings for, these usually disreputable or useless websites. Although not really harmful, splogs are another unwanted form of content that continues to grow like weeds on the web.

Podcasts and Webcasts

What is a podcast? A **podcast** is a form of digital media comprised of a series of audio or video files that are distributed over the Internet. There are podcasts for radio shows, audiobooks, magazines, and even educational programs, which you can download to any device that can play audio files. What makes podcasts different from other audio files found on the web is that podcasts deliver their content using **Really Simple Syndication (RSS)**. RSS is a format that sends the latest content of the podcast series automatically to an **aggregator** such as iTunes or Feedspot. An aggregator locates all the RSS series to which you've subscribed and automatically downloads only the new content to your computer or media player. If you have several favorite websites or podcasts, rather than checking each site for updated content, aggregators collect all the site updates in one place. These updates or changes to the content are then delivered automatically if you subscribe to the podcast, instead of you having to search for the latest content and download it manually.

Where can I find podcasts? Most online news and radio sites offer podcasts of their programs. Although many podcasts are news related, others offer entertaining and educational content. For example, you can access lessons on yoga, foreign language classes, or DIY tips. Many schools supply students with course content updates through podcasts, and instructors sometimes create podcasts of their lectures. Figure 3.7 lists some websites where you can find podcasts.

Can I create my own podcast? It's simple to create a podcast. To record the audio content all you need is a computer with a microphone, and if you want to make a video podcast, you also need a webcam or video camera. Although high-end equipment will produce more sophisticated output, you certainly can use whatever equipment you might own. You may also need additional software to edit the audio and video

FIGURE 3.7

Podcast Directories and Aggregators

iTunes (itunes.com)

- Software makes it easy to play, manage, and share your favorite podcasts

Podfeed (podfeed.net)

- Broad collection of podcasts

Stitcher (stitcher.com)

- Customize podcast playlists

YouTube (youtube.com)

- Good source for video blogs (vlogs)

content, depending on how professional you wish the podcast to be. After you've recorded and edited the podcast content, you need to export it to MP3 format. The free program Audacity (**audacity.sourceforge.net**) lets you both edit audio files and export them to MP3 format. All that's left is for you to create an RSS feed (tricky, but doable) and then upload the content to a site that hosts podcasts, such as iTunes, Podfeed, or Stitcher.

What's a webcast? A **webcast** is the (usually live) broadcast of audio or video content over the Internet. Unlike podcasts, which are prerecorded and made available for download, most webcasts are distributed in "real time," meaning that they're live or one-time events. Some webcasts are archived so they can be viewed at a later date. Webcasts are not updated automatically like podcasts, but some, such as Microsoft's On-Demand Webcasts, are RSS feeds.

Webcasts use continuous audio and video feeds, which let you view and download large audio and video files. Webcasts can include noninteractive content such as a simultaneous broadcast of a radio or television program, but more recent webcasts invite interactive responses from the viewing or listening audience. For example, ORLive (**orlive.com**) provides surgical webcasts that demonstrate the latest surgical innovations and techniques. Webcasts also are used in the corporate world to broadcast annual meetings and in the educational arena to transmit seminars.

Figure 3.8 lists the popular methods of online communication that we've discussed. ■

FIGURE 3.8

Methods of Online Communication

SOCIAL NETWORKING	E-MAIL	INSTANT MESSAGING
• Web 2.0 technology • Lets you build an online network of friends • Lets you share media content	• Most common form of online communication • Asynchronous (not having to be done at the same time)	• Real-time exchange • Can be used with multiple persons simultaneously • Video/audio chats available

WIKIS	BLOGS	PODCASTS	WEBCASTS
• Great collaborative tool • Content updated by many users • Historical content kept, so you can revert to past versions	• Written by a single author • Chronologic entries • Searchable content • May include images, audio, and video	• Audio/video files delivered via RSS • New RSS content collected with aggregator • Can download and view content on portable media player	• Most often live, streamed broadcasts

web
ENTERTAINMENT

When you think of how you use the Internet for entertainment purposes, what comes to mind? Streaming audio and video, Internet radio, MP3s, interactive gaming, and smart TV are all favorite responses. What makes all these forms of web entertainment so popular is their multimedia content. **Multimedia** is anything that involves one or more forms of media in addition to text. It includes the following:

* *Graphics* such as drawings, charts, and photos (the most basic form of multimedia)
* *Audio files* such as the clips you hear when you visit websites, MP3 files you download, podcasts and webcasts, and live broadcasts you can listen to through Internet radio
* *Video files* ranging from simple, short video clips on sites such as YouTube (**youtube.com**) to movies and television shows on sites such as Hulu (**hulu.com**)

What is streaming media?
Streaming media is multimedia (audio and video) that is continuously fed to your browser so you avoid having to wait for the entire file to download completely before listening to or watching it. Without streaming media, you wouldn't be able to watch movies on Netflix or on demand from your cable provider, listen to live audio broadcasting, or even play some online games. Internet radio also uses streaming media to present a continuous stream of audio to its listeners. Pandora (**pandora.com**) enables you to personalize your audio stream by specifying a favorite artist, song, or composer that you want to hear. Then the service picks music with the same characteristics. In addition to Internet radio service, Spotify (**spotify.com**) lets you pick your own songs, build playlists, and share your playlists with others.

Do I need anything besides a browser to view or hear multimedia on the web?
Most graphics on the web will appear in your browser without any additional software. However, to view and hear some multimedia files—for example, podcasts, YouTube videos, and audio files—you might need a **plug-in** (or **player**)—a special software component that adds a specific feature to an existing software program. Figure 3.9 lists the most popular plug-ins.

FIGURE 3.9

Popular Plug-Ins and Players and Their Uses		
PLUG-IN NAME	**WHERE YOU GET IT**	**WHAT IT DOES**
Adobe Reader	adobe.com	Views and prints portable document format (PDF) files
Flash Player	adobe.com	Plays animation and movies through web browsers
QuickTime Player	apple.com	Plays MP3, animation, music, musical instrument digital interface (MIDI), audio, and video files
Shockwave Player	adobe.com	Plays interactive games, multimedia, graphics, and streaming audio and video on the web
Silverlight	microsoft.com	Similar to Flash; plays web-based animations and videos
Windows Media Player	microsoft.com	Plays MP3 and WAV music files, movies, and live audio and video on broadcasts on the web

(NetPhotos3/Alamy; NetPhotos3/Alamy; NetPhotos3/Alamy; NetPhotos3/Alamy; Shutterstock; Nicemonkey/Shutterstock)

BITS&BYTES

HTML5 Versus Flash

Adobe's Flash is a plug-in you're no doubt familiar with that is designed to run multimedia through web browsers. Flash has been the multimedia standard for decades and was at one time used with all browsers. However, in 2007, a controversy between Flash and HTML5 began when the Apple iPhone was introduced—and this controversy continued with the later introduction of the iPad. What was the problem? Both the iPhone and the iPad ran with an operating system that supported HTML5 rather than Flash. Flash-based YouTube videos, for example, would not play on an iPhone or an iPad.

Why would Apple choose HTML5 over Flash? HTML5—the fifth revision of the HTML standard—is open-source code, meaning the program code is available to the general public to use or modify, unlike Flash, which is owned by one company. The goal of HTML5 is to ease the handling of multimedia and graphical content on the web, to reduce or eliminate the need for plug-ins, and to become device independent. Adobe discontinued development of Flash for mobile devices several years ago and has reoriented its efforts in helping to improve HTML5 so that it becomes as fully functional as Flash.

Because Flash had been dominant for so long, it's taken a while for the HTML5 standard to catch on. But even Flash stalwarts such as YouTube, which was solely Flash dependent, added capability to run HTML5 video in 2011. Similarly, most Flash-dependent websites have incorporated HTML5 players or extensions to run on mobile devices and browsers. While the Flash Player plugin is still installed and used in the majority of desktop browsers, HTML5 will undoubtedly become the standard for mobile devices and browsers.

How do I get players and plug-ins? If you purchased your computer within the past several years, most popular plug-ins probably came preinstalled on your computer. If a website requires a plug-in not installed on your computer, you are usually automatically directed to a site where you can download the plug-in free of charge. For example, to use streaming video, your browser might send you to the Adobe website, where you can download Flash Player.

Is there any way to get multimedia web content to load faster? When you're on the Internet, your browser keeps track of the sites you've visited so that it can load them faster the next time you visit them. This *cache* (temporary storage place) of the text pages, images, and video files from recently visited websites can make your web surfing more efficient, but it can also slow down your hard drive. Additionally, if you don't have your cache settings configured to check for updates to the web page, your browser may not load the most recent content. To keep your system running efficiently, consider doing the following:

- Delete your temporary Internet cache every month or so, depending on your usage.
- To ensure the most recent website content is displayed, click Refresh or press the F5 key if you revisit a site in the same browsing session.
- Clear your Internet cache manually or adjust the setting in your web browser so that it clears the cache automatically every time you exit the browser. ■

conducting business over the internet:
E-COMMERCE

It's hard to believe that only a few years ago, many people were scared to buy things online. Today, there is little hesitation, and you can buy nearly anything on the web, including big-ticket items such as homes and cars. **E-commerce**—short for **electronic commerce**—is the process of conducting business online. Figure 3.10 shows the most common items purchased through e-commerce transactions.

Are there different types of e-commerce? There are three types of e-commerce business models:

1. **Business-to-consumer (B2C)** transactions take place between businesses and consumers. Such transactions include those between customers and completely online businesses (such as **Amazon.com**) and those between customers and stores that have both an online and a physical presence, such as Target (**target.com**). Such businesses are referred to as *click-and-brick* businesses. Some click-and-bricks allow online purchases and in-store pickups and returns.

2. **Business-to-business (B2B)** transactions occur when businesses buy and sell goods and services to other businesses. An example is Omaha Paper Company (**omahapaper.com**), which distributes paper products to other companies.

3. **Consumer-to-consumer (C2C)** transactions occur when consumers sell to each other through sites such as eBay (**ebay.com**), Craigslist (**craigslist.org**), and Etsy (**etsy.com**).

Consumer electronics

Books

Athletic apparel and sporting goods

Shoes

Pet supplies

FIGURE 3.10 Top Five Online Consumer Purchases.

Social commerce is a subset of e-commerce that uses social networks to assist in marketing and purchasing products. If you're on Facebook, you've no doubt noticed the many businesses that have Facebook pages asking you to "Like" them. Consumers are voicing their opinions on Facebook and other sites about products and services by providing ratings and reviews, and studies show that such peer recommendations have a major influence on buying behavior. When you see your friend on Facebook recommend a product or service, you're more likely to click through to that retailer and check out the product.

For example, after implementing the Facebook "Like" button, American Eagle noticed that Facebook-referred visitors spent 57 percent more than other online shoppers. Other peer-influenced e-commerce trends include group-buying and individual customization. Groupon and LivingSocial are two popular deal-of-the-day group purchase websites that require a certain number of people to buy the discounted deal before the deal can go through. CafePress and Zazzle sell T-shirts and other items that are customized with your own graphic designs.

But e-commerce encompasses more than just shopping opportunities. Today, anything you can do inside your bank you can do online, and approximately 80 percent of U.S. households do some form of online banking. Many people use online services to check their account balances, pay bills online, and check stock and mutual fund performance. Credit card companies allow you to view, schedule, and pay your credit card bill; brokerage houses allow you to conduct investment activities online.

E-Commerce Safeguards

Just how safe are online transactions? When you buy something online, you may use a credit card; therefore, money is exchanged directly between your credit card company and the online merchant's bank. Because online shopping eliminates a salesclerk or other human intermediary from the transaction, it can actually be safer than traditional retail shopping.

What precautions should I take when shopping online? In addition to using some basic common computing sense such as having a firewall and up-to-date antivirus

 ACTIVE HELPDESK
Doing Business Online

In this Active Helpdesk, you'll play the role of a helpdesk staffer, fielding questions about e-commerce and e-commerce safeguards.

software on your computer, and using strong passwords for all your online accounts, there are several important guidelines to follow to ensure your online shopping experience is a safe one (see Figure 3.11):

- **Look for visual indicators that the website is secure.** Check that the beginning of the URL changes from "http://" to "https://"—with the *s* standing for secure, indicating that the **secure sockets layer** protocol has been applied to manage the security of the website. Also, look for a small icon of a closed padlock in the toolbar (in both Internet Explorer and Firefox) and a green-colored address bar, indications that the site may be secure. (However, note that even if a site has these indicators, it still might not be safe. Consider the validity of the site before making a purchase.)

- **Shop at well-known, reputable sites.** If you aren't familiar with a site, investigate it with the Better Business Bureau (**bbb.org**) or at bizrate (**bizrate.com**). Make sure the company has a phone number and street address in addition to a website. You can also look for third-party verification such as that from TRUSTe or the Better Business Bureau. But let common sense prevail. Online deals that seem too good to be true are generally just that—and may be pirated software or illegal distributions.

- **Pay by credit card, not debit card.** Federal laws protect credit card users, but debit card users don't have the same level of protection. If possible, reserve one credit card for Internet purchases only; even better, use a prepaid credit card that has a small credit limit. For an extra layer of security, find out if your credit card company has a service that confirms your identity with an extra password or code that only you know to use when making an online transaction or that offers a one-time-use credit card number. Also, consider using a third-party payment processor such as PayPal or Google Wallet. PayPal also offers a security key that provides additional security to your PayPal account.

- **When you place an order, check the return policy, save a copy of the order, and make sure you receive a confirmation number.** Make sure you read and understand the fine print on warranties, return policies, and the retailer's privacy statements. If the site disappears overnight, this information may help you in filing a dispute or reporting a problem to a site such as the Better Business Bureau.

- **Avoid making online transactions when using public computers.** Public computers may have *spyware*

(Beboy/Shutterstock; Roy Wylam/Alamy; Photoinnovation/Shutterstock; KRT/Newscom; Maxx-Studio/Shutterstock; Isak55/Shutterstock; Alhovik/Shutterstock; Iqoncept/Shutterstock)

FIGURE 3.11

Online Shopping Precautions

When shopping at home, use a firewall and antivirus software for general computer protection.

Don't shop on public WiFi networks, as they may contain spyware.

Check for visual indicators such as https:// in the URL, a closed padlock icon, and a green address bar.

Look for third-party verification from TRUSTe or the Better Business Bureau symbol.

Use a credit card, not a debit card, to protect transactions, or use a third-party payer such as PayPal or Google Wallet.

Create a strong password for all online accounts (one that includes numbers and other symbols such as @).

Deals that are too good to be true are usually just that.

Read and understand the fine print on warranties, return policies, and the retailer's privacy statements.

installed, which are programs that track and log your keystrokes and can retrieve your private information. Similarly, unless you have specific protection on your own notebook computer, avoid making wireless transactions on public hotspots.

Whether you're doing business, playing games, or communicating with friends or colleagues, the Internet makes these activities more accessible. The Internet can potentially make these experiences and activities more enriched as well, although you must take precautions for the safest of experiences. ■

> **Before moving on to Part 2:**
> - **Watch Replay Video 3.1** ⊙ .
> - Then check your understanding of what you've learned so far.

BITS&BYTES

Making Safe Payments Using PayPal and Apple Pay

When people first began making online purchases, many were not comfortable buying from sites like eBay because the sites required them to give personal financial information such as credit card numbers to strangers. PayPal (**paypal.com**) resolved that issue by serving as a payment intermediary that allows anyone to pay with credit cards and bank accounts without sharing their financial information. PayPal is now a standard means of payment for many online merchants and offers buyer protection and dispute resolution services. Figure 3.12 shows how PayPal works.

Apple Pay is aiming to change customers' payment habits by having them pay merely by using their iPhone or iWatch. Apple Pay uses security features that shield your credit card information from merchants (and Apple!), making it a safer payment method than handing over a credit card to be swiped. So forget fumbling for your credit card—just wave your phone!

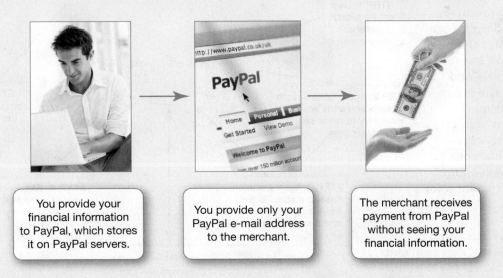

| You provide your financial information to PayPal, which stores it on PayPal servers. | You provide only your PayPal e-mail address to the merchant. | The merchant receives payment from PayPal without seeing your financial information. |

FIGURE 3.12 How PayPal Works. *(Yuri Arcurs/Shutterstock; AKP Photos/Alamy; Happydancing/Shutterstock)*

Think about all the types of data on the web that you access manually, such as appointment times, transportation and entertainment schedules, and store locations and hours. It would seem that computers would be helpful in plugging through all this web data, but oddly, that is not the case. Web pages are designed for people to read, not for computers to manipulate. As yet, no reliable way exists for computers to process the meaning of data on a web page so that it can be used to see relationships or make decisions.

The **semantic web** (or **Web 3.0**) is an evolving extension of the web in which data is defined in such a way to make it more easily processed by computers. Right now, search engines function by recognizing keywords such as *office hours* and *dentist*, but they can't determine, for example, in which office and on what days Dr. Smith works and what his available appointment times are. By using a so-called "agent," the semantic web would enable computers to find that type of information, coordinate it with your other schedules and preferences, and then make the appointment for you.

The semantic web would also assist you in comparing products, prices, and shipping options by finding the best product option based on specified criteria and then placing the order for you. Additionally, the agent would record the financial transaction into your personal bookkeeping software and arrange for a technician to help install the software, if needed.

For the semantic web to work, businesses, services, and software would all use the same categorization structures so that similar information would share the same attributes, ensuring consistency of metadata throughout the web. The semantic web would build on this type of capability so that each website would have text and pictures (for people to read) and metadata (for computers to read) describing the information on the web (see Figure 3.13).

Although some of the semantic web's functionalities are beginning to emerge in technologies such as Siri in the current iPhone operating system, the majority of its functionality and implementation are still in development. The greatest challenge is recoding all the information currently available on the web into the type of metadata that computers can recognize. The very grandeur of that task means that we will not see a fully functional semantic web until sometime in the distant future. In the meantime, we can continue to benefit from each small step toward that goal.

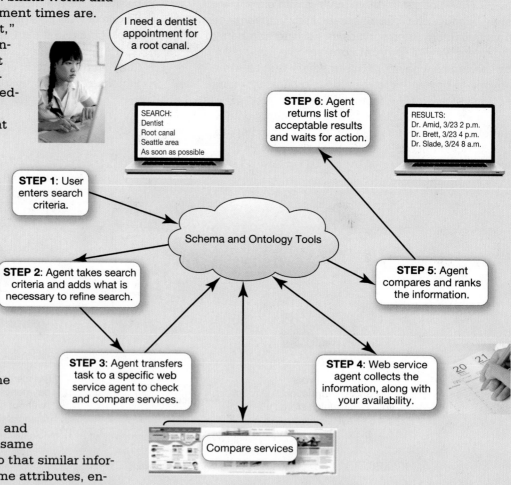

I need a dentist appointment for a root canal.

SEARCH:
Dentist
Root canal
Seattle area
As soon as possible

STEP 1: User enters search criteria.

STEP 2: Agent takes search criteria and adds what is necessary to refine search.

STEP 3: Agent transfers task to a specific web service agent to check and compare services.

Schema and Ontology Tools

Compare services

STEP 4: Web service agent collects the information, along with your availability.

STEP 5: Agent compares and ranks the information.

STEP 6: Agent returns list of acceptable results and waits for action.

RESULTS:
Dr. Amid, 3/23 2 p.m.
Dr. Brett, 3/23 4 p.m.
Dr. Slade, 3/24 8 a.m.

FIGURE 3.13 The Semantic Web.

check your understanding// review & practice

For a quick review to see what you've learned so far, answer the following questions. Visit **pearsonhighered.com/ techinaction** to check your answers.

multiple choice

1. Which is NOT an event associated with the beginning of the Internet?

   a. The U.S. Department of Defense creates ARPA.

   b. TCP/IP protocol was developed that allowed different computers to communicate with each other.

   c. Amazon.com was one of the first websites on the Internet.

   d. The first e-mail program was written by Ray Tomlinson.

2. What do you need if you want to read, send, and organize e-mail from *any* computer connected to the Internet?

   a. an e-mail client program

   b. an e-mail server

   c. an e-mail aggregator

   d. a web-based e-mail account

3. Which is NOT an example of Web 2.0 technology?

   a. e-mail   **c.** blogging

   b. social networking   **d.** wiki

4. Which of the following is NOT a characteristic of a blog?

   a. Blogs are used to express opinions.

   b. Blogs are generally written by a single author.

   c. Blogs are private and require password access.

   d. Blogs are arranged as a listing of entries.

5. Which of the following would be the correct classification for Etsy.com?

   a. B2B

   b. C2C

   c. B2C

   d. Click-and-brick business

To take an autograded version of this review, please go to the companion website at **pearsonhighered.com/techinaction**, or go your MyITLab course.

Continue

TRY THIS

Create a OneDrive Account to Store and Share Your Files in the Cloud

You probably have your favorite ways of moving your files around. Perhaps you have a USB drive or you e-mail files to yourself, or maybe you have a portable external hard drive. With any of these solutions, there can be confusion as to which is the most current version of the file if you have worked on it on multiple devices at different times. You also run the risk of losing your USB drive or deleting the e-mail attachment by mistake. These methods also make exchanging files difficult if you want to share your files or collaborate with a group.

A simpler solution is to use a web-based or cloud storage and sharing service such as OneDrive or Dropbox. OneDrive is part of Microsoft's Office Online. With 15 GB of free storage space for new users, you can store thousands of files and get to them anytime you're online.

Step 1 Sign in to OneDrive: Go to **onedrive.com**. Sign in to your Microsoft account. If you don't have a Microsoft account, creating one is easy. A Microsoft account will give you access to services such as OneDrive, Xbox LIVE, and **Outlook.com**.

Step 2 Create a Folder and Add Files: Once you're in OneDrive, you can create a folder and then begin to add files.

- To create a folder: Click **Create** at the top of the page, click **Folder**, and then give your new folder a name. Click the new folder to open it.
- To add a file: Click **Upload** at the top of the page, then locate the file and click **Open**. To upload more than one file, hold the **Ctrl key** while you select each file.

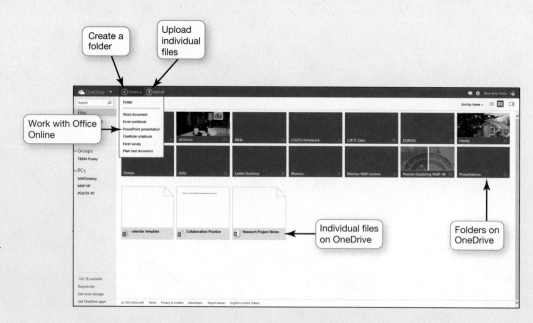

Step 3 Share a File or Folder:
To share a file or folder, do the following:

- Right-click the file or folder that you want to share, and click **Share**.
- Fill in the e-mail form.
- Establish editing privileges by clicking the **Recipients can only view** link. Then change to **Recipients can edit**, if desired, then click **Share**.
- To see what files that have been shared with you, click **Shared** in the left menu.

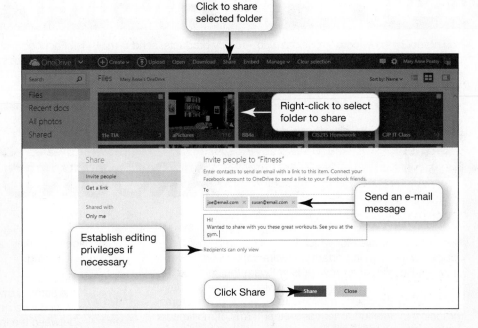

Click to share selected folder

Right-click to select folder to share

Send an e-mail message

Establish editing privileges if necessary

Click Share

Make This

TOOL: App Inventor 2

MAKE: A Web-Capable App

Want your app to be able to display a web page?

In this exercise, you'll continue your mobile app development by adding a new power to your apps: web browsing.

It's as easy as using the WebViewer component in **App Inventor**. Drag a WebViewer component onto your Designer screen, then control it with the Blocks for WebViewer. These allow you to go back, forward, to the home page, or to any specific URL.

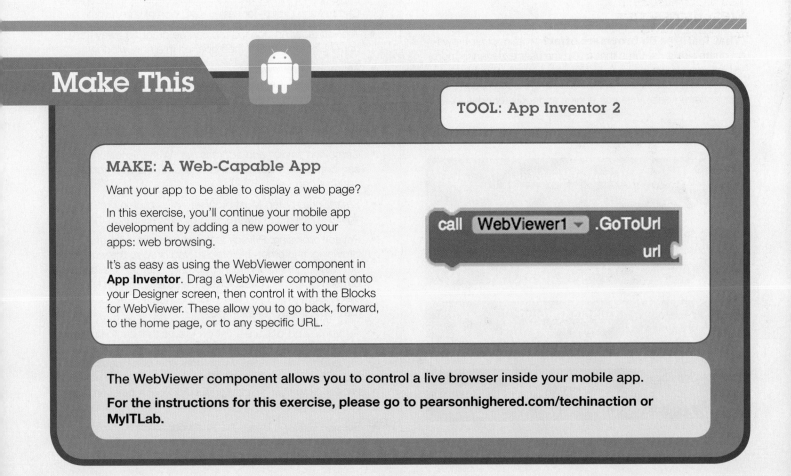

call WebViewer1 .GoToUrl
url

The WebViewer component allows you to control a live browser inside your mobile app.

For the instructions for this exercise, please go to pearsonhighered.com/techinaction or MyITLab.

Using the Web Effectively

You no doubt know how to use the web—to buy products, send e-mail, visit Facebook, and use Google—but do you know how to use it effectively? In this section, we'll look at ways to make your online experience more enjoyable, more productive, and even more efficient.

accessing and moving
AROUND THE WEB

None of the activities for which we use the web could happen without an important software application: a web browser. Recall that a browser is software that lets you locate, view, and navigate the web. Most browsers today are *graphical* browsers, meaning they can display pictures (graphics) in addition to text and other forms of multimedia such as sound and video. The most common browsers are displayed in Figure 3.14.

Web Browsers

What features do browsers offer? Most popular browsers share similar features that make the user experience more efficient (as shown in Figure 3.15). For example, most browsers include a built-in search box in which you can designate your preferred default search engine and tools for printing,

page formatting, and security settings. Other features include the following:

- *Tabbed browsing:* Web pages are loaded in "tabs" within the same browser window. Rather than having to switch among web pages in several open windows, you can flip between the tabs in one window. You may also save a group of tabs as a Favorites group if there are several tabs you often open at the same time.

- *Pinned tabs:* You can "dock" tabs to the taskbar (in Internet Explorer) or minimize and save them permanently (Google Chrome and Firefox) for easier navigation of your favorite sites.

- *Tear-off tabs:* An opened tab can be dragged away from its current window so it's then opened in a new window.

- *Thumbnail previews:* Another convenient navigation tool that most browsers share is providing thumbnail previews of all open web pages in open tabs.

- *Tab isolation:* With this feature, tabs are independent of each other, so if one crashes, it does not affect the other tabs.

- *Combined search and address bar:* With this feature, you can both type a website URL or search the web from the address bar.

- *SmartScreen filter:* Most browsers offer built-in protection against phishing, malware, and other web-based threats.

- *Privacy browsing:* Privacy features (such as InPrivate Browsing in Internet Explorer) let you browse the web without retaining a history trail, temporary Internet files, cookies, or usernames and passwords. These features are especially helpful when you use public computers at college or the public library, for example.

- *Add-ons:* Add-ons are small programs that customize and increase the functionality of the browser. Examples include Video DownloadHelper, which converts web videos, like those found on YouTube, to files you can save, as well as a Facebook toolbar that integrates Facebook functionality into your browser.

- *Session Restore:* Brings back all your active web pages if the browser or system shuts down unexpectedly.

Internet Explorer
A very popular browser by Microsoft

Firefox
Open source
Has strong following

Google Chrome
Newest browser
Quickly gaining popularity

Safari
Developed by Apple for Macs
Has a Windows version for PCs

(Pablo Fonseca O./La Nacion de Costa Rica/Newscom; Lucia Lanpur/Alamy Tommy (Louth)/Alamy 2020WEB/Alamy)

FIGURE 3.14 Common Web Browsers

FIGURE 3.15 Like most of the popular web browsers, Internet Explorer and Google Chrome include tabbed and privacy browsing and an address bar that doubles as a search bar. Pinned tabs make accessing your favorite sites even easier. *(Internal Revenue Service; NASA)*

BITS&BYTES

Maxthon: A Great Alternative Browser

Not well known in the United States but quite popular elsewhere globally, Maxthon is a web browser that rivals our U.S. favorites. Maxthon has the convenient features of tabbed browsing, bookmarking capabilities, thumbnails of previously viewed sites, and privacy viewing, so you'll feel quite at home rather quickly. Since Maxthon is a cloud-based browser, when you access the browser on any device, all your settings are synced. Maxthon does have some unique features, such as Maxthon's dock—a sidebar that resides in the desktop, with customizable shortcut icons to your favorite websites. In addition, Maxthon enables you to use mouse gestures so that you can match a specific mouse movement with a specific command. In addition, super drag and drop enables you to drag and drop a link, image, or highlighted text into the search box rather than typing the content; night mode adjusts the brightness of the screen; "snap" enables you to take screen grabs; and SkyNote lets you save and access notes. If you haven't already, you may enjoy taking Maxthon for a test drive.

URLs, Protocols, and Domain Names

What do all the parts of a URL mean? You gain initial access to a particular **website** by typing its unique address, or **Uniform Resource Locator** (**URL**, pronounced "you-are-ell"), in your browser. A website is comprised of many different web pages, each of which is a separate document with its own unique URL. Like a regular street address, a URL is comprised of several parts that help identify the web document it stands for (see Figure 3.16):

- the *protocol* (set of rules) used to retrieve the document;
- the **domain name**; and
- the *path* or subdirectory

Although every part of a URL is important information that ensures the web page you requested actually displays in your

FIGURE 3.16 The Parts of a URL

FIGURE 3.17

Common Top-Level Domains and Their Authorized Users

DOMAIN NAME	WHO CAN USE IT
.biz	Businesses
.com	Originally for commercial sites, but now can be used by anyone
.edu	Degree-granting institutions
.gov	Local, state, and federal U.S. governments
.info	Information service providers
.mil	U.S. military
.net	Originally for networking organizations, but no longer restricted
.org	Organizations (often not-for-profits)

browser, you don't have to type in every part in the location or address bar of the browser. Most current browsers no longer require you to enter the http:// protocol or the "www," and most don't even require the domain if it's a .com—the browser will enter those automatically.

What's the protocol? You're probably most familiar with URLs that begin with *http*, which is short for **Hypertext Transfer Protocol (HTTP)**. HTTP is the protocol that allows files to be transferred from a **web server**—a computer that hosts the website you're requesting—so that you can see it on your computer. The HTTP protocol is what the web is based on.

Is HTTP the only protocol I need to use? HTTP is the most common protocol, but it's not the only one. HTTP is part of the Internet protocol suite, a group of protocols that govern how information is exchanged on a network. Another protocol in that group is the **File Transfer Protocol (FTP)**. As its name implies, FTP was originally designed, before the HTTP protocol was developed, to transfer files from your computer to a web server. Today, FTP is often used when you have large files to upload or download. To connect to most FTP servers, you need a user ID and password. To upload and download files from FTP sites, you can use a browser or file transfer software such as WS_FTP, Fetch, or FileZilla.

BitTorrent, like FTP, is a protocol used to transfer files, though it's not part of the Internet protocol suite. To use BitTorrent, you install a software client program. It uses a *peer-to-peer networking system,* so that sharing occurs between connected computers that also have the BitTorrent client installed. BitTorrent was developed in 2001 and has been gaining popularity, especially among users who want to share music, movies, and games. Use caution, however, when accessing BitTorrent content. Because it is a peer-to-peer system, it's possible for copyrighted material to be shared illegally.

What's in a domain name? The domain name identifies the site's **host**, the location that maintains the computers that store the website files. For example, **www.berkeley.edu** is the domain name for the University of California at Berkeley website. The suffix in the domain name after the dot (such as "com" or "edu") is called the **top-level domain**. This suffix indicates the kind of organization to which the host belongs. Figure 3.17 lists the most frequently used top-level domains.

Each country has its own top-level domain. These are two-letter designations such as .za for South Africa and .us for the United States. A sampling of country codes is shown in Figure 3.18. Within a country-specific domain, further subdivisions can be made for regions or states. For instance, the .us domain contains subdomains for each state, using the two-letter abbreviation of the state. For example, the URL for Pennsylvania's website is **www.state.pa.us**.

What's the information after the domain name that I sometimes see? When the URL is the domain name, such as **www.nytimes.com**, you're requesting a site's home page. However, sometimes a forward slash and additional text follow the domain name, such as in **www.nytimes.com/pages/crosswords**. The information after each slash indicates a particular file or **path** (or **subdirectory**)

FIGURE 3.18

Examples of Country Codes

COUNTRY CODE	COUNTRY
.au	Australia
.ca	Canada
.jp	Japan
.uk	United Kingdom

Note: For a full listing of country codes, refer to **iana.org/domains/root/db/**.

FIGURE 3.19 Navigating a Web Page *(U.S. Small Business Administration)*

within the website. In Figure 3.16, you would connect to the crossword page on the *New York Times* site.

Hyperlinks and Beyond

What's the best way to get around in a website?
As its name implies, the web is a series of interconnected paths, or links. You've no doubt moved around the web by clicking on **hyperlinks**, specially coded elements that let you jump from one web page to another within the same website or to another site altogether (see Figure 3.19). Generally, text that operates as a hyperlink appears in a different color (often blue) and is usually underlined, but sometimes images also act as hyperlinks. When you hover your cursor over a hyperlink, the cursor changes to a hand with a finger pointing upward.

What other tools can I use to navigate a website?
To move back or forward one page at a time, you can use the browser's Back and Forward buttons (see Figure 3.19).

To help navigate more quickly through a website, some sites provide a **breadcrumb trail**—a navigation aid that shows users the path they have taken to get to a web page, or where the page is located within the website. It usually appears at the top of a page. Figure 3.19 shows

an example of a breadcrumb trail. "Breadcrumbs" get their name from the fairy tale "Hansel and Gretel," in which the characters drop breadcrumbs on the trail to find their way out of a forest. By clicking on earlier links in a breadcrumb trail, you can go directly to a previously visited web page without having to use the Back button to navigate back through the website.

The History list on your browser's toolbar is also a handy feature. The History list shows all the websites and pages you've visited over a certain period of time. These sites are organized according to date and can go back as far as three weeks, depending on your browsing activity. To access the History list in Internet Explorer, click the star in the upper right-hand corner of the browser window and then click the History tab.

 SOUND BYTE
Welcome to the Web

In this Sound Byte, you'll visit the web in a series of guided tours of useful websites. This tour serves as an introductory guide for web newcomers but is also a great resource for more experienced users.

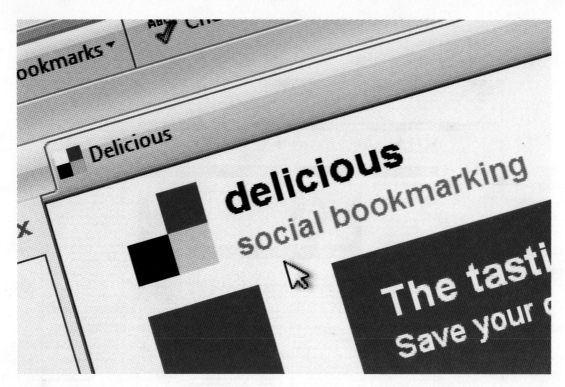

FIGURE 3.20 Delicious is a social bookmarking website that allows you to organize and share your favorite websites. *(Delicious Science, LLC, www.delicious.com)*

Favorites, Live Bookmarks, and Tagging

What's the best way to mark a site so I can return to it later? If you want an easy way to return to a specific web page, you can use your browser's **Bookmarks** feature (Internet Explorer calls this feature **Favorites**). This feature places a marker of the site's URL in an easily retrievable list in your browser's toolbar. To organize the sites into categories, most browsers offer tools to create folders.

Favorites and Bookmarks are great for quickly locating those sites you use most, but they're accessible to you only when you're on your own computer. Although most browsers provide features that let you export the list of bookmarks to a file you can import to another computer or another browser, another way to access your Bookmarks and Favorites from any computer is to use MyBookmarks (**mybookmarks.com**), a free Internet service that stores your Bookmarks and Favorites online.

What are live bookmarks? Live bookmark is a feature in Firefox that adds the technology of RSS feeds to bookmarking. Safari and Internet Explorer also have built-in RSS readers, while Chrome requires that you add on an extension. Because the web is constantly changing, the site you bookmarked last week may subsequently change and add new content. Traditionally, you would notice the change only the next time you visited the site. Live bookmarks deliver content updates to you as soon as they become available using RSS, the same technology that updates blogs and podcasts that we described earlier in the chapter. Live bookmarks and RSS feeds are useful if you're interested in the most up-to-date news stories, sports scores, or stock prices.

What is tagging? Tagging, also known as **social bookmarking**, is like bookmarking your favorite website, but instead of saving it to your browser for only you to see, you're saving it to a social bookmarking site so that you can share it with others. A social bookmark or tag is a **keyword** or term that you assign to a web page, digital image, or video. A tag can be something you create to describe the digital content, or it can be a suggested term provided by the website. For example, as you were surfing the web you came across a web page with a great article on inexpensive places to go for spring break. You might tag the article with the term *vacations*. Others on the same social bookmarking site who are looking for websites about vacations may use *vacations* as the search term and find the article you tagged.

Delicious (**delicious.com**) is one of the original social bookmarking sites (see Figure 3.20). Delicious lets you group related links and organize them into "bundles." So if you've collected several links to websites about different places to go to over spring break, you can collect all those links into one bundle about vacations. Or if you want to see what links others may have found about interesting vacations, you could search Delicious with the term *vacations* to see other vacation-related bundles.

Another social bookmarking site is Diigo (**diigo.com**). Diigo differs from Delicious by allowing you to annotate the pages with highlights and sticky notes. Through Diigo, you can archive web pages so they are always available. ∎

trends in IT

Doing Business on a Shoestring—Thanks to the Internet

Let's say you think that flip-flops in school colors would be a popular product. Your school's bookstore carries everything else with the school's colors and logo, but not flip-flops. You've asked your friends and several classmates, and most of them say they would buy flip-flops in the school's colors. So what do you do next? How do you move from product concept to selling a physical product?

Before the Internet, it would have been much more difficult and expensive to get your product produced and distributed. First, you would have had to find someone to design your flip-flops. Then, to make the flip-flops, you would have had to find a manufacturer, who may have required a high minimum order (maybe tens of thousands of pairs of flip-flops). You also would have needed a package design, marketing brochures, a company logo, a storage facility, and more. Finally, the largest hurdle would have been to convince a brick-and-mortar retailer, such as your campus bookstore, to carry your product.

Today, however, the Internet brings the power of the global economy right to your door (see Figure 3.21). For product design and manufacturing, you can visit a site like Alibaba (**alibaba.com**), which helps entrepreneurs locate manufacturers of all sorts of products. Many manufacturers are happy to work with small business owners to custom-design products. So if you find a flip-flop style you like, you probably can get it customized with your school colors.

But what happens if the bookstore doesn't want to sell your flip-flops? If this happens, you can set up a website to sell them yourself. Of course, you may need help doing this, in which case you can locate skilled professionals by using sites such as Guru (**guru.com**) or Elance (**elance.com**). You simply create a description of the job you need done (such as logo design for a flip-flop company), post it on the site, and invite freelancers to bid on your job. You then contact the freelancers who look promising, review samples of their work, and decide on someone who can help you—and at a competitive price. After your website is designed and up and running, you can place your business on social networking sites, such as Facebook, to help potential customers discover your product

and spread the word about your great flip-flops. You probably already have lots of friends on Facebook who attend your school and would be good potential customers.

Another hurdle is determining where you'll store your product and who will package and ship it to customers. If your parents' basement isn't large enough, you can outsource warehousing and order fulfillment to **Amazon.com**. Amazon will (for a fee) warehouse your inventory and then package and ship it when customer orders are received. Orders don't have to come through Amazon's site (although that is an option); you can provide ordering information collected on your site to Amazon, and Amazon will take care of the rest.

Although there is always a cost to starting up a business, up-front costs are much lower when you take advantage of the global marketplace and the Internet. So, take that brilliant idea you have and turn it into a business today!

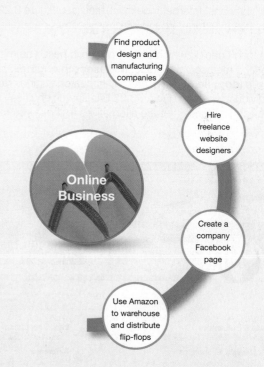

FIGURE 3.21 By using the services of only a few websites, you can create and distribute products, such as your own line of custom flip-flops.

searching the web
EFFECTIVELY

You've most likely "Googled" something today, and if you did, your search is one of over five billion daily searches. Google is the world's most popular **search engine**—a set of programs that searches the web for keywords (specific words you wish to look for or *query*) and then returns a list of the sites on which those keywords are found. In fact, Google has become so popular that its name is synonymous with looking for information on the web. Other popular search engines include Yahoo!, Bing, and Ask.com. But there are even more options for searching the web.

For some web searches, it might be better to use a **subject directory**, which is a structured outline of websites organized by topics and subtopics. By drilling down through the topics and subtopics, you can narrow down to a list of meaningful websites to look through. For example, if you wanted to know about exhibits of 3-D photography, you might click Arts>Visual Arts>Photography>3-D>Exhibits in a subject directory. In Yahoo's subject directory (**dir.yahoo.com**), the result would be a list of relevant websites about 3-D photography exhibits. The website ipl2 (**ipl2.org**) has a subject directory that combines resources from the Internet Public Library and the Librarians' Internet Index websites (see Figure 3.22). (ipl2 also has a feature through which you can ask a librarian a question.)

If you can't decide which search engine is best, you may want to try a metasearch engine. **Metasearch engines**, such as Dogpile (**dogpile.com**), search other search engines rather than individual websites. Figure 3.23 lists search engines and subject directories that are alternatives to those you might use most often.

Using Search Engines Effectively

How do search engines work? Search engines have three components:

1. The first component is a program called a *spider,* which constantly collects data on the web, following links in websites and reading web pages. Spiders get their name because they crawl over the web using multiple "legs" to visit many sites simultaneously.
2. As the spider collects data, the second component of the search engine, an *indexer program*, organizes the data into a large database.
3. When you use a search engine, you interact with the third component: the *search engine software*. This software searches the indexed data, pulling out relevant information according to your search.

The resulting list appears in your web browser as a list of hits—sites that match your search.

Why don't I get the same results from all search engines? Each search engine uses a unique formula, or *algorithm*, to formulate the search and create the resulting index of related sites. In addition, search engines differ in how they rank the search results. Most search engines rank their results based on the frequency of the appearance of your queried keywords in websites as well as the location of those words in the sites. This means that sites that include the keywords in their URL or site name will most likely appear at the top of the results list. An important part of a company's marketing

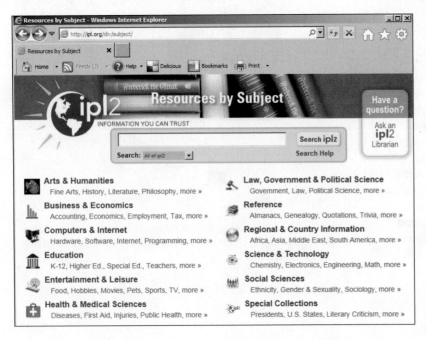

FIGURE 3.22 There are good alternatives to Google. ipl2 (**ipl2.org**) is a subject directory that lists resources by subject. Other alternatives are metasearch engines and specialty search engines.

FIGURE 3.23

Alternative Search Engines and Subject Directories

Bing **bing.com**	Web search engine from Microsoft
BrightPlanet **brightplanet.com**	"Deep web" directory that searches databases not normally searched by typical search engines.
ChaCha **chacha.com**	Uses live people who help you search; free of charge. Also available by texting your questions to 242242.
Dogpile **dogpile.com**	Metasearch engine that searches Google, Yahoo!, and Bing.
Excite **excite.com**	Website that in addition to having keyword search capabilities includes subject directory links to information on a wide variety of topics including travel, weather, concert tickets, and top news items.
Info.com **info.com**	Metasearch engine that searches Google, Yahoo!, Bing, and Yandex (a Russian search engine).
InfoMine **infomine.com**	Subject directory of academic resources with keyword search engine capabilities.
ipl2 **ipl2.org**	Subject directory that combines resources from the Internet Public Library and the Librarians' Internet Index websites.
Google Images **google.com/images**	Visual search engine that displays images rather than text as a result of a keyword search.
Open Directory Project **dmoz.org**	Human-edited subject directory with keyword search capabilities. Maintained by a global community of volunteer editors.
Yippy **yippy.com**	Metasearch engine that groups similar results into topics called clusters (for example, NBA, College Basketball, Photo Gallery, and Articles would be some resulting clusters if you use the search term *basketball*). Clicking on any of these clusters results in listing those sites specific to that subset of basketball.

Note: For a complete list of search engines, go to **searchengineguide.com**

strategy is search engine optimization, which is designing the corporate website to ensure it ranks near the top of a search.

Search engines also differ as to which sites they search. For instance, Google and Bing search nearly the entire web, whereas specialty search engines search only sites that are relevant to a particular topic or industry. Specialty search engines exist for almost every industry or interest. DailyStocks (**dailystocks.com**) is a search engine used primarily by investors that searches for corporate information. Search Engine Watch (**searchenginewatch.com**) has a list of many specialty search engines, organized by industry.

Can I use a search engine to search just for images and videos? With the increasing popularity of multimedia, search engines such as Google, Bing, and Yahoo! let you search the web for digital images and audio and video files. After putting in your search term, select Video from Google's top menu to display only the search results that are videos. You can further narrow down the video selection by using the filtering tools. Blinkx (**blinkx.com**) is a video search engine that helps you sift through all the video posted on the web (see Figure 3.24).

How can I refine my searches for better results? You've probably searched for something on Google and gotten back a list of hits that includes thousands—even millions—of web pages that have no relevance to the topic you're interested in. Initially, Boolean operators were needed to help refine a search. **Boolean operators** are words such as *AND, NOT,* and *OR* that describe the relationships between keywords in a search. With the simple addition of a few words or constraints, you can narrow your search results to a more manageable and more meaningful list.

Are there other helpful search strategies? Other strategies can help refine your searches when entering your search keywords:

- **Search for a phrase.** To search for an exact phrase, place quotation marks around your keywords. The search engine will look for only those websites that contain the words in *that exact order*. For example, if you want information on the movie *The Green Hornet* and you type these words without

 ACTIVE HELPDESK
Getting Around the Web
In this Active Helpdesk, you'll play the role of a helpdesk staffer, fielding questions about web browsers, URLs, and how to use hyperlinks and other tools to get around the web.

quotation marks, your search results will contain pages that include either of the words *Green* and *Hornet*, although not necessarily in that order. Typing *"The Green Hornet"* in quotation marks guarantees that search results will include this exact phrase.

- **Search within a specific website.** To search just a specific website, you can use the search keyword, then *site:* followed by the website's URL. For example, searching with *processor site:* www.wired.com returns results about processors from the Wired. com website. The same method works for entire classes of sites in a given top-level domain or country code.

- **Use a wild card.** The asterisk ("*") is a wild card, or placeholder, feature that is helpful when you need to search with unknown terms. Another way to think about the wild card search feature is as a "fill in the blank." For example,

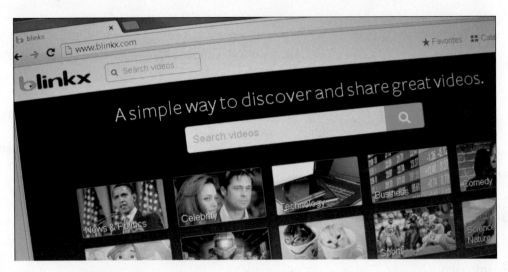

FIGURE 3.24 Blinkx is a video search engine that helps you sift through the increasing number of videos on the web. *(blinkx, LLC)*

searching with *Congress voted * on the * bill* might bring up an article about the members of Congress who voted *no* on the *healthcare* bill or a different article about the members of Congress who voted *yes* on the *energy* bill.

How else can I customize my searches? Many other specialty search strategies and services are available. By clicking on Search tools in Google's menu at the top of a Google search, you can restrict search results by time, location, and even reading level (see Figure 3.25). You can also click on the Apps button in Google's main page, then click the "More" and "Even more from Google" options for all the specialized search products Google offers (see Figure 3.26):

- *Scholar* searches scholarly literature such as peer-reviewed papers, theses, and publications from academic organizations. Each search result contains bibliographic information as well.

- *Custom Search* lets you create a customized search engine to search only a selected set of sites tailored to your needs. You can add this specialized search engine to a website or blog or design it for a specific organization.

- *Google Shopping* lets you search by product rather than by company. So if you're interested in buying a digital camera, Google Shopping lists cameras by popularity and provides information on the stores that carry the cameras, along with the average price.

- *Alerts* let you know by e-mail when content that you specify has been updated, so you can monitor a developing news story or be aware of breaking news about your favorite sports team, for example.

BITS&BYTES

Searching to Do Good

Wouldn't it be great to benefit others just by searching the web? Now there's an easy way to "do good" with every search. Goodsearch (**goodsearch.com**) is a Yahoo!-powered search engine that donates half of its revenues (approximately a penny per search) to approved U.S. charities and schools that users designate. The money Goodsearch donates comes from the site's advertisers. More than 100,000 charitable organizations are being helped by Goodsearch, but if the organization you're interested in isn't on the list, as long as it's a registered U.S. not-for-profit organization, you can apply to have it added. Goodsearch has expanded its program to online shopping and dining out.

You can also contribute to your favorite charity by shopping online through Goodshop (**goodshop.com**). Instead of going directly to your favorite online store, go to Goodshop first, find and click through to the store of your choice, and start shopping. Participating stores donate up to 30% of the purchased amount. Similarly, through the GoodDining program, dine at a participating restaurant and a percentage of your bill will go to your cause. So, search, shop, and eat—and do some good!

Evaluating Websites

How can I make sure a website is appropriate to use for research? When you're using the Internet for research, you shouldn't assume that everything you find is

FIGURE 3.25 Use Google's search tools to restrict the time frame, the location, and even the reading level of your search results. *(Google, Inc.)*

accurate and appropriate to use. The following is a list of questions to consider before you use an Internet resource; the answers to these questions will help you decide whether you should consider a website to be a good source of information:

- **Authority:** Who is the author of the article or the sponsor of the site? If the author is well known or the site is published by a reputable news source (such as the *New York Times*), then you can feel more confident using it as a source than if you are unable to locate such information. *Note:* Some sites include a page with information about the author or the site's sponsor.

- **Bias:** Is the site biased? The purpose of many websites is to sell products or services or to persuade rather than inform. These sites, though useful in some situations, present a biased point of view. Look for sites that offer several sets of facts or consider opinions from several sources.

- **Relevance:** Is the information on the site current? Material can last a long time on the web. Some research projects (such as historical accounts) depend on older records. However, if you're writing about cutting-edge technologies, you need to look for the most recent sources. Therefore,

look for a date on information to make sure it is current.

- **Audience:** For what audience is the site intended? Ensure that the content, tone, and style of the site match your needs. You probably wouldn't want to use information from a site geared toward teens if you're writing for adults, nor would you use a site that has a casual style and tone for serious research.

- **Links:** Are the links available and appropriate? Check out the links provided on the site to determine whether they're still working and appropriate for your needs. Don't assume that the links provided are the only additional sources of information. Investigate other sites on your topic, as well. You should also be able to find the same information on at least three different websites to help verify the information is accurate. ■

 ACTIVE HELPDESK
Evaluating Websites

In this Active Helpdesk, you'll play the role of a helpdesk staffer, fielding questions about how websites can be evaluated as appropriate to use for research.

 SOUND BYTE
Finding Information on the Web

In this Sound Byte, you'll learn how and when to use search engines and subject directories. Through guided tours, you'll learn effective search techniques, including how to use Boolean operators and metasearch engines.

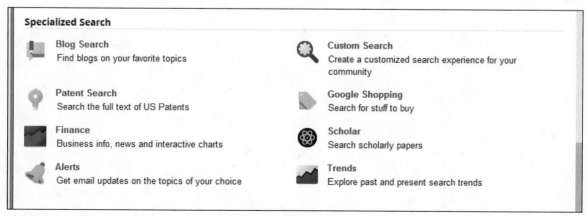

FIGURE 3.26 Google's Specialized Search Tools. *(Google, Inc.)*

Despite having so much information easily available on the web, using it without receiving proper permissions is not only wrong but can also be illegal. So what can you borrow from the web and what must you seek permission to use? Consider these scenarios:

1. You find a political cartoon that would be terrific in a PowerPoint presentation you're creating for your civics class. You copy it into your presentation.

2. Your hobby is writing children's books, which you later sell online. Most of what you create is your content, but sometimes you borrow story ideas from other children's books and just change a few characters or situations. You do not obtain permission from the originators of the story ideas you borrow.

3. You're pressed for time and need to do research for a paper due tomorrow. You find information on an obscure website and copy it into your paper without documenting the source.

4. You download a song from the Internet and incorporate it into a PowerPoint presentation for a school project. Because you assume everyone knows the song, you don't credit it in your sources.

Which of the preceding scenarios represent copyright violations? Which represent plagiarism? The distinctions between these scenarios are narrow in some cases, but it's important to understand the differences.

Plagiarism occurs when you use someone else's ideas or words and represent them as your own.

In today's computer society, it's easy to copy information from the Internet and paste it into a Word document, change a few words, and call it your own. To avoid plagiarism, properly credit all information you obtain from the Internet by using quotation marks around all words you borrow directly, and credit your sources for any ideas you paraphrase or borrow.

WriteCheck (**writecheck.com**) is a website specifically for students to help check for plagiarism violations (see Figure 3.27). The site compares your document to a database of publications, books, and web content and identifies possible plagiarism violations. Although some common phrasing may be truly coincidental, real and purposeful plagiarism is reasonably easy to identify. Students can use WriteCheck before submitting an assignment to ensure their papers are free from plagiarism and avoid the serious consequences of this offense.

Copyright violation is more serious because it, unlike plagiarism, is punishable by law. Copyright law assumes that all original work is copyrighted even if the work does not display the copyright symbol (©). Copyright violation occurs when you use another person's material for your own personal economic benefit or when you take away from the economic benefit of the originator. In most cases, citing the source is not sufficient; you need to seek and receive written permission from the copyright holder.

There are exceptions to this rule. There is no copyright on government documents, so you can download and reproduce material from any government website. The British Broadcasting Corporation (BBC) is also beginning to digitize and

FIGURE 3.27 Students can compare their work to a database of publications in sites such as WriteCheck to check for unintended plagiarism. *(Keith Morris/Alamy)*

make available its archives of material to the public without copyright restrictions. Teachers and students receive special consideration that falls under a provision called *academic fair use*. As long as the material is being used for educational purposes only, limited copying and distribution is allowed.

One standard applied to academic fair use is the effect the use has on the potential market. For example, a student can include a cartoon in a PowerPoint presentation without seeking permission from the artist. However, to avoid plagiarism, you still must credit your sources of information.

So, do you now know which of the four scenarios above are plagiarism or copyright violations? Let's review them.

1. You are not in violation because the use of the cartoon is for educational purposes and falls under the academic fair use provision. You must still credit the source, however.

2. You are in violation of copyright laws because you are presenting others' ideas for children's stories as your own and receiving personal economic benefit from them.

3. You are guilty of plagiarism because you copied content from another source and implied it was your own work.

4. Again, because your copying is for a school project, you are not in violation of copyright laws because of the academic fair use provision. However, it's always important to document your sources.

Before moving on to the Chapter Review:
- **Watch Replay Video 3.2** ▶.
- Then check your understanding of what you've learned so far.

check your understanding // review & practice

For a quick review to see what you've learned so far, answer the following questions. Visit **pearsonhighered.com/techinaction** to check your answers.

multiple choice

1. What is the navigation aid that shows users the path they have taken to get to a web page located within a website?

   a. favorites   **c.** bookmarks

   b. breadcrumb trail   **d.** social bookmarks

2. Which is NOT a component of a search engine?

   a. social bookmarking site

   b. indexer program

   c. subject directory

   d. live bookmark site

3. When using the Internet for research, you

   a. can assume that everything you find is accurate and appropriate.

   b. should evaluate sites for bias and relevance.

   c. can assume the author is an authority on the subject matter.

   d. can assume that the links provided on the site are the only additional sources of information.

4. Which of the following is not an Internet protocol?

   a. ARPANET

   b. HTTP

   c. FTP

   d. BitTorrent

5. Country codes are what part of a URL?

   a. sub-top-level domain

   b. top-level domain

   c. path

   d. protocol

To take an autograded version of this review, please go to the companion website at **pearsonhighered.com/techinaction**, or go your MyITLab course.

Continue

3 Chapter Review

The Internet and How It Works

1. What is the origin of the Internet?

- The Internet is the largest computer network in the world, connecting millions of computers.
- Government and military officials developed the early Internet as a reliable way to communicate in the event of war. Eventually, scientists and educators used the Internet to exchange research.
- Today, we use the Internet and the web (which is a part of the Internet) to shop, research, communicate, and entertain ourselves.

2. How does data travel on the Internet?

- A computer (or other device) connected to the Internet acts as either a client (a computer that asks for information) or a server (a computer that receives the request and returns the information to the client).
- Data travels between clients and servers along a system of communication lines or pathways. The largest and fastest of these pathways form the Internet backbone.
- To ensure that data is sent to the correct computer along the pathways, IP addresses (unique ID numbers) are assigned to all computers connected to the Internet.

Communicating and Collaborating on the Web

3. How can I communicate and collaborate using Web 2.0 technologies?

- Web 2.0 can be described as the social web, in which the user is also a participant.
- Examples of Web 2.0 technologies include social networking, blogs, wikis, podcasts, and webcasts.
- Social networking enables you to communicate and share information with friends as well as meet and connect with others.
- Blogs are journal entries posted to the web that are generally organized by a topic or area of interest and are publicly available.

- Video logs are personal journals that use video as the primary content in addition to text, images, and audio.
- Wikis are a type of website that allows users to collaborate on content—adding, removing, or editing it.
- Podcasts are audio or video content that is available over the Internet. Users subscribe to receive updates to podcasts.
- Webcasts are broadcasts of audio or video content over the Internet.

4. How can I communicate using e-mail and instant messaging?

- E-mail allows users to communicate electronically without the parties involved being available at the same time, whereas instant-messaging services are programs that enable you to communicate in real time with others who are online.

Web Entertainment

5. What multimedia files are found on the web, and what software is needed to access those files?

- Multimedia is anything that involves one or more forms of media in addition to text, such as graphics, audio, and video clips.
- Sometimes you need a special software program called a *plug-in* (or *player*) to view and hear multimedia files.

Conducting Business over the Internet: E-Commerce

6. What is e-commerce, and what online safeguards are available?

- E-commerce is the business of conducting business online.
- E-commerce includes transactions between businesses (B2B), between consumers (C2C), and between businesses and consumers (B2C).
- Because more business than ever before is conducted online, numerous safeguards have been put in place to ensure that transactions are protected.

Accessing and Moving Around the Web

7. What is a web browser, and what are a URL and its parts?

- Once you're connected to the Internet, in order to locate, navigate to, and view web pages, you need to install special software called a web browser on your system.
- The most common web browsers are Internet Explorer, Firefox, Google Chrome, and Safari.
- You gain access to a website by typing in its address, called a Uniform Resource Locator (URL).
- A URL is comprised of several parts, including the protocol, the domain, the top-level domain, and paths (or subdirectories).

8. How can I use hyperlinks and other tools to get around the web?

- One unique aspect of the web is that you can jump from place to place by clicking on specially formatted pieces of text or images called *hyperlinks*.
- You can also use the Back and Forward buttons, History lists, breadcrumb trails, and Favorites or Bookmarks to navigate the web.
- Favorites, live bookmarks, and social bookmarking help you return to specific web pages without having to type in the URL and help you organize the web content that is most important to you.

Searching the Web Effectively

9. How do I search the Internet effectively, and how can I evaluate websites?

- A search engine is a set of programs that searches the web using specific keywords you wish to query and then returns a list of the websites on which those keywords are found.
- Search engines can be used to search for images, podcasts, and videos in addition to traditional text-based web content.
- A subject directory is a structured outline of websites organized by topic and subtopic. Metasearch engines search other search engines.
- To evaluate whether it is appropriate to use a website as a resource, determine whether the author of the site is reputable and whether the site is intended for your particular needs. In addition, make sure that the site content is not biased, the information on the site is current, and all the links on the site are available and appropriate.

> Be sure to check out the companion website for additional materials to help you review and learn, including a Tech Bytes Weekly newsletter—
> **pearsonhighered.com/techinaction**.
> And don't forget the Replay Videos ▶ .

key terms //

aggregator **83**

blog (weblog) **83**

Bookmarks **98**

Boolean operators **101**

breadcrumb trail **97**

business-to-business (B2B) **87**

business-to-consumer (B2C) **87**

client **78**

client/server network **78**

consumer-to-consumer (C2C) **87**

domain name **95**

e-commerce (electronic commerce) **87**

e-mail (electronic mail) **79**

e-mail client **80**

Favorites **98**

File Transfer Protocol (FTP) **96**

host **96**

hyperlink **97**

Hypertext Transfer Protocol (HTTP) **96**

instant messaging (IM) **81**

Internet **76**

Internet backbone **78**

Internet Protocol (IP) address **78**

keyword **98**

live bookmark **98**

metasearch engine **100**

multimedia **85**

path (subdirectory) **96**

plug-in (player) **85**

podcast **83**

Really Simple Syndication (RSS) **83**

search engine **100**

secure socket layer **88**

semantic web (Web 3.0) **90**

server **78**

social commerce **87**

social networking **79**

streaming media **85**

subject directory **100**

tagging (social bookmarking) **98**

top-level domain **96**

Uniform Resource Locator (URL) **95**

video log (vlog or video blog) **83**

Web 2.0 **79**

web-based e-mail **80**

web browser (browser) **77**

webcast **84**

web server **96**

website **95**

wiki **81**

World Wide Web (WWW or the web) **77**

chapter quiz// assessment

For a quick review to see what you've learned, answer the following questions. Submit the quiz as requested by your instructor. If you are using MyITLab, the quiz is also available there.

multiple choice

1. The Internet was created to provide:
   a. a secure form of communications.
   b. a common communications means for all computers.
   c. both A and B.
   d. neither A or B.

2. Which of the following describes an IP address?
   a. It is referred to as a dotted quad.
   b. It identifies any computer connecting to the Internet.
   c. It identifies a website.
   d. All of the above.

3. Which of the following is an installed e-mail client?
   a. Outlook
   b. Windows Messenger
   c. Gmail
   d. Yahoo! mail

4. What web browser feature would be particularly useful when using public computers?
   a. Pinned tabs
   b. Session restore
   c. Privacy browsing
   d. All of the above

5. In the URL http://www.whitehouse.gov/blog, which part is considered the path or subdirectory?
   a. http
   b. .gov
   c. www.whitehouse.gov
   d. /blog

6. Search engines that search other search engines are called
   a. metasearch engines.
   b. betasearch engines.
   c. gigasearch engines.
   d. megasearch engines.

true–false

_____ 1. A search engine that searches other search engines is called a SuperSearch engine.

_____ 2. Webcasts are only delivered as prerecorded audio and video content.

_____ 3. The "s" in HTTPS stands for secure and indicates that the secure sockets layer protocol has been applied to the website.

_____ 4. IP addresses are used to identify computers connected to the Internet.

critical thinking

1. **The Power of Google**

   Google is the largest and most popular search engine on the Internet today. Because of its size and popularity, some people claim that Google has enormous power to influence a web user's search experience solely by its website-ranking processes. What do you think about this potential power? How could it be used in negative or harmful ways?

   a. Some websites pay search engines to list them near the top of the results pages. These sponsors therefore get priority placement. What do you think of this policy?

   b. What effect (if any) do you think that Google has on website development? For example, do you think website developers intentionally include frequently searched words in their pages so that they will appear in more hit lists?

2. **Mobile E-Commerce Safety**

   The text lists several ways to ensure your online transactions are secure and to reduce the risk of things going awry as you shop and sell online. However, surveys indicate that many feel that shopping from a mobile device, such as a smartphone, presents additional risks. Do you agree there are additional risks when conducting e-commerce from a mobile device? Why or why not?

team time //

Collaborating with Technology

Problem

Collaborating on projects with team members is a regular part of business and academia. Many great tools are available that facilitate online collaboration, and it's important to be familiar with them. In this Team Time, each team will create a group report on a specific topic, using online collaboration tools, and compare and rate the tools and the collaboration process.

Process

Split your group into teams. To appreciate fully the benefits of online collaboration, each team should have at least five or six members. Each group will create a team report on a topic that is approved by your instructor. As part of the report, one group member should record the process the group took to create the report, including a review of the tools used and reflections on the difficulties encountered by the group.

1. Conduct a virtual meeting. Agree on an online meeting and video collaboration tool such as Skype, Google+ Hangouts, ooVoo, or Tinychat and conduct a group chat. In this phase, outline your group project strategy and delegate work responsibilities.

2. Share documents and collaborate online. Your group must create one document that is accessible to every member at all times. Explore document-sharing sites such as Google Drive, Evernote, OneDrive, or Dropbox and collaboratively create your group document. All members are responsible for reviewing the entire document.

Conclusion

After all the team group reports have been completed and shared, discuss the following with your class: What is the benefit of using online collaboration technology to create group projects? How did collaboration technologies help or hinder the team process?

ethics project //

Plagiarism

In this exercise, you'll research and then role-play a complicated ethical situation. The role you play may or may not match your own personal beliefs, but your research and use of logic will enable you to represent whichever view is assigned. An arbitrator will watch and comment on both sides of the arguments, and together the team will agree on an ethical solution.

Problem

Plagiarism, or portraying another's work as your own, has been around for a long time and extends well beyond the classroom. For example, Nick Simmons, the son of Gene Simmons (from KISS) and a member of A&E's *Family Jewels* reality series, created a comic book series, *Incarnate*. Radical Publishing picked up the series but quickly stopped publication when Internet messages accused the author of copying from other similar series. Similarly, the Australian band Men at Work was cited for copying a melody from "Kookaburra Sits in the Old Gum Tree" for its 1980s hit "Down Under" and owes the owner years of royalties.

Research Areas to Consider

- Plagiarism violations
- Comic book series *Incarnate*
- Australian band Men at Work
- Plagiarism consequences

Process

1. Divide the class into teams. Research the areas cited above and devise a scenario in which someone has violated plagiarism rules.

2. Team members should write a summary that provides background information for their character—for example, author, publisher, or arbitrator—and that details their character's behaviors to set the stage for the role-playing event. Then team members should create an outline to use during the role-playing event.

3. Team members should arrange a mutually convenient time to meet for the exchange, using a virtual meeting tool or by meeting in person.

4. Team members should present their case to the class or submit a PowerPoint presentation for review by the rest of the class, along with the summary and resolution they developed.

Conclusion

As technology becomes ever more prevalent and integrated into our lives, more and more ethical dilemmas will present themselves. Being able to understand and evaluate both sides of an argument, while responding in a personally or socially ethical manner, will be an important skill.

Create a Report: Conducting Research on the Web

You and a partner have been asked to write a report on alternatives to using the Google search engine, as well as how to evaluate a website for a research paper. The paper needs to cite references within the body of the text, and include a list of your works cited at the end of the report. Your partner has begun the report. You are going to modify what has been started.

You will use the following skills as you complete this activity:	
• Use Find and Replace	• Insert a Hyperlink
• Format Bulleted Lists	• Add Sources
• Insert SmartArt	• Insert Citations and Bibliography

Instructions:

1. Start Word. Open *TIACh3_Start.docx* and save it as **TIACh3_LastFirst.docx**, using your last and first name.

2. Using Find and Replace, find all instances of *metasearch* and replace them with **meta-search**.

3. At the blank paragraph after the end of the second paragraph of text under *Alternative Search Engines*, insert a Vertical Box List SmartArt graphic. Open the text pane, if necessary. Place the cursor after the first bullet, and enter **Google Scholar**. (Do not include the period.) Press Enter, press Tab and then type **Searches scholarly literature**. (Do not include the period.)

   Repeat these steps to add the following information for the next two bullets:
   Dogpile
       Meta-search engine that searches Google, Yahoo!, and Bing
   Yippy
       Meta-search engine that groups similar results into topics
   Press Enter, press Shift +Tab, and then type **InfoMine**
   Press Enter, then press Tab and type **Subject directory of academic resources using keywords**

   Hint: To insert a SmartArt graphic, on the INSERT tab, in the Illustrations group, click SmartArt.

4. Change the SmartArt graphic colors to Colorful—Accent. Move the Google Scholar box and bullet point to the bottom of the SmartArt. Change the SmartArt Style to Intense Effect.

   Hint: To change the colors, on the SMARTART DESIGN tab, in the SmartArt Styles group, click Colors. To move the box and bullet point, in the Create Graphic group, click Move Down. To change the style, in the SmartArt Styles group, click the more button for Styles.

5. In the second to last sentence of the first paragraph in the Alternative Search Engines section, select the text *list of subject directories*. Then, create a hyperlink to the web page **http://hanlib.sou.edu/searchtools.subjdir.html**. (Do not include the period.)

6. At the end of the first paragraph in the *Evaluating Websites* section, immediately to the left of the period, insert a citation to a new Web Site source using the following information:
   Author: **Kapoun, Jim**
   Name of Web Page: **Five criteria for evaluating Web pages**
   Name of Web Site: **Olin & Uris Libraries, Cornell University**
   Year: **2010**
   Month: **May**
   Day: **10**
   URL: **http://olinuris.library.cornell.edu/ref/research/webcrit.html**

   Hint: To display the URL field, click the checkbox for Show All Bibliography Fields.

7. In the Evaluating Websites section, create a bulleted list with the five points beginning with *Authority, Bias or Objectivity, Relevance, Audience,* and *Coverage*. Use a checkmark as the bullet point.

8. Press CTRL + End to go to the end of the document, press Enter, and then insert a Works Cited Bibliography. Change the citation style to **APA Sixth Edition**.

   Hint: To create a Works Cited Bibliography, on the REFERENCES tab, in the Citations & Bibliography group, click Bibliography. To change the citation style, click the more button for Style.

9. Save the document, and then close Word.

10. Submit the document as directed.

Technology in Focus

The History of the Personal Computer

Ever wonder how big the first personal computer was or how much the first laptop weighed? Computers are such an integral part of our lives that we don't often stop to think about how far they've come or where they got their start. In just 40 years, computers have evolved from expensive, huge machines that only corporations could own to small, powerful devices that almost anyone can have. In this Technology in Focus feature, we look at the history of the personal computer.

FIGURE 1 Timeline of Early Personal Computer Development

The Altair 8800

- Only 256 bytes of memory
- No keyboard or monitor
- Switches on front used to enter data in machine code (1s and 0s)
- Lights on front indicated results of a program

1975

Commodore PET

- Featured in *Popular Science* magazine
- Popular in business settings in Europe

October 1977

1976

Apple I

Steve Jobs and Steve Wozniak form Apple Computer

June 1977

- Featured color monitor, sound, and game paddles
- 4 KB of RAM
- Operating system stored in ROM
- Optional floppy disk to load programs (mostly games)

Apple II

(AP Photo/Heinz Nixdorf Museumsforum; SSPL/The Image Works; Marilyn K. Yee/New York Times Co./Getty Images; AP Photo/Steve Castillo; SSPL/Getty Images; Jerry Mason/Photo Researchers, Inc.)

The First Personal Computer: The Altair

Our journey through the history of the personal computer starts in 1975. At that time, most people weren't familiar with the mainframes and supercomputers that large corporations and the government owned. With price tags exceeding the cost of buildings, and with few if any practical home uses, these monster machines weren't appealing to or attainable by average Americans.

However, in 1975, the first personal computer, the **Altair 8800** (see Figure 1), was born. At $395 for a do-it-yourself kit or $498 for a fully assembled unit (about $2,236 in today's dollars), the price was reasonable enough that computer fanatics could finally own their own computers.

The Altair was primitive by today's standards—no keyboard, no monitor, and completely not user friendly. Despite its limitations, computer enthusiasts flocked to the machine. Many who bought it had been taught to program, but until that point, they had access only to big, clumsy computers at their jobs. With the Altair, they could create their own programs. Within three months, 4,000 orders were placed for the machine.

The release of the Altair marked the start of the personal computer boom. In fact, two men whose names you might have heard were among the first Altair owners: Bill Gates and Paul Allen were so enamored by the "minicomputer" that they wrote a compiling program (a program that translates user commands into commands the computer can understand) for it. The two later convinced the Altair's developer to buy their program, marking the start of a company called Microsoft. We'll get to that story later. First, let's see what their rivals were up to.

The Apple I and II

Around the time the Altair was released, **Steve Wozniak**, an employee at Hewlett-Packard, was dabbling with his own computer design. **Steve Jobs**, who was working for computer game manufacturer Atari at the time, liked Wozniak's prototypes and made a few suggestions. Together, the two built a personal computer, the **Apple I**, in Wozniak's garage (see Figure 1) and formed the Apple Computer Company in 1976.

A year later, in 1977, the **Apple II** was born (see Figure 1). The Apple II included a color monitor, sound, and game

TRS-80

- Introduced by Radio Shack
- Monochrome display
- 4 KB of RAM
- Circuitry hidden under keyboard
- Wildly popular with consumers—sold 10,000 units in the first month

November 1977

IBM PC (5150)

- Marketed to businesses and consumers
- 64 KB to 256 KB of RAM
- Floppy disk drives optional
- Hard disks not supported in early models

August 1981

April 1981

- First "portable" computer
- Weighed 24.5 pounds
- 5-inch screen
- 64 kilobytes of RAM
- Two floppy disk drives
- Preinstalled with spreadsheet and word processing software

Osbourne

(Interfoto/Alamy; Interfoto/Alamy; Science & Society Picture Library/Contributor/Getty Images)

paddles. Priced around $1,300 (about $5,206 in today's dollars), one of its biggest innovations was that the operating system was stored in read-only memory (ROM). Previously, the operating system had to be rewritten every time the computer was turned on. The friendly features of the Apple II operating system encouraged less technically oriented computer enthusiasts to write their own programs.

An instant success, the Apple II would eventually include a spreadsheet program, a word processor, and desktop publishing software. These programs gave personal computers like the Apple functions beyond gaming and special programming and led to their popularity.

Enter the Competition

Around the time Apple was experiencing success with its computers, a number of competitors entered the market. The largest among them were Commodore, Radio Shack, Osborne, and IBM. The **Commodore PET** (see Figure 1) was aimed at the business market and did well in Europe, while Radio Shack's **TRS-80** (see Figure 1) was clearly aimed at the U.S. consumer market. Just one month after its release in 1977, it had sold about 10,000 units.

The Osborne: The Birth of Portable Computing

The Osborne Company introduced the first portable computer, the **Osborne**, in 1981 (see Figure 1). Although portable, the computer weighed 24.5 pounds. It featured a minuscule 5-inch screen and carried a price tag of $1,795 (about $4,704 today). The Osborne was an overnight success, and its sales quickly reached 10,000 units per month. However, despite the computer's popularity, the Osborne Company eventually closed. Compaq bought the Osborne design and in 1983 produced its own portable computer.

IBM PCs

Until 1980, IBM primarily made mainframe computers, which it sold to large corporations, and hadn't taken the personal

computer seriously. In 1981, however, IBM released its first personal computer, the **IBM PC** (see Figure 1). Because many companies were familiar with IBM mainframes, they adopted the IBM PC. The term *PC* soon became the term used to describe all personal computers.

IBM marketed its PC through retail outlets such as Sears to reach home users, and it quickly dominated that market. In January 1983, *Time* magazine, playing on its annual person of the year issue, named the computer "1982 Machine of the Year."

Other Important Advancements

It wasn't just personal computer hardware that was changing. At the same time, advances in programming languages and operating systems and the influx of application software were leading to more useful and powerful machines.

The Importance of BASIC

The software industry began in the 1950s with programming languages such as FORTRAN, ALGOL, and COBOL. These languages were used mainly by businesses to create financial, statistical, and engineering programs. However, the 1964 introduction of **Beginners All-Purpose Symbolic Instruction Code (BASIC)** revolutionized the software industry. BASIC was a language that beginning programming students could easily learn. It thus became enormously popular—and the key language of the PC. In fact, **Bill Gates** and **Paul Allen** (see Figure 2) used BASIC to write their program for the Altair. As we noted earlier, this program led to the creation of **Microsoft**, a company that produced computer software.

FIGURE 2 Bill Gates and Paul Allen are the founders of Microsoft. *(Doug Wilson/CORBIS)*

The Advent of Operating Systems

Because data on the earliest personal computers was stored on audiocassettes, many programs weren't saved or reused. This meant that programs had to be rewritten whenever they were needed. In 1978, Steve Wozniak designed a 5.25-inch floppy disk drive so that programs could be saved easily and operating systems developed.

Operating systems are written to coordinate with the specific processor chip that controls the computer. At that time, Apples ran on a Motorola chip, whereas PCs (IBMs and so on) ran on an Intel chip. **Disk Operating System (DOS)**, developed by Wozniak and introduced in 1977, was the OS that controlled the first Apple computers. The **Control Program for Microcomputers (CP/M)**, developed by Gary Kildall, was the OS designed for the Intel 8080 chip (the processor for PCs).

In 1980, when IBM was entering the personal computer market, it approached Bill Gates at Microsoft to write an OS program for the IBM PC. Gates recommended that IBM investigate the CP/M OS, but IBM couldn't arrange a meeting with the founder, Gary Kildall. Microsoft reconsidered the opportunity to write an OS program and developed **MS-DOS** for IBM computers. Eventually, virtually all PCs running on the Intel chip used MS-DOS as their OS. Microsoft's reign as one of the dominant players in the personal computer landscape had begun.

The Software Application Explosion: VisiCalc and Beyond

Because the floppy disk was a convenient way to distribute software, its inclusion in personal computers set off an application software explosion. In 1978, Harvard Business School student Dan Bricklin recognized the potential for a personal computer spreadsheet program. He and his friend Bob Frankston created the program **VisiCalc**, which became

FIGURE 3 This 1983 Hewlett-Packard computer used an early version of the MS-DOS operating system as well as the Lotus 1-2-3 spreadsheet program. *(Everett Collection / SuperStock)*

FIGURE 4

YEAR	APPLICATION
1978	**VisiCalc:** First electronic spreadsheet application **WordStar:** First word processing application
1980	**WordPerfect:** Best DOS-based word processor, was eventually sold to Novell and later acquired by Corel
1983	**Lotus 1-2-3:** Added integrated charting, plotting, and database capabilities to spreadsheet software **Word for MS-DOS:** Introduced in the pages of *PC World* magazine on the first magazine-inserted demo disk
1985	**Excel:** One of the first spreadsheets to use a graphical user interface **PageMaker:** The first desktop publishing software

Application Software Development

an instant success. Finally, ordinary home users could see the benefit of owning a personal computer. More than 100,000 copies of VisiCalc were sold in its first year.

After VisiCalc, other electronic spreadsheet programs entered the market. **Lotus 1-2-3** came on the market in 1983 (see Figure 3), and **Microsoft Excel** entered the scene in 1985. These products became so popular that they eventually put VisiCalc out of business.

Meanwhile, word processing software was also gaining a foothold in the industry. Until then, there were separate, dedicated word processing machines; personal computers, it was believed, were for computation and data management only. However, once **WordStar**, the first word processing application, became available for personal computers in 1979, word processing became another important use for the personal computer. Competitors such as **Word for MS-DOS** (the precursor to Microsoft Word) and **WordPerfect** soon entered the market. Figure 4 lists some of the important dates in application software development.

The Graphical User Interface

Another important advancement in personal computers was the introduction of the **graphical user interface (GUI)**, which allowed users to interact with the computer more easily. Until that time, users had to use complicated command- or menu-driven interfaces. Apple was the first company to take full commercial advantage of the GUI, but the GUI was not invented by a computer company.

Xerox: Birth of the GUI

In 1972, a few years before Apple launched its first personal computer, photocopier manufacturer **Xerox** was designing

FIGURE 5 The Alto was the first computer to use a GUI, and it provided the basis for the GUI that Apple used. However, because of marketing problems, the Alto never was sold. *(Josie Lepe/MCT/Newscom)*

FIGURE 6 The Lisa was the first computer to introduce a GUI to the market. Priced too high, it never gained the popularity it deserved. *(SSPL/The Image Works)*

a personal computer of its own. Named the **Alto** (see Figure 5), the computer included a word processor, based on the What You See Is What You Get (WYSIWYG) principle, that incorporated a file management system with directories and folders. It also had a mouse and could connect to a network. None of the other personal computers of the time had these features. For a variety of reasons, Xerox never sold the Alto commercially. Several years later, it developed the Star Office System, which was based on the Alto. Despite its convenient features, the Star never became popular because no one was willing to pay the $17,000 asking price.

The Lisa and the Macintosh

Xerox's ideas were ahead of their time, but many of the ideas present in the Alto and Star would soon catch on. In 1983, Apple introduced the **Lisa**, the first successful personal computer brought to market that used a GUI (see Figure 6). Legend has it that Jobs had seen the Alto during a visit to Xerox in 1979 and was influenced by its GUI. He therefore incorporated a similar user interface into the Lisa, providing features such as windows, drop-down menus, icons, a file system with folders and files, and a point-and-click device called a mouse. The only problem with the Lisa was its price. At $9,995 (about $23,866 in today's dollars), few buyers were willing to take the plunge.

A year later, in 1984, Apple introduced the **Macintosh**, shown in Figure 7. The Macintosh was everything the Lisa was and then some, at about a third of the cost. The Macintosh was also the first personal computer to utilize 3.5-inch floppy disks with a hard cover, which were smaller and sturdier than the previous 5.25-inch floppies.

The Internet Boom

The GUI made it easier for users to work on the computer. The Internet provided another reason for people to buy computers. Now people could conduct research and communicate in a new way. In 1993, the web browser **Mosaic** was introduced. This browser allowed users to view multimedia on the web, causing Internet traffic to increase by nearly 350%.

FIGURE 7 The Macintosh became one of Apple's best-selling computers, incorporating a GUI along with other innovations such as the 3.5-inch floppy disk drive. *(Ed Kashi/CORBIS)*

Meanwhile, companies discovered the Internet as a means to do business, and computer sales took off. IBM-compatible PCs became the computer system of choice when, in 1995, Microsoft introduced **Internet Explorer**, a browser that integrated web functionality into Microsoft Office applications, and **Windows 95**, the first Microsoft OS designed to be principally a GUI OS.

About a year earlier, in 1994, a team of developers launched the **Netscape** web browser, which soon became a predominant player in browser software. However, pressures from Microsoft became too strong, and in 1998, Netscape announced it would no longer charge for the product and would make the code available to the public.

Making the Personal Computer Possible: Early Computers

Billions of personal computers have been sold over the past three decades. But the computer is a compilation of parts, each of which is the result of individual inventions. Let's look at some early machines that helped to create the personal computer we know today.

The Pascalene Calculator and the Jacquard Loom

From the earliest days of humankind, we have been looking for a more systematic way to count and calculate. Thus, the evolution of counting machines led to the development of the computer we know today. The **Pascalene** was the first accurate mechanical calculator. This machine, created by the French mathematician **Blaise Pascal** in 1642, used revolutions of gears, like odometers in cars, to count by tens. The Pascalene could be used to add, subtract, multiply, and divide. The basic design of the Pascalene was so sound that it lived on in mechanical calculators for more than 300 years.

Nearly 200 years later, **Joseph Jacquard** revolutionized the fabric industry by creating a machine that automated the weaving of complex patterns. Although not a counting or calculating machine, the **Jacquard loom** (shown in Figure 8) was significant because it relied on stiff cards with punched holes to automate the weaving process. Much later, this punch-card process would be adopted as a means for computers to record and read data.

Babbage's Engines

In 1834, **Charles Babbage** designed the first automatic calculator, called the **Analytical Engine** (see Figure 9). The machine was actually based on another machine called the **Difference Engine**, which was a huge steam-powered mechanical calculator that Babbage designed to print astronomical tables. Although the Analytical Engine was never developed, Babbage's detailed drawings and descriptions of the machine include components similar to those found

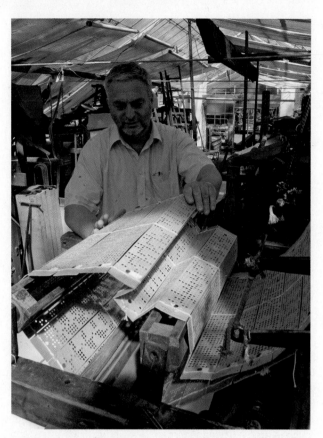

FIGURE 8 The Jacquard loom used holes punched in stiff cards to make complex designs. This technique would later be used in punch cards that controlled the input and output of data in computers. *(JANEK SKARZYNSKI/AFP/Getty Images/Newscom)*

in today's computers, including the store (akin to RAM) and the mill (a central processing unit) as well as input and output devices. This invention gave Charles Babbage the title of the "father of computing."

Meanwhile, Ada Lovelace, who was the daughter of poet Lord Byron and a student of mathematics (which was unusual for women of the time), was fascinated with Babbage's Engines. She translated an Italian paper on Babbage's machine and, at the request of Babbage, added her own extensive notes. Her efforts are thought to be the best description of Babbage's Engines.

The Hollerith Tabulating Machine

In 1890, **Herman Hollerith**, while working for the U.S. Census Bureau, was the first to take Jacquard's punch-card concept and apply it to computing with his **Hollerith Tabulating Machine**. Until that time, census data had been tabulated manually in a long, laborious process. Hollerith's tabulating machine automatically read data that had been punched onto small punch cards, speeding up the tabulation process. Hollerith's machine became so successful that he left the Census Bureau in 1896 to start the Tabulating

FIGURE 9 The Analytical Engine, designed by Charles Babbage, was never fully developed but included components similar to those found in today's computers. *(Chris Howes/Wild Places Photography/Alamy)*

Machine Company. His company later changed its name to International Business Machines, or IBM.

The Z1 and the Atanasoff–Berry Computer

German inventor **Konrad Zuse** is credited with a number of computing inventions. His first, in 1936, was a mechanical calculator called the **Z1**. The Z1 is thought to be the first computer to include certain features integral to today's systems, such as a control unit and separate memory functions.

In 1939, John Atanasoff, a professor at Iowa State University, and his student Clifford Berry built the first electrically powered digital computer, called the **Atanasoff–Berry Computer (ABC)**, shown in Figure 10. The computer was the first to use vacuum tubes, instead of the mechanical switches used in older computers, to store data. Although revolutionary at the time, the machine weighed 700 pounds, contained a mile of wire, and took about 15 seconds for each calculation. (In comparison, today's personal computers can perform billions of calculations in 15 seconds.) Most importantly, the ABC was the first computer to use the binary system and to have memory that repowered itself upon booting.

The design of the ABC would be central to that of future computers.

The Harvard Mark I

From the late 1930s to the early 1950s, **Howard Aiken** and **Grace Hopper** designed the Mark series of computers used by the U.S. Navy for ballistic and gunnery calculations. Aiken, an electrical engineer and physicist, designed the computer, while Hopper did the programming. The **Harvard Mark I**, finished in 1944, could add, subtract, multiply, and divide.

However, many believe Hopper's greatest contribution to computing was the invention of the **compiler**, a program that translates English-language instructions into computer language. The team was also responsible for a common computer-related expression. Hopper was the first to "debug" a computer when she removed a moth that had flown into the Harvard Mark I and had caused the computer to break down (see Figure 11). After that, problems that caused a computer not to run were called *bugs*.

The Turing Machine

Meanwhile, in 1936, British mathematician **Alan Turing** created an abstract computer model that could perform logical operations. The **Turing Machine** was not a real machine but rather a hypothetical model that mathematically defined a mechanical procedure (or algorithm). Additionally, Turing's concept described a process by which the machine

FIGURE 10 The Atanasoff–Berry Computer laid the design groundwork for many computers to come. *(AP Photo/Frederick News-Post)*

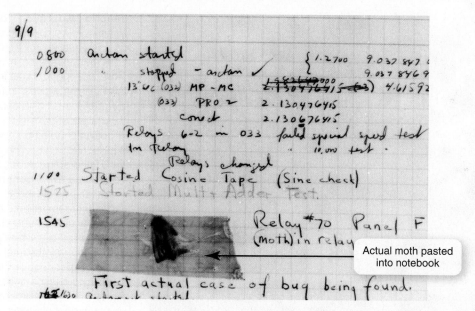

FIGURE 11 Grace Hopper coined the term *computer bug* when a moth flew into the Harvard Mark I, causing it to break down. *(Naval History and Heritage Command, photo # NH 96566)*

could read, write, or erase symbols written on squares of an infinite paper tape. This concept of an infinite tape that could be read, written to, and erased was the precursor to today's RAM.

The ENIAC

The **Electronic Numerical Integrator and Computer (ENIAC)**, shown in Figure 12, was another U.S. government–sponsored machine developed to calculate the settings used for weapons. Created by **John W. Mauchly** and **J. Presper Eckert** at the University of Pennsylvania, it was put into operation in 1944. Although the ENIAC is generally thought of as the first successful high-speed electronic digital computer, it was big and clumsy. The ENIAC used nearly 18,000 vacuum tubes and filled approximately 1,800 square feet of floor space. Although inconvenient, the ENIAC served its purpose and remained in use until 1955.

The UNIVAC

The **Universal Automatic Computer**, or **UNIVAC**, was the first commercially successful electronic digital computer. Completed in 1951, the UNIVAC operated on magnetic tape (see Figure 13), setting it apart from its competitors, which ran on punch cards. The UNIVAC gained notoriety when, in a 1951 publicity stunt, it was used to predict the outcome of the Stevenson–Eisenhower presidential race. After analyzing only 5% of the popular vote, the UNIVAC correctly identified Dwight D. Eisenhower as the victor. After that, UNIVAC soon became a household word. The UNIVAC and computers like it were considered **first-generation computers** and were the last to use vacuum tubes to store data.

Transistors and Beyond

Only a year after the ENIAC was completed, scientists at the Bell Telephone Laboratories in New Jersey invented

FIGURE 12 The ENIAC took up an entire room and required several people to manipulate it. *(University of Pennsylvania/AP Images)*

FIGURE 13 UNIVACs were the first computers to use magnetic tape for data storage. *(CBS/Landov)*

second-generation computers. Still, transistors were limited as to how small they could be made.

A few years later, in 1958, **Jack Kilby**, while working at Texas Instruments, invented the world's first **integrated circuit**, a small chip capable of containing thousands of transistors. This consolidation in design enabled computers to become smaller and lighter. The computers in this early integrated-circuit generation were considered **third-generation computers**.

Other innovations in the computer industry further refined the computer's speed, accuracy, and efficiency. However, none was as significant as the 1971 introduction by the Intel Corporation of the **microprocessor chip**, a small chip containing millions of transistors (see Figure 15). The microprocessor functions as the central processing unit (CPU), or brains, of the computer. Computers that use a microprocessor chip are called **fourth-generation computers**. Over time, Intel and Motorola became the leading manufacturers of microprocessors. Today, the Intel Core i7 is one of Intel's most powerful processors.

As you can see, personal computers have come a long way since the Altair and have a number of inventions and people to thank for their amazing popularity. What will the future bring? ■

the **transistor**, another means to store data (see Figure 14). The transistor replaced the bulky vacuum tubes of earlier computers and was smaller and more powerful than tubes. It was used in almost everything, from radios to phones. Computers that used transistors were referred to as

FIGURE 14 Transistors were 1/10 the size of vacuum tubes, faster, and produced much less heat. *(borissos/Fotolia)*

FIGURE 15 Today's microprocessors can contain billions of transistors. *(Tudor Voinea/Shutterstock)*

check your understanding// review & practice

For a quick review of what you've learned, answer the following questions. Visit **pearsonhighered.com/techinaction** to check your answers.

multiple choice

1. What was the name of the first web browser?

   a. Mosaic

   b. Internet Explorer

   c. Netscape

   d. Firefox

2. Which programming language revolutionized the software industry?

   a. ALGOL

   b. BASIC

   c. COBOL

   d. FORTRAN

3. Which invention enabled computers to be made smaller and lighter?

   a. the integrated circuit

   b. the transistor

   c. the microprocessor chip

   d. magnetic tape

4. Which computer was touted as the first personal computer?

   a. Altair

   b. Commodore PET

   c. Lisa

   d. Osborne

5. What was the importance of the Turing machine to today's computers?

   a. It described a system that was a precursor to today's notebook computer.

   b. It was the first electronic calculator and a precursor to the computer.

   c. It was the first computer to have a monitor.

   d. It described a process to read, write, and erase symbols on a tape and was the precursor to today's RAM.

6. Which computer first stored its operating system in ROM?

   a. Apple I

   b. Apple II

   c. Lisa

   d. Macintosh

7. What was the first spreadsheet application?

   a. Lotus 1-2-3

   b. Excel

   c. WordStar

   d. VisiCalc

8. Which components are a characteristic of third-generation computers?

   a. transistors

   b. vacuum tubes

   c. integrated circuits

   d. microprocessor chips

9. For what is the UNIVAC computer best known?

   a. It was the first computer used to tabulate U.S. census data.

   b. It was the first computer to use the binary system.

   c. It was the first computer to incorporate a magnetic tape system.

   d. It was the first computer used as a mechanical calculator.

10. Who are the founders of Apple?

    a. Paul Allen and Bill Gates

    b. Steve Jobs and Steve Wozniak

    c. Steve Jobs and Bill Gates

    d. Bill Gates and Steve Wozniak

To take an autograded version of this review, please go to the companion website at **pearsonhighered.com/techinaction**, or go your MyITLab course.

4

Application Software: Programs That Let You Work and Play

Programs That Let You Work

The Nuts and Bolts of Software

OBJECTIVES

1. What's the difference between application software and system software? **(p. 124)**

2. What are the different ways I can access and use software? **(pp. 124–125)**

Productivity and Business Software

OBJECTIVES

3. What kinds of applications are included in productivity software? **(pp. 126–134)**

4. What kinds of software do small and large businesses use? **(pp. 134–135)**

Programs That Let You Play

Multimedia and Entertainment Software

OBJECTIVE

5. What different types of multimedia and entertainment software are available? **(pp. 140–145)**

🔊 **Sound Byte:** Enhancing Photos with Image-Editing Software

🔒 **Active Helpdesk:** Choosing Software

Managing Your Software

OBJECTIVES

6. What's important to know when buying software? **(pp. 146–149)**

7. How do I install and uninstall software? **(pp. 149–150)**

🔒 **Active Helpdesk:** Buying and Installing Software

Make This: Explore an App Builder Skill on **page 139**

For all media in this chapter go to **pearsonhighered.com /techinaction** or **MyITLab**.

Norebbo/Shutterstock; Mnaxer/Shutterstock; Iko/Shutterstock; Timo Darco/Fotolia

HOW COOL IS THIS?

Scan here for more info

Ever watch a video on your smartphone only to **fall asleep** or to be interrupted and miss part of it? **Eye-tracking software** has been around for a while. It's been used with desktop computers to help the disabled and in some high-end cars to warn drivers of dozing off. And FocusAssist for iPad from Mindflash is meant to help you **focus and pay attention** during training videos. These uses are only the tip of the iceberg, and experts agree that eye tracking has the potential to **transform** the way users interact with their mobile devices. With a **blink of an eye**, you could open or close apps, scroll through a webpage, take a picture, and so on. What possibilities do you see this technology presenting? *(Ra2 Studio/Fotolia)*

Programs That Let You Work

A computer without software is like a sandwich without filling. Although a computer's hardware is critical, a computer system does nothing without software. In this section, we'll look at programs created to help you work more effectively and efficiently. First, let's check out some software basics.

the nuts and bolts of
SOFTWARE

Technically speaking, the term **software** refers to a set of instructions that tells the computer what to do. An instruction set, also called a **program**, provides a means for us to interact with and use the computer, even if we lack specialized programming skills. Your computer has two main types of software:

1. **Application software** is the software you use to do tasks at home, school, and work. Figure 4.1 shows the various types of application software we'll discuss in this chapter.

2. **System software** includes software that helps run the computer and coordinate instructions between application software and the computer's hardware devices. System software includes the operating system (such as Windows and OS X) and utility programs (programs in the operating system that help manage system resources). We discuss system software in detail in Chapter 5.

Other types of software, such as web browsers, virus protection, and backup and recovery software, are used every day. We'll discuss these types of software elsewhere in this book.

What software do I need to install on my computer? Virtually every new computer comes with software preinstalled, including an operating system and some application software, depending on which computer you buy. If you need to add other software to your system, you'll need either to

install the software yourself or to access it from the web. There are two types of software you can install on your computer:

1. **Proprietary (or commercial) software** is software you buy, such as the Microsoft Office applications you're probably familiar with. You can download proprietary software directly from the Internet, or you can buy it on a DVD.

2. **Open source software** is free software that is available with few licensing and copyright restrictions. One advantage of open source software is that a community of users continues to make changes to the software, keeping

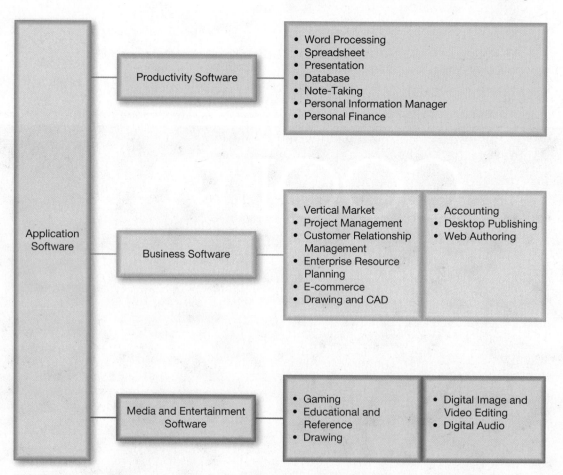

FIGURE 4.1 Application software lets you perform a variety of tasks.

- Word Processing
- Spreadsheet
- Presentation
- Database
- Note-Taking
- Personal Information Manager
- Personal Finance

Productivity Software

- Vertical Market
- Project Management
- Customer Relationship Management
- Enterprise Resource Planning
- E-commerce
- Drawing and CAD
- Accounting
- Desktop Publishing
- Web Authoring

Business Software

- Gaming
- Educational and Reference
- Drawing
- Digital Image and Video Editing
- Digital Audio

Media and Entertainment Software

Application Software

trends in IT

Mobile Commerce: What Have You Bought with Your Phone Lately?

Most people own a mobile device, so it's no surprise that companies regard *mobile commerce* (or m-commerce)—using applications on smartphones and tablets to buy and sell products—as a trend that shouldn't be ignored.

Although mobile commerce hasn't taken over traditional methods of e-commerce just yet, the number of purchases from mobile devices continues to rise. Some studies indicate that in a few years, the number of mobile online retail transactions in the United States will double and account for nearly a quarter of all e-commerce retail activity. The emergence of tablets and better functioning m-commerce apps has improved the mobile shopping experience. Consider two trends that have facilitated the growing acceptance of m-commerce:

1. *Mobile payments:* Instead of using your credit card or debit card to buy something, some retailers such as Starbucks and Target have mobile apps that enable you to pay just by showing your smartphone. Mobile wallets, such as Google Wallet and Square Wallet, have been slow to catch on. Apple is hoping that Apple Pay can become the digital payment leader. Regardless, industry experts anticipate that mobile wallets will become the primary payment method of the future.

2. *Mobile coupons and barcodes:* Many consumers use mobile device apps to look up information by scanning special quick response (QR) codes (such as the one shown on page 123) on products. Many stores also have virtual store loyalty cards on their apps that let you access coupons, product information, and store discount programs.

Although many mobile device owners feel it's not as safe to use their mobile devices to make purchases, it's just as safe as making purchases with your computer on the web. Time and education will help to relieve those fears.

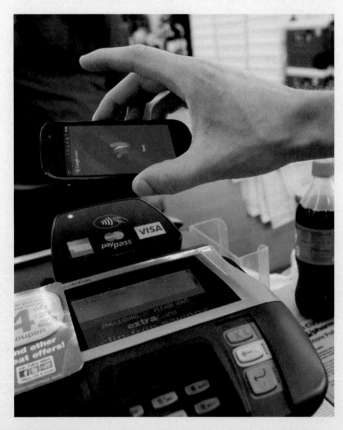

FIGURE 4.2 Have you made a payment using your smartphone instead of a credit card yet? (*Dai Sugano/San Jose Mercury News/MCT/Newscom*)

it current without needing to wait for periodic updates. However, unlike Microsoft Office and other proprietary applications, open source applications offer little or no formal support. Instead, they're supported from their community of users across websites and newsgroups.

Can I use software directly from the web? Another way to obtain software is through **Software as a Service** **(SaaS)**, in which the vendor hosts the software online and you access and use the software over the Internet without having to install it on your computer. With these **web-based applications**, you can collaborate online with others, avoiding the coordination mess that often occurs when transferring documents via e-mail. Although many web-based applications are not as fully featured as their installable counterparts, most work with files from other applications. ∎

productivity and business
SOFTWARE

One reason computers are invaluable is that they make it easier to complete our daily tasks. **Productivity software** includes programs that let you perform various tasks required at home, school, and business and includes word processing, spreadsheet, presentation, database, and personal information manager programs.

Bundled Productivity Software

Is it better to buy software individually or in a bundled package? For proprietary software, it's cheaper to buy a **software suite** than to buy each program individually. Software suites are available for all types of software. Productivity software suites include:

- *Microsoft Office:* the standard proprietary software suite for Windows. A version is also available for Apple computers.
- *Apache OpenOffice:* an open source productivity suite that provides functionality similar to that of Microsoft Office. You can download the installation file you'll need to run OpenOffice at **openoffice.org**.
- *Apple iWork:* a productivity suite made especially for Apple computers.

Microsoft Office Online and Google Drive are examples of web-based productivity suites. Microsoft Office Online includes online versions of Word, Excel, PowerPoint, and OneNote but with less functionality than the installed versions. Google Drive (**drive.google.com**) includes word processing, spreadsheet, and presentation functionality, as well as forms and drawing applications. If you're looking for basic productivity software that you can access from any computer, either online suite is sufficient. Figure 4.3 lists examples of productivity software suites, along with the individual applications each suite offers.

The individual programs within a suite work well together because they share common features, toolbars, and menus. For example, when using applications in the Microsoft Office suite, you can seamlessly create a spreadsheet in Excel, import it into Access, and then link an Access query to a Word document. It would be much harder to do the same thing using different applications from a variety of software developers.

Word Processing Software

What are the most common word processing applications? You've probably used **word processing software** to create and edit documents such as research papers, class notes, and résumés. Microsoft Word is the most popular word processing program that you can buy and install on your computer. If you're looking for a more affordable alternative, you might want to try an open source alternative such as Writer, a word processing program from the Apache OpenOffice suite (**openoffice.org**). Writer is similar to Microsoft Word. When saving a document in Writer, the default file format has an OpenDocument file (.odt) extension. However, by using

FIGURE 4.3

Productivity Software Suites

PRODUCTIVITY SUITE	WORD PROCESSING	SPREADSHEET	PRESENTATION	DATABASE	NOTE-TAKING	PIM/E-MAIL
Installed: Proprietary						
Microsoft Office	Word	Excel	PowerPoint	Access	OneNote	Outlook
Apple iWork	Pages	Numbers	Keynote			
Installed: Open Source						
Apache OpenOffice	Writer	Calc	Impress	Base		
Web-Based						
Microsoft Office Online	Word	Excel	PowerPoint		OneNote	Outlook
Google Drive	Documents	Spreadsheets	Presentation			Gmail
Zoho	Writer	Sheet, Books	Show	Creator	Notebook	
ThinkFree	Document	Spreadsheet	Presentation		Note	

the Save As command, you can save files in other formats, such as .docx for Word.

What special tools do word processing programs have that I might not know about? You're probably familiar with the basic tools of word processing software, such as the spelling and grammar checking tools, the thesaurus, and the find-and-replace tool. But did you know you can translate words or phrases into another language or automatically correct your spelling as you type? You also can automatically summarize key points in a text document, add bibliographical references, and include illustrations with different picture styles.

How can I make my documents look more professional? With word processing software, you can easily change fonts, font styles, and sizes; add colors to text; adjust margins; add borders to portions of text or to entire pages; insert bulleted and numbered lists; and organize your text into columns. You also can insert pictures from your own files or from a gallery of images and graphics, such as clip art and SmartArt, which are included with the software.

You also can enhance the look of your document by creating an interesting background or by adding a "theme" of coordinated colors and styles. Figure 4.4 shows what a document can look like when you apply formatting options found in many word processing applications. (Note that although many of the open source and web-based applications have great formatting capabilities, most are not as fully featured as the installed version of Microsoft Word.)

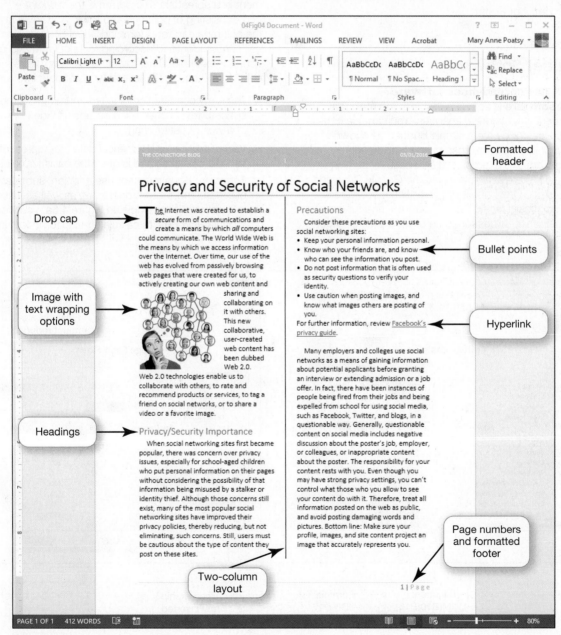

FIGURE 4.4 Nearly every word processing application has formatting features that let you give your documents a professional look.

BITS&BYTES

Finding the Right Software

There are millions of applications, and new ones are developed and released every day. How can you find the right ones to meet your needs? What are the cool new applications or the ones that just don't work? The editors and analysts at *PC Magazine* have put together AppScout (**appscout.pcmag.com**), a site that provides reviews of the best software, websites, and web applications. Next time you're looking for a new application, check out AppScout.

Spreadsheet Software

Why would I use spreadsheet software?

Spreadsheet software is software that lets you make calculations and perform numerical analyses. You can use it to track your expenses or create a simple budget, as shown in Figure 4.5a, for example. Microsoft Excel and Apache OpenOffice Calc are two examples of spreadsheet software. (Web-based options are available within the Google Drive and Office Online suites.) One benefit of spreadsheet software is that it can automatically recalculate all formulas and functions in a spreadsheet when values for some of the inputs change.

For example, as shown in Figure 4.5b, you can insert an additional row in your budget ("Membership") and change a value (for September Financial aid), and the results for "Total Expenses" and "Net Income" recalculate automatically.

Because automatic recalculation lets you immediately see the effects different options have on your spreadsheet, you can quickly test different assumptions. This is called *what-if analysis*. Look again at Figure 4.5b and ask, "If I don't get as much financial aid next semester, what impact will that have on my total budget?" The recalculated cells in rows 18 and 19 help answer your question. In addition to financial analysis, many spreadsheet applications have limited database capabilities to sort, filter, and group data.

How do I use spreadsheet software? The basic element in a spreadsheet program is the *worksheet,* which is a grid consisting of columns and rows. As shown in Figure 4.5a, the columns and rows form individual boxes called *cells*. Each cell can be identified according to its column and row position. For example, a cell in column A, row 1 is referred to as cell A1. You can enter several types of data into a cell:

- *Text:* Any combination of letters, numbers, symbols, and spaces. Text is often used as labels to identify the contents of a worksheet or chart.

- *Values and Dates:* Numerical data that represents a quantity or a date/time and is often the basis for calculations.

- *Formulas:* Equations that use addition, subtraction, multiplication, and division operators, as well as values and cell references. For example, in Figure 4.5a, you would use the formula =D8-D17 to calculate net income for November.

FIGURE 4.5 Spreadsheet software lets you easily calculate and manipulate numerical data with the use of built-in formulas.

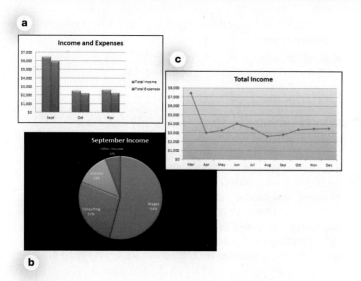

FIGURE 4.6 (a) Column charts show comparisons.
(b) Pie charts show how parts contribute to the whole.
(c) Line charts show trends over time. *(Column charts show comparisons., N/A; Pie charts show how parts contribute to the whole., N/A; Line charts show trends over time.,)*

- *Functions:* Formulas that are preprogrammed into the spreadsheet software. Functions help you with calculations ranging from the simple (such as adding groups of numbers) to the complex (such as determining monthly loan payments), without requiring you to know the exact formula. In Figure 4.5a, to calculate the total of all expenses for September, you could use the built-in addition function, which would look like this: =SUM(B10:B16).

What kinds of graphs and charts can I create with spreadsheet software? As shown in Figure 4.6, most

	Current	1 Year History		
		Trend	High	Low
Microsoft	$ 25.79		30.54	20.26
Apple	$ 255.96		261.09	125.83
Intel	$ 20.95		22.84	15.72
Hewlett Packard	$ 46.05		53.15	34.35
Dell	$ 13.24		16.2	11.57

Sparklines

FIGURE 4.7 Sparklines are tiny graphs that fit into a single cell. *(Sparklines are tiny graphs that fit into a single cell., N/A)*

spreadsheet applications let you create a variety of charts, including basic column charts, pie charts, and line charts, with or without 3-D effects. In addition to these basic charts, you can make stock charts (for investment analysis) and scatter charts (for statistical analysis) or create custom charts. A newer feature in Excel is *sparklines*—small charts that fit into a single cell and make it easy to show data trends (see Figure 4.7).

Presentation Software

How can software help with my presentations?
You've no doubt sat through presentations where the speaker used **presentation software** such as Microsoft PowerPoint (see Figure 4.8) to create a slide show. Because these applications are simple to use, you can produce high-quality presentations without a lot of training. With some of the capabilities in PowerPoint, you can embed online videos, add effects, and even trim video clips without the need for a separate video-editing program.

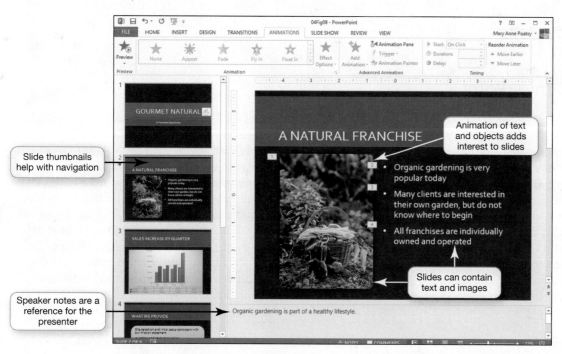

FIGURE 4.8 You can use Microsoft PowerPoint to create dynamic presentations.

What are some tips to make a great presentation?
Undoubtedly, you've seen at least one bad presentation. Don't make your audience suffer through another one! Here are some tips for designing good presentations:

- *Be careful with color:* Choose dark text on a light background or light text on a dark background. Avoid using clashing text and background colors.

- *Use bullets for key points:* Limit the number to four to six bulleted points per slide. Avoid full sentences and paragraphs.

- *Use images:* Images can convey a thought or illustrate a point. Make sure any text over an image can be read easily.

- *Consider font size and style:* Keep the font size large enough to read from the back of the room. Avoid script or fancy font styles. Use only one or two font styles per presentation.

- *Keep animations and/or background audio to a minimum:* They can be distracting (see Figure 4.9).

Database Software

Why is database software useful? Database software such as Oracle, MySQL, and Microsoft Access are powerful applications that let you store and organize data. As mentioned earlier, spreadsheet applications are easy to use for simple tasks such as sorting, filtering, and organizing data. However, you need to use a more robust, fully featured database application to manage larger and more complicated data that is organized in more than one table; to group, sort, and retrieve data; and to generate reports. Traditional databases are organized into *fields, records,* and *tables,* as shown in Figure 4.10.

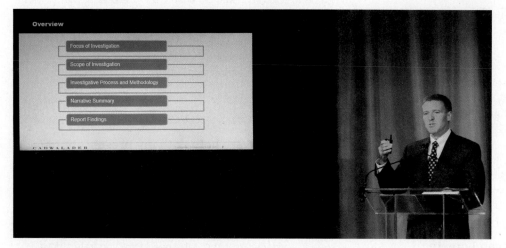

FIGURE 4.9 PowerPoint is a tool that, when used properly, can add organization and clarity to a presentation.

BITS&BYTES

Alternatives to PowerPoint

PowerPoint is generally the go-to application for creating presentation visual aids. But there are several applications that offer a compelling alternative to PowerPoint that are worth a closer look. One cool alternative is Prezi (**prezi.com**), a web-based program that uses an innovative way to produce presentations. Rather than using a set of slides, Prezi uses a large canvas in which you connect ideas. By using the zoom and navigation features, you can move over the canvas, focusing on individual aspects, then zoom in on the finer details and zoom out to see the bigger concept. You can add videos as well as rotate the canvas for added visual interest.

Since images often make the presentation, consider using HaikuDeck (**www.haikudeck.com**). This app has search tools that match your slide content to a wealth of free art to illustrate your presentations. PowToon (**www.powtoon.com**) provides a library of cartoon-like characters that are easily animated to give your presentations more of a "storytelling" aspect rather than fact delivery. PowToon can be converted to video clips and then displayed on the web. Apache OpenOffice Impress and Zoho Show (**www.zoho.com**) are good open source and web-based alternatives, respectively, and are fairly similar to PowerPoint.

FIGURE 4.10 In databases, information is organized into fields, records, and tables.

How do businesses use database software?

Websites like Amazon, iTunes, eBay, and Pandora all rely on databases to keep track of products, clients, invoices, and personnel information. Often, some of that information is available to a home computer user. For example, at Amazon, you can access the history of all the purchases you've ever made on the site. FedEx, UPS, and other shipping companies also let you search their online databases for tracking numbers, allowing you to get instant information on the status of your packages.

OneNote, and you can search for a term across all the digital notebooks you created during the semester to find common ideas such as key points that might appear on a test. There is also a OneNote app for the iPhone and iPad.

Several very good and functional free and online note-taking options are also available to help you take notes or to just jot down a quick reminder. Evernote (**evernote.com**), for example, lets you take notes via

Note-Taking Software

Is there software to help me take notes?

Microsoft OneNote is a popular note-taking and organizational tool you can use for research, brainstorming, and collaboration, as well as just organizing random bits of information. Using OneNote, you can organize your notes into tabbed sections (see Figure 4.11). In addition, you can access your OneNote notes from other Microsoft Office applications. For example, if you're writing a research paper in Word, click the OneNote icon in the Word ribbon to open OneNote, where you can add your notes—perhaps a reference to a website where you found some interesting research. Later, if you open OneNote and click on that reference, it will bring you to the exact spot in the Word document where you made the reference.

You can also add audio or video recordings of lectures to

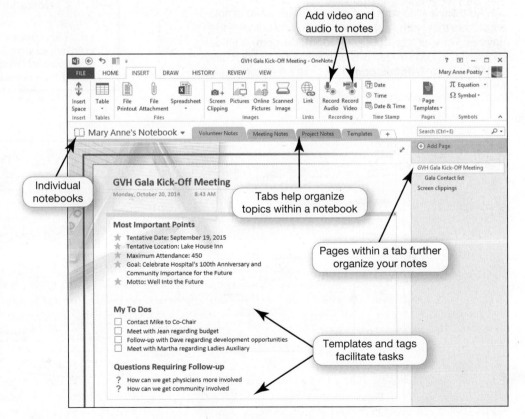

FIGURE 4.11 Microsoft OneNote is a great way to collect and organize notes and other information. The files are readily searchable and easy to share.

the web, your phone, or your computer and then sync your notes between your devices. You can then share your notes with other Evernote users for easy collaboration. Figure 4.12 lists some popular alternative note-taking applications.

Personal Information Manager Software

How can software help me manage my e-mail, time, contact lists, and tasks? Most productivity suites contain some form of **personal information manager (PIM) software** to help you manage e-mail, contacts, calendars, and tasks in one place. Microsoft Outlook (see Figure 4.13) is the most widely used PIM program. If you share a network at home or at work and are using the same PIM software as others on a common network, a PIM program simplifies sharing calendars and scheduling meetings.

Many web-based e-mail clients, such as Yahoo! and Google, also include coordinating calendar and contacts similar to Microsoft Outlook. Yahoo! includes Notepad for jotting down notes and tasks. Google's calendar and contacts sync with Outlook so you can access your Outlook calendar information by logging into Google. This gives you access to your schedule anywhere you have access to a computer and an Internet connection.

There are a wide variety of other to-do lists and simple organizers that work with all your mobile and computing devices. For example, Toodledo (**toodledo.com**) is a free program that coordinates well with Microsoft Outlook, and OmniFocus (**omnifocus.com**) is a more full-featured option for Mac devices.

FIGURE 4.12

Beyond Microsoft OneNote: Alternative Note-Taking Applications

Evernote (evernote.com)
- Web-based
- Notes can be shared for easy collaboration
- Syncs notes between all devices

AudioNote (luminantsoftware.com)
- Synchronized note taking and audio recording
- Allows text or handwritten notes
- Highlights notes during playback

Simplenote (simplenote.com)
- Web-based, open source
- Notes organized by tags
- Mobile apps available

Noteability (gingerlabs.com)
- PDF annotations
- Advanced word processing
- Linked audio recordings to notes
- Auto-sync notes between devices

FIGURE 4.13 Microsoft Outlook includes common PIM features, such as a summary of appointments, a list of tasks, and e-mail messages.

BITS&BYTES

Productivity Software Tips and Tricks

Looking for tips on how to make better use of your productivity software? Some websites send subscribers periodic e-mails full of tips, tricks, and shortcuts for their favorite software programs:

- Microsoft's website includes many tips and tricks for its Office applications (**office.microsoft.com**).
- MakeTechEasier (**maketecheasier.com**) has tidbits for a variety of applications, including Windows and Mac products, Apache OpenOffice, and cellphone applications.
- GCFLearnFree.org (**gcflearnfree.org**) offers free instructional tutorials on a variety of technology topics, including Microsoft Office applications.
- You can also find tips as videos online. To take any videos from YouTube, TED, and other websites on the road with you for future off-line reference, check out Video Downloader (**appsneon.com**) to download, convert, and copy videos to your personal media player.

Microsoft Office Productivity Software Features

What tools can help me work more efficiently with productivity software? Whether you're working on a word processing document, spreadsheet, database, or slide presentation, you can make use of several tools to increase your efficiency:

- A **wizard** walks you through the steps necessary to complete a complicated task. At each step, the wizard asks you questions. Based on your responses, the wizard helps you complete that portion of the task. When you install software, you're often guided by a wizard.
- A **template** is a predesigned form. Templates are included in many productivity applications. They provide the basic structure for a particular kind of document, spreadsheet, database, or presentation. Templates can include specific page layout designs, formatting and styles relevant to that particular document, and automated tasks (macros).
- A **macro** is a small program that groups a series of commands so that they will run as a single command. Macros are best used to automate a routine task or a complex series of commands that must be run frequently. For example, a teacher may write a macro to sort the grades in her grade book in

descending order and to highlight grades that add up to less than a C average. Every time she adds the results of an assignment or a test, she can set up the macro to run through this series of steps.

Personal Financial Software

How can I use software to keep track of my finances? Financial planning software helps you manage your daily finances. Financial planning programs include electronic checkbook registers and automatic bill payment tools. With these features, you can make recurring monthly payments, such as rent or student loans, with automatically scheduled online payments. The software records all transactions, including online payments, in the checkbook register. In addition, you can assign categories to each transaction and then use these categories to create budgets and analyze your spending patterns.

Intuit's installed and web-based products, Quicken and Mint (**mint.com**), respectively, are the market leaders in financial planning software (see Figure 4.14). Both are great at tracking and analyzing your spending habits and at offering advice on how to better manage your finances. With either, you also can track your investment portfolio. With Mint, you can monitor and update your finances from any computer with a private and secure setting. You can also access Mint on a smartphone or tablet, so your information is conveniently accessible. Mint also provides access to a network of other users with whom to exchange tips and advice.

What software can I use to prepare my taxes? Tax preparation software, such as Intuit TurboTax and H&R Block At Home, lets you prepare your state and federal taxes on your own instead of hiring a professional. Both programs offer a complete set of tax forms and instructions, as well as videos that contain expert advice on how to complete each form. Each company also offers free web-based versions of federal forms and instructions. In addition, error-checking features are built into the programs to catch mistakes. TurboTax

FIGURE 4.14 Mint (**mint.com**) is an online financial management tool. An extensive online community provides helpful tips and discussions with other people in similar situations. *(Reprinted with permission © Intuit Inc. All rights reserved.)*

As noted in the chapter, when you purchase software, you're purchasing a license to use it rather than purchasing the actual software. That license tells you how many times you can install the software, so it is important to read it. If you make more copies of the software than the license permits, you're participating in **software piracy** (see Figure 4.15). Historically, the most common way software has been pirated has been by borrowing installation CDs from others and installing the software on other computers. Larger-scale illegal duplication and distribution by counterfeiters are quite common as well. In addition, the Internet provides various ways to copy and distribute pirated software illegally.

Is it really a big deal to copy a program or two? As reported by the Business Software Alliance, nearly half of all software used is pirated. Not only is pirating software unethical and illegal, the practice has financial impacts on all software consumers. The financial loss to the software industry is estimated to be over $50 billion. This loss decreases the amount of money available for further software research and development, while increasing the up-front costs to legitimate consumers.

To determine whether you have a pirated copy of software installed on your computer, conduct a software audit. The Business Software Alliance website (**bsa.org**) has several free third-party software audit tools that help you identify and track software installed on your computer and networks. These programs check the serial numbers of the software installed on your computer against software manufacturer databases of officially licensed copies and known fraudulent copies. Any suspicious software installations are flagged for your attention.

As of yet, there's no such thing as an official software police force, but if you're caught with pirated software, severe penalties do exist. A company or individual can pay up to $150,000 for each software title copied. In addition, you can be criminally prosecuted for copyright infringement, which carries a fine of up to $250,000, a five-year jail sentence, or both.

Efforts to stop groups involved with counterfeit software are in full force. Software manufacturers also are becoming more aggressive in programming mechanisms into software to prevent illegal installations. For instance, with many Microsoft products, installation requires you to activate the serial number of your software with a database maintained at Microsoft. This is different from the traditional "registration" that enrolled you voluntarily and allowed you to be notified of product updates. Failure to activate your serial number or attempting to activate a serial number used previously results in the software going into a "reduced functionality mode" after the 50th time you use it. Therefore, without activation or after activating a used serial number, you would not be able to save documents in Office.

FIGURE 4.15 Making more copies than the software license permits is pirating and is illegal. (*Gor Prole/Getty Images*)

can also run a check for audit alerts, file your return electronically, and offer financial planning guidance to help you plan and manage your financial resources effectively in the following year (see Figure 4.16).

Some financial planning applications also coordinate with tax preparation software. Both Quicken and Mint, for example, integrate seamlessly with TurboTax, so you never have to go through your debit card statements and bills to find tax deductions, tax-related income, or expenses. Many banks and credit card companies also offer online services that download a detailed monthly statement into Quicken and Mint. Remember, however, that the tax code changes annually, so you must obtain an updated version of the software each year.

Small Business Software

What kinds of software are helpful for small business owners? If you have a small business or a hobby that produces income, you know the importance of keeping good records and tracking your expenses and income. **Accounting software** helps small business owners manage their finances more efficiently by providing tools for tracking accounts receivable and accounts payable. In addition, these applications offer inventory management, payroll, and billing tools. Examples of accounting applications are Intuit QuickBooks and Sage 50. Both programs include templates for invoices, statements, and financial reports so that small business owners can create common forms and reports.

If your business requires the need for newsletters, catalogs, annual reports, or other large, complicated publications, consider using **desktop publishing (DTP) software**. Although many word processing applications include some of the features that are hallmarks of desktop publishing, specialized DTP software, such as Microsoft Publisher,

QuarkXPress, and Adobe InDesign, allows professionals to design books and other publications that require complex layouts.

What software do I use to create a web page? **Web authoring software** allows even the novice to design interesting and interactive web pages without knowing any HTML code. Web authoring applications often include wizards, templates, and reference materials to help novices complete most web authoring tasks. More experienced users can take advantage of these applications' advanced features to make the web content current, interactive, and interesting. Microsoft Expression Web and Adobe Dreamweaver are two programs that both professionals and casual web page designers use.

Note that if you need to produce only the occasional web page, you'll find that many applications include features that let you convert your document into a web page. For example, in some Microsoft Office applications, you can choose to save a file as a web page.

Software for Large and Specialized Businesses

What types of software do large businesses use? There is an application for almost every aspect of business. There are specialized programs for project management software, customer relationship management (CRM), enterprise resource planning (ERP), e-commerce, marketing and sales, finance, point of sale, security, networking, data management, and human resources, to name just a few. Figure 4.17 lists many of the common types of business-related software. Some applications are tailored to the specific needs of a particular company or industry. Software designed for a specific industry, such as property management software for real estate professionals, is called **vertical market software**.

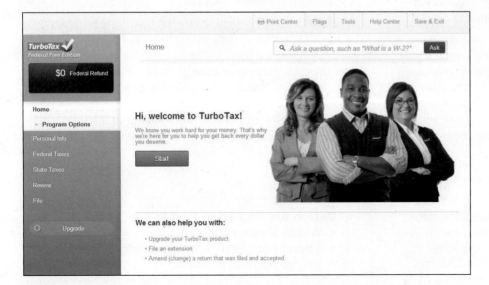

What software is used to make 3-D models? Engineers use **computer-aided design (CAD)** programs such as Autodesk's AutoCAD to create automated designs, technical drawings, and 3-D model visualizations. Here are some cool applications of CAD software:

- Architects use CAD software to build virtual models of their plans and readily visualize all aspects of design before actual construction.

- Engineers use CAD software to design everything from factory components to bridges. The 3-D nature of these programs lets engineers rotate their models and adjust their designs if necessary, eliminating costly building errors.

- CAD software also is used in conjunction with GPS devices for accurate placement of fiber optic networks around the country.

FIGURE 4.16 Tax preparation software such as Intuit TurboTax lets you prepare and file your taxes using a guided, systematic process. *(Reprinted with permission © Intuit Inc. All rights reserved.)*

FIGURE 4.17

Common Types of Large Business–Related Software

PROJECT MANAGEMENT	CUSTOMER RELATIONSHIP MANAGEMENT (CRM)	ENTERPRISE RESOURCE PLANNING (ERP)
Creates scheduling charts to plan and track specific tasks and to coordinate resources	Stores sales and client contact information in one central database	Controls many "back office" operations and processing functions such as billing, production, inventory management, and human resources management

E-COMMERCE	COMPUTER-AIDED DESIGN (CAD)	VERTICAL MARKET
Facilitates website creation and hosting services, shopping cart setup, and credit card–processing services	Creates automated designs, technical drawings, and 3-D model visualizations for architecture, automotive, aerospace, and medical engineering industries	Addresses the needs of businesses in a specific industry or market such as the real estate, banking, and automotive industries

John T Takai/Shutterstock; Eltoro69/Shutterstock; Designdepot Ltd/Shutterstock; Helder Almeida/Shutterstock; Cybrain/Shutterstock; Nmedia/Shutterstock

BITS&BYTES

Need to Work on Files Together? Try These Real-Time Collaboration Tools

You're part of a group working together on a project. You could share files via e-mail, but you've found that can lead to confusion, with multiple versions of the document being revised at the same time. Consider some of these other methods to share and collaborate on files:

- Skype (**skype.com**) lets users work together through video calling and share desktops remotely with other Skype users. This lets two users view the same file at the same time, and the remote user can follow the cursor on the screen of the host user to see exactly what the host user is doing, just as if they were working together in the same room.

- Google Drive (**drive.google.com**), Office Online, and wikis allow multiple users to work together in real time on the same document and to communicate with project members via live text chat.

- Scribblar (**scribblar.com**) is a multiuser whiteboard with live audio chat, which is great for holding virtual brainstorm sessions.

- Dropbox (**dropbox.com**), OneDrive (**onedrive .com**), and Google Drive (**drive.google.com**) are online file storage systems that enable you to share files with others in addition to keeping files synced with any Internet-connected device.

- The medical engineering community uses CAD software to create anatomically accurate solid models of the human body, developing medical implants quickly and accurately.

The list of CAD applications keeps growing as more and more industries realize the benefits CAD can bring to their product development and manufacturing processes. ■

Before moving on to Part 2:
- **Watch Replay Video 4.1** ▶.
- **Then check your understanding of what you've learned so far.**

check your understanding // review & practice

For a quick review to see what you've learned so far, answer the following questions. Visit **pearsonhighered.com /techinaction** to check your answers.

multiple choice

1. Software that is available on demand via the Internet is called

   a. proprietary software.

   b. Software as a Service (SaaS).

   c. productivity software.

   d. open source software.

2. Software that allows an individual to track financial transactions is called

   a. checking software.   **c.** personal financial software.

   b. tax planning software.   **d.** small business accounting software.

3. Which type of program takes advantage of automatic recalculation and what-if analysis?

   a. spreadsheet   **c.** CAD/CAM

   b. database   **d.** project management

4. Which of the following is true about open source software?

   a. The program code is confidential.

   b. The program can be changed and is freely distributed.

   c. The program can be freely distributed as long as the program code is not changed.

   d. The program code is subject to copyright protection.

5. Which program can you use to take notes in class?

   a. Noteability

   b. Evernote

   c. OneNote

   d. all of the above

To take an autograded version of this review, please go to the companion website at **pearsonhighered.com/techinaction**, or go your MyITLab course.

Continue

TRY THIS

Citing Website Sources

You've been assigned a research paper, and your instructor requires citations and a bibliography. In the past, you might have resorted to using websites such as Son of Citation Machine (**citationmachine.net**) or EasyBib (**easybib.com**) to create your citations and generate a bibliography. But did you know there are tools built right into Microsoft Word that do the same thing?

To Add a New Citation and Source to a Document:

Step 1 Click at the end of the sentence or phrase that you want to cite.

Step 2 On the References tab, in the Citations & Bibliography group, click **Insert Citation**.

Step 3 To add the source information, click **Add New Source**.

Note: To create a citation and fill in the source information later, click **Add New Placeholder**.

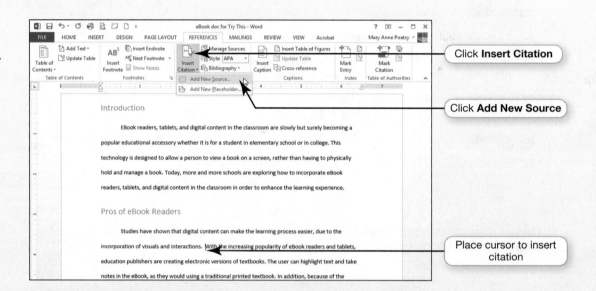

Click **Insert Citation**

Click **Add New Source**

Place cursor to insert citation

Step 4 Begin to fill in the source information by clicking the arrow next to Type of Source.

Fill out the fields in the Create Source dialog box

Step 5 The citation will appear in your document.

Studies have shown that digital content can make the learning process easier, due to the incorporation of visuals and interactions. (Andrews, 2013) With the increasing popularity of eBook readers and tablets, education publishers are creating electronic versions of textbooks. The user can highlight text and take notes in the eBook, as they would using a traditional printed textbook. In addition, because of the software used with eBook readers and tablets, users can more easily search

The citation displays in text

To Create a Bibliography:

You can create a bibliography at any point after you insert one or more sources in a document. Click where you want to insert a bibliography, usually at the end of the document. Then do the following:

Step 1 On the References tab, in the Citations & Bibliography group, click **Bibliography**.

Step 2 Click a predesigned bibliography format to insert the bibliography into the document. The bibliography is automatically generated.

Click Bibliography

Choose a built-in bibliography style

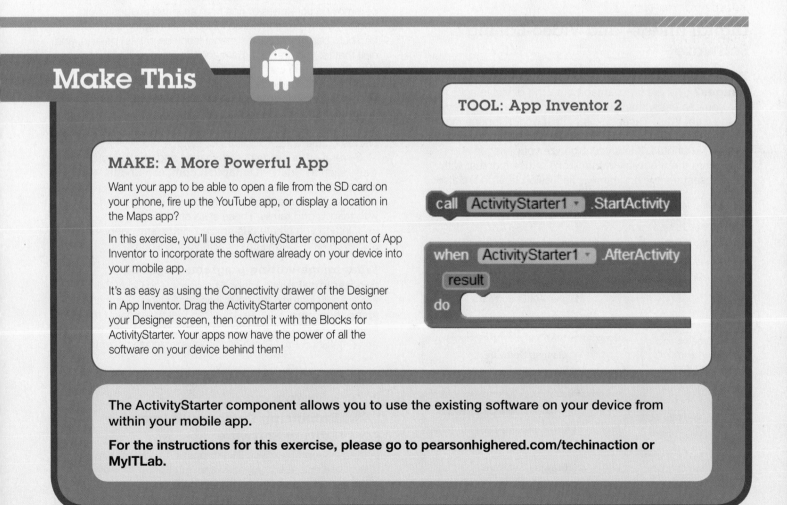

Make This

TOOL: App Inventor 2

MAKE: A More Powerful App

Want your app to be able to open a file from the SD card on your phone, fire up the YouTube app, or display a location in the Maps app?

In this exercise, you'll use the ActivityStarter component of App Inventor to incorporate the software already on your device into your mobile app.

It's as easy as using the Connectivity drawer of the Designer in App Inventor. Drag the ActivityStarter component onto your Designer screen, then control it with the Blocks for ActivityStarter. Your apps now have the power of all the software on your device behind them!

The ActivityStarter component allows you to use the existing software on your device from within your mobile app.

For the instructions for this exercise, please go to pearsonhighered.com/techinaction or MyITLab.

Programs That Let You Play

While many programs help you be more productive, there are also programs that entertain you with audio, video, and digital images and through games, animations, and movies. Regardless of whether the software helps you work or play, it's important to know how to work with and manage the software so that you install it correctly and use it legally. This section discusses multimedia and entertainment software, as well as how to manage any type of software.

multimedia and entertainment
SOFTWARE

From movies and television to music and photography, the entertainment world is vastly digital. **Multimedia software** includes digital image- and video-editing software, digital audio software, and other specialty software required to produce computer games, animations, and movies. In this section, we look at several popular types of multimedia and entertainment software, as shown in Figure 4.18.

Digital Image- and Video-Editing Software

How can I edit, share, and organize digital images? One great advantage of taking digital images is that you can easily manipulate them and then share them on the web. While Facebook is a great option for sharing images, Flickr (**flickr.com**) is a website specifically designed for sharing photos. It lets you organize your images and then share them publicly with millions of users or just with your closest friends and family. Discussion boards are also available so that people can leave comments about the images.

If you want to edit your photos before sharing, Adobe Photoshop Elements is **image-editing software** geared to the casual photographer. Image-editing software includes tools for basic modifications to digital photos such as removing red-eye; modifying contrast, sharpness, and color casts; or removing scratches or rips from scanned images of old photos. Many programs also include painting tools such as brushes, pens, and artistic media (such as paints, pastels, and oils) that let you create realistic-looking images. Some include templates so you can insert your favorite pictures into preformatted pages for digital scrapbooks or greeting cards. Google Picasa (**picasa.google.com**) is a popular application that not only lets you edit images but also helps to organize and share your digital images (see Figure 4.19). Picasa also stores your photos on the web.

Several other online photo-sharing and photo-storing sites, such as Snapfish (**snapfish.com**) and Shutterfly (**shutterfly.com**), let you upload your digital images from your computer, create photo albums, and share them with friends and family. These sites offer printing services as well, letting you create customized cards, stationery, books, and even smartphone cases with your images.

What image-editing programs might a professional use? Adobe Photoshop and Corel PaintShop Pro are fully featured image-editing applications. Gimpshop (**gimpshop.com**) is a free download that has most of the features offered by the for-pay applications, such as Photoshop and PaintShop Pro. These offer sophisticated tools for tasks

Multimedia and Entertainment Software	Digital Image- and Video-Editing Software
	Digital Audio Software
	Gaming Software
	Educational and Reference Software
	Drawing Software

FIGURE 4.18 There are many varieties of multimedia and entertainment software.

SOUND BYTE
Enhancing Photos with Image-Editing Software

In this Sound Byte, you'll learn tips and tricks on how to best use image-editing software. You'll learn how to remove the red-eye from photos and to incorporate borders, frames, and other enhancements to produce professional effects.

Image-editing tools

Images placed here and arranged in collage

E-mail, print, and export tools

FIGURE 4.19 You can create collages of your favorite images using Google Picasa. *(Google, Inc.)*

like layering images and masking images (hiding parts of layers to create effects such as collages). Designers use these more sophisticated tools to create the enhanced digital images used commercially in logos, in advertisements, and on book and CD covers.

What software do I need to edit digital videos?

While it's easy to upload videos directly to YouTube or Facebook unedited, you can use **digital video–editing software** to help refine your videos. Although the most expensive products (such as Adobe Premiere Pro and Apple's Final Cut Pro) offer the widest range of special effects and tools, some moderately priced video-editing programs have enough features to keep the casual user happy. Windows Movie Maker and iMovie have intuitive drag-and-drop features that make it simple to create professional-quality movies with little or no training (see Figure 4.20).

Window used to view or edit movie clips

Video clips in clips pane

Movie clips display in clip viewer

Transition icon controls transition effects between clips

FIGURE 4.20 Video-editing programs such as Apple iMovie make it easy to create and edit movies. *(Anthony Devlin/EMPPL PA Wire/AP Images)*

Have you ever done any of the following?

- Posted pictures on Facebook that your friends accessed from their iPhone
- Used Dropbox or OneDrive to store your files instead of carrying around a flash drive
- Used Google Drive or Microsoft Office Online to collaborate on a team project
- Used Carbonite to back up your data online

By doing any of these activities, you have participated in cloud computing. So what exactly is **cloud computing**?

Cloud computing refers to storing data, files, and applications on the web and being able to access and manipulate these files and applications from any Internet-connected device. Being able to work from the cloud eliminates the need to have everything stored on your own computer's drives and lets you access your pictures, music, files, and programs from any device as long as you have access to the Internet. In addition, cloud computing makes it easier to collaborate and communicate with others, and it can cut down on administrative tasks for organizations maintaining large amounts of computer hardware and software.

There are two sides to cloud computing:

1. The *front end* is the side we see as users. It involves a web browser like Internet Explorer, Firefox, or Google Chrome.
2. The *back end* consists of various data centers and server farms that house the files and programs you access "on the cloud" (see Figure 4.21). These data centers and server farms are warehouses full of computers and servers, and they are being created all over the world, providing us with "cloud storage." The computers in the data centers or server farms are designed to work together, adjusting to the varying degrees of demand placed on them at any time.

Google is one of the first true explorers in the cloud, building applications such as Google Drive, Gmail, and the Chrome web browser in an effort to create a completely virtual operating environment. A fully functioning operating environment would enable users to sign in on any computer and have "their" computer setup (desktop configurations and images, programs, files, and other personalized settings) display. Additionally, cloud computing would reduce the need for all of us to have the fastest computers with the most memory and storage capabilities. Instead, we could all have simple front-end terminals with basic input and output devices because the computers on the back end will be providing all the computing muscle.

The Chromebook is Google's first attempt at a notebook where all the applications and files are stored on the web. Nothing is installed or saved to a hard drive, not even the operating system! All programs are accessed and all work is done through the web-based browser, so sending e-mail, editing photos, and working on documents are all done via web-based applications. Since the Chromebook requires an Internet connection to get most tasks done, users must be near a WiFi connection or pay for a data plan.

FIGURE 4.21 There are two sides to cloud computing: the side we see as users and the banks of computers and servers that house the files and programs we access.

There are some considerations with cloud computing of which you need to be aware:

- *Security and privacy:* Right now, the security of information stored on the web is built on trusting that the passwords we set and the security systems that the data centers put in place are able to keep our information away from unauthorized users. Caution is always warranted, as nothing is completely safe and private.

- *Backup:* Because even the devices in these large data centers and server farms inevitably will break down, the cloud computing systems have redundant systems to provide backup. However, for critical files that you must have, it might be a good idea not to completely rely on the cloud but to have your own offline backup system, as well.

- *Access issues:* With cloud computing, you access your files and programs only through the Internet. If you couldn't access the Internet due to a power failure or system failure with your Internet service provider, you wouldn't be able to access your files. Storing your most critical files and programs offline will help reduce the inconvenience and loss of productivity while access to the Internet is being restored.

Before relying on cloud computing, consider the above concerns against the advantages of the convenience of having your information when and where you want it and the ability to promote better collaboration.

Digital Audio Software

What's the difference between all the digital audio file types on my computer? You probably have a variety of digital audio files stored on your computer, such as downloaded music files, audiobooks, or podcasts. These types of audio files have been *compressed* so they're more manageable to transfer to and from your computer and over the Internet. MP3, short for MPEG-1 Audio Layer 3, is a type of audio compression format and is the most common compressed digital format, but there are other compressed formats, such as AAC and WMA.

You may also see *uncompressed* audio files on your computer, such as WAV or AIFF files. Uncompressed files—the files found on audio CDs, for example—have not had any data removed, so the quality is a perfect representation of the audio as it was recorded. Unfortunately, the file size is much larger than that of compressed files. Compressed formats remove data such as high frequencies that the human ear does not hear in order to make the files smaller and easier to download and store. MP3 format, for example, makes it possible to transfer and play back music on smartphones and other music players. A typical CD stores between 10 and 15 songs in uncompressed format, but with files in MP3 format, the same CD can store between 100 and 180 songs. The smaller file size not only lets you store and play music in less space, it also allows quick and easy distribution over the Internet. Ogg Vorbis (or just Ogg) is a free, open source audio compression format alternative to MP3. Some say that Ogg produces a better sound quality than MP3.

What do I use to create my own audio files? There are many digital audio applications that let you create and record your own audio files. With programs such as MAGIX Music Maker or Apple GarageBand, you can compose your own songs or soundtracks with virtual instruments, voice recorders, synthesizers, and special audio effects, and these will end up as uncompressed MIDI files. Other programs, such as Audacity and Cakewalk SONAR, let you record audio files.

Can I edit audio files? Audio-editing software includes tools that make editing audio files as easy as editing text files. Software such as the open source Audacity (**audacity.sourceforge.net**) and Sony Sound Forge Pro (**sonycreativesoftware.com**) lets you perform such basic

BITS&BYTES

Mirror, mirror…

Sometimes when you download software, especially open source software, you must choose a download location. Each location in the list is a mirror site. A mirror site is a copy of a website or set of files hosted at a remote location. Software developers sometimes use geographically distributed mirror sites so that users can choose the mirror site closest to their location to expedite the download time. Mirror sites are also used as backups, so if a server goes down for some reason, users can access the software from a different site, ensuring the software is always accessible. Developers also use mirror sites to help offset issues associated with a sudden influx of traffic that would otherwise overload a single server.

 ACTIVE HELPDESK
Choosing Software

In this Active Helpdesk, you'll play the role of a helpdesk staffer, fielding questions about the different kinds of multimedia software, educational and reference software, and entertainment software.

editing tasks as cutting dead air space from the beginning or end of a song or clipping a portion from the middle. You can also add special sound effects, such as echo or bass boost, and remove static or hiss from MP3 files. AudioAcrobat (**audioacrobat.com**), a web-based program, makes it easy to record and stream audio and video and hosts your audio files. These applications support recording sound files from a microphone or any source you can connect through the input line of a sound card.

Gaming Software

Can I make video games? Now that video games represent an industry that generates billions in revenue each year, designing and creating video games is emerging as a desirable career opportunity. Professionally created video games involve artistic storytelling and design, as well as sophisticated programming. Major production houses such as Electronic Arts use applications not easily available to the casual home enthusiast. However, you can use the editors and game engines available for games such as EverQuest, Oblivion, and Unreal Tournament to create custom levels and characters to extend the game.

If you want to try your hand at creating your own video games, multimedia applications such as Unity, Adobe Flash, and RPG Maker VX provide the tools you need to explore game design and creation. The program GameMaker (**yoyogames .com**) is a free product that lets you build a game without any programming; you drag and drop key elements of the new game creation into place. Alice (**alice.org**) is another free environment to check out; it lets you easily create 3-D animations and simple games (see Figure 4.22). You can also make games for your phone. Try the Make This exercise to see how easy it can be. Also see the Sound Byte on 3-D Programming the Easy Way in Chapter 10.

Educational and Reference Software

What fun educational and reference software should I check out? If you want to learn more about a subject, you can turn to the web for many instructional videos and documents. But sometimes, it's best to use software for more complete or detailed instructions. Educational and reference software is available to help you master, study, design, create, or plan. As shown in Figure 4.23, there are software products that teach new skills such as typing, languages, cooking, and playing the guitar.

Students who will be taking standardized tests like the SAT often use test preparation software. In addition, many computer and online brain-training games and programs are designed to improve the health and function of your brain. Lumosity (**lumosity.com**) is one such site that has a specific "workout" program that you can play on your PC or smartphone. Brain Age[2] (**brainage.com**) has software for the Nintendo DS and is designed for players of all ages.

What types of programs are available to train people to use software or special machines? Many programs provide tutorials for popular computer applications (you may even use one in your course provided with MyITLab). These programs use illustrated systematic instructions to guide users through unfamiliar skills in an environment that acts like the actual software, without the software actually being installed.

Some training programs, known as **simulation programs**, allow you to experience or control the software as if it were an actual event. Such simulation programs include commercial and military flight training, surgical instrument training, and machine operation training. One benefit of simulated training programs is that they safely allow you to experience potentially dangerous situations such as flying a helicopter during high winds. Consequently, users of these training programs are more likely to take risks and learn from their mistakes—something they could not afford to do in real life. Simulated training programs also help prevent costly errors. Should something go awry, the only cost of the error is restarting the simulation program.

Do I need special software to take courses online? Although some courses are run from an individually developed website, many online courses are run using **course management software** such as Blackboard, Moodle, and Canvas. In addition to traditional classroom tools such as calendars and grade books, these programs provide special areas for students and instructors to exchange ideas and information through chat rooms, discussion forums, and e-mail. In addition, collaboration tools such as whiteboards and desktop sharing facilitate virtual office hour sessions. Depending on the content and course materials, you may need a password or special plug-ins to view certain videos or demos.

Drawing Software

What kind of software should I use to create illustrations? Drawing software (or **illustration software**) lets you create or edit 2-D, line-based drawings. You can use it to create technical diagrams or original nonphotographic drawings, animations, and illustrations using standard tools such as pens, pencils, and paintbrushes. You also can drag geometric objects from a toolbar onto the canvas area to create images and can use paint bucket, eyedropper, and spray can tools to add color and special effects to the drawings.

FIGURE 4.22 Software programs such as that from Alice.org help students learn how to program as well as create 3-D animations and simple games. (*Carnegie Mellon University Press*)

FIGURE 4.23

Educational and Reference Software: A Sample of What's Available

Test Preparation

Designed to improve your performance on standardized tests

Simulation

Allows you to experience a real situation through a virtual environment

Instructional

Designed to teach you almost anything from playing a musical instrument to learning a language or cooking

Trip Planning

Generates maps and provides driving instructions; some incorporate hotel, restaurant, and other trip information

Home Design/ Improvement

Provides 2-D or 3-D templates and images to let you better visualize indoor and outdoor remodeling projects and landscaping ideas

Course Management

Web-based software system that creates a virtual learning experience, including course materials, tests, and discussion boards

Brain Training

Features games and activities to exercise your brain to improve your memory, processing speed, attention, and multitasking capabilities

Genealogy

Helps chart the relationships between family members through multiple generations

(Amy Cicconi/Alamy; Greg Pease/Getty images; Iqoncept/Shutterstock; Almagami/Shutterstock; Zack Clothier/Shutterstock; Scott Maxwell/LuMaxArt/Shutterstock; Julien Tromeur/Fotolia, Sassyphotos/Fotolia

Adobe Illustrator includes tools that let you create professional-quality creative and technical illustrations such as muscle structures in the human body. Its warping tool allows you to bend, stretch, and twist portions of your image or text. Because of its many tools and features, Illustrator is the preferred drawing software program of most graphic artists.

What kind of software can be used for home or landscape planning?

There are many software packages to help plan the layout of homes and landscapes, such as those offered by Broderbund. A simple, web-based and fairly full-featured free 3-D modeling application is Trimble's SketchUp (formerly owned by Google). SketchUp (**sketchup.com**) lets you create a 3-D image of your dream home (see Figure 4.24). ■

FIGURE 4.24 SketchUp is a free, web-based 3-D modeling application. *(Archipoch/ Shutterstock)*

managing your
SOFTWARE

It's important to know how to pick out the best software for your computer, how to get it onto your computer correctly, and how to take it off. We discuss all of these topics next.

Getting Software

Is discounted software for students available?
If you're a student, you can sometimes buy substantially discounted software that is no different from regularly priced software. Campus computer stores and college bookstores offer discounted prices to students who possess a valid student ID. Online software suppliers such as Journey Education Marketing (**journeyed.com**) and Academic Superstore (**academicsuperstore.com**) also offer popular software to students at reduced prices. Software developers, such as Microsoft and Apple, often offer their products to students at a discount so it's always good to check their websites before purchasing software or hardware.

Can I get software for free legally? In addition to open source software, discussed previously in this chapter,

freeware is copyrighted software that you can use for free. Explore sites like FileHippo (**filehippo.com**) and MajorGeeks (**majorgeeks.com**) to see how many good freeware programs are available. However, while much legitimate freeware exists, some unscrupulous people use freeware to distribute viruses and malware. Be cautious when installing freeware, especially if you're unsure of the provider's legitimacy.

Can I try new software before it's released?
Some software developers offer beta versions of their software free of charge. A **beta version** is an application that is still under development (see Figure 4.25). By distributing free beta versions, developers hope users will report errors, or bugs, they find in their programs. Many beta versions are available for a limited trial period and are used to help developers respond to issues before they launch the software on the market.

Are there risks associated with installing beta versions, freeware, or downloading software from the Internet? By their very nature, beta products are unlikely to be bug free, so you always run the risk of something

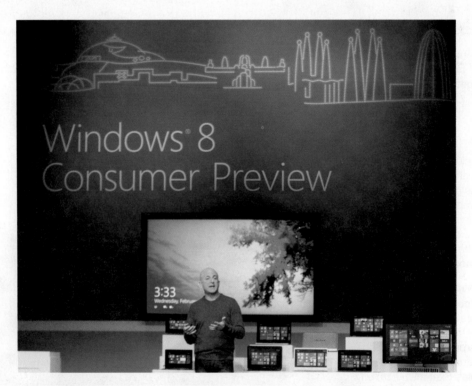

FIGURE 4.25 Prior to releasing Windows 8, Microsoft released the beta version, named Consumer Preview, for users to try. *(Gustau Nacarino/Reuters/Corbis)*

BITS&BYTES

How to Open Unknown File Types

Normally, when you double-click a file to open it, the program associated with the file runs automatically. For example, when you double-click a file with a .doc or .docx extension, the file opens in Microsoft Word. However, if the file has no extension or Windows has no application associated with that file type, an "Open with" dialog box appears and asks what program you want to use to open the file. In other cases, a document may open with a program other than the one you wanted to use. This is because many applications can open several file types, and the program you expected the file to open in is not currently the program associated with that file type. To assign a program to a file type or to change the program to open a particular file type, follow these instructions:

1. Use the search and navigation tools in File Explorer (previously called Windows Explorer) to locate the file you want to change. (For example, you can search for all Word files by searching for *.doc or *.docx.) Right-click on the file, and then point to **Open With**.

2. A list of programs installed on your computer appears. Click the program you want to use to open this file type. If you're sure the selected program is the one that should always be used for this file type, then instead select **Choose default program**, and make sure to check "**Use this app for all [extension] files**," and click the default program from the list.

When you double-click that file in the future, the file will open in the program you selected.

going awry with your system by installing and using beta versions. Unless you're willing to deal with potential problems, it may be best to wait until the last beta version is released—often referred to as the *gold version*. By that time, most of the serious bugs have been worked out.

As a precaution, you should be comfortable with the reliability of the source before downloading a freeware or beta version of software. If it's a reliable developer whose software you're familiar with, you can be more certain that a serious bug or virus isn't hiding in the software. Similarly, you should be sure that the software you're downloading is meant for your system and that your system has met all the necessary hardware and operating system requirements.

Before installing any software, it's always good to make sure your virus protection software is up to date. It's equally important that you back up your system as well as create a *restore point*. That way, if something does go awry, you can return your system to the way it was before you started. You can create a restore point by using Windows 8 System protection tools. To access the System protection tools, click System and Security from the Control Panel, and then click System. In the left pane, click System protection to display the System Properties dialog box. On the System Protection tab, click the Create button, and type a description for the restore point (such as "Before installing [name of software]") and click Create. You will be notified when the restore point is created.

Software Licenses

Don't I own the software I buy? Most people don't understand that, unlike other items they purchase, the software they buy doesn't belong to them. The only thing they're actually purchasing is a license that gives them the right to use the software for their own purposes as the *only* user of that copy. The application is not theirs to lend.

A **software license**, also known as an **End User License Agreement (EULA)**, is an agreement between you, the user, and the software company (see Figure 4.26). You accept this agreement before installing the software on your machine. It's a legal contract that outlines the acceptable uses of the program and any actions that violate the agreement. Generally, the agreement states who the ultimate owner of the software is, under what circumstances copies of the software can be made, and whether the software can be installed on any other machine. Finally, the license agreement states what, if any, warranty comes with the software.

FIGURE 4.26 You must accept the terms of the software license before using the product.

BITS&BYTES

Run versus Save When Downloading Software

When you download software from the web, often you're given the choice to run or save it (see Figure 4.27). What's the difference? When you select Run, the program is downloaded to your machine and generally stored in Temporary Internet Files. Then the file is "run," meaning that it is loaded into memory and the operating system runs it. Use the Run option when you need to use the downloaded file on a limited basis, such as a song or video that you only plan to watch once or twice. Some installation programs instead install the software on your machine in a permanent location when Run is selected.

When you select Save (or sometimes Save As) on a download, the file will be copied to your hard disk. There may be an AutoRun program associated with the file that starts the installation automatically. Otherwise, you may need to navigate to the stored location and execute (or run) the file independently. The big difference is that the saved file is not downloaded into a temporary location. Use Save when you want to keep the file for a longer period of time or when you want to control where the file or program is saved.

Do you want to run or save **ChromeSetup.exe** (722 KB) from **dl.google.com**?   Run   Save ▼   Cancel   ✕

Google, Inc.

FIGURE 4.27 When downloading software, you have the choice to Run or Save.

Does a license only cover one installation? Some software is purchased with a single license to cover one person's specific use. You can't share these licenses, and you can't "extend" the license to install the software on more than one of your computers. Many manufacturers are now offering licensing bundles to allow several computers in one household to be installed with a legal copy. For example, Apple offers a Family Pack Software License Agreement that permits a user to install the purchased software legally on as many as five computers in the same household, and some versions of Microsoft Office come with the ability to install the software on multiple computers in the same household.

Businesses and educational institutions often buy multiuser licenses that allow more than one person to use the software. Some multiuser licenses are per-seat and limit the number of users overall, whereas others, called *concurrent licenses,* limit the number of users accessing the software at any given time.

Does open source software require a license?
As you learned earlier, anyone using open source software has access to the program's code. Therefore, open source software programs can be tweaked by another user and redistributed. A free software license, the *GNU General Public License,* is required and grants the recipients the right to modify and redistribute the software. Without such a license, the recipient would be in violation of copyright laws. This concept of redistributing modified open source software under the same terms as the original software is known as **copyleft**. Thus, all enhancements, additions, and other changes to copyleft software must also be distributed as free software.

Getting the Right Software for Your System

How do I ensure the software I buy will work on my computer? Every software program has a set of **system requirements** that specify the minimum recommended standards for the operating system, processor, primary memory (random access memory, or RAM), and hard drive capacity. Sometimes there are other specifications for the video card, monitor, optical drive, and other peripherals. These requirements are printed on the software packaging or are available at the manufacturer's website. Before installing software on your computer, ensure that your system setup meets the minimum requirements as specified by the developer.

When is it worth buying a newer version?
Periodically, software developers improve the functionality of their software by releasing a software upgrade. Although software developers suggest otherwise, there's no need to rush out and buy the latest version of a software program every time one is available. Depending on the software, some upgrades may not be sufficiently different from the previous version to make it cost-effective for you to buy the newest version. Unless the upgrade adds features that are important to you, you may be better off waiting to upgrade every other release. You also should consider whether you use the software frequently enough to justify an upgrade and whether your current system can handle the new system requirements of the upgraded version. In between

upgrades, developers will make available software updates (sometimes referred to as software patches). Updates are usually downloaded and provide smaller enhancements to the software or fix program bugs.

If I have an older version of software and someone sends me files from a newer version, can I still open them? Software vendors recognize that people work on different versions of the same software. Vendors, therefore, make new versions backward compatible, meaning that the new versions can recognize (open) files created with older versions. However, some software programs are not forward compatible, so these older versions are not able to recognize files created on newer versions of the same software. Files created on newer versions of software can be recognized by older versions if the correct file extension is chosen under Save As Type. For example, a .docx can be recognized by an older version of Microsoft Word if it is saved as .doc (Word 97-2003 document).

Installing and Uninstalling Software

What's the difference between a custom installation and a full installation? Before you use most software, you must permanently place it, or install it, on your system. The installation process may differ slightly depending on whether you're installing the software from a DVD or downloading it from the web. One of the first steps in the installation wizard asks you to decide between a full installation and a custom installation. A **full installation** (often referred to as a *typical installation*) copies all the most commonly used files and programs from the distribution disc to your computer's hard drive. By selecting **custom installation**, you can decide which features you want installed on your hard drive. Installing only the features you want saves space on your hard drive.

How do I start my programs in Windows 8? Every program you install on your system gets a tile on the Start screen. The simplest way to start an application is by clicking the program tile on the Start screen. Alternatively, you can work from the desktop view in Windows 8. To easily access commonly used programs or newly installed programs, you can pin a shortcut to a program on the taskbar or to the Start screen. To place a program on the taskbar or pin it to the Start screen, right-click the program icon on your desktop or right-click the program tile on the Start screen. From the options that are displayed, select Pin to Taskbar or Pin to Start. Windows then places an icon for this program on the taskbar or a tile on the Start screen (see Figure 4.28). To uninstall a pinned icon from Start, right-click the icon and select Unpin from Start.

How do I uninstall a program? An application contains many different files—library files, help files, and other text files—in addition to the main file you use to run the program. By deleting only the main file, you're not ridding your system of all the pieces of the program. Windows 8 makes it easy to uninstall a program: Simply right-click on the program icon on the Start screen, then click Uninstall. To uninstall a program from the desktop view in Windows 8.1, open the

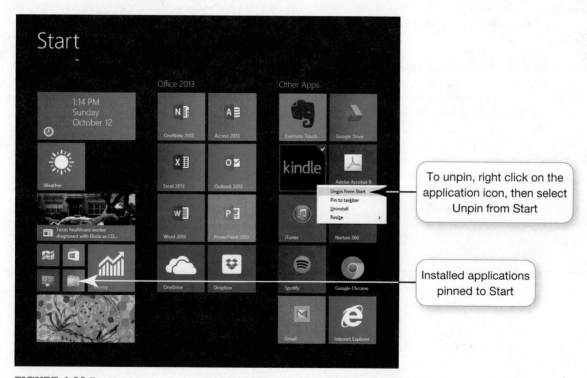

FIGURE 4.28 By pinning an application to the Start screen in Windows 8.1, you have easy access to your most frequently used programs.

BITS&BYTES

Ridding Your Computer of "Bloat"

Manufacturers often include software on new computers that you don't want or need. Called *bloatware*, this software can slow down your computer and degrade its performance. How do you get rid of it? Install an application such as PC Decrapifier (**pcdecrapifier .com**), or, if you'd rather do it yourself, consider some of these tips:

- *Uninstall preinstalled antivirus software:* If you have antivirus software on your old computer, you may be able to transfer the unexpired portion of your software license to your new computer. If this is the case, you can uninstall the preinstalled trial version on your new computer.

- *Uninstall unwanted toolbars:* Many computers come with Google, Bing, and other toolbars preinstalled. Go through Programs and Features in the Control Panel to uninstall any toolbars you don't want.

- *Remove manufacturer-specific software:* Some computer manufacturers install their own software. Some of these programs can be useful, but others are help features and update reminders that are also found in your operating system. You can remove any or all of these support applications and instead just check the manufacturer's website periodically for updates or new information.

Control Panel, select Programs from the Control Panel, then click Uninstall a program. Select the program you want to uninstall from the list, then click Uninstall.

If my computer crashes, can I get the preinstalled software back? Although some preinstalled software is not necessary to replace if your computer crashes, other software such as the operating system is critical to reinstall. Most manufacturers use a separate partition on the hard drive to hold an image, or copy, of the preinstalled software. However, it's not always possible to reboot from the partitioned hard drive, especially when your computer crashes, so one of the first things you should do after you purchase a new computer is create a recovery drive. Generally, the manufacturer will

have placed a utility on your system, or you can use the Recovery utility included in Windows to create a recovery drive. You can access the Advanced Recovery tools in Windows 8.1 from the Control Panel by typing Recovery in the search box, and then clicking Create a recovery drive under System. Then, to create the recovery drive, insert a blank flash drive in a USB port and follow the steps in the wizard. Once the recovery drive has been made, label the flash drive and put it away in a safe place.

There is an application for almost anything you want or need to do on your computer, whether it is school or work related or just for entertainment purposes. And there are a variety of types of applications, such as proprietary, open source, web-based, and freeware. Have fun exploring all the various possibilities! ■

ACTIVE HELPDESK
Buying and Installing Software

In this Active Helpdesk, you'll play the role of a helpdesk staffer, fielding questions about how to best purchase software or to get it for free, how to install and uninstall software, and where you can go for help when you have a problem with your software.

> **Before moving on to the Chapter Review:**
> - **Watch Replay Video 4.2** .
> - **Then check your understanding of what you've learned so far.**

check your understanding // review & practice

For a quick review to see what you've learned so far, answer the following questions. Visit **pearsonhighered.com /techinaction** to check your answers.

multiple

1. The minimum set of recommended standards for a program is known as the

   a. operating system.   **c.** setup guide.

   b. system requirements. **d.** installation specs.

2. Which of the following statements about compressed audio files is FALSE?

   a. Compressed audio files have a smaller file size than uncompressed audio files.

   b. The sound is noticeably different on compressed audio files than on uncompressed audio files.

   c. WAV is a compressed audio file format.

   d. Downloaded songs are compressed audio files.

3. Which of the following is considered a benefit of using simulation programs?

   a. They allow users to experience potentially dangerous situations without risk.

   b. They help to prevent costly errors.

   c. They allow users to train on software that is not installed on their systems.

   d. All of the above

4. Which of the following is NOT necessary to do before installing beta software?

   a. creating a restore point

   b. backing up your system

   c. defragging the hard drive

   d. ensuring your virus protection software is updated

5. Which software is best to use if you want to change the looks of your digital pictures?

   a. image-editing program

   b. video-editing program

   c. media management software

   d. All of the above

To take an autograded version of this review, please go to the companion website at **pearsonhighered.com/techinaction**, or go your MyITLab course.

 Continue

4 Chapter Review

The Nuts and Bolts of Software

1. What's the difference between application software and system software?

- The term *software* refers to a set of instructions that tells the computer what to do.
- Application software is the software you use to do everyday tasks at home, school, and work. Application software includes the following:

  o Productivity software, such as word processing, finance, and personal information management programs
  o Business software for small and large businesses
  o Multimedia software, such as applications used for image and video editing, recording and editing digital audio, and gaming software
  o Educational and reference software

- System software is the software that helps run the computer and coordinates instructions between application software and the computer's hardware devices. System software includes the operating system and utility programs.

2. What are the different ways I can access and use software?

- Some software comes preinstalled on your computer. You will need to add other software by installing the software or accessing the software from the web. There are two types of software that you can install on your computer:

  1. Proprietary (or commercial) software is software you buy.
  2. Open source software is program code that is free and publicly available with few licensing and copyright restrictions. The code can be copied, distributed, or changed without the stringent copyright protections of software products you purchase.

- Web-based applications are those that are hosted online by the vendor and made available to the customer over the Internet. This web-based distribution model is also referred to as Software as a Service

(SaaS). Web-based applications are accessed via an Internet connection to the site that hosts the software.

Productivity and Business Software

3. What kinds of applications are included in productivity software?

- Productivity software programs include the following:

  o Word processing: to create and edit written documents
  o Spreadsheet: to do calculations and numerical and what-if analyses easily
  o Presentation: to create slide presentations
  o Database: to store and organize data
  o Note-taking: to take notes and easily organize and search them
  o Personal information manager (PIM): to keep you organized by putting a calendar, address book, notepad, and to-do lists within your computer

- Individuals can also use productivity software to help with business-like tasks such as managing personal finances and preparing taxes.

4. What kinds of software do small and large businesses use?

- Businesses use software to help them with the following tasks:

  o Finances and accounting
  o Desktop publishing
  o Web page authoring
  o Project management
  o Customer Relationship Management (CRM)
  o Enterprise Resource Planning (ERP)
  o E-commerce

- Businesses may use specialized business software (or vertical market software) that is designed for their specific industry.
- Some businesses also use specialized drawing software to create technical drawings and computer-aided design (CAD) software to create 3-D models.

Multimedia and Entertainment Software

5. What types of multimedia and entertainment software are available?

- Multimedia software is software for playing, copying, recording, editing, and organizing multimedia files. Multimedia software includes the following:

  o Digital image- and video-editing software
  o Digital audio software
  o Specialty software to produce computer games

- Educational and reference software is available to help you master, study, design, create, or plan.

  o Simulation (training) programs let users experience or control the software as if it were the actual software or an actual event. Simulated programs safely allow users to experience potentially dangerous situations without the risks of experiencing the same situations in real life.
  o Course management software provides traditional classroom tools such as discussion areas, assignment features, and grade books over the Internet.
  o Drawing software includes a wide range of software programs that help you create and edit simple line-based drawings or create more-complex designs for both imaginative and technical illustrations.

Managing Your Software

6. What's important to know when buying software?

- You must purchase software unless it is freeware or open source.
- When you purchase software, you're actually purchasing the license to use it and therefore must abide by the terms of the licensing agreement you accept when installing the program.
- Before installing software on your computer, ensure that your system setup meets the system

requirements that specify the minimum recommended standards for the operating system, processor, primary memory (RAM), and hard drive capacity. Sometimes, there are other specifications for the video card, monitor, optical drive, and other peripherals.

7. How do I install and uninstall software?

- When installing software, you are often given the choice between a full (typical) or custom installation.

  o A full installation copies all the files and programs from the distribution disc to your computer's hard drive.
  o A custom installation lets you decide which features you want installed on your hard drive.

- When uninstalling software, it's best to use the uninstall feature that comes with the operating system.

  o In Windows 8.1, right-click on the program tile on the Start screen, then select Uninstall from the shortcut menu that displays.
  o Using the uninstall feature of the operating system when uninstalling a program will help you ensure that all additional program files are removed from your computer.

- Your system comes with preinstalled software, such as the operating system and possibly some files from the manufacturer.
- One of the first things you should do after you purchase a new computer is create a recovery drive that you can use to reboot the computer after a system failure and return the computer to the condition it was in when you first purchased it.

Be sure to check out the companion website for additional materials to help you review and learn, including a Tech Bytes Weekly newsletter—
pearsonhighered.com/techinaction.
And don't forget the Replay Videos .

key terms //

chapter quiz// assessment

For a quick review to see what you've learned, answer the following questions. Submit the quiz as requested by your instructor. If you are using MyITLab, the quiz is also available there.

multiple choice

1. Which software application would you use to calculate and manipulate numerical data?

   a. Microsoft Office Excel

   b. Apple iWork Numbers

   c. Apache OpenOffice Calc

   d. All of the above

2. PowToon and HaikuDeck are alternatives to

   a. Microsoft Word.

   b. Microsoft PowerPoint.

   c. Adobe InDesign.

   d. Apple iWork Pages.

3. Calendars, tasks, and e-mail will be found in which application?

   a. Excel

   b. One Note

   c. Outlook

   d. Access

4. Which of the following describes copyleft?

   a. Terms enabling redistributing proprietary software

   b. Terms enabling redistributing open source software

   c. Terms enabling free use of software content

   d. Terms restricting free use of software content

5. What is often distributed prior to a final release of software?

   a. Alpha prerelease

   b. Open source release

   c. Beta version

   d. Freeware version

6. What should you check first to ensure software will work on your computer?

   a. The type of operating system

   b. The amount of available RAM

   c. The available hard drive capacity

   d. All of the above

true–false

_____ 1. Productivity software suites are not available as web-based software.

_____ 2. A wizard is a software tool that offers a step-by-step guide through complicated tasks.

_____ 3. Removing red-eye, cropping, and altering pictures with pen- and brush-like tools are features of image-editing software.

_____ 4. When you buy software, you then own it and can do anything you'd like with it, including giving it to friends to install on their machines.

critical thinking

1. **Living on the Cloud**

   Cloud computing is becoming more popular, and many users are working from the cloud and not even realizing it. Open Google Drive and Office Online and compare one of the applications in these online suites with an installed counterpart (e.g., Excel Online and Google Spreadsheets vs. Excel). What similarities and differences do you find between the online applications and the installed version? Envision a time when all software is web-based and describe how being totally on the cloud might be an advantage. What disadvantages might a cloud-based environment present?

2. **Windows 8 Modern Apps**

   With the launch of Windows 8 came Modern Apps. Modern Apps are designed primarily to work well on touchscreen devices and are more streamlined than desktop applications. Some software, such as Skype and Internet Explorer, have separate versions that run both as a Modern App and a desktop application. Why do you think Microsoft developed Modern Apps? Do you think having two versions of the same software might be helpful or confusing? Explain your answer.

team time//

Software for Startups

Problem

You and your friends have decided to start Recycle Technology, a not-for-profit organization that would recycle and donate used computer equipment. In the first planning session, your group recognizes the need for certain software to help you with various parts of the business such as tracking inventory, designing notices, mapping addresses for pickup and delivery, and soliciting residents by phone or e-mail about recycling events, to name a few.

Task

Split your class into as many groups of four or five as possible. Make some groups responsible for locating free or web-based software solutions and other groups responsible for finding proprietary solutions. Another group could be responsible for finding mobile app solutions. The groups will present and compare results with each other at the end of the project.

Process

1. Identify a team leader who will coordinate the project and record and present results.

2. Each team is to identify the various kinds of software that Recycle Technology needs. Consider software that will be needed for all the various tasks required to run the organization such as communication, marketing, tracking, inventory management, and finance.

3. Create a detailed and organized list of required software applications. Depending on your team, you will specify either proprietary software or open source software.

Conclusion

Most organizations require a variety of software to accomplish different tasks. Compare your results with those of other team members. Were there applications that you didn't think about, but that other members did? How expensive is it to ensure that even the smallest company has all the software required to carry out daily activities, or can the needs be met with free, open source products?

ethics project//

Open Source Software

Ethical conduct is a stream of decisions you make all day long. In this exercise, you'll research and then role-play a complicated ethical situation. The role you play might or might not match your own personal beliefs, but your research and use of logic will enable you to represent the view assigned. An arbitrator will watch and comment on both sides of the arguments, and together, the team will agree on an ethical solution.

Topic: Proprietary Software Versus Open Source Software

Proprietary software has set restrictions on use and can be very expensive, whereas open source software is freely available for users to use as is or to change, improve, and redistribute. Open source software has become acceptable as a cost-effective alternative to proprietary software—so much so that it is reported that the increased adoption of open source software has caused a drop in revenue to the proprietary software industry. But determining which software to use involves more than just reducing the IT budget.

Research Areas to Consider

- Open source software
- Proprietary software
- Copyright licensing
- Open source development

Process

1. Divide the class into teams.
2. Research the areas cited above and devise a scenario in which someone is a proponent for open source software but is being rebuffed by someone who feels that "you get what you pay for" and is a big proponent of using proprietary software.
3. Team members should write a summary that provides background information for their character—for example: open source proponent, proprietary developer, or arbitrator—and that details their character's behaviors to set the stage for the role-playing event. Then, team members should create an outline to use during the role-playing event.
4. Team members should present their case to the class or submit a PowerPoint presentation for review by the rest of the class, along with the summary and resolution they developed.

Conclusion

As technology becomes ever more prevalent and integrated into our lives, more and more ethical dilemmas will present themselves. Being able to understand and evaluate both sides of the argument, while responding in a personally or socially ethical manner, will be an important skill.

Analyzing Benchmark Data

You work for a design firm that uses many of the software applications in the Adobe Creative Suite, especially Photoshop, Illustrator, and InDesign. You have been asked to evaluate whether it would be worthwhile to upgrade the software to the latest version. In addition to reviewing any new or revised features, you also want to provide an analysis on any improvements in product efficiency and performance, so you have repeated doing the same skills with the current and new data and have recorded the results. Now you just need to analyze it.

You will use the following skills as you complete this activity:	
• AutoFill Data	• Align and Wrap Text
• Insert AVERAGE Function	• Apply Conditional Formatting
• Add Borders	• Create Bar Chart

Instructions:

1. Open *TIA_Ch4_Start* and save as **TIA_Ch4_LastFirst**.
2. In cell F1, enter **Current Average**, and in cell J1 enter **New Average**
3. In cell F2, use the AVERAGE function to compute the average of the range C2:E2. In cell J2, use the AVERAGE function to compute the average of the range G2:I2.
4. Select cell F2, then drag the Fill Handle to cell F13. Select cell J2, then drag the Fill Handle to cell J13.
5. Select the cells in C2:J13, then format the cell contents with Number format with one decimal.
6. Select cell A2, and Merge and Center across cells A2:A5. Then adjust the orientation of the text to Rotate Text Up (90 degrees). Middle Align cell contents and Bold text.
7. Use Format Painter to copy these formats to cell A6 and cell A10.
8. Select range A2:J5, then apply Thick Box Border. Repeat with ranges A6:J9 and A10:J13.
9. Select range F1:F13, then apply Thick Box Border. Repeat with range J1:J13.
10. Select J2:J13, then apply a Conditional Format that will format cells that are Less Than those cells in range F2:F13 with Green Fill and Dark Green Text.
    a. Hint: In the Format cells that are LESS THAN box enter =F2 (*not* F2). The rest of the cells in the range will update automatically.
11. Create a Clustered Bar Chart using ranges B1:B13, F1:F13, J1:J13.
    a. Hint: Hold down the CTRL button as you select ranges F1:F13 and J1:J13.
12. Modify the Clustered Bar Chart with a title "Benchmark Comparison: New and Current Versions of CS Software", add a title to the Horizontal Axis that reads "Seconds". Position and resize chart so it fits A16:J34.
13. Save the workbook, and submit based on your instructor's directions.

5

System Software: The Operating System, Utility Programs, and File Management

Understanding System Software

Operating System Fundamentals

OBJECTIVES

1. What software is included in system software? **(p. 160)**

2. What are the different kinds of operating systems? **(pp. 160–163)**

3. What are the most common operating systems? **(pp. 162–165)**

◀❙▶ **Sound Byte:** Customizing Windows

What the Operating System Does

OBJECTIVES

4. How does the operating system provide a means for users to interact with the computer? **(p. 166)**

5. How does the operating system help manage resources such as the processor, memory, storage, hardware, and peripheral devices? **(pp. 167–171)**

6. How does the operating system interact with application software? **(p. 171)**

The Boot Process: Starting Your Computer

OBJECTIVE

7. How does the operating system help the computer start up? **(pp. 172–174)**

🛱 **Active Helpdesk:** Starting the Computer: The Boot Process

Using System Software

The Windows Interface

OBJECTIVE

8. What are the main features of the Windows interface? **(pp. 178–183)**

Organizing Your Computer: File Management

OBJECTIVE

9. How does the operating system help me keep my computer organized? **(pp. 184–188)**

◀❙▶ **Sound Byte:** File Management

🛱 **Active Helpdesk:** Organizing Your Computer: File Management

Utility Programs

OBJECTIVE

10. What utility programs are included in system software and what do they do? **(pp. 189–195)**

🛱 **Active Helpdesk:** Using Utility Programs

◀❙▶ **Sound Byte:** File Compression

◀❙▶ **Sound Byte:** Hard Disk Anatomy

◀❙▶ **Sound Byte:** Letting Your Computer Clean Up After Itself

Make This: Explore an App Builder Skill on **page 177**

The information in this text is written for Windows 8.1, Update 2. If you are still running a different version of Windows 8, your screens and task instructions may vary slightly.

For all media in this chapter go to **pearsonhighered.com/techinaction** or **MyITLab**.

(Mary Anne Poatsy; Ferenc Szelepcsenyi/Shutterstock; Revers/Shutterstock; Stanislav Popov/Shutterstock; Reji/Fotolia)

HOW COOL IS THIS?

Scan here for more info

Thought watches were going the way of the dinosaurs? Think again! Fumbling for your smartphone in your pocket is so yesterday. **Android Wear smartwatches** are the wave of the future. Android Wear devices aim to **simplify your life** by freeing up your hands and allowing you to make more face-to-face contact with your friends. Running to board your flight with your hands full of carryon luggage? **Your watch can flash a QR code** to the boarding attendant. Need some quick info? **OK Google is on your watch,** so just say "Ok Google, what's the score in the Villanova game?" and you'll have the answer. Always forgetting your phone when you run (or wondering where to put it)? Your smartwatch is always on your wrist so it can **host apps that are constantly monitoring your physical activity.** So leave that phone in your pocket—Android Wear has you covered! *(Koya979/Fotolia; Google, Inc.)*

Understanding System Software

As discussed in the previous chapter, your computer uses two basic types of software: application software and system software. **Application software** is the software you use to do everyday tasks at home and at work. **System software** is the set of programs that helps run the computer and coordinates instructions between application software and the computer's hardware devices. From the moment you turn on your computer to the time you shut it down, you're interacting with system software.

 ## operating system
FUNDAMENTALS

System software consists of two primary types of programs: the *operating system* and *utility programs*. The **operating system (OS)** is a group of programs that controls how your computer functions. The OS:

- Manages the computer's hardware, including the processor, memory, and storage devices, as well as peripheral devices such as the printer;
- Provides a consistent means for application software to work with the central processing unit (CPU); and
- Is responsible for the management, scheduling, and coordination of tasks

You interact with your OS through the **user interface**—the *desktop, icons,* and *menus* that let you communicate with your computer.

A **utility program** is a small program that performs many of the general housekeeping tasks for your computer, such as system maintenance and file compression. A set of utility programs is bundled with each OS, but you can also buy stand-alone utility programs that often provide more features.

Do all computers have operating systems? Every computer, from the smallest laptop to the largest supercomputer, has an OS. Even cell phones, game consoles, cars, and some appliances have operating systems. The role of the OS is critical; the computer can't operate without it.

Are all operating systems alike? You're probably familiar with Microsoft Windows, Apple OS X, and perhaps the Android operating system if it's on your phone, but many other operating systems exist. Laptops, tablet computers, and smartphones all need specific operating systems designed to take advantage of their unique characteristics. However, as devices begin to converge in terms of functionality, and operating systems continue to become more powerful, developers such as Microsoft and Apple are making operating systems that have similar functionality (such as OS X and iOS) or single operating systems (such as Windows 8) that can run on multiple devices. Figure 5.1 lists a number of common operating systems.

When operating systems were originally developed, they were designed for a single user performing one task at a time

FIGURE 5.1

Common Operating Systems

OS NAME	DEVELOPED BY	AVAILABLE ON
Windows Windows 8	Microsoft	Laptops, tablets, desktops, all-in-ones, cell phones
OS X	Apple	Laptops, desktops, all-in-ones
iOS	Apple	Tablets, iPhones, iPod Touches
Android	Google	Cell phones, tablets
Linux	Open source	Laptops, desktops

(© MONICA M. DAVEY/epa/Corbis; Pawan Kumar/Alamy Kevork Djansezian/Getty Images; Denis Doyle/Bloomberg/Getty Images; Tbbbb/Fotolia)

(that is, they were *single-user, single-task operating systems*). However, modern operating systems allow a single user to **multitask**—to perform more than one process at a time. And operating systems such as Windows and OS X provide networking capabilities as well, essentially making them *multiuser, multitasking operating systems*.

Operating systems can be categorized by the type of device in which they're installed, such as robots and specialized equipment with built-in computers, mainframes and network computers, mobile devices, and personal computers. Next, we'll look at these different types of operating systems.

Real-Time Operating Systems

Why do machines with built-in computers need an OS? Machinery that performs a repetitive series of specific tasks in an exact amount of time requires a **real-time operating system (RTOS)**. Also referred to as *embedded systems,* RTOSs require minimal user interaction. This type of OS is a program with a specific purpose, and it must guarantee certain response times for particular computing tasks; otherwise, the machine is useless. The programs are

written specifically for the needs of the devices and their functions. Therefore, there are no commercially available standard RTOS software programs. Devices that must perform regimented tasks or record precise results—such as measurement instruments found in the scientific, defense, and aerospace industries—require RTOSs. Examples include digital storage oscilloscopes and the Mars Reconnaissance Orbiter.

Where else are RTOSs used today? You also encounter RTOSs every day in devices such as fuel-injection systems in car engines, automobile "infotainment" systems, and some common appliances. RTOSs are also found in many types of robotic equipment. Television stations use robotic cameras with RTOSs that glide across a suspended cable system to record sports events from many angles (see Figure 5.2).

Operating Systems for Networks, Servers, and Mainframes

What kind of operating systems do networks use? A **multiuser operating system** (or **network operating system**) lets more than one user access the computer system at a time by handling and prioritizing requests from multiple users. Networks (groups of computers connected to each other so that they can communicate and share resources) need a multiuser OS because many users simultaneously access the server (the computer that manages network resources such as printing and communications). The latest versions of Windows and OS X can be considered network operating systems: They enable users to set up basic networks in their homes and small businesses.

In larger networks, a more robust network OS is installed on servers and manages all user requests. For example, on a network where users share a printer, the network OS ensures that the printer prints only one document at a time in the order the requests were made. Examples of network operating systems include Windows Server, Linux, and UNIX.

What is UNIX? UNIX is a multiuser, multitasking OS that is used as a network OS, although it can also be found on PCs. Developed in 1969 by Ken Thompson and Dennis Ritchie of AT&T's Bell Labs, the UNIX code was initially not proprietary—in other words, no company owned it. Rather, any programmer was allowed to use the code and modify it to meet his or her needs. UNIX is now a brand that belongs to the company The Open Group, but any vendor that meets testing requirements and pays a fee can use the UNIX name. Individual vendors then modify the UNIX code to run specifically on their hardware.

What other kinds of computers require a multiuser OS? Mainframes and supercomputers also require multiuser operating systems. Mainframes routinely support hundreds or

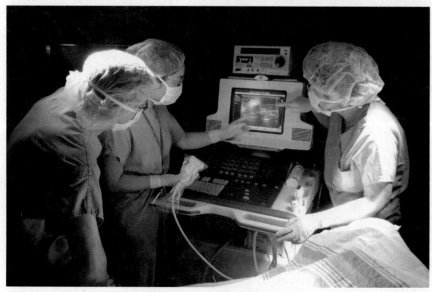

FIGURE 5.2 Devices such as TV sky cameras, cars, and medical equipment use RTOSs. *(John Pyle/Cal Sport Media/Newscom; Mark Gail/The Washington Post/Getty Images; David Elfstrom/Getty Images)*

thousands of users at time, and supercomputers are often accessed by multiple people working on complex calculations. Examples of mainframe operating systems include UNIX, Linux on System z, and IBM's z/OS, whereas the vast majority of supercomputers use Linux.

Operating Systems for Mobile Devices

What kind of OS does a smartphone use? Figure 5.3 shows the most common operating systems found on smartphones such as the iPhone. Most smartphones have at least modest multitasking capabilities, such as letting you check e-mail while you're on a phone call. More advanced smartphones provide greater multitasking, such as letting you talk and use apps at the same time.

What OS do tablets use? Popular tablet operating systems include iOS, Android, and Windows (see Figure 5.4). iPads use iOS, whereas a number of different tablets (such as the Samsung Galaxy Tab and the Google Nexus) use versions of Android. The Kindle Fire also runs a customized version of Android. Until the release of Windows 8 in 2012, Microsoft didn't have a popular tablet OS, but the company has managed to grab a 5% market share releasing Windows 8, which is optimized for tablet devices.

Do gaming consoles and iPods use an OS? Gaming systems such as Microsoft's Xbox 360, the Nintendo Wii, and the Sony PlayStation, as well as personal media players such as the iPod, all require system software developed specifically for the particular device. The system software controls the physical aspects of the device (such as game controllers) as well as other application programs that come with the device. For example, the operating systems on gaming consoles control web browsing and file storage of media and photos as well as playing of DVDs and games.

Operating Systems for Personal Computers

What are the most popular operating systems for personal computers? Microsoft Windows, OS X, and Linux (an open source OS) are the top three operating systems for personal computers. Although they share similar features, each is unique.

What's special about Windows? Microsoft **Windows** is an operating environment that incorporates a user-friendly, visual interface like the one that was first introduced with Apple's OS. Over time, improvements in Windows have concentrated on increasing user functionality and friendliness, improving Internet capabilities, supporting home networks, and enhancing file privacy and security. The newest release of Microsoft's OS, **Windows 8**, provides a new interface optimized for touch-screen devices.

What's the difference between the various editions of Windows 8 operating systems? Windows 8 simplifies consumer choices because it's offered in only two versions: Windows 8 and Windows 8 Pro. For most users, Windows 8 is sufficient, as it now includes

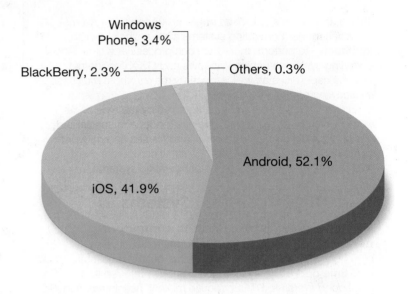

FIGURE 5.3 Popular Smartphone Operating Systems

many features (such as remote access) that weren't included in Windows 7 Home Premium. However, Windows 8 doesn't include Media Center, which you may be used to seeing in previous versions of Windows. Media Center is now available only as an add-on package for Windows 8 Pro. Windows 8.1 is the latest release currently available of the Windows 8 OS.

What's special about the Mac OS? In 1984, **Mac OS** became the first commercially available OS to incorporate a **graphical user interface**, or **GUI**, with user-friendly point-and-click technology. Many Mac users have switched from Windows because of the "coolness" of the Mac OS, OS X. With the release of the Mountain Lion version, Apple added many of the popular and innovative features loved by iOS

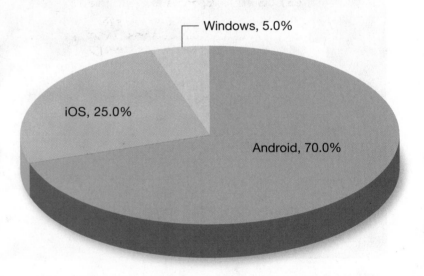

FIGURE 5.4 Popular Tablet Operating Systems

users, such as messages, reminders, notes, and a notification center. The latest version, Yosemite, was released in fall 2014 and features interface and usability enhancements designed to dovetail with the iOS 8 upgrade released just a few months earlier. If you've been using Windows for a while, you shouldn't have any problems making the transition to OS X. You'll notice immediately that OS X uses the same desktop metaphors as Windows, including icons for folders and a Trash Can (similar to a Recycle Bin) for deleted documents. OS X also includes a window-based interface like the one in Windows.

OS X is based on the UNIX operating system, which is exceptionally stable and reliable. However, just as with any other OS, you still need to install updates as they become available and protect yourself from viruses, spyware, and other malicious software.

What is Linux? Linux is an open source OS designed for use on personal computers and as a network OS. Open source software is freely available for anyone to use or modify as he or she wishes. Linux began in 1991 as a part-time project of Finnish university student Linus Torvalds. It has since been tweaked by scores of programmers as part of the Free Software Foundation GNU Project (**gnu.org**).

Linux has a reputation as a stable OS that is not subject to crashes or failures. Because the code is open and available to anyone, Linux can be modified or updated quickly by hundreds of programmers around the world.

What computers use Linux? Linux is gaining popularity among computer manufacturers, which have begun to ship it with some of their latest PCs. Android, the tablet and phone OS, is Linux based. Because the overall size of Android is much smaller than that of Windows, some ultrabook users choose to use it in place of the factory-installed Windows OS (see Figure 5.5). Some Linux-based operating systems have been modified to run on iPods and gaming systems.

Where can I get Linux? Linux is available for download in various packages known as **distributions**, or **distros**. Distros include the underlying Linux kernel (the code that provides Linux's basic functionality) and special modifications to the OS, and may also include additional open source software (such as OpenOffice). A good place to start researching distros is **distrowatch.com**. This site tracks Linux distros and provides helpful tips for beginners on choosing one.

BITS&BYTES

Upgrading Your Operating System

If you've had your computer for a year or two, you may be wondering whether you should upgrade to the newest release of your OS (such as going from Windows 7 to Windows 8.1). Here are a few key things to consider before taking the plunge:

- **Is your current OS still supported?** When the company deploys new versions of operating systems, it may stop supporting older versions. If your current version will no longer be supported, it's best to upgrade to a newer version.
- **Are there significant features in the new version that you want?** Operating systems are often upgraded to provide extra security, better performance, and additional features intended to make your computer experience more efficient, and perhaps even more fun. But if the only features the new version offers are ones you don't need, you should reconsider upgrading.
- **Will your hardware work with the new version of the OS?** Check the minimum operating requirements (required RAM, processor speed, hard drive space, etc.) of the new version to ensure that your computer can handle the workload of the new OS. You'll also need to make sure drivers for the

new OS are available for all your hardware devices and peripherals to ensure they'll work with it. Microsoft has made this easy with Windows 8.1 Upgrade Assistant, which you can download from Microsoft's website. The Upgrade Assistant scans your hardware, devices, and installed programs for compatibility, advises you on how to resolve any issues, and recommends what you should do before upgrading.

- **Is your application software compatible with the new version of the OS?** Usually, application software works fine with a new version of an OS. Sometimes it doesn't. Check with software vendors regarding compatibility. Most programs that run under Windows 7 will run from the desktop in Windows 8.1. And Windows 8.1 has an upgrade option in its install program that lets you install Windows 8.1 over an existing installation of Windows 7. This relieves you from having to install all your application software after upgrading.

Before starting the upgrade, back up all your data files so you won't lose anything accidentally during the upgrading process. File Recovery and other backup features in Windows make this job less of a hassle.

Does it matter what OS is on my computer? An OS is designed to run on specific CPUs. CPUs have different designs, which can require modifying the OS software to allow it to communicate properly with each CPU. The combination of an OS and a specific processor is referred to as a computer's **platform**.

For user convenience, computers and other devices usually come with an OS already installed. However, with some PCs, you can specify which OS you'd like installed when you order your device. For example, Windows and Linux can run on most of the hardware being sold today. Your choice of an OS in this case is mostly a matter of price and personal preference. However, Apple equipment—computers, iPhones, iPads, and iPod Touches—comes with Apple operating systems preinstalled.

Note that most *application software* is OS dependent. You need to make sure you get the correct version of the application software for your OS, such as Microsoft Office 2013 for Windows and Microsoft Office 2011 for OS X.

Can I have more than one OS on my computer?

Many people run more than one OS on their computers because different operating systems offer different features. For example, Windows and Linux both run well on Apple computers. A standard utility included in OS X called Boot Camp lets you boot into either Windows or OS X. And if you want to run both OS X and Windows OS at the same time, you can create "virtual drives" using virtualization software such as Parallels or VMware Fusion.

FIGURE 5.5 Developed by Google, the Android OS is based on Linux and runs easily on laptops and tablets. *(Andrew Rubtsov/Alamy)*

In Windows, you can create a separate section of your hard drive (called a *partition*) and install another OS on it while leaving your original Windows installation untouched. After installing the second OS, when your computer starts, you're offered a choice of which OS to use.

How do operating systems use the "cloud"?

Now that broadband Internet access and providing computer resources via the Internet (so-called *cloud computing*) are becoming more commonplace, operating systems have features that are tied to cloud computing. Here are a few examples:

- Windows 8 features tighter integration with the cloud. Using your *Microsoft account,* Windows 8 stores your settings and keeps track of applications you've purchased from the Windows store online. You can easily access and store files online in your *OneDrive account*. You can also log into your Windows account from any Windows 8 machine and be able to see your familiar desktop and applications.

- Similarly, OS X allows you to sign in with your *Apple ID,* which provides access to Apple's *iCloud* system. iCloud stores your content online and automatically pushes it out to all your Apple devices.

- Google has launched the *Google Chrome OS* (see Figure 5.6), which is a web-based OS. With the Chrome OS, virtually no files are installed on your computing device. Rather, the main functionality of the OS is provided by accessing the web through a web browser. Chrome OS is only available on certain hardware from Google's manufacturing partners, and these devices are called *Chromebooks*. The Chrome OS should not be confused with the *Google Chrome browser*. The browser is application software that can run in many different operating systems.

Another pioneer in accessing cloud-based storage and applications with a browser is the open source product eyeOS (**eyeos.com**). eyeOS allows companies to set up private clouds containing data and applications that can be accessed by their employees, partners, or customers. Using almost any computing device with a browser, users can access their data and applications through an Internet connection. ∎

SOUND BYTE
Customizing Windows

In this Sound Byte, you'll find out how to customize your desktop. You'll learn how to configure the desktop, set up a screen saver, change pointer options, customize the Start screen, and manage user accounts.

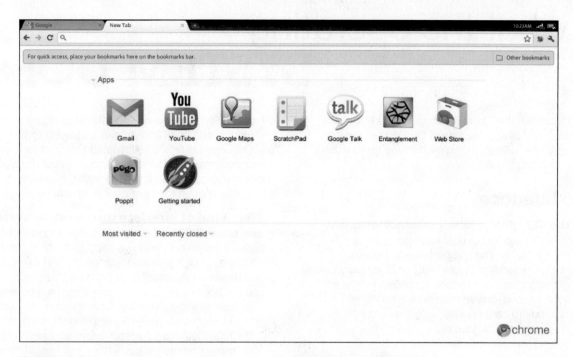

FIGURE 5.6 The Google Chrome OS has a very minimalist look. *(Courtesy of Google, Inc.)*

BITS&BYTES

OS Market Share Battle: It's Still a Windows World

So who is winning the OS market share war? It depends on the type of device. For conventional desktop and laptop computers, hands down the winner is still various versions of Windows, with 91.6% of the market (see Figure 5.7). But as of July 2014, Windows only had a 3.4% market share on smartphones vs. Android's 52.1%. Clearly Microsoft is losing the phone OS wars.

Linux, 1.68%
Mac OS X, 4.12%
Windows Vista, 3.05%
Others, 2.63%
Windows 8, 8.1 12.48%
Windows 7, 51.22%
Windows XP, 24.82%

FIGURE 5.7 Desktop/Laptop Operating Systems

what the operating
SYSTEM DOES

As shown in Figure 5.8, the OS is like an orchestra's conductor. It coordinates and directs the flow of data and information through the computer system. In this section, we explore the operations of the OS in detail.

The User Interface

How does the OS control how I interact with my computer? The OS provides a user interface that lets you interact with the computer. The first personal computers used *Microsoft Disk Operating System* (*MS-DOS,* or just *DOS*), which had a command-driven interface, as shown in Figure 5.9a. A **command-driven interface** is one in which you enter commands to communicate with the computer system. The DOS commands were not always easy to understand; as a result, the interface proved to be too complicated for the average user. Therefore, PCs were used primarily in business and by professional computer operators.

The command-driven interface was later improved by incorporating a menu-driven interface, as shown in Figure 5.9b. A **menu-driven interface** is one in which you choose commands from menus displayed on the screen. Menu-driven interfaces eliminated the need for users to know every command because they could select most of the commonly used commands from a menu. However, they were still not easy enough for most people to use.

What kind of interface do operating systems use today? Current personal computer operating systems such as Microsoft Windows and OS X use a graphical user interface, or GUI (pronounced "gooey"). Unlike command- and menu-driven interfaces, GUIs display graphics and use the point-and-click technology of the mouse and cursor (or human finger), making them much more user-friendly.

Linux-based operating systems do not have a single default GUI interface. Instead, users are free to choose among many commercially available and free interfaces, such as GNOME and KDE, each of which provides a different look and feel.

Processor Management

Why does the OS need to manage the processor? When you use your computer, you're usually asking the processor (also called the CPU) to perform

Manages computer hardware and peripherals

Provides a user interface

The Operating System

Provides a consistent interaction between applications and the CPU

Manages memory and storage

Manages the processor

FIGURE 5.8 The OS is the orchestra conductor of your computer, coordinating its many activities and devices.

FIGURE 5.9 (a) A command-driven interface. (b) A menu-driven interface.

several tasks at once. For example, you might be printing a Word document, chatting with your friends on Facebook, and watching a movie using the Blu-ray drive—all at the same time, or at least what appears to be at the same time. Although the CPU is powerful, it still needs the OS to arrange the execution of all these activities in a systematic way.

To do so, the OS assigns a slice of its time to each activity that requires the processor's attention. The OS must then switch among different processes millions of times a second to make it appear that everything is happening seamlessly. Otherwise, you wouldn't be able to watch a movie and print at the same time without experiencing delays in the process.

How exactly does the OS coordinate all the activities? When you create and print a document in Word while also watching a Blu-ray movie, for example, many different devices in the computer are involved, including your keyboard, mouse, Blu-ray drive, and printer. Every keystroke, every mouse click (or touch on the screen), and each signal to the printer and from the Blu-ray drive creates an action, or **event**, in the respective device (keyboard, mouse, Blu-ray drive, or printer) to which the OS responds.

Sometimes these events occur sequentially (such as when you type characters one at a time), but other events involve two or more devices working concurrently (such as the printer printing while you type and watch a movie). Although it looks as though all the devices are working at the same time, the OS in fact switches back and forth among processes, controlling the timing of events on which the processor works.

For example, assume you're typing and want to print a document. When you tell your computer to print your document, the printer generates a unique signal called an **interrupt** that tells the OS that it's in need of immediate attention. Every device has its own type of interrupt, which is associated with an **interrupt handler**, a special numerical code that prioritizes the requests. These requests are placed in the interrupt table in the computer's primary memory (RAM).

The OS processes the task assigned a higher priority before processing a task assigned a lower priority. This is called **preemptive multitasking**.

In our example, when the OS receives the interrupt from the printer, it suspends the CPU's typing activity and Blu-ray activity and puts a "memo" in a special location in RAM called a *stack*. The memo is a reminder of what the CPU was doing before it started to work on the printer request. The CPU then retrieves the printer request from the interrupt table and begins to process it. On completion of the printer request, the CPU goes back to the stack, retrieves the memo it placed about the keystroke or Blu-ray activity, and returns to that task until it is interrupted again, in a very quick and seamless fashion, as shown in Figure 5.10.

What happens if more than one document is waiting to be printed? The OS also coordinates multiple activities for peripheral devices such as printers. When the processor receives a request to send information to the printer, it first checks with the OS to ensure that the printer is not already in use. If it is, the OS puts the request in another temporary storage area in RAM, called the *buffer*. The request then waits in the buffer until the **spooler**, a program that helps coordinate all print jobs currently being sent to the printer, indicates the printer is available. If more than one print job is waiting, a line (or *queue*) is formed so that the printer can process the requests in order.

Memory and Storage Management

Why does the OS have to manage the computer's memory? As the OS coordinates the activities of the processor, it uses RAM as a temporary storage area for instructions and data the processor needs. The processor then accesses these instructions and data from RAM when it's ready to process them. The OS is therefore responsible for coordinating the space allocations in RAM to ensure there's

STEP 2: CPU receives an interrupt request from the printer

STEP 1: CPU is playing a movie

STEP 4: CPU executes printing

STEP 6: CPU resumes playing the movie

CPU Processing Activity

STEP 3: Memo about movie stored in stack

Stack

STEP 5: Memo about movie retrieved from stack

RAM

FIGURE 5.10 How Preemptive Multitasking Works

What happens if my computer runs out of RAM? When there isn't enough RAM for the OS to store the required data and instructions, the OS borrows from the more spacious hard drive. This process of optimizing RAM storage by borrowing hard drive space is called **virtual memory**. As shown in Figure 5.11, when more RAM is needed, the OS swaps out from RAM the data or instructions that haven't recently been used and moves them to a temporary storage area on the hard drive called the **swap file** (or **page file**). If the data or instructions in the swap file are needed later, the OS swaps them back into active RAM and replaces them in the hard drive's swap file with less active data or instructions. This process of swapping is known as **paging**.

Can I ever run out of virtual memory? Only a portion of the hard drive is allocated to virtual memory. You can manually change this setting to increase the amount of hard drive space allocated, but eventually your computer will become sluggish as it is forced to page more often. This condition of excessive paging is called **thrashing**. The solution to this problem is to increase the amount of RAM in your computer so that it won't be necessary for it to send data and instructions to virtual memory.

enough space for all the pending instructions and data. The OS then clears the items from RAM when the processor no longer needs them.

Can my OS ever run out of RAM? RAM has limited capacity. Like most users, you'll add new software and peripherals to your computer over time. Most computers sold for home use have between 4 and 16 GB of RAM. If you have an older computer system with less RAM, it might be time to consider buying a new computer or adding more RAM. As you add and upgrade software and increase your usage of the computer system, you might find that the amount of RAM you have is no longer sufficient for your needs.

How does the OS manage storage? If it weren't for the OS, the files and applications you save to the hard drive and other storage locations would be an unorganized mess. Fortunately, the OS has a file-management system that keeps track of the name and location of each file you save and the programs you install. We'll talk more about file management later in this chapter.

RAM

Data and instructions not recently used

Operating System

Data and instructions needed now

Location of the swap file

FIGURE 5.11 Virtual memory borrows excess storage capacity from the hard drive when there isn't enough capacity in RAM. *(brontazavra/ Shutterstock; aPERFECT/Fotolia; Tim Dobbs/Shutterstock)*

Hardware and Peripheral Device Management

How does the OS manage the hardware and peripheral devices? Each device attached to your computer comes with a special program called a **device driver** that facilitates communication between the device and the OS. Because the OS must be able to communicate with every device in the computer system, the device driver translates the device's specialized commands into commands the OS can understand, and vice versa. Devices wouldn't function without the proper device drivers because the OS wouldn't know how to communicate with them.

Do I always need to install drivers? Today, most devices, such as flash drives, mice, keyboards, and digital cameras, come with the driver already installed in Windows. The devices whose drivers are included in Windows are called Plug and Play devices. **Plug and Play (PnP)** is a software and hardware standard designed to facilitate the installation of new hardware in PCs by including in the OS the drivers these devices need in order to run. Because the OS includes this software, incorporating a new device into your computer system seems automatic. PnP lets you plug a new device into your computer, turn it on, and immediately play (use) the device (see Figure 5.12).

What happens if the device is not PnP? Sometimes you may have a device that is so new the drivers aren't yet available automatically in Windows. You'll then be prompted to insert the driver that was provided with the device or downloaded

FIGURE 5.12 A Windows message showing a successful driver installation the first time an external hard drive was connected to the computer.

from the Internet. If you obtain a device secondhand and don't receive the device driver, or if you're required to update the device driver, you can often download the necessary driver from the manufacturer's website. You can also go to websites such as DriverZone (**driverzone.com**) to locate drivers.

Can I damage my system by installing a device driver? Occasionally, when you install a driver your system may become unstable (that is, programs may stop responding, certain actions may cause a crash, or the device or the entire system may stop working). Although this is uncommon, it can happen. Fortunately, to remedy the problem, Windows has a Roll Back Driver feature that removes a newly installed driver and replaces it with the last one that worked (see Figure 5.13).

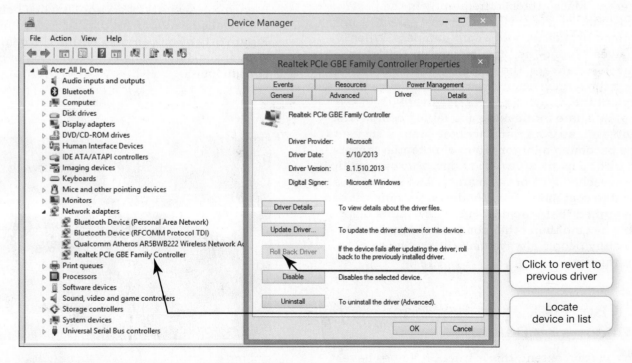

FIGURE 5.13 The Roll Back Driver feature in Windows removes a newly installed driver and replaces it with the last one that worked.
>*To access the Device Manager window, navigate to the desktop, right-click the Start button to display the shortcut menu, and select* **Device Manager**. *To display the Properties dialog box, double-click on a device. Click the* **Driver** *tab.*

Many Mac users feel they are impervious to viruses and malware (software that can disable or interfere with the use of a computing device) because those are "just Windows problems." This means that Mac users often run their computers with only the basic protection provided by Apple in its operating system software. Are Mac users wild risk takers, or are they actually safe from hackers? As with many issues, it's a little bit of both.

Threats Are Out There

Windows users have been bombarded by malware and virus attacks for decades. When you bought your last Windows machine, it invariably came with a trial version of third-party antivirus/anti-malware software. Running a Windows computer without antivirus/anti-malware software is just asking for trouble.

However, over the last several years, the attacks against Macs have also increased. Why weren't Macs attacked frequently in the past? Most malware is designed to steal sensitive information such as credit card numbers. When thieves expend the time, money, and effort to develop malware, they want to ensure that it targets the largest population of potential victims. Up until recently, Windows had over 90% of the market share for desktop and laptop computers. However, as OS X gains market share, Mac users are becoming a larger group of potential targets. In fact, in many affluent nations, Mac ownership has reached 20% of the market. And since Macs tend to cost more than Windows machines, it can be argued that Mac users may have more disposable income than other computer buyers. And wealthy people always make attractive targets for thieves.

But Isn't OS X Just Safer Than Windows by Design?

To a certain extent, this is true. OS X does have certain design features that tend to prevent the installation and spread of malware. Apple has also designed current versions of iOS and OS X to prevent the installation of unapproved software (i.e., software not available on Apple's approved online outlets like the App Store). In addition, apps sold on the App Store are required to be designed using the access control technology known as *App Sandbox*.

When most software programs or apps are running, they have broad latitude to interact with the OS (such as Windows or OS X). Usually they have all the rights that the user has over the OS. So if hackers can design an exploit that takes advantage of a security flaw in an app, they can potentially gain extensive control over the computer using the access that the user has to the OS. As noted, Apple requires all approved apps to be "sandboxed" (developed to run in the App Sandbox environment). When an app is sandboxed, the developer defines what the app needs to do in order to interact with the OS. The OS then grants only those specific rights and privileges to the app and nothing else. By doing this, it severely limits what hackers can do in an OS if they breach the security of an app. It's like being in a high-walled sandbox (or playpen) as a child (see Figure 5.14). You can play within the confines of your space, but you can't make mischief outside certain limits.

FIGURE 5.14 Just as sandboxes are designed to constrain children, toys, and sand to a specific area, Mac apps are also designed to limit access to the OS. *(EduardSV/Fotolia)*

So I'll Buy a Mac and Be Safe Forever, Right?

Alas, it's not that simple. Although it's more difficult to design exploits for OS X and iOS, it's not impossible. And a great deal of cybercrime relies on social engineering techniques like those used in scareware scams. *Scareware* is software designed to make it seem as if there is something wrong with your computer. The author of the scareware program then "persuades" you to buy a solution to the problem, acquiring your credit card number in the process. Scareware victims can be both Mac and PC users, so even if you own a Mac, you need to be aware of such scams and avoid falling prey to them (see Chapter 9).

The Solution: Extra Security Precautions!

The current versions of OS X, iOS, and Windows all include some level of security tools and precautions.

But there are a few things you should do to protect yourself:

1. **Make sure your software is set to download and install updates automatically**—As OS developers discover holes in their software's security, they provide updates to repair these problems.

2. **Use third-party antivirus/anti-malware software (even on a Mac).** Although no product will detect 100% of malware, detecting some is better than detecting none.

3. **Be aware of social engineering techniques.** Use vigilance when surfing the Internet so you don't fall prey to scams.

So, no OS is 100% safe. But if you're informed and proceed with caution, you can avoid a lot of schemes perpetrated by hackers and thieves.

Software Application Coordination

How does the OS help application software run on the computer? Every computer program, no matter what its type or manufacturer, needs to interact with the CPU using computer code. For programs to work with the CPU, they must contain code the CPU recognizes. Rather than having the same blocks of code for similar procedures in each program, the OS includes the blocks of code—each called an **application programming interface (API)**—that application software needs in order to interact with the CPU. Microsoft DirectX, for example, is a group of multimedia APIs built into the Windows OS that improves graphics and sounds when you're playing games or watching videos on your PC.

What are the advantages of using APIs? To create applications that can communicate with the OS, software programmers need only refer to the API code blocks when they write an application. They don't need to include the entire code sequence. APIs not only prevent redundancies in software code, they make it easier for software developers to respond to changes in the OS. Software companies also take advantage of APIs to make applications in software suites (such as Microsoft Office) that have a similar interface and functionality. And since these applications share common APIs, data exchange is facilitated between two programs, such as inserting a chart from Excel into a Word document. ∎

the boot process: starting
YOUR COMPUTER

Many things happen quickly between the time you turn on your computer and the time it's ready for you to start using it. As we discussed earlier, all data and instructions (including the OS) are stored in RAM while your computer is on. When you turn off your computer, RAM is wiped clean of all its data (including the OS). How does the computer know what to do when you turn it on if there is nothing in RAM? It runs through a special boot process (or start-up process) to load the OS into RAM. The term *boot,* from *bootstrap loader* (a small program used to start a larger program), alludes to the straps of leather, called *bootstraps,* that people used to use to help them pull on their boots. This is also the source of the expression "pull yourself up by your bootstraps."

What are the steps involved in the boot process? As illustrated in Figure 5.15, the **boot process** consists of four basic steps. Let's look at each step in detail.

Step 1: Activating BIOS

What's the first thing that happens after I turn on my computer? In the first step of the boot process, the CPU activates the **basic input/output system (BIOS)**. BIOS is a program that manages the exchange of data between the OS and all the input and output devices attached to the system. BIOS is also responsible for loading the OS into RAM from its permanent location on the hard drive. BIOS itself is stored on a read-only memory (ROM) chip on the motherboard. Unlike data stored in RAM, data stored in ROM is permanent and is not erased when the power is turned off.

CPU

ROM chip

STEP 1: CPU activates BIOS
- Basic input/output system
- Stored permanently in ROM

STEP 2: Power-on self-test (POST)
- Tests components of the computer
- Compares results with configuration information in CMOS

STEP 3: Load OS to RAM
- OS loaded from hard drive
- Kernel is *memory resident*

STEP 4: Configuration and customization settings checked and Start screen displays

FIGURE 5.15 The Boot Process

Step 2: Performing the Power-On Self-Test

How does the computer determine whether the hardware is working properly? The first job BIOS performs is to ensure that essential peripheral devices are attached and operational—a process called the **power-on self-test**, or **POST**. The BIOS compares the results of the POST with the various hardware configurations permanently stored in CMOS (pronounced "see-moss"). CMOS, which stands for *complementary metal-oxide semiconductor,* is a special kind of memory that uses almost no power. A small battery provides enough power so that the CMOS contents won't be lost after the computer is turned off. CMOS contains information about the system's memory, types of disk drives, and other essential input and output hardware components. If the results of the POST compare favorably with the hardware configurations stored in CMOS, the boot process continues.

Step 3: Loading the OS

How does the OS get loaded into RAM? Next, BIOS goes through a preconfigured list of devices in its search for the drive that contains the **system files**, the main files of the OS. When it is located, the OS loads into RAM from its permanent storage location on the hard drive.

Once the system files are loaded into RAM, the **kernel** (or **supervisor program**) is loaded. The kernel is the essential component of the OS. It's responsible for managing the processor and all other components of the computer system. Because it stays in RAM the entire time your computer is powered on, the kernel is said to be *memory resident.* Other, less critical, parts of the OS stay on the hard drive and are copied over to RAM on an as-needed basis so that RAM is managed more efficiently. These programs are referred to as *nonresident.* Once the kernel is loaded, the OS takes over control of the computer's functions.

Step 4: Checking Further Configurations and Customizations

Is that it? Finally, the OS checks the registry for the configuration of other system components. The **registry** contains all the different configurations (settings) used by the OS and by other applications. It contains the customized settings you put

ACTIVE HELPDESK
**Starting the Computer:
The Boot Process**

In this Active Helpdesk, you'll play the role of a helpdesk staffer, fielding questions about how the operating system helps the computer start up.

into place, such as mouse speed, as well as instructions as to which programs should be loaded first.

Why do I sometimes need to enter a login name and password at the end of the boot process? The verification of your login name and password is called **authentication**. The authentication process blocks unauthorized users from entering the system. You may have your home computer set up for authentication, especially if you have multiple users accessing it. All large networked environments, like your college, require user authentication for access.

On a Windows 8 computer, the default setting is to input a password to log in to your **Microsoft account** after your computer has completely booted up. Because configuration settings are stored online and associated with a particular Microsoft account, this makes it easy for multiple people to share any Windows 8 computer while maintaining access to their individual settings and preferences.

How do I know if the boot process is successful? The entire boot process takes only a few minutes to complete. If the entire system is checked out and loaded properly, the process completes by displaying the login screen or the Start screen. The computer system is now ready to accept your first command.

Handling Errors in the Boot Process

What should I do if my computer doesn't boot properly? Sometimes problems occur during the boot process. Here are some suggestions for solving a boot problem:

- If you've recently installed new software or hardware, try uninstalling it. (Make sure you use the Uninstall a program feature in the Control Panel to remove the software.) If the problem no longer occurs when rebooting, you can reinstall the device or software.
- Try accessing the Windows Advanced Options Menu (accessible by pressing the F8 key during the boot process). If Windows detects a problem in the boot process, it will add Last Known Good Configuration to the Windows Advanced Options Menu. Every time your computer boots successfully, a configuration of the boot process is saved. When you choose to boot with the Last Known Good Configuration, the OS starts your computer by using the registry information that was saved during the last shut down.
- Try refreshing your computer (new in Windows 8).

What happens when a PC is "refreshed"? Sometimes Windows does not boot properly or the system does not respond properly. You may even see messages related to "fatal exceptions." **Refresh your PC** is a new utility

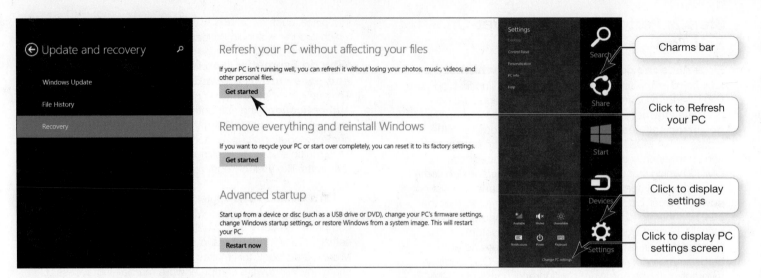

FIGURE 5.16 The Update and recovery screen (an option on the PC settings screen) in Windows 8.1 provides access to the Refresh your PC option. *To access the Update and recovery screen, display the Charms bar on the Start screen (swipe from right, or point cursor to upper-right corner of screen), click* **Settings**, *then click* **Change PC settings**. *On the PC settings screen, click* **Update and recovery**, *then select* **Recovery**.

program in Windows 8 that attempts to diagnose and fix errors in your Windows system files that are causing your computer to behave improperly (see Figure 5.16). When a PC is refreshed, the following occurs:

- Your data files (documents, music, videos, etc.) and personalization settings are not removed or changed.

- Apps that you have downloaded from the Windows Store are kept intact.

- Apps that you have downloaded from the Internet or installed from DVDs will be removed from your PC. Therefore, you'll need to reinstall them after the refresh.

It's recommended that you back up your PC prior to refreshing it as a precautionary measure. Finally, if all other attempts to fix your computer fail, try a System Restore to roll back to a past configuration. System Restore is covered in more detail later in this chapter.

What should I do if my keyboard or another device doesn't work after I boot my computer? Sometimes during the boot process, BIOS skips a device (such as a keyboard) or improperly identifies it. Your only indication that this problem has occurred is that the device won't respond after the system has been booted. When that happens, try rebooting. If the problem persists, check the OS's website for any patches (or software fixes) that may resolve the issue. If there are no patches or the problem persists, you may want to get technical assistance. ■

> **Before moving on to Part 2:**
> - **Watch Replay Video 5.1** ▶ .
> - Then check your understanding of what you've learned so far.

check your understanding // review & practice

For a quick review to see what you've learned so far, answer the following questions. Visit **pearsonhighered.com /techinaction** to check your answers.

multiple choice

1. Which is NOT an example of a network operating system?

   a. Linux   **c.** Android

   b. UNIX   **d.** Windows

2. You are most likely to find an RTOS

   a. in a robotic camera.

   b. on a supercomputer.

   c. on a mainframe.

   d. on an iPad.

3. Which of the following is an example of a web-based OS?

   a. OS X

   b. Windows

   c. Linux

   d. Chrome

4. Early operating systems such as MS-DOS used a _____ interface.

   a. command-driven

   b. graphical user

   c. menu-driven

   d. magnetic tape–based

5. The OS can optimize RAM storage by using

   a. thrashing.

   b. virtual memory.

   c. an interrupt handler.

   d. a spooler.

To take an autograded version of this review, please go to the companion website at **pearsonhighered.com/techinaction**, or go your MyITLab course.

TRY THIS

Organizing Tiles on the Start Screen in Windows 8.1

The Start screen in Windows 8.1 is similar to the desktop in Windows 7 in that you can arrange the tiles on the Start screen to suit your needs, much like you can move around the icons on the Windows 7 desktop. You can even create groups of tiles and give each group a name. On a busy Start screen, this helps you keep your tiles organized so you can find the right app quickly. Let's create a small group for app tiles that take us out to the Internet.

Step 1 Locate the OneDrive tile on your Start screen. Left-click the tile (or press and hold) and drag it to the space between two groups of tiles. A faint vertical bar will appear, indicating that you wish to place that tile in its own group. Release the mouse button (or stop touching the screen). The One-Drive tile should now be alone in its own group.

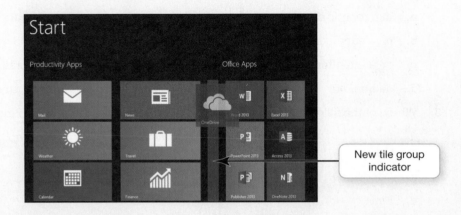

New tile group indicator

Step 2 Locate the Internet Explorer and Store tiles. Left-click and drag (or press and drag) these tiles so they are in close proximity to the OneDrive tile. Release the mouse button (or stop pressing the screen) and these tiles should join the OneDrive tile in their own group. To name the group, right-click on a blank area of the Start screen and select **Name groups**. In the **Name group box** that appears above the group, enter *Internet Apps*. Left-click (or press) on any blank area of the Start screen.

Name group box

Step 3 Perhaps you use OneDrive quite frequently. You may wish to make that tile larger. Right-click (or press and hold) the OneDrive tile to select it. From the shortcut menu that displays, select **Resize**, and then **Wide**. Notice that the OneDrive icon is now twice the size of the other two icons.

Right-click to select

Select to enlarge tile

Make This

TOOL: App Inventor 2

MAKE: A Notification Alert

Does your app need to communicate with or provide feedback to the user? With the Notifier component of **App Inventor**, you can make your program generate message boxes or ask for a response from the user.

In this exercise, you'll use the Notifier component of **App Inventor** to show a message box, post a user choice with two buttons for response, or post an alert. Your apps can now use more of the features of the Android operating system to communicate!

The *Notifier component allows you to communicate with alerts, message boxes, and text choice popups within your mobile app.*

For the instructions for this exercise, please go to pearsonhighered.com/techinaction or MyITLab.

Using System Software

Now that you know how system software works, let's explore how specific operating systems and their tools function.

 the windows
INTERFACE

As we mentioned earlier, Windows 8 is a departure from previous versions of Windows because it's designed for a variety of devices, including laptops, phones, and tablets. To enable Windows 8 to function on all types of devices, there are often three different ways to accomplish tasks in Windows 8:

1. Using a mouse
2. Touching the screen (on touch-enabled devices)
3. Using keystrokes

Which method you use depends on the type of device you're using and, to a large extent, on your personal preferences.

The **Start screen** is the first interaction you have with the OS and the first image you see on your display. As its name implies, the Start screen is the place where you begin all of your computing activities. The Windows 8 Start screen provides you with access to your most used applications in one convenient screen.

How do Windows 8 "optimized" programs differ from older Windows apps? Windows 8 apps are applications specifically designed to run in the interface of Windows 8.

The **Windows 8 interface** features large type with clean, readable block images inspired by metropolitan service signs such as those found on bus stations and subways.

Windows 8 apps either are preinstalled with Windows 8 (such as Photos, Messaging, and Calendar) or are available for download from the Windows Store (Microsoft's apps marketplace). You can launch Windows 8 apps by clicking or tapping on their icons on the Start screen.

Windows 8 apps are displayed full screen, without the distractions of borders or controls (such as toolbars or menus). For example, Figure 5.17 shows Internet Explorer 11, which is a Windows 8 app. Notice that unlike older versions of Internet Explorer, there are no window borders or menus visible (see Figure 5.17a), as the application fills the entire screen. Controls and settings are contained on **app bars**, such as the Tabs bar (see Figure 5.17b), that float on the screen above the app when you summon them or you need them. Right-clicking on a Windows 8 app screen (or swiping up from the bottom) usually displays the app bars.

What are the main features of the Windows 8 Start screen? The Start screen is based on the interface for Windows smartphones. The most useful feature of the Start

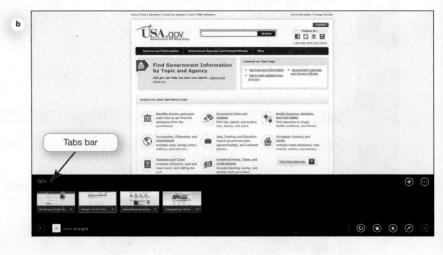

FIGURE 5.17 (a) Internet Explorer 11, a Windows 8 app, displays full screen. (b) Right-clicking on the Internet Explorer 11 screen displays the open Tabs bar.

screen is that it lets you customize it to meet your needs. (For more on customizing the Start screen, see the Try This feature on pages 176–177.) As such, the Start screen on your computer may be different from the Start screen on your friend's computer. And because your Windows 8 settings and preferences are saved in your Microsoft account, when you log on to any Windows 8 computer, you'll see your own personal settings, preferences, and applications reflected on the Start screen (see Figure 5.18).

For performing common tasks, such as searching or sharing information, Windows 8 has created special shortcuts called **charms**. Charms are located on the *Charms bar* (see Figure 5.18b), which you access by moving your cursor to the upper-right corner of the screen, swiping in from the right edge of the screen, or pressing the Windows key+C.

Why can't I see tiles for certain applications on my Start screen? Not all the Windows 8 apps and programs installed on your computer are visible on the Start screen. You can choose which applications are visible on the Start screen through a process called **pinning**. Usually, when you install a Windows 8 app or any other program on your computer, it pins the program (displays it) on the Start screen by default. If there is a tile on the Start screen you don't need, just right-click on it (or touch and hold) and select the Unpin from Start option that appears on the shortcut menu.

If you want to see all the applications installed on your computer, not just the ones pinned to your Start screen, click the All programs (apps) button that appears at the bottom of the

Start screen (see Figure 5.18a). This displays the Apps screen (see Figure 5.19), which shows all Windows 8 apps and other programs installed on your computer.

What happened to the Start button from Windows 7? When using Windows 8.1 for the first time, you might be looking for the Start button, which is not initially displayed on the Start screen. If you leave the Start screen and go to the desktop, you will see the Start button (represented by the Windows 8 logo) in its familiar spot on the taskbar. However, this does not have the functionality of the old Windows 7 Start button. Instead of displaying a list of installed applications, the new Start button merely returns you to the Start screen. Once you have returned to the Start screen from the desktop, moving your cursor to the lower left-hand corner of the Start screen will display the Start button.

How can I quickly access useful programs and tools that were available from the Windows 7 Start button? Right-clicking on the Windows 8.1 Start button displays a menu of quick links to common administrative tasks and programs, such as Control Panel, File Explorer, and shutdown options.

Where is the Windows desktop? If you've been using versions of Windows prior to Windows 8, you're used to the desktop being the first screen you see on your computer. The desktop from Windows 7 still exists, just in a slightly modified version. You can access the Windows 8 desktop via the

a

b

FIGURE 5.18 (a) The Windows 8 Start screen is the new point of entry to the OS. (b) The Charms bar provides access to common tasks.

Search box for apps

Return to Start screen

FIGURE 5.19 The Windows 8 Apps screen shows all Windows 8 apps and other programs installed on your computer.

Desktop icon on the Start screen or by pressing the Windows key+D. Programs that have not been designed to run in the Windows 8 interface (like Microsoft Office 2013) will run on the Windows 8 desktop.

The desktop still has features like the taskbar. The **taskbar** displays open and favorite applications for easy access. You can point to an icon to preview windows of open files or programs, or move your mouse over a thumbnail to preview a full-screen image. Or, you can right-click an icon to view a Jump List—the most recently or commonly used files or commands for that application.

How can I switch between apps in Windows 8? If you want to go back to the last program you were using, just point your cursor to the upper-left corner of the screen and drag (or swipe) from the left. Drag the thumbnail image of your previous program to the middle of your screen and it will be available. Repeatedly swiping from the left will scroll backward through all your open programs.

For a list of open programs—so you can jump right to the correct one—position your cursor in the upper-left corner until the thumbnail appears, then move the cursor down (or swipe in from the left, and before you let go, swipe out again) to display a list of thumbnails of previous programs called a *switch list* (see Figure 5.20). Alternatively, pressing and holding the Alt key and then pressing the Tab key repeatedly also allows you to scroll through open apps.

How can I see more than one Windows 8 app on my screen at a time? Windows 8 apps can snap into place on either the left or right side of the screen, so you can easily display two (or more) apps at the same time. Just display the thumbnail list of running apps and click and drag the thumbnail of the second app you want to display to the left or right side of the screen. The app will snap into place while

FIGURE 5.20 Thumbnails of open programs allow you to switch quickly between them.

BITS&BYTES

Touch Language for Windows 8

Because the main thrust of Windows 8 is to optimize Windows for touch-screen devices, the Windows developers needed to agree on a set of touch interactions they would use when programming Windows 8.

If you're using Windows 8 on a touch-screen device, you may want to learn the gestures shown in Figure 5.21.

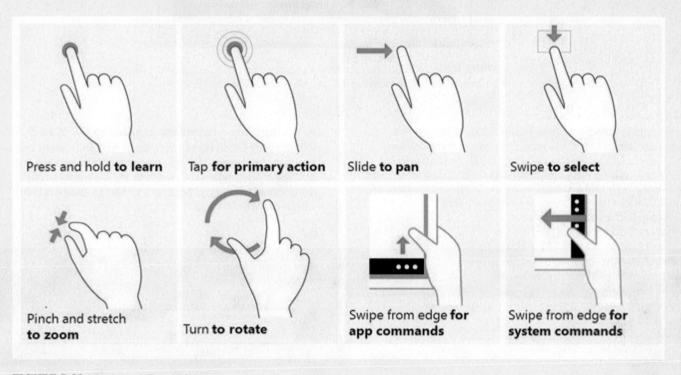

Press and hold **to learn** Tap **for primary action** Slide **to pan** Swipe **to select**

Pinch and stretch **to zoom** Turn **to rotate** Swipe from edge **for app commands** Swipe from edge **for system commands**

FIGURE 5.21 Windows 8 Touch Gestures

still leaving the other app you had running visible, with each one taking up half the screen. You can resize the apps as necessary to allow one to take up more screen space than the other. Depending on your screen resolution, you may be able to display up to four apps at the same time using snap.

How do I close a Windows 8 app? When Windows 8 apps aren't displayed on the screen, Windows will suspend them temporarily so they don't use much memory or power. Therefore, theoretically, you don't ever need to shut down Windows 8 apps. However, most people prefer not to have endless apps running, and it may be inconvenient to scroll through a huge list of running apps to find the one you want. To close a Windows 8 app from within the app, press

Alt+F4. Alternatively, you can move your cursor to the top of the screen until the title bar displays, then click the close button (X). Right-clicking on a thumbnail of the app on the switch list also allows you to close an app, as does swiping from the top of the screen to the bottom with your finger.

How does the Mac user interface compare with Windows 8? Although the OS X and the Windows operating systems aren't compatible, they're extremely similar in terms of functionality. For example, as is the case with Windows, OS X programs appear in resizable windows and use menus and icons. However, instead of the Start screen, OS X features a Dock with icons on the bottom for your

MacBook Air

FIGURE 5.22 OS X Yosemite continues Apple's goal of making a seamless OS experience no matter what device you are using. *(Apple, Inc.)*

most popular programs (see Figure 5.22). Yosemite, the latest version of OS X, features tight integration between OS X and portable devices running iOS 8. Apple wants to make transferring data and tasks from one device to another seamless.

Is a Linux user interface similar to OS X and Windows? Different distros of Linux feature different user interfaces. But most of them, like Ubuntu (see Figure 5.23), are based on familiar Windows and OS X paradigms, such as using icons to launch programs and having apps run in a window environment. ∎

FIGURE 5.23 The Ubuntu Linux user interface resembles the Windows desktop. *(Mozilla, Firefox)*

Proprietary software such as Microsoft Windows and Apple's OS X is developed by corporations and sold for profit. This means that the **source code**, the actual lines of instructional code that make the program work, is not accessible to the general public. Without being able to access the source code, it's difficult for a user to modify the software or see exactly how the program author constructed various parts of the OS.

Restricting access to the source code protects companies from having their programming ideas stolen, and it prevents customers from using modified versions of the software. However, in the late 1980s, computer specialists became concerned that large software companies (such as Microsoft) were controlling a large portion of market share and driving out competitors. They also felt that proprietary software was too expensive and contained too many bugs (errors).

These people felt that software should be developed without a profit motive and distributed with its source code free for all to see. The theory was that if many computer specialists examined, improved, and changed the source code, a more full-featured, bug-free product would result. Hence, the open source movement was born.

So, if an OS such as Linux is free and relatively bug-free, why does Windows, which users must pay for, have such a huge market share? One reason is that corporations and individuals have grown accustomed to one thing that proprietary software makers can provide: technical support. It's almost impossible to provide technical support for open source software because anyone can freely modify it; thus, there is no specific developer to take responsibility for technical support. Similarly, corporations have been reluctant to install open source software extensively because of the cost of the internal staff of programmers that must support it.

Companies such as Red Hat, Ubuntu, and Xandros have been combating this problem. Red Hat offers a free, open source OS called Fedora (see Figure 5.24). In addition, Red Hat has modified the original Linux source code and markets a version, Red Hat Enterprise Linux, as a proprietary program. Fedora is the testing ground for what eventually goes into this proprietary program. Red Hat Enterprise Linux comes in versions for servers and desktops. Purchasers of Red Hat Enterprise Linux receive a warranty and technical support. Packaging open source software in this manner has made its use much more attractive to businesses. As a result, many web servers are hosted on computers running Linux.

FIGURE 5.24 Companies like Red Hat provide free or low-cost Linux software, such as Fedora, but technical support is often not available (or not free). *(Paul Sakuma/AP Images)*

organizing your computer:
FILE MANAGEMENT

So far we've discussed how the OS manages the processor, memory, storage, and devices, and how it provides a way for applications and users to interact with the computer. An additional function of the OS is to enable **file management**, which provides an organizational structure to your computer's contents. In this section, we discuss how you can use this organizational structure to make your computer more organized and efficient.

Organizing Your Files

How does the OS organize files? Windows organizes the contents of your computer in a hierarchical **directory** structure composed of *drives, libraries, folders, subfolders,* and *files*. The hard drive, represented as the C: drive, is where you permanently store most of your files. Each additional storage drive (optical drive, flash drive, or external hard drive) is given a unique letter (*D, E, F,* and so on). The C: drive is like a large filing cabinet in which all files are stored. As such, the C: drive is the top of the filing structure of your computer and is referred to as the **root directory**. All other folders and files are organized within the root directory. There are areas in the root directory that the OS has filled with files and folders holding special OS files. The programs within these files help run the computer and generally shouldn't be accessed.

What exactly are files and folders? In an OS, a **file** is a collection of program instructions or data that is stored and treated as a single unit. Files can be generated from an application such as a Word document or an Excel workbook. In addition, files can represent an entire application, a web page, a set of sounds, or an image. Files can be stored on the hard drive, a flash drive, online, or on any other permanent storage medium. As the number of files you save increases, it becomes more important to keep them organized in folders and libraries. A **folder** is a collection of files.

How does the library work? In Windows, a **library** gathers categories of files from different locations and displays them as if they were all saved in a single folder, regardless of where they are physically stored. For example, you might have pictures stored all over your computer, including your external hard drive. Rather than looking through each separate location to view your pictures, you can access all of them more easily by looking in the Pictures library. There are four default libraries: Documents, Music, Pictures, and Videos.

How can I easily locate and see the contents of my computer? In Windows, **File Explorer** (previously called Windows Explorer) is the main tool for finding, viewing, and managing the contents of your computer. It shows the location and contents of every drive, folder, and file. As illustrated in Figure 5.25, File Explorer is divided into two panes, or sections:

1. The *navigation pane* on the left shows the contents of your computer. It displays commonly accessed areas, organized by Favorites and Libraries (Documents, Music, Pictures, and Videos).
2. When you select a Favorite, Library, drive, or Homegroup, the files and folders of that particular area are displayed in the *details pane* on the right.

BITS&BYTES

How to Get the Most from Windows Libraries

To get the most out of using Windows libraries, consider the following tips:

- **Display libraries:** In Windows 8.1, Libraries are not displayed by default in File Explorer. To display Libraries, right-click on a blank space in the Navigation Pane and select *Show libraries* from the shortcut menu.

- **Add a new library:** To add a new library (such as one for your games), open File Explorer. In the Navigation Pane on the left side of the window, right-click on Libraries, click New, and then click Library. Type in a name for the new library. To add new locations to the library, open the new library, and click on Include a Folder.

- **Share or collaborate with libraries:** Say you have pictures saved on your laptop, your dad's desktop, and your mom's laptop. As long as all three computers are on the same Homegroup network, you can share each other's libraries by right-clicking the library name, pointing to Share With, and then clicking one of the two Homegroup options, depending on whether you want to allow editing privileges to those with whom you're sharing the library.

- **Create a backup library:** Do you store important data in a variety of folders on your computer? Even though it's best to back up your entire system, you might only need to back up specific folders. In that case, create a new library and call it "Backup." Add the folders you want to ensure are backed up to the library, and then point your backup software to that library.

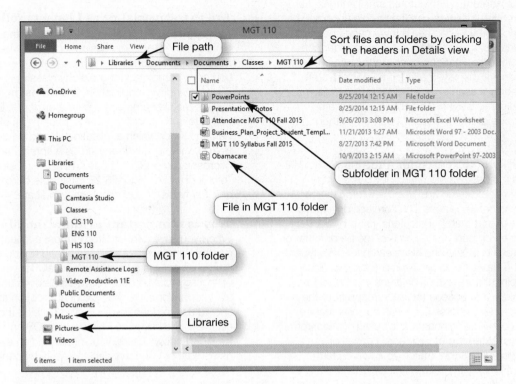

FIGURE 5.25 File Explorer lets you see the contents of your computer.
> *Right-click on the Start button to display the menu, and then select* **File Explorer**.

What are some tips on how best to organize my files? Creating folders is the key to organizing files because folders keep related documents together. For example, you might create one folder called "Classes" to hold your class work. Inside the "Classes" folder, you could create subfolders for each of your classes (such as ENG 110 and MGT 110). Inside each of those subfolders, you could create further subfolders for each class's assignments, homework, and so on.

Grouping related files into folders makes it easier for you to identify and find files. Which would be easier—going to the MGT 110 folder to find a file or searching through the hundreds of individual files in the Documents library hoping to find the right one? Grouping files in a folder also allows you to

move files more efficiently, so you can quickly transfer critical files needing frequent backup, for instance.

Viewing and Sorting Files and Folders

Are there different ways I can view and sort my files and folders? When you open any folder in File Explorer, the ribbon at the top displays a View tab. Clicking on the View tab offers you different ways to view the folders and files. In some views, the folders are displayed as *Live Icons*. Live Icons allows you to preview the actual contents of a specific file or folder without actually opening the file. Live Icons can be displayed in a variety of views. Here are the two most useful views for students:

1. **Details view:** This is the most interactive view. As shown in Figure 5.25, files and folders are displayed in list form, and the additional file information is displayed in columns alongside the name of the file. You can sort and display the contents of the folder by any of the column headings, so you can sort the contents alphabetically by name or type, or hierarchically by date last modified or file size. Right-click the column heading area to modify the display of columns.

 SOUND BYTE
File Management

In this Sound Byte, you'll examine the features of file management and maintenance. You'll learn the various methods of creating folders, how to turn a group of unorganized files into an organized system of folders with related files, and how to maintain your file system.

2. **Large Icons view:** As shown in Figure 5.26, Large Icons view shows the contents of folders as small images. Large Icons view is the best view to use if your folder contains picture files because you can see a few images peeking out of the folder. It's also good to use if your folder contains PowerPoint presentations because the title slide of the presentation will display, making it easier for you to distinguish among presentations. Additionally, a preview pane is available in this view. The preview pane lets you view the first page of the selected document without having to open it.

What's the best way to search for a file? In Windows 8, the Search app is the best way to search for files and the contents of folders. The Search app searches through your hard drive or other storage devices (DVD or flash drive) to locate files and folders that match the criteria you provide. Your search can be based on part of the name of the file or folder or just a word or phrase in it. You can also search for a file type by representing the file name as an asterisk (called a wildcard character) and typing the file extension (such as "*.xlsx" to search for Excel files). You access the Search app from the Charms bar or from File Explorer. OS X has a similar feature called Spotlight. Make sure to change the search option from Everywhere to Files (at the top of the Search panel) or you'll also see a list of web pages that match your search term.

Naming Files

Are there special rules I have to follow when I name files? The first part of a file, or the **file name**, is generally the name you assign to the file when you save it. For example, "bioreport" may be the name you assign a report you have completed for a biology class.

In a Windows application, an **extension**, or **file type**, follows the file name and a period or dot (.). Like a last name, this extension identifies what kind of family of files the file belongs to, or which application should be used to read the file. For example, if "bioreport" is a spreadsheet created in Microsoft Excel 2013, it has an .xlsx extension, and its name is "bioreport.xlsx." Figure 5.27 lists some common file extensions and the types of documents they indicate.

Why is it important to know the file extension? When you save a file created in most applications running under the Windows OS, you don't need to add the extension to the file name; it is added automatically for you. Mac and Linux operating systems don't require file extensions. This is because the information as to the type of application the computer should use to open the file is stored inside the file itself. However, if you're using the Mac or Linux OS and will be sending files to Windows users, you should add an extension to your file name so that Windows can more easily open your files.

FIGURE 5.26 The Large Icons view is a good way to display the contents of files and folders. The Preview pane on the right lets you see the first page of your document without first opening it.
> *To access Large Icons view, click the* **View** *tab from the ribbon in File Explorer, and then select* **Large Icons** *view. To access the Preview pane, click that icon on the View tab of the ribbon.*

FIGURE 5.27

Common File Name Extensions

EXTENSION	TYPE OF DOCUMENT	APPLICATION
.docx	Word processing document	Microsoft Word 2007 and later
.xlsx	Workbook	Microsoft Excel 2007 and later
.accdb	Database	Microsoft Access 2007 and later
.pptx	Presentation	Microsoft PowerPoint 2007 and later
.pdf	Portable Document Format	Adobe Acrobat or Adobe Reader
.rtf	Text (Rich Text Format)	Any program that can read text documents
.txt	Text	Any program that can read text documents
.htm or .html	HyperText Markup Language (HTML) for a web page	Any program that can read HTML
.jpg	Joint Photographic Experts Group (JPEG) image	Most programs capable of displaying images
.zip	Compressed file	Various file compression programs

Have you ever been sent a file by e-mail and couldn't open it? Most likely, that was because your computer didn't have the program needed to open the file. Sometimes, similar programs that you already have installed can be used to open the file, so it's helpful to know what the file extension is. Sites such as FILExt (**filext.com**) can help you identify the source program.

Are there things I shouldn't do when naming my files? Each OS has its own naming conventions, or rules, which are listed in Figure 5.28. Beyond those conventions, it's important that you name your files so that you can easily identify them. Files names can have as many as 255 characters, so don't be afraid to use as many characters as you need. A file name such as "BIO 101 Research Paper First Draft.docx" makes it very clear what that file contains.

Keep in mind, however, that all files must be uniquely identified, unless you save them in different folders or in different locations. Therefore, although files may share the same file name (such as "bioreport.docx" or "bioreport.xlsx") or share the same extension ("bioreport.xlsx" or "budget.xlsx"), no two files stored in the same folder can share *both* the same file name and the same extension.

How can I tell where my files are saved? When you save a file for the first time, you give the file a name and designate where you want to save it. For easy reference, the OS includes libraries where files are saved unless you specify otherwise. In Windows, the default libraries are Documents for files, Music for audio files, Pictures for graphics files, and Videos for video files.

You can determine the location of a file by its **file path**. The file path starts with the drive in which the file is located and includes all folders, subfolders (if any), the file name, and the extension. For example, if you were saving a picture of Andrew Carnegie for a term paper for a U.S. History course, the file path might be C:\Documents\HIS182\Term Paper\Illustrations\ACarnegie.jpg.

As shown in Figure 5.29, "C:" is the drive on which the file is stored (in this case, the hard drive), and "Documents" is the file's primary folder. "HIS182," "Term Paper," and "Illustrations" are successive subfolders within the "Documents" main folder. Last comes the file name, "ACarnegie," separated from the file extension (in this case, "jpg") by a period. The backslash characters (\), used by Windows, are referred to as **path separators**. OS X files use a colon (:), whereas UNIX and Linux files use the forward slash (/) as the path separator.

FIGURE 5.28

File-Naming Conventions

	OS X	WINDOWS
File and folder name length	As many as 255 characters*	As many as 255 characters
Case sensitive?	Yes	No
Forbidden characters	Colon (:)	" / \ * ? <> | :
File extensions needed?	No	Yes

Note: Although OS X supports file names with as many as 255 characters, many applications running on OS X still support only file names with a maximum of 31 characters.

 ACTIVE HELPDESK

Organizing Your Computer: File Management

In this Active Helpdesk, you'll play the role of a helpdesk staffer, fielding questions about the desktop, window features, and how the OS helps keep the computer organized.

C:\Documents\HIS182\Term Paper\Illustrations\ACarnegie.jpg

Drive | Primary Folder | Subfolders | File Name | Extension

FIGURE 5.29 Understanding File Paths

Working with Files

How can I move and copy files? Once you've located your file with File Explorer, you can perform many other file-management actions such as opening, copying, moving, renaming, and deleting files. You open a file by double-clicking the file from its storage location. You can copy a file to another location using the Copy command. To move a file from one location to another, use the Cut command. You can access both of these commands easily by right-clicking on a file's name, which displays a shortcut menu.

Where do deleted files go? The **Recycle Bin** is a folder on the desktop, represented by an icon that looks like a recycling bin, where files deleted from the hard drive reside until you permanently purge them from your system. Unfortunately, files deleted from other drives don't go to the Recycle Bin but are deleted from the system immediately. In addition, files stored in the cloud are not cycled through the Recycle Bin. When you delete a file from a thumb drive or a network drive, consider it gone forever!

Mac systems have something similar to the Recycle Bin, called Trash, which is represented by a wastebasket icon. To delete files on a Mac, drag the files to the Trash icon.

How do I permanently delete files from my system? Files placed in the Recycle Bin or the Trash remain in the system until they're permanently deleted. To delete files from the Recycle Bin permanently, select Empty Recycle Bin after right-clicking the desktop icon. On Macs, select Empty Trash from the Finder menu in OS X.

What happens if I need to recover a deleted file? Getting a file back after the Trash has been emptied still may be possible using one of two methods:

- File History is a Windows 8 utility that automatically backs up files (see page 196 for a further explanation of File History) and saves previous versions of files to a designated drive (such as an external hard drive). If you're using File History, you can restore previously deleted files or even previous versions of files you've changed.

- When the Trash is emptied, only the reference to the file is deleted permanently, so the OS has no easy way to find the file. The file data actually remains on the hard drive until it's written over by another file. You may be able to use a program such as FarStone's RestoreIT or Norton Online Backup to try to retrieve files you think you've permanently deleted. These programs reveal files that are still intact on the hard drive and help you recover them. This is how they do it on *CSI*! ■

BITS&BYTES

Save Files in the Cloud Right from Your Apps

When you sign up for a Windows account, you automatically get free storage on OneDrive, Microsoft's cloud storage site. Taking advantage of this free storage space helps ensure that you have files available to you whenever you need them and have access to the Internet.

Fortunately, it's easy to save files to OneDrive in Windows 8. When you use the Save As command in an application, OneDrive shows up as a location (see Figure 5.30) to which you can save files (assuming you're connected to the Internet). So instead of saving your research paper to the Documents folder on your C: drive, save it to a folder called Documents on OneDrive. Initially there won't be any folders in your OneDrive account, but just create any that you need. Using OneDrive will ensure the availability of your files when you need them.

FIGURE 5.30 OneDrive appears as a location in which you can create folders and save files.

utility PROGRAMS

The main component of system software is the OS. However, *utility programs*—small applications that perform special functions on the computer—are also an essential part of system software. Utility programs come in three flavors:

1. Those that are included with the OS (such as System Restore)
2. Those sold as stand-alone programs (such as Norton antivirus)
3. Those offered as freeware (such as anti-malware software like Ad-Aware from Lavasoft)

Figure 5.31 lists some of the various types of utility programs available within the Windows OS as well as some alternatives available as stand-alone programs. In general, the basic utilities designed to manage and tune your computer hardware are incorporated into the OS. The stand-alone utility programs typically offer more features or an easier user interface for backup, security, diagnostic, or recovery functions. For some Windows programs, like Task Manager and Resource Monitor, no good stand-alone alternatives exist.

Display Utilities

How can I change the appearance of my Start screen and desktop? You can personalize the Start screen and the lock screen (the screen that forces you to enter a password to resume using your computer) to suit your tastes.

To do so, display the Charms bar, select Settings, and then choose Personalize. This provides you with access to personalization options such as changing pictures, colors, and backgrounds. This also provides you with access to the features you need to change the appearance of your desktop if you access the Charms bar from that screen.

The Programs and Features Utility

What's the correct way to add new programs to my system? When you download Windows 8 apps from the Windows Store, they automatically install on your computer. If you install non-Windows 8 programs, the program usually automatically runs a *wizard* that walks you through the installation process. If a wizard doesn't start automatically, open the Control Panel, click Programs, then click Programs and Features. This prompts the OS to look for the setup program of the new software, and it starts the installation wizard.

 ACTIVE HELPDESK
Using Utility Programs

In this Active Helpdesk, you'll play the role of a helpdesk staffer, fielding questions about the utility programs included in system software and what these programs do.

FIGURE 5.31

Utility Programs Available Within Windows and as Stand-Alone Programs

WINDOWS UTILITY PROGRAM	STAND-ALONE ALTERNATIVES	WHAT IT DOES
File Explorer File Compression	WinZip, StuffIt	Reduces file size
Disk Cleanup	McAfee Total Protection	Removes unnecessary files from your hard drive
Error-Checking	SeaTools (free download from **seagate.com**)	Checks your hard drive for unnecessary or damaged files
Task Manager and Resource Monitor	None	Displays performance measures for processes; provides information on programs and processes running on your computer
Disk Defragmenter	Norton Utilities, iDefrag	Rearranges files on your hard drive to allow for faster access of files
System Restore	FarStone RestoreIT, Acronis True Image	Restores your system to a previous, stable state
File History, File Recovery	Acronis True Image, Norton Online Backup	Backs up important files, makes a complete mirror image of your current computer setup

In this section, we explore many of the utility programs you'll find installed on a Windows 8 OS. Unless otherwise noted, you can find Windows utilities in the Control Panel. We'll discuss antivirus and personal firewall utility programs in Chapter 9.

File Compression Utilities

Why would I want to use a file compression utility? File compression makes a large file more compact, making it easier and faster for you to send large attachments by e-mail, upload them to the web, or save them onto a disc. As shown in Figure 5.32, Windows has a built-in **file compression utility** that takes out redundancies in a file (zips it) to reduce the file size. You can also obtain several stand-alone freeware and shareware programs, such as WinZip (for Windows) and StuffIt (for Windows or Mac), to compress your files.

How does file compression work? Most compression programs look for repeated patterns of letters and replace these patterns with a shorter placeholder. The repeated patterns and the associated placeholder are cataloged and stored temporarily in a separate file called the *dictionary*. For example,

in the following sentence, you can easily see the repeated patterns of letters.

The rain in Spain falls mainly on the plain.

Although this example contains obvious repeated patterns (ain and the), in a large document, the repeated patterns may be more complex. The compression program's algorithm (a set of instructions designed to complete a solution in a step-by-step manner) therefore runs through the file several times to determine the optimal repeated patterns needed to obtain the greatest compression.

SOUND BYTE
File Compression

In this Sound Byte, you'll learn about the advantages of file compression and how to use Windows to compress and decompress files. This Sound Byte also teaches you how to find and install file compression shareware programs.

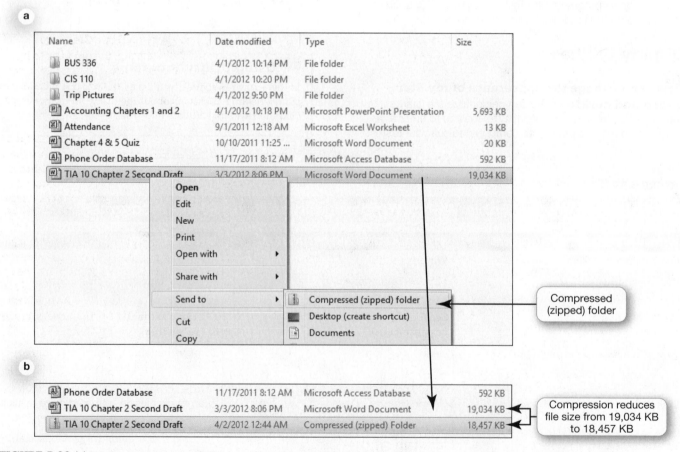

FIGURE 5.32 (a) File compression is a built-in utility of the Windows OS. (b) Compressing the Word document reduces the file size from 19,034 KB to 18,457 KB.
> *To access the Windows file compression utility, right-click the file or folder that you want to compress, select* **Send to** *from the shortcut menu, and then select* **Compressed (zipped) folder**.

STEP 1: Right-click zipped folder

TIA 10 Chapter 2 Second Draft

Open
Open in new window
Pin to Start
Extract All...
Open with...
Share with
Send to

STEP 2: Select Extract All...

Chapter 4 & 5

Extract Compressed (Zipped) Folders

Select a Destination and Extract Files

Files will be extracted to this folder:

C:\Users\Alan\Documents\TIA 10 Chapter 2 Second Draft   Browse...

☐ Show extracted files when complete

STEP 3: Browse to storage location

Libraries ▸ Documents ▸

☆ Favorites
🖥 Desktop
📥 Downloads
📦 Dropbox
📍 Recent places

📚 Libraries
📄 Documents
🎵 Music

Name	Date modified
BUS 336	4/1/2012 10:14 PM
CIS 110	4/1/2012 10:20 PM
TIA 10 Chapter 2 Second Draft	4/2/2012 12:59 AM
Trip Pictures	4/1/2012 9:50 PM
Accounting Chapters 1 and 2	4/1/2012 10:18 PM
Attendance	9/1/2011 12:18 AM
Chapter 4 & 5 Quiz	10/10/2011 11:25 ...
Phone Order Database	11/17/2011 8:12 AM

Extract   Cancel

STEP 4: Extracted file displays in selected location

FIGURE 5.33 The Extraction Wizard in Windows makes unzipping compressed folders and files easy.

How effective are file compression programs?

Current compression programs can reduce text files by 50% or more, depending on the file. However, some files, such as PDF files, already contain a form of compression, so they don't need to be compressed further. Image files such as JPEG, GIF, and PNG files discard small variations in color that the human eye might not pick up. Likewise, MP3 files permanently discard sounds that the human ear can't hear. These graphic and audio files don't need further compression.

How do I decompress a file I've compressed? When

you want to restore the file to its original state, you need to *decompress* the file. Generally, the program you used to compress the file can decompress the file as well (see Figure 5.33).

System Maintenance Utilities

What utilities can make my system work faster?

Disk Cleanup is a Windows utility that removes unnecessary files from your hard drive. These include files that have accumulated in the Recycle Bin as well as temporary files—files created by Windows to store data temporarily while a program is running. Windows usually deletes these temporary files when you exit the program, but sometimes it forgets to do this or doesn't have time because your system freezes or incurs a problem that prevents you from properly exiting a program.

Disk Cleanup also removes temporary Internet files (web pages stored on your hard drive for quick viewing) as well as offline web pages (pages stored on your computer so you can view them without being connected to the Internet). If not deleted periodically, these unnecessary files can slow down your computer.

How can I control which files Disk Cleanup

deletes? When you run Disk Cleanup, the program scans your hard drive to determine which folders have files that can be deleted and calculates the amount of hard drive space that will be freed up by doing so. You check off which type of files you would like to delete, as shown in Figure 5.34.

How can I diagnose potential errors or damage on

my hard drive? Error-checking is a Windows utility that checks for lost files and fragments as well as physical errors on your hard drive. Lost files and fragments of files occur as you save, resave, move, delete, and copy files on your hard drive. Sometimes the system becomes confused, leaving references on the **file allocation table**, or **FAT** (an index of all sector numbers in a table), to files that no longer exist or have been moved. Physical errors on the hard drive occur when the mechanism that reads the hard drive's data (which is stored as *1*s or *0*s) can no longer determine whether the area holds a *1* or a *0*. These areas are called *bad sectors*. Sometimes Error-checking can recover the lost data, but more often, it deletes the files that are taking up space.

Error-checking also makes a note of any bad sectors so that the system won't use them again to store data. To locate Error-checking in Windows 8.1, display File Explorer, right-click the disk you want to diagnose, select Properties, and select the Tools tab. On Macs, you can use the Disk Utility to test and repair disks. Disk Utility is located in the Utilities subfolder in the Applications folder on your hard drive.

How can I check on a program that's stopped

running? If a program has stopped working, you can use the Windows **Task Manager** utility (see Figure 5.35) to check on the program or to exit the nonresponsive program.

FIGURE 5.34 Using Disk Cleanup will help free space on your hard drive.
> *Disk Cleanup is accessed by displaying File Explorer, right-clicking on the disk you wish to clean, selecting **Properties** from the shortcut menu, and then clicking the **Disk Cleanup** button on the General tab.*

In Windows 8.1, the Processes tab of Task Manager lists all the programs you're using and indicates their status. "Not responding" will be shown next to a program that stopped improperly. If the status section is blank (Figure 5.35), then the program is working normally. You can terminate programs that aren't responding by right-clicking the app name and selecting End Task from the shortcut menu.

System Restore and Backup Utilities

Is there an undo command for the system? Suppose you've just installed a new software program and your computer freezes. After rebooting the computer, when you try to start the application, the system freezes once again. You uninstall the new program, but your computer continues to freeze after rebooting. What can you do now?

SOUND BYTE
Hard Disk Anatomy

In this Sound Byte, you'll watch a series of animations that show various aspects of a hard drive, including the anatomy of a hard drive, how a computer reads and writes data to a hard drive, and the fragmenting and defragmenting of a hard drive.

FIGURE 5.35 You can use Windows 8.1 Task Manager to close nonresponsive programs.
> *Task Manager is accessed by holding down **Ctrl**, **Alt**, and **Del** or by right-clicking on the taskbar at the bottom of the desktop.*

Disk defragmenting programs group together related pieces of files on the hard drive, allowing the OS to work more efficiently. To understand how disk defragmenter utilities work, you first need to understand the basics of how a hard disk drive stores files. A hard disk drive is composed of several platters, or round, thin plates of metal, covered with a special magnetic coating that records the data. The platters are about 3.5 inches in diameter and are stacked onto a spindle. There are usually two or three platters in any hard disk drive, with data stored on one or both sides. Data is recorded on hard disks in concentric circles called **tracks**. Each track is further broken down into pie-shaped wedges, each called a **sector** (see Figure 5.36). The data is further identified by **clusters**, which are the smallest segments within the sectors.

FIGURE 5.36 On a hard disk platter, data is recorded onto tracks, which are further divided into sectors and clusters.

When you want to save (or write) a file, the bits that make up your file are recorded onto one or more clusters of the drive. To keep track of which clusters hold which files, the drive also stores an index of all sector numbers in a table. To save a file, the computer looks in the table for clusters that aren't already being used. It then records the file information on those clusters. When you open (or read) a file, the computer searches through the table for the clusters that hold the desired file and reads that file. Similarly, when you delete a file, you're actually not deleting the file itself but rather the reference in the table to the file.

So, how does a disk become fragmented? When only part of an older file is deleted, the deleted section of the file creates a gap in the sector of the disk where the data was originally stored. In the same way, when new information is added to an older file, there may not be

FIGURE 5.37 Defragmenting the hard drive arranges file fragments so that they are located next to each other. This makes the hard drive run more efficiently.

space to save the new information sequentially near where the file was originally saved. In that case, the system writes the added part of the file to the next available location on the disk, and a reference is made in the table as to the location of this file fragment. Over time, as files are saved, deleted, and modified, the bits of information for various files fall out of order and the disk becomes fragmented.

Disk fragmentation is a problem because the OS isn't as efficient when a disk is fragmented. It takes longer to locate a whole file because more of the disk must be searched for the various pieces, slowing down your computer.

Defragmenting tools take the hard drive through a defragmentation process in which pieces of files scattered over the disk are placed together and arranged sequentially on it. Also, any unused portions of clusters that were too small to save data in before are grouped, increasing the available storage space on the disk. Figure 5.37 shows before and after shots of a fragmented disk that has gone through the defragmentation process.

The disk defragmentation utility in Windows 8 is set by default to automatically defragment the hard drive on a regular basis. Macs don't have a defragmentation utility built into the system. Those users who feel the need to defragment their Mac can use iDefrag, an external program from Coriolis Systems.

For more about hard disks and defragmenting, check out the Sound Byte "Hard Disk Anatomy."

Windows has a utility called **System Restore** that lets you roll your system settings back to a specific date when everything was working properly. A **system restore point**, which is a snapshot of your entire system's settings, is generated prior to certain events, such as installing or updating software, or automatically once a week if no other restore points were created in that time. You also can create a restore point manually at any time.

Should problems occur, if the computer was running just fine before you installed new software or a hardware device, you could restore your computer to the settings that were in effect before the software or hardware installation (see Figure 5.38). System Restore doesn't affect your personal data files (such as Word documents or e-mail), so you won't lose changes made to these files.

How can I protect my data in the event something malfunctions in my system? When you use the Windows 8.1 **File History** utility, you can have Windows automatically create a duplicate of your libraries, desktop, contacts, and favorites and copy it to another storage device, such as an external hard drive (see Figure 5.39). A backup copy protects your data in the event your hard drive fails or files are accidentally erased. File History also keeps copies of different versions of your files. This means that if you need to go back to the second draft of your history term paper, even though you are now on your fifth draft, File History should allow you to recover it. File History needs to be turned on by the user and requires an external hard drive (or network drive) that is always connected to the computer to function.

Windows 8 also includes recovery tools that allow you to complete backups of your entire system (system image) that you can later restore in the event of a major hard drive crash.

OS X includes a backup utility called Time Machine that automatically backs up your files to a specified location. Apple also offers backup hardware called Time Capsules, which are hard disk drives with wireless connectivity, designed to work with Time Machine and record your backup data. Because Time Machine makes a complete image copy of your system, it can also be used to recover your system in the case of a fatal error. (For more information on backing up your files, see Chapter 9.)

Accessibility Utilities

What utilities are designed for users with special needs? Microsoft Windows includes an Ease of Access Center, which is a centralized location for assistive technology and tools to adjust accessibility settings. In the Ease of

SOUND BYTE
Letting Your Computer Clean Up After Itself

In this Sound Byte, you'll learn how to use the various maintenance utilities within the OS. You'll also learn why maintenance tasks should be done on a routine basis to make your system more efficient.

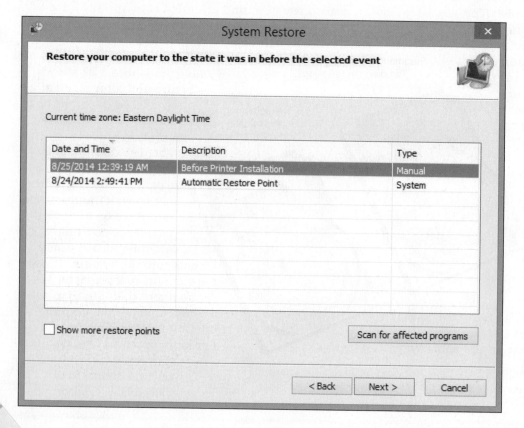

FIGURE 5.38 This System Restore Wizard shows both a restore point set manually by a user and one that was created automatically by Windows before a backup was run. Setting a restore point is good practice before installing any hardware or software.
> *The System Restore Wizard is found by right-clicking the* **Start** *button, choosing* **System**, *selecting the* **System Protection** *link, and then clicking the* **System Restore** *button. The* **System Restore Wizard** *appears, with the restore points shown on the second page of the Wizard.*

FIGURE 5.39 Windows 8.1 File History set up to back up files to an external hard drive.

>*To access File History, display the Charms bar, choose* **Settings**, *select* **Change PC settings**, *choose* **Update and recovery**, *and then select* **File History**.

Access Center, which is accessible from the Control Panel, you can find the tools to help users with disabilities, shown in Figure 5.40. The tools shown in the figure are just a sampling of the available tools. If you're not sure where to start or what settings might help, a questionnaire asks you about routine tasks and provides a personalized recommendation for settings that will help you better use your computer.

Whether you use Windows, OS X, Linux, or another operating system, a fully featured OS is available to meet your needs. As long as you keep the operating system updated and regularly use the available utilities to fine-tune your system, you should experience little trouble from your OS. ■

Before moving on to the Chapter Review:
- **Watch Replay Video 5.2** ▷ .
- **Then check your understanding of what you've learned so far.**

FIGURE 5.40

Windows Ease of Access Tools

MAGNIFIER	NARRATOR
• Creates a separate window that displays a magnified portion of the screen	• Reads what is on screen • Can read the contents of a window, menu options, or text you have typed

SPEECH RECOGNITION	ON-SCREEN KEYBOARD	HIGH CONTRAST
• Allows you to dictate text and control your computer by voice	• Allows you to type with a pointing device	• Color schemes invert screen colors for vision-impaired individuals
		Easier to Read!

(Imagery Majestic/Fotolia; Anatoly Maslennikov/Fotolia; Gilles Lougassi/Fotolia)

>*The Ease of Access Center is found by accessing the Control Panel and clicking* **Ease of Access**.

check your understanding // review & practice

For a quick review to see what you've learned so far, answer the following questions. Visit **pearsonhighered.com/techinaction** to check your answers.

multiple choice

1. Which of the following is NOT considered to be a utility program?

   a. Internet Explorer

   b. Disk Cleanup

   c. Task Manager

   d. System Restore

2. The process of adding a Windows 8 app to the Start screen is known as

   a. clipping.

   b. visualizing.

   c. pinning.

   d. screening.

3. The Windows app used for locating files and folders is

   a. Disk Manager.   **c.** File Explorer.

   b. Finder.   **d.** Library Explorer.

4. Which of the following is NOT a common file name extension?

   a. .docx

   b. .jpg

   c. .pptx

   d. .zipped

5. The _____ utility can free up space on the hard drive.

   a. Task Manager

   b. Disk Cleanup

   c. System Refresh

   d. File Explorer

To take an autograded version of this review, please go to the companion website at **pearsonhighered.com/techinaction**, or go your MyITLab course.

Continue

5 Chapter Review

Operating System Fundamentals

1. What software is included in system software?

- System software is the set of software programs that helps run the computer and coordinates instructions between application software and hardware devices. It consists of the operating system (OS) and utility programs.
- The OS controls how your computer system functions.
- Utility programs are programs that perform general housekeeping tasks for the computer, such as system maintenance and file compression.

2. What are the different kinds of operating systems?

- There are many different kinds of operating systems.
- Real-time operating systems (RTOSs) require no user intervention.
- A multiuser operating system (network operating system) provides access to a computer system by more than one user at a time.
- Smartphones have their own specific operating systems, which allow the user to multitask.
- Tablets use operating systems that allow interaction with touch-screen interfaces.
- Gaming consoles use operating systems developed specifically for those particular devices.

3. What are the most common operating systems?

- Microsoft Windows is the most popular OS. The most recent release is Windows 8.1.
- Another popular OS is the Mac OS, which is designed to work on Apple computers.
- Linux is an open source OS based on UNIX and designed primarily for use on personal computers.

What the Operating System Does

4. How does the operating system provide a means for users to interact with the computer?

- The OS provides a user interface that enables users to interact with the computer.
- Most OSs today use a graphical user interface (GUI). Common features of GUIs include windows, menus, and icons.

5. How does the operating system help manage resources such as the processor, memory, storage, hardware, and peripheral devices?

- When the OS allows you to perform more than one task at a time, it is multitasking. To provide for seamless multitasking, the OS controls the timing of the events on which the processor works.
- As the OS coordinates the activities of the processor, it uses RAM as a temporary storage area for instructions and data the processor needs. The OS is therefore responsible for coordinating the space allocations in RAM to ensure that there is enough space for the waiting instructions and data. If there isn't sufficient space in RAM for all the data and instructions, then the OS allocates the least necessary files to temporary storage on the hard drive, called *virtual memory*.
- The OS manages storage by providing a file-management system that keeps track of the names and locations of files and programs.
- Programs called *device drivers* facilitate communication between devices attached to the computer and the OS.

6. How does the operating system interact with application software?

- All software applications need to interact with the CPU. For programs to work with the CPU, they must contain code that the CPU recognizes.
- Rather than having the same blocks of code appear in each application, the OS includes the blocks of code to which software applications refer. These blocks of code are called *application programming interfaces* (APIs).

The Boot Process: Starting Your Computer

7. How does the operating system help the computer start up?

- When you start your computer, it runs through a special process called the *boot process*.
- The boot process consists of four basic steps: (1) The basic input/output system (BIOS) is activated when the user powers on the CPU. (2) In the POST check, the BIOS verifies that all attached devices are in place. (3) The OS is loaded into RAM. (4) Configuration and customization settings are checked.

The Windows Interface

8. What are the main features of the Windows interface?

- In Windows 8, the Start screen provides your first interaction with the OS and with access to your computer's apps, tools, and commonly used programs.
- The Windows 8 interface is designed for touch-screen devices.
- Windows 8 apps run full screen and feature commands hidden in app bars.
- Non-Windows 8 programs run on the desktop.

Organizing Your Computer: File Management

9. How does the operating system help me keep my computer organized?

- The OS allows you to organize the contents of your computer in a hierarchical structure of directories that includes files, folders, libraries, and drives.

- File Explorer helps you manage your files and folders by showing the location and contents of every drive, folder, and file on your computer.
- Creating folders is the key to organizing files.

Utility Programs

10. What utility programs are included in system software and what do they do?

- Some utility programs are incorporated into the OS; others are sold as stand-alone off-the-shelf programs.
- Common Windows utilities include those that enable you to adjust your display, add or remove programs, compress files, clean unnecessary files off your system, check for lost files and errors, restore your system to an earlier setting, back up your files, and check on programs that have stopped running.

> Be sure to check out the companion website for additional materials to help you review and learn, including a Tech Bytes Weekly newsletter—**pearsonhighered.com/techinaction**. And don't forget the Replay Videos ▷ .

key terms//

chapter assessment // quiz

For a quick review to see what you've learned, answer the following questions. Submit the quiz as requested by your instructor. If you are using MyITLab, the quiz is also available there.

multiple choice

1. Which of the following is an OS that is NOT used on tablet computers?

   a. iOS

   b. BlackBerry

   c. Android

   d. Windows

2. Borrowing hard drive space to optimize RAM storage is known as

   a. authentication.

   b. virtual memory.

   c. paging.

   d. multitasking.

3. An example of an open source OS is

   a. Windows.

   b. OS X.

   c. Linux.

   d. DOS.

4. Which of the following is not considered an accessibility utility?

   a. System Restore

   b. Magnifier

   c. Narrator

   d. Speech Recognition

5. Apps specifically designed for Windows 8.1

   a. run on the desktop.

   b. run full screen.

   c. can't be closed down once started.

   d. use a large amount of RAM.

6. The Windows app used for file management is

   a. Disk Manager.

   b. Task Manager.

   c. File Explorer.

   d. Library Explorer.

true–false

_____ **1.** Different versions of Linux are known as "distros."

_____ **2.** The third step of the boot process is the power-on self-test (POST).

_____ **3.** System restore points can only be created by Windows automatically on a regular schedule.

_____ **4.** The Windows 8 desktop no longer includes the taskbar.

critical thinking

1. **Protecting Embedded Systems**

   As more devices and appliances make use of RTOSs, the necessity of protecting them from hackers becomes increasingly critical. Developers are working to improve the security of the software and to safeguard communications between such devices. How concerned are you about the security of RTOSs in cars, smart homes, and wearable technology? Is enough being done to ensure the safety of these devices? What else could be done?

2. **Ease of Access**

   Windows 8 and Mac OS X both include a number of features and utilities designed for users with special needs. Compare the offerings of each OS. Are there options offered by one OS that are not available in the other? Which OS do you think has the best selection? Can you think of any areas that have not been addressed by this assistive technology? Research software from third-party developers to see if there are other tools that would also be useful. Should these tools be included in the OS? Why or why not?

team time //

Choosing the Best OS

Problem

You're the owner of a technology consulting firm. Your current assignments include advising start-up clients on their technology requirements. The companies include a nonprofit social service organization, a small interior design firm, and a social media advertising agency. Obviously, one of the critical decisions for each company is the choice of OS.

Task

Recommend the appropriate OS for each company.

Process

1. Break up into teams that represent the three primary operating systems: Windows, Mac, or Linux.
2. As a team, research the pros and cons of your OS. What features does it have that would benefit each

company? What features does it not have that each company would need? Why would your OS be the appropriate (or inappropriate) choice for each company?

3. Develop a presentation that states your position with regard to your OS. Your presentation should have a recommendation and include facts to back it up.
4. As a class, decide which OS would be the best choice for each company.

Conclusion

Because the OS is the most critical piece of software in the computer system, the selection should not be taken lightly. The OS that is best for a nonprofit social service organization may not be best for an interior design firm. A social media advertising agency may have different needs altogether. It is important to make sure you consider all aspects of the work environment and the type of work being done to ensure a good fit.

ethics project //

OS Upgrades

In this exercise, you'll research and then role-play a complicated ethical situation. The role you play may or may not match your own personal beliefs, but your research and use of logic will enable you to represent whichever view is assigned. An arbitrator will watch and comment on both sides of the arguments, and together, the team will agree on an ethical solution.

Problem

Software developers spend millions of dollars developing new versions of their OS products. Developers argue that new OS versions are needed to meet consumer demands for popular features. Consumers, however, often resent the constant cycle of upgrades, which require them to learn the new features and pay for new software. Most schools feel they need to teach the current version of an OS but sometimes can't afford the upgrades.

Research Areas to Consider

- Windows 8 features vs. Windows 7 features
- Software licensing agreements
- Costs for Windows 8 upgrades
- Costs for adding touch-screens to existing desktop computers

Process

1. Divide the class into teams.
2. Research the areas cited above and devise a scenario in which a college is considering upgrading to Windows 8 from Windows 7 and needs to justify an increase in student fees to accomplish the upgrade.
3. Team members should write a summary that provides background information for their character—for example, representative of Microsoft, student, parent, teacher, or arbitrator—and that details their character's behaviors to set the stage for the role-playing event. Then, team members should create an outline to use during the role-playing event.
4. Team members should present their case to the class or submit a PowerPoint presentation for review by the rest of the class, along with the summary and resolution they developed.

Conclusion

As technology becomes ever more prevalent and integrated into our lives, more and more ethical dilemmas will present themselves. Being able to understand and evaluate both sides of the argument, while responding in a personally or socially ethical manner, will be an important skill.

Mobile Operating Systems: Changing Market Share

Using Excel 2013, you will display the market share statistics of both mobile and desktop operating systems using line, column, and pie charts.

You will use the following skills as you complete this activity:	
• Create a Line Chart	• Add Shape to Chart
• Create and Format a Pie Chart	• Insert Sparklines
• Create and Format a Column Chart	

Instructions:

1. Open *TIA_Ch5_Start* and save as **TIA_Ch5_LastFirst.**

2. In cell B3 type **2011**. Create a line chart from the range A3:E9. Modify the chart as follows:

   a. Add a title: **Change in Mobile OS Market Share 2011–2014**. *2011–2014* should be on a separate line. Change the font size of *2011–2014* to 10.

   b. Move the chart to a separate worksheet. Rename the new worksheet **Line Chart**, and place after the Data worksheet.

   c. Filter out the *Symbian and Others* data so only *Android*, *iOS*, *Windows*, and *Blackberry* data displays.

   e. Add a **Line Callout 1** shape to the chart with the line pointing between the 2013 and 2014 Android data. Add text to the callout: **Looks like Android market share will surpass iOS market share in 2015.**

   Hint: Line Callout 1 is in the Callouts section in the Insert Shape group on the FORMAT CHART TOOLS tab.

3. Create a pie chart from the ranges A3:A9 and E3:E9.

   Hint: Use the CTRL button to select non-adjacent ranges. Modify the chart as follows:

   a. Add a title: **2014 Mobile OS Market Share**

   b. Use **Quick Layout 1** to add data % and Series data labels to each data point.

   c. Resize the chart so it fits in the range A14:H30.

4. Create a clustered column chart that compares just Android and iOS data for 2011-2014. Modify the chart as follows:

   a. Add a title: **Android vs. iOS Market Share**

   b. Format the chart with **Style 8**.

   c. Move the chart to a separate worksheet. Rename the new worksheet **Column Chart**, and place it after the *Line Chart* worksheet.

5. Add a **Line Sparkline** to cell F4 using the data in range B4:E4. Using the **Fill Handle**, copy the Sparkline to range F5:F9. Add a **High Point** to each Sparkline.

6. **Save** the document and submit based on your instructor's directions.

Information Technology Ethics

The ethical choices we make have a far-reaching impact on our lives. In this Technology in Focus feature, we examine how technology and ethics affect each other. We'll discuss several key issues related to technology and ethics, including the following:

- Social justice
- Intellectual property
- Privacy
- E-commerce
- Electronic communication
- Computer abuse

But first, let's get started by asking an important question: What is ethics?

What Is Ethics?

Ethics is the study of the general nature of morals and of the specific moral choices individuals make. Morals involve conforming to established or accepted ideas of right and wrong (as generally dictated by society) and are usually viewed as being black or white. Ethical issues often involve subtle distinctions, such as the difference between fairness and equity. Ethical principles are the guidelines you use to make decisions each day.

For example, say you stop to use a photocopier on campus. You discover a copy of the upcoming final exam for your psychology course that your teacher left behind. Do you give it back to your professor without looking at the questions? Do you share it with your friends so you can all get good grades on the final? Do you give a copy to your friend who really needs to pass the course in order to prevent losing his or her financial aid?

Doesn't everyone have the same basic ethics?
There are many systems of ethical conduct. Figure 1 lists the five major ethical systems.

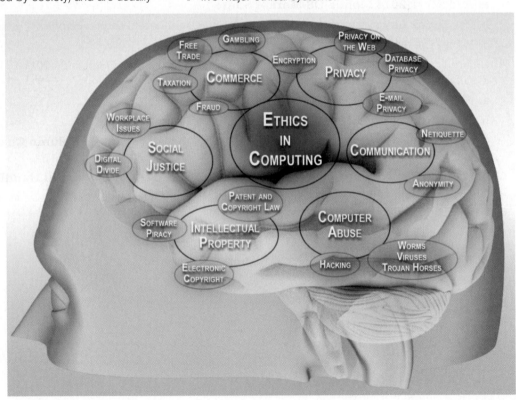

FIGURE 1

Systems of Ethics

ETHICAL SYSTEM	BASIC TENETS	EXAMPLES
Relativism	• No universal moral truth • Moral principles dictated by cultural tastes and customs	Topless bathing is prevalent in Europe but generally banned on public beaches in the United States
Divine Command Theory	• God is all-knowing and sets moral standards • Conforming to God's law is right; breaking it is wrong	Christians believe in rules such as the Ten Commandments
Utilitarianism	• Actions are judged solely by consequences • Actions that generate greater happiness are judged to be better than actions that lead to unhappiness • Individual happiness is not important—consider the greater good	Using weapons of mass destruction ends a war sooner and therefore saves lives otherwise destroyed by conventional fighting
Virtue Ethics	• Morals are internal • Strive to be a person who behaves well spontaneously	A supervisor views the person who volunteered to clean up a park as a better person than the workers who are there because of court-ordered community service
Deontology (Duty-Based)	• Focus on adherence to moral duties and rights • Morals should apply to everyone equally	Human rights (like freedom of religion) should be respected for all people because human rights should be applied universally

Aren't laws meant to guide people's ethical actions? Laws are formal, written standards designed to apply to everyone. Laws are enforced by government agencies and interpreted by the courts. However, it's impossible to pass laws that cover every possible behavior in which humans can engage. Therefore, ethics provide a general set of unwritten guidelines for people to follow.

Is unethical behavior the same as illegal behavior? Unethical behavior isn't necessarily illegal. Take the death penalty. In many U.S. states, putting convicted criminals to death for certain crimes is legal. However, many people consider it unethical to execute a human for any reason.

Not all illegal behavior is unethical, though. Civil disobedience, which is manifested by intentionally refusing to obey certain laws, is used as a form of protest to effect change. Gandhi's nonviolent resistance to the British rule of India, which led to India's establishment as an independent country, is an example of civil disobedience. Is it ever ethical for one country to control another country's people?

Note that there is also a difference between *unethical* behavior and *amoral* behavior:

- *Unethical behavior* can be defined as not conforming to a set of approved standards of behavior. For instance, using your phone to text message a test answer to your friend during an exam is unethical.

- *Amoral behavior* occurs when a person has no sense of right and wrong and no interest in the moral consequences of his or her actions, such as when a murderer shows no remorse for his or her crime.

Which system of ethics works best? There is no universal agreement on which is the best system of ethics. Most societies use a blend of different systems. Regardless of the ethical system of the society in which you live, all ethical decisions are greatly influenced by personal ethics.

Personal Ethics

What are personal ethics? Every day you say and do certain things, and each time, you're making decisions. As you choose your words and actions, you're following a set of **personal ethics**—a set of formal or informal ethical principles you use to make decisions in your life. Some people have a clear, well-defined set of principles they follow.

FIGURE 2 It would be nice if there were signposts to ethical conduct, but the issues are complex. *(IQoncept/Shutterstock)*

Others' ethics are inconsistent or are applied differently in different situations.

It can be challenging to adhere to your own ethical principles if the consequences of your decisions might lead to an unhappy result. For example, to get the job of your dreams, should you say on your résumé that you've already finished your degree, even though you're still one credit short? Is this lying? Is such behavior justified in this setting? After all, you do intend to finish that last credit, and you would work really hard for this company if you were hired. If you tell the truth and state that you haven't finished college yet, you might be passed over for the position. Making this choice is an ethical decision (see Figure 2).

How do a person's ethics develop? Naturally, your family plays a major role in establishing the values you cherish in your own life, and these might include a cultural bias toward certain ethical positions (see Figure 3). Your religious affiliation is another major influence on your ethics because most religions have established codes of ethical conduct. How these sets of ethics interact with the values of the larger culture is often challenging. Issues such as abortion, the death penalty, and war often create conflict between personal ethical systems and the larger society's established legal–ethical system.

As you mature, your life experiences also affect your personal ethics. Does the behavior you see around you make sense within the ethical principles that your family, your church, or your first-grade teacher taught you? Has your experience led you to abandon some ethical rules and adopt others? Have you modified how and when you apply these laws of conduct depending on what's at stake?

What if I'm not sure what my personal ethics are? When you have a clear idea of what values are important to you, it may be easier to handle situations in your life that demand ethical action. Follow these steps to help define a list of personal values:

1. **Describe yourself.** Write down words that describe who you are, based on how others view you. Would a friend describe you as honest, or helpful, or kind? These keywords will give you a hint as to the values and behaviors that are important to you.

2. **List the key principles you believe in.** Make a list of the key principles that influence your decisions. For example, would you be comfortable working in a lab that used animals for medical research? If not, is it because

FIGURE 3 Many different forces shape your personal ethics. *(Noam Armonn/Shutterstock; Rachel Donahue/Getty Images; Rob Marmion/Shutterstock; Shutterstock)*

you value protecting any living being? How important is it to you that you never tell a lie? Or do you feel it is kind to lie in some situations? List the key ideas you believe to be important in conducting your life. Do you always behave this way, or are you "flexible"? Are there situations in which your answers might change (say, if the medical research was to cure cancer or the lie was to protect someone's feelings)?

3. **Identify external influences.** Where did your key principles come from—your parents? Your friends? Spiritual advisors? Television and movies? You may want to question some of your beliefs once you actually identify where they came from.

4. **Consider "why."** After writing down your beliefs, think about *why* you believe them. Have you accepted them without investigation? Do they stand up in the context of your real-world experiences?

5. **Prepare a statement of values.** Distill what you have written into a short statement. By having a well-defined statement of the values you hold most important in your own life, which you can refer to in times of challenge, it will be easier for you to make ethical decisions.

What are the benefits to ethical living? Society has established its own set of rules of conduct in the form of laws. Ignoring or being inconsistent in following these rules can have an immediate impact. And more and more research is showing

the health benefits of ethical living. When your day-to-day decisions are in conflict with your ethical principles, you often develop stress and anger.

Perhaps even happiness itself is a result of living ethically (see Figure 4). **Positive psychology** is a new focus in the field of psychology. Pioneered by Dr. Martin Seligman of the University of Pennsylvania, this field works to discover the *causes* of happiness instead of addressing the treatment of mental dysfunctions. Dr. Seligman's research has shown that by identifying your personal strengths and values and then aligning your life so that you can apply them every day, you can be happier (and suffer less depression)—an effect equivalent to that of antidepressant medication and therapy. Thus, finding a way to identify and then apply your ethics and values to your daily life can impact your health and happiness.

Personal Ethics and Your Work Life

How do employers affect personal ethics? You may have a set of personal ethics that guide your behavior, but do your ethics change when you go to work? Of course, your employer expects you to follow the rules of conduct established for the business. However, this doesn't mean you need to blindly follow corporate practices that you feel are unethical or detrimental to society (see Figure 5).

Cheating
Stealing
Selfishness
Lying

Generosity
Honesty
Trust

FIGURE 4 The field of positive psychology shows that living and working ethically affects your happiness. *(Shutterstock; Shutterstock)*

If you spot unethical behavior at your company, what do you do? Whistle-blowers are people who report businesses to regulatory agencies for committing illegal acts or who expose unethical (but still legal) acts committed by their employers by publicizing unethical behavior through

FIGURE 5 How should you respond if you see people in authority at work behaving unethically? *(Corbis)*

various media outlets. The Sarbanes–Oxley Act of 2002 requires companies to provide mechanisms for employees and third parties to report complaints, including ethics violations, anonymously. In addition, many businesses are using their websites to allow whistle-blowers to report wrongdoing anonymously, replacing previously used e-mail and telephone hotline systems, which did not shield employees from being identified. With an online system, it's easier for a company to sort and classify complaints and designate them for appropriate action.

Should your employer have control over your conduct outside of the office? Do behavior, integrity, and honesty off the job relate to job performance? They might. But even if they don't, from your employer's perspective, your actions could reflect poorly on your employer. Consider the employee of Memorial Hermann Southeast (a Houston hospital) who was fired from her job after making an allegedly racist comment about the unrest in Ferguson, Missouri, on her Facebook page. The hospital administration felt that her comment was contrary to the hospital's mission of serving all members of the community. Therefore, although your ethics might dictate one mode of behavior, you need to consider how your employer might view your actions.

How does making ethical choices in a business setting differ from making personal ethical choices? Most personal ethical decisions involve few people. However, before making an ethical choice for a business, you need to consider the effect your choice will have on all of the business's stakeholders. **Stakeholders** are those people or entities who are affected by the operations of a business. Typical business stakeholders include customers, suppliers, employees, investors (shareholders), financial lenders, and society at large.

For instance, suppose you decide to cut costs in your restaurant by hiring workers "off the books" by paying them in cash. Although doing so might boost profits in the short term, the long-term impact on stakeholders can be severe. If you're caught avoiding paying payroll taxes by paying workers in cash, fines will be levied against your business, which may cause investors to lose money and may affect the company's ability to repay lenders. The negative publicity from being caught doing something illegal may cause a downturn in business, which, in turn, might force layoffs of employees or even closure of the business. Your simple decision on cutting costs isn't as simple as it may seem.

In summary, in a business environment, your behavior is guided by the ethical principles defined by the business owner or management, but you're ultimately guided by your own personal ethics.

Technology and Ethics: How One Affects the Other

Because technology moves faster than rules can be formulated to govern it, how technology is used is often left up to the individual and the guidance of his or her personal ethics. In the rest of this Technology in Focus feature, we explore situations in which ethics and technology affect each other: social justice (brain technology), intellectual property (international piracy), privacy (personal privacy and technology), e-commerce (geolocation), electronic communication (free speech), and computer abuse (cyberbullying).

Ethical considerations are never clear-cut. They're complex, and reasonable people can have different, yet equally valid, views. We present alternative viewpoints in each setting for you to consider and discuss. Figure 6 summarizes the issues we'll be discussing.

FIGURE 6

Ethics in Computing

TOPIC	ETHICAL DISCUSSION	DEBATE ISSUE
Social justice	Should the ethics of robotic systems be programmable by individuals?	Should manufacturers, the government, or individuals set the ethical parameters of robotic systems?
Intellectual property	Do entire countries support software piracy?	Can we impose our values and intellectual property laws on the world?
Privacy	Can employers peer into your personal profiles on social media sites?	Should personal privacy be protected?
E-commerce	Do geolocation devices and applications threaten privacy?	Do the benefits of geolocation devices and applications outweigh the risks?
Electronic communication	When does big business limit free speech?	Should companies allow the Chinese government to dictate when to curtail free speech?
Computer abuse	Whose responsibility is it to monitor cyberbullying?	Should parents bear all the responsibility of monitoring cyberbullying, or should it be in the hands of public officials?

SOCIAL JUSTICE

Who Sets the Ethics for Robots?

Summary of the Issue

The rise of the Internet of Things means that more embedded computers and robotics are being included in devices every year. Personal robots in households are not far off. But who controls the ethical constraints by which robotic machinery operates?

Automobiles now contain sophisticated robotic systems to exercise control over the vehicle and respond faster than humans can. Using radar, accident-avoidance systems can apply the brakes and even change lanes to help drivers avoid accidents. In the coming years, these systems may exercise even more control of your vehicle.

Consider this scenario: You come up over the crest of a hill. A school bus is disabled in your lane and you are traveling too fast to brake in time to avoid hitting it. To the left is a lane of oncoming traffic. To the right is a large grove of trees. A robotic system controlling your car has three options: (1) Apply the brakes to slow the vehicle. You will hit the school bus but at a lower speed. You will survive, but some occupants of the bus may be killed. (2) Swerve to the left into oncoming traffic to avoid hitting the school bus. You may hit another car, but the risk of loss of human life is limited to just the occupants of two vehicles. (3) Swerve to the right into the trees. Only you are at risk of being killed if your car hits a tree. So which scenario does the robotic system controlling your car choose?

At this point, automobile manufacturers program robotic devices when they build the cars. But should owners have a choice of overriding the programming in their vehicles and adjust the ethical parameters of the robotic systems? If an owner was selfless, he or she could program the car to always make decisions that resulted in less harm to others (option 3 above). Alternatively, he or she could program the car to choose option 1, which minimizes his or her chance of injury.

And what would you as a manufacturer do until laws are passed regarding robotic ethics? If you program the car to protect the driver's life at all costs and the accident described above results in children on the bus dying, you could be sued by the families of the bus occupants. On the other hand, if you programmed the car to minimize harm to others, you could be sued by the driver's family when the car swerves into the woods and crashes into a tree killing the driver.

What is best for society as a whole? The answer is not very clear cut but is one we will need to wrestle with in the coming years.

Questions to Think About and Research

1. Who should be responsible for controlling the ethics of robotic systems? Why?
2. If a collision avoidance system in an automobile takes control of the vehicle to avoid an accident and a death results, who is responsible—human or machine?
3. When do the benefits of robotic controls outweigh the risks of the technology taking ethical decisions out of the hands of human beings?
4. Does relying on robots to make ethical decisions make us less human?

POINT

Individuals Should Have the Right to Set Ethics for Robotic Systems They Own

Advocates of individual choice over robotic ethics feel that just as individuals are free to make choices in their own lives, these choices should be extended to robots that they own.

1. Society dictates what is legal and illegal by passing laws. As long as choices over robotic ethics don't violate laws, they should be in the hands of individual owners.

2. Individuals should have the right to set ethical parameters for their robots because they may wish to be even more selfless than society dictates (i.e., by having the robots protect other people's lives, even at the cost of their own life).

3. When devices such as automobiles don't have robotic systems, individuals make ethical decisions in times of crisis. Robotic systems should be an extension of the individual's ethical values.

COUNTERPOINT

Robotic Ethics Should Be Controlled by the Government or Manufacturers

Critics maintain that individuals cannot be trusted to make decisions on robotic ethics that will benefit society as a whole. The greater good is served by making universal ethics programming decisions at the point of manufacture.

1. If robots do not contain ethical constraints that prevent harm to human beings, human lives may be lost.

2. Robots must have ethical programming that allows them to make decisions regarding the best possible outcomes in life and death situations.

3. Allowing individuals to adjust the ethics of robotic devices exposes society to risks from careless, thoughtless, or psychotic individuals.

FIGURE 7 Who should set the ethics for robotic systems? Individuals? Manufacturers? The government? *(Dolphfyn/Alamy)*

INTELLECTUAL PROPERTY

International Pirates

Summary of the Issue

Intellectual property (such as music, writing, and software) is protected by copyright law. But there have been challenges in enforcing these standards in other countries. What happens to fair trade if some countries refuse to enforce copyright laws? How should the trade partners of these countries respond?

The Business Software Alliance estimated that in 2013, 69% of computers in the Philippines and 74% of the computers in China ran on pirated software. For comparison, the estimated piracy levels in the United States and Sweden are 18% and 23%, respectively. This discrepancy means that many businesses in the Philippines and China don't have to spend money for operating system or productivity software, which gives them an advantage in the international marketplace. Although some companies, like Microsoft, continue to do business in China and the Philippines despite the high levels of piracy, smaller companies often can't survive there. For example, Tom Adams, chief executive of Rosetta Stone, pulled his company and its language training software products out of China. He describes China as a "kleptocratic society" and worries about the amount of theft of his software in that environment.

In fact, the chief executives of 12 major software companies—Microsoft, Adobe, Autodesk, Symantec, and others—have lobbied the U.S. administration and lawmakers to continue to put pressure on China to crack down on illegal copying. With a potential market of more than one billion people, and an increasing number of technology-hungry purchasers, companies dread the idea of missing out on the Chinese market. In 2010, talks between the United States and China resulted in promises by the Chinese government of stricter enforcement of antipiracy laws and implementation of aggressive antipiracy media campaigns. But to date, software companies have failed to see any significant increases in software sales in China, indicating the Chinese government's actions have been ineffective. Even though the Philippines government stepped up enforcement of copyright laws (see Figure 8) in an effort to get off the U.S. government's intellectual property watch list, they haven't made much progress in slowing piracy.

Many countries, such as Pakistan, Bangladesh, Nicaragua, Algeria, and Vietnam, have higher rates of piracy than China and the Philippines. The Business Software Alliance estimates the monetary losses from software piracy at more than $63 billion worldwide for 2013, although there is debate around the exact value.

Most people have had the opportunity to participate in the piracy of copyrighted materials through illegal peer-to-peer sharing and the use of torrents. This behavior is now multiplied to the level of nations, and the consequences are still being explored.

Questions to Think About and Research

1. Should a government be penalized for failing to actively enforce the laws it has enacted within its own country? If so, what should the penalties be, and how should they be enforced?

2. Does each government have the right to make its own decision on a stand against piracy?

3. How can other countries respond to international piracy?

4. Does individual piracy have any connection to the enforcement of copyright laws on an international level?

POINT

International Copyright Protections Need to Be Vigorously Enforced

Artists and software developers depend on the integrity of the protection of intellectual property, both within the United States and internationally, to make a fair profit on their work.

1. If other countries do not fight piracy, artists and developers have a disadvantage in the marketplace.
2. By allowing massive piracy, some countries are stealing from others.
3. Every country needs to have a common understanding and enforcement of intellectual property laws for trade to be fair and beneficial to everyone.

COUNTERPOINT

Global Business Demands Understanding Other Cultures

Most countries have laws on their books regarding intellectual property. It is not the job of the United States to tell a foreign government how to conduct its internal affairs.

1. The existing laws on intellectual property have worked to serve the interests of these countries. If U.S. companies do not want to sell to the billion-person market of China, then that is their choice.
2. Piracy exists within the United States, so it is hypocritical to be chastising foreign governments for software piracy.
3. Companies can pursue restitution for piracy through the foreign court systems.

FIGURE 8 Despite public crackdowns on pirated media, the Philippines still hasn't made much progress on decreasing instances of pirating.
(Rolex Dela Pena/epa/Corbis)

Should Employers Peer into Your Personal Life?

Summary of the Issue

Like respect and dignity, privacy is a basic human right. What, exactly, is privacy? Simply stated, privacy is the right to be left alone to do as one pleases. The idea of privacy is often associated with hiding something (a behavior, a relationship, or a secret). However, privacy really means not being required to explain your behavior to others. But social media sites such as Facebook are inherently about sharing information with others. Does this mean there is no such thing as personal privacy (see Figure 9) on social media sites?

Facebook and other social media allow you to set privacy filters on your personal information. You can choose to share information publically, share it with just with your friends, or keep it totally private. Employers now routinely check social media sites to gather publically shared information on prospective employees. But recently, many government agencies, such as police departments and some private employers, have been asking job seekers for access to their *private* Facebook information, as well.

Sometimes this is blatant, such as what happened to a Maryland corrections officer who was seeking reinstatement. During an interview, he was asked for his Facebook password. The interviewer then proceeded to log on to his account, purportedly to see if he had any gang affiliations.

Although this might seem like a legitimate reason for a prison system to screen candidates, the U.S. Senate disagrees. In 2012 and 2013, legislators proposed the Password Protection Act to prevent employers from demanding passwords to private sites from employees. The 2012 bill died in committee, and the 2013 bill was still in committee as of late 2014. The state governments are acting, however, and over a dozen states, including Maryland, New Jersey, and California, have enacted similar legislation. Employers are currently prohibited from asking prospective employees information related to their gender, race, religion, age, and sexual orientation, but this information is often found in social media site profiles. Facebook has also warned employers against this practice, as it violates the terms-of-use agreement for the site.

Often, however, employer research is more subtle. For example, employers often encourage prospective employees to "friend" them on Facebook. Although these company profiles are set up specifically so that prospective employees can learn information about the company, once prospective employees "friend" the company, company representatives can often see more information about these would-be employees than what is visible in their public profile.

The American Civil Liberties Union (ACLU) and other privacy advocates have begun voicing opposition to these practices, citing erosion of personal privacy rights. You wouldn't give a prospective employer the keys to your house so they could poke around in your personal life. But doesn't it have almost the same effect if you let them see your private information in a social media profile?

Employers—especially small businesses—argue that hiring decisions are so critical that they need to gather as much information as possible and that people voluntarily surrendering passwords is not a violation of prospective employees' rights. But critics of these practices say that job seekers may feel powerless to refuse these invasions of their privacy for fear they'll be turned down for a job.

The control and privacy of information will continue to be a fine balancing act for the foreseeable future, with employers trying to gather intelligence while appeasing the concerns of privacy advocates. Leaving a trail of electronic breadcrumbs is to a certain extent inevitable. But cleaning up or hiding your "trail" is still important to many users, not because they're trying to hide something but because they value their basic right to privacy.

Questions to Think About and Research

1. Should you be able to decide exactly what information on a social networking site you share with others? Would you be willing to pay for this privilege?

2. Do you know what your privacy settings are on the social media sites you use? Is there any information being shared publicly that you weren't aware was being shared?

3. Should employers be allowed to ask prospective employees for their passwords to social media sites? In which states is this currently illegal?

4. Is there any information on sites you use that you want to restrict potential employers from seeing? Do these sites allow you to restrict the information you wish to protect?

POINT

Employers Have No Right to Job Seekers' Private Social Media Information

The advocates of protecting privacy in the United States argue that the right to privacy is a basic human right that should be afforded to everyone. Personal privacy concerns should outweigh the business needs of a corporation.

1. Social media sites have an inherent duty to protect the data of their users.
2. If employers are screening private information, they might misuse or lose control of the data or violate current employment law.
3. Default privacy settings on social media sites should all be opt-in, allowing users the ultimate control over who views their data.

COUNTERPOINT

Employers Are Entitled to Gather Personal Information Directly Related to Employment

Advocates for unrestricted sharing of information feel that business concerns outweigh privacy concerns. Businesses should have the right to screen all data in social media sites to determine the character and fitness of employment candidates.

1. Volunteering password information does not violate an individual's right to privacy.
2. Users can make their own privacy decisions and choose not to post or share sensitive information (opt out).
3. In the digital age, loss of a certain amount of privacy is inevitable.

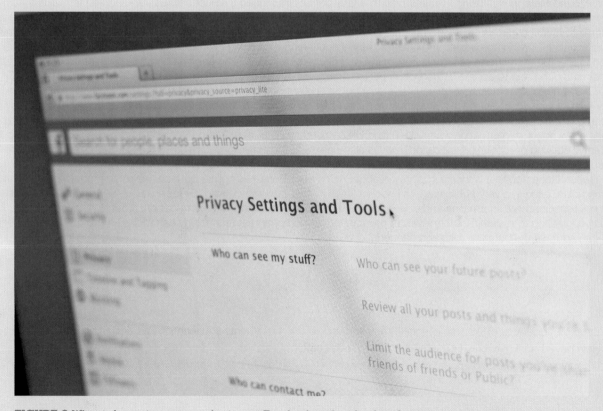

FIGURE 9 What information are you sharing on Facebook and with whom? *(Dolphfyn/Alamy)*

Geolocation: Who Knows Where You Are?

Summary of the Issue

"Where are you?" is the burning social networking question these days, and your smartphone probably has the answer. The technology is called geolocation (see Figure 10), and smartphones have a GPS chip that can calculate your exact position. Services such as Foursquare, Gowalla, Brightkite, and Loopt are all hoping you'll use their geolocation services to find your friends or let your friends find you. Through the apps, you can receive recommendations of places to visit or things to do nearby. Businesses are using geolocation apps to promote their products and offer rewards for "checkins" to help drive customers to their location.

When you sign up on Foursquare and other social media sites, you can choose what information is publically available, such as your location or your Facebook profile. Foursquare is designed to make it convenient to see where your friends are and who's in the venue where you're currently "checked in." You might be cautious and choose to make personal and location information only accessible to your friends—or it might all be public. But what if another app you know nothing about is using your information in a way never intended by the social media sites you joined?

Consider the controversy that erupted around the iPhone app Girls Around Me. When the app was first launched, it used data from Foursquare to create a local map that showed how many individuals logged into Foursquare were in geographic locations near you. It also allowed you to view Facebook profiles of people around you if they had their Facebook profiles linked to their Foursquare account. The app developer, i-Free, promoted the app as a tool to see what was happening in a wider range of locations instead of just one at a time. It viewed its tool as a way to let users identify "hot spots" of activity that had a lot of people checked in. i-Free said the app was just like looking in the window of a location to see how crowded it was, but it was also aggregating publically available information provided by other social media services.

Critics of the app decried it as a tool for stalkers that provided more information than people could gain by glancing in a window. They argued that the app violated the privacy of Foursquare users because they had no knowledge of how the Girls Around Me app was using their information. Many detractors argued that just because you agreed to make certain information public on Foursquare doesn't mean you automatically agree to the use of that same information on other apps that might function in a different (and perhaps objectionable) way. Foursquare claimed that i-Free was violating the terms of its information-sharing agreement and changed its application programming interfaces (APIs) to effectively disable the Girls Around Me app. i-Free removed the app from the App Store for retooling. The app has been reintroduced, and Foursquare is permitting the app to access some of their users' information once again.

But the question remains, when you leave your home and announce your constant whereabouts through tweets and checkins, do you lose your privacy in exchange for fun and convenience? Although you can set certain levels of privacy in the apps, there is still the potential for someone with bad intentions (stalkers, robbers) to follow your updates. And do you really know how the information you make public will be used by other app creators? In addition to opening yourself up to potential stalking or robbery, geolocation devices also can track the activities you might not want publicized and that once documented can later be used against you.

It wasn't long ago that we were concerned about using our real names online, but now we're comfortable with sharing our exact location in a very public way. As Facebook CEO Mark Zuckerberg said, "People have really gotten comfortable not only sharing more information and different kinds, but more openly and with more people." But does such acceptance justify neglecting to maintain certain levels of privacy? Again, it seems that technology has moved more quickly than society can address the potential risks and dangers.

Questions to Think About and Research

1. Do the benefits of geolocation outweigh the risks?
2. What other devices besides cell phones track and record our movements and locations as digital records?
3. How have social networks increased the risks of geolocation?
4. What risks do geolocation pose for college students? How can users mitigate those risks?

POINT

Geolocation Devices Do Not Threaten Privacy

The advocates of using geolocation devices with minimal concern for threatened privacy are those who believe the social norm has shifted and people have become comfortable with sharing more information.

1. Businesses are adopting geolocation apps as a part of their social media strategy in order to drive customers to their business. They would lose revenue if such activities ceased.

2. As the devices and apps become better and more precise, they may become useful as public safety and news-gathering devices.

3. Society may need to reevaluate its views about how much privacy is needed in people's digital lives, as well as the degree of an individual's responsibility for making sensible decisions about sharing information through the Internet.

COUNTERPOINT

Geolocation Devices Are a Threat to Privacy

The advocates for tighter privacy controls and awareness campaigns about the potential risks of using geolocation devices suggest that the threats are too big to ignore. Society has become too complacent with privacy issues.

1. Privacy settings on apps and GPS devices should be more restrictive in order to avoid broadcasting one's location and risking personal assault.

2. Laws and regulations will need to be created as to the use and distribution of digital location information.

3. Consumers need to be educated about geolocation and the ways it can affect them so that they are able to make informed choices.

FIGURE 10 Geolocation applications help you find cool places and businesses. But who do you want to find you with geolocation? *(Cseke Timea/Fotolia)*

ELECTRONIC COMMUNICATION

Does Free Speech Have a Price?

Summary of the Issue

In early 2006, when Google launched its search engine services in China, it conceded to the Chinese government's demands that it self-censor its search engine, restricting search results for sensitive information such as the details of the Tiananmen Square protests and of human rights groups. This decision prompted much discussion, with some condemning Google's decision for putting business profits over what they saw as basic human rights (see Figure 11). Google justified its actions by stating that a company must operate within the rules of the market in which it operates and that the benefits of increased access to information for people in China "outweighed our discomfort in agreeing to censor some results." And, compared with search results from **Baidu.com**, the leading Chinese search engine, Google was not censoring all information.

However, in 2010, Google announced that it was no longer willing to censor search results and moved the site to Hong Kong, where it hoped there would be less censorship. The departure was a reaction to a sophisticated, targeted cyberattack that Google believes was done to gather information on Chinese human rights activists. At that time, Google had about a 35% market share.

Microsoft had only a 1% share of the market, so it decided to partner with **Baidu.com** to provide English-language search results for China's largest search engine. Microsoft stated it would agree to abide by Chinese censorship laws (so search terms like *freedom* and *democracy* deliver filtered results), thereby respecting the laws of the countries where it operates. However, before honoring any censor requests, Microsoft insisted that Chinese authorities made legally binding requests in writing.

So how did it all work out? As of the first quarter of 2014, Google's market share has dropped to 1.5% in China, whereas **Baidu.com** has increased its market share to 58%. Microsoft's decision to keep censoring its searches appears to have paid off—at least from a monetary perspective. But is the financial result more important than the social implications of its behavior?

Questions to Think About and Research

1. Is there anything else that Google could have done that would have a major impact on China's censorship laws?
2. Has Microsoft's compliance with censorship laws furthered the Chinese government's cooperation in combating software piracy in China? Are Microsoft's financial incentives even deeper than just Internet market share?
3. Can the U.S. government compel technology companies to take a firmer stance on free speech in China and elsewhere by instituting criminal charges if U.S. companies do not take reasonable steps to protect human rights?

POINT

U.S. Companies Should Comply with Local Laws in Foreign Countries

Those in favor of Microsoft's actions to remain in China feel that if a company chooses to operate in a foreign country, it knows the local laws and should be prepared to work within those laws as it does business. It is not the place of a company to try to change laws of foreign countries.

1. Microsoft conducts businesses in other countries that have censorship laws, so why not participate in China?
2. Working in China does not mean a company supports all of China's policies.
3. Microsoft's presence continues to advance the progress the Chinese government is making toward democracy. U.S. companies can ethically stay in China if they make an effort to improve human rights there. U.S. companies operating in China should agree on guidelines that respect human rights.
4. A U.S. company's presence has no impact on reform—reform must come from within.

COUNTERPOINT

U.S. Companies Should Put What Is Right Ahead of What Is Financially Expedient

Those in favor of Google's actions believe that international corporations should begin to take a firm stance against governments that do not promote basic human rights.

1. China will never change unless there are financial and political incentives to do so. Google's departure helps pressure the Chinese government.
2. Google's withdrawal from China threatens the viability of many advertising resellers in China. Will this added pressure help or hinder human rights efforts?
3. Google's decision to leave helps put pressure on China's government to play by global standards. China cannot expect to compete in the global marketplace while refusing to have a global exchange of ideas.

FIGURE 11 Is free speech possible in countries (such as China) where information availability is restricted by law? *(Kentoh/Shutterstock)*

COMPUTER ABUSE

Cyberbullying: Who Should Protect Children from Each Other?

Summary of the Issue

Cyberbullying is just like normal bullying, but it involves the use of digital technologies such as the Internet, cell phones, or video (see Figure 12). There are many types of cyberbullying, some of which might result in criminal charges depending on the type of incident:

- Bombarding a victim with harassing instant messages or text messages
- Stealing a password and then using the victim's account to embarrass the victim by sending harassing, threatening, or lewd messages while pretending to be the victim
- Spreading rumors or lies on social networking sites
- Posting embarrassing photos or videos on the web
- Infecting the victim's computer with malware, usually to spy on the victim

The effects of cyberbullying can be devastating. Infamous cases include Hannah Smith, the English girl who at 14 committed suicide after being repeatedly taunted on social networking sites, and Tyler Clementi, a Rutgers freshman who committed suicide after his roommate showed fellow students videos of him having sex.

Signs that a child is a victim of cyberbullying are often the same as the signs of depression. A child may:

- Suddenly lose interest in normal activities
- Be reluctant to go to school
- Lose his or her appetite
- Have trouble sleeping
- Appear upset after using the Internet
- Experience unusual mood swings (such as bursting into tears for no apparent reason)

Signs that a child might be perpetrating cyberbullying include the following:

- Using the Internet excessively
- Sending large volumes of text messages
- Clearing the computer screen when others enter a room
- Conducting clandestine Internet activities (refusal to say what he or she is doing)

Vigilance over children's online activities is obviously key to spotting both victims and perpetrators of cyberbullying.

But who is responsible for monitoring children? Parents obviously need to protect their children, but bullying usually doesn't happen until children are exposed to other children, such as in school. So should teachers shoulder the responsibility for detecting, reporting, and mitigating cyberbullying? Children often spend more time in school during the day than under the supervision of their parents. But cyberbullying activities don't just take place in school. Most children have access to the Internet at home and can carry on campaigns of terror from their bedrooms.

There is currently no federal law prohibiting cyberbullying, but the recently passed law against cyberstalking may cover this area. According to the Cyberbullying Research Center (**cyberbullying.us**), as of August 2014, 49 states had antibullying laws on the books. However, only 48 state laws cover electronic harassment, and a mere 20 state laws cover cyberbullying. Many legislatures are reluctant to pass laws that instruct parents on how to raise their children because this tends to raise issues about personal freedom. Therefore, anti-cyberbullying laws tend to place the burden of detection on the schools. For instance, the Massachusetts law requires schools to provide age-appropriate education on bullying to students, to train school employees in detection and prevention of bullying, and to have plans developed for detecting and reporting bullying.

Questions to Think About and Research

1. What level of responsibility should school employees have for protecting children from cyberbullying?
2. Should there be federal laws that make cyberbullying a crime? If so, how would these laws be enforced?
3. What types of education for children would be beneficial in preventing cyberbullying? When should these programs begin, and how often should children be required to participate?

POINT

Parents Must Protect Their Children from Cyberbullying

Proponents of parental responsibility for detecting and preventing cyberbullying feel that it's a personal behavior issue. Individuals are responsible for their own behavior as long as it doesn't harm others. Parents should be allowed to educate their children according to their own standards of behavior and preferences in terms of moral behavior (such as religion).

1. Parents are ultimately responsible for protecting their children.

2. Bullying is a personal behavior issue, and all decisions regarding personal freedom and behavior should be made by parents.

3. Because educating children about bullying is key to preventing it, the content of such training needs to be controlled by parents.

COUNTERPOINT

Schools Must Bear the Responsibility for Protecting Students from Cyberbullying

Cyberbullying affects society because it can severely damage an individual's self-esteem. Cyberbullying is similar to other hate crimes and should enlist public officials (such as educators) in enforcement of the laws.

1. Parents do not supervise their children 24/7 and therefore require help from other responsible adults to protect their children.

2. Parents need to be assured that publicly funded institutions such as schools and libraries are "safe havens" where their children will not be exposed to malicious activities.

3. Educators have better resources than most parents for teaching children about the serious effects of cyberbullying.

FIGURE 12 Cyberbullying involves the use of digital technologies both to bully and to disseminate acts of bullying. *(Rawdon Wyatt/Alamy)*

Using Computers to Support Ethical Conduct

Although there are many opportunities to use computers and the Internet unethically, we can also use technology to support ethical conduct. For example, many charitable organizations use the Internet and other technology tools for fundraising. When severe flooding wiped out 1,600 homes in Colorado in September 2013, the Salvation Army and other charities received many pledges via their websites.

Google Crisis Response is a project sponsored by Google that helps disseminate information before and after a crisis to coordinate relief efforts and provide updates to the public (see Figure 13). Google Person Finder, part of Google Crisis Response, helps individuals and organizations to provide information and updates on persons missing (or located) after a disaster.

Computing devices and the Internet provide many opportunities for you to start or get involved in ethical initiatives. Consider the Empty Bowls movement that was started by students at Wichita State University students. Local potters, students, and educators worked to create bowls and then guests were invited to consume a simple meal of bread and soup from them. For a donation to help local organizations feed the hungry, donors were encouraged to keep the bowls as a reminder of all the empty bowls in the world. This movement is now spreading across the United States through the website **emptybowls.net**. What can you and your fellow students do in your community?

Throughout your life, you'll encounter many ethical challenges relating to information technology. Your personal ethics—combined with the ethical guidelines your company provides and the general ethical environment of society—will guide your decisions.

For further information on ethics, check out the following websites:

- Ethics in Computing (**ethics.csc.ncsu.edu**)
- The Center for Ethics in Science and Technology (**ethicscenter.net**)
- Business Ethics: The Magazine of Corporate Responsibility (**business-ethics.com**)
- Council for Ethical Leadership at Capital University (**businessethics.org**)

FIGURE 13 Tools provided by Google Crisis Response help disseminate information and locate lost individuals after a disaster such as the tornado in Moore, Oklahoma, in 2013. *(Google, Inc.)*

check your understanding// review & practice

For a quick review of what you've learned, answer the following questions. Visit **pearsonhighered.com/techinaction** to check your answers.

multiple choice

1. Which theory states that there is no universal moral truth?

   a. deontology

   b. divine command theory

   c. utilitarianism

   d. relativism

2. The ethical theory that states that individual happiness is not important is known as

   a. utilitarianism.

   b. virtue ethics.

   c. deontology.

   d. divine command theory.

3. Which ethical philosophy states that morals are internal?

   a. deontology

   b. virtue ethics

   c. relativism

   d. divine command theory

4. Which of the following statements is *false*?

   a. Individuals who have no sense of right or wrong exhibit amoral behavior.

   b. Ethical decisions are usually influenced by personal ethics.

   c. Unethical behavior is always illegal.

   d. Life experience affects an individual's personal ethics.

5. Unethical behavior

   a. is the same as illegal behavior.

   b. is based on civil disobedience.

   c. is different from illegal behavior.

   d. is governed by specific laws passed by legislative bodies.

6. The field of psychology that theorizes that happiness results from ethical living is known as

   a. principled psychology.

   b. positive psychology.

   c. moral psychology.

   d. affirmative psychology.

7. Which system of ethics is most widely agreed on to be the best system?

   a. utilitarianism

   b. relativism

   c. virtue ethics

   d. There is no universally agreed-on best system.

8. What should you do if you spot unethical behavior at your workplace?

   a. Nothing, as long as the behavior is legal.

   b. Report it to the police immediately.

   c. Follow company procedures for reporting unethical behavior.

   d. Start looking for a new job.

9. Which of the following actions would NOT help to identify your personal ethics?

   a. Describe yourself.

   b. Identify the influences of your work environment.

   c. Conduct a genealogic study of your extended family.

   d. Prepare a list of values that are most important to you.

10. Ethical decisions in business affect which of the following?

    a. the employees

    b. the business's clients and customers

    c. the suppliers and financial lenders

    d. all stakeholders

6

Understanding and Assessing Hardware: Evaluating Your System

Evaluating Key Subsystems

Your Ideal Computing Device

OBJECTIVE

1. What kind of computing device is best for me? **(pp. 224–225)**

Evaluating the CPU Subsystem

OBJECTIVE

2. What does the CPU do, and how can I evaluate its performance? **(pp. 226–229)**

🔊 Sound Byte: Using Windows to Evaluate CPU Performance

Evaluating the Memory Subsystem

OBJECTIVES

3. How does memory work in my computer? **(pp. 230–231)**

4. How do I evaluate how much memory I need? **(p. 232)**

🔊 Sound Byte: Memory Hierarchy Interactive

👤 Active Helpdesk: Evaluating Your CPU and RAM

🔊 Sound Byte: Installing RAM

Evaluating the Storage Subsystem

OBJECTIVES

5. What are the computer's storage devices? **(pp. 233–236)**

6. How do I evaluate my storage devices? **(pp. 236–238)**

🔊 Sound Byte: Optical Media Reading and Writing Interactive

🔊 Sound Byte: Installing an SSD Drive

Evaluating Other Subsystems and Making a Decision

Evaluating the Video and Audio Subsystems

OBJECTIVES

7. What components affect the quality of video on my computer? **(pp. 242–244)**

8. How do I know if I need better video performance? **(p. 244)**

9. What components affect my computer's sound quality? **(pp. 246–247)**

👤 Active Helpdesk: Evaluating Computer System Components

Evaluating System Reliability and Making a Final Decision

OBJECTIVE

10. How can I improve the reliability of my system? **(pp. 248–249)**

Make This: Explore an App Builder Skill on **page 241**

For all media in this chapter go to **pearsonhighered.com/techinaction** or MyITLab.

(Radius Images/Alamy; Nigel James/Alamy; Joppo/Fotolia; Oleksiy Mark/Shutterstock; Leigh Prather/Shutterstock; SSilver/Fotolia; Ivelin Radkov/Alamy)

ow COOL IS THIS?

to create something really cool? The **Arduino microcontroller project** has
an abundance of DIY (do-it-yourself) electronics projects and created an energized
nunity of do-it-yourselfers. This **small printed circuit board** is based on a
controller and includes everything you need: You **just plug it in and begin
DIY project**. The open-source hardware is licensed under the Creative Commons
se, so schematics are freely available to be changed or re-created as you wish.

ilyPad variation of the Arduino, designed by MIT engineer Leah Buechley, is
used to create wearable projects. Conductive thread runs from the Arduino output
o LEDs, and the **finished garments are washable**. One project is this turn-
biking jacket. The Arduino LilyPad fires up an LED turn signal on your back to
you visible on the road.

Evaluating Key Subsystems

It can be tough to know if your computer is the best match for your needs. New technologies emerge so quickly, and it's hard to determine whether they're expensive extras or tools you need. Do you need USB 3.0 instead of USB 2.0? Doesn't it always seem like your friend's computer is faster than yours anyway? Maybe you could get more out of newer technologies, but should you upgrade the system you have or buy a new machine? In this chapter, you'll learn how to measure your system's performance and gauge your needs so that you end up with a system you love.

 your ideal
COMPUTING DEVICE

When is the best time to buy a new computer?
There never seems to be a perfect time to buy. It seems that if you can just wait a year, computers will be faster and cost less. But is this actually true?

As it turns out, it is true. In fact, a rule of thumb often cited in the computer industry called **Moore's Law** describes the pace at which central processing units (CPUs) improve. Named for Gordon Moore, the cofounder of the CPU chip manufacturer Intel, this rule predicts that the number of transistors inside a CPU will increase so fast that CPU capacity will double about every two years. (The number of transistors on a CPU chip helps determine how fast it can process data.)

This rule of thumb has held true for over 45 years. Figure 6.1 shows a way to visualize this kind of exponential growth. If CPU capacity were put into terms of population

growth, a group of 2,300 people at the start of CPU development would now be a country of over one billion! Moore himself has predicted that around the year 2020, CPU chips will be manufactured in a different way, thus changing or eliminating the effects of Moore's Law altogether.

In addition to the CPU becoming faster, other system components also continue to improve dramatically. For example, the capacity of memory chips such as dynamic random access memory (DRAM)—the most common form of memory found in personal computers—increases about 60% every year. Meanwhile, hard drives have been growing in storage capacity by some 50% each year.

OK, things change fast. How do I know what's best for me? Consider what kind of user you are and

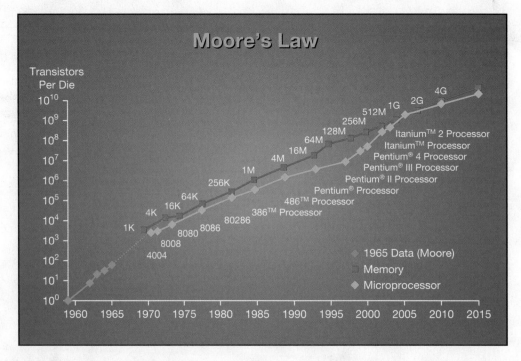

FIGURE 6.1 Moore's Law illustrates the amazing pace of growth in CPU capabilities.

FIGURE 6.2

What Kind of Technology User Are You?

Casual User
- Uses the computer primarily for Internet access
- Uses some software applications locally, like Microsoft Office
- Uses videos and software but does not create them

Power User
- Needs fast, powerful processing
- Needs fast storage and lots of it
- Creates videos and software programs

Mobile User
- Needs a lightweight device
- Needs a long battery life
- Is happy to sacrifice some capabilities for less weight

(Ilaszlo/Shutterstock; ColorBlind Images/Iconica/Getty Images; olly/Shutterstock)

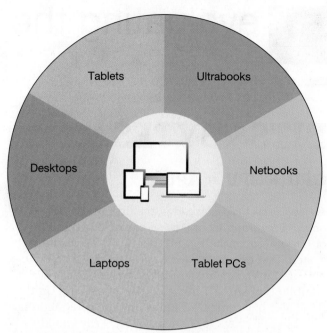

FIGURE 6.3 Range of Computing Devices

what needs you have. For example, are you a power user who wants a machine for doing video editing and high-end gaming? Are you a more casual user, mainly using a device for word processing and Internet access? Are you on the move and need to bring your computer with you everywhere? Figure 6.2 shows a few different types of users—which type (or types) are you?

Now ask yourself, does your current computer match your needs? As we evaluate the pieces of your system, it'll become clear whether you need a few upgrades or perhaps a new machine better suited to you.

How do I pick from all the types of devices available? A huge number of choices are on the market (see Figure 6.3):

- Tablets (like the iPad or Galaxy)
- Ultrabooks (like the MacBook Air)
- Netbooks (like the Chromebook)
- Tablet PCs (which have a touch-enabled screen and a full keyboard)
- Laptops (or notebooks)
- Desktops

The main distinction among the available options is based on your need for mobility versus your need for processing power. If you're on the move all the time and have to have the lightest solution possible, an ultrabook may be best for you. At less than 3 pounds, they're great on weight but don't include an optical drive for DVDs/Blu-rays or much storage space. Even lighter are tablets like the iPad, but they also lack optical drives and may not be able to run all the software you need.

Why would I consider buying a desktop? Desktop systems are invariably a better value than lighter, more mobile computers. You'll find you get more computing power for your dollar, and you'll have more opportunity to upgrade parts of your system later. In addition, desktops often ship with a 24-inch or larger monitor, whereas lighter computers offer screens between 10 and 17 inches.

Desktop systems are also more reliable. Because of the vibration that a laptop experiences and the added exposure to dust, water, and temperature fluctuations that portability brings, laptops often have a shorter lifespan than desktop computers. You'll have less worry over theft or loss with a desktop, too. Manufacturers do offer extended warranty plans that cover laptop computers for accidental damage and theft; however, such plans can be costly.

How long should I plan on keeping my computing device? You should be able to count on two years, and maybe even four or five years. The answer depends in part on how easy it is to upgrade your system. Take note of the maximum amount of memory you can install in your device. Also, check whether you can upgrade your device's graphics capabilities down the road.

How can I tell if my current system is good enough? We'll begin by conducting a **system evaluation**. To do this, we'll look at your computer's subsystems, see what they do, and check how they perform during your typical workday. Then we'll compare that with what is available on the market, and the path forward for you will become clearer. Even if you're not in the market for a new computer, conducting a system evaluation will help you understand what you might want down the road. ■

evaluating the
CPU SUBSYSTEM

BITS&BYTES

CPU + GPU = APU

A new trend has emerged in the design of CPU chips: The graphics processor can now be built into, or integrated, onto the CPU itself. This allows for a system that does not need a separate video card. One manufacturer, Advanced Micro Devices, calls this combination an APU (Accelerated Processing Unit). (Intel also has some CPU chips that are designed this way but still refers to them as CPUs.) Why wouldn't everyone use an integrated GPU? Because integrated GPUs offer only lower-end graphics capabilities, so many people still prefer to use a separate video card with its own higher-performance GPU.

Let's start by considering your system's processor, or CPU. The CPU is located on the system motherboard and is responsible for processing instructions, performing calculations, and managing the flow of information through your computer. The dominant processors on the market are the Core family from Intel, featuring the i7, i5, and i3 (see Figure 6.4).

FIGURE 6.4 The Intel i5 and i7 CPU chips run many of the laptop and desktop offerings on the market today. *(David Caudery/PC Format Magazine/Getty Images)*

How can I find out what CPU my computer has? If you have a PC, System Properties will show you the type of CPU you have installed. For example, the CPU in the computer in Figure 6.5 is an Intel i5 running at 2.6 GHz. AMD is another popular manufacturer of CPUs; you may have one of its processors, such as the FX-8150 or the Phenom X4. But more detailed information about your CPU, such as its number of cores and amount of cache memory, is not shown on this screen. Let's dive into that.

FIGURE 6.5 The System Properties window identifies your computer's CPU as well as its speed. This computer has an Intel i5 running at 2.6 GHz.

>*To access your system settings, right-click the **Start** button. From the menu that displays, choose **System**.*

How the CPU Works

How does the CPU actually work? The CPU is composed of two units: the *control unit* and the *arithmetic logic unit (ALU)*. The control unit coordinates the activities of all the other computer components. The ALU is responsible for performing all the arithmetic calculations (addition, subtraction, multiplication, and division). It also makes logic and comparison decisions, such as comparing items to determine if one is greater than, less than, or equal to another.

Every time the CPU performs a program instruction, it goes through the same series of steps:

1. It *fetches* the required piece of data or instruction from random access memory (RAM), the temporary storage location for all the data and instructions the computer needs while it's running.
2. It *decodes* the instruction into something the computer can understand.
3. It *executes* the instruction.
4. It *stores* the result to RAM before fetching the next instruction.

This process is called a **machine cycle**. (We discuss the machine cycle in more detail in the Technology in Focus feature "Under the Hood" on page 303.)

CPU Factors

What makes one CPU different from another? You pay more for a computer with an Intel i7 than one with an i5 because of its increased processing power. A CPU's processing power is determined by the following:

- Its *clock speed*
- Whether it has multiple *cores*
- Its amount of *cache memory*

How does a CPU with a higher clock speed help me? The **clock speed** of a CPU dictates how many instructions the CPU can process each second. It is measured in gigahertz (GHz), or billions of steps per second. The faster the clock speed, the more quickly the next instruction is processed. CPUs currently have clock speeds between 2.1 and 4 GHz. There is a huge difference between a computer with a 2.1 GHz CPU and one with a 4 GHz CPU.

Some users push their hardware to perform faster, **overclocking** their processor. Overclocking means that you run the CPU at a faster speed than the manufacturer recommends. It produces more heat, meaning a shorter lifetime for the CPU, and usually voids any warranty, but in gaming systems, you'll see this done quite often.

How does a multi-core CPU help me? A **core** on a CPU contains the parts of the CPU required for processing. As shown in Figure 6.6a, with multiple-core technology, two or more complete processors live on the same chip, enabling the independent execution of two sets of instructions at the same time. If you had a clone of yourself sitting next to you working, you could get twice as much done: That is the idea of multi-core processing. With multi-core

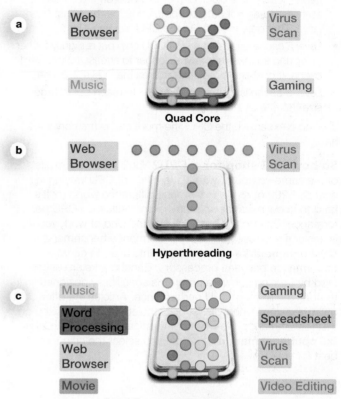

FIGURE 6.6 (a) Intel Quad Core processors have four cores that are able to run four programs simultaneously. (b) Hyperthreading allows work on two processes to happen in one core at the same time. (c) So, a four-core hyperthreaded processor can be working on eight programs at one time.

processing, applications that are always running behind the scenes, such as virus protection software and your operating system (OS), can have their own dedicated processor, freeing the other processors to run other applications more efficiently. This results in faster processing and smoother multitasking.

CPUs began to execute more than one instruction at a time when **hyperthreading** was introduced in 2002. Hyperthreading provides quicker processing of information by enabling a new set of instructions to start executing *before the previous set has finished*. As shown in Figure 6.6b, hyperthreading allows two different programs to be processed at one time, but they're sharing the computing resources of the chip.

All of the Intel Core processors have multiple cores *and* hyperthreading (see Figure 6.6c). The Intel i7-990X has six cores, each one using hyperthreading, so it simulates having 12 processors!

How does more cache memory help me? The CPU's **cache memory** is a form of RAM that gets data to the CPU for processing much faster than bringing the data in from the computer's RAM. There are three levels of cache memory, defined by their proximity to the CPU:

- *Level 1 cache* is a block of memory built on the CPU chip itself for storage of data or commands that have just been used. That gets the data to the CPU blindingly fast!
- *Level 2 cache* is located on the CPU chip but is slightly farther away and so takes somewhat longer to access than Level 1 cache. It contains more storage area than Level 1 cache.
- *Level 3 cache* is slower for the CPU to reach but is larger in size than Level 2 cache.

The more expensive the CPU, the more cache memory it will have.

So how do I shop for a CPU? You'll often see models of the same computer with just a different CPU varying in cost by $200 or more. Is the price difference worth it? It's hard to know because so many factors influence CPU performance. Picking the best CPU for the kind of work you do is easier if you research some performance benchmarks. **CPU benchmarks** are measurements used to compare performance between processors. Benchmarks are generated by running software programs specifically designed to push the limits of CPU performance. Articles are often published comparing CPUs, or complete systems, based on their benchmark performance. Investigate a few, using sites like **cpubenchmark.net**, before you select the chip that's best for you.

Measuring the CPU

How can I tell whether my current CPU is meeting my needs? One way to determine whether your CPU is right for you is to watch how busy it is as you work. You can do this by checking out your **CPU usage**—the percentage of time your CPU is working.

Your computer's OS has utilities that measure CPU usage. These are incredibly useful, both for considering whether you should upgrade and for investigating if your computer's performance suddenly seems to drop off for no apparent reason.

On Windows systems, Task Manager lets you access this data (see Figure 6.7). The **CPU usage graph** records your CPU usage for the past minute. (Note that if you have multiple cores and hyperthreading, you'll see only one physical processor listed, but it will show that you have several virtual processors.) Of course, there will be periodic peaks of high CPU usage, but if your CPU usage levels are greater than 90% during most of your work session, a faster CPU will contribute a great deal to your system's performance.

To walk through using the Task Manager, check out the Try This on pages 240–241 and watch the "Using Windows to Evaluate CPU Performance" Sound Byte. Mac OS X has a

FIGURE 6.7 The Performance tab of the Windows Task Manager utility shows you how busy your CPU is.

>*To access the Performance tab, right-click the* **Start** *button. From the menu, select* **Task Manager**, *and then click the* **Performance** *tab.*

BITS&BYTES

The Haswell Boost

The amount of power a CPU requires is very important to designers looking to extend the battery life of an ultrabook or tablet. Intel's newest generation of the Core CPU line, its fourth-generation processors, nicknamed "Haswell," gives systems up to a 50% boost in battery life. Since Haswell-based computers also see about a 40% increase in graphics performance, look for the fourth-generation Intel CPU for a system that is fast and can make it through the day on a single charge.

similar utility named Activity Monitor, which is located in the Utilities folder in the Applications subfolder.

How often do I have to be watching the CPU load?
Keep in mind that the workload your CPU experiences depends on how many programs are running at one time. Even though the CPU may meet the specs for each program separately, how you use your machine during a typical day may tax the CPU. If you're having slow response times or decide to measure CPU performance as a check, open the Task Manager and leave it open for a full day.

Check in at points when you have a lot of open windows and when you have a lot of networking or disk-usage demand.

So a better CPU means a better performing system? Your CPU affects only the *processing* portion of the system performance, not how quickly data can move to or from the CPU. Your system's *overall* performance depends on many factors, including the amount of RAM installed as well as hard drive speed. Your selection of CPU may not offer significant improvements to your system's performance if there is a bottleneck in processing because of insufficient RAM or hard drive performance, so you need to make sure the system is designed in a balanced way. Figure 6.8 lists factors to consider as you decide which specific CPU is right for you. ■

◀)) SOUND BYTE
Using Windows to Evaluate CPU Performance

In this Sound Byte, you'll learn how to use the utilities provided by Windows to evaluate your CPU's performance. You'll also learn about shareware utilities (software that you can install and try before you purchase it) that expand on the capabilities the Task Manager utility provides.

FIGURE 6.8

Evaluating the CPU

- Power users: Clock speed is very important; consider whether overclocking is worth sacrificing CPU longevity
- Casual/Mobile users: Clock speed is not as important

- Power users: Get as many cores as possible
- Casual users: Fewer cores is acceptable
- Mobile users: Low power draw is more critical than number of cores

Clock Speed

Multiple Cores

CPU

Cache Memory

CPU Benchmarks

- Power users: Paying for more cache memory is a good investment
- Casual/Mobile users: Save your money

- Use benchmarks to get an exact measure of the difference between two CPUs

evaluating the
MEMORY SUBSYSTEM

Random access memory (RAM) is your computer's temporary storage space. Although we refer to RAM as a form of storage, it really is the computer's short-term memory. It remembers everything that the computer needs in order to process data into information, such as data that has been entered and software instructions, but only when the computer is on. RAM is an example of **volatile storage**. When the power is off, the data stored in RAM is cleared out. This is why, in addition to RAM, systems always include **nonvolatile storage** devices for permanent storage of instructions and data. Read-only memory (ROM), for example, holds the critical start-up instructions. Hard drives provide the largest nonvolatile storage capacity in the computer system.

Why not use a hard drive to store the data and instructions? It's about one million times faster for the CPU to retrieve a piece of data from RAM than from a mechanical hard drive. The time it takes the CPU to grab data from RAM is measured in nanoseconds (billionths of seconds), whereas pulling data from a fast mechanical hard drive takes an average of 10 milliseconds (ms), or thousandths of seconds.

Figure 6.9 shows the various types of memory and storage distributed throughout your system: memory that is actually part of the CPU (such as CPU registers and cache), RAM, virtual memory, optical drives, and SSD and mechanical hard drives. Each of these has its own tradeoff of speed versus price. Because the fastest memory is so much more expensive, systems are designed with much less of it. This principle is influential in the design of a balanced computer system and can have a tremendous impact on system performance.

The RAM in Your System

Are there different types of RAM? Yes, but in most current systems, the type of RAM used is double data rate 3 (DDR3) memory modules, available in several different speeds (1066 MHz, 1333 MHz, 1600 MHz). The higher the speed, the better the performance. DDR5 (double data rate 5) memory, which has an even faster data transfer rate, is seen in high-performance video graphics cards.

RAM appears in the system on **memory modules** (or **memory cards**), small circuit boards that hold a series of RAM chips and fit into special slots on the motherboard. Most memory modules in today's systems are packaged as a *dual inline memory module (DIMM)*, a small circuit board that holds several memory chips (see Figure 6.10).

How can I tell how much RAM is installed in my computer? The amount of RAM actually sitting on memory

FIGURE 6.9 A computer system's memory has many different levels, ranging from the small amounts in the CPU to the much slower but more plentiful storage of a mechanical hard drive.

FIGURE 6.10 A DIMM memory module holds a series of RAM chips. *(Hugh Threlfall/Alamy)*

modules in your computer is your computer's **physical memory**. The easiest way to see how much RAM you have is to look in the System Properties window. (On a Mac, choose the Apple menu and then About This Mac.) This is the same window you looked in to determine your system's CPU type and speed, and is shown in Figure 6.5. RAM capacity is measured in gigabytes (GB), and most machines sold today have at least 4 GB of RAM.

 SOUND BYTE
Memory Hierarchy Interactive
In this Sound Byte, you'll learn about the different types of memory used in a computer system.

How can I tell how my RAM is being used? To see exactly how your RAM is being used, open the Resource Monitor and click on the Memory tab (see Figure 6.11). The Resource Monitor gives additional details on CPU, disk, network, and memory usage inside your system, and you can use it to see how you're using all the RAM you paid for!

Windows uses a memory-management technique known as **SuperFetch**. SuperFetch monitors the applications you use the most and preloads them into your system memory so that they'll be ready to be used when you want them. For example, if you have Microsoft Word running, Windows stores as much of the information related to Word in RAM as it can, which speeds up how fast your application responds. This is because pulling information from RAM is much faster than pulling it from the hard drive. You can watch this process at work using the Resource Monitor. Figure 6.11 shows how the 8 GB of installed RAM is being used:

- 1.5 GB is running programs.
- 2.15 GB is holding cached data and files ready for quick access.
- 4.4 GB is currently unused.

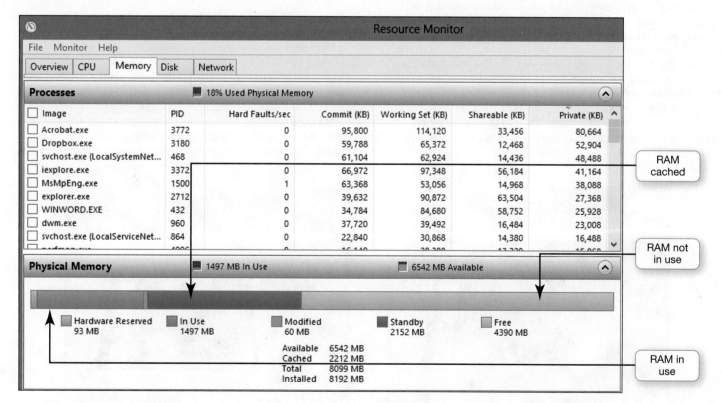

FIGURE 6.11 The Resource Monitor's Memory tab shows a detailed breakdown of how the computer is using memory.

>*To access the Resource Monitor, in the Task Manager, click the* **Performance** *tab, click* **Open Resource Monitor***, and then click the* **Memory** *tab.*

How much RAM do I need? At a minimum, your system needs enough RAM to run the OS. Running the 64-bit version of Windows 8.1 requires a minimum of 2 GB of RAM. However, because you run more applications at one time than just the OS, you'll want to have more RAM than just what's needed for the OS. For example, Figure 6.12 shows how much RAM is recommended for the OS, a web browser, and some software.

It's a good idea to have more than the minimum amount of RAM you need now so you can use more programs in the future. Remember, too, that "required" means these are the *minimum values* recommended by manufacturers; having more RAM often helps programs run more efficiently. New systems today ship with at least 4 GB of RAM, and high-end systems can come with 24 GB. The rule of thumb: When buying a new computer, buy as much RAM as you can afford.

FIGURE 6.12

Sample RAM Allocation	
APPLICATION	**RAM RECOMMENDED**
Windows 8.1 (64 bit)	2 GB
Microsoft Office Professional 2013	2 GB
Internet Explorer 11	2 GB
iTunes 11	1 GB
Adobe Photoshop Elements 12	2 GB
Total RAM recommended to run all programs simultaneously	**9 GB**

Adding RAM

Is there a limit to how much RAM I can add to my computer? The motherboard is designed with a specific number of slots into which the memory cards fit, and each slot has a limit on the amount of RAM it can hold. To determine your specific system limits, check the system manufacturer's website.

In addition, the OS running on your machine imposes its own RAM limit. For example, the maximum amount of RAM for the 32-bit version of Windows 8.1 is 4 GB, whereas the maximum memory limit using the 64-bit version of Windows 8.1 Pro is 512 GB.

Is it difficult or expensive to add RAM? Adding RAM is fairly easy (see Figure 6.13). Be sure that you purchase a memory module that's compatible with your computer. Also be sure to follow the installation instructions that come with the RAM module. Typically, you simply line up the notches and gently push the memory module in place.

RAM is a relatively inexpensive system upgrade. The cost of RAM does fluctuate in the marketplace as much as 400% over time, though, so if you're considering adding RAM, you should watch the prices of memory in online and print advertisements. ∎

FIGURE 6.13 Adding RAM to a computer is quite simple and relatively inexpensive. On a laptop, you often gain access through a panel on the bottom. *(Editorial Image, LLC/Alamy)*

evaluating the
STORAGE SUBSYSTEM

Remember, there are two ways data is stored on your computer: temporary storage and permanent storage. RAM is a form of temporary (or volatile) storage. The information residing in RAM is not stored permanently. It's critical to have the means to store data and software applications permanently.

Fortunately, several storage options exist. Storage devices include internal hard drives, SSDs, optical drives, and external hard drives. When you turn off your computer, the data that has been written to these devices will be available the next time the machine is powered on. These devices therefore provide *nonvolatile* storage.

Mechanical Hard Drives

What makes the hard drive such a popular storage device? With storage capacities exceeding 4 terabytes (TB), a mechanical **hard drive** has the largest capacity of any storage device. And because it offers the most storage per dollar, the hard drive is also a more economical device than other options.

Today, most desktop system units are designed to support more than one internal hard drive. The Apple Mac Pro has room for four hard drives, and the Thermaltake Level 10 can support six hard drives. Each one simply slides into place when you want to add more storage.

How is data stored on a hard drive? A hard drive is composed of several coated, round, thin plates of metal stacked on a spindle. Each plate is called a **platter**. When data is saved to a hard drive platter, a pattern of magnetized spots is created on the iron oxide coating of each platter. When the spots are aligned in one direction, they represent a *1*; when they're aligned in the other direction, they represent a *0*. These

*0*s and *1*s are *bits* (or *binary digits*) and are the smallest pieces of data that computers can understand. When data stored on the hard drive platter is retrieved (or read), your computer translates these patterns of magnetized spots into the data you have saved.

How quickly does a hard drive find information? The hard drive's **access time**, the time it takes a storage device to locate its stored data and make it available for processing, is faster than optical drives. Mechanical hard drive access times are measured in milliseconds (ms), meaning thousandths of seconds. For large-capacity drives, access times of approximately 12 to 13 milliseconds are typical. For comparison, a DVD drive can take over 150 milliseconds to access data.

Solid-State Drives

Do mechanical hard drives have the fastest access times? A **solid-state drive (SSD)** uses electronic memory and has no mechanical motors or moving parts. Having no mechanical motors allows SSDs to offer incredibly fast access times, reaching data in only a tenth of a millisecond (0.1 ms). That's about 100 times faster than mechanical hard drives (see Figure 6.14)! SSDs also have a great advantage when booting up since a mechanical hard drive has to wait for motors to bring the plates up to the final rotation speed. The start-up time of SSDs is so fast, in fact, that most desktop and laptop systems offer an option to use at least one SSD. This "system drive" may only be 20 GB large, but it holds the operating system and means the wake-up time for the system will be very fast. In addition, SSDs run with no noise, generate very little heat, and require very little power, making them a popular option in ultrabooks.

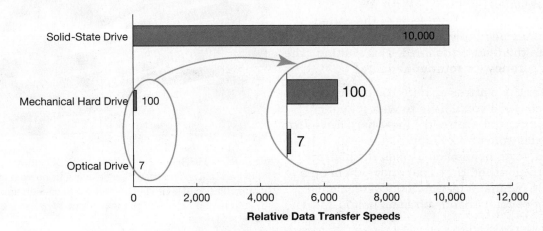

FIGURE 6.14 Relative Data Transfer Speeds for Nonvolatile Storage Options

The thin metal platters that make up a mechanical hard drive are covered with a special magnetic coating that enables the data to be recorded onto one or both sides of the platter. Hard drive manufacturers prepare the disks to hold data through a process called *low-level formatting*. In this process, concentric circles, each called a **track**, and pie-shaped wedges, each called a **sector**, are created in the magnetized surface of each platter, setting up a gridlike pattern that identifies file locations on the hard drive. A separate process called *high-level formatting* establishes the catalog that the computer uses to keep track of where each file is located on the hard drive. More detail on this process is presented in the Dig Deeper feature "How Disk Defragmenter Utilities Work" in Chapter 5.

Hard drive platters spin at a high rate of speed, some as fast as 15,000 revolutions per minute (rpm). Sitting between the platters are special "arms" that contain read/write heads (see Figure 6.15). A **read/write head** moves from the outer edge of the spinning platter to the center, as frequently as 50 times per second, to retrieve (read) and record (write) the magnetic data to and from the hard drive platter. As noted earlier, the average total time it takes for the read/write head to locate the data on the platter and return it to the CPU for processing is called its *access time*. A new hard drive should have an average access time of approximately 12 ms.

Access time is mostly the sum of two factors—seek time and latency:

1. The time it takes for the read/write heads to move over the surface of the disk, moving to the correct track, is called the **seek time**. (Sometimes people incorrectly refer to this as access time.)
2. Once the read/write head locates the correct track, it may need to wait for the correct sector to spin to the read/write head. This waiting time is called **latency** (or **rotational delay**).

The faster the platters spin (or the faster the rpm), the less time you'll have to wait for your data to be accessed. Currently, most hard drives for home systems spin at 7,200 rpm.

The read/write heads don't touch the platters of the hard drive; rather, they float above them on a thin cushion of air at a height of 0.5 microinches. As a matter of comparison, a human hair is 2,000

microinches thick and a particle of dust is larger than a human hair. Therefore, it's critical to keep your hard drive free from all dust and dirt because even the smallest particle could find its way between the read/write head and the disk platter, causing a **head crash**—a stoppage of the hard drive that often results in data loss.

SSDs free you from worry about head crashes at all. The memory inside an SSD is constructed with electronic transistors, meaning there are no platters, no motors, and no read/write arms. Instead, a series of cells are constructed in the silicon wafers. If high voltage is applied, electrons move in and you have one state. Reverse the voltage and the electrons flow in another direction, marking the cell as storing a different value. The limiting factor for an SSD's lifespan is how many times data can be written to a cell. But the current generation of SSDs is proving to have very strong performance over time. Intel, one manufacturer of SSDs, says its drives will last five years when being written to heavily (20 GB per day).

Capacities for mechanical hard drives can exceed 4,000 GB (4 TB) and SSD drives are now storing 1 TB. Increasing the amount of data stored in these mechanical drives is achieved either by adding more platters or by increasing the amount of data stored on each platter. SSD capacities continue to increase as the density of transistors on silicon wafers increases. Modern technology continues to increase the quantities of data that can be stored in small places.

FIGURE 6.15 The hard drive is a stack of platters enclosed in a sealed case. Special arms fit between each platter. The read/write heads at the end of each arm read data from and save data to the platters. *(Skaljac/Shutterstock)*

Storage capacities for SSDs now range up to 2 TB, but such a large SSD is very expensive. Systems now often offer an SSD of 128 GB or 256 GB and then a mechanical hard drive, or two, to provide TBs of inexpensive slower storage space.

Optical Drives

How do optical drives work? Optical drives are disc drives that use a laser to store and read data. Data is saved to a compact disc (CD), digital video disc (DVD), or Blu-ray disc (BD) (called **optical media**) within established tracks and sectors, just like on a hard drive. But optical discs store data as tiny pits that are burned into the disc by a high-speed laser. These pits are extremely small, less than 1 micron (a millionth of a meter).

Figure 6.16 shows how data is read from a disc by a laser beam, with the pits and nonpits (called *lands*) translating into the *1*s and *0*s of the binary code that computers understand. CDs and DVDs use a red laser to read and write data. Blu-ray discs get their name because they are read with a blue laser light, which has a shorter wavelength and can focus more tightly and pack more information on a disc. Blu-ray drives are the fastest optical devices on the market and deliver the high-definition quality video that larger displays and monitors demand.

Why can I store data on some optical discs but not others? All forms of optical media come in three formats:

1. *Prerecorded* discs are read-only (ROM), meaning you can't save any data onto them.
2. *Recordable* (R) formats allow you to write data to them, but only once.
3. *Rewriteable* (RW) discs let you write and rewrite data to them many times.

Should I bother having an optical disc drive? Traditionally, optical media delivered music and movies, but these are now available through streaming services. Likewise, in the past, software was often installed from a DVD, but now you can buy almost all software online. Therefore, many lightweight systems have stopped including optical drives. For example, ultrabooks are so thin and lightweight they often leave out an optical drive but may include a slot for an SD memory card to allow you to transfer files. You can

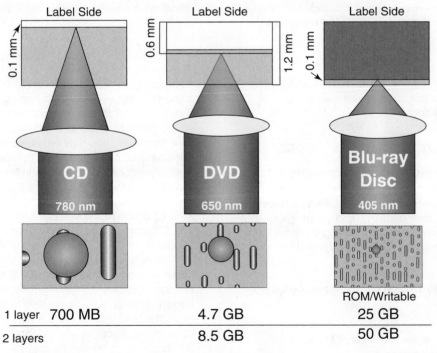

FIGURE 6.16 Blu-ray lasers have a shorter wavelength and so can store a much higher density of information than CDs and DVDs.

FIGURE 6.17 In Windows, the free and used capacity of each device in the computer system is shown in the Computer window. The General tab of the Properties dialog box gives you more-detailed information.

>*To view the Computer window, launch File Explorer (previously called Windows Explorer), and then click* **This PC***. To view the pie chart, right-click the* **C drive***, and select* **Properties***.*

buy external optical drives, but if you have a need for optical drives, you're probably better off purchasing a laptop computer with an optical drive.

Your Storage Capacity and Needs

How do I know how much storage capacity I have? Typically, hard drive capacity is measured in gigabytes (GB) or terabytes (1 TB = 1,000 GB). Windows displays the hard drives, their capacity, and usage information, as shown in Figure 6.17. To get a slightly more detailed view, select a drive and then right-click and choose Properties.

How much storage do I need? You need enough space to store the following:

- The OS
- The software applications you use, such as Microsoft Office, music players, and games
- Your data files
- Your digital music library, photos, videos of television shows and movies, and so on

Figure 6.18 shows an example of storage calculation. If you plan to have a system backup on the same drive, be sure to budget for that room as well. However, note that if you're going to store your data files online instead of on your computer, you may not need much hard drive space. For example, if you stream all the movies you watch from Netflix, keep all your data files in Microsoft OneDrive, and use online software like Google Docs to edit, you may need very little hard drive space. Most ultrabooks like the Dell XPS 13 or the Apple MacBook Air are configured with 128-GB drives. In fact, many Chromebooks have only a 16-GB drive.

Also note that you don't need to meet all your storage needs with an internal hard drive. You can also add an external hard drive to your system, many of which use a USB port to connect. If you're looking to buy an external hard drive, the USB 3.0 standard is about 10 times faster than USB 2.0, so if your system supports USB 3.0, that's the better choice.

Is it better to have one huge drive or several smaller drives? It depends on what's important to you: speed or security. If you purchase two smaller drives, you can

FIGURE 6.18

Sample Hard Drive Space Requirements

APPLICATION/DATA	HARD DRIVE SPACE REQUIRED	HEAVY CLOUD STORAGE USER
Windows 8 (64 bit)	20 GB	20 GB
Microsoft Office 2013 Professional	3.5 GB	3.5 GB
Adobe Photoshop Elements 12	4 GB	4 GB
Adobe Premiere Pro CC	10 GB	10 GB
Video library of movies	80 GB (about 40 HD movies)	Streamed through online services
Music library	50 GB (about 7,000 songs)	Stored in cloud (iCloud or Amazon Cloud Drive)
Photographs	5 GB	Stored in iCloud or Dropbox
Total storage in use	**172.5 GB**	**37.5 GB**
Full backup	172.5 GB	Stored in cloud using Carbonite
Total required	**345 GB**	**37.5 GB**

combine them using RAID technology. **RAID (redundant array of independent disks)** is a set of strategies for using more than one drive in a system (see Figure 6.19). RAID 0 and RAID 1 are the most popular options for consumer machines.

- When you run two hard drives in **RAID 0**, the time it takes to write a file is cut in half. If disk performance is very important—for example, when you're doing video editing

or sound recording—using two files in RAID 0 could be important. RAID 0 is faster because every time data is written to a hard drive, it's spread across the two physical drives (see Figure 6.19a). The write begins on the first drive, and while the system is waiting for that write to be completed, the system jumps ahead and begins to write the next block of data to the second drive. This makes writing information to disk almost twice as fast as using

FIGURE 6.19 (a) A RAID 0 configuration speeds up file read/write time. (b) A RAID 1 configuration gives you an instant backup.

BITS&BYTES

How Much Storage to Buy?

No matter what kind of device you purchase, you'll have to decide how much storage you're willing to pay for. Does your Nexus 7 tablet need 16 GB? 32 GB? Should the SSD drive in your ultrabook be 128 GB? 256 GB? 512 GB? When you make your decision, keep in mind two factors:

1. Check whether you can add storage later using an SD card. If you can use a few SD cards to store music or photos, that will be a cheaper option.

2. Check how much usable storage is available in the device. For example, a 128-GB drive provides less than 128 GB of available storage space after the operating system, the manufacturer software, and backup storage space are accounted for.

just one hard drive. The downside is that if either of these disks fail, you lose all your data because part of each file is on each drive. So RAID 0 is for those most concerned with performance.

- If you're really paranoid about losing data, you should consider having two drives in RAID 1. In a **RAID 1** configuration, all the data written to one drive is instantly perfectly mirrored and written to a second drive (see Figure 6.19b). This provides you with a perfect, instant-by-instant backup of all your work. It also means that if you buy two 1-TB drives, you only have room to store 1 TB of data because the second 1-TB drive is being used as the "mirror."

RAID 0 and RAID 1 configurations are available on many desktop systems and are even beginning to appear on laptop computers.

So how do my storage devices measure up?
Figure 6.20 summarizes the factors you should consider in evaluating your storage subsystem. ■

> **Before moving on to Part 2:**
> - **Watch Replay Video 6.1** ▷.
> - **Then check your understanding of what you've learned so far.**

FIGURE 6.20

Evaluating Storage

- How much storage space do you need?
- Do you need a RAID 0 configuration for better performance?
- Do you want a RAID 1 configuration for immediate constant backup?

- Do you need to read or produce DVD/CDs?
- Do you need to read Blu-ray discs?
- Do you need to produce Blu-ray discs?

Mechanical Hard Drive

Storage

Optical Drive

Solid–State Drive

- Do you want very fast start-up of the system at boot-up and from sleep mode?
- Are you okay having a second hard disk drive for larger storage space?

(Maxim_Kazmin/Fotolia)

check your understanding// review & practice

For a quick review to see what you've learned so far, answer the following questions. Visit **pearsonhighered.com/techinaction** to check your answers.

multiple choice

1. Which statement about ultrabook computers is FALSE?

   a. Ultrabooks have the fastest optical drives.

   b. Ultrabooks are equipped with SSD drives for fast start-up.

   c. Ultrabooks typically weigh less than 3 pounds.

   d. Ultrabooks are available for either Windows or the OS X operating systems.

2. SSDs are classified as what type of storage?

   a. volatile   c. video

   b. nonvolatile   d. cache

3. When would you want to consider RAID 1 technology?

   a. When you need the fastest solution for writing data

   b. When you need an instant backup of your work

   c. If you think that SSDs are too expensive

   d. When you only want to have one hard disk drive

4. The limit to how much RAM you can add to your system

   a. depends on the design of the motherboard.

   b. depends on the operating system running on your system.

   c. depends on the amount of memory each memory card slot supports.

   d. all of the above.

5. SuperFetch is a memory-management technique that

   a. determines the type of RAM your system requires.

   b. makes the boot-up time for the system very quick.

   c. preloads the applications you use most into system memory.

   d. defragments the hard drive to increase performance.

To take an autograded version of this review, please go to the companion website at **pearsonhighered.com/techinaction**, or go your MyITLab course.

Continue

TRY THIS

Measure Your System Performance

Using the Windows Task Manager and the Resource Monitor can provide you with a lot of useful information about your computer system. Let's make sure you can use these Windows tools to keep an eye on your system performance.

Step 1   Hold the Windows key and press X. From the pop-up menu, select **Task Manager**. Click **More Details** and then the **Performance** tab.

Step 2   If you leave this window open while you work, you can pop in and check the history of how your CPU, disk, memory, and network are performing. Let's start by looking at **CPU** utilization.

This computer is only occasionally going over 50%, so the system isn't limited by CPU performance.

Step 3   Clicking on **Memory** in the left panel shows that we have 8 GB of memory installed in this computer.

Notice that memory usage is consistent at about 4 GB. We have plenty of available memory so this system isn't limited by memory capacity.

Step 4 Clicking on **Disk** in the left panel shows that here we have one disk drive, a 1 TB internal hard drive. The lower graph shows the history of data moving back and forth to the disk, the disk transfer rate. The larger upper graph shows how active the disk is—what percentage of time it is reading and writing. If that is consistently high, upgrading to a faster, larger disk will have a big performance impact.

Make This

TOOL: App Inventor 2

MAKE: A Location-Aware App

Your smartphone comes equipped with a number of built-in sensors that can, for example, read accelerations (to tell if your phone is shaking), location (using GPS satellites), and even atmospheric pressure. App Inventor can work with sensor data and supports a wide set of sensors used in the Lego Mindstorms kits to recognize color or respond to touch and sound.

In this exercise, you'll use the LocationSensor component in App Inventor to combine information about your environment into your apps.

The LocationSensor component allows you to work with live GPS data within your mobile app.

For the instructions for this exercise, please go to pearsonhighered.com/techinaction or MyITLab.

Evaluating Other Subsystems and Making a Decision

The audio and video subsystems of your computer affect much of your enjoyment of the machine. Let's evaluate those subsystems and consider what state-of-the-art audio/video would add to your computing experience. Then let's consider how to make sure your system is reliable—nothing interferes with enjoying technology like a misbehaving computer!

 evaluating the
VIDEO SUBSYSTEM

How video is displayed depends on two components: your video card and your monitor. If you're considering using your computer to display complex graphics, edit high-definition videos, or play graphics-rich games with a lot of fast action, you may want to consider upgrading your video subsystem.

Video Cards

What exactly is a video card? A **video card** (or **video adapter**) is an expansion card that's installed inside the system unit to translate binary data into the images you view on your monitor. Modern video cards like the ones shown in Figures 6.21 and 6.22 let you connect video equipment using a number of different ports:

- *DVI ports* for digital LCD monitors
- *HDMI ports* for high-definition TVs, Blu-ray players, or gaming consoles
- *DisplayPort adapters,* a newer style port that can connect to digital monitors or projectors

How much memory does my video card need? All video systems include their own RAM, called **video memory**. Several standards of video memory are available, including graphics double data rate 3 (GDDR3) memory and the newer **graphics double data rate 5 (GDDR5)** memory.

The amount of video memory on your video card makes a big impact on the resolution the system can support and on how smoothly and quickly it can render video. Most new laptop computers come with video cards equipped with a minimum of 1 GB of video memory. For the serious gamer, 2 GB or more is essential, and cards with 3 GB are available. These high-end video cards allow games to generate smoother animations and more sophisticated shading and texture.

How can I tell how much memory my video card has? You'll find information about your system's video card in the Advanced Settings of the Screen Resolution window.

Processor covered by heat sink and fan

Clips into motherboard

DisplayPort adapter

HDMI port to digital monitor

Digital Video Interface (DVI) port to digital monitor

Video memory chip

Video memory chips

FIGURE 6.21 Video cards have grown to be highly specialized subsystems.

FIGURE 6.22 Video card processors produce so much heat that video cards have their own fan—or two. *(Nikkytok/Fotolia)*

To get to the Screen Resolution window, right-click on your desktop and select Screen resolution. In the Screen Resolution window, click the Advanced settings link. A dialog box will appear that shows you the type of video card installed in your system, as well as its memory capacity.

How does the CPU handle intensive video calculations? Because displaying graphics demands a lot of computational work from the CPU, video cards come with their own **graphics processing unit (GPU)**. The GPU is a separate processing chip specialized to handle 3-D graphics and image and video processing with incredible efficiency and speed. When the CPU is asked to process graphics, it redirects those tasks to the GPU, significantly speeding up graphics processing. Figure 6.23 shows how the CPU can run much more efficiently when a GPU does all the graphics computations.

In addition, special lighting effects can be achieved with a modern GPU. Designers can change the type of light, the texture, and the color of objects based on complex interactions. Some GPU designs incorporate dedicated hardware to allow high-definition movies to be decoded or special physics engines to model water, gravity, and rigid body movements.

Why do some people use more than one video card in the same system? For users who are primarily doing text-based work, one video card is certainly enough. Computer gamers and users of high-end visualization software, however, often take advantage of the ability to install more than one video card at a time. Two or even three video cards can be used in one system.

The two major video chip set manufacturers, Nvidia and AMD, have each developed their own standards supporting the combining of multiple video cards. For Nvidia, this standard is named SLI; for AMD, it is called CrossFire X. When the system is running at very high video resolutions, such as 1920 x 1200 or higher, multiple video cards working together provide the ultimate in performance. If you're buying a new system and might be interested in employing multiple video cards, be sure to check whether the motherboard supports SLI or CrossFire X.

Can I run a few monitors from one video card? Working with multiple monitors is useful if you often have more than one application running at a time (see Figure 6.24) or even if you just want to expand your gaming experience. Some video cards can support up to six monitors from a

 ACTIVE HELPDESK
Evaluating Computer System Components

In this Active Helpdesk, you'll play the role of a helpdesk staffer, fielding questions about the computer's storage, video, and audio devices and how to evaluate whether they match your needs as well as how to improve the reliability of your system.

Without a GPU

With a GPU

FIGURE 6.23 The GPU is specialized to handle processing of photos, videos, and video game images. It frees up the CPU to work on other system demands.

single card. The AMD Radeon graphics card, for example, lets you merge all six monitors to work as one screen or to combine them into any subset—for example, displaying a movie on two combined screens, Excel on one monitor, Word on another, and a browser spread across the final two.

Can I have a 3-D experience from a computer monitor? 3-D panels are available for desktop monitors and for some laptops. Using the 3-D wireless vision glasses included with the panels, the glasses make existing games or 3-D movies display in stereoscopic 3-D.

How do I know if I'm putting too much demand on my video card? If your monitor takes a while to refresh when you're editing photos or playing a graphics-rich game, then the video card could be short on memory

or the GPU is being taxed beyond its capacity. You can evaluate this precisely using the software that came with your card. For example, AMD Overdrive software monitors the GPU usage level, the current temperature, and the fan speed.

Review the considerations listed in Figure 6.25 to see if it might be time to upgrade your video card. On a desktop computer, replacing a video card is fairly simple: Just insert the new video card in the correct expansion slot on the motherboard. The video card in a laptop is more difficult to upgrade since the display and keyboard usually have to be removed to replace the video card. Note that some very basic laptop systems have video adapters integrated into the motherboard, so these video cards can't be upgraded. ∎

BITS&BYTES

Where's the Free TV?

Most major networks are streaming content for free so that you can catch episodes of most TV series on the go. Subscription channels like HBO and Showtime all give subscribers free streaming. If you have HBO at home, you can watch any show from the HBO GO website. If you're interested in more international viewing, head to Squid TV and select broadcasts from around the world. If you're looking for homemade shows, sites like Twitch.tv and Ustream are filled with live and archived video webcasts. And if you want to make TV instead of just watching, you can webcast your own show from the Ustream webapp using your webcam or smartphone video camera.

FIGURE 6.25

Evaluating the Video Card

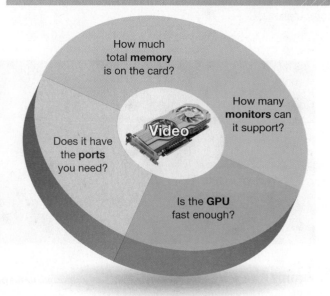

How much total **memory** is on the card?

How many **monitors** can it support?

Does it have the **ports** you need?

Is the **GPU** fast enough?

Video

trends in IT

Thunderbolt: The New Standard for Data Transfer

Faster is always better, and the newest input/output standard, Thunderbolt, is faster than anything seen before. And speed isn't its only advantage.

Intel used fiber optics—the transmission of digital data through pure glass cable as thin as human hair—to develop the new input/output technology named Thunderbolt. Thunderbolt supports blazingly fast transfer rates of 10 Gb/s, zooming past even the theoretical limit of the new USB 3.0, which is 4.8 Gb/s. How fast is that? Intel says that Thunderbolt could transfer a full-length HD movie in under 30 seconds or in just 10 minutes copy a library of music that would take a solid year to play through. And Thunderbolt can supply much more power to devices than the USB standard allows. It also has a very slim connector design, allowing laptop designers to make their systems even thinner (see Figure 6.26).

But one of the greatest hopes that comes with Thunderbolt is that the technology will be able to replace a number of different ports, cleaning up the cluttered design we see now on the sides of laptops and the backs of desktop units. Apple has introduced Thunderbolt ports on its full line of systems. A Thunderbolt port looks like a single thin port that supports both the video standard DisplayPort and the bus standard PCI Express (see Figure 6.27). So Thunderbolt can connect monitors

USB port   Thunderbolt port

FIGURE 6.26 Thunderbolt ports are very thin, allowing for new design options.

to computers using VGA, DisplayPort, DVI, or HDMI and can connect systems to external hard drives that use USB, FireWire, or eSATA. One Thunderbolt port can support several devices because the cables can be daisy-chained (connected one after another in a serial fashion), so having just one Thunderbolt port on a laptop allows you to connect up to six different peripherals to your system.

Thunderbolt technology also gives you a two-for-one deal, because each connector can support two separate channels to send and receive data, each one still operating at the full 10 Gb/s bandwidth.

What will this mean to laptop designers? Some speculate we'll see the heavy, heat-producing video cards currently integrated into gaming laptops become external graphics boxes. An incredibly thin, light laptop design would let you be wonderfully mobile all day, and then when you come home, you'd attach one cable. It would run from your Thunderbolt port to your 60-inch HDTV and then continue on to a separate graphics processor box. That same laptop would then be running a huge high-definition monitor with a high-resolution graphics and physics engine.

Apple is not the only company that uses the Intel technology. Hard-drive companies like LaCie and Western Digital, as well as audio/video processing companies like Avid and Apogee, now offer Thunderbolt products. The USB community may put up a bit of a fight to keep their standard around, but the allure of incredible speed, great versatility, and small, thin packaging is going to make the Thunderbolt technology a trend to watch.

Could Thunderbolt make USB a thing of the past?

PCI Express — Thunderbolt™ Cable — PCI Express

DisplayPort   DisplayPort

Thunderbolt Controller   Thunderbolt Controller

FIGURE 6.27 Thunderbolt can carry two channels of information on the same connector.

evaluating the
AUDIO SUBSYSTEM

For many users, a computer's preinstalled speakers and sound card are adequate. However, if you often use your computer to play games, music, and video, you may want to upgrade your speakers or your sound card.

What does the sound card do? Like a video card, a **sound card** is an expansion card that attaches to the motherboard inside your system unit. A sound card enables the computer to drive the speaker system. Most desktop systems have a separate sound card, although low-end computers often have integrated the job of managing sound onto the motherboard itself.

What does a basic sound card do for me? Many computers ship with a **3-D sound card**. 3-D sound technology is better at convincing the human ear that sound is omnidirectional, meaning that you can't tell from which direction the sound is coming. This tends to produce a fuller, richer sound than stereo sound. However, 3-D sound is not surround sound.

What is surround sound, then? **Surround sound** is a type of audio processing that makes the listener experience sound as if it were coming from all directions by using multiple speakers. The current surround-sound standard is from Dolby. There are many formats available, including Dolby Digital EX and Dolby Digital Plus for high-definition audio. Dolby TrueHD is the newest standard. It features high-definition and lossless technology, which means that no information is lost in the compression process.

To create surround sound, another standard, Dolby Digital 7.1, takes digital sound from a medium (such as a Blu-ray disc) and reproduces it in eight channels. Seven channels cover the listening field with placement to the left front, right front, left rear, right rear, and center of the audio stage, as well as two extra speakers to the side, as shown in Figure 6.28. The eighth channel holds extremely low-frequency (LFE) sound data and is sent to a subwoofer, which can be placed anywhere in the room.

The name 7.1 surround indicates that there are seven speakers reproducing the full audio spectrum and one speaker handling just lower frequency bass sounds. There is also a 5.1 surround-sound standard, which has a total of six speakers—one subwoofer, a center speaker, and four speakers for right/left in the front and the back. If you have a larger space or want precise location of sounds, use the newer 7.1 system.

To set up surround-sound on your computer, you need two things:

1. A set of surround-sound speakers and, for the greatest surround-sound experience,
2. A sound card that is Dolby Digital compatible

Does it matter what kind of speakers my laptop has? The limited size for speakers in a laptop

FIGURE 6.28 Dolby Digital 7.1 surround sound gives you a better quality audio output. *(Dolby Laboratories, Inc.)*

FIGURE 6.29 Sample Home Recording Studio Setup *((Fotolia; Aleksangel/Fotolia; Maksym Yemelyanov/Fotolia; Sashkin/Fotolia; Mariusz Blach/Fotolia; AbsentAnna/Fotolia; Nakov/Fotolia))*

and the added weight of circuitry to drive them means most people use headphones or ear buds for great audio instead of speakers. However, some laptops have built-in higher-quality speakers, like the Alienware line featuring Klipsch speakers and the HP series offering Beats speakers.

What setup do I need if I want to use my computer for recording my band? You can connect MIDI instruments, high-quality microphones, and recording equipment to your computer through an **audio MIDI interface** box. MIDI is an electronics standard that allows different kinds of electronic instruments to communicate with each other and with computers. The audio interface box attaches to your computer through a USB port and adds jacks for connecting guitars and microphones. You can edit and mix tracks through many different software packages, like Ableton Live or GarageBand. Figure 6.29 shows a simple home recording studio setup.

Figure 6.30 lists the factors to consider when deciding whether your audio subsystem meets your needs. ∎

FIGURE 6.30

Evaluating the Audio Subsystem

Do you want to upgrade your **speaker** quality?

Do you want 7.1 or 5.1 **surround sound?**

Do you need an **audio MIDI interface** box?

Audio

evaluating system
RELIABILITY

Many computer users decide to buy a new system because they're experiencing problems such as slow performance, freezes, and crashes. Over time, even normal use can cause your computer to build up excess files and to become internally disorganized. This excess, clutter, and disorganization can lead to deteriorating performance or system failure. If you think your system is unreliable, see if the problem is one you can fix before you buy a new machine. Proper upkeep and maintenance also may postpone an expensive system upgrade or replacement.

What can I do to ensure my system stays reliable? Here are several procedures you can follow to ensure your system performs reliably (see also Figure 6.31):

- **Clear out unnecessary files.** Temporary Internet files can accumulate quickly on your hard drive, taking up unnecessary space. Running the Disk Cleanup utility is a quick and easy way to ensure your temporary Internet files don't take up precious hard drive space. Likewise, you should delete any unnecessary files from your hard drive regularly because they can make your hard drive run more slowly.

- **Install a reliable antivirus package.** Make sure it's set to update itself automatically and to run a full system scan frequently.

- **Run spyware and adware removal programs.** These often detect and remove different pests and should be used in addition to your regular antivirus package.

- **Run the Disk Defragmenter utility on your hard drive.** When your hard drive becomes fragmented, its storage capacity is negatively affected. When you defragment (defrag) your hard drive, files are reorganized, making the hard drive work more efficiently. But remember that this only makes sense for mechanical drives. With no motors, there is no need to defrag an SSD drive.

- **Automate the key utilities.** The utilities that need to be run more than once, like Disk Cleanup, Disk Defragmenter, and the antivirus, adware, and spyware programs, can

be configured to run automatically at any time interval you want. You can use Windows Task Scheduler or third-party programs like Norton Security Suite to set up a sequence of programs to run one after the other every evening while you sleep, so you can wake up each day to a reliable, secure system.

What can I do when my system crashes? Computer systems are complex. It's not unusual to have your system stop responding occasionally. If rebooting the computer doesn't help, you'll need to begin troubleshooting:

1. **Check that you have enough RAM.** You learned how to do this in the "Evaluating the Memory Subsystem" section earlier in this chapter (page 230–232). Systems with insufficient RAM often crash.

2. **If your system isn't responding, try a System Restore.** Windows 8 automatically creates restore points before any major change to the system takes place, such as when you install a new program or change a device driver. You can also click on System and Security and manually create a restore point at any time. You can then select any restore point and bring your system back to the state it was in at that point. Open the Control Panel, click on System, and then select System Protection to learn more about System Restore.

   For Mac systems, the Mac OS X Time Machine, shown in Figure 6.32, provides automatic backup and enables you to look through and restore (if necessary) files, folders, libraries, or the entire system.

3. **If a System Restore wasn't enough to fix the problem, consider a Windows Refresh on your system.** This Windows 8 utility removes all the changes you've made to the system and brings it back to the state it came to you from the factory. It removes all the applications from third-party vendors, but it won't remove personal files like your music, documents, or videos.

FIGURE 6.31

Utilities to Keep Your System Reliable

TO AVOID THIS PROBLEM	USE THIS TOOL	FOR MORE INFO
Your hard drive is running low on space, making it run slowly	Disk Cleanup utility	Chapter 5
Your system is slowing down; browsers or other programs are behaving strangely	Antivirus software Spyware and adware removal software	Chapter 9
Files are spread across many spots on the hard drive, making the hard drive run slowly	Disk Defragmenter utility	Chapter 5
System not responding	Windows Refresh	Chapter 5

FIGURE 6.32 Mac's Time Machine keeps copies of files, folders, and libraries and can restore your system back to any previous point in time. *(Screen shot(s) reprinted with permission from Apple Inc.)*

4. **If you see an error code in Windows, visit the Microsoft Knowledge Base (support.microsoft.com).** This online resource helps users resolve problems with Microsoft products. For example, it can help you determine what an error code indicates and how you may be able to solve the problem.

5. **Search Google.** If you don't find a satisfactory answer in the Knowledge Base, try copying the entire error message into Google and searching the larger community for solutions.

Can my software affect system reliability? Having the latest version of software makes your system much more reliable. You should upgrade or update your OS, browser software, and application software as often as new patches (or updates) are reported for resolving errors. Sometimes these errors are performance related; sometimes they're potential system security breaches.

If you're having a software problem that can be replicated, use the Steps Recorder to capture the exact steps that lead to it. In Windows 8.1, display the Charms bar, select Search, then type "ste" in the search box. Now run the Steps Recorder and go through the exact actions that create the problem you're having. At any particular step, you can click the Add Comment button and add a comment about any part of the screen. The Steps Recorder then produces a documented report, complete with images of your screen and descriptions of each mouse movement you made. You can then e-mail this report to customer support to help technicians resolve the problem.

How do I know whether updates are available for my software? You can configure Windows so that it automatically checks for, downloads, and installs any available updates for itself, Internet Explorer, and other Microsoft applications such as Microsoft Office. From the Windows Control Panel, open System and Security and then Windows Update. Click Change Settings.

Many other applications now also include the ability to check for updates. Check under the Help menu of the product, and you'll often find a Check for Updates command.

What if none of this helps? Is buying a new system my only option? If your system is still unreliable after these changes, consider upgrading your OS to the latest version. There are often substantial increases in reliability with a major release of a new OS. However, upgrading the OS may require hardware upgrades such as additional RAM, an updated graphics processor, and even a larger hard drive. When you launch the Windows 8 upgrade from the web, it determines whether your hardware, applications, and devices will work with the new OS. ∎

making a final
DECISION

Now that you've evaluated your computer system, you need to shift to questions of *value*. How close does your system come to meeting your needs? How much would it cost to upgrade your current system to match what you'd ideally like your computer to do, not only today but also a few years from now? How much would it cost to purchase a new system that meets these specifications?

To know whether upgrading or buying a new system would have better value for you, you need to price both scenarios. Conduct a thorough system evaluation (Figure 6.33) to gather the data to help you decide. Purchasing a new system is an important investment of your resources, and you want to make a well-reasoned, well-supported decision.

Getting Rid of Your Old Computer

What should I do with my old computer? Before you get rid of your computer, be sure to consider what benefit you might obtain by having two systems. Would you have a use for the older system? Would you be able to donate it?

FIGURE 6.33

Key Items in System Evaluation

CPU
- What is your CPU usage level?

RAM
- Do you have at least 4 GB?

Storage
- Do you need an SSD start-up drive?
- Do you have a fast-access mechanical drive for large storage space?
- Do you need RAID 0 or RAID 1 storage drives for extra-fast performance or mirroring?

Video
- Do you have enough graphics memory?
- Is your GPU powerful enough?
- Do you have HDMI ports?
- How many monitors do you need to run simultaneously?

Audio
- Do you have 7.1 or 5.1 surround sound?

Also, before you decide to throw it away, consider the environmental impact (Figure 6.34). Mercury in LCD screens, cadmium in batteries and circuit boards, and flame retardants in plastic housings all are toxic. An alarming, emerging trend is that discarded machines are beginning to create an e-waste crisis.

So how can I recycle my old computer? Instead of throwing your computer away, you may be able to donate it to a nonprofit organization. Here are a few ways to do this:

- Many manufacturers, such as Dell, offer recycling programs and have formed alliances with nonprofit organizations to help distribute your old technology to those who need it.
- Sites like Computers with Causes (**computers withcauses.org**) organize donations of both working and nonworking computers, printers, and mice.
- You can also take your computer to an authorized computer-recycling center in your area. The Tele-communications Industry Association provides an e-cycling information site you can use to find a local e-cycling center (**ecyclingcentral.com**).

For companies that need to retire large quantities of computers, the risk of creating an environmental hazard is serious. Firms like GigaBiter (**gigabiter.com**) offer a solution. GigaBiter eliminates security and environmental risks associated with electronic destruction by first delaminating the hard drive and then breaking down the computer e-waste into recyclable products. The result of the final step is a sand-like substance that is 100% recyclable.

Can I donate a computer safely, without worrying about my personal data? Before donating or recycling a computer, make sure you carefully remove all data from your hard drive. Built into Windows 8 is an option to help with this, Remove everything and reinstall Windows. It removes all user-installed applications and all of your personal data, and resets your PC settings back to the default values.

Becoming a victim of identity theft is a serious risk. Credit card numbers, bank information, Social Security numbers, tax records, passwords, and personal identification numbers (PINs) are just some of the types of sensitive information that we casually record to our computers' hard drives. Just deleting files that contain proprietary personal information is not protection enough. Likewise, reformatting or erasing your hard drive does not totally remove data, as was proved by two MIT graduate students. They bought more than 150 used hard drives from various sources. Although some of the hard drives had been reformatted or damaged so that the data was supposedly nonrecoverable, the two students were able to retrieve medical records, financial information, pornography, personal e-mails, and more than 5,000 credit card numbers!

The open source software movement has flourished over the past decade. In response to increasing prices and the limitations placed on commercially available software, programmers began to donate time to design, develop, and support software systems. These products, like Gimp (a photo-editing tool), were then made freely available.

In the world of hardware, a similar but different approach called the open source hardware movement has flourished. Because hardware projects require materials and tools to assemble, products distributed as open source are not free in terms of cost, but they are free from any restrictions on how you modify them. Inexpensive hardware devices now span the range from the Digispark, a $9 microcontroller the size of a quarter, to the $40 Raspberry Pi, a full Linux-based computer the size of a credit card. Sample open source hardware projects include video game systems, 3-D printers, and even do-it-yourself medical devices.

Is open hardware good for the world? Does it undermine the intellectual property of others who want to create hardware resources and sell them for a profit? What is the impact on developing countries if they have immediate access to hardware designs instead of being required to purchase these items from a for-profit company? Follow the future of open source hardware by keeping an eye on ezines like Make (**makezine.com**), developer and supplier sites like Adafruit (**adafruit.com**), and tutorial headquarters like Instructables (**instructables.com**).

FIGURE 6.34 An electronics garbage dump can cause environmental concerns, like the leaching of lead and mercury into the ground.
(Ton Koene/AGE Fotostock)

The U.S. Department of Defense suggests a seven-layer overwrite for a "secure erase." This means that you fill your hard drive seven times over with a random series of *1*s and *0*s. Fortunately, several programs exist for doing this. For PCs running Windows, look for utility programs like File Shredder or Eraser. Wipe is available for Linux, and ShredIt X can be used for Mac OS X. These programs provide secure hard drive erasures, either of specific files on your hard drive or of the entire hard drive. ∎

Before moving on to the Chapter Review:
- **Watch Replay Video 6.2** ▷.
- Then check your understanding of what you've learned so far.

check your understanding// review & practice

For a quick review to see what you've learned so far, answer the following questions. Visit **pearsonhighered.com/techinaction** to check your answers.

multiple choice

1. Dolby Digital 7.1 creates
   a. ultra-sharp high-def video.
   b. a digital signal from an audio input.
   c. 8-channel surround sound.
   d. 7-channel surround sound.

2. Which is NOT a type of video port?
   a. HDMI
   b. DVI
   c. USB 3.0
   d. DisplayPort

3. When a computer is no longer useful, it can be
   a. securely donated.
   b. recycled.
   c. turned into a sand-like substance.
   d. all of the above.

4. To improve video performance, modern computers have a _____ in addition to the CPU.
   a. GPU
   b. VPU
   c. DPU
   d. APU

5. The faster data transfer port for computers today is the _____ port
   a. USB 3.0
   b. HDMI
   c. Thunderbolt
   d. DisplayPort

To take an autograded version of this review, please go to the companion website at **pearsonhighered.com/techinaction**, or go your MyITLab course.

 Continue

summary //

Your Ideal Computing Device

1. What kind of computer is best for me?

- Review the types of computer devices available and consider what your needs are for weight, screen size, and processing power.
- Evaluate your computer system so you have clear data on what you currently have. Then you can compare it with what is on the market and make a decision to upgrade or purchase a new device.

Evaluating the CPU Subsystem

2. What does the CPU do, and how can I evaluate its performance?

- You can find out what processor you have using the System Properties window.
- The CPU works by running a series of four steps: fetch, decode, execute, and store.
- CPUs are compared based on their clock speed, the number of cores they have, and their amount of cache memory.
- CPU benchmarks help you compare the overall performance of different CPUs.
- The CPU performance can be measured and recorded using the CPU usage graph of the Resource Monitor.

Evaluating the Memory Subsystem

3. How does memory work in my computer?

- RAM is used to hold instructions and data because the CPU can access RAM much faster than it can access the hard drive.
- Memory modules are small circuit boards that hold a series of RAM chips in your system.

4. How do I evaluate how much memory I need?

- The System Properties window shows how much physical memory you have installed.
- The Resource Monitor shows how the installed RAM is being used by your system.
- You can easily install RAM in your system, though each system has a limit on how much RAM it can hold.

Evaluating the Storage Subsystem

5. What are the computer's storage devices?

- Data is stored on mechanical hard drives, solid-state drives, and optical drives.
- There is a wide range of difference in access times and cost between different storage solutions, so most systems have a combination of types.

6. How do I evaluate my storage devices?

- The Properties dialog box in File Explorer (previously called Windows Explorer) displays information on the amount of storage available in your system.
- Compute the amount of storage you need for the software and data files you want to keep locally.
- Decide how many drives you want, what type each should be, and how you will configure them. RAID 0 is an option for combining drives for optimal performance. RAID 1 is an option for combining drives for immediate backup.

Evaluating the Video and Audio Subsystems

7. What components affect the quality of video on my computer?

- The video card is key to video quality. Be aware of how much video memory is installed and what kind of GPU is used on the card.
- Some users install multiple video cards for high-end graphics performance.
- With only one card, you can run multiple monitors.

8. How do I know if I need better video performance?

- If you see long refresh times, you may want an upgraded video card. The software that comes with the card can run performance testing to give you specific data on how the card is doing.

9. What components affect my computer's sound quality?

- The sound card and speakers control the sound quality in your system.
- If you want surround sound, you may want to invest in a new sound card and additional speakers.

Evaluating System Reliability and Making a Final Decision

10. How can I improve the reliability of my system?

- To make sure your system stays reliable, clear out unnecessary files, run antivirus software, run spyware and adware removal programs, run the Disk Defragmenter on mechanical hard drives, and use the Task Scheduler to automate these tasks.

- If your system is crashing often, check that you have enough RAM. Then consider a system restore or even a system refresh.
- Keep your software updated. Use the Steps Recorder to capture problems as they happen and report them to the manufacturer.

> Be sure to check out the companion website for additional materials to help you review and learn, including a Tech Bytes Weekly newsletter—
> **pearsonhighered.com/techinaction**
> And don't forget the Replay Videos .

key terms//

chapter quiz // assessment

For a quick review to see what you've learned, answer the following questions. Submit the quiz as requested by your instructor. If you are using MyITLab, the quiz is also available there.

multiple choice

1. Moore's law refers to:

   a. the amount of memory on a memory chip.

   b. the overall system processing capability.

   c. the number of transistors inside a CPU chip.

   d. the speed of DRAM.

2. Which of the following is true?

   a. RAM is where the CPU is located.

   b. Intel is the only manufacturer of CPUs.

   c. The CPU contains the ALU.

   d. The Windows System Properties window tells you how much memory you should buy.

3. Computers are designed with

   a. volatile memory.

   b. non-volatile memory.

   c. both volatile and non-volatile memory.

   d. neither volatile nor non-volatile memory.

4. The amount of time your current CPU is working is called

   a. CPU usage.

   b. Task Manager.

   c. virtual processing.

   d. system performance.

5. The amount of video memory in a modern video card is

   a. different from one model of card to the next.

   b. determined by the operating system.

   c. related to the size of the SSD drive.

   d. set by the CPU speed.

6. Windows creates "restore points" so that you can

   a. extend your warranty.

   b. add additional hard disk storage space.

   c. return your system to the way it was before you installed new software.

   d. protect your system from viruses.

true/false

_____ **1.** RAID 0 cuts the time it takes to write a file to disk in half.

_____ **2.** SuperFetch is a memory-management technique that pulls info from your hard drive into RAM.

_____ **3.** In Windows, the Refresh procedure is the same as the Restore procedure.

_____ **4.** GDDR5 memory is often used in external hard drives.

critical thinking

1. Measure Up

Briefly describe the way you would evaluate whether the CPU, memory, and storage of your system was meeting your needs. What tools would you need? What operating system programs help you evaluate performance?

2. A Green Machine

Review the impacts on the environment of your computer during its entire life-cycle. How do the production, transportation, and use of the computer affect the increase of greenhouse gas emissions? How does the selection of materials and packaging impact the environment? What restricted substances (like lead, mercury, cadmium, and PVC) are found in your machine? Could substitute materials be used? How would the ultimate "green machine" be designed?

Many Different Devices for Many Different Needs

Problem

Even within one discipline, there are needs for a variety of types of computing solutions. Consider the Communications Department in a large university. There are some groups involved in video production, some groups producing digital music, and some groups creating scripts.

Process

1. Split the class into teams. Select one segment of the Communications Department that your team will represent: video production, digital music, or scripting. The video production team requires its labs to be able to support the recording, editing, and final production and distribution of digital video. The digital music group wants to establish a recording studio (after the model of the Drexel University recording label, Mad Dragon Records, at **maddragonmusic. com**). The scripting group needs to support a collaborative community of writers and voice-over actors.

2. Analyze the computing needs of that segment, with particular focus on how it needs to outfit its computer labs.

3. Price the systems you would recommend and explain how they will be used. What decisions have you made in order to guarantee they will still be useful in three years?

4. Write a report that summarizes your findings. Document the resources you used and generate as much enthusiasm as you can for your recommendations.

Conclusion

Being able to evaluate a computer system and match it to the current needs of its users is an important skill.

Benchmarking

In this exercise, you'll research and then role-play a complicated ethical situation. The role you play might not match your own personal beliefs; regardless, your research and use of logic will enable you to represent the view assigned. An arbitrator will watch and comment on both sides of the arguments, and together, the team will agree on an ethical solution.

Problem

We've seen that for complex systems like computers, performance often is determined by using benchmarks, software suites that test a full area of performance. The results of these tests become a major force in marketing and selling the product.

There have been a number of claims of unethical conduct in the area of benchmarking. Companies have been accused of using out-of-date testing software to skew their results. Some companies have manipulated the settings on the machine to artificially raise their score (for example, turning off the display before testing for battery life). Some companies make sure the systems sent out to magazines and other evaluators have better-performing components than you might get off the shelf. Where is the line between gaining a competitive edge and lying when it comes to hardware assessment?

Research Areas to Consider

- SysMark2002
- BAPCo
- MobileMark
- 2009 Nobel Prize for Physics

Process

1. Divide the class into teams. Research the areas cited above from the perspective of either an Intel engineer working on a new CPU, an engineer working on a competing CPU, or a benchmark designer.

2. Team members should write a summary that provides documentation for the positions their character takes around the issue of equitable testing of hardware. Then, team members should create an outline to use during the role-playing event.

3. Team members should present their case to the class or submit a PowerPoint presentation for review, along with the summary they developed.

Conclusion

As technology becomes ever more prevalent and integrated into our lives, more and more ethical dilemmas will present themselves. Being able to understand and evaluate both sides of the argument, while responding in a personally or socially ethical manner, will be an important skill.

Laptop Alternatives

You are in need of a new laptop that is lightweight but that has enough power to edit the videos you produce for your YouTube channel. You have asked a few of your friends for some suggestions. One friend put together a list of possible computers in an Excel workbook; the other friend created a list as a text file. You will import the text file into the Excel 2013 table, sort the data, then filter the data to display only those computers you are interested in. Using Excel 2013 you will use tables to sort, filter, and display data.

You will use the following skills as you complete this activity:	
• Import Data from Text File	• Apply Filters
• Format as Table	• Change Cell Fill Color
• Sort Data	

Instructions:

1. Open *TIA_Ch6_Start.xlsx*, and save as **TIA_Ch6_ LastFirst.xlsx**.

2. Select cell A30, then import the text file, *TIA_Ch6_TableText,* accepting all defaults.

   a. To Import a text file, on the DATA tab, in the Get External Data group, click From Text. You will end up with 40 rows of data.

3. Format the range A1:M41 as a table, with Table Style Medium 13. Select Yes when asked to convert the selection to a table and remove all external connections.

   a. To format a range as a table, on the HOME tab, in the Styles group, select Format as Table, then select the desired style.

4. Sort the data by Style (A to Z), then by Processor Speed (Largest to Smallest), then by RAM (Largest to Smallest)

   a. To Sort data with multiple levels, on the DATA tab, in the Sort & Filter group, click Sort, then click Add level. Select the desired column in each sort drop down list. Make sure *My data has headers* checkbox is selected.

5. Filter the data to display Ultrabooks with Intel Core i5 processors and Solid-State Drives (SSDs).

   a. To Filter data, on the DATA tab, in the Sort & Filter group, click Filter. Then click the arrow for each column to be filtered, and then add or delete checkmarks for the desired category.

6. Copy the header row and four rows that display after all filters have been applied. Open a new worksheet, and paste the copied data. Rename the worksheet Choices.

7. Select cells A1:M1, and Wrap Text. Resize the width of column D, E, G, and M to 12.

8. Select cells A3:M3, and change the Fill Color to Yellow.

9. In cell A8, type **The HP Ultrabook is my choice, as it has the most RAM, greatest storage capacity, and the best wireless standard of the four choices.**

10. Save and submit based on your instructor's directions.

7

Networking: Connecting Computing Devices

How Networks Function

Networking Fundamentals

OBJECTIVE

1. What is a network, and what are a network's advantages and disadvantages? **(pp. 260–261)**

🔒 **Active Helpdesk:** Understanding Networking

Network Architectures and Components

OBJECTIVES

2. What are the different ways to classify networks? **(pp. 262–264)**

3. Which type of network is most commonly found in the home? **(p. 264)**

4. What are the main components of every network? **(pp. 265–268)**

Connecting to the Internet

OBJECTIVE

5. What are my options for connecting to the Internet? **(pp. 269–272)**

🔊 **Sound Byte:** Connecting to the Internet

🔒 **Active Helpdesk:** Connecting to the Internet

Your Home Network

Installing and Configuring Home Networks

OBJECTIVES

6. How do I tell if my home network is up to date, and how do I identify the devices on the network? **(pp. 276–277)**

7. Besides computers, what other devices can I connect to a home network? **(pp. 277–284)**

8. How do I configure the software on my computer and set up other devices to get my network up and running? **(pp. 284–286)**

9. What problems might I encounter when setting up a wireless network? **(p. 286)**

🔊 **Sound Byte:** Installing a Home Computer Network

Securing Wireless Networks

OBJECTIVE

10. Why are wireless networks more vulnerable to security risks than wired networks, and what special precautions are required to ensure my wireless network is secure? **(pp. 288–289)**

🔊 **Sound Byte:** Securing Wireless Networks

Make This: Explore an App Builder Skill on **page 275**

For all media in this chapter go to **pearsonhighered.com/techinaction** or **MyITLab**.

(Sergey Nivens/Fotolia; AKS/Fotolia; Ktsdesign/Shutterstock; Norebbo/Shutterstock; Maksim Kabakou/Shutterstock)

HOW COOL IS THIS?

Scan here for more info

Many of us have multiple wireless devices but often **no access to WiFi**, or we're too near the limit on our mobile device data plan to do what we want without costing a small fortune. Now, using **Karma WiFi**, you can travel with your own **personal hot spot**, and you can share the connection while **earning more data** as you do. All you need to do is buy a Karma device and set up an account. You get 1 GB of data, which is enough to watch a two-hour movie or listen to eight hours of music. When you've used that up, you can purchase more—no subscription needed. And you can stretch how often you need to buy more data by **sharing your connection**. As others connect to your Karma hot spot, you each earn a free 100 MB. You only share the connection—not your data—so the more you share, the more free bandwidth you accumulate. The benefits of social networking have come to WiFi! *(Mathisworks/Getty Images)*

How Networks Function

You access wired and wireless networks all the time—when you use an ATM, print out a document, or use the Internet (the world's largest network). It's important to understand the fundamentals of networking, such as how networks are set up, what devices are necessary to establish a network, and how you can access a network so that you can share, collaborate, and exchange information among your friends, family, and colleagues.

 networking
FUNDAMENTALS

Many of today's homes have more than one computing device capable of connecting to the Internet. A typical family engages in many activities that involve sharing and accessing files over and from the Internet and using a variety of Internet-connected devices (see Figure 7.1). What makes all this technology transfer and sharing possible? A computer network!

A computer **network** is simply two or more computers that are connected via software and hardware so they can communicate with each other. Each device connected to a network is referred to as a **node**. A node can be a computer, a peripheral such as a printer or a game console, or a network device such as a router.

What are the benefits of networks? There are several benefits to having computers networked:

- *Sharing an Internet connection:* A network lets you share the high-speed Internet connection coming into your home.

- *Sharing printers and other peripherals:* Networks let you share printers and other peripheral devices. For example, say you have a laptop that isn't connected to a printer. To print a document from your laptop without a network, you would need to transfer the file using a flash drive or other device to another computer that's connected

Jackie watches a video she took while on vacation

Andy plays PlayStation online and uploads a video he made for school

Mom watches a lecture from her online course while she prepares a snack

Dad watches a streaming movie and checks fantasy football scores on his iPad

Andrea takes pictures of her dog and uploads them directly to Facebook

FIGURE 7.1 With a home network, all family members can connect their computing devices whenever and wherever they want.

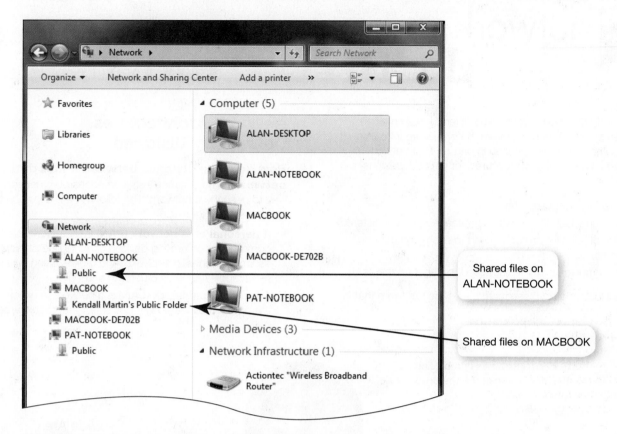

Shared files on
ALAN-NOTEBOOK

Shared files on MACBOOK

FIGURE 7.2 File Explorer (previously called Windows Explorer) shows five networked computers set up for sharing.

to a printer or carry your laptop to the printer and connect your laptop to it. With a network, you can print directly from your device even if it's not physically connected to the printer.

- *Sharing files:* You can share files between networked computers without having to use portable storage devices such as flash drives to transfer the files. In addition, you can set sharing options in Windows or OS X that let the user of each computer on the network access files stored on any other computer on the network. For example, the Windows network in Figure 7.2 has five computers attached to it. ALAN-DESKTOP, ALAN-NOTEBOOK, and PAT-NOTEBOOK are running Windows. The two MACBOOKs are running OS X. The Public folders enable file sharing because the user of any computer on the network can access the Public folder's contents.
- *Common communications:* As illustrated in Figure 7.2, computers running different operating systems can communicate on the same network.

Are there disadvantages to setting up networks?
Fortunately, after most home networks have been set up, there isn't much else that needs to be done to maintain or administer the network; therefore, the benefits of using a network outweigh the disadvantages. However, large networks involve an initial purchase of equipment to set them up. They also need to be administered, which can be costly and time consuming. **Network administration** involves tasks such as:

- Installing new computers and devices
- Monitoring the network to ensure it's performing efficiently
- Updating and installing new software on the network, and
- Configuring, or setting up, proper security for a network.

How fast does data move through networks?
Data transfer rate (also called **bandwidth**) is the maximum speed at which data can be transmitted between two nodes on a network. **Throughput** is the actual speed of data transfer that is achieved. Throughput is always less than or equal to the data transfer rate. Data transfer rate and throughput are usually measured in *megabits per second (Mbps)*. A megabit is one million bits. One of the main factors that determines how fast data moves is the type of network, which we'll discuss later in this chapter. ■

 ACTIVE HELPDESK
Understanding Networking
In this Active Helpdesk, you'll play the role of a helpdesk staffer, fielding questions about home networks—their advantages, their main components, and the most common types—as well as about wireless networks and how they are created.

network ARCHITECTURES

The network you have in your home differs greatly in terms of its size, structure, and cost from the one on your college campus. This difference is based in part on their network architectures. **Network architectures**, or network designs, are classified according to:

- The distance between nodes
- The way in which the network is managed (or administered)
- The set of rules (or *protocol*) used to exchange data between network nodes, and
- The communications medium used to transport the data

Next we'll look at all of these factors plus the hardware that is often used on networks.

Network Architectures Defined by Distance

How does the distance between nodes define a network? The distance between nodes on a network is one way to describe a network. The following are common types of networks (see Figure 7.3):

- A **personal area network (PAN)** is a network used for communication among devices close to one person, such as smartphones, notebooks, and tablets using wireless technologies such as Bluetooth and WiFi.
- A **local area network (LAN)** is a network in which the nodes are located within a small geographic area.

FIGURE 7.3 Networks can be classified by the distance between their nodes. *(SiuWing/ Shutterstock)*

WAN
Wide Area
Network

MAN
Metropolitan
Area Network

HAN
Home Area
Network

LAN
Local Area
Network

PAN
Personal Area
Network

Examples include a network in a computer lab at school or at a fast-food restaurant.

- A **home area network (HAN)** is a specific type of LAN located in a home. HANs are used to connect all of a home's digital devices, such as computers, peripherals, phones, gaming devices, digital video recorders (DVRs), and televisions.

- A **metropolitan area network (MAN)** is a large network designed to provide access to a specific geographic area, such as an entire city. Many U.S. cities are now deploying MANs to provide Internet access to residents and tourists. Some MANs employ WiMAX wireless technology that extends local WiFi networks across greater distances.

- A **wide area network (WAN)** spans a large physical distance. The Internet is the largest WAN, covering the globe. A WAN is also a networked collection of LANs. If a school has multiple campuses located in different towns, each with its own LAN, connecting the LANs of each campus by telecommunications lines allows the users of the LANs to communicate. All the connected LANs would be described as a single WAN.

Network Architectures Defined by Levels of Administration

How does the level of administration define a network? A network can be administered, or managed, in two main ways—centrally or locally (see Figure 7.4):

- *Central administration:* In a centrally administered network, tasks performed from one computer can affect the other computers on the network. A **client/server network** is an example. In a client/server network, a *client* is a computer on which users accomplish tasks and make requests, whereas the *server* is the computer that provides information or resources to the client computers as well as central administration for network functions such as printing. Most networks that have 10 or more nodes are client/server networks.

- *Local administration:* In a locally administered network, the configuration and maintenance of the network must be performed on each individual computer attached to the network. A **peer-to-peer (P2P) network** is an example. In a P2P network, each node connected on the network

Client/Server Network	Peer-to-Peer (P2P) Network

Server

Client

Client

Client

Peer (node)

Peer (node)

Peer (node)

Peer (node)

Peer (node)

FIGURE 7.4 Client/Server and P2P Networks. *(Oleksiy Mark/Fotolia; Oleksiy Mark/Fotolia; Sashkin/Fotolia; Maksym Dykha/Fotolia; Oleksiy Mark/Fotolia; Tuulijumala/Fotolia)*

BITS&BYTES

PAN Clothing: Organization and Power for Portable Gear

Now that people carry so many portable computing devices, clothing designers are starting to offer clothing that facilitates the storage, transportation, charging, and networking of their digital gadgets. The SCOTTeVEST is one of a line of vests and jackets designed to hold iPods, smartphones, and even iPads. It also features a built-in PAN to help maintain connectivity of your devices. And because all the devices in your PAN need power, accessories such as the Voltaic Backpack (shown in Figure 7.5) help recharge your digital devices using renewable energy sources. So don't forget to consider the perfect fashion accessory for your latest digital acquisition!

FIGURE 7.5 The Voltaic Backpack recharges your mobile devices using solar cells. *(Ashley Cooper pics/ Global Warming Images/Alamy)*

can communicate directly with every other node on the network. Thus, all nodes on this type of network are peers (equals). When printing, for example, a computer on a P2P network doesn't have to go through the computer that's connected to the printer. Instead, it can communicate directly with the printer. Because they're simple to set up, cost less than client/server networks, and are easier to configure and maintain, P2P networks are the most common type of home network. Very small schools and offices may also use P2P networks.

Ethernet Protocols

What network standard is used in my home network? The vast majority of home and corporate networks are Ethernet networks. An **Ethernet network** is so named because it uses the Ethernet protocol as the means (or standard) by which the nodes on the network communicate.

The Ethernet protocol was developed by the Institute of Electrical and Electronics Engineers (IEEE), which develops many standard specifications for electronic data transmission that are adopted throughout the world. Establishing standards for networking is important so that devices from different manufacturers will work well together. The standard for wired Ethernet networks is 802.3. The standard for wireless Ethernet networks, also known as **wireless fidelity (WiFi)**, is 802.11. The current version of wireless Ethernet is 802.11ac. Previous versions included 802.11n, 802.11g, 802.11b, and 802.11a.

How is the 802.11ac version different from the previous versions? The current wireless Ethernet

standard, 802.11ac, is faster and has a better signal range than the earlier 802.11n standard. The 802.11n standard operates at either a 2.4 GHz or a 5 GHz frequency, and prior standards operated only at the 2.4 GHz frequency that many other wireless devices (such as wireless land line phones) run on. The 802.11ac standard operates at a 5 GHz frequency. This means the 802.11ac standard is more resistant to signal interference. 802.11ad, also known as WiGig, is still an emerging standard. WiGig is expected to deliver even faster speeds at 60 GHz frequencies. It will allow devices, including video devices, to communicate wirelessly at multi-gigabit speeds.

Will my devices using older WiFi standards still work on a newer network? Devices using older standards, such as 802.11n, will still work with newer 802.11ac networks, but they'll operate with slower data transfer rates and may run into some frequency interference. The ability of current devices to use earlier standards in addition to the current standard is known as **backward compatibility**.

Are there different standards for wired Ethernet? The most commonly used wired Ethernet standard for home networks is the **gigabit Ethernet** standard. A data transfer rate of up to 1 gigabit per second (Gbps) is possible using this standard. Computers generally ship with gigabit Ethernet cards installed in them.

For even faster data transfer speeds, *10 gigabit Ethernet* is available. It provides a maximum data transfer rate of 10 Gbps. But 10 gigabit Ethernet networks are primarily used in businesses with large data throughput needs. ∎

network
COMPONENTS

To function, all networks must include:

- A means of connecting the nodes on the network (cables or wireless technology)
- Special hardware devices that allow the nodes to communicate with each other and to send data
- Software that allows the network to run (see Figure 7.6)

Transmission Media

How do nodes connect to each other? All network nodes are connected to each other and to the network by transmission media. **Transmission media** can be either wired or wireless; they establish a communications channel between the nodes on a network. The media used depend on the requirements of a network and its users.

What transmission media is used on a wired network? Wired networks use various types of cable (wire) to connect nodes (see Figure 7.7). The type of network and the distance between nodes determines the type of cable used:

- **Twisted-pair cable** is made up of copper wires that are twisted around each other and surrounded by a plastic jacket. Normal telephone cable is a type of twisted-pair cable, although phone cable won't work for connecting a LAN or HAN. A slightly different type of twisted-pair cable, called **unshielded twisted-pair (UTP) cable**, is used for networks. UTP is composed of four pairs of wires twisted around each other to reduce electrical interference.
- **Coaxial cable** consists of a single copper wire surrounded by layers of plastic. If you have cable TV, the cable running into your TV or cable box is most likely coaxial cable.
- **Fiber-optic cable** is made up of plastic or glass fibers that transmit data at extremely fast speeds.

What type of cable is used in most wired home networks? The most popular transmission media option for wired Ethernet networks is UTP cable. You can buy UTP cable in varying lengths with Ethernet connectors (called RJ-45 connectors) already attached. Ethernet connectors resemble standard phone connectors (called RJ-11 connectors) but are slightly larger and have contacts for eight wires (four pairs) instead of four wires.

FIGURE 7.6 Network Components. *(ifong/Shutterstock; Sergii Korolko/Shutterstock; Courtesy of Epson America, Inc; vectorlib .com/Shutterstock; Adrian Lyon/Alamy; Norman Chan/Shutterstock)*

FIGURE 7.7

Wired Transmission Media

Twisted-pair cable

Coaxial cable

Fiber-optic cable

Deepspacedave/Shutterstock; Zwola Fasola/Shutterstock; Zentilia/Shutterstock

Do all wired Ethernet networks use the same kind of UTP cable? The three main types of UTP cable you would consider using in wired Ethernet home networks and their data transfer rates are as follows (also see Figure 7.8):

1. *Cat 5E:* Although Cat 5E cable is the cheapest of the three types and is sufficient for many home networking tasks, it was designed for 100 Mbps–wired Ethernet networks that were popular before gigabit Ethernet networks became the standard. Therefore, you should probably not install Cat 5E cable even though it's still available in stores.

2. *Cat 6:* Because **Cat 6 cable** is designed to achieve data transfer rates that support a gigabit Ethernet network, it's probably the best choice for home networking cable, though it's more expensive and more difficult to work with than Cat 5E cable.

3. *Cat 6a:* Cat 6a cable is designed for ultrafast Ethernet networks that run at speeds as fast as 10 Gbps. Installing a 10 gigabit Ethernet network in the home is probably unnecessary

because today's home applications (even gaming and streaming media) don't require this rate of data transfer.

What transmission media is used to connect nodes on a wireless network? As noted earlier, *WiFi* is a standard for wireless transmissions using radio waves to connect computing devices to wireless networks and the Internet. With so many portable devices being connected to networks, a network with wireless connectivity is used in businesses as well as in most homes. However, note that wireless networks generally have decreased throughput compared with that of wired networks.

Why are wireless networks slower than wired networks? Some common reasons why wireless signals may have decreased throughput are:

- Wireless signals are more susceptible to interference from magnetic and electrical sources.
- Other wireless networks (such as your neighbor's network) can interfere with the signals on your network.

FIGURE 7.8 The three main UTP cable types used in home networks have different data transfer rates. *(Deepspacedave/Shutterstock; Zwola Fasola/Shutterstock; Zentilia/Shutterstock)*

- Certain building materials (such as concrete and cinder-block) and metal (such as a refrigerator) can decrease throughput.
- Throughput varies depending on the distance between your networking equipment.
- Wireless networks usually use specially coded signals to protect their data, whereas wired connections don't protect their signals. This process of coding signals can slightly decrease throughput, although once coded, data travels at usual speeds.

Can I have both wired and wireless nodes on the same network? One network can support nodes with both wireless and wired connections. Most people use wireless connections for portable devices such as laptops. However, many of the devices connected to a network, such as printers and TVs, usually stay in one location. Although these devices probably feature wireless connectivity, hooking them up to wired connections lets you take advantage of the faster throughput achieved by wired connectivity. In situations where you want to achieve the highest possible throughput on your portable device, you may want to use a wired connection temporarily.

Basic Network Hardware

What hardware is needed for different nodes on the network to communicate? For the different nodes on a network to communicate with each other and access the network, each node needs a **network adapter**. All desktop and laptop computers as well as smartphones, tablets, and many peripherals sold today contain network adapters installed *inside* the device. This type of integrated network adapter is referred to as a **network interface card (NIC)**. Different NICs are designed to use different types of transmission media. Most NICs included in computing devices today are built to use wireless media, but many can use wired media as well.

What equipment do I need in order to hook up to broadband? A broadband Internet connection requires a modem. Depending on the type of broadband service you have, you'll have either a cable modem or a DSL modem. Often, your Internet service provider will rent the appropriate modem to you or specify what type of modem you have to buy to work properly with the Internet service provider's technology. The modem translates the broadband signal into digital data and back again.

What hardware is necessary to transmit data through a network? Data is sent through a network in bundles called **packets**. For computers to communicate, these packets of data must be able to flow between network nodes. **Network navigation devices**, such as a router or a switch, facilitate and control the flow of data through a network:

- A **router** transfers packets of data between two or more networks. On a home network, you need a router to transfer data between your home network and the Internet, which is considered a separate network. To add WiFi to your home network, you need a router that features wireless capabilities.
- A **switch** acts like a traffic signal on a network (see Figure 7.9). All routers sold for home use have integrated

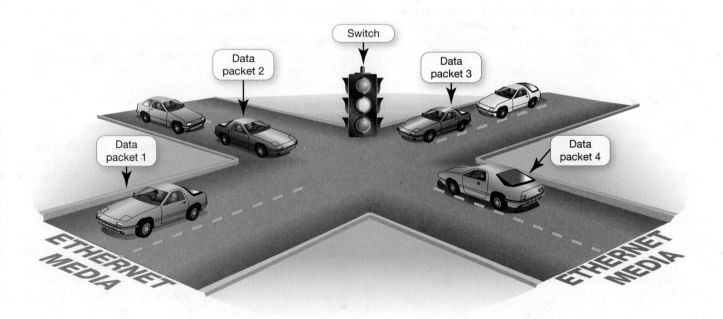

FIGURE 7.9 A simplified explanation of the function of switches is that, together with NICs, they act like traffic signals or traffic cops. They enforce the rules of the data road on an Ethernet network and help prevent data packets from crashing into each other. *(Luca di Filippo, iStockphoto)*

Internet

Wired/Wireless Modem Router

Tablet

HDTV

Laptop

FIGURE 7.10 A small network with a wired/wireless modem router attached. *(Beboy/Shutterstock; Laurentiu Iordache/Fotolia; Iko/Shutterstock; Sergey Peterman/Shutterstock; Oleksiy Maksymenko/Alamy)*

switches. Switches receive data packets and send them to their intended nodes on the same network (not between different networks). During the transmission process, data packets can suffer collisions; subsequently, the data in them is damaged or lost and the network doesn't function efficiently. The switch keeps track of the data packets and, in conjunction with NICs, helps the data packets find their destinations without running into each other. The switch also keeps track of all the nodes on the network and sends the data packets directly to the node for which they're headed. This keeps the network running efficiently.

Where should you place the router on your network? Most routers today have integrated modems, so only one device is needed (see Figure 7.10). The modem router should connect directly to the Ethernet cable, and all computer devices—such as an HDTV, a tablet, and a laptop—are connected to the modem router via a wired or wireless connection.

Network Software

What network software do home networks require? Because home networks are P2P networks, they need operating system software that supports P2P networking. Windows, OS X, and Linux all support P2P networking. You can connect computers running any of these operating systems to the same home network.

Is the same network software used in client/server networks? As opposed to P2P networks, the nodes on a client/server network don't communicate directly with each other; rather, they communicate through a centralized server. Communicating through a server is more efficient in a network with a large number of nodes, but it requires more complex software than is necessary for P2P networks. Therefore, the servers on client/server networks have specialized **network operating system (NOS)** software installed. This software handles requests for information, Internet access, and the use of peripherals for the rest of the network nodes. Examples of NOS software include Windows Server and SUSE Linux Enterprise Server. ■

connecting
TO THE INTERNET

One of the main reasons for setting up a network is to share an Internet connection. Some businesses and large organizations have a dedicated connection to the Internet, but other businesses and homeowners purchase Internet access from **Internet service providers (ISPs)**. ISPs may be specialized providers, like Juno, or companies like Comcast that provide additional services, such as phone and cable TV. Broadband is the preferred way to access the Internet, but in some situations, cellular or dial-up access may be necessary.

Wired Broadband Internet Connections

What exactly is broadband Internet access?
Broadband, often referred to as high-speed Internet, refers to a type of connection that offers a means to connect to the Internet with faster throughput. Broadband has a data transmission rate that ranges from 1 to 500 Mbps. This high rate of access is in contrast to dial-up Internet access, which has a maximum transmission speed of 56 Kbps (kilobits per second).

What types of broadband are available? As shown in Figure 7.11, the standard wired broadband technologies in most areas are *cable*, *DSL (digital subscriber line)*, and *fiber-optic service*. *Satellite broadband* is used mostly in rural or mountain areas that can't get DSL, cable, or fiber-optic service.

There are also wireless broadband options. *Mobile broadband* is offered through many cell-phone service providers through 3G and 4G networks. *Wireless Internet* is also available via WiFi radio waves. We'll discuss these options later in the chapter.

How does cable Internet work? Cable Internet is a broadband service that transmits data over the coaxial cables that also transmit cable television signals; however, cable TV and cable Internet are separate services. Cable TV is a one-way service in which the cable company feeds programming signals to your television. To bring two-way Internet connections to homes, cable companies had to upgrade their networks with two-way data-transmission capabilities.

How does DSL work? DSL (digital subscriber line) uses twisted-pair cable, the same as that used for regular telephones, to connect your computer to the Internet. The bandwidth of the wires is split into three sections, like a three-lane highway. One lane is used to carry voice data. DSL uses the remaining two lanes to send and receive data separately at much higher frequencies than voice data. Although DSL uses a standard phone line, having a traditional phone line in your house doesn't mean you have access to DSL service. Your local phone company must have special DSL technology to offer you the service.

How does fiber-optic service work? Fiber-optic service uses fiber-optic lines, which are strands of optically

FIGURE 7.11

Comparing Common Wired Broadband Internet Connection Options			
BROADBAND TYPE	**TRANSMISSION MEDIUM**	**SPEED CONSIDERATIONS**	**AVERAGE AND MAXIMUM DOWNLOAD SPEEDS**
Cable	Coaxial cable, similar to cable TV wire	Cable connections are shared, so speed can drop during high-usage periods	Average speed of 10 Mbps, with maximum of 30 Mbps
DSL (Digital Subscriber Line)	Copper wire phone line	Speed drops as distance from the main signal source increases	Average speed of 3.7 Mbps, with maximum of 15 Mbps
Fiber-Optic	Strands of optically pure glass or plastic	Transmits data via light signals, which do not degrade over long distances	Average speed of 50 Mbps, with maximum of 500 Mbps

pure glass or plastic that are as thin as a human hair. They're arranged in bundles called *optical cables* and transmit data via light signals over long distances. Because light travels so quickly, this technology can transmit an enormous amount of data at superfast speeds. When the data reaches your house, it's converted to electrical pulses that transmit digital signals your computer can "read." Fiber-optic cable is not usually run inside the home. On a fiber-optic network, twisted-pair or coaxial cable is still used inside the home to transport the network signals.

How does satellite Internet work? To take advantage of **satellite Internet**, you need a satellite dish (see Figure 7.12), which is placed outside your home and connected to your computer with coaxial cable, the same type of cable used for cable TV. Data from your computer is transmitted between your personal satellite dish and the satellite company's receiving satellite dish by a satellite that sits in a geosynchronous orbit thousands of miles above the Earth.

How do I choose which broadband connection option is best for me? Depending on where you live, you might not have a choice of the broadband connection available. Check with your local cable TV provider, phone company, and satellite TV provider(s) to determine what broadband options are available and what the transfer rates are in your area.

Often, the most difficult decision is choosing between high-speed plans offered by the same company. For instance, at the time of printing, Verizon offered several fiber-optic plans that featured download speeds from 25 to 500 Mbps. Although 25 Mbps is fine for every day browsing, e-mail, and shopping, it may not be fast enough for streaming HD movies or satisfying the needs of multiple devices on the Internet

FIGURE 7.12 ISPs that offer satellite Internet can provide Internet access even in remote areas. *(Ilene MacDonald/Alamy)*

BITS&BYTES

The Net Neutrality Debate

If you posted a blog on the Internet, it would have the same opportunity of being accessed as a new on-demand movie from Verizon or an online sale at Target. This is because data on the Internet is treated equally. There has been no differentiation by the type of user, the content that is being uploaded, or by the mode of communication. This is the concept of *net neutrality*.

However, big Internet service providers, such as Comcast, Verizon, and Time Warner Cable, would like to change that. In their perfect world, the Internet would be transformed into a tiered structure in which large users that "hog" the Internet, such as Netflix, Google, and Facebook, would have to pay for priority,

faster access, whereas smaller users for whom paying for priority access would be difficult or impossible would have less priority, slower access. The Internet service providers claim that this type of tiered priority system would promote competition and innovation. Companies like Netflix and Google claim that having to pay for faster access would put small startups at a disadvantage and ultimately stifle innovation. The government is proposing to classify Internet service providers as utilities, similar to electricity providers, and regulating them accordingly.

The debate continues. Where do you stand on net neutrality?

at the same time. Finally, you may also need to consider what other services you want bundled into your payment, such as phone or TV. Consulting with friends and neighbors about the plan they have and whether it's meeting their needs can help you decide on the right plan for you.

Wireless Internet Access

How can I access the Internet wirelessly at home? To access the Internet wirelessly at home, you need to establish WiFi on your home network by using a router that features wireless capabilities. You also need the right equipment on your mobile device. Virtually all laptops, smartphones, game systems, and personal media players sold today are WiFi enabled and come with wireless capability built in.

How can I access WiFi when I'm away from home? When you're away from home, you need to find a WiFi hotspot. Many public places, such as libraries, hotels, airports, and fast-food and coffee shops, offer WiFi access. Most locations are free, though a few still charge or require a special password to access the connection. Websites like Wi-Fi-FreeSpot (**wififreespot.com**) or apps such as WiFiGet help you locate a free hotspot wherever you're planning to go. When you have to buy WiFi access, you can pay for a single session or a monthly membership through services such as Boingo (**boingo.com**). Boingo has over 1 million hotspots worldwide, including airports, hotels, and restaurants.

Even wireless in-flight Internet service is available! Gogo (**gogoair.com**) is a wireless broadband network that provides coverage on participating airlines across the continental United States. So, when you are cleared to use your portable electronic devices, you can comfortably access wireless Internet while in the air.

How can I access the Internet when WiFi isn't available? There are often occasions when you're not in a WiFi hotspot but still need to access the Internet. In these instances, you may want to consider signing up for mobile broadband. **Mobile broadband** connects you to the Internet through the same cellular network that cell phones use to get 3G or 4G Internet access.

3G and 4G can be thought of as "WiFi everywhere" in that they provide Internet access to your mobile devices in the same way they provide voice service to your mobile phone. *3G* and *4G* refer to the third and fourth generations, respectively, of cell-phone networks. **4G** is the latest service standard and offers the fastest data-access speeds over cell-phone networks. To utilize the 3G or 4G capabilities of a mobile device, you

need to sign up for an access plan with a mobile data provider such as Verizon or AT&T.

How does mobile broadband Internet compare with wired Internet access? 3G performs similarly to a standard DSL connection (roughly 3 Mbps). According to the standards set for 4G, the data transfer rate you would get while in a moving vehicle is approximately 100 Mbps; from a fixed location, you can expect up to a 1 Gbps data transfer rate. Some of the early 4G systems released in the market support less than the required 1 Gbps rate and are not fully compliant with the 4G standards, and so are being tagged as 4G LTE. They are still faster than 3G, however.

How can I get 3G/4G service if my device doesn't have the right equipment? Many devices such as the iPad, Kindle Fire, Chromebook, and some laptops are available with built-in 3G or 4G capabilities. If your device doesn't have built-in 3G or 4G equipment, you can buy a *USB modem*. USB modems fit into a USB port on your device and let you access 3G or 4G networks. Like a smartphone, they also require a service plan.

Alternatively, instead of buying a USB modem that works on one device, you can buy a *mobile hotspot* (see Figure 7.13). These mobile hotspots let you connect more than one device

FIGURE 7.13 A MiFi device turns your phone signal into a 4G LTE mobile hotspot for you and four of your friends. (*Anonymous/PRNewsFoto/Verizon Wireless/AP Images*)

BITS&BYTES

The Internet of Things

FIGURE 7.14 The Internet of Things has resulted in more devices—like smoke detectors, dishwashers, and pacemakers—using the Internet more than people do.

(zonadearte/Getty Images)

Have you ever heard of the **Internet of Things (IoT)?** It's not a new concept—it has been around since the new millennium. The IoT is defined as the interconnection of uniquely identifiable embedded computing devices that transfer data over a network without requiring human-to-human or human-to-computer interaction. "Things" can be anything—machines, appliances, buildings, vehicles, even animals, people, plants, and soil. In addition to all the "smart" TVs, refrigerators, and thermostats we hear so much about, a thing can be a person with a heart monitor implant that can warn of an oncoming problem or a device in an automobile that monitors driving behaviors so insurance companies can better assess risk. Ultimately, the Internet of Things is about connecting companies, people, and technology in real-time via an extension of the Internet into the physical world. By the year 2020, there will be an estimated 50 billion connected devices. How do you think the IoT will impact you?

---

to the Internet with either WiFi or mobile broadband. Mobile hotspots require you to purchase a data plan, but the monthly fee may be less than paying for individual monthly plans on multiple devices. So, if you have several mobile devices that need wireless Internet access, this may be the most economical and functional way to access the Internet while on the road.

Dial-Up Connections

Why would I ever want to consider a dial-up connection to the Internet? Although about 70% of Internet users in the United States use high-speed Internet connections such as DSL, cable, or fiber-optic, there are still some areas (usually rural) where broadband service isn't available. A dial-up connection needs only a standard phone line and a modem to access the Internet. Therefore, some people choose to use a dial-up connection when there's no high-speed service in their area. Additionally, a dial-up connection

is the least costly way to connect to the Internet, so for those who don't use the Internet frequently, the extra cost of broadband may be unnecessary.

What are the disadvantages of dial-up? The major downside to dial-up is speed. Dial-up modems transfer data about 600 times slower than a fiber-optic broadband connection. Also, dial-up uses a traditional phone line to connect to the Internet; therefore, unless you have a separate phone line just for your dial-up connection, when you're using dial-up, you tie up your phone line. ■

> **Before moving on to Part 2:**
> • **Watch Replay Video 7.1** ▶.
> • **Then check your understanding of what you've learned so far.**

check your understanding// review & practice

For a quick review to see what you've learned so far, answer the following questions. Visit **pearsonhighered.com /techinaction** to check your answers.

multiple choice

1. The current standard for home wireless Ethernet networks is

   a. WiGig.

   b. 802.3.

   c. 802.11ac.

   d. all of the above.

2. The type of network used for communication among a laptop and smartphone using Bluetooth is a

   a. WAN.

   b. PAN.

   c. LAN.

   d. MAN.

3. The fastest broadband Internet service is usually

   a. fiber-optic.

   b. DSL.

   c. cable.

   d. satellite.

4. Which network device acts as a traffic signal on a network?

   a. network operating software

   b. transmission media

   c. a network navigation device

   d. a switch

5. The device used to move data between two networks is called a

   a. gateway.

   b. switch.

   c. wireless range extender.

   d. router.

To take an autograded version of this review, please go to the companion website at **pearsonhighered.com/techinaction**, or go your MyITLab course.

Continue

TRY THIS

Testing Your Internet Connection Speed

Your ISP may have promised you certain downloading and uploading data speeds. How can you tell if you're getting what was promised? Numerous sites on the Internet, such as **speedtest.net** and **broadband.gov**, test the speed of your Internet connection. You can then see how your results compare with others, as well as determine whether you're getting the results promised by your ISP.

Step 1 Go to **speedtest.net**, then click **Begin Test**.
(Courtesy of Ookla.)

Go to speedtest.net, and click Begin Test

Step 2 The program will display a "signal" being sent as a small data file which is downloaded from a remote server to your location. Then the speed is measured as a data file which is uploaded back from your location to the remote server. When the test is done, your results display, along with the location of the server that was used in the test. *(Courtesy of Ookla.)*

Upload Speed: Time taken to move data from your computer to the server

Download Speed: Time taken to move data from the server to your computer

Ping: Measures the time it takes to get a response from the server

Location of the remote server used in the test

Step 3 You can access more information about your results and how they compare with global averages by clicking the My Results link at the top of the test screen. Note that many factors can influence your Internet speeds, so be sure to run the test at several different times of the day over the course of a week before complaining to your ISP about not getting your promised speed. *(Courtesy of Ookla.)*

Best results

Comparison of your results vs. global averages

Results of various tests are displayed

Make This

TOOL: Ping and Telnet

MAKE: Networked Devices

One of the nice features of programming in **App Inventor** is that you can instantly see changes on your target device as you work. The two devices connect using WiFi. But what is going on behind the scenes to allow this?

In this exercise, you'll explore how the AI Companion software works with the AI program to connect your systems. You'll see how useful networking utilities like Ping and Telnet are to investigate how network firewalls are set up.

Network Server

IP Address of PC

IP Address of phone/tablet

The App Inventor Companion app and program communicate across WiFi to make your programming easier.

For the instructions for this exercise, please go to pearsonhighered.com/techinaction or MyITLab.

Your Home Network

You know what a network is and the advantages of having one. In this section, we look at installing or updating a home network and keeping it safe.

 installing and configuring
HOME NETWORKS

Now that you understand the basic components of a network and your Internet connection options, you're ready to install a network in your home. If you already have a network in your home, it's useful to examine your network settings and configuration to make sure they're still meeting your needs, especially if you've added new devices.

Only a few years ago, most home networks included just a few computers and a printer. However, a network that can manage those devices is often very different from one that can support the smartphones, gaming consoles, tablets, and smart TVs many homes have added to their networks since. If you're using any of these additional devices and you haven't updated your network equipment or setup in a while, it may be time to do so.

Planning Your Home Network

Where do I start? One of the first things you should do to evaluate your network is list all the devices you're using, as well as any devices you think you may add in the near future. Then determine whether your network is sufficiently up to date to support all your devices.

What wireless Ethernet standard should my network be using? For a home network to run most efficiently and to provide the fastest experience, it's best that all network nodes—computers, network adapters (NICs), routers, and so on—use the latest Ethernet standard. Devices that support the 802.11n standard have been around for a while, so if you've bought a laptop or other portable device in the past few years, it most likely has an 802.11n NIC. Your router may also be supporting the 802.11n standard.

However, many newer devices support the 802.11ac standard. If you have the fastest 802.11ac NIC in your laptop but the router is the slower 802.11n standard, then data will be sent at the speeds supported by the lower standard. If you haven't updated your router in a while, you may want to consider getting an 802.11ac router (Figure 7.15) to get the fastest connection speeds.

Additionally, the higher standard gives your wireless signal more range, so if you feel that some of your devices aren't connecting properly to the Internet from certain parts of your home, you may want to upgrade to the higher standard.

How can I tell what wireless standard my router supports? You may be able to tell whether your router is supporting the faster 802.11ac standard just by looking at it. Many routers have the wireless standard indicated on the device. If you're still not sure, you can search for more information on your router by entering the model number into a search engine. If your router is provided by your ISP and it's an older standard, you should consider having your ISP provide you with a new router.

How can I tell what network adapters are installed in my computer? To see which network adapters are installed in your Windows computer, use the Device Manager utility (see Figure 7.16), which lists all the adapters. If you can't tell which wireless standard the adapter supports from the list, search the Internet for information on your specific adapter to determine its capability. The Device Manager can also alert you if there's a problem with the adapter.

FIGURE 7.15 802.11ac wireless routers offer the fastest connection speeds and a greater wireless signal range. *(Oleksiy Mark/Shutterstock)*

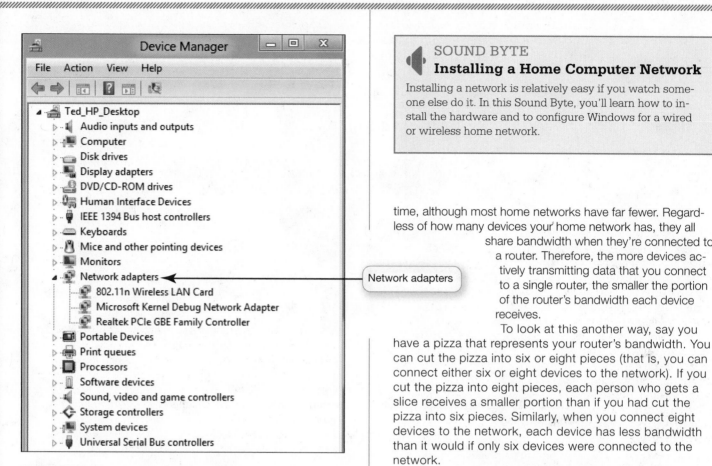

FIGURE 7.16 The Windows Device Manager shows the wireless and wired network adapters installed on a computer.

> To access the Device Manager, right-click the Start button to display the shortcut menu, and select **Control Panel***. Then click* **Hardware and Sound***, and select* **Device Manager** *from the* **Devices and Printers** *group.*

Connecting Devices to a Router

How can I directly connect multiple devices to my router? Most home routers have three or four Ethernet ports on the back to support wired connections. If you have a lot of devices (such as a game console, an HDTV, and a laptop) in your home that you use at the same time, you might want to connect some of them via a wired connection to increase the bandwidth to each device.

If you need additional ports for plugging in wired connections to your network, you can buy a stand-alone switch and plug that into one of the ports on your router (see Figure 7.17). This will give you additional ports for making wired connections. However, don't mistakenly buy another router with an embedded switch and try adding that to your network. The two routers will cause conflicts as they fight for control over network navigation.

How many wireless devices can connect to a router in a home network? Most home wireless routers can support up to 253 wireless connections at the same

time, although most home networks have far fewer. Regardless of how many devices your home network has, they all share bandwidth when they're connected to a router. Therefore, the more devices actively transmitting data that you connect to a single router, the smaller the portion of the router's bandwidth each device receives.

To look at this another way, say you have a pizza that represents your router's bandwidth. You can cut the pizza into six or eight pieces (that is, you can connect either six or eight devices to the network). If you cut the pizza into eight pieces, each person who gets a slice receives a smaller portion than if you had cut the pizza into six pieces. Similarly, when you connect eight devices to the network, each device has less bandwidth than it would if only six devices were connected to the network.

Are wireless routers for Windows and OS X networks different? All routers that support the 802.11n standard and the newer 802.11ac standard should work with computers running Windows or OS X. However, Apple has designed routers that are optimized for working

Router

Switch

FIGURE 7.17 You can add additional ports to your network by connecting a switch to your router. *(Alarich/Shutterstock)*

FIGURE 7.18 The AirPort Express router can be used for home networks to support devices running iOS, OS X, and Windows. *(Handout/MCT/Newscom)*

with Apple computers. So if you're connecting Apple computers to your network, you may want to use the Apple Air-Port Extreme router for larger home networks, or the AirPort Express for smaller networks (see Figure 7.18). Windows devices can also connect to an AirPort router, so it's a great choice for households with both Apples and PCs. The AirPort Extreme uses the newest 802.11ac technology for the fastest data transfers. In addition, it offers the option of creating a guest network, which can use a different password or no password at all, keeping all your networked devices and files secure.

How do I know what's connected to my router?
To determine what's connected to your router, you need to log in to an account associated with your router's IP address. You can find your router's IP address on the router manufacturer's website. Once you know it, type it into a web browser. You may need to enter a user name and password, but eventually you'll get to a configuration page that lists what wired and wireless devices are in your network. You may be surprised at all the various devices associated with your network.

Figure 7.19 shows a router network listing with wired (desktop computer) and wireless (TiVo DVR, laptop, iPhone, and iPads) devices connected in a home network. You'll notice that each device also has an IP address. You can think of your network as an apartment building. The router's IP address is the building's street address, while the IP addresses of the individual devices connected to the router are the apartment numbers. Each device needs an IP address so the router knows to which device to send information.

FIGURE 7.19 Wired and wireless connections can use the same router.

BITS&BYTES

Mesh Networks: An Emerging Alternative

Have you ever heard of a *mesh network*? This emerging technology uses small radio transmitters instead of wireless routers as its network nodes. What is so great about mesh networks is that only one node needs to physically connect to a network connection, and then all other nodes can share wirelessly with each other. This connection sharing between nodes can extend almost endlessly, since one wired node can share its Internet connection wirelessly with other nearby nodes, and then those nodes can share their connection wirelessly with nodes closest to them—thus creating a "mesh" of connectivity. The truly wireless aspect of mesh networks poses several advantages to the wireless networks that are in place today: they are easier to install since few wires need to be run; they can accommodate more nodes; and they enable wireless networks to be created in outdoor and unstructured venues.

In developing nations as well as in some areas in the United States, mesh networks have helped to provide access to the Internet in a much more timely and inexpensive manner than waiting for the physical connections to be established. Mesh networks also can help promote cellular communications during times of disasters when traditional communications are halted. And if you have an Android mobile phone, you can participate in the "Serval Mesh," which allows users to send and receive information without depending on established cellular networks.

Network-Attached Storage Devices

What can I attach to my network to facilitate file sharing and backup of data?
Network-attached storage (NAS) devices are specialized devices designed to store and manage all network data. Although data can always be stored on individual hard drives in computers on a network, NAS devices provide for centralized data storage and access.

Popular for years on business networks, NAS devices are now being widely marketed for home networks (see Figure 7.20). You can think of them as specialized external hard drives, and many of them actually resemble external hard drives. NAS devices connect directly to the network through a router or switch. Specialized software is installed on computers attached to the network to ensure that all data saved to an individual computer is also stored on the NAS device as a backup.

For Apple computers, the AirPort Time Capsule is a wireless router combined with a hard drive that facilitates the backup of all computers connected to the network. The AirPort Time Capsule looks very similar to the AirPort router, and it works in conjunction with the Time Machine backup feature of OS X. If you buy an AirPort Time Capsule, you won't need to buy an AirPort router (or other router) because the AirPort Time Capsule also fulfills this function on your network. When the AirPort Time Capsule is installed on your network, Macs connected to the network will ask the user if they want to use the AirPort Time Capsule as their source for Time Machine backups. The AirPort Time Capsule is another type of NAS device.

FIGURE 7.20 A network-attached storage device provides centralized data storage and access. *(Leslie Wilk/Alamy)*

trends in IT

Where Should You Store Your Files? The Cloud Is Calling!

You need to store your files where they're backed up regularly and securely. You also need to access your files whenever you need them. So should you store your files on your home network? That might work if your network-attached storage is accessible via the Internet. The latest trend, however, is to store your files in the cloud. Deciding which cloud option to use depends on a number of factors.

For Files Currently Being Used

Having the latest version of a file accessible on any device you use is important. However, constantly saving a file on multiple devices or carrying around a flash drive can be cumbersome and time consuming. When you store your files on the cloud, you avoid the hassle of saving the same file on multiple devices.

A popular web-based application for storing files on the cloud is Dropbox. Dropbox supports computers running Windows, OS X, and Linux, as well as many smartphones and tablets. After installing the Dropbox software on your devices, any files you save in the Dropbox folder are accessible to all your other devices via the Internet. You can also share folders in Dropbox with other Dropbox users, making it ideal for group projects.

FIGURE 7.21 MediaFire offers free storage and file sharing. *(MediaFire)*

Other cloud services include Google Drive, Microsoft OneDrive, Apple iCloud, and Amazon Cloud Drive. They have both free and paid levels of service.

For Media on the Go

You might like to view or listen to your media on the go, and storing it out in the cloud and streaming it over the Internet to your device may make a lot of sense. All the companies mentioned above let you store your media files on their servers. However, since each service offers limited amounts of space for free, these might not be the best options for large media collections.

For Large Media Collections That Need to Be Shared

For large media collections that you want to share with others, sites like ADrive and MediaFire (Figure 7.21) are popular choices. Both MediaFire and ADrive offer storage for free. You can easily share files with other people on either site. The advantage of these sites is the amount of free storage and the sharing and social media capabilities. All these sites offer greater storage capacities and other features with a paid account. You can also post links to the files directly to Facebook or Twitter from MediaFire.

When you choose which option is best for you, make sure to carefully investigate the site's file backup policies. Some free accounts don't feature guaranteed backups of your media, or the site might delete files that you haven't accessed for a certain period of time. The pay accounts generally guarantee that the files are backed up regularly. So don't ignore backup policies—you want your files to be there when you need them!

Home Network Servers

Besides external hard drives, are there other NAS devices I could use on my network? A more sophisticated type of NAS device is a **home network server**. Home network servers are specialized devices designed to store files, share files across the network, and back up files on computers connected to the network. All computers connected to the network can access the server.

Home network servers (see Figure 7.22) often look like oversized external hard drives. They are configured with operating systems like Windows Server 2012 Essentials and connect directly as a node on your network. Home servers have more sophisticated functionality than NAS devices and often handle the following tasks:

- Automatically back up all computers connected to the network
- Act as a repository for files to be shared across the network
- Function as an access gateway to allow any computer on the network to be accessed from a remote location via the Internet (see Figure 7.23)

Note that even though these devices are servers, they don't convert a home P2P network into a client/server network because these servers don't perform all the functions performed on client/server networks. Also note that you can access the media stored on your Windows Server 2012 Essentials server through your Xbox One as long as the Xbox is also connected to your home network.

FIGURE 7.22 Home network servers can perform a variety of tasks that simplify file management on a home network. *(Sashkin/Fotolia)*

Digital Entertainment Devices on a Network

What kinds of digital entertainment devices can connect directly to the network? A **network-ready device** (or Internet-ready device) can be connected directly to a network, either through a wired or wireless connection. Most game consoles, Blu-ray players, and DVRs, as well as many televisions (smart TVs) and home theater systems, are network ready. A device that is not network ready requires that the device be connected directly to another computer via a cable on the network.

Why should I connect digital entertainment devices to my network? One reason for connecting entertainment devices to your network is to access and share digital content between devices on your network. Connecting these devices to your network also connects them to the Internet so you can access a lot of entertainment content, including movies, videos, and music available online.

FIGURE 7.23 Windows Server 2012 Essentials home page. *(ItGroove Professional Services, Ltd.)*

You can also use gaming devices to play multiplayer games with players in the next room or all over the world. The content you access is either downloaded or streamed to your devices. Newer smart TVs and other smart devices (such as Blu-ray players, game consoles, and home theater systems) are continually adding apps and video services so that you can play games, view on-demand and online videos, listen to Internet radio, and access social networking sites (see Figure 7.24). Some smart devices also feature an integrated web browser that lets you access the web directly, without the use of apps.

What if I don't have a smart TV?
You can get the same services on your existing television by using a Blu-ray player that features integrated wireless connectivity to receive streaming media from various ISPs. For best video viewing, look for a Blu-ray player that has high-definition resolution and the capability to display 3-D video. Some set-top boxes also provide the same types of connectivity as a Blu-ray player. Alternatively, you can use devices such as Apple TV or Google Chromecast that enable you to send Internet-based media to your traditional TV.

Why should I connect my DVR to my network?
You may have a DVR, like the TiVo Premiere, which you use to record HDTV programs. Connecting your TiVo to your network makes it possible to receive downloads of movies

FIGURE 7.24 Smart TVs have their own apps and let you directly access the web so you can play games, connect with your social networking accounts, and view on-demand and online videos. *(Stanca Sanda/Alamy)*

directly to your TiVo from services such as Netflix and Amazon Instant Video. And some home network servers, like the Hewlett Packard MediaSmart servers, now work in conjunction with TiVo devices to provide them with additional storage. The TiVo Desktop software (see Figure 7.25), which you download from **tivo.com**, lets you transfer

FIGURE 7.25 The TiVo Desktop software facilitates the transfer of recorded shows to portable devices so you can enjoy your content on the go. *(TiVo® and the TiVo logo are trademarks of TiVo Inc. and its subsidiaries worldwide)*

FIGURE 7.26 The Remote Play feature of the PS Vita 4 lets you access PS4 features, like the PlayStation Store, directly from your Vita. *(Kyodo/AP Images)*

shows recorded on your TiVo to your computer or portable devices.

Why should I connect my gaming consoles to my home network? Current gaming systems, like the PlayStation 4 (PS4), can function as a total entertainment platform when connected to the Internet through your network. The PS4 has a built-in Blu-ray drive and can play Blu-ray discs, DVDs, and music files. You can download movies, games, and videos from the Internet directly to the PS4. You can also use it to share media across your network and to import photos or video from cameras and phones.

If you have a PS Vita, you can use an application called Remote Play (see Figure 7.26) to access features of your PS4 from your Vita. You can use the Vita to turn your PS4 on and off; access photos, music, and video files; play games; and browse the Internet. Media is transmitted from your PS4 and displayed on the Vita screen.

Specialized Home-Networking Devices

How can I use my home network to share photos? Digital picture frames that display photos are popular, and some come with built-in wireless adapters for easy connection to home networks. Featuring a touch-screen interface, this frame can access photos stored on your network or on an online photo-sharing site and display them. You can even set up an e-mail address for the picture frame so that friends and family can e-mail pictures directly to the frame.

How can I use my home network to enhance my home security? Monitoring cameras, both for indoor and outdoor use, are now available for the home that feature wireless connectivity so you can keep track of your home while you're away. You can connect these cameras to your network and monitor them in real time through software and portable devices such as an iPhone or Android phone (see Figure 7.27).

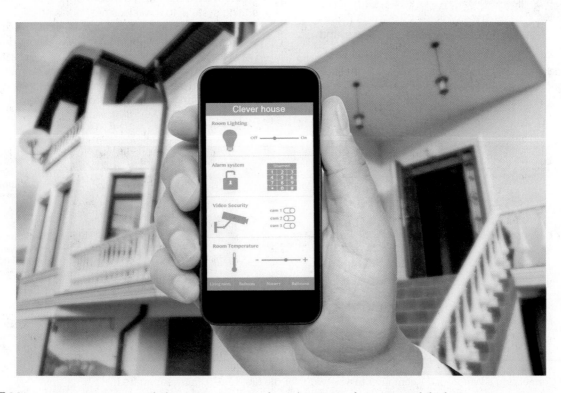

FIGURE 7.27 Many security systems can help you monitor your home's security from your mobile devices. *(Logitech)*

The software can be configured to alert you via e-mail or text message when the cameras detect movement, such as a vehicle entering your driveway. Some systems also allow you to receive alerts when there is a lack of movement. This can be useful for monitoring an aging relative or for monitoring the arrival of children coming home from school.

As time goes on, many more types of entertainment devices and home gadgets will be connected to your home network.

Configuring Software for Your Home Network

How do I set up a Windows home network for the first time? In Windows, the process of setting up a network is fairly automated, especially if you're using the same version of Windows on all your computers. The Windows examples in this section assume all computers are running Windows 8.1. You can launch the Windows network setup wizards from the Network and Sharing Center, which you access via the Network and Internet group in the Control Panel. Before configuring the computers to the network, do the following:

1. Make sure there are network adapters on each node.
2. For any wired connections, plug all the cables into the router, nodes, and so on.
3. Make sure your broadband modem is connected to your router and that the modem is connected to the Internet.
4. Turn on your equipment in the following order (allowing the modem and the router about one minute each to power up) and configure:
   a. Your broadband modem
   b. Your router
   c. All computers and peripherals (printers, scanners, and so on)

You can add other devices, such as TVs, Blu-ray players, and gaming consoles, to the network after you configure the computers.

After you've completed the previous steps, open the Network and Sharing Center from the Control Panel (see Figure 7.28):

- If your computer has a wired connection to the network, you should automatically be connected. You should give the network the same secured name you give to your router (see *Troubleshooting Wireless Network Problems on page 286*).
- If you're connecting wirelessly, click Connect to a Network in the Network and Sharing Center. The Networks panel opens on the right side of your screen, displaying the wired and wireless connection options. You will need to enter your security passphrase to connect to your wireless network initially.

How do I share files with other computers on my network? For ease of file and peripheral sharing, Windows 7 created a feature known as *homegroup* that has carried over to Windows 8. The homegroup is a software device that makes it easier to allow computers on a Windows 8 network to share peripherals and information. To create a homegroup after connecting your first Windows 8 computer to your network, complete the steps outlined in Figure 7.29.

What if I don't have the same version of Windows on all my computers? Computers with various versions of Windows can coexist on the same network. Always set up the computers running the newest version of Windows first. Then consult the Microsoft website for guidance on how to configure computers with previous versions of Windows.

How do I connect a mobile device to a wireless network? Connecting a mobile device, regardless of its operating system, to a wireless network is an easy process these days. When you boot up your device, your device will display a list of available networks that the NIC in your device detects. On Macs, the list pops up in the network login screen. On Windows 8 devices, you can click on the Internet access icon in the system tray to display available networks, or click the Settings charm in Windows 8, to display network connections.

FIGURE 7.28 Connecting a Windows 8.1 computer to a network for the first time is fairly automated.

FIGURE 7.29

Creating a Homegroup in Windows 8

CREATING A HOMEGROUP IN WINDOWS 8

Step 1: Click **Create a homegroup** in the HomeGroup window (accessed from the Network and Internet group in the Control Panel).

Step 2: Choose the sharing options for computers that belong to the homegroup. You can choose to share pictures, music, videos, documents, and printers with other Windows computers that belong to the homegroup. Although these are global settings for every computer in the homegroup, you can change these settings on individual computers if you wish.

Step 3: Windows generates a password. All other computers added to the network will need this password to join the homegroup. Once you've created the homegroup on the first computer, it will belong to that homegroup. You can then begin connecting other Windows computers to the network and join them to the homegroup you created.

BITS&BYTES

Analyzing Network Problems

If you have areas in your home where you have little or no WiFi coverage, try using a WiFi analyzer to gather information before embarking on ways to improve your coverage. There are free apps such as WiFi Analyzer (Android) or Wi-Fi Inspector (Windows) that provide signal strength and other details that will be helpful in remedying the problem.

If there is a padlock icon next to the network name, this means that the network is secure and will require a password. Enter the password for the network in the password box, and click the Join button. For unsecure networks, you don't need a password. Checking the "Remember this network" check box will make any network a preferred network, enabling the computer to connect to the network automatically when that network is available. You can have multiple preferred networks, such as your home, school, work, and local coffee shop networks.

Troubleshooting Wireless Network Problems

What types of problems can I run into when installing wireless networks? The maximum range of 802.11n or 802.11ac wireless devices is about 350 feet. But as you go farther away from your router, the throughput you achieve decreases. Obstacles between wireless nodes also decrease throughput. Walls, floors, and large metal objects (such as refrigerators) are the most common sources of interference with wireless signals.

What if a node on the network seems slow? Repositioning the node within the same room (sometimes even just a few inches from the original position) can affect communication between nodes. If this doesn't work, move the device closer to the router or to another room in your house. If these solutions don't work, consider using a dual-band N router or adding a wireless range extender to your network.

What's a dual-band N router? A dual-band N router allows for simultaneous support for both 2.4 GHz and 5 GHz frequency bands for 802.11n and all prior 802.11 standards (a, b, and g). Traditional routers only support one signal band at a time, so they're more likely to experience interference by outside devices (such as cell phones or microwave ovens) using the same bandwidth. Dual-band N routers allow for simultaneous access to both frequencies and therefore provide maximum flexibility in setting up a home network. For example, data transfers can be set to run on the 2.4 GHz side without impacting the performance of 802.11n clients that might be streaming video on the 5 GHz band.

What's a wireless range extender? A **wireless range extender** is a device that amplifies your wireless signal to extend to parts of your home that are experiencing poor connectivity. For example, as shown in Figure 7.30, Laptop C on the back porch can't connect to the wireless network even though Computer B in the den can. By placing a range extender in the den, where there is still good connectivity to the wireless network, the wireless signal is amplified and beamed farther out to the back porch. This allows Laptop C to make a good connection to the network. ■

FIGURE 7.30 Because a wireless range extender is installed in the den, Laptop C on the back porch can now connect to the wireless network.

ethics in IT

Sharing Your Internet Connection with Your Neighbors: Legal? Ethical? Safe?

With the advances in wireless equipment, signals can travel well beyond the walls of your home. This makes it possible for a group of neighbors to share a wireless signal and potentially save money by splitting the cost of one Internet connection among them. However, before jumping into this venture, you need to weigh a few issues carefully:

- **State and local laws:** You probably aren't legally prohibited from sharing an Internet connection, but check on state and local laws. Most laws are designed to prohibit piggy using a network without the network owner's consent. However, if you're giving neighbors permission to share your connection, you probably aren't violating any piggybacking laws.

- **ISP restrictions:** The terms of your agreement with your ISP might prohibit you from sharing your connection with people outside your household. If you aren't allowed to share the type of account you have now, your ISP probably offers an account (such as a small business account) that lets you share a connection, but it will most likely be more expensive. You might be able to share a personal account without being detected by your ISP, but that would be unethical because you should be paying for a higher level of access.

- **Range of access:** You also need to consider whether the shared access should be open to all neighbors or just to the neighbors contributing to the cost of the Internet connection (see Figure 7.31). You could leave the connection open, like the connections at your local coffee shop, and let anyone who finds it log on and surf. You could register your free hotspot with a service like NinthDecimal (**ninthdecimal.com**) and then people would be able to find it. However, neighbors who are helping pay for the connection might not want to fund free surfing for everyone. Make sure you work this out before proceeding.

- **Security:** If you're going to host a free and open hotspot, you need to make sure you set it up safely. You want to maintain a secure network for you and your neighbors while still allowing the occasional visiting surfer to use the connection. There are WiFi sharing services such as

Fon (**corp.fon.com**) and Chillifire (**chillifire.net**) that provide hardware and software that let you configure your hotspot so your network remains secure.

Although offering free access to anyone will earn you lots of good karma, additional risks exist because you don't know what mischief or criminal activities someone might engage in while connected to the Internet through your account. Think carefully before you proceed down the sharing path, and make sure you set up your hotspot to protect your internal network.

FIGURE 7.31 The first network listed is the home network; the other networks are from neighbors (and have much weaker signals).

securing wireless
NETWORKS

All computers that connect to the Internet, whether or not they're on a network, need to be secured from intruders. This is usually accomplished by using a firewall, which is a hardware or software solution that helps shield your network from prying eyes. (We discuss firewalls at length in Chapter 9.) Wireless networks present special vulnerabilities; therefore, you should take additional steps to keep your wireless network safe. If you're setting up a new network, it's wise to take these precautions *as you set up your network*. If you have a network already installed, check to be sure you've followed the guidelines discussed here.

Why is a wireless network more vulnerable than a wired network? With a wired network, it's fairly easy to tell if a **hacker**, someone who breaks into computer systems to create mischief or steal information, is using your network. However, the newer wireless 802.11 networks have wide ranges that may extend outside your house. This makes it possible for a hacker to access your network without your knowledge.

Also, in some areas where residences are close together, wireless signals can reach a neighbor's residence. Most wireless network adapters are set up to access the strongest wireless network signal detected. **Piggybacking** is connecting to a wireless network without the permission of the owner. This practice is illegal in many jurisdictions but often happens inadvertently between neighbors.

Why should I be worried about someone logging onto my wireless network without my permission? If your neighbor is using your network connection, his or her usage could be slowing down your connection speed. Some neighbors might even be computer savvy enough to penetrate your unprotected wireless network and steal personal information, just as any other hackers would. And any cyberattacks or illegal behavior a hacker initiates from your wireless network could get you in trouble with the authorities.

How is my wireless network vulnerable? Packets of information on a wireless network are broadcast through the airwaves. Savvy hackers can intercept and decode information from your transmissions that may allow them to bypass standard protections, such as a firewall, that you

---

SOUND BYTE
Securing Wireless Networks
In this Sound Byte, you'll learn some simple steps to secure your wireless network against intruders.

---

have set up on your network. Therefore, to secure a wireless network, take the additional precautions described in the Sound Byte "Securing Wireless Networks" and summarized as follows:

1. **Change your network name (SSID).** Each wireless network has its own name to identify it, known as the **service set identifier (SSID)**. Unless you change this name when you set up your router, the router uses a default network name that all routers from that manufacturer use (such as "Wireless" or "Netgear"). Hackers know the default names and access codes for routers. If you haven't changed the SSID, it's advertising the fact that you probably haven't changed any of the other default settings for your router either.

2. **Disable SSID broadcast.** Most routers are set up to broadcast their SSIDs so that other wireless devices can find them. If your router supports disabling SSID broadcasting, turn it off. This makes it more difficult for a hacker to detect your network and nearly impossible for a neighbor to inadvertently connect to your network.

3. **Change the default password on your router.** Routers have default user names and passwords. Hackers can use these to access your router and break into your network. Change the password on your router to something hard to guess. Use at least eight characters that are a combination of letters, symbols, and numbers.

4. **Turn on security protocols.** Most routers ship with security protocols such as Wired Equivalent Privacy (WEP) or Wi-Fi Protected Access (WPA). Both use encryption (a method of translating your data into code) to protect data in your wireless transmissions. WPA is a much stronger protocol than WEP, so enable WPA if you have it; enable WEP if you don't.

5. **Create a passphrase.** When you enable these protocols, you're forced to create a security encryption key (passphrase). When you attempt to connect a node to a security-enabled network for the first time, you're required to enter the security key. The security key or passphrase (see Figure 7.32) is the code that computers on your network need to decrypt (decode) data transmissions. Without this key, it's extremely difficult, if not impossible, to decrypt the data transmissions from your network. The Windows 8 Networks panel shows all wireless networks within range. Moving your cursor over the network name will reveal details about the network such as whether it's a secured network. Clicking on a network name allows you to connect to it or prompts you for more information such as the SSID name and security key.

FIGURE 7.32 By accessing your router, you can configure the security protocols available on your router and change the SSID. *(Courtesy of the Mozilla Foundation)*

6. **Implement media access control.** Each network adapter on your network has a unique number (like a serial number) assigned to it by the manufacturer. This is called a media access control (MAC) address, and it's a number printed right on the network adapter. Many routers allow you to restrict access to the network to only certain MAC addresses. This helps ensure that only authorized devices can connect to your network.

7. **Limit your signal range.** Many routers allow you to adjust the transmitting power to low, medium, or high. Cutting down the power to low or medium could prevent your signal from reaching too far away from your home, making it tougher for interlopers to poach your signal.

8. **Apply firmware upgrades.** Your router has read-only memory that has software written to it. This software is known as **firmware**. As bugs are found in the firmware (which hackers might exploit), manufacturers issue patches, just as the makers of operating system software do. Periodically check the manufacturer's website and apply any necessary upgrades to your firmware.

If you follow these steps, you'll greatly improve the security of your wireless network. In Chapter 9, we'll explore many other ways to keep your computer safe from malicious individuals on the Internet and ensure that your digital information is secure. ■

Before moving on to the Chapter Review:
- **Watch Replay Video 7.2** ↻ .
- Then check your understanding of what you've learned so far.

check your understanding// review & practice

For a quick review to see what you've learned so far, answer the following questions. Visit **pearsonhighered.com /techinaction** to check your answers.

multiple choice

1. What would you use to see what network adapters are installed in your Windows computer?

   a. the Device Manager utility

   b. the Programs and Utilities manager

   c. the Ethernet Manager utility

   d. the Home Network manager

2. All of the following are methods to secure your wireless network except

   a. disabling SSID broadcast.

   b. creating a passphrase.

   c. changing your network name (SSID).

   d. disabling WEP.

3. Which network-ready device facilitates file sharing and data backup?

   a. home network server

   b. AirPort Time Capsule

   c. network-attached storage

   d. all of the above

4. To share files between computers on a Windows home network, you must

   a. enable groupsharing.

   b. create a homegroup.

   c. enable Windows sharing.

   d. none of the above.

5. How can you tell what wireless devices are connected to your router?

   a. Look at the router itself.

   b. Log in to the router's IP address and check the configuration page.

   c. Look at the device's wireless settings.

   d. All of the above.

To take an autograded version of this review, please go to the companion website at **pearsonhighered.com/techinaction**, or go your MyITLab course.

Continue

Networking Fundamentals

1. What is a network, and what are a network's advantages and disadvantages?

- A computer network is simply two or more computers that are connected using software and hardware so they can communicate.
- Advantages of networks include allowing users to
  - share an Internet connection,
  - share printers and other peripheral devices,
  - share files, and
  - communicate with computers regardless of their operating system.
- Disadvantages for larger networks are that they require administration and that they may require costly equipment.

Network Architecture and Components

2. What are the different ways to classify networks?

- Networks can be defined by the distance between nodes:
  - A personal area network (PAN) is used for communication among personal mobile devices using Bluetooth or WiFi wireless technologies.
  - A local area network (LAN) connects nodes that are located in a small geographic area.
  - A home area network (HAN) is a specific type of LAN located in a home.
  - A metropolitan area network (MAN) is a large network in a specific geographic area.
  - A wide area network (WAN) spans a large physical distance.
- Networks are classified by administration:
  - Central: A client/server network contains two types of computers: a client computer on which users perform specific tasks and a server computer that provides resources to the clients and central control for the network. Most networks that have 10 or more nodes are client/server networks.
  - Local: Peer-to-peer (P2P) networks enable each node connected to the network to communicate directly with every other node. Most home networks are P2P networks.

3. Which type of network is most commonly found in the home?

- Ethernet networks are the most common networks used in home networking.
- Most Ethernet networks use a combination of wired and wireless connections, depending on the data throughput required. Wired connections usually achieve higher throughput than wireless connections.
- Wired Ethernet home networks use the gigabit Ethernet standard.
- Wireless Ethernet networks are identified by a protocol standard: 802.11 a/b/g/n/ac.
  - 802.11ac is the newest standard.
  - WiGig (802.11ad) is a new wireless link between devices. WiGig is similar to but faster than Bluetooth.

4. What are the main components of every network?

- To function, any network must contain a number of components:
  - A means of connecting the nodes on the network (cables or wireless technology)
  - Special hardware devices that allow the nodes to communicate with each other and to send data
  - Software that allows the network to run

Connecting to the Internet

5. What are my options for connecting to the Internet?

- Wired networks use various types of cable to connect nodes. The type of network and the distance between the nodes determines the type of cable used. Broadband connections include the following types:
  - Cable transmits data over coaxial cable, which is also used for cable television.
  - DSL uses twisted-pair wire, similar to that used for telephones.
  - Fiber-optic cable uses glass or plastic strands to transmit data via light signals.
  - Satellite is a connection option for those who do not have access to faster broadband technologies. Data is transmitted between a satellite dish and a satellite that is in a geosynchronous orbit.

- WiFi allows users to connect to the Internet wirelessly but is not as fast as a wired connection.
- Mobile broadband is a 3G or 4G service delivered by cell-phone networks.
- Dial-up is the cheapest means of accessing the Internet, but it is also the slowest.

Installing and Configuring Home Networks

6. How do I tell if my home network is up to date, and how do I identify the devices on the network?

- Most home network routers should support both wireless and wired access to the Internet.
- For a home network to run efficiently, all nodes such as NICs and routers should use the same Ethernet standard.
- The Device Manager utility in Windows lists all adapters installed on your computer.

7. Besides computers, what other devices can I connect to a home network?

- All devices are connected to your router, either wirelessly or with a wired connection. Wired connections deliver better throughput than wireless.
- To add additional ports to your network, you can connect a switch to your router.
- Network-attached storage (NAS) devices let you store and share data files such as movies and music, as well as provide a central place for file backups. Home network servers can be used instead of an NAS device if your needs require more sophisticated functionality than NAS devices.
- Connecting digital entertainment devices (such as gaming consoles) lets you stream movies and other entertainment directly from the Internet.

8. How do I configure the software on my computer and set up the devices required to get my network up and running?

- The latest versions of Windows make it easy to set up wired and wireless networks.
  - Plug in the modem, the router, and all cables, and then switch on the modem, router, and computers (in that order).
  - Launch the Network and Sharing Center, and select the appropriate links for setup.
  - Make sure each computer has a distinct name, and ensure that all computers are in the same homegroup.

- Devices such as gaming consoles each have their own setup procedures for connecting to wireless networks but usually require the same information as that needed for connecting a computer to a secured wireless network.

9. What problems might I encounter when setting up a wireless network?

- You may not get the throughput you need through a wireless connection. Therefore, you may need to consider a wired connection for certain devices.
- Distance from the router, as well as walls, floors, and large metal objects between a device and the router, can interfere with wireless connectivity.
- To solve connectivity problems, dual-band N routers allow for simultaneous support for devices running on both the 2.4 GHz and 5 GHz frequency bands for 802.11n and earlier standards. Wireless range extenders can amplify signals to improve connectivity in areas of poor signal strength.

Securing Wireless Networks

10. Why are wireless networks more vulnerable to security risks than wired networks, and what special precautions are required to ensure my wireless network is secure?

- Wireless networks are even more susceptible to hacking than wired networks because the signals of most wireless networks extend beyond the walls of your home.
- Neighbors may unintentionally (or intentionally) connect to the Internet through your wireless connection, and hackers may try to access it.
- To prevent unwanted intrusions into your network, you should change the default password on your router to make it tougher for hackers to gain access, use a hard-to-guess SSID (network name), disable SSID broadcasting to make it harder for outsiders to detect your network, enable security protocols such as WPA or WEP, create a network passphrase, implement media access control, limit your signal range, and apply firmware upgrades.

> Be sure to check out the companion website for additional materials to help you review and learn, including a Tech Bytes Weekly newsletter—**pearsonhighered.com/techinaction**. And don't forget the Replay Videos ▶.

key terms//

chapter quiz // assessment

For a quick review to see what you've learned, answer the following questions. Submit the quiz as requested by your instructor. If you are using MyITLab, the quiz is also available there.

multiple choice

1. Which of the following would NOT be a benefit of networking computers?

   a. sharing an Internet connection

   b. sharing printers and other peripherals

   c. sharing files

   d. sharing software licenses

2. Bethany is in her home, watching a video she took on vacation, while her brother is playing FIFA Soccer on his Xbox, and her dad is checking stock quotes on his iPad. What kind of network does this family have?

   a. P2P network

   b. client/server network

   c. both A and B

   d. neither A and B

3. What two devices are often combined into one device in a small network to connect the home network to the Internet and to share the connection between devices on the network?

   a. router hub and switch

   b. switch and router

   c. modem and router

   d. modem and switch

4. To determine what devices are connected to your router, you should

   a. log into an account associated with your router's IP address.

   b. view My Computer properties.

   c. look to see if the device's IP address matches the router's IP address.

   d. all of the above.

5. Which of the following is NOT a reason to connect your digital entertainment device to your home network?

   a. You can access digital content stored on other network devices.

   b. You can share digital content between network devices.

   c. Your stored entertainment files are more secure when connected to a home network.

   d. You can easily download entertainment content from the Internet.

6. Which of the following might cause interference or poor connectivity between nodes on a wireless network?

   a. concrete walls   c. some appliances

   b. nodes that are too   d. all of the above
      far apart

true/false

_____ 1. 802.11ac is the current wireless Ethernet standard.

_____ 2. With a home network, you can share digital entertainment content between devices.

_____ 3. Actual data throughput is usually higher on wired networks than on wireless networks.

_____ 4. Client-server networks are the type of network used mainly in homes.

critical thinking

1. **Using Online Storage**

   Sneakernet is jargon for physically transporting files from one location to another, as in using a flash drive. Think about the advantages and disadvantages of using flash drives versus online storage systems, such as Dropbox, Google Drive, and OneDrive. Defend your preferred method of storing and sharing files.

2. **Internet of Things**

   Think about the term "Internet of Things" in which things (objects, animals, people) are connected to the Internet and can automatically transfer data over a network. Our society is already filled with many examples of "smart nodes"—such as cars, appliances, and entertainment devices—that are connected to the Internet. What are the advantages and disadvantages of developing a more robust Internet of Things and continuing to add more smart nodes?

Providing Wireless Internet Access to the Needy

Problem

Not everyone can afford wireless Internet access, and this can put families, especially ones with school-aged children, at a disadvantage.

Task

You're volunteering for a charity that wants to install wireless networks in the homes of needy families. The project is funded by charitable grants with the objective of providing basic broadband Internet access and networking capabilities at no cost to the recipients.

Process

Break the class into three teams. Each team will be responsible for investigating one of the following issues:

1. **Internet service providers:** Research ISPs that serve the town where your school is located. Compare maximum upload and download speeds as well as costs. Be sure to consider the cost of the modems—whether they're purchased or rented. Select what your group considers the best deal.

2. **Networking equipment and network-ready peripherals:** Each home needs to be provided with an 802.11ac-capable wireless router and a network-ready all-in-one printer. Research three options for these devices, considering price as well as functionality.

3. **Security:** Work in conjunction with the group researching routers to determine the best router to purchase since it needs to support a security protocol such as WPA. Consider other types of protection needed, such as antivirus software and firewalls.

Present your findings to your class and come to a consensus about the solution you would propose for the charity.

Conclusion

Providing technology to underserved populations on a cost-effective basis will go a long way toward closing the digital divide.

Firing Employees for Expressing Views on Social Media Sites

In this exercise, you'll research and then role-play a complicated ethical situation. The role you play may or may not match your own personal beliefs; regardless, your research and use of logic will enable you to represent the view assigned. An arbitrator will watch and comment on both sides of the arguments, and together the team will agree on an ethical solution.

Problem

Employers often are intolerant of employees who express negative opinions or expose inside information about their employers on social media sites. Given that most jurisdictions in the United States use the doctrine of employment at will (employees can be fired at any time for any reason), many employers are quick to discipline or terminate employees who express opinions with which the company disagrees. When such cases come to court, the courts often find in favor of the employers.

Research Areas to Consider

- Ellen Simonetti and Delta Airlines
- Fired for blogging about work
- Free speech
- Joyce Park or Michael Tunison

Process

1. Divide the class into teams. Research the areas above and devise a scenario in which someone has complained about an employee blogging about an issue such as cleanliness at a food manufacturing facility.

2. Team members should write a summary that provides background information for their character—for example, employee, human resources manager, or arbitrator—and that details their character's behaviors to set the stage for the role-playing event. Then, team members should create an outline to use during the role-playing event.

3. Team members should present their case to the class or submit a PowerPoint presentation for review, along with the summary and resolution they developed.

Conclusion

As technology becomes ever more prevalent and integrated into our lives, more and more ethical dilemmas will present themselves. Being able to understand and evaluate both sides of the argument, while responding in a personally or socially ethical manner, will be an important skill.

Home Networking Guide

You write a newsletter, **The Everyday Technologist**, which specializes in technology tips and tricks for the casual everyday technology user. Your current newsletter is a guide to home networks. The basic document has been created, and now using Word 2013 you need to add formatting and images to make the guide more visually appealing.

You will use the following skills as you complete this activity:	
• Apply Text Effects	• Insert Column Break
• Insert Word Art	• Insert Images
• Insert Columns	• Apply Text Wrapping
• Insert Section Breaks	• Use Custom Margins

Instructions:

1. Open *TIA_Ch7_Start.docx*, and save as **TIA_Ch7_ LastFirst.docx.**

2. Select the title Home Networking Guide, and convert the text to a Word Art Object using Gradient Fill – Blue, Accent 1, Reflection.

3. Click Layout Options , and select Top and Bottom. Then, click See More... at the bottom of the Layout Options window, and in the Layout dialog box, in the Horizontal section, select the Alignment option, and then choose Centered from the dropdown box.

4. Apply the Fill – Orange, Accent 2, Outline – Accent 2 Text Effect to the three headings: Hardware, Wireless vs. Wired, and Powerline Adapters. Increase the font size of each heading to 18.

5. Create custom margins with so all margins are .7".

6. Position the cursor before the heading Hardware. Insert a Section Break (Continuous), and then apply Two Column formatting.

7. Place the cursor at the end of the second bullet point paragraph in the Hardware section. Insert the image TIA_Ch7_Modem Router. Change the Layout Option of the image to Square. Resize the image so the height is .9" and the width is 1.2", then move the image so that the two top lines of the Router paragraph display above the image, and the left side of the image is flush with the left margin.

8. Place the cursor at the beginning of the Powerline Adapters paragraph. Insert the image TIA_Ch7_Powerline. Change the Layout Option to Tight. Change the height of the image to 1", and then move the image so the right side is flush with the right margin of the document and centered vertically in the Powerline Adapter paragraph.

9. Place the cursor at the beginning of Current Wireless (Wi-Fi) Standards. Insert a Column Break. Format the text with Bold and Italics.

10. Save and submit for grading.

Technology in Focus

Under the Hood

Some people are drawn to understanding things in detail; others are happy just to have things work. If you use a computer, you may not have been tempted to "look under the hood." However, if you can understand the hardware inside a computer, you'll have some real advantages:

- You won't have to pay a technician to fix or upgrade your computer. You'll be able to fine-tune it yourself, and you'll be able to make your investment in your computer last longer.
- You'll be able to evaluate new advances in technology. For example, what's the impact of a new type of memory or a new processor?
- If you're a programmer, you'll be able to write more efficient and faster programs.

And if you're preparing for a career in information technology, understanding computer hardware is critical for you. In this Technology in Focus feature, we'll build on what you've learned about computer hardware in other chapters and go "under the hood" to look at the components of your system unit in more detail. Let's begin by looking at the building blocks of computers: switches.

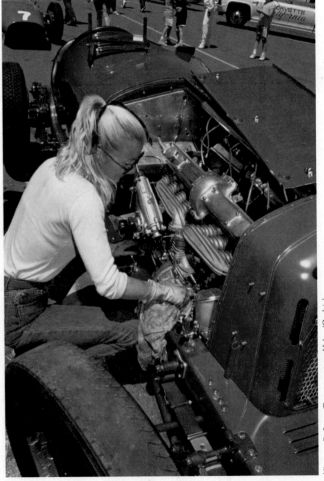

(George D. Lepp/Documentary Value/Corbis)

Switches

How does a computer process the data you input? A computer system can be viewed as an enormous collection of on/off switches. These simple on/off switches are combined in different ways to perform addition and subtraction and to move data around the system.

Electrical Switches

To process data into information, computers need to work in a language they understand. Computers understand only two states of existence: on and off. Inside a computer, these two possibilities, or states, are defined using the two numbers 1 and 0; the language represented by these numbers is called **binary language** because just two numbers are used. Everything a computer does, such as processing data or printing a report, is broken down into a series of 0s and 1s. **Electrical switches** are the devices inside the computer that are flipped between the two states of 1 and 0, signifying "on" and "off."

You use various forms of switches every day. The light switch in your kitchen either is ON, allowing current to flow to the light bulb, or OFF. Another switch you use each day is

FIGURE 1 Water faucets can be used to illustrate binary switches.

a water faucet. As shown in Figure 1, shutting off the faucet so that no water flows could represent the value 0, whereas turning it on could represent the value 1.

Computers are built from a huge collection of electrical switches. The history of computers is really a story about creating smaller and faster sets of electrical switches so that more data can be stored and manipulated quickly.

Vacuum Tubes. The earliest generation of electronic computers used **vacuum tubes** as switches. Vacuum tubes act as switches by allowing or blocking the flow of electrical current. The problem with vacuum tubes is that they take up a lot of space, as shown in Figure 2. The first high-speed digital computer, the Electronic Numerical Integrator and Computer (ENIAC), was deployed in 1945. It used nearly 18,000 vacuum tubes as switches and was about half the size of a basketball

court! In addition to being large, the vacuum tubes produced a lot of heat and burned out frequently.

Since the introduction of ENIAC's vacuum tubes, two major revolutions have occurred in the design of switches, and consequently computers, to make them smaller and faster:

1. The invention of the *transistor*
2. The fabrication of *integrated circuits*

Transistors. Transistors are electrical switches built out of layers of a special type of material called a **semiconductor**. A semiconductor is any material that can be controlled either to conduct electricity or to act as an insulator (to prohibit electricity from passing through). Silicon, which is found in common sand, is the semiconductor material used to make transistors (see Figure 3).

By itself, silicon doesn't conduct electricity particularly well, but if specific chemicals are added in a controlled way to the silicon, it begins to behave like a switch. The silicon allows electrical current to flow easily when a certain voltage is applied; otherwise, it prevents electrical current from flowing, thus behaving as an on/off switch. This kind of behavior is exactly what's needed to store digital information—the *0*s (off) and *1*s (on) of binary language.

The first transistors were much smaller than vacuum tubes, produced little heat, and could quickly be switched from on to off, thereby allowing or blocking electrical current. They also were less expensive than vacuum tubes.

It wasn't long, however, before transistors reached their limits. Continuing advances in technology began to require more transistors than circuit boards could reasonably handle. Something was needed to pack more transistor capacity into a smaller space. Thus, integrated circuits, the next technical revolution in switches, were developed.

Integrated Circuits. Integrated circuits (or **chips**) are tiny regions of semiconductor material that support a huge number of transistors (see Figure 4). Most integrated circuits are no more than a quarter inch in size yet can hold billions of transistors.

This advancement has enabled computer designers to create small yet powerful **microprocessors**, which are the chips that contain a central processing unit (CPU). The Intel 4004, the first complete microprocessor to be located on a single integrated circuit, was released in 1971, marking the beginning of the true miniaturization of computers. The Intel 4004 contained slightly more than 2,300 transistors. Today, more than 2 billion transistors can be manufactured in a space as tiny as the nail of your little finger!

Number Systems

How can simple switches be organized so that they let you use a computer to pay your bills online or write an essay? How can a set of switches describe a number or a word or

FIGURE 2 Early computers were constructed using vacuum tubes (see inset). The difference in size achieved by moving from tubes to transistors allowed computers to become desktop devices instead of room-sized machines. *(Historical/Corbis)*

FIGURE 3 This silicon wafer has the transistor circuitry for hundreds of devices etched on it. *(Justin Sullivan/Getty Images)*

give a computer the command to perform addition? Recall that to manipulate the on/off switches, the computer works in binary language, which uses only two digits, *0* and *1*. Let's look at how numbering systems work so that we can begin to understand this more deeply.

The Base-10 Number System

A **number system** is an organized plan for representing a number. Although you may not realize it, you're already familiar with one number system. The **base-10 number system**, also known as **decimal notation**, is the system you use to represent all of the numeric values you use each day. It's called base 10 because it uses 10 digits—0 through 9—to represent any value.

To represent a number in base 10, you break the number down into groups of ones, tens, hundreds, thousands, and so on. Each digit has a place value depending on where it appears

in the number. For example, using base 10, in the whole number 6,954 there are 6 sets of thousands, 9 sets of hundreds, 5 sets of tens, and 4 sets of ones. Working from right to left, each place in a number represents an increasing power of 10, as follows:

$$6,954 = (6 * 1,000) + (9 * 100) + (5*10) + (4*1)$$
$$= (6 * 10^3) + (9 * 10^2) + (5 * 10^1) + (4 * 10^0)$$

Note that in this equation, the final digit *4* is represented as $4 * 10^0$ because any number raised to the zero power is equal to 1.

The Base-2 (or Binary) Number System

Anthropologists theorize that humans developed a base-10 number system because we have 10 fingers. However, computer systems are not well suited to thinking about numbers in groups of 10. Instead, computers describe a number in powers of 2 because each switch can be in one of two positions: on or off (see Figure 5). This numbering system is referred to as the **binary number system**.

The binary number system is also referred to as the **base-2 number system**. Even with just two digits, the binary number system can still represent all the values that a base-10 number system can. Instead of breaking the number down into sets of ones, tens, hundreds, and thousands, as is done in base-10 notation, the binary number system describes a number as the sum of powers of 2—ones, twos, fours, eights, and sixteens. Binary numbers are used to represent every piece of data stored in a computer: all of the numbers, all of the letters, and all of the instructions that the computer uses to execute work.

FIGURE 4 An integrated circuit is packaged in a small case but holds billions of transistors. *(Edelweiss/Fotolia)*

FIGURE 5 Computer humor—binary has only two digits: 0 and 1! *(ThinkGeek, Inc.; Larry Lambert/Cartoonstock)*

Representing Integers. In the base-10 number system, a whole number is represented as the sum of *1s, 10s, 100s,* and *1,000s*—that is, sums of powers of 10. The binary system works in the same way, but describes a value as the sum of groups of *1s, 2s, 4s, 8s, 16s, 32s, 64s,* etc.—that is, powers of 2: 1, 2, 4, 8, 16, 32, 64, and so on.

Let's look at the number 67. In base 10, the number 67 would be six sets of *10s* and seven sets of *1s,* as follows:

Base 10: 67 = (6 * 10^1) + (7 * 10^0)

One way to figure out how 67 is represented in base 2 is to find the largest possible power of 2 that could be in the number 67. Two to the eighth power is 256, and there are no groups of 256 in the number 67. Two to the seventh power is 128, but that is bigger than 67. Two to the sixth power is 64, and there is a group of 64 inside a group of 67.

67 has	1	group of	64	That leaves 3 and
3 has	0	groups of	32	
	0	groups of	16	
	0	groups of	8	
	0	groups of	4	
	1	group of	2	That leaves 1 and
1 has	1	group of	1	Now nothing is left

So, the binary number for 67 is written as 1000011 in base 2:

Base 2: 67 = 64 + 0 + 0 + 0 + 0 + 2 + 1
$$= (1 * 2^6) + (0 * 2^5) + (0 * 2^4) + (0 * 2^3) +$$
$$(0 * 2^2) + (1 * 2^1) + (1 * 2^0)$$
$$= (1000011)_{base\ 2}$$

It's easier to have a calculator do this for you! Some calculators have a button labeled DEC (for decimal) and another labeled BIN (for binary). Using Windows 8, you can access the Scientific Calculator that supports conversion between decimal (base 10) and binary (base 2) by accessing Search from the Charms bar and typing "calc" on the Start screen. From the App search results, choose the first Calculator on the search results. From the Calculator menu, select View and then Programmer. You can enter your calculation in decimal and instantly see the binary representation in 64 bits, as shown in Figure 6.

SOUND BYTE
Where Does Binary Show Up?

In this Sound Byte, you'll learn how to use tools to work with binary, decimal, and hexadecimal numbers. (These tools come with the Windows operating system.) You'll also learn where you might see binary and hexadecimal values when you use a computer.

FIGURE 6 The Windows Calculator in Programmer mode instantly converts values from decimal to binary.

Hexadecimal Notation. A large integer value becomes a very long string of *1s* and *0s* in binary! For convenience, programmers often use **hexadecimal notation** to make these expressions easier to use. Hexadecimal is a base-16 number system, meaning it uses 16 digits to represent numbers instead of the 10 digits used in base 10 or the 2 digits used in base 2. The 16 digits it uses are the 10 numeric digits, 0 to 9, plus six extra symbols: A, B, C, D, E, and F. Each of the letters A through F corresponds to a numeric value, so that A equals 10, B equals 11, and so on (see Figure 7). Therefore, the value 67 in decimal notation is 1000011 in binary or 43 in hexadecimal notation. It is much easier for computer scientists to use the 2-digit 43 than the 7-digit string 1000011. The Windows Calculator in Programmer view also can perform conversions to hexadecimal notation. (You can watch a video that shows you how to perform conversions between bases using the Windows Calculator in the Sound Byte titled, "Where Does Binary Show Up?")

Representing Characters: ASCII. We've just been converting integers from base 10, which *we* understand, to base 2 (binary state), which the computer understands. Similarly, we need a system that converts letters and other symbols that *we* understand to a binary state the computer understands. To provide a consistent means for representing letters and other characters, certain codes dictate how to represent characters in binary format. Most of today's personal computers use the American National Standards Institute (ANSI, pronounced "AN-see") standard code, called the **American Standard Code for Information Interchange** (ASCII, pronounced "AS-key"), to represent each letter or character as an 8-bit (or 1-byte) binary code.

Each binary digit is called a **bit** for short. Eight binary digits (or bits) combine to create one **byte**. We've been converting base-10 numbers to a binary format. In such cases, the binary format has no standard length. For example, the binary format for the number *2* is two digits (10), whereas the binary

FIGURE 7

Sample Hexadecimal Values

DECIMAL NUMBER	BINARY VALUE	HEXADECIMAL VALUE
00	0000	00
01	0001	01
02	0010	02
03	0011	03
04	0100	04
05	0101	05
06	0110	06
07	0111	07
08	1000	08
09	1001	09
10	1010	A
11	1011	B
12	1100	C
13	1101	D
14	1110	E
15	1111	F

format for the number *10* is four digits (1010). Although binary numbers can have more or fewer than 8 bits, each single alphabetic or special character is 1 byte (or 8 bits) of data and consists of a unique combination of a total of eight *0*s and *1*s.

The ASCII code represents the 26 uppercase letters and 26 lowercase letters used in the English language, along with many punctuation symbols and other special characters, using 8 bits. Figure 8 shows several examples of the ASCII code representation of printable letters and characters.

Representing Characters: Unicode. Because it represents letters and characters using only 8 bits, the ASCII code can assign only 256 (or 2^8) different codes for unique characters and letters. Although this is enough to represent English and many other characters found in the world's languages, ASCII code can't represent all languages and symbols,

FIGURE 8

ASCII Standard Code for a Sample of Letters and Characters

ASCII CODE	REPRESENTS THIS SYMBOL	ASCII CODE	REPRESENTS THIS SYMBOL
01000001	A	01100001	a
01000010	B	01100010	b
01000011	C	01100011	c
01011010	Z	00100011	#
00100001	!	00100100	$
00100010	"	00100101	%

Note: For the full ASCII table, see **ascii-code.com**.

(Courtesy of the American National Standards Institute)

because some languages require more than 256 characters and letters. Thus, a new encoding scheme, called **Unicode**, was created. By using 16 bits instead of the 8 bits used in ASCII, Unicode can represent nearly 1,115,000 code points and currently assigns more than 96,000 unique character symbols (see Figure 9).

The first 128 characters of Unicode are identical to ASCII, but because of its depth, Unicode is also able to represent the alphabets of all modern and historic languages and notational systems, including such languages and writing systems as Tibetan, Tagalog, and Canadian Aboriginal syllabics. As we continue to become a more global society, it's anticipated that Unicode will replace ASCII as the standard character formatting code.

Representing Decimal Numbers. The binary number system can also represent a decimal number. How can a string of *1*s and *0*s capture the information in a value such as 99.368? Because every computer must store such numbers in the same way, the Institute of Electrical and Electronics Engineers (IEEE) has established a standard called the *floating-point standard* that describes how numbers with fractional parts should be represented in the binary number system. Using a 32-bit system, we can represent an incredibly wide range of numbers.

The method dictated by the IEEE standard works the same for any number with a decimal point, such as the number −0.75. The first digit, or bit (the sign bit), is used to indicate whether the number is positive or negative. The next 8 bits store the magnitude of the number, indicating whether the number is in the hundreds or millions, for example. The standard says to use the next 23 bits to store the value of the number.

Interpretation. *All* data inside the computer is stored as bits:

- **Positive and negative integers** can be stored using signed integer notation, with the first bit (the sign bit) indicating the sign and the rest of the bits indicating the value of the number.

FIGURE 9 The written languages of the world require thousands of different characters. The Unicode Code Chart (**unicode.org/charts**) shows how Unicode provides a system allowing digital representation of over 1,100,000 unique characters.

- **Decimal** numbers are stored according to the IEEE floating-point standard.
- **Letters and symbols** are stored according to the ASCII code or Unicode.

These number systems and codes exist so that computers can store different types of information in their on/off switches. No matter what kind of data you input in a computer—a color, a musical note, or a street address—that data will be stored as a pattern of *1*s and *0*s. The important lesson is that the interpretation of *0*s and *1*s is what matters. The same binary pattern could represent a positive number, a negative number, a fraction, or a letter.

How does the computer know which interpretation to use for the *1*s and *0*s? When your mind processes language, it takes the sounds you hear and uses the rules of English, along with other clues, to build an interpretation of the sound as a word. If you're in New York City and hear someone shout, "Hey, Lori!" you expect that someone is saying hello to a friend. If you're in London and hear the same sound—"Hey! Lorry!"—you jump out of the way because a truck is coming at you! You knew which interpretation to apply to the sound because you had some other information—the fact that you were in England.

Likewise, the CPU is designed to understand a specific language or set of instructions. Certain instructions tell the CPU to expect a negative number next or to interpret the following bit pattern as a character. Because of this extra information, the CPU always knows which interpretation to use for a series of bits.

How the CPU Works

Any program you run on your computer is actually a long series of binary code describing a specific set of commands the CPU must perform. These commands may be coming from a user's actions or may be instructions fed from a program while it executes. Each CPU is somewhat different in the exact steps it follows to perform its tasks, but all CPUs must perform a series of similar general steps. These steps, also illustrated in Figure 10, are referred to as a CPU **machine cycle (or processing cycle)**:

1. **Fetch:** When any program begins to run, the *1*s and *0*s that make up the program's binary code must be "fetched" from their temporary storage location in random access memory (RAM) and moved to the CPU before they can be executed.

2. **Decode:** Once the program's binary code is in the CPU, it is decoded into commands the CPU understands.

3. **Execute:** Next, the CPU actually performs the work described in the commands. Specialized hardware on the CPU performs addition, subtraction, multiplication, division, and other mathematical and logical operations.

4. **Store:** The result is stored in one of the **registers**, special memory storage areas built into the CPU, which are the most expensive, fastest memory in your computer. The CPU is then ready to fetch the next set of bits encoding the next instruction.

No matter what program you're running and no matter how many programs you're using at one time, the CPU performs these four steps over and over at incredibly high speeds. Shortly, we'll look at each stage in more detail. But first, let's examine components that help the CPU perform its tasks.

The Control Unit

The CPU, like any part of the computer system, is designed from a collection of switches. How can the simple on/off switches of the CPU "remember" the fetch-decode-execute-store sequence of the machine cycle?

The **control unit** of the CPU manages the switches inside the CPU. It is programmed by CPU designers to remember the sequence of processing stages for that CPU and how each switch in the CPU should be set (i.e., on or off) for each stage. With each beat of the system clock, the control unit moves each switch to the correct on or off setting and then performs the work of that stage.

FIGURE 10 The CPU Machine Cycle

The System Clock

To move from one stage of the machine cycle to the next, the motherboard uses a built-in **system clock**. This internal clock is actually a special crystal that acts like a metronome, keeping a steady beat and controlling when the CPU moves to the next stage of processing.

These steady beats or "ticks" of the system clock, known as the **clock cycle**, set the pace by which the computer moves from process to process. The pace, known as **clock speed**, is measured in hertz (Hz), which describes how many times something happens per second. Today's system clocks are measured in gigahertz (GHz), or a billion clock ticks per second. Therefore, in a 3 GHz system, there are 3 billion clock ticks each second.

Let's now look at each of the stages in the machine cycle in a bit more depth.

(Steve Young/Fotolia LLC)

Stage 1: The Fetch Stage

The data and program instructions the CPU needs are stored in different areas in the computer system. Data and program instructions move between these areas as they're needed by the CPU for processing. Programs are permanently stored on the hard drive because it offers nonvolatile storage. However, when you launch a program, it—or sometimes only its essential parts—is transferred from the hard drive into RAM.

The program moves to RAM because the CPU can access the data and program instructions stored in RAM more than 1 million times faster than if they're left on the hard drive. In part, this is because RAM is much closer to the CPU than the hard drive is. Another reason for the delay in transmission of data and program instructions from the hard drive to the CPU is the relatively slow speed of mechanical hard drives. The read/write heads have to sweep over the spinning platters, which takes time. Even nonmechanical SSD hard drives have slower access speeds than RAM. RAM is a type of memory that gives very fast direct access to data.

As specific instructions from the program are needed, they're moved from RAM into registers (the special storage areas located on the CPU itself), where they wait to be executed.

The CPU's storage area isn't big enough to hold everything it needs to process at the same time. If enough memory were located on the CPU chip itself, an entire program could be copied to the CPU from RAM before it was executed. This

would add to the computer's speed and efficiency because there would be no delay while the CPU stopped processing operations to fetch instructions from RAM to the CPU. However, including so much memory on a CPU chip would make these chips extremely expensive. In addition, CPU design is so complex that only a limited amount of storage space is available on the CPU itself.

Cache Memory. The CPU doesn't actually need to fetch every instruction from RAM each time it goes through a cycle. Another layer of storage, called **cache memory**, has even faster access to the CPU than RAM. Cache memory consists of small blocks of memory located directly on and next to the CPU chip. These memory blocks are holding places for recently or frequently used instructions or data that the CPU needs the most. When these instructions or data are stored in cache memory, the CPU can retrieve them more quickly than if it had to access them in RAM.

Modern CPU designs include several types of cache memory:

- **Level 1 cache:** If the next instruction to be fetched isn't already located in a CPU register, instead of looking directly to RAM to find it, the CPU first searches Level 1 cache. **Level 1 cache** is a block of memory built onto the CPU chip to store data or commands that have just been used.

- **Level 2 cache:** If the command is not located in Level 1 cache, the CPU searches Level 2 cache. Depending on the design of the CPU, **Level 2 cache** is either located on the CPU chip but slightly farther away from the CPU than Level 1 or is located on a separate chip next to the CPU and therefore takes somewhat longer to access. Level 2 cache contains more storage area than Level 1 cache. For the Intel Core i7, for example, Level 1 cache is 64 kilobytes (KB) and Level 2 cache is 1 megabyte (MB).

  Only if the CPU doesn't find the next instruction to be fetched in either Level 1 or Level 2 cache will it make the long journey to RAM to access it.

- **Level 3 cache:** The current direction of processor design is toward increasingly large multilevel CPU cache structures. Today, CPUs such as Intel's Core i7 processors have an additional third level of cache memory storage called **Level 3 cache**. On computers with Level 3 cache, the CPU checks this area for instructions and data after it looks in Level 1 and Level 2 cache but before it makes the longer trip to RAM (see Figure 11). Level 3 cache holds between 2 and 12 MB of data. With 12 MB of Level 3 cache, there is storage for some entire programs to be transferred to the CPU for execution.

As an end user of computer programs, you do nothing special to use cache memory. The advantage of having more cache memory is that you'll experience better performance because the CPU won't have to make the longer trip to RAM to get data and instructions as often. Unfortunately, because it's built into the CPU chip or motherboard, you can't upgrade cache; it's part of the original design of the CPU. Therefore, as with RAM, when buying a computer, it's important to consider the one with the most cache memory, everything else being equal.

(Andrea Danti/Fotolia LLC)

| ADD | R1,R2 |
| STORE | R7 |

Stage 2: The Decode Stage

The main goal of the decode stage is for the CPU's control unit to translate (or **decode**) the program's instructions into commands the CPU can under-stand. The collection of commands that a specific CPU can execute is called the **instruction set** for that system. Each CPU has its own unique instruction set. For example, the AMD FX 8350 eight-core processor in a Gamer Mage system has a different instruction set than the fourth-generation Intel Core i5 used in a Dell Inspiron notebook. The control unit interprets the code's bits according to the instruction set the CPU designers laid out for that particular CPU. The control unit then knows how to set up all the switches on the CPU so that the proper operation will occur.

Because humans are the ones who write the initial instructions, all the commands in an instruction set are written in a language called **assembly language**, which is easier for humans to work with than binary language. Many CPUs have similar assembly commands in their instruction sets, including the following commands:

CPU INSTRUCTION	FUNCTION
ADD	Add
SUB	Subtract
MUL	Multiply
DIV	Divide
MOVE	Move data to RAM
STORE	Move data to a CPU register
EQU	Check if equal

CPUs differ in the choice of additional assembly language commands selected for the instruction set. Each CPU design team works to develop an instruction set that is both powerful and speedy.

However, because the CPU knows and recognizes only patterns of 0s and 1s, it can't understand assembly language directly, so these human-readable instructions are translated into binary code. The control unit uses these long strings of binary code called **machine language** to set up the hardware in the CPU for the rest of the

BITS&BYTES

Using a Little Hideaway

Taking data you think you'll be using soon and storing it nearby is a simple but powerful idea. This strategy shows up in places in your computer system other than cache memory. For example, when you're browsing web pages, it takes longer to download images than text. Your browser software automatically stores images on your hard drive so that you don't have to download them again if you want to go back and view a page you've already visited. Although this cache of files is not related to the cache storage space designed into the CPU chip, the idea is the same. The word cache is derived from the French word cacher, which means "to hide." A little bit of memory space used as a hideaway can give performance a big boost.

operations it needs to perform. Machine language is a binary code for computer instructions, much like the ASCII code is a binary code for letters and characters. Similar to each letter or character having its own unique combination of 0s and 1s assigned to it, a CPU has a table of codes consisting of combinations of 0s and 1s for each of its commands. If the CPU sees a particular pattern of bits arrive, it knows the work it must do. Figure 12 shows a few commands in both assembly language and machine language.

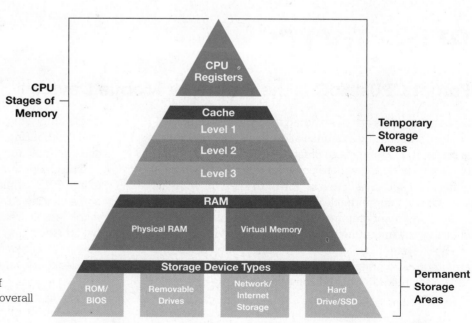

FIGURE 11 The CPU has multiple stages of internal memory, which is just a part of the overall hierarchy of a computer's memory storage.

FIGURE 12

Representations of Sample CPU Commands		
HUMAN LANGUAGE FOR COMMAND	CPU COMMAND IN ASSEMBLY LANGUAGE (LANGUAGE USED BY PROGRAMMERS)	CPU COMMAND IN MACHINE LANGUAGE (LANGUAGE USED IN THE CPU'S INSTRUCTION SET)
Add	ADD	1110 1010
Subtract	SUB	0001 0101
Multiply	MUL	1111 0000
Divide	DIV	0000 1111

Stage 3: The Execute Stage

(Taras Livyy/Fotolia LLC)

The **arithmetic logic unit (ALU)** is the part of the CPU designed to perform mathematical operations such as addition, subtraction, multiplication, and division and to test the comparison of values such as *greater than, less than,* and *equal to*. For example, in calculating an average, the ALU is where the addition and division operations would take place.

The ALU also performs logical OR, AND, and NOT operations. For example, in determining whether a student can graduate, the ALU would need to ascertain whether the student had taken all required courses AND obtained a passing grade in each of them. The ALU is specially designed to execute such calculations flawlessly and with incredible speed.

The ALU is fed data from the CPU's registers. The amount of data a CPU can process at a time is based in part on the amount of data each register can hold. The number of bits a computer can work with at a time is referred to as its **word size**. Therefore, a 64-bit processor can process more information faster than a 32-bit processor.

Stage 4: The Store Stage

(John Takai/Fotolia LLC)

In the final stage, the result produced by the ALU is stored back in the registers. The instruction itself will explain which register should be used to store the answer.

Once the entire instruction has been completed, the next instruction will be fetched, and the fetch-decode-execute-store sequence will begin again.

Making CPUs Even Faster

Knowing how to build a CPU that can run faster than the competition can make a company rich. However, building a faster CPU isn't easy. A new product launch must take into

BITS&BYTES

Forget CPUs: SoC Is the Future for Mobile Devices!

Since consumers are demanding more powerful mobile devices such as smartphones and tablets, the pressure is on for chip designers to create smaller chips. But the chips also need to be more powerful than the previous generation and consume less power to keep up with software and communication demands.

Intel and other chip manufacturers have risen to the challenge by migrating away from CPUs and introducing SoC (system on a chip) architecture. Whereas CPU architecture requires additional chips to support the CPU, SoC integrates all the computer circuitry into a

single chip. This is essential for making the "brains" of small computing devices such as tablets, smartphones, and wearable technology.

The Quark line of SoCs from Intel was introduced in late 2013. While not as powerful as some previous chips like the Atom processor, Quark chips consume much less power. Low power consumption is essential for extending battery life for mobile and wearable devices. Thanks to SoC design, the future is getting smaller every year!

consideration the time it will take to design, manufacture, and test that processor. When the processor finally hits the market, it must be faster than the competition if the manufacturer hopes to make a profit. To create a CPU that will be released 36 months from now, it must be built to perform at least twice as fast as anything currently available.

Processor manufacturers can increase CPU performance in many different ways:

- Using *pipelining*
- Designing the CPU's instruction set so that it contains *specialized instructions for handling multimedia and graphics*
- Including *multiple independent processing paths* inside the CPU

Let's explore each of these methods in more detail.

Pipelining

As an instruction is processed, the CPU runs sequentially through the four stages of processing: fetch, decode, execute, and store. **Pipelining** is a technique that allows the CPU to work on more than one instruction (or stage of processing) at the same time, thereby boosting CPU performance.

For example, without pipelining, it may take four clock cycles to complete one instruction (one clock cycle for each of the four processing stages). However, with a four-stage pipeline, the computer can process four instructions at the same time. The ticks of the system clock (the clock cycle) indicate when all instructions move to the next process. Using pipelining, a four-stage processor can potentially run up to four times faster because some instruction is finishing every clock cycle rather than

waiting four cycles for each instruction to finish. In Figure 13a, a non-pipelined instruction takes four clock cycles to be completed, whereas in Figure 13b, the four instructions have been completed in the same time using pipelining.

There is a cost to pipelining a CPU, however. The CPU must be designed so that each stage (fetch, decode, execute, and store) is independent. This means that each stage must be able to run at the same time that the other three stages are running. This requires more transistors and a more complicated hardware design.

Specialized Multimedia Instructions

Each design team that develops a new CPU tries to imagine what users' greatest needs will be in four or five years. Currently, several processors on the market reflect this consideration by incorporating specialized multimedia instructions into the basic instruction set.

Hardware engineers have redesigned the chip so that the instruction set contains new commands customized to speed up the work needed for video and audio processing. For example, Intel has integrated into its second-generation Core processor the Advanced Encryption Standard (AES) instruction set. These seven new instructions work to allow the CPU to deliver faster data protection.

Multiple Processing Efforts

Many high-end server systems use a set of completely separate CPU chips on one motherboard. These server

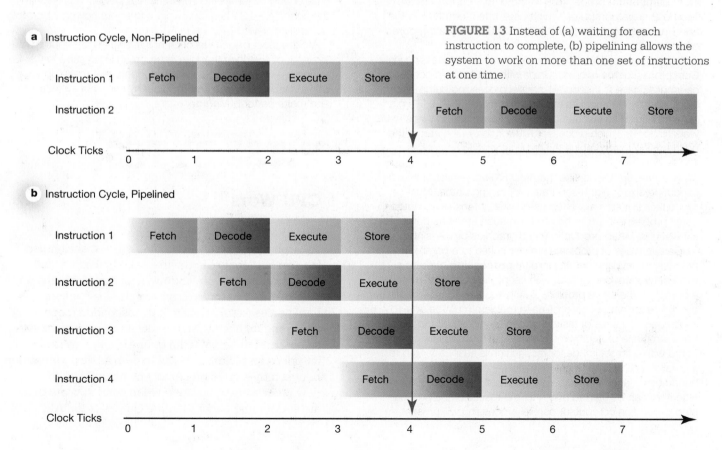

a Instruction Cycle, Non-Pipelined

| Instruction 1 | Fetch | Decode | Execute | Store |

| Instruction 2 | | | | | Fetch | Decode | Execute | Store |

Clock Ticks: 0 1 2 3 4 5 6 7

FIGURE 13 Instead of (a) waiting for each instruction to complete, (b) pipelining allows the system to work on more than one set of instructions at one time.

b Instruction Cycle, Pipelined

Instruction 1	Fetch	Decode	Execute	Store
Instruction 2		Fetch	Decode	Execute	Store
Instruction 3			Fetch	Decode	Execute	Store
Instruction 4				Fetch	Decode	Execute	Store

Clock Ticks: 0 1 2 3 4 5 6 7

BITS&BYTES

Today's Supercomputers: Faster than Ever

Supercomputers are the biggest and most powerful type of computer. Scientists and engineers use these computers to solve complex problems or to perform massive computations. Some supercomputers are single computers with multiple processors, whereas others consist of multiple computers that work together.

The Tianhe-2 was recently ranked as the world's fastest supercomputer. It features a whopping 3,120,000 cores and runs the Linux operating system. Tianhe-2 is deployed at the National Supercomputer Center in Guangzho, China. Since it was developed by the National University of Defense Technology, the assumption is that it will be used primarily for weapons system research.

The rankings of supercomputers change frequently as new models are deployed or older models are upgraded. You can keep up with the rankings at **top500.org**.

FIGURE 14 The Tianhe-2 in China is the world's faster supercomputer . . . for now! Check **top500.org** for the latest rankings. *(Long Hongtao/Xinhua Press/Corbis)*

systems can later be scaled so that they can accommodate large numbers of processors with multiple cores, like the Tianhe-2 supercomputer, which uses Intel Xeon Ivy Bridge and Phi processors to provide 3,120,000 computing cores of power!

In personal computers, Intel uses *multi-core processing* in its Core processor line of chips. Chips with quad-core processing capabilities have four separate parallel processing paths inside them, so they're almost as fast as four separate CPUs. It's not quite four times as fast because the system must do some extra work to decide which processor will work on which part of the problem and to recombine the results each CPU produces.

Six-core processors, like the Intel i7 Extreme Edition, and even eight-core CPUs (like the AMD FX) are available as well, executing six (or eight) separate processing paths. Multi-processor systems are often used when intensive computational problems need to be solved in such areas as computer simulations, video production, and graphics processing.

Certain types of problems are well suited to a parallel-processing environment. In **parallel processing**, there is a large network of computers, with each computer working on a portion of the same problem simultaneously. To be a good candidate for parallel processing, a problem must be able to be divided into a set of tasks that can be run simultaneously. For example, a problem where millions of faces are being compared with a target image for recognition is easily adapted to a parallel setting. The target face can be compared with many hundreds of faces at the same time. But if the next step of an algorithm can be started only after the results of the previous step have been computed, parallel processing will present no advantages.

In the future, you can expect CPUs to continue to get smaller and faster and to consume less power. This fits with the current demands of consumers for more powerful portable computing devices.

At the most basic level of binary *1*s and *0*s, computers are systems of switches that can accomplish impressive tasks. By understanding the hardware components that make up your computer system, you can use your system more effectively and make better buying decisions.

BITS&BYTES

CPU Wars

The ARM processor, which is used in tablets and smartphones, was a CPU contender that challenged Intel for supremacy in the market. Microsoft even released a version of Windows 8 for the ARM processor, since it consumes less power and is cheaper than Intel processors. However, Intel responded recently by launching its line of Quark processors, which are even smaller and more powerful than ARM processors. Look for prices on tablets to begin to drop as the competition between these two processors heats up! And expect new processors to be launched in coming years that are smaller and faster than the Quarks or the ARMs.

check your understanding // review & practice

For a quick review of what you've learned, answer the following questions. Visit **pearsonhighered.com /techinaction** to check your answers.

multiple choice

1. Which part of the CPU is specifically designed to perform mathematical operations?

   a. fetch module

   b. ALU

   c. registers

   d. cache memory

2. What is another name for the base-10 number system?

   a. decimal notation

   b. binary number system

   c. hexadecimal notation

   d. integer system

3. Which encoding scheme can represent the alphabets of all modern and historic languages?

   a. base-2 number system

   b. Unicode

   c. ASCII

   d. scientific

4. A multi-core processor like the Intel i7 is

   a. one physical chip.

   b. several chips joined together on the motherboard.

   c. two separate cards installed in your system.

   d. a software setting you can use to speed up CPU processing.

5. To regulate the internal timing of a computer system, the motherboard uses

   a. a system clock.

   b. software simulation.

   c. RAM.

   d. a register.

6. Special areas of memory storage built into the CPU are known as

   a. switches.

   b. semiconductors.

   c. registers.

   d. DIMMs.

7. Which is the correct set and order of steps in the machine cycle?

   a. execute, store, fetch, decode

   b. store, fetch, execute, decode

   c. execute first instruction, execute second instruction, execute third instruction

   d. fetch, decode, execute, store

8. All data inside the computer is stored as

   a. words.

   b. numbers.

   c. binary patterns.

   d. cache memory.

9. Which statement about pipelining is TRUE?

   a. Pipelining does not boost CPU performance.

   b. Pipeline design is only used in computers in conjunction with parallel processing.

   c. Pipelining allows a less complicated hardware design.

   d. Pipelining allows the computer to process multiple instructions simultaneously.

10. From fastest to slowest, which is the fastest sequence of accessing memory?

    a. registers, RAM, Level 1 cache, Level 2 cache

    b. registers, Level 1 cache, Level 2 cache, RAM

    c. Level 1 cache, Level 2 cache, RAM, registers

    d. Level 2 cache, Level 1 cache, registers, RAM

8

Digital Devices and Media: Managing a Digital Lifestyle

Make This: Explore an App Builder Skill on **page 93**

For all media in this chapter go to **pearsonhighered.com /techinaction** or MyITLab.

(Kuroji/Fotolia; Oleksiy Mark/Fotolia; Frankie Angel/Alamy; Tetra Images/Getty Images;

HOW COOL IS THIS?

Scan here for more info

Ever heard of **3D printing**? If not, you soon will, as it is maturing into a technology that is set to launch a **hardware revolution**. First-generation 3D printing consisted of "extruded plastic printing"—melting plastic down and then pushing it into a mold to shape it. Newer 3D printers go beyond the extruded plastic of first generation 3D printing using a new, more accurate technique. The printer's laser draws on the surface of a pool of **liquid plastic resin**. The small spots where the laser hits harden. Layer by layer, a specific shape can be formed. The accuracy and resolution of this approach far exceeds earlier 3D printers, and **different colors, transparencies, and flexibility** can be incorporated to create much more sophisticated printable parts. Visit sites like Thingiverse to see the growing collection of objects you can print out at home. *(Miguel Navarro/Getty Images)*

Mobile Devices

For many of us, our phone is our lifeline to the world, and if not our phone, then our laptop or iPad. We live in a digital world, and our devices have evolved to let us communicate anywhere we go, 24/7. In this section, we'll check out a number of mobile devices and their features. But first, we look at digital convergence.

 digital
CONVERGENCE

Digital convergence, the use of a single unifying device to handle media, Internet, entertainment, and telephony needs, is exemplified in the range of devices now on the market. You see digital convergence in the evolution of smartphones, which now let you do just about anything a computer can do. The push to digital convergence is seen in the migration of digital devices into environments like the cabin of your car. The Tesla S features a 17-inch touch-screen display, shown in Figure 8.1a, that controls all of the electronics systems of the car, including a high-definition camera watching as you back up, and provides Internet access, mobile communications, and navigation. Even some refrigerators, like the one shown in Figure 8.1b, now include LCD touch-screen displays and network adapters so that they can play music and display family photos and recipes from websites such as **epicurious.com**.

In fact, devices are beginning to converge so much that an organization has been created to standardize them. The Digital Living Network Alliance (**dlna.org**) is an organization working to standardize different kinds of appliances and network devices used in our homes. As our appliances, cars, and homes become designed to communicate over a common network, how we manage our media, control our living spaces, and communicate with our families will continue to change.

How have mobile devices converged? As more and more computing power is available in mobile processors, mobile devices have evolved to be able to do multiple tasks. Smartphones can now videoconference like laptops. Tablets such as the iPad are touch sensitive like smartphones. Netbooks and ultrabooks both run traditional desktop operating systems and are lightweight. All these devices have significant overlap in the tasks they can perform, so learning the differences will be important in finding the device that's just right for you. Let's start by taking a look at smartphones. ■

FIGURE 8.1 (a) Auto electronics have now converged with tablet technology. The Tesla S features a 17-inch touch display. (b) Some refrigerators are now equipped with touch screens that connect to the Internet. *(Kyodo/AP Images; Steve Marcus/Reuters/Landov LLC; Steve Marcus/Reuters/Landov LLC)*

telephony: smartphones
AND BEYOND

Communication has changed radically in the digital age. Chapter 3 discussed the use of wikis, blogs, and other web-based tools for connecting people and their ideas. All of these software applications are dependent on digital information.

Hardware devices that support communication also have evolved because of digital technologies. **Telephony**, the use of equipment to provide voice communications over a distance, has shifted from an analog science to a digital one. In this section, we examine smartphones and Voice over Internet Protocol (VoIP) devices to see how they're changing to meet modern communication needs.

Smartphone Basics

What makes a smartphone a smartphone? A smartphone does more than let you make and answer phone calls. In fact, smartphones illustrate the power of digital convergence (see Figure 8.2). They incorporate functions and features, such as the following, that used to be available only in separate, dedicated devices:

- Internet access
- Personal information management (PIM) features
- Voice recording features
- The ability to play and organize music files
- GPS services
- Digital image and video capture
- Computing power to run programs like word processors or even video-editing software

Examples of smartphones include the iPhone and the Samsung Galaxy.

Isn't every phone a smartphone now? All phones that use mobile, cellular technology can be called **cellular (cell) phones**. Although many cell phones on the market are considered smartphones, less powerful cell phones are available. Called **feature phones**, these inexpensive phones have modest processors, simpler interfaces, and often no touch screen. As more features are integrated into every cell phone product, though, it becomes difficult to distinguish a smartphone from a feature phone. Most providers, like AT&T or Verizon, label a smartphone as one that has sufficient power so that you can use Internet features easily. In addition, you often have to purchase a data plan with a smartphone. In this chapter, we'll use the term *cell phone* to refer to all cellular phones and *smartphones* to refer to the more powerful type of cell phone that can run more complex applications.

Smartphone Components

Are smartphones computers? All cell phones—smartphones and feature phones—have the same components as any computer: a processor (central processing unit, or CPU), memory, and input and output devices, as shown in Figure 8.3. Cell phones require their own operating system (OS) software and have their own application software. So, in effect, all cell phones are computers.

Smartphones use a CPU and an interface so powerful that they can take on many of the same tasks as much more expensive computers: videoconferencing, recording and editing high-definition (HD) video, and broadcasting live-streaming video.

(F5ketch/Fotolia; Maxx-Studio/Shutterstock; MrGarry/Shutterstock; Frank Peters/Shutterstock; You can more/Shutterstock; Gielmichal/Shutterstock; Bartosz Zakrzewski/Shutterstock)

FIGURE 8.2 Digital convergence has brought us single devices like smartphones that play the role of many separate devices.

LED display

CPU

Memory

Camera module

Audio interface

Touch-screen controller

Battery

FIGURE 8.3 Inside your smartphone, you'll find a CPU; a memory chip; input devices such as a microphone, a camera, and a touch screen; and output devices such as a display screen. *(© 2014 iFixit)*

What kind of processor is inside a smartphone?
Although the processor in a cell phone is not as fast or as high-powered as the processor in a desktop computer, it's still responsible for a great number of tasks. The processor coordinates sending all of the data among the other electronic components inside the phone. It also runs the cell phone's OS, which provides a user interface so that you can change phone settings, store information, play games, and so on. Popular processors for smartphones include the Qualcomm Snapdragon and the Apple A7. These use dual-core processing technology, which used to be reserved for high-end computer systems.

Is there a standard OS for smartphones? There are a number of operating systems in the smartphone market now. Many smartphones use the Android OS. Apple's iPhone uses iOS, a version of the OS X operating system used in Apple's computers. Microsoft is also now in the running with the Windows Phone mobile OS. These operating systems are required to translate the user's commands into instructions for the processor. Figure 8.4 illustrates some of the user interfaces featured among smartphone operating systems.

What does the memory inside a smartphone do?
Your phone's memory stores all of the phone's information and programs. The OS is stored in read-only memory (ROM), the phone's permanent memory, because the phone would be useless without that key piece of software. Other phone data, such as ring tones and contact lists, is stored in separate internal memory chips.

Many smartphones let you add additional memory through micro SD flash cards (see Figure 8.5). Micro SD cards are easy to install inside a phone, and some models have external slots for an SD card. Not all smartphones

FIGURE 8.4

Mobile Operating Systems

OPERATING SYSTEM	MANUFACTURER	USER INTERFACE
Android	Used by HTC, Samsung	
iOS	Apple	
Windows Phone	Microsoft	
BlackBerry OS	BlackBerry	

(Manaemedia/123RF; Oleksiy Mark/Shutterstock; Torian Dixon/123RF;

allow memory upgrades in this way, however. For example, iPhones don't let you add memory.

What input and output devices do smartphones use? The primary input devices for a smartphone are its microphone and touch pad. Some phones, such as the BlackBerry Porsche (see Figure 8.6), offer both a touch screen and a built-in keyboard. The Apple iPhone provides a software-based keyboard that supports more than 40 languages. And a smartphone's digital camera is also an input device, capturing photos and video.

Cell-phone output devices include a speaker and a liquid crystal display (LCD). Higher-end models include full-color, high-resolution LCD screens. Newer on the market are OLED (organic light-emitting diode) displays, which allow very bright, sharp imaging and draw less power than LCD screens.

What smartphone software is available? A smartphone OS comes with a standard collection of software, such as a to-do list, contact manager, and calendar. Modified

FIGURE 8.5 Micro SD flash cards add memory to some phones. *(Andrey Pavlov/123RF)*

versions of application software such as Microsoft Word, Excel, Outlook, and PowerPoint are available for some high-end smartphones. Manufacturers also have web-based software stores, like the App Store for the Apple iPhone and the Windows store for Win 8–based devices (see Figure 8.7). Software applications are available for Android through Google Play. The Android developer community holds competitions to spur the creation of new software applications for Android-based phones.

How Cell Phone Technology Works

What's "cellular" about a cell phone? As noted earlier, the term *cell phone* is short for *cellular phone*. A set of connected "cells" makes up a cellular network. Each cell is a geographic area centered on a **base transceiver station**, which is a large communications tower with antennas, amplifiers, receivers, and transmitters. When you place a call on a cell phone, a base station picks up the request for service. The station then passes the request to a central location called a **mobile switching center**. The reverse process occurs when you receive an incoming call. A telecommunications company builds its network by constructing a series of cells that overlap in an attempt to guarantee that its cell-phone customers have coverage no matter where they are.

As you move during your phone call, the mobile switching center monitors the strength of the signal between your cell phone and the closest base station. When the signal is no longer strong enough between your cell phone and the base station, the mobile switching center orders the next base station to take charge of your call. When your cell phone "drops out," it may be because the distance between base stations is too great to provide an adequate signal.

FIGURE 8.6 Many smartphones have touch screens and built-in keyboards. Some support more than 40 languages! *(BlackBerry/MarketFotoPress EPN/Newscom)*

FIGURE 8.7 Google Play, the Windows Store, and Apple's App Store are some of the many online stores delivering software for mobile devices. *(Google Inc/AP Images; Kevin Britland/ Alamy; Anatolii Babii/Alamy)*

BITS&BYTES

Bluetooth and LE Beacons

More mobile devices are coming equipped to work with low-energy Bluetooth signals. This allows you to interact with small devices, called *beacons*, that can be mounted on any surface and run for years on a single coin battery. Beacons can recognize your device from up to 50 feet away. Sets of these can pinpoint your location to exactly where in a store you're standing. The beacon can then wake up a specific app on your phone and push you information. So as you walk toward the bakery department, the store app could pop open and give you a cupcake coupon!

How do cell phones use digital signals? When you speak into a cell phone, a series of digital processing steps occur:

1. Sound enters the microphone as a sound wave. Because these sound waves need to be *digitized* (that is, converted into a sequence of *1*s and *0*s that the cell phone's processor can understand), an **analog-to-digital converter chip** converts your voice's sound waves into digital signals.

2. Next, the digital data must be *compressed*, or squeezed, into the smallest possible space so that it will transmit more quickly to another phone. The processor can't perform the mathematical operations required at this stage quickly enough, so there's a specialized chip called the **digital signal processor** included in the cell phone that handles the compression work.

3. Finally, the digital data is *transmitted* as a radio wave through the cellular network to the destination phone.

When you receive an incoming call, the digital signal processor decompresses the incoming message. An amplifier boosts the signal to make it loud enough, and it is then passed on to the speaker.

Synchronizing

What's the best way to synchronize data between my phone and computer? The process of updating your data so your to-do lists, schedules, and other files on your cell phone and computer are the same is called **synchronizing,** or **syncing**. There are two main ways to transfer information between your phone and computer:

1. *Wired:* Use a micro SD card or a USB cable to directly transfer data.
2. *Wireless:* Use a wireless connection to transfer data.

How does a wired transfer of data work? Almost all phones are designed with a USB port. Some have a mini-USB connector, while other models require a special cable to connect the phone to a standard USB port. Once connected using a USB data cable, your phone will appear on your computer like an additional flash drive, and you can drag and drop files to it. You can also charge your phone through the USB cable.

If your phone supports a high-density micro SD card, you can easily remove the card and slip it directly into a flash card reader in your computer.

How do I transfer information to and from my phone wirelessly? Most smartphones on the market today are Bluetooth-enabled, meaning they include a small Bluetooth chip that allows them to transfer data wirelessly to any other Bluetooth-enabled device. **Bluetooth** technology uses radio waves to transmit data signals over distances up to approximately 300 feet (for Bluetooth 4). Bluetooth 4 devices are the newest on the market and are almost twice as fast as Bluetooth 3 devices.

Another way to wirelessly transfer data to your phone is to use a wireless connection to a cloud service. A number of web services are now available to synchronize your e-mail, files, contacts, and calendars instantly and wirelessly. IFTTT, for example, wirelessly syncs folders of data and photos on your Android phone to your home computers automatically (see Figure 8.8). These web services follow the model of cloud computing, where Internet-based services and resources are distributed to users instead of being installed as an application on the user's computer. Apple's iOS has cloud support integrated into applications like Calendar, iTunes, PhotoStream, Contacts, and Mail. A photo taken on your iPhone will automatically be transferred to your iPad and your home Windows or Mac computer, for example.

There are other providers of wireless synchronization for mobile devices. Google Sync works with a range of devices. All of your Google e-mail, calendar events, and contacts are automatically backed up online instantly on the Google servers. Even the Amazon Kindle uses wireless synchronization so that if you read a bit further in your e-book on your phone, when you get to your office the Kindle software on your PC will have automatically updated to bookmark the new page you're on.

SOUND BYTE
Connecting with Bluetooth
In this Sound Byte, you'll learn what freedoms Bluetooth affords you and how to use Bluetooth devices.

ACTIVE HELPDESK
Keeping Your Data on Hand
In this Active Helpdesk, you'll play the role of a helpdesk staffer assisting people with management of their cloud storage accounts.

Text Messaging

What does SMS stand for?
Short message service (SMS)—often just called *text messaging*—is a technology that lets you send short text messages (up to 160 characters) over cellular networks. You can send SMS messages to other mobile devices or to any e-mail address.

Companies now support texting in many ways—for example, your bank may allow you to text commands to request account balances or details about your last transaction and the bank will text the requested information back to you.

How does SMS work? SMS uses the cell-phone network to transmit messages. When you send an SMS message, an SMS calling center receives the message and delivers it to the appropriate mobile device using something called *store-and-forward* technology. This technology allows users to send SMS messages to any other SMS device in the world.

Is the same technology used to send and receive photos and videos? SMS technology lets you send only text messages. However, an extension of SMS called **multimedia message service (MMS)** lets you send messages that include text, sound, images, and video clips to other phones or e-mail addresses. MMS messages actually arrive as a series of messages; you view the text, then the image, then the sound, and so on. You can then choose to save just one part of the message (such as the image), all of it, or none of it. MMS users can subscribe to financial, sports, and weather

FIGURE 8.8 A cloud service lets you keep the information on your phone instantly in sync with your other computing devices.

services that will "push" information to them, sending it automatically to their phones in MMS format.

Mobile Internet

What's the best way to connect my smartphone to the Internet?
There are two ways smartphones (and most mobile devices) can connect to the Internet:

1. Using a WiFi network
2. Using the cellular phone system (a 3G or 4G connection)

A major advantage of WiFi is that it offers a faster data-transfer speed. However, there may not always be a WiFi signal available where you are. Cellular networks are much more widely available, whether you're in your car or just walking down the street.

For devices like tablets, manufacturers will offer one model that can only connect to the Internet using WiFi and another model that costs more but can connect with either WiFi or cellular 3G/4G.

Who sells cellular Internet service for my smartphone? Just as you have an Internet service provider (ISP) for Internet access for your desktop or laptop computer, you must have a **wireless Internet service provider** (or **wireless ISP**) to connect your smartphone to the Internet. Phone companies (such as T-Mobile, Verizon, and AT&T) double as wireless ISPs. Most wireless ISPs also offer free login to their network of WiFi hotspots if you're a cellular customer.

How do I purchase Internet time? Providers measure your Internet usage not according to how much time you're on the Internet but according to how much data you download and upload. An Internet connectivity plan is known as a **data plan**. You pay one monthly price and are allowed data transfers up to some fixed limit per month, such as 2 GB or 500 MB. If you exceed your data limit in a month, the fee for the extra data usage is usually very expensive.

Understanding your data usage is complicated. A cellular data plan is for Internet data transfer, not texting. Providers require a separate texting plan. Note that all the data transfer you do using WiFi (instead of the 3G/4G network) does not count as part of your data plan usage.

How big a data plan do I need to buy? Before subscribing to a data plan, you should assess your needs:

- How often will you be able to use WiFi access, and how often will you need to use the cellular network?
- How often do you download apps, stream music, or play online games?
- Do you use your phone to watch streaming video?
- Do you use your smartphone's Internet access to download files attached to e-mails or from your company website?

BITS&BYTES

Texting for Change

Can texting impact social change? Texting is now being used to address serious social issues because it is the choice communication mode of people age 14 to 30. Studies show that texts reach the teenage population at 11 times the effectiveness of e-mail. The average number of monthly texts a teenager sends and receives is over 3,500 a month. This holds true across a wide range of socioeconomic categories.

Crisis texting hotlines are opening to reach and respond to the violence, rape, and bullying that young people experience. The site DoSomething.org (**dosomething.org**) opened a Crisis Text Line to organize their response to crisis text messages they were receiving. In addition, police around the country are establishing anonymous texting tip lines to take advantage of the prevalence of texting.

Begin by estimating how much data you transfer up and down from the Internet each month. To do so, you can use an online estimator supplied by your provider like the one shown in Figure 8.9. Apps such as My Data Usage Pro or 3G Watchdog are also available for any smartphone to keep track of data usage for you. Some mobile operating systems, like Android, allow you to see a graph of your data usage and set alarms at specific levels.

Be sure you select a plan that provides adequate service at a good price. Remember, most providers require each device using cellular Internet to be covered by a data plan.

At what speed is digital information transferred to my smartphone? Although broadband speeds of 50 megabits per second (Mbps) are achievable at home using a cable or fiber-optic connection, your smartphone will connect at a much lower speed. The exact speed will depend on which technology you're using: WiFi, 3G cellular, or 4G cellular (see Figure 8.10).

We discussed WiFi networks in depth in Chapter 7. These networks typically run at speeds of 4 to 5 Mbps. Currently, there are two cellular data-transfer standards:

1. *3G:* 3G brought mobile device data-transfer rates as high as 3.8 Mbps (or more, under ideal conditions). 3G is more reliable than WiFi and is less susceptible to interference. 3G blankets most major urban areas with connectivity.

2. *4G:* 4G networks are now rolling out across the United States. The promise of 4G is incredible: mobile connection speeds of up to 100 Mbps! Currently, most providers can't deliver true 4G speeds; their 4G networks deliver speeds of 6 Mbps to 13 Mbps. These options, often named "4G LTE," are faster than 3G but don't meet the rate required to be true 4G, so they're referred to as "near 4G" networks. The expansion of 4G will usher in a new generation of mobile devices.

How do I set my phone to use a WiFi connection? It will be slightly different for each mobile OS, but in general,

FIGURE 8.9 Online tools can help you estimate your monthly data usage. *(Courtesy of AT&T)*

you turn on the setting that allows your phone to look for a network. If a network is found, the phone will try to log in. If the network has security protection, you'll be prompted for a password before joining. Most smartphones then display a special icon to show that you're using a WiFi connection instead of a 3G/4G signal.

FIGURE 8.10 The range of speeds you achieve when connecting to the Internet with your smartphone or mobile device depends on the type of connection.

BITS&BYTES

Want to Read That Voicemail?

Consider using Google Voice. Google Voice automatically transcribes your voice messages to text so if you're at a noisy concert, you can still check in on that last call. The transcription makes it easy to search for information left in a voice message. If you want, the transcribed calls can be e-mailed to you and you can text back a response right from the e-mail. You can sign up for a free Google Voice phone number at **google.com/voice**.

Some people choose to leave their phone in the mode where it's looking for a WiFi network so it will always use a WiFi signal if it is available, saving them on data plan usage. This does use more battery life, though, so turn off WiFi detection if you're trying to extend your battery.

Can I use my 3G/4G signal to create a WiFi hotspot for my other devices? As mentioned in Chapter 7, if a WiFi spot isn't available, there are devices that will instantly create a mobile hotspot for you. MiFi (pronounced "my fy") devices are often available free with a new account from major Internet providers like Verizon and AT&T. These devices connect to the Internet through the wireless phone network and then distribute the WiFi signal over an area of 30 feet. These personal hot spots can then support up to 10 WiFi-enabled devices.

Another approach is **tethering**, which makes sure that as long as you have a 3G/4G signal, your computer can access the Internet even when it tells you there are no available wireless networks. Several phones offer this capability. For example, an iPhone can connect to your notebook computer through wireless Bluetooth and then provide Internet access through its 4G network signal. Check with your provider, though, because they may charge an extra fee for tethering.

Smartphone Security

Can I get a virus on my smartphone? Viruses can indeed infect smartphones. Over half of users say they send confidential e-mails using their phones, and one-third of users access bank account or credit card information on their phones, so smartphones are the next most likely realm of attack by cybercriminals. Although viruses plaguing smartphones have not yet reached the volume of viruses attacking PC operating systems, with the proliferation of mobile devices, virus attacks are expected to increase.

Kaspersky, McAfee, and F-Secure are among leading companies currently providing antivirus software for mobile devices. Products are designed for specific operating systems; for example, Kaspersky Mobile Security has versions for Android phones and tablets, Windows phones, and BlackBerry devices. Often, businesses will have their information technology department install and configure an antivirus solution like this for all the phones used in the organization.

If no antivirus program is available for your phone's OS, the best precautions are commonsense ones. Check the phone manufacturer's website frequently to see whether your smartphone needs any software upgrades that could patch security holes. In addition, remember that you shouldn't download ring tones, games, or other software from unfamiliar websites.

How do I keep my phone number private? If you're concerned about widely distributing your phone number and potentially inviting lots of unwanted calls, consider using a virtual phone number. A virtual phone number is a phone number you create that can be assigned to ring on existing phone numbers. Companies such as Telusion (**tossabledigits.com**) will sell you a virtual number. Then, when you're filling out a registration form for some web service, you can input your virtual phone number in the web form instead of giving out your number. When you set up the virtual account, you can restrict the hours that you will receive calls from that number, and if you're receiving many unwanted calls, you can disable the virtual number without affecting your cell- or smartphone service.

VoIP

Is the cellular network the only way to place phone calls? Cell phone service is still not 100% reliable, and dropped calls and poor reception are a problem in some areas. As an alternative, a fully digital phone service called **Voice over Internet Protocol (VoIP)** is available.

How is VoIP different from regular telephone service? VoIP is a form of voice-based Internet communication that turns a standard Internet connection into a means to place phone calls, including long-distance calls (see Figure 8.11). Traditional telephone communications use analog voice data and telephone connections. In contrast, VoIP uses technology similar to that used in e-mail to transmit your voice data digitally over the Internet.

Who are some VoIP providers? Skype is one very well-known provider. Creating a VoIP account with Skype (**skype.com**) is simple (see the Try This in Chapter 1, pages 12–13).

FIGURE 8.11 VoIP technology lets your computing device behave like a phone or video phone, using the Internet instead of the telephone system to transmit data. *(David Malan/Getty Images)*

Skype requires that both callers and receivers have the company's free software installed on their device (computer, tablet, or phone). With Skype you can place a phone call, make an HD-video call, and even share screens between users. Calls to other Skype users are free, and you can place low-cost calls to non-Skype users. Major ISPs, like Comcast and Verizon, also provide VoIP phone services as an option you can package with your Internet or cable television plan.

What do I need to use VoIP? VoIP calls can be placed from anywhere you have Internet access. Any Android or iOS phone or tablet can also be used as a VoIP device. There are also standalone VoIP phones sold, sometimes called *IP phones*.

What are the advantages and disadvantages of VoIP? For people who make many long-distance phone calls, the advantage of VoIP is that it's free or low cost. Portability is another advantage: As long as you're connected to the Internet, you can sign on to your VoIP service and make your call.

Although VoIP is affordable and convenient, it does have drawbacks:

- Some people regard sound quality and reliability issues as VoIP's primary disadvantages.
- Another drawback when using VoIP at home is the loss of service if power is interrupted.
- Another issue with VoIP is security risks. Having a hacker break in to a VoIP system to make unauthorized calls is a serious but avoidable problem. Encryption services that convert data into a form not easily understood by unauthorized people are being deployed to help protect calls made over the Internet.

VoIP continues to enjoy explosive growth, and the technology will continue to improve.

What new features come with using VoIP? If you set up a VoIP service as your home telephone system, you can have your telephone messages automatically bundled up as e-mails and sent to your account. If you're watching television and a call comes in, it can be displayed on the screen with caller ID information. Some learning management systems also use VoIP. For example, if you're using MyITLab with this course, you can call your professor through VoIP without having his or her personal phone number.

Smartphone GPS

Does my smartphone contain a GPS chip? Today every cell- and smartphone has to include a GPS chip. The Federal Communications Commission (FCC) mandated this to enable the complete rollout of the Enhanced 911 (E911) program. E911 automatically gives dispatchers precise location information for any 911 call. It also means your phone records may include this precise tracking information, which indicates where you are when you make a call.

How does GPS work? Built and operated by the U.S. Department of Defense, the **global positioning system (GPS)** is a network of 21 satellites (plus 3 working spares) that constantly orbits the Earth. GPS devices use an antenna to pick up the signals from these satellites and use special software to transform those signals into latitude and longitude. Using the information obtained from the satellites, GPS devices determine geographical location anywhere on the planet to within 3 feet (see Figure 8.12). The exact accuracy depends on such things as atmospheric conditions and interference from obstacles like mountains or buildings.

Can I track a family member using the GPS chip in his or her phone? Cell-phone providers offer plans (for a monthly fee) that allow you to track where a phone is at any given time. For example, AT&T's Family Map service lets parents track all the phones on their family plan in real time. Locations of all phones are displayed over the web on a map or to an app for your phone, or the service will send an automatic text message alert with the phones' locations at a specific time each day. So a parent could have a text or e-mail sent with his or her daughter's phone location each day at 3 p.m. to be sure she made it home from school. The person being tracked can't turn off the service. ■

FIGURE 8.12 GPS computes your location anywhere on Earth from a system of orbiting satellites. *(Evgeny Terentev/Getty Images)*

tablets, netbooks, and
ULTRABOOKS

The best way to navigate all the mobile devices on the market is to be aware of the boundaries between types of devices. In this section, we'll look at what changes when you move from one type of device to another.

Tablets

How do tablets compare with smartphones? *Tablets* are very light, very portable devices. The top-selling tablets include the Apple iPad and the Samsung Galaxy, but there are over 75 tablets on the market (see Figure 8.13). The main difference between any tablet and a smartphone is screen size. Whereas smartphones usually have displays that are less than 5 inches, tablets come with screen sizes between 7 and 10 inches. But manufacturers are beginning to make even larger phones, offering a "phablet" model of phone, with screen sizes almost 6 inches. The larger screen allows for a larger virtual keyboard and higher resolution.

In most other regards, smartphones and tablets are similar. They have the following features:

- Similar operating systems: Whether iOS or Android, common operating systems operate on smartphones and tablets.
- Similar processors: The processing power of smartphones and tablets is often the same.
- Touch-screen interfaces: Smartphones and tablets are both equipped with touch-screen interfaces.

FIGURE 8.13 iPad...Nexus...Galaxy? There are over 75 tablets on the market now. Finding the right digital device can be a challenge. *(John Lamb/Getty Images)*

- Long battery life: Most tablets and smartphones run at least 10 hours on a single charge.
- Similar software applications: Most apps available for one device are available for the other.
- Similar Internet connectivity: Both offer 3G/4G as well as WiFi connectivity.
- Bluetooth: Both can be connected over Bluetooth to printers, keyboards, and other peripherals.

Can tablets function as a communication device? Although tablets are currently not able to make cell-phone calls, they can easily place audio or video phone calls if connected to a WiFi network. A VoIP application like Skype is required for that. There are also apps available that allow tablets to handle texting. HeyWire, for example, supports free national and international texting from a range of devices, including tablets as well as phones.

Netbooks

Why would I want a netbook instead of a tablet? A tablet runs a mobile OS. A *netbook*, on the other hand, uses a full traditional OS, like Windows 8. This means you can't run programs like Microsoft Office on a tablet, but you can on a netbook. In addition, a netbook has a physical keyboard. Netbooks weigh 2 pounds or less and are inexpensive compared with both tablets and ultrabooks, so they are a good option if you're looking for value. Many models are available for under $300.

Why wouldn't I want a netbook? The processing power and memory on a netbook makes it difficult to run software that does a lot of computation. Netbooks also have very small screens (usually 10 inches or less). The screen resolution and small keyboard may not work for your needs, so be sure to try one out before making a purchase.

Ultrabooks

How are ultrabooks different from laptops? *Ultrabooks* are a newer category of full-featured computers that focus on offering a very thin, lightweight computing solution. Ultrabooks don't offer optical drives, for example, allowing a very thin profile. Most ultrabooks offer SSD drives and so have very fast response times on boot up and restoring from hibernation. They weigh in at under 3 pounds even though they feature the same operating systems and CPUs as heavier, larger laptops. They also include full-size keyboards and

13- to 15-inch screens. Examples include the Apple Macbook Air and the Asus Zenbook.

How are ultrabooks different from tablets? Whereas tablets share a lot in common with smartphones, ultrabooks are lightweight laptops. They are good choices when you want to run a traditional OS, have a lot of computing power. Figure 8.14 summarizes how tablets and ultrabooks compare.

Making a Choice

With all these choices, how do I know which device is best for me? Use these guidelines to determine what best fits your personal needs for this particular device. Consider the following:

- **Screen size and style of keyboard:** You can adapt these with accessories (add a Bluetooth keyboard or connect to a larger external monitor), but most of the time these will determine how you interact with your device. Do you want a touch-based interface? Is a physical keyboard important, or is a software keyboard sufficient?
- **Weight:** Does an additional 2 pounds matter? The price of an ultrabook is several hundred dollars more than an equivalent laptop.
- **Number of devices:** Is this your only computing device? As technology prices fall, you may be able to have more than one device. You might find an affordable solution that includes both a very mobile device and a second more powerful one.

Figure 8.15 summarizes several different mobile device categories. ■

FIGURE 8.14

Tablets Versus Ultrabooks

FEATURE	TABLET	ULTRABOOK
Operating System	Mobile OS (iOS, Android, Windows)	Traditional OS (Windows or OS X)
Interface	Touch screen	Some have non-touch screens; have full-size keyboards
Screen Size	7 to 10 inches	13 to 15 inches
Processing Power	Mobile processor	Full quad-core Intel i5, i7
Storage	≤ 128 GB	128 to 500 GB
Software	Specialized applications custom designed for touch interface	Standard versions of software for desktop environments (Microsoft Office, etc.)

BITS&BYTES

The Fabulous Phablet

You may have noticed that the screens of smartphones are growing. In fact, the latest generation has grown into a cross between a phone and a tablet, creating a new category (and a new word): the *phablet*. These touch-screen phones sport screens larger than 5.5 inches. Especially in emerging global markets in China and India, the phablet is increasingly the tool of choice because one device is taking the place of having both a phone and a separate home computer.

(Peter Dazeley/Getty Images; Chris Tzou/Bloomberg/Getty Images; Ethan Miller/Getty Images; Josep Lago/AFP/Getty Images; Sean Gallup/Getty Images)

Laptop
* 5 to 8 lbs
* Traditional OS

Ultrabook
* Less than 3 lbs
* Traditional OS

Netbook
• 1 to 3 lbs
• Traditional OS

Tablet
• Less than 2 lbs
• Mobile OS

Smartphone
• 0.25 lbs
• Mobile OS

FIGURE 8.15 A full spectrum of mobile devices is available.

Before moving on to Part 2:
• **Watch Replay Video 8.1** ⊙.
• **Then check your understanding of what you've learned so far.**

check your understanding// review & practice

For a quick review to see what you've learned so far, answer the following questions. Visit **pearsonhighered.com /techinaction** to check your answers.

multiple choice

1. The operating system on your cell phone

   a. can be changed from iOS to Android.

   b. is a version of Android if you are using an iPhone.

   c. is stored on the SD card in the phone.

   d. None of the above.

2. VoIP is a phone service that

   a. requires a fiber-optic connection.

   b. works over an Internet connection.

   c. is only available for calls within the United States.

   d. has extremely high quality but is very expensive.

3. Which service allows you to use your cell phone or smartphone to send messages that contain images?

   a. MMS

   b. ISP

   c. SMS

   d. MiFi

4. When there are no available wireless networks, your phone

   a. cannot reach the Internet.

   b. can use Bluetooth technology to connect to the Internet.

   c. can use VoIP to still send e-mail.

   d. can use tethering to connect your computer to the Internet .

5. There are several categories of mobile devices because

   a. we do not yet have digital convergence.

   b. there is a range of trade-offs between weight and performance.

   c. everyone wants the fastest processor.

   d. no one has designed a digital device that works well for travel.

To take an autograded version of this review, please go to the companion website at **pearsonhighered.com/techinaction**, or go your MyITLab course.

Continue

You've just taken some fantastic video and photos on a trip to the zoo, and you'd like to organize the media and put it on your Facebook page. What should you do? Try Movie Maker!

Before You Start

a. Before starting, make sure you have several video clips and photos available. If you don't have any of your own, you can use the sample photos and video clips provided with Windows.

b. Movie Maker is part of the Windows Essentials package that is an add-on to Windows (this means it does not come preinstalled in Windows). To install Movie Maker, go to Microsoft's Windows Essentials website (**windows.microsoft.com/en-US/windows-live/essentials-home**) and click the **Download now** link. Once installed, there should be a tile on the Windows 8 Start Screen for Movie Maker. Click (or touch) this tile to launch Movie Maker.

Step 1   The first step is to import your video clips and photos to Movie Maker. On the **Home tab** of the Ribbon, click the **Add Videos and Photos** icon.

Step 2   In the dialog box that appears, browse to where your media files are saved, select the files you wish to import, and then click the **Open** button. The files you've added will appear in the Media window.

Step 3   In your movie, the video clips and pictures will display in the order shown in the media window (timeline). Click and drag your media to the spot in the timeline where you want it to appear.

Step 4   On the **Home tab** of the Ribbon, click the **Add music** icon and browse to a location on your storage device where you have music files. Select the music file you wish to add as a soundtrack for your movie, and then click the **Open** button.

Step 5   AutoMovie themes will add transitions between clips and title or credit slides based on prede-signed templates. Just click on one of the available themes in the **AutoMovie themes** group on the **Home tab** to apply that theme to your movie.

Step 6   Alternatively, you can manually add a title slide or credit slides by clicking on the appropriate icons on the **Home tab**. Just click on the slide in the preview window to enter a title for your slide.

Step 7   To preview your movie, click the **Play** button under the Preview window. When you're satisfied with your movie, go to the **Home tab** and click the **Save movie** icon to save it.

Step 8   To publish your movie on Face-book, go to the **Home tab**, and click the **Facebook** icon in the Share group. Select a resolution for your movie, and log on to Facebook (if neces-sary). Movie Maker will add your movie to your Facebook page.

Make This

TOOL: AI VideoPlayer

MAKE: A Video-Playing App

Do you want to run video clips inside your app?

In this exercise, you'll continue your mobile app development by using the Video Player compo-nent in **App Inventor** to run video clips inside your app. Using the component, you can play clips stored on your device, clips that you've recorded with the built-in camera, or clips on the Internet.

The Video Player has controls to pause, play, and fast forward or rewind and lets you ma-nipulate the size of the video screen as well as the volume. So decide how you will make your applications more media-intensive using the Video Player component in App Inventor!

The Video Player component allows you to display video inside your app.

For the instructions for this exercise, please go to pearsonhighered.com/techinaction or MyITLab.

The Digital Information Age

Do you really understand how all the digital technology you use every day actually works? Do you realize how many revolutionary changes are happening in all kinds of media as we continue to use digital formats? Let's take a closer look at what it means to be "digital" and the advantages it brings us.

 digital
DEFINED

Today, no matter what you're interested in—music, movies, TV, radio, stock prices—digital information is the key. All forms of entertainment have migrated to the digital domain (see Figure 8.16). Phone systems and TV signals are now digital streams of data. MP3 files encode digital forms of music, and digital cameras and video cameras are now commonplace. In Hollywood, feature films are being shot entirely with digital equipment, and many movie theaters use digital projection equipment. Satellite radio systems such as SiriusXM satellite radio and HD Radio are broadcast in digital formats.

How is digital different from analog? Any kind of information can be digitized (measured and converted to a stream of numeric values). Consider sound. It's carried to your ears by sound waves, which are actually patterns of pressure changes in the air. Images are our interpretation of the changing intensity of light waves around us. These sound and light waves are called **analog** waves or continuous waves. They illustrate the loudness of a sound or the brightness of the colors in an image at a given moment in time. They're continuous signals because you would never have to lift your pencil off the page to draw them; they are just long, continuous lines.

First-generation recording devices such as vinyl records and analog television broadcasts were designed to reproduce these sound and light waves. A needle in the groove of a vinyl record vibrates in the same pattern as the original sound wave. Analog television signals are actually waves that tell an analog TV how to display the same color and brightness as is seen in the production studio.

However, it's difficult to describe a wave, even mathematically. The simplest sounds, such as that of middle C on a piano, have the simplest shapes, like the one shown in Figure 8.17a. However, something like the word *hello* generates a highly complex pattern, like the one shown in Figure 8.17b.

What advantages do digital formats have over analog ones? Digital formats describe signals as long strings of numbers. This digital representation gives us a simple way to describe sound and light waves exactly so that sounds and images can be reproduced perfectly any time they're wanted. In addition, we already have easy ways to distribute digital information, such as streaming movies or attaching files to a Facebook message. Thus, digital information can be reproduced exactly and distributed easily; both these reasons give digital huge advantages over an analog format.

How can a sequence of numbers express complicated analog shapes? The answer is provided by something called *analog-to-digital conversion*. In analog-to-digital conversion, the incoming analog signal is measured many times each second. The strength of the signal at each measurement is recorded as a simple number. The series of numbers produced by the analog-to-digital conversion process gives us the digital form of the wave. Figure 8.18 shows analog and digital versions of the same wave. In Figure 8.18a, you see the original, continuous analog wave. You could draw that wave without lifting your pencil from the page. In

FIGURE 8.16

Analog Versus Digital Entertainment

	ANALOG	DIGITAL
Publishing	Magazines, books	E-books, e-zines
Music	Vinyl record albums and cassette tapes	CDs, MP3 files, and streaming music stations
Photography	35-mm single-lens reflex (SLR) cameras Photos stored on film	Digital cameras, including digital SLRs Photos stored as digital files
Video	8-mm, VHS, and Hi8 camcorders Film stored on tapes	HD digital video (DV) cameras Film stored as digital files; distributed on DVD and Blu-ray discs and streamed
Radio	AM/FM radio	HD Radio, SiriusXM satellite radio
Television	Analog TV broadcast	High-definition digital television (HDTV)

FIGURE 8.17 (a) This is an analog wave showing the simple, pure sound of a piano playing middle C. (b) This is the complex wave produced when a person says "Hello."

Figure 8.18b, the wave has been digitized and is no longer a single line; instead, it is represented as a series of points or numbers.

How has the change from analog to digital technologies affected our lifestyles? When the market for communication devices for entertainment media—like photos, music, and video—switched to a digital standard, we began to have products with new and useful capabilities. Small devices can now hold huge collections of a variety of types of information. We can interact with our information any time we like in ways that, prior to the conversion to digital media, had been too expensive or too difficult to learn. The implications of the shift to digital media are continually evolving. ■

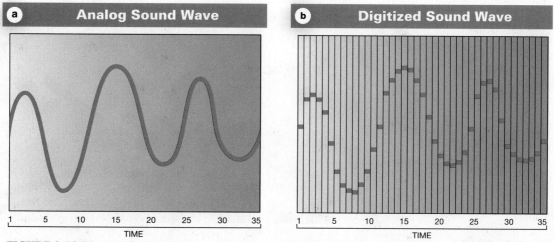

FIGURE 8.18 (a) A simple analog wave. (b) A digitized version of the same wave. (*Courtesy of SONY Creative Software.; Courtesy of SONY Creative Software.*)

Your mobile device performs many tasks, and now, thanks to near field communication (NFC) technology, it will feature yet another form of convergence: the integration of your wallet into your phone. How so? NFC technology allows a device with an NFC chip (such as a smartphone) to communicate with another NFC device (such as a checkout machine) with a single touch. In fact, with NFC, you can forget your wallet: Financial transactions can be processed just by bringing the devices within an inch of each other.

Because NFC has such a short range (up to 1.5 inches), it is being used for secure credit card transactions. Both MasterCard and Visa are piloting programs that would allow cell phones to "tap and go," meaning phone owners would no longer need to carry physical credit cards. Instead, they could simply tap their phone near an NFC checkout device and have it automatically transmit the proper loyalty card information, select and process any coupon offers, and pay all at once (see Figure 8.19).

In countries like Japan, Spain, and Germany, NFC ticketing programs are already in place. The Deutsche Bahn rail system allows users to tap their phones to an NFC tag when they get on the train and to another on departing. The fare is automatically calculated and billed to their credit card monthly. Marketing agencies are also using NFC.

An NFC chip can be stored inside a poster, for example. When a passerby touches his or her phone to a specific spot, a coupon or a website address can be transmitted.

NFC can handle identification verification as well. The swipe cards that verify your identity for entry into secure areas can be replaced using NFC to exchange stored virtual credentials. The same technology can be used to open door locks or any system where a user name and password are used. So, opening a cabinet or logging into a computer can all be managed with a tap of your NFC-enabled phone.

Several mobile applications, such as Apple Pay and Google Wallet, are available for NFC sales transactions. These programs conduct NFC transactions as well as collect your loyalty cards, gift cards, receipts, boarding passes, tickets, and keys within your phone. Currently not all service providers will enable the NFC chip on your smartphone, however, so check before you buy a new phone.

Imagine a time soon when you're out to dinner with friends and need to split the bill. Your NFC phone is already linked to your credit card, and you simply tap your friend's phone to transfer him his share of the bill. Some are predicting the worldwide NFC market will grow to be worth $50 billion over the next few years, making this a trend to watch.

FIGURE 8.19 NFC-equipped phones will shift how we handle financial transactions and identify ourselves.

(File/AP Images)

digital
MEDIA

The entertainment industry has become an all-digital field. The publishing industry, the music recording industry, photography, and film production have all seen radical changes in how content is created and how it is distributed to an audience. Let's look at these forms of entertainment and how they affect you.

Digital Publishing

Are printed books dead? The publishing industry is migrating to digital materials. **Electronic text (e-text)** is textual information captured digitally so that it can be stored, manipulated, and transmitted by electronic devices. With the increasing usage of e-text, the market for printed materials is changing dramatically. In fact, Amazon now sells more Kindle e-books than printed books each year. Several authors, such as Stieg Larsson and James Patterson, have each sold over one million e-books.

What electronic devices are trying to replace books? **E-readers** (see Figure 8.20) are devices that can display e-text and have supporting tools, like note taking, bookmarks, and integrated dictionaries. They are selling at a brisk pace with a dizzying range of offerings in the market, including the Amazon Kindle and Fire, Barnes and Noble NOOK, and Sony Reader.

FIGURE 8.20 E-readers are popularizing the digital e-book. *(Kristoffer Tripplaar/Alamy)*

Tablets are also helping to popularize the digitized e-book and electronic versions of major magazines and newspapers. In the U.S. book market, e-books seem to be settling in at between 20 to 30% of total book sales.

What features make e-readers popular? One big allure of digital publishing is distribution. Ease of access to digital books is very attractive. Even a 1,000-page book can be delivered to your e-reader in under a minute. An incredible array of titles is available—over one million books are available in the Amazon Kindle store alone. In addition, there are millions of texts without copyright that are available for free.

The basic features of e-readers offer many advantages over paper books:

- Integrated dictionaries pull up a definition just by your highlighting a word. The Kindle, for example, can work with both English and German dictionaries—a help in reading foreign works.
- Note taking and highlighting are supported, and you can search the text for your own notes or for specific terms. You can also easily share the notes you make on the book with others.
- URL links or links to a glossary are often live in the book.
- Bookmarks are immediately pushed through cloud technology so you can read on one device and pick up with the most current bookmark on another device.

Do I need a dedicated device just for reading e-texts? There are free software download versions of the Kindle and the NOOK that run on either PC or Apple computers. You can also download certain texts that have no copyrights and read them directly on a computer either as a PDF file or by using browser add-ons like MagicScroll.

How is digital text displayed? There are two popular technologies used for representing digital text:

1. *Electronic ink:* **Electronic ink (E Ink)** is a very crisp, sharp grayscale representation of text. The "page" is composed of millions of microcapsules with white and black particles in a clear fluid. Electronic signals can make each spot appear either white or black. E Ink devices reflect the light that shines on the page, like ordinary paper. E Ink gives great contrast and is much easier to read in direct sunlight. Examples of devices using E Ink include high-contrast screens like the Amazon Kindle Paperwhite (see Figure 8.21a) and the Barnes and Noble NOOK.

2. *Backlit monitors:* Another option for presenting e-text is the high-resolution backlit monitors seen in readers like the iPad or the Amazon Fire (see Figure 8.21b). These screens illuminate themselves instead of depending on

FIGURE 8.21 The two main technologies for e-text display are (a) E Ink grayscale displays, like on the Amazon Kindle, and (b) high-resolution backlit color screens, like on the Amazon Fire. *(David McNew/Getty Images; Emmanuel Dunand/AFP/Getty Images)*

room lighting conditions. They display color materials, like magazines, with great clarity and full color. The glass does reflect glare, though, which makes them hard to use in bright, direct sunlight. Some people experience more fatigue when reading from a backlit device than when using E Ink. Also note that E Ink readers have a battery life of a month or two on a charge, whereas high-resolution color readers hold a charge for 8 to 10 hours.

Be sure to try both under a variety of conditions before you make a purchasing decision.

What kinds of file formats are used in electronic publishing? Digital formats for publishing vary. Amazon uses a proprietary format (.azw extension), so books purchased for a Kindle are not transportable to a non-Kindle device. An open format also exists, ePub. Some e-readers support the ePub file format. There is an ePub reader plugin available for the browser Firefox and several stand-alone software ePub readers like Stanza.

Where do I buy e-books? There are a number of vendors associated with e-reader devices:

- Amazon sells the Kindle device, and it connects directly to the Amazon Kindle store.
- The Barnes and Noble NOOK device works with the Barnes and Noble e-bookstore.
- There are many publishers selling e-books online that can be read on any kind of device.
- Textbooks can be purchased in e-book format directly from the publisher; for example, the technology publisher O'Reilly has an online e-bookstore. Another option is a company like CourseSmart, which offers a year-long

subscription to a digital text that times out and disappears from your device after your subscription is up.

What if I just want to borrow a book from a library? Libraries are now including e-book and audio book lending as part of their mission (see Figure 8.22). There is never a late fee; the book just times out and disappears from your device when the borrowing period expires. Products like the Overdrive Media Console (**overdrive.com**) let you search to find which area library has the book you want. When you log in to the library website, you can download a text any time of day or night. Libraries have a specific number of copies of each e-book title available, so you may be added to a waiting list if all the copies are checked out, just like with paper books. However, there is a lot of friction between publishers and libraries on how to handle the impact of lending electronically. It's so convenient that some publishers are refusing to allow their e-books to be distributed through libraries.

Can I borrow an e-book from a friend? Lending of e-books is now becoming a popular feature of e-reader systems. The Barnes & Noble NOOK, for example, has a Lend Me feature on certain books. An eligible book can be loaned once for a period of 14 days.

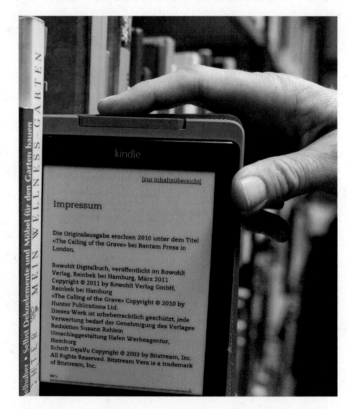

FIGURE 8.22 E-books and audio books can be borrowed for free at most public libraries. *(Alex Ehlers/dpa/picture-alliance/Newscom)*

Where can I find free e-books? A great source of free reading is Project Gutenberg (**gutenberg.org**). This repository site is a collection of over 42,000 free books in ePub, Kindle, and PDF formats. It contains books that are free in the United States because their copyrights have expired. The catalog includes many classic titles like *War and Peace* by Leo Tolstoy or mystery novels by Agatha Christie.

How can I publish my own works? Self-publishing is much easier in the age of digital texts. There are many options available:

- Self-publish into the *Amazon Kindle Store* in a matter of minutes and earn up to a 70% royalty on sales.
- Use a company like *Smashwords* (**smashwords.com**). It accepts a Microsoft Word document from you and then makes your book available through a number of vendors like the Apple iBooks store, Barnes & Noble, and the Sony Reader store. Your book can also be distributed as an app to mobile marketplaces like Google Play or the Apple App Store.
- Use a site like *Lulu* (**lulu.com**) to do social marketing for your book so that you can promote it. In addition, it offers services from editors, designers, and marketers.

Digital Music

How is digital music created? The sound waves created by instruments need to be turned into a string of digital information to record digital music. Figure 8.23 shows the process of digitally recording a song:

1. Playing music creates analog waves.
2. A microphone feeds the sound waves into a chip called an *analog-to-digital converter (ADC)* inside the recording device.
3. The ADC digitizes the waves into a series of numbers.
4. This series of numbers can be recorded onto CDs or DVDs, saved in a file, or sent electronically.
5. On the receiving end, a playback device such as a mobile device or a DVD player is fed that same series of numbers. Inside the playback device is a *digital-to-analog converter (DAC)*, a chip that converts the digital numbers to a continuous analog wave.
6. That analog wave tells the receiver how to move the speaker cones to reproduce the original waves, resulting in the same sound as the original.

More precisely, the digital wave will be *close* to exact. How accurate it is, or how close the digitized wave is in shape to the original analog wave, depends on the sampling rate of the ADC. The **sampling rate** specifies the number of times the analog wave is measured each second. The higher the sampling rate, the more accurately the original wave can be recreated. The improved sound quality higher sampling can afford also depends on the quality of the output device and

FIGURE 8.23 During the complete recording process, information changes from analog form to digital data and then back again to analog sound waves. *(Ben Chams/Fotolia)*

speakers, of course. However, higher sampling rates also produce much more data and therefore result in bigger files. For example, sound waves on CDs are sampled at a rate of approximately 44,000 times a second. This produces a huge list of numbers for even a single minute of a song.

What file types store digital music? You're no doubt familiar with the MP3 file format used to store digital music, but many others exist, such as AAC and WMA. If you buy a song from the iTunes Store, for example, you receive an AAC-format file. There are also many formats, such as DivX, MPEG-4 (which usually has an .mp4 extension), WMV, and XviD, which hold both video and audio information. All file formats compete on sound and video quality and *compression*, which relates to how small the file can be and still provide high-quality play-back. Be sure to check what kind of files your audio device understands before you store music on it.

How do I know how much digital media my device can hold? The number of songs or hours of video a device like an iPod can hold depends on how much storage space it has. Less expensive mobile devices use built-in flash memory ranging from 2 to 64 GB, whereas more expensive models use built-in hard drives, which provide as much as 160 GB of storage.

Another factor that determines how much music a player can hold is the quality of the MP3 music files. The size of an MP3 file depends on the digital sampling of the song. The same song could be sampled at a rate anywhere between 64 kbps and 320 kbps. The size of the song file will be five times larger if it is sampled at 320 kbps rather than the lower sampling rate of 64 kbps. The higher the sampling rate, the better quality the sound—but the larger the file size.

How do you control the size of an MP3 file? If you are *ripping*, or converting, a song from a CD to a digital MP3 file, you can select the sampling rate yourself. You decide by considering what quality sound you want, as well as how many songs you want to fit onto your MP3 player. For example, if your player has 1 GB of storage and you have ripped songs at 192 kbps, you could fit about 694 minutes of music onto the player. The same 1 GB could store 2,083 minutes of music if it were sampled at 64 kbps. Whenever you are near your computer, you can connect your player and download a different set of songs, but you always are limited by the amount of storage your player has.

What if I want to access more music than my device has room for? Some of the devices that use flash memory allow you to add storage capacity by purchasing removable flash memory cards. You can also use a service that streams the music to you over WiFi or 3G/4G networks. Services like Spotify and GooglePlay have subscription plans that let you listen to any of the millions of tracks in their catalog. The music is not yours to own, however—if you cancel your subscription, you no longer have access to the music.

But because it's streamed to you, it doesn't take up space on your device drive. Some streaming services offer options that also let you download music so that you can still play the songs on your playlist even if you're not in range of Internet access.

How do I transfer files to my music device? To move large volumes of data between your computer and your music device, you want a high-speed port. Most devices use a USB port, which lets you transfer files quickly. Cloud services are appearing that automatically push music to your mobile device. Apple's iOS operating system supports iCloud technology. This means that as soon as you purchase a new song from iTunes, it's automatically pushed to all your registered iTunes devices—your Mac, your PC, your iPad and iTouch, and your iPhone.

What if I want a lot of people to listen to my digital music? You have a number of options for listening to your music other than with headphones:

- Many audio receivers now come with a port or a dock so that you can connect a mobile device directly to them as another audio input source.
- Networked audio/video receivers have the hardware and software required to connect to your home network and use streaming services like Pandora or Spotify to play music (see Figure 8.24).
- Most new cars are equipped with an auxiliary input to the speaker system to support connecting a mobile device; others have a fully integrated software system that displays and runs your playlists. Many Ford models use the Microsoft Sync system that allows you to navigate through your playlists with just voice commands.

FIGURE 8.24 Networked audio receivers can run Internet streaming services like Spotify and can connect to home servers.
(Anton Mishchenko/123RF)

FIGURE 8.25 Sonos is a multiroom system that streams music wirelessly throughout your home.
(Robert Schlesinger/dpa/picture-alliance/Newscom)

- There are systems, like Sonos (see Figure 8.25), that can mate wirelessly with a mobile device and broadcast sound throughout the house.

If I don't pay for a music download, is it illegal?
Although you need to pay for most music you download, some artists post songs for free. Business models are still evolving as artists and recording companies try to meet audience needs while also protecting their own intellectual property rights. Several different approaches exist. One is to deliver something called *tethered downloads*, in which you pay for the music and own it but are subject to restrictions on its use.

Another approach is to offer *DRM-free* music, which is music without any **digital rights management (DRM)**. DRM is a system of access control that allows only limited use of material that's been legally purchased. It may be that the song can only run on certain devices or a movie can only be viewed a certain number of times. A DRM-free song can be placed on as many computers or players as you wish. These song files can be moved freely from system to system.

Will streaming music services eliminate radio stations? The Internet allows artists to release new songs to their fans immediately (on sites such as Facebook) and without relying on radio airtime. This opens up new channels for artists to reach an audience and changes the amount of power radio stations have in the promotion of music. Many radio stations have increased listenership by making their stations available through Internet sites and by broadcasting in high-definition quality.

What if I want to publicize my band's music?
Digital music has made distributing your own recordings very simple. You can make your own creations available using sites like SoundCloud (**soundcloud.com**) and ReverbNation (**reverbnation.com**). You can quickly create a web page for your band, post your songs, and start building a fan base through Facebook. ReverbNation will send you reports detailing who's listening to your music and what they're saying about it. ReverbNation is also a way to connect with independent recording labels and to find places that want to book your band.

BITS&BYTES

Need Money for Your Band? Try Indiegogo

What if your band has already built up a fan base but just needs to have the up-front money to go into the studio to record? Indiegogo (**indiegogo.com**) is a crowd-funding website specializing in creative projects and causes. Musicians have a platform to go to their fan base and raise money before a recording session or a tour, or even when tragedy strikes. When cellist Mike Block had a serious accident, he used Indiegogo to raise money to pay off his medical bills. Mike offered copies of an upcoming album or personal lessons as rewards to funders. He raised over $48,000 using Indiegogo and was able to repay years of accumulated medical expenses.

Digital Photography

What is "analog" photography? Before digital cameras hit the market, most people used some form of 35-mm single-lens reflex (SLR) camera. When you take a picture using a traditional SLR camera, a shutter opens, creating an aperture (a small window in the camera) that allows light to hit the 35-mm film inside. Chemicals coating the film react when exposed to light. Later, additional chemicals develop the image on the film, and the image is printed on special light-sensitive paper. A variety of lenses and processing techniques, special equipment, and filters are needed to create printed photos taken with traditional SLR cameras.

What's different about digital photography? Digital cameras do not use film. Instead, they capture images on electronic sensors called *charge-coupled device (CCD) arrays* and then convert those images to digital data, long series of numbers that represent the color and brightness of millions of points in the image. Unlike traditional cameras, digital cameras allow you to see your images the instant you shoot them. Most camera models can now record digital video as well as digital photos.

DIG DEEPER

The Shift to Digital Music: A Bumpy Ride

The shift to digital music wasn't an easy transition for the recording industry. The initial MP3 craze was fueled by sites such as MP3.com, which originally stored its song files on a public server with the permission of the original artists or recording companies. Therefore, you weren't infringing on a copyright by downloading songs from sites such as MP3.com.

Napster was a file-exchange site created to correct some of the annoyances found by users of MP3.com (see Figure 8.26). One such annoyance was the limited availability of popular music in MP3 format. Napster differed from MP3.com because songs or locations of songs were not stored in a central public server but instead were "borrowed" directly from other users' computers. This process of users transferring files between computers is referred to as **peer-to-peer (P2P) sharing**. Napster also provided a search engine dedicated to finding specific MP3 files. This direct search and sharing eliminated the inconvenience of searching links only to find them unavailable.

The problem with Napster was that it was so good at what it did. The rapid acceptance and use of Napster—at one point, it had nearly 60 million users—led the music industry to sue the site for copyright infringement, and Napster was closed in June 2002. Napster has since merged with Rhapsody as a streaming music service.

The music industry has needed to reinvent itself since the demise of Napster. The initial reaction of the recording industry was to continue to enforce its absolute ownership over digital forms of its music. The industry even filed legal actions against individuals who had downloaded large amounts

FIGURE 8.26 Napster was one of the original P2P music-sharing sites. *(Mike Fanous/Gamma-Rapho/Getty Images)*

of music from Internet sites. This heavy-handed reaction to the new era of digital music ultimately backfired and left the music industry scrambling. Overall music sales have dropped significantly each year for the last decade. The recording industry is still trying to counter losing CD sales. The approach they took early on did not allow them to adapt quickly enough to the new business models required by the shift to digital technologies.

P2P sharing sites are still operating today. Napster was "easy" to shut down because it used a central index server that queried other Napster computers for requested songs. Current P2P protocols (such as BearShare) differ from Napster in that they don't limit themselves to sharing only MP3 files. Video files are easily obtainable on P2P sites. More importantly, these sites don't have a central computer acting to index all this information. Instead, they operate in a true P2P sharing environment in which computers connect directly to other computers. This makes them a prime source of unwanted viruses and spyware.

The argument these P2P networks make to defend their legality is that they do not run a central server like the original Napster but only facilitate connections between users. Therefore, they have no control over what the users choose to trade. As the digital music industry matures, new avenues of distribution are appearing. BT Bundles are packages of free audio, video, and print content downloaded from the musician through Bit Torrent. You can unlock additional content by paying or supplying your e-mail address. Tracks that are easy to remix are provided so fans can create and share their own extensions to the work.

How do I select a digital camera? The first question to answer is whether you want a compact "point-and-shoot" camera or a more expensive digital SLR. If you decide you want a digital SLR, you have a number of options. Some digital SLRs let you switch among different lenses, as shown in Figure 8.27, and offer features important to serious amateur and professional photographers. Although having such flexibility in selection of lenses is a great advantage, most of these cameras are also larger, heavier, and use more battery power than the fixed-lens models. Think about how you'll be using your camera and decide which model will serve you best in the long run. One great resource to use is Digital Photography Review (**dpreview.com**), a site that compares cameras and provides feedback from owners.

What determines the image quality of a digital camera? The overall image quality is determined by many factors:

- The quality of the lenses used
- The image sensor size
- The file format and compression used
- The color management software included
- The camera's **resolution**, or the number of data points it records for each image captured

A digital camera's resolution is measured in megapixels (MP). The word *pixel* is short for *picture element*, which is a single dot in a digital image. Point-and-shoot models typically offer resolutions from 12 to 20 MP. Professional digital SLR cameras, such as the Nikon D800, can take photos at resolutions as high as 36 MP.

If you're interested in making only 5" × 7" or 8" × 10" prints, a lower-resolution camera is fine. However, low-resolution images become grainy and pixelated when pushed to larger size. For example, if you tried to print an 11" × 14" enlargement from an 8 MP image taken using your smartphone's camera, the image would look grainy; you would see individual dots of color instead of a clear, sharp image. The 16 to 24 MP cameras on the market now have plenty of resolution to guarantee sharp, detailed images even with enlargements as big as 11" × 14".

But the size of the image sensor that actually captures the light is also very critical. Larger sensors demand larger cameras and larger lenses. Professional digital cameras use a full-frame sensor, the size of a 35 mm negative. Smartphones need to use a very compact sensor (typically about 4.5 mm) and pair that with a wider angle lens to be able to capture the full scene.

What file formats are used for digital images? To fit more photos on the same size flash memory card, digital cameras let you choose from several different file types in order to compress the image data into less memory space. When you choose to compress your images, you'll lose some of the detail, but in return you'll be able to fit more images on

your flash card. The most common file types supported by digital cameras are raw uncompressed data (RAW) and Joint Photographic Experts Group (JPEG):

- *RAW files* have different formats and extensions depending on the manufacturer of a particular camera. The RAW file records all of the original image information, so it's larger than a compressed JPEG file.
- *JPEG files* can be compressed just a bit, keeping most of the details, or compressed a great deal, losing some detail. Most cameras let you select from a few different JPEG compression levels.

Often, cameras also support a very low-resolution storage option that provides images that aren't useful for printing but are so small that they're easy to e-mail. Even people who have slow Internet connections are able to quickly download and view such images on screen.

Why not just use the camera on my smartphone? The cameras on smartphones are improving in resolution—Nokia now offers a 41 MP camera phone—but they often employ smaller image sensors and inferior lenses compared to stand-alone cameras. In addition, many features that photographers rely on often aren't available in smartphone cameras, such as different types of autofocus, image stabilization algorithms, and smile shutter, which waits to take a shot until your subject is smiling.

What's the best way to transfer my photos to my computer? Digital cameras have a built-in USB port you can use to copy the image files to your computer. Another option is to transfer the flash card from your camera directly to a built-in memory card reader on your computer. Some camera models support wireless network connections so that you can transfer the images without the fuss of connecting any cables.

FIGURE 8.27 Digital SLR cameras can accommodate a range of separate auto-focus lenses. *(Brandon Alms/123RF)*

Can I make my old photos digital? You can use a scanner to turn your hand-drawn sketches or old photos into digital files. Most scanner software lets you store the converted images as TIFF files or in compressed form as JPEG files. Some scanners include hardware that lets you scan film negatives or slides as well or even insert a stack of photos to be scanned in sequence.

Scanner quality is measured by its resolution, which is given in dots per inch (dpi). Most modern scanners can digitize a document at resolutions as high as 9600 × 9600 dpi in either color or grayscale mode. Scanners also typically support optical character recognition (OCR). OCR software converts pages of handwritten or typed text into electronic files. You can then open and edit these converted documents with word processing programs such as Microsoft Word.

How can I share my digital photos? You've probably shared a number of photos on Facebook or Instagram already. Other options include creating online albums at sites such as Picasa, which let you share your photos without having to print them. You can also design electronic scrapbooks on a number of digital scrapbooking sites such as **cottagearts.net**.

Of course, you can carry and display your photos on your tablet and smartphone. You can also connect your iPad wirelessly to your TV and deliver slide shows of your photos, complete with musical soundtracks you've selected. If you have networked your home, a TV connected to your network can display all the photos and videos stored on your computer.

What are the best options for printing digital photos? If you want to print photos, you have two main options:

1. **Use a photo printer:** The most popular and inexpensive ones are inkjet printers. Some inkjet printers can print high-quality color photos, although they vary in speed, quality, and features. Dye-sublimation printers are another option. If you're interested in a printer to use for printing only photos, a dye-sublimation printer is a good choice. However, some models print only specific sizes, such as 4" × 6" prints, so be sure the printer you buy will fit your long-term needs.

2. **Use a photo-printing service:** Most photo-printing labs, including the film-processing departments at stores such as Target, offer digital printing services. The paper and ink used at these labs are higher quality than what is available for home use and produce heavier, glossier prints that won't fade. You can send your digital photos directly to local merchants such as CVS and Walgreens for printing using Windows Photo Gallery. Online services, such as Flickr (**flickr.com**) and Shutterfly (**shutterfly.com**), store your images and allow you to create hard-copy prints, albums, mugs, T-shirts, or calendars.

Digital Video

What devices, sites, and other sources provide digital video content? Digital video surrounds us:

- Television is broadcast in digitally formatted signals.
- The Internet delivers a huge amount of digital video through YouTube, communities like Vimeo (**vimeo.com**), and webcasting sites like Ustream (**ustream.tv**).
- Sites like Hulu (**hulu.com**) rebroadcast many current television shows as well as films and movie trailers.
- Many pay services are available to deliver digital video to you. These include on-demand streaming from cable providers, iTunes, Netflix's Instant Watch films, and Amazon's Instant Video download service.
- And, of course, you can create your own digital video. Although you can buy dedicated digital camcorders to record digital video, many smartphones now record HD video. Webcams also work as inexpensive devices for creating digital video.

How do I record my own digital video? Video equipment for home use stores information in a digital video format. Such cameras don't require any tapes; they store hours of video on built-in hard drives or flash cards. Some models even record directly to DVD. You can easily transfer video files to your computer and, using video-editing software, edit the video at home. You can save (or write) your final product on a CD or DVD and play it in your home DVD system or on your computer. For true videophiles, cameras and burners are available for HD video format.

What if I decide to add special effects and a sound track? Video-editing software presents a storyboard or timeline with which you can manipulate your video file, as shown in Figure 8.28. You can review your clips frame by frame or

FIGURE 8.28 Adobe Premiere allows you to build a movie from video clips and to add sound tracks and special effects. (*Adobe Premiere screenshot(s) reprinted with permission from Adobe Systems Incorporated*)

FIGURE 8.29

Typical File Formats for Digital Video

FORMAT	FILE EXTENSION	NOTES
QuickTime	.qt .mov	You can download the QuickTime player without charge from **apple.com/quicktime**. The Pro version allows you to build your own QuickTime files.
Moving Picture Experts Group (MPEG)	.mpg .mpeg .mp4	The MPEG-4 video standard was adopted internationally in 2000; it's recognized by most video player software.
Windows Media Video	.wmv	This is a Microsoft file format recognized by Windows Media Player (included with the Windows OS).
Microsoft Video for Windows	.avi	This is a Microsoft file format recognized by Windows Media Player (included with the Windows OS).
RealMedia	.rm	This format is from RealNetworks and is popular for streaming video. You can download the player for free at **real.com**.
Adobe Flash Video	.flv	This is the Adobe Flash video format, sometimes embedded in Shockwave files (*.swf).

trim them at any point. You can add titles, audio tracks, and animations; order each segment on the timeline in whichever sequence you like; and correct segments for color balance, brightness, or contrast. Examine online tutorial resources such as Izzy Video podcasts (**izzyvideo.com**) to learn how to make the most impact with the editing and effects you apply to your raw video footage.

What kinds of files will I end up with? Once you're done editing your video file, you can save or export it in a variety of formats. Figure 8.29 shows some of the popular video file formats in use today, along with the file extensions they use.

Your choice of file format for your finished video will depend on what you want to do with the video. For example, the QuickTime streaming file format is a great choice if your file is really large and you plan to post it on the web. The Microsoft AVI format is a good choice if you're sending your file to a wide range of users because it's the standard video format for Windows Media Player.

Different compression algorithms will have different results on your particular video. Try several to see which one does a better job of compressing your particular file. A **codec** (*compression/decompression*) is a rule, implemented in either software or hardware, that squeezes the same audio and video information into less space. Some information will be lost using compression, and there are several different codecs to choose from, each claiming better performance than its competitors. Commonly used codecs include MPEG-4, H.264, and DivX. There's no one codec that's always superior—a codec that works well for a simple interview may not do a good job compressing a live-action scene.

What if I want to produce a DVD with a full menuing system? You can use special authoring software such as Pinnacle Studio HD or Adobe Encore. These DVD/

Blu-ray software packages often include preset selections for producing video for specific mobile devices. These programs can also create final discs that have animated menu systems and easy navigation controls, allowing the viewer to move quickly from one movie or scene to another. Home DVD and Blu-ray players, as well as gaming systems such as PlayStation and Xbox, can read these discs.

What's the quickest way to get my video out to viewers? The quickest way to get your video content out is to broadcast. Webcasting, or broadcasting your video live to an audience, is an option that has become simple to do. All you need is a webcam (see Figure 8.30), and sites like **justin.tv** or **ustream.tv** will let you quickly set up to webcast

FIGURE 8.30 Webcams are small enough to make them part of any activity. (*ZUMA Press/Alamy*)

Digital Media   **337**

You just returned from your trip to the Grand Canyon, and your friends are raving about the photos you took. You decide to put them on Flickr so others can see them. You also think that someone might see your photos and want to use them in a commercial publication such as a magazine. Because you own the copyright to your photos, you control how they can be used—and you want to protect your rights. You add a disclaimer to Flickr indicating that all rights are reserved on your photos. Anyone who wants to use them will need to contact you and request permission.

All of a sudden, you're bombarded by requests for permission to use your photos. A high school student in Illinois wants to feature one on her travel blog. A church in Georgia wants to use a photo for its newsletter. An ad agency in Seattle wants to modify your sunrise photo and use it in an ad. How are you going to manage all these permission requests?

Copyleft, a play on the word *copyright*, is designed for this situation. *Copyleft* is a term for various licensing plans that enable copyright holders to grant certain rights to the work while retaining other rights. Creative Commons (**creativecommons.org**), a nonprofit organization, has developed various licenses you can use based on the rights you wish to grant. Simply decide which type of license best fits your goals for the work, and Creative Commons provides you with HTML you can use to add the specific licensing information to your site.

The advantage to using Creative Commons licenses is that people won't constantly send you permission requests to use your work. The licenses explain how your work can be used. Also, many advocates of copyleft policies feel that creativity is encouraged when people are free to modify other people's work instead of worrying about infringing on copyright.

Opponents of Creative Commons licenses complain that the licenses have affected their livelihoods. If millions of images are out on Flickr with Creative Commons licenses that permit free commercial use, professional photographers might have a tougher time selling their work. Furthermore, Creative Commons licenses are irrevocable. If you make a mistake and select the wrong license for your work, or you later find out a work is valuable and you've already selected a license that allows commercial use, you're out of luck.

Each of us needs to carefully consider the value of our intellectual property and decide how best to conduct our digital livelihood. Understanding the meaning of copyright, and copyleft, is both important so that you respect the rights of others and so that you can simplify your life in granting permission rights to the works you create.

---

your video as it is captured to a live Internet audience. You can also display an interactive chat next to the video feed. Both the chat and the video are captured and archived for viewers who missed the live broadcast. Most smartphones record video at a quality good enough to directly webcast from your phone, and most laptops have an integrated webcam.

You may want to take time and produce a more polished video. When you have it just right, you can upload it to video-sharing sites like YouTube or Metacafe.

Of course, it's illegal for you to upload videos you don't own. You also can't take a piece of a copyrighted video and post it publicly. The Ethics in IT section in this chapter presents several legal and ethical situations that are important for you to be aware of as a content creator in the digital age.

How is HD different from "plain" digital? *HD* stands for **high definition**. It is a standard of digital television signal that guarantees a specific level of resolution and a specific *aspect ratio*, which is the rectangular shape of the image. A 1080 HDTV displays 1,920 vertical lines and 1,080 horizontal lines of video on the screen, which is over six times as many pixels as a standard definition TV. The aspect ratio used is 16:9, which makes the screen wider, giving it the same proportions as the rectangular shape of a movie theater screen (see Figure 8.31). This allows televisions to play movies in the widescreen format for which they were created, instead of "letterboxing" the film with black bars on the top and the bottom of the screen.

What types of connectivity are provided on modern TV sets? A typical HDTV set has multiple HDMI connectors, allowing game consoles, Blu-ray players, and cable boxes to be connected and to produce the highest-quality output. HDMI is a single cable that carries all of the video and all of the audio information.

FIGURE 8.31 (a) Standard-definition TV has a more "square" aspect ratio, whereas (b) HDTV matches the 16:9 ratio used in the motion picture industry without resorting to (c) letterboxing. *(Pichugin Dmitry/Shutterstock)*

Many TV sets have a built-in SD card reader. This allows users to display slide shows of photographs captured by their digital cameras. A PC VGA port is also included on most sets to allow you to feed your computer's output video signal directly to the television. There are ways to connect wirelessly from your mobile or computer device to your TV as well. Apple TV and Google's Chromecast let you view content from your device on the big screen without connecting cables.

FIGURE 8.32 Slingbox can send your digital television content to your tablet, notebook, or smartphone, wherever you may be. *(Handout/MCT/Newscom)*

What are the advantages to watching digital video on my TV? Other information services can be integrated with the broadcast; so, for example, if a telephone call came through during the show, a pop-up could appear identifying the caller. Additional content can be delivered in real time with the broadcast, explaining the background of characters or pulling up behind-the-scenes info. In the future, there will be more interactivity integrated so you can participate in live polls or chats on screen as the show is broadcast.

Can I record the digital video that comes over my TV? There are a variety of digital video recorders (DVRs) available that record in HD. Models like TiVo even recommend new shows you might like based on what you've been watching. You can also install personal video recording (PVR) software on your computer. Programs like Kodi (**xbmc.org**) let you use your computer to view the schedule program guide, select shows to record (without commercials), and then watch them from anywhere you have Internet access.

Can I get digital video to watch on my portable device? Many DVR units, like TiVo, support software that lets you transfer recorded shows to files on your PC and format them for viewing on a mobile device. There are also devices like Slingbox that take the video from your TV and broadcast it to you over the Internet. With Slingbox, you can be in another room, or another country, and control and watch your home TV on your notebook or your smartphone (see Figure 8.32). ∎

> **Before moving on to Chapter Review:**
> • **Watch Replay Video 8.2** ▷ .
> • **Then check your understanding of what you've learned so far.**

check your understanding // review & practice

For a quick review to see what you've learned so far, answer the following questions. Visit **pearsonhighered.com /techinaction** to check your answers.

multiple choice

1. Which is *not* a factor that determines the quality of images taken with a digital camera?

   a. lens quality

   b. resolution

   c. file format

   d. type of battery

2. An audio interface unit can

   a. connect a computer to musical instruments and microphones.

   b. provide Dolby surround sound.

   c. create electronic drum sounds.

   d. convert between different audio file formats.

3. P2P is an acronym for

   a. packet-to-packet networking.

   b. peer-to-peer sharing.

   c. person-to-person texting.

   d. power-to-people delivery.

4. An analog signal is different from a digital signal because

   a. it is continuous.

   b. it has only specific discrete values.

   c. it is easier to duplicate.

   d. it is easier to transmit.

5. The open format for publishing of e-books that is optimized for mobile devices is

   d. ePub.

   b. raw.

   c. azw.

   d. pdf.

To take an autograded version of this review, please go to the companion website at **pearsonhighered.com/techinaction**, or go your MyITLab course.

Continue

summary //

Digital Convergence

1. How is the trend of digital convergence seen in the market?

- Digital convergence has brought us single devices with the capabilities that used to require four or five separate tools.

Telephony: Smartphones and Beyond

2. What hardware and software comprise a typical smartphone?

- Like a traditional computer, a smartphone has a central processor, memory, and an OS. These components work in the same way as in a computer to process information and support communications, software applications, and other services.

3. How do I synchronize information between my phone and my computer, and how do mobile Internet data plans work?

- Information can be synched between devices using either wired or wireless solutions.
- A wired sync requires either a micro SD card or a USB cable to connect the device directly to the computer.
- A wireless sync can be done using Bluetooth or WiFi or by connecting to a cloud service.
- Mobile data plans allow your device to have access at almost any location.
- Data transfers occur at either 3G or 4G speeds, depending on your device and provider. Fees are tied to the amount of data you transfer each month.

4. What do I need to keep my smartphone secure?

- Viruses can infect smartphones, so using an antivirus software package is important. Check the manufacturer's website frequently for updates and practice safe habits by not downloading or opening files from unknown sources.

5. How does digital telephony support VoIP services?

- VoIP allows inexpensive communication using a computer or a WiFi-enabled phone. Because it's based on a digital format for information, it can support services like automatic delivery of phone messages to an e-mail account or texts to a mobile device.

Tablets, Netbooks, and Ultrabooks

6. What distinguishes the performance of tablets, netbooks, and ultrabooks?

- Mobile devices differ in terms of size and weight, input (physical keyboard, software keyboard on a touch screen), and OS (mobile OS or traditional OS).
- Netbooks and ultrabooks can run traditional software packages like Microsoft Office, whereas tablets run new versions of productivity software made to take advantage of the features of the tablet.

Digital Defined

7. What advantage do digital formats have over analog signals?

- Digital media is based on a series of numeric data, i.e., number values that were measured from the original analog waveform. As a string of numbers, a digital photo or video file can be easily processed by modern computers.

Digital Media

8. How is the digital format changing the way media is created and distributed?

- The increased use of digital information has led to a period of greater creativity and control of our data. In a digital format, information is easy to carry, manipulate, and exchange. This has led to revolutionary changes in communication, entertainment media, and mobile computing.
- Digital publishing is allowing a variety of new distribution methods into the industry. E-readers and online bookstores are bringing changes to the models of how to sell printed materials.

- Digital music is created by combining pure digital sounds with samples of analog sounds. It has meant changes for the recording industry, for performers, and for music listeners. It's now inexpensive to carry a music library, to create new songs, and to distribute them worldwide.

9. How do I work with digital images and video?

- Digital cameras allow you to instantly capture and transfer images to your devices, computers, and cloud storage sites.
- Using software for video production, you can create polished videos with titles, transitions, a sound track, and special effects and distribute them on DVDs.
- You can also use a webcam to stream live video to sites that will "broadcast" it over the Internet.

> Be sure to check out the companion website for additional materials to help you review and learn, including a Tech Bytes Weekly newsletter—**pearsonhighered.com/techinaction**. And don't forget the Replay Videos ▶ .

key terms//

chapter quiz// assessment

For a quick review to see what you've learned, answer the following questions. Submit the quiz as requested by your instructor. If you are using MyITLab, the quiz is also available there.

multiple choice

1. A cell phone is cellular because

   a. software can be plugged in or removed.

   b. phones have become so small in size.

   c. it uses a network made up of cells or base transceiver stations.

   d. of the pattern on the screen of the device.

2. Which of the following is FALSE?

   a. Bluetooth technology uses radio waves.

   b. An analog-to-digital converter chip converts your voice into digital signals.

   c. Your phone can only be connected to the Internet if there is a WiFi network available.

   d. SMS is an acronym for short message service, also called text messaging.

3. Which of the following is NOT a mobile device?

   a. base transceiver station

   b. phablet

   c. tablet

   d. ultrabook

4. DRM is an acronym for

   a. Digital Role Maker.

   b. Digital Real Movie.

   c. Distribution Regional Media.

   d. Digital Rights Management.

5. Streaming music services allow you to

   a. subscribe monthly and have access to millions of songs.

   b. purchase audio CDs.

   c. make your own music available to your friends.

   d. avoid digital rights management.

6. A digital camera's resolution

   a. is measured in megapixels (MP).

   b. only matters for analog cameras.

   c. depends on the camera's lens.

   d. tells you how to transfer images to your printing service.

true–false

_____ 1. Every smartphone contains a GPS chip.

_____ 2. A WiFi network is always faster than a 4G network.

_____ 3. Digital video can be stored in an .mpg file, an .mpeg file, or an .mp4 file.

_____ 4. HDMI is a single cable that carries both high-definition video as well as audio signals.

critical thinking

1. **Mobile Sensors**

   Smartphones have many built-in sensors, some of which measure acceleration, location, and pressure. What kind of sensors would you add to a smartphone to make it more useful?

2. **Self-Publishing**

   What impact will the availability of self-publication have on the writing and recording industries? Will it promote a greater amount of quality content or a flood of amateur work? How could this be managed?

"And One Will Rule Them All"

Problem

Digital convergence posits the dream of one device that can do it all, for everyone. But there are so many different mobile devices saturating the market that many people are left in a state of confusion.

Task

For each client scenario described as follows, the group will select the minimum set of devices that would support and enhance the client's life.

Process

1. Consider the following three clients:
   - A retired couple who now travels for pleasure a great deal. They want to be involved in their grandchildren's lives and will need support for their health, finances, and personal care as they age.
   - A young family with two children, two working parents, and a tight budget.
   - A couple in which each individual is a physician and each adores technology.

2. Make two recommendations for your clients in terms of digital technologies that will enhance their business or their lifestyle. Discuss the advantages and disadvantages of each technology. Consider value, reliability, computing needs, training needed, and communication needs as well as expandability for the future.

3. As a group, prepare a final report that considers the recommendations you have made for your clients.

Conclusion

Digital information has allowed the development of a new style of living, both at home and at work. With so many digital solutions on the market, recommending digital options needs to focus on converging to the minimum set of tools that will enhance life without adding complication to it.

When Everyone Has a Voice

In this exercise, you'll research and then role-play a complicated ethical situation. The role you play might or might not match your own personal beliefs; in either case, your research and use of logic will enable you to represent the view assigned. An arbitrator will watch and comment on both sides of the arguments, and together the team will agree on an ethical solution.

Background

Much of the world's population is now equipped with Internet-ready camera phones. Sensors on these phones could measure for viruses or compute pollution indexes, while the cameras could be used to document a range of human behavior. This could create changes in political movements, art, and culture as everyone's experience is documented and shared.

Research Areas to Consider

- Evgeny Morozov RSA Animate
- Mobilebehavior.com
- The Witness Project
- Center for Embedded Networked Sensing

Process

1. Divide the class into teams.
2. Research the areas cited above and devise a scenario in which mobile access could make an impact politically or environmentally, positively or negatively.
3. Team members should write a summary that provides background information for their character—for example, business owner, politician, reporter, or arbitrator—and that details their character's behaviors to set the stage for the role-playing event. Then team members should create an outline to use during the role-playing event.
4. Team members should arrange a mutually convenient time to meet for the exchange, using a virtual meeting tool or by meeting in person.
5. Team members should present their case to the class or submit a PowerPoint presentation for review by the rest of the class, along with the summary and resolution they developed.

Conclusion

As technology becomes ever more prevalent and integrated into our lives, more and more ethical dilemmas will present themselves. Being able to understand and evaluate both sides of the argument, while responding in a personally or socially ethical manner, will be an important skill.

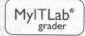
Estimating Cellular Data Usage

You want to determine how much data you need for your cellular data plan. You have tracked your usage for the past several weeks. You will determine your average weekly usage, then estimate your average monthly usage. Using data guidelines from your local carrier, you determine your total monthly data usage. Lastly, you calculate the percent of total usage each activity uses.

You will use the following skills as you complete this activity:	
• Use Absolute Cell References	• Apply a Custom Header and Footer
• Create an IF Function	• Insert Dates and Use Date Math
• Use the ROUNDUP Function	• Use the AVERAGE Function

Instructions:

1. Open the TIA_Ch8_Start file, and save as TIA_Ch8_LastFirst.

2. In cell B14, enter today's date. In cell C14, create a formula that adds 7 days to cell B14, then using the Fill Handle, copy the results in cell C14 to the range D14:H14. Format the results, if necessary, as Short Date.

3. In the range H15:H21, enter data that reflects an estimate of your own smartphone activity usage. (For example, in cell H15, enter the number of emails you would send in a week, and in cell H16, enter the number of hours you would spend streaming music in a week).

4. In cell B24, compute the average weekly usage for the range B15:H15. Use the Fill Handle to copy the results to the range B25:B30.

5. In cell C24, compute the average monthly usage by multiplying cell B24 by 4. Using the Fill Handle, copy the results to the range C25:C30.

6. In cell D24, calculate the estimated usage by multiplying C24 by B3. Using the Fill Handle, copy the results in cell D24 to the range D25:D30. Format the results in the range B24:D30 as Number with two decimal places.

7. In cell H8, type **Total Estimated Monthly Data Usage (MB)**. Bold, and right align the text. Then in cell I8, create a function that totals data in the range D24:D30.

8. In cell H9, type **Total Estimated Monthly Data Usage (GB)**. Bold and right align the text. Then in cell I9 divide I8 by 1024 to convert the results in megabytes (MB) to results in gigabytes (GB).

9. In cell H10, type **Minimum Data Required by Plan**. Bold and right align the text. Then in cell I10, use the ROUNDUP function to round the results in cell I9 to a whole number.

   a. Hint: The formula will be = ROUNDUP(I9,0)

10. In cell H11, type **Would selected plan work with 20% increase in usage?**. Bold and right align the text. Then in cell I11, use the IF function to determine whether or not a 20% increase to the results in cell I9 would be greater or equal to the results in cell I10. Use "YES" if the statement is true, and "NO" if the statement is false.

    a. Hint: The formula is: =IF(I9*1.2<=I10,"YES","NO")

11. In cell E23, type **% of Total Usage**, then in cell E24, create a formula that computes the percent of total usage for Emailing by dividing D24 by I8. Format results as Percentage with no decimals. Using the Fill Handle, copy the results to the range E25:E30.

    a. Hint: Make sure you use the absolute cell reference.

12. Insert a custom header that displays your First and Last name in the top right of the page, and a custom footer that displays the date in the bottom left of the page, and the file name in the bottom right of the page.

13. Change the orientation to Landscape.

14. Save and submit the file as directed by your instructor.

9

Securing Your System: Protecting Your Digital Data and Devices

Major Threats to Your Digital Assets

Cybercrime and Identity Theft

OBJECTIVE

1. What is cybercrime, and who perpetrates it? **(pp. 348–349)**

Protecting Yourself from Computer Viruses

OBJECTIVES

2. What are the types of viruses from which I need to protect my computer? **(pp. 350–352)**

3. What can I do to protect my computer from viruses? **(pp. 353–355)**

🔖 **Active Helpdesk:** Avoiding Computer Viruses

🔊 **Sound Byte:** Protecting Your Computer

Protecting Digital Assets from Hackers

OBJECTIVES

4. How can hackers attack my computing devices, and what harm can they cause? **(pp. 356–359)**

5. What is a firewall, and how does it keep my computer safe from hackers? **(pp. 360–362)**

6. How do I create secure passwords and manage all of my passwords? **(pp. 362–364)**

7. How can I surf the Internet anonymously and use biometric authentication devices to protect my data? **(pp. 364–366)**

🔖 **Active Helpdesk:** Understanding Firewalls

🔊 **Sound Byte:** Installing a Personal Firewall

Protecting Your Digital Property from Yourself

Managing Online Annoyances

OBJECTIVE

8. How do I manage online annoyances such as spyware and spam? **(pp. 370–375)**

Keeping Your Data Safe

OBJECTIVES

9. What data do I need to back up, and what are the best methods for doing so? **(pp. 376–380)**

10. What is social engineering, and how do I avoid falling prey to phishing? **(pp. 381–383)**

🔊 **Sound Byte:** Managing Computer Security with Windows Tools

Protecting Your Physical Computing Assets

OBJECTIVE

11. How do I protect my physical computing assets from environmental hazards, power surges, and theft? **(pp. 384–386)**

🔊 **Sound Byte:** Surge Protectors

Make This: Explore an App Builder Skill on **page 369**

HOW COOL IS THIS?

Scan here for more info

Biometrics authentication for Barclay's bank customers is getting a major upgrade. Starting in 2015, the bank will be offering scanners based on Hitachi's VeinID **finger vein authentication technology**. The scanners read the vein patterns inside your finger, which are unique, to **verify your identity**. How does this improve upon fingerprint scans? Fingerprint scanning technology has flaws—impressions of your fingerprints can be left on scanner surfaces and can be duplicated to fool security devices. However, because your veins are inside your body, **they don't leave residue on scanners**. This technology will probably be rolled out to consumers in the coming years. *(Nerthuz/Fotolia; Hitachi, Ltd)*

Major Threats to Your Digital Assets

The media is full of stories about malicious computer programs damaging computers, criminals stealing people's identities online, and attacks on corporate websites bringing major corporations to a standstill. These are examples of cybercrime. In this part of the chapter, we'll discuss the three most serious types of cybercrime you need to worry about: identity theft, computer viruses, and hackers.

 cybercrime and
IDENTITY THEFT

Cybercrime is any criminal action perpetrated primarily through the use of a computer. The existence of cybercrime means that computer users must take precautions to protect themselves. The FBI maintains a website (**www.fbi.gov /about-us/investigate/cyber**) specifically to inform the public about types of cybercrimes and methods of protecting yourself.

Who perpetrates computer crimes? Cybercriminals are individuals who use computers, networks, and the Internet to perpetrate crime. Anyone with a computer and the where-withal to arm him- or herself with the appropriate knowledge can be a cybercriminal.

What kinds of cybercrimes are conducted over the Internet? The Internet Crime Complaint Center (IC3) is a partnership between the FBI and the National White Collar Crime Center (NW3C). In 2013 (the latest year for which data was available at this book's publication), the IC3 received almost 263,000 complaints related to Internet crime. Four common categories of complaints received are shown in Figure 9.1. FBI–related scams involve people pretending to represent official organizations, such as the FBI or Home-land Security, to defraud. Nonauction scams involve running auctions of merchandise that does not really exist, wherein the perpetrators just collect funds and disappear without delivering the promised goods. Advance fee fraud involves

FIGURE 9.1

Common Types of Cybercrimes Reported to the IC3 in 2013

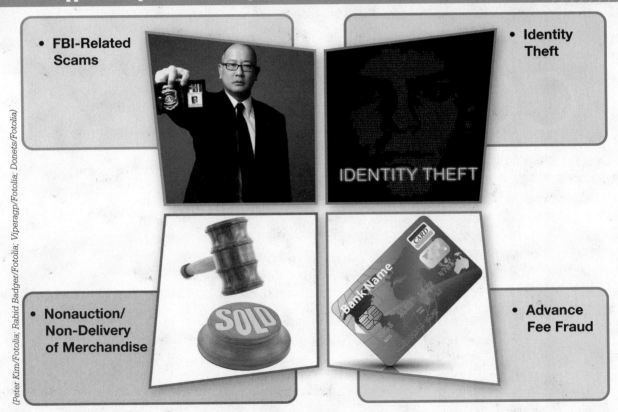

- **FBI-Related Scams**
- **Identity Theft**
- **Nonauction/ Non-Delivery of Merchandise**
- **Advance Fee Fraud**

IDENTITY THEFT

SOLD

(Peter Kim/Fotolia; Rabid Badger/Fotolia; Viperagp/Fotolia; Donets/Fotolia)

348 **Chapter 9** Securing Your System: Protecting Your Digital Data and Devices

convincing individuals to send money as a "good faith" gesture to enable them to receive larger payments in return. The scammers then disappear with the advance fees. Although these complaints relate to some type of fraud, other complaints received involve equally serious matters such as computer intrusions (hacking), child pornography, and blackmail.

What is the most financially damaging cybercrime plaguing individuals? Theft of personal data such as bank account numbers and credit/debit card numbers is of most concern to individuals because this information is usually used for fraudulent purposes. **Identity theft** occurs when a thief steals personal information such as your name, address, Social Security number, birth date, bank account number, and credit card information and runs up debts in your name. Many victims of identity theft spend months, or even years, trying to repair their credit and eliminate fraudulent debts.

What types of scams do identity thieves perpetrate? The nefarious acts cover a wide range:

- Counterfeiting your existing credit and debit cards
- Requesting changes of address on your bank and credit card statements, which makes detecting fraudulent charges take longer
- Opening new credit cards and bank accounts in your name and then writing bad checks and not paying off the credit card balances (ruining your credit rating in the process)
- Obtaining medical services under your name (you might lose coverage later if the thief's treatment exceeds the limits of your policy's covered services)
- Buying a home with a mortgage in your name, then reselling the house and absconding with the money (leaving you with the debt)

Many people believe that the only way your identity can be stolen is by a computer. However, the Federal Trade Commission (**ftc.gov**) has identified other methods thieves use to obtain others' personal information:

- Stealing purses and wallets, in which people often keep personal information such as their ATM PIN codes
- Stealing mail or looking through trash for bank statements and credit card bills
- Posing as bank or credit card company representatives and tricking people into revealing sensitive information over the phone
- Installing skimming devices on ATM machines that record information, such as account numbers and passcodes

Although foolproof protection methods don't exist, there are precautions that will help you minimize your risk, which we'll discuss later in this chapter.

With all the news coverage about identity theft and other cybercrimes, aren't people being more cautious? Although most people are aware of spam, a survey by the Messaging, Malware and Mobile Anti-Abuse Working Group (M³AAWG) found that half of e-mail users in North America and Europe have opened spam, some of which are designed to trick you into divulging sensitive information. The M³AAWG also discovered that 46% of people who opened spam did so intentionally—out of idle curiosity, to follow links to unsubscribe to unwanted e-mails (which only brings more spam), or because they are interested in the product being touted.

Does cybercrime include the theft of computing devices? Although theft of computer equipment is not classified as a cybercrime (it is considered larceny), the theft of tablets, smartphones, notebook computers, and other portable computing devices is on the rise. The resale value for used electronic equipment is high, and the equipment can be easily sold online. ■

computer
VIRUSES

A computer **virus** is a computer program that attaches itself to another computer program (known as the *host* program) and attempts to spread to other computers when files are exchanged. Creating and disseminating computer viruses is one of the most widespread types of cybercrimes. Some viruses cause only minor annoyances, whereas others cause destruction or theft of data. Many viruses are designed to gather sensitive information such as credit card numbers.

Why are viruses such a threat to my security? Computer viruses are threatening because they are engineered to evade detection. Viruses normally attempt to hide within the code of a host program to avoid detection. And viruses are not just limited to computers. Smartphones, tablet computers, and other devices can be infected with viruses. Viruses such as SpyEye Mobile Banking are used to trick users into downloading an infected file to their phones, which then steals their online banking information.

I have an Apple computer, so I don't need to worry about viruses, do I? This is a popular misconception! Everyone, even Apple users, needs to worry about viruses. As the OS X and iOS operating systems have gained market share, the amount of virus attacks against Apple operating systems is on the rise.

What do computer viruses do? A computer virus's main purpose is to replicate itself and copy its code into as many other host files as possible. This gives the virus a greater chance of being copied to another computer system so that it can spread its infection. However, computer viruses require human interaction to spread. Although there might be a virus in a file on your computer, a virus normally can't infect your computer until the infected file is opened or executed.

Although virus replication can slow down networks, it's not usually the main threat. The majority of viruses have secondary objectives or side effects, ranging from displaying annoying messages on the computer screen to destroying files or the contents of entire hard drives.

Catching a Virus

How does my computer catch a virus? If your computer is exposed to a file infected with a virus, the virus will try to copy itself and infect a file on your computer.

Downloading infected audio and video files from peer-to-peer file-sharing sites is a major source of virus infections. Shared flash drives are also a common source of virus infection, as is e-mail. Just opening an e-mail message usually won't infect your computer with a virus, although some new viruses are launched when viewed in the preview pane of your e-mail software. Downloading and running (executing) a file that's attached to the e-mail are common ways that your computer becomes infected. Thus, be extremely wary of

e-mail attachments, especially if you don't know the sender. Figure 9.2 illustrates the steps by which computer viruses are often passed from one computer to the next:

1. An individual writes a virus program, attaches it to a music file, and posts the file to a file-sharing site.
2. Unsuspecting Bill downloads the "music file" and infects his computer when he listens to the song.
3. Bill sends his cousin Fred an e-mail with the infected "music file" and contaminates Fred's tablet.
4. Fred syncs his phone with his tablet and infects his phone when he plays the music file.
5. Fred e-mails the file from his phone to Susan, one of his colleagues at work. Everyone who copies files from Susan's infected work computer, or whose computer is networked to Susan's computer, risks spreading the virus.

What types of viruses exist? Although thousands of computer viruses and variants exist, they can be grouped into six broad categories based on their behavior and method of transmission.

Boot-Sector Viruses

What are boot-sector viruses? A **boot-sector virus** replicates itself onto a hard drive's master boot record. The **master boot record** is a program that executes whenever a computer boots up, ensuring that the virus will be loaded into memory immediately, even before some virus protection programs can load. Boot-sector viruses are often transmitted by a flash drive left in a USB port. When the computer boots up with the flash drive connected, the computer tries to launch a master boot record from the flash drive, which is usually the trigger for the virus to infect the hard drive.

Logic Bombs and Time Bombs

What are logic bombs and time bombs? A **logic bomb** is a virus that is triggered when certain logical conditions are met, such as opening a file or starting a program a certain number of times. A **time bomb** is a virus that is triggered by the passage of time or on a certain date. For example, the Michelangelo virus was a famous time bomb that was set to trigger every year on March 6, Michelangelo's birthday. The effects of logic bombs and time bombs range from the display of annoying messages on the screen to the reformatting of the hard drive, which causes complete data loss.

Worms

What is a worm? Although often called a virus, a **worm** is subtly different. Viruses require human interaction to spread, whereas worms take advantage of file transport methods, such

STEP 1: Virus creation

Hacker's computer

File-sharing server

STEP 2: Initial virus infection

Bill's computer

STEP 3: Virus spreads to another computer

Susan's work computer

Fred's smartphone

STEP 4: Fred infects his cell phone

Fred's tablet

STEP 5: Other computers susceptible to infection

FIGURE 9.2 Computer viruses are passed from one unsuspecting user to the next. *(Vovan/Shutterstock)*

as e-mail or network connections, to spread on their own. A virus infects a host file and waits until that file is executed to replicate and infect a computer system. A worm, however, works independently of host file execution and is much more active in spreading itself. Recently developed worms, like The Moon, even attack peripheral devices such as routers. Worms can generate a lot of data traffic when trying to spread, which can slow down the Internet.

Script and Macro Viruses

What are script and macro viruses? Some viruses are hidden on websites in the form of scripts. A **script** is a series of commands—actually, a miniprogram—that is executed without your knowledge. Scripts are often used to perform useful, legitimate functions on websites, such as collecting name and address information from customers. However, some scripts are malicious. For example, you might click a link to display a video on a website, which causes a script to run that infects your computer with a virus.

A **macro virus** is a virus that attaches itself to a document that uses macros. A *macro* is a short series of commands that usually automates repetitive tasks. However, macro languages are now so sophisticated that viruses can be written with them. In 1999, the Melissa virus became the first major macro virus to cause problems worldwide.

E-Mail Viruses

What is an e-mail virus? In addition to being a macro virus, the Melissa virus was the first practical example of an e-mail virus. **E-mail viruses** use the address book in the victim's e-mail system to distribute the virus. In the case of the

Melissa virus, anyone opening an infected document triggered the virus, which infected other documents on the victim's computer. Once triggered, the Melissa virus sent itself to the first 50 people in the e-mail address book on the infected computer.

Encryption Viruses

What are encryption viruses? When **encryption viruses** (also known as ransomware) infect your computer, they run a program that searches for common types of data files, such as Microsoft Word files, and compresses them using a complex encryption key that renders your files unusable. You then receive a message that asks you to send payment to an account if you want to receive the program to decrypt your files. The flaw with this type of virus, which keeps it from being widespread, is that law enforcement officials can trace the payments to an account and may possibly be able to catch the perpetrators. Figure 9.3 summarizes the major categories of viruses.

Additional Virus Classifications

How else are viruses classified? Viruses can also be classified by the methods they take to avoid detection by antivirus software:

- A **polymorphic virus** changes its own code or periodically rewrites itself to avoid detection. Most polymorphic viruses infect a particular type of file such as .EXE files, for example.

- A **multipartite virus** is designed to infect multiple file types in an effort to fool the antivirus software that is looking for it.

FIGURE 9.3

Major Categories of Viruses

Boot-sector Viruses
Execute when a computer boots up

Logic Bombs/Time Bombs
Execute when certain conditions or dates are reached

Worms
Spread on their own with no human interaction needed

Script and Macro Viruses
Series of commands with malicious intent

E-mail Viruses
Spread as attachments to e-mail, often using address books

Encryption Viruses
Hold files "hostage" by encrypting them; ask for ransom to unlock them

(Tribalium81/Fotolia; LoopAll/Fotolia; Ded Mazay/Fotolia; Theo Malings/Fotolia; Beboy/Fotolia; Andrea Danti/Fotolia)

- **Stealth viruses** temporarily erase their code from the files where they reside and then hide in the active memory of the computer. This helps them avoid detection if only the hard drive is being searched for viruses. Fortunately, current antivirus software scans memory as well as the hard drive.

Virus Symptoms

How can I tell if my computer is infected with a virus? Sometimes it can be difficult to definitively tell whether your computer is infected with a virus. However, if your computer displays any of the following symptoms, it may be infected with a virus:

1. Existing program icons or files suddenly disappear. Viruses often delete specific file types or programs.
2. You start your browser and it takes you to an unusual home page (i.e., one you didn't set) or it has new toolbars.
3. Odd messages, pop-ups, or images are displayed on the screen, or strange music or sounds play.
4. Data files become corrupt. (However, note that files can become corrupt for reasons other than a virus infection.)
5. Programs stop working properly, which could be caused by either a corrupted file or a virus.
6. Your system shuts down unexpectedly, slows down, or takes a long time to boot up. ∎

ACTIVE HELPDESK
Avoiding Computer Viruses

In this Active Helpdesk, you'll play the role of a helpdesk staffer, fielding questions about different types of viruses and what users should do to protect their computer from them.

BITS&BYTES

CAPTCHA: Keeping Websites Safe from Bots

Automated programs called *bots* (or web robots) are used to make tasks easier on the Internet. For example, search engines use bots to search and index web pages. Unfortunately, bots can also be used for malicious or illegal purposes because they can perform some computing tasks faster than humans. For example, bots can be used on ticket-ordering sites to buy large blocks of high-demand concert tickets. They are also often used to post spam in the comment sections of blogs. Fortunately, website owners can deploy CAPTCHA software (see Figure 9.4) to prevent such bot activities.

CAPTCHA (Completely Automated Public Turing Test to Tell Computers and Humans Apart) programs generate distorted text and require that it be typed into a box. Because bots can't yet be programmed to read distorted text, which most people can, the CAPTCHA program can verify that a human is performing

FIGURE 9.4 CAPTCHA programs like this one verify that a human, not a bot, is performing the requested task. *(Courtesy of the Carnegie Mellon University Press)*

the task being tested. If you want to try integrating a CAPTCHA program into your website (to protect your e-mail address), go to **google.com/recaptcha**, which offers free CAPTCHA tools to help you protect your data.

preventing virus
INFECTIONS

Antivirus software is specifically designed to detect viruses and protect your computer and files from harm. Symantec, Kaspersky, AVG, and McAfee are among the companies that offer highly rated antivirus software packages. Antivirus protection is also included in comprehensive Internet security packages such as Norton Internet Security, Kaspersky Internet Security, and McAfee Total Protection. These software packages also help protect you from threats other than computer viruses. For example, Windows 8 includes Windows Defender, which defends against malware as well as viruses.

Antivirus Software

How often do I need to run antivirus software?

Although antivirus software is designed to detect suspicious activity on your computer at all times, you should run an active virus scan on your entire system at least once a week. By doing so, all files on your computer will be checked for undetected viruses.

Current antivirus programs run scans in the background when your CPU is not being heavily utilized. But you can also configure the software to run scans at times when you aren't using your system—for example, when you're asleep (see Figure 9.5). (However, it's important to note that your computer has to be on and not in sleep mode for these virus scans to take place.) Alternatively, if you suspect a problem, you can launch a scan and have it run immediately.

How does antivirus software work? The main functions of antivirus software are as follows:

- *Detection:* Antivirus software looks for virus signatures in files. A **virus signature** is a portion of the virus code that's unique to a particular computer virus. Antivirus software scans files for these signatures when they're opened or executed and identifies infected files and the type of virus infecting them.

- *Stopping virus execution:* If the antivirus software detects a virus signature or suspicious activity, such as the

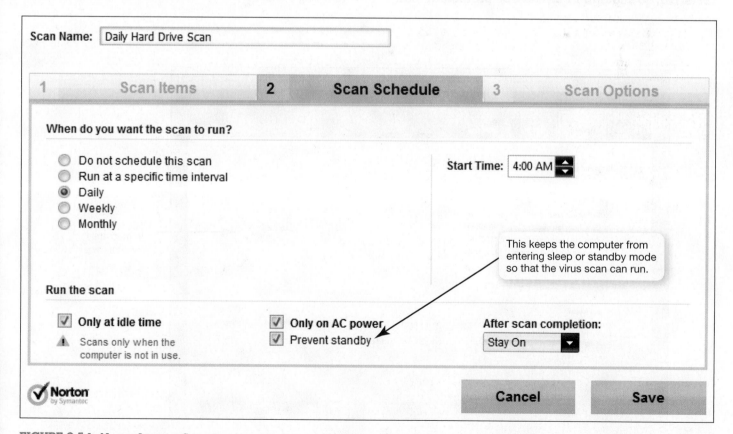

FIGURE 9.5 In Norton Internet Security, you can set up virus scans to run automatically. This computer will be scanned every day at 4 a.m. *(Reprinted with permission of Symantec Corporation)*

launch of an unknown macro, it stops the execution of the file and virus and notifies you that it has detected a virus. It also places the virus in a secure area on your hard drive so that it won't spread to other files; this procedure is known as **quarantining**. Usually, the antivirus software then gives you the choice of deleting or repairing the infected file. Unfortunately, antivirus programs can't always fix infected files to make them usable again. You should keep backup copies of critical files so that you can restore them in case a virus damages them irreparably.

- *Prevention of future infection:* Most antivirus software will also attempt to prevent infection by inoculating key files on your computer. In **inoculation**, the antivirus software records key attributes about your computer files, such as file size and date created, and keeps these statistics in a safe place on your hard drive. When scanning for viruses, the antivirus software compares the attributes of the files with the attributes it previously recorded to help detect attempts by virus programs to modify your files.

Does antivirus software always stop viruses?
Antivirus software catches *known* viruses effectively. However, new viruses are written all the time. To combat unknown viruses, modern antivirus programs search for suspicious virus-like activities as well as virus signatures. To minimize your risk, you should keep your antivirus software up to date.

My new computer came with antivirus software installed, so shouldn't I already be protected? Most

new computers do come with antivirus software preinstalled. However, these are usually trial versions of the software that only provide updates to the software for a limited period of time, usually 90 or 180 days. After that, you have to buy a full version of the software to ensure you remain protected from new viruses.

How do I make sure my antivirus software is up to date? Most antivirus programs have an automatic update feature that downloads updates for virus signature files every time you go online (see Figure 9.6). Also, the antivirus software usually shows the status of your update subscription so that you can see how much time you have remaining until you need to buy another version of your software.

What should I do if I think my computer is infected with a virus? Boot up your computer using the antivirus installation disc. This should prevent most virus programs from loading and will allow you to run the antivirus software directly from your disk drive. (*Note:* If you download your antivirus software from the Internet, copy it to a DVD in case you have problems in the future.) If the software does detect viruses, you may want to research them further to determine whether your antivirus software will eradicate them completely or whether you'll need to take additional manual steps to eliminate the viruses. Most antivirus company websites, such as the Symantec site (**symantec.com**), contain archives of information on viruses and provide step-by-step solutions for removing them.

FIGURE 9.6 Antivirus software, such as Windows Defender, provides for automatic updates but also allows manual updates.

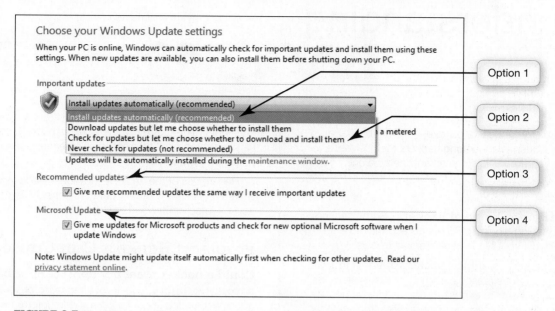

FIGURE 9.7 The Windows Update screen makes it easy for users to configure Windows to update itself.

>To enable automatic updates, access the Control Panel, select **System and Security**, *click the* **Windows Update** *link, and then click the* **Change Settings** *link.*

How do I protect my phone from viruses? Because smartphones and other mobile devices run operating systems and contain files, they are susceptible to infection by viruses. Cybercriminals are now hiding viruses in legitimate-looking apps for download to mobile devices. Most antivirus software companies now offer antivirus software specifically designed for mobile devices, such as Kaspersky Internet Security for Android, designed to protect phones and tablets.

Software Updates

Why does updating my operating system (OS) software help protect me from viruses? Many viruses exploit weaknesses in operating systems. Malicious websites can be set up to attack your computer by downloading harmful software onto your computer. According to research conducted by Google, this type of attack, known as a **drive-by download**, affects almost 1 in 1,000 web pages. To combat these threats, make sure your OS is up to date and contains the latest security patches. You can update your Windows OS with an automatic update utility called Windows

 SOUND BYTE
Protecting Your Computer

In this Sound Byte, you'll learn how to use a variety of tools to protect your computer, including antivirus software and Windows utilities.

Update. When you enable automatic updates, your computer searches for updates on the Microsoft website every time it connects to the Internet. Mac OS X has a similar utility for gathering updates.

Do OS updates only happen automatically? The default option in Windows is to receive updates automatically. There are several other options you can choose from in Windows, as shown in Figure 9.7. The following options are noteworthy:

- *Option 1: Install updates automatically.* Selecting this option will automatically download and install updates at a time you have specified. *We strongly recommend that you select this option.*

- *Option 2: Check for updates but let me choose whether to download and install them.* This is an appropriate choice only if you have low bandwidth Internet access. Because downloads over dial-up can take a long time, you need to control when they will occur. But you need to be extra vigilant with this option because you may forget to install important updates.

- *Option 3: Give me recommended updates.* This option ensures you receive recommended (optional) updates as well as critical (necessary) updates.

- *Option 4: Microsoft Update.* This option ensures you receive updates for other Microsoft products besides Windows, such as Microsoft Office.

If you keep both your antivirus and OS software up to date, you'll help prevent viruses from infecting your computer. ∎

understanding
HACKERS

Although there's a great deal of disagreement as to what a hacker actually is, especially among hackers themselves, a **hacker** is most commonly defined as anyone who unlawfully breaks into a computer system—either an individual computer or a network (see Figure 9.8).

Are there different kinds of hackers? Some hackers are offended by being labeled as criminals and therefore attempt to classify different types of hackers as follows:

- **White-hat hackers** (or **ethical hackers**) break in to systems for nonmalicious reasons, such as to test system security vulnerabilities or to expose undisclosed weaknesses. They believe in making security vulnerabilities known either to the company that owns the system or software or to the general public, often to embarrass a company into fixing a problem.
- **Black-hat hackers** break into systems to destroy information or for illegal gain. The terms *white hat* and *black hat* are references to old Western movies in which the heroes wore white hats and the outlaws wore black hats.
- **Grey-hat hackers** are a bit of a cross between black and white—they often illegally break into systems merely to

flaunt their expertise to the administrator of the system they penetrated or to attempt to sell their services in repairing security breaches.

Regardless of the hackers' opinions, the laws in the United States and in many other countries consider *any* unauthorized access to computer systems a crime.

Problems Hackers Can Cause

Could a hacker steal my debit card or bank account number? Hackers often try to break in to computers or websites that contain credit card information. If you perform financial transactions online, such as banking or buying goods and services, you probably do so using a credit or debit card. Credit card and bank account information can thus reside on your hard drive or an online business's hard drive and may be detectable by a hacker.

Aside from your home computer, you have personal data stored on various websites. For example, many sites require that you provide a login ID and password to gain access. Even if this data isn't stored on your computer, a hacker may be able to capture it when you're online by using a *packet analyzer (sniffer)* or a *keylogger* (a program that captures all keystrokes made on a computer).

What's a packet analyzer? Data travels through the Internet in small pieces called *packets*. The packets are identified with an IP address, in part to help identify the computer to which they are being sent. Once the packets reach their destination, they're reassembled into cohesive messages.

A **packet analyzer (sniffer)** is a program deployed by hackers that looks at (or sniffs) each packet as it travels on the Internet—not just those addressed to a particular computer, but all packets coming across a particular network. For example, a hacker might sit in a coffee shop and run a packet sniffer to capture sensitive data (such as debit/credit card numbers) from patrons using the coffee shop's free wireless network. Wireless networks such as these can be particularly vulnerable to this type of exploitation if encryption of data isn't enabled when the networks are set up. (This topic was covered in more detail in Chapter 7.)

What do hackers do with the information they "sniff"? Once a hacker has your debit/credit card information, he or she can use it to purchase items illegally or can sell the number to someone who will. If a hacker steals the login ID and password to an account where you have your bank card information stored (such as eBay or Amazon), he or she can also use your account to buy items and have them shipped to him- or herself instead of to you. If hackers can gather enough information in conjunction with your credit card information, they may be able to commit identity theft.

"Oh, we used to use a crystal ball, but hacking into your credit files is much more informative!"

FIGURE 9.8 Hackers can find lots of personal information about you on the Internet. *(Wildt, Chris/Cartoonstock)*

Although this sounds scary, you can easily protect yourself from packet sniffing by installing a firewall (which we discuss later in this chapter) and using data encryption on a wireless network (which was covered in Chapter 7).

Trojan Horses and Rootkits

Besides stealing information, what other problems can hackers cause if they break into my computer? Hackers often use individuals' computers as a staging area for mischief. To commit widespread computer attacks, for example, hackers need to control many computers at the same time. To this end, hackers often use Trojan horses to install other programs on computers. A **Trojan horse** is a program that appears to be something useful or desirable, like a game or a screen saver, but while it runs it does something malicious in the background without your knowledge (see Figure 9.9).

What damage can Trojan horses do? Often, the malicious activity perpetrated by a Trojan horse program is the installation of a backdoor program or a rootkit. **Backdoor programs** and **rootkits** are programs (or sets of programs) that allow hackers to gain access to your computer and take almost complete control of it without your knowledge. Using a backdoor program, hackers can access and delete all the files on your computer, send e-mail, run programs, and do just about anything else you can do with your computer. A computer that a hacker controls in this manner is referred to as a **zombie**. Zombies are often used to launch *denial-of-service attacks* on other computers.

Denial-of-Service Attacks

What are denial-of-service attacks? In a **denial-of-service (DoS) attack**, legitimate users are denied access to a computer system because a hacker is repeatedly making requests of that computer system through a computer he or she has taken over as a zombie. A computer system can handle only a certain number of requests for information at one time. When it is flooded with requests in a DoS attack, it shuts down and refuses to answer any requests for information, even if the requests are from a legitimate user. Thus, the computer is so busy responding to the bogus requests for information that authorized users can't gain access.

Couldn't a DoS attack be traced back to the computer that launched it? Launching a DoS attack on a computer system

from a single computer is easy to trace. Therefore, most savvy hackers use a **distributed denial-of-service (DDoS) attack**, which launches DoS attacks from more than one zombie (sometimes thousands of zombies) at the same time.

Figure 9.10 illustrates how a DDoS attack works. A hacker creates many zombies and coordinates them so that they begin sending bogus requests to the same computer at the same time. Administrators of the victim computer often have a great deal of difficulty stopping the attack because it comes from so many computers. Often, the attacks are coordinated automatically by botnets. A **botnet** is a large group of software programs (called *robots* or *bots*) that runs autonomously on zombie computers. Some botnets have been known to span millions of computers.

Because many commercial websites receive revenue from users, either directly (such as via subscriptions to on-line games) or indirectly (such as when web surfers click on advertisements), DDoS attacks can be financially distressing for the owners of the affected websites.

How Hackers Gain Computer Access

How exactly does a hacker gain access to a computer? Hackers can gain access to computers directly or indirectly:

- Direct access involves sitting down at a computer and installing hacking software. It's unlikely that such an attack would occur in your home, but it's always a wise precaution to set up your computer so that it requires a password for a user to gain access.

  - The most likely method a hacker will use to access a computer is to enter indirectly through its Internet connection.

Many people forget that their Internet connection is a two-way street. Not only can you access the Internet, but people on the Internet can access your computer. Think of your computer as a house. Common sense tells you to lock your home's doors and windows to deter theft when you aren't there. Hooking your computer up to the Internet without protection is like leaving the front door to your house wide open. Your computer obviously doesn't have doors and windows like a house, but it does have logical ports.

FIGURE 9.9 The term *Trojan horse* derives from Greek mythology and refers to the wooden horse that the Greeks used to sneak into the city of Troy and conquer it. Therefore, computer programs that contain a hidden, and usually dreadful, "surprise" are referred to as Trojan horses. *(Ralf Kraft/ Fotolia)*

Hacker launches DDoS by activating zombies (red lines)

Hacker's computer

Academic computer (zombie)

Government computer (zombie)

Home computer (zombie)

Internet Service Provider computer (zombie)

Corporate computer (zombie)

Zombie computers attack target system (blue lines)

Victim of DDoS

FIGURE 9.10 Zombie computers are used to facilitate a DDoS attack. *(Vovan/Shutterstock; Nicholas Monu/Getty)*

BITS&BYTES

Are Your Photos Helping Criminals Target You?

All cell phones today contain GPS chips. The cameras in phones often use information gathered from the GPS chips to encode information onto photos in the form of geotags. A **geotag** is a piece of data attached to a photo that indicates your latitude and longitude when you took the photo. Geotagging is useful for applications that can take advantage of this information, but problems arise when you share geotagged photos on the web.

If you post a lot of photos, cybercriminals and cyberstalkers can use the information from the geotags on your photos to figure out the patterns of your movements. They may be able to ascertain when you're at work or that you're currently on vacation, which leads them to determine prime times for burglarizing your

home. Some sites such as Facebook and Twitter have measures in place to limit the amount of geotagged information that can be seen in photos in order to prevent their users from unwittingly revealing personal information. However, many photo-sharing sites don't have such protections in place.

The safest thing to do is not tag your photos with geotags in the first place. It's usually easy to disable location tracking on your smartphone. For instance, on the iPhone, on the Settings screen, select General, then Location Services, and choose Off. So stop geotagging your photos, and make it tougher for the cybercriminals to figure out your movements. For photos that already have geotags, you can remove them using software such as BatchPurifier or Geotag Remover.

FTP (Port 21)

E-mail (Port 25)

YOUR COMPUTER

HTTP (Port 80)

DNS (Port 53)

Telnet (Port 23)

WEBSITE REQUEST

FIGURE 9.11 Open logical ports are an invitation to hackers.

What are logical ports? Logical ports are virtual—that is, not physical—communications gateways or paths that allow a computer to organize requests for information, such as web page downloads or e-mail routing, from other networks or computers. Unlike physical ports, such as USB ports, you can't see or touch a logical port; it's part of a computer's internal organization.

Logical ports are numbered and assigned to specific services. For instance, logical port 80 is designated for hypertext transfer protocol (HTTP), the main communications protocol for the web. Thus, all requests for information from your browser to the web flow through logical port 80. Open logical ports, like open windows in a home, invite intruders, as illustrated in Figure 9.11. Unless you take precautions to restrict access to your logical ports, other people on the Internet may be able to access your computer through them.

Fortunately, you can thwart most hacking problems by installing a firewall, which we discuss next. ■

restricting access to your
DIGITAL ASSETS

Keeping hackers at bay is often just a matter of keeping them out. You can achieve this by:

- Preventing hackers from accessing your computer (usually through your Internet connection)
- Protecting your digital information in such a way that it can't be accessed (by using passwords, for example)
- Hiding your activities from prying eyes

In this section, we explore strategies for protecting access to your digital assets and keeping your Internet-surfing activities from being seen by the wrong people.

Firewalls

What is a firewall? A **firewall** is a software program or hardware device designed to protect computers from hackers. It's named after a housing construction feature that slows the spread of fires from house to house. A firewall specifically designed for home networks is called a **personal firewall**. By using a personal firewall, you can close open logical ports to invaders and potentially make your computer invisible to other computers on the Internet.

Which is better, a software firewall or a hardware firewall? Both hardware and software firewalls will protect you from hackers. One type isn't better than the other. Although installing either a software or a hardware firewall on your home network is probably sufficient, you should consider installing both for maximum protection. This will provide you with additional safety, just as wearing multiple layers of clothing helps keep you warmer in the winter than a single layer.

Types of Firewalls

What software firewalls are there? Both Windows and OS X include reliable firewalls. The Windows Action Center is a good source of information about the security settings on your computer (see Figure 9.12), including the status of your firewall. Security suites such as Norton Internet Security, McAfee Internet Security, and ZoneAlarm Internet Security

FIGURE 9.12 The security section of the Windows Action Center provides the status of programs protecting your computer.

>*To view the Action Center, access the Control Panel, select* **System and Security**, *and then click the* **Action Center** *link.*

Suite also include firewall software. Although the firewalls that come with Windows and OS X will protect your computer, firewalls included in security suites often come with additional features such as monitoring systems that alert you if your computer is under attack.

If you're using a security suite that includes a firewall, the suite should disable the firewall that came with your OS. Two firewalls running at the same time can conflict with each other and cause your computer to slow down or freeze up.

What are hardware firewalls? You can also buy and configure hardware firewall devices. Many routers sold for home networks include firewall protection. Just like software firewalls, the setup for hardware firewalls is designed for novices, and the default configuration on most routers keeps unused logical ports closed. Documentation accompanying routers can assist more-experienced users in adjusting the settings to allow access to specific ports if needed.

How Firewalls Work

How do firewalls protect you from hackers? Firewalls are designed to restrict access to a network and its computers. Firewalls protect you in two major ways:

1. By blocking access to logical ports and
2. By keeping your computer's network address secure

How do firewalls block access to your logical ports? Certain logical ports are very popular in hacker attacks. To block access to logical ports, firewalls examine data packets that your computer sends and receives. Data packets contain information such as the address of the sending and receiving computers and the logical port that the packet will use. Firewalls can be configured so that they filter out packets sent to specific logical ports in a process known as **packet filtering**. Firewalls are also often configured to ignore requests that originate from the Internet asking for access to certain ports. This process is referred to as **logical port blocking**. By using filtering and blocking, firewalls keep hackers from accessing your computer (Figure 9.13).

How do firewalls keep your network address secure? Every computer connected to the Internet has a unique address called an *Internet Protocol address (IP address)*. Data is routed to the correct computer on the Internet based on the IP address. This is similar to how a letter finds its way to your mailbox. You have a unique postal address for your home. If a hacker finds out the IP address of your computer, he or she can locate it on the Internet and try to break into it. This is similar to how a conventional thief might target your home after finding out you collect antique cars by using your street address to locate your house.

Your IP address for your home network is assigned to your router by your Internet service provider (ISP), but each device

on your home network also has an IP address. Firewalls use a process called **network address translation (NAT)** to assign internal IP addresses on a network. The internal IP addresses are used only on the internal network and therefore can't be detected by hackers. For hackers to access your computer, they must know your computer's internal IP address. With a NAT–capable router/firewall installed on your network, hackers are unable to access the internal IP address assigned to your computer, so your computer is safe. You can use NAT in your home by purchasing a hardware firewall with NAT capabilities. Many routers sold for home use are also configured as firewalls, and many feature NAT.

Knowing Your Computer Is Secure

How can I tell if my computer is at risk? For peace of mind, you can visit websites that offer free services that test your computer's vulnerability. One popular site is Gibson Research Corporation (**grc.com**). The company's ShieldsUP and LeakTest programs are free and easy to run and can pinpoint security vulnerabilities in a system connected to the Internet. If you get a clean report from these programs, your

FIGURE 9.13 Firewalls use filtering and blocking to keep out unwanted data and keep your network safe. *(Intelligent Computer Solutions)*

system is probably not vulnerable to attack. See the Try This section in this chapter (page 368) for instructions on how to test your system.

What if I don't get a clean report from the testing program? If the testing program detects potential vulnerabilities and you don't have a firewall, you should install one as soon as possible. If the firewall is already configured and common ports (such as those shown in Figure 9.14) are identified as being vulnerable, consult your firewall documentation for instructions on how to close or restrict access to those ports.

Password Protection and Password Management

How can I best use passwords to protect my computer? You no doubt have many passwords you need to remember to access your digital life. However, creating strong passwords—ones that are difficult for hackers to guess—is an essential piece of security that people sometimes overlook. Password-cracking programs have become more sophisticated. In fact, some commonly available programs can test more than one million password combinations per second! Creating a secure password is therefore more important than ever.

Many people use extremely weak passwords. The Imperva Application Defense Center, a computer-security research organization, conducted a review of 32 million passwords that were used at the website **rockyou.com**. More than 345,000 people were using "12345," "123456," or "123456789" as their password. And almost 62,000 people were using "password"! Passwords such as these are easy for hackers to crack.

FIGURE 9.14

Common Logical Ports

PORT NUMBER	PROTOCOL USING THE PORT
21	FTP (File Transfer Protocol) control
23	Telnet (unencrypted text communications)
25	SMTP (Simple Mail Transfer Protocol)
53	DNS (domain name system)
80	HTTP (Hypertext Transfer Protocol)
443	HTTPS (HTTP with Transport Layer Security [TLS] encryption)

Websites that need to be very secure, such as those for financial institutions, usually have strong defenses to prevent hackers from cracking passwords. But sites that need less security, such as casual gaming or social networking sites, might have less protection. Hackers attack poorly defended sites for passwords because many people use the same password for every site they use. So if a hacker can get your password from a poorly secured gaming site, they might be able to access your bank account with the same password.

Creating Passwords

What constitutes a strong password? Strong passwords are difficult for someone to guess. Follow these guidelines to create strong passwords (see Figure 9.15):

- Don't use easily deduced components related to your life, such as parts of your name, your pet's name, your street address, or the name of the website or institution for which you are creating the password (i.e., don't use "Citibank" for your online banking password).
- Use a password that is at least 14 characters long. Longer passwords are more difficult to deduce. Consider using a passphrase that is even longer (see the Bits & Bytes on page 364).
- Don't use words found in the dictionary.
- Use a mix of upper- and lowercase letters and symbols (such as # or %).
- Never tell anyone your password or write it down in a place where others might see it, like in your wallet or purse.
- Change your passwords on a regular basis, such as monthly or quarterly. Your school or your employer probably requires you to change your password regularly. This is also a good idea for your personal passwords.
- Don't use the same password for every account you have.

If you have trouble thinking of secure passwords, there are many password generators available for free, such as the Strong Password Generator (**strongpasswordgenerator .com**).

How can I check the strength of my passwords? You can use online password strength testers, such as the Password Meter (**passwordmeter.com**), to evaluate your passwords. The Password Meter provides guidelines for good passwords and shows you how integrating various elements, such as symbols, affects the strength score of your password.

How do I restrict access to my computer? Windows, OS X, and most other operating systems have built-in password (or passcode) protection for files as well as the entire desktop. After a certain period of idle time, your computer is automatically password locked, and your password must be entered to gain access to the computer. This provides excellent protection from casual snooping if you need to walk away from your computer for a period of time. If someone attempts to log on to your computer without your password, that person won't be able to gain access. It's an especially good idea to use passwords on laptop computers, smartphones, and

FIGURE 9.15

Strong and Weak Password Candidates

PASSWORD	RATING	GOOD POINTS	BAD POINTS
Joysmithl022	Poor	• Contains upper- and lowercase letters • Contains letters and numbers	• Less than 14 characters • Contains name and birth date
test44drive6car	Mediocre	• 15 characters in length	• Contains three words found in the dictionary • Numbers repeated consecutively
8$RanT%5ydTTtt&	Better	• Good length • Contains upper- and lowercase letters • Contains symbols	• Upper- and lowercase letters repeated consecutively • Still contains one dictionary word (rant)
7R3m3mB3R$5%y38	Best	• All good points from above • Dictionary word (remember) has 3s instead of Es	• None

tablets because this provides additional protection of your data if your device is lost or stolen.

Windows 8 allows you to use picture passwords. You select a picture and then draw three gestures on it—either straight lines, circles, or taps. This picture then works as an additional method for accessing your computer. You just unlock your computer by repeating the gestures (see Figure 9.16). But if you forget your gestures, you can always access your computer via the conventional password.

Managing Your Passwords

How can I remember all of my complex passwords? Good security practices suggest that you have different passwords for all the different websites that you access and that you change your passwords frequently. The problem with well-constructed passwords is that they can be hard to remember.

Fortunately, password-management tools are now available. They take the worry out of forgetting passwords because the password-management software does the remembering for you.

Where can I obtain password-management software? Most current Internet security suites and web browsers make it easy to keep track of passwords by providing password-management tools. For example, Internet Explorer (IE) will remember passwords for you. When you go to a website that requires a login, IE will display a dialog box prompting you to have IE remember the password for the site (see Figure 9.17). Then, when you return to the site and type in your user name, IE will fill in the password information for you using a process known as auto complete. However, there are some passwords that you shouldn't have your browser remember, such as your online banking password. So be selective when using this feature.

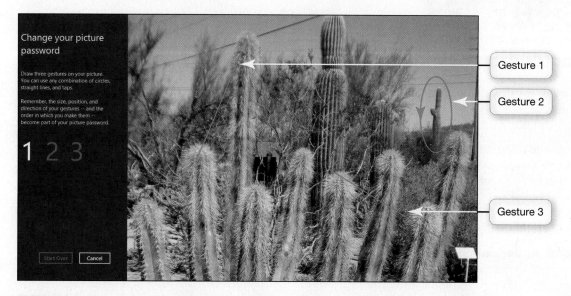

FIGURE 9.16 Drawing three gestures on your picture (and repeating them once) sets your picture password options in Windows 8.

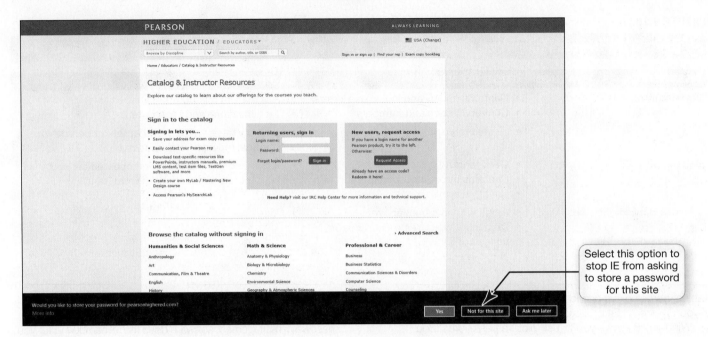

FIGURE 9.17 The password bar in IE 11 displays whenever you type in a password for a website for which IE hasn't yet stored the password.

Anonymous Web Surfing: Hiding from Prying Eyes

Should I be concerned about surfing the Internet on shared, public, or work computers? If you use shared computers in public places such as libraries, coffee shops, or student unions, you never know what nefarious tools have been installed by hackers on a public computer. When you browse the Internet, traces of your activity are left behind

on that computer, often as temporary files. A wily hacker can glean sensitive information long after you've finished your surfing session. In addition, many employers routinely review the Internet browsing history of employees to ensure workers are spending their time on the Internet productively.

What tools can I use to keep my browsing activities private when surfing the Internet? The current versions of Google Chrome, Firefox, and Internet Explorer include privacy tools (called Incognito,

BITS&BYTES

Multi-Factor Authentication: Don't Rely Solely on Passwords!

Computer system security depends on authentication—proving the user is who they say they are. There are three independent authentication factors:

- Knowledge factor: Something the user knows (password, PIN)
- Possession factor: Something the user has (ATM card, mobile phone)
- Inherence factor: Something only the user is (biometric characteristics, such as fingerprints)

Multi-factor authorization requires two of the three above factors be demonstrated before authorization is granted. At the bank's ATM machine, you present an ATM card (something you have) and then use a

PIN code (something you know) to access your account.

For online access, multi-factor authentication often relies on the use of mobile phones. For instance, when you register a Google account, you supply your mobile phone number. If you then want to make changes to your account, you supply the password (something you know). The second step of authentication is Google sending an SMS message with a unique code to your mobile phone. Retrieving the code and entering it online proves you have the phone (something the user has) and serves as the second authentication step.

Multi-factor authentication is much safer than single-factor authentication. So make use of it when it is offered to you to enhance your account security.

Private Browsing, and InPrivate, respectively) that help you surf the web anonymously (see Figure 9.18). When you choose to surf anonymously, all three browsers open special versions of their browser windows that are enhanced for privacy. When surfing in these windows, records of websites you visit and files you download don't appear in the web browser's history files. Furthermore, any temporary files generated in that browsing session are deleted when you exit the special window.

Are there any other tools I could use to protect my privacy? Portable privacy devices, such as the Ironkey Personal Flash Drive (**ironkey.com**), provide an even higher level of surfing privacy. Simply plug the device into an available USB port on the machine on which you'll be working. All sensitive Internet files, such as cookies, passwords, Internet history, and browser caches, will be stored on the privacy device, not on the computer you're using. Privacy devices such as these often come preloaded with software designed to shield your IP address from prying eyes, making it difficult (if not impossible) for hackers to tell where you're surfing on the Internet. These privacy devices also have password-management tools that store all of your login information and encrypt it so it will be safe if your privacy device falls into someone else's hands.

Is there anything else I can do to keep my data safe on shared computers? Another free practical solution is to take the Linux OS with you on a flash drive and avoid using the public or work computer's OS. The interfaces of many Linux distros look almost exactly like Windows and are easy to use. There are several advantages to using a Linux-based OS on a public or work computer:

- Your risk of picking up viruses and other malicious programs is significantly reduced because booting a computer from a flash drive completely eliminates any interaction with the computer's OS. This, in turn, significantly reduces the chance that your flash drive will become infected by any malware running on the computer.
- Virus and hacking attacks against Linux are far less likely than attacks against Windows. Because Windows has about 90% of the OS market, people who write malware tend to target Windows systems.
- When you run software from your own storage medium, such as a flash drive, you avoid reading and writing to the hard disk of the computer. This significantly enhances your privacy because you don't leave traces of your activity behind.

Pendrivelinux (**pendrivelinux.com**) is an excellent resource that offers many different versions of Linux for download and includes step-by-step instructions on how to install them

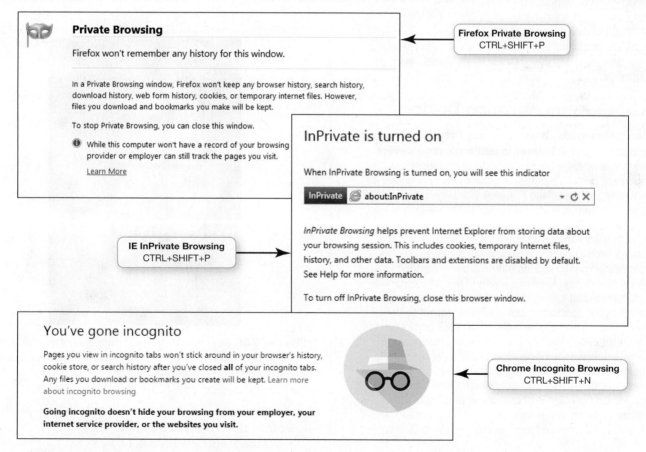

FIGURE 9.18 The recent versions of the Firefox, Internet Explorer, and Google Chrome browsers all feature privacy tools for web surfing. *((a) Courtesy of the Mozilla Foundation; (c) Courtesy of the Mozilla Foundation)*

on your flash drive (see Figure 9.19). If you're a Mac user, the gOS version of Linux provides a close approximation of OS X, so you can feel right at home.

Do I need to take special precautions with my tablet devices? Tablets like the iPad run their own proprietary operating systems that differ from the operating systems deployed on laptop and desktop computers. Although tablet operating systems do contain security features, they may not be robust enough to satisfy business users who have a great deal of confidential information on their tablets, especially when the devices are connected to wireless networks. Third-party software developers are now offering many apps to enhance tablet security. Comprehensive suites like IPVanish (**ipvanish.com**) offer features such as government-grade encryption of data, enhanced e-mail security, and anonymous web surfing. So look for security apps that are specifically designed for your tablet device if you often deal with sensitive data on your tablet, such as online banking.

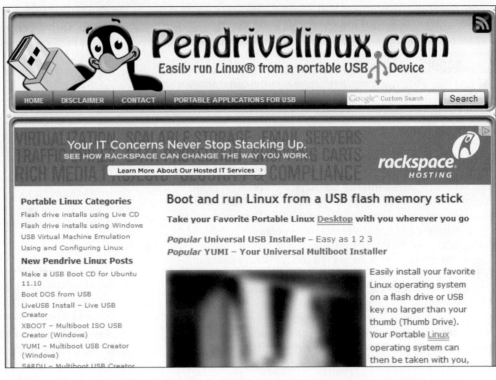

FIGURE 9.19 **Pendrivelinux.com** can help you load a version of Linux onto a flash drive. *(Courtesy of USB Pen Drive Linux)*

Biometric Authentication Devices

Besides passwords, how else can I restrict the use of my computer? A **biometric authentication device** is a device that reads a unique personal characteristic such as a fingerprint or the iris pattern in your eye and converts its pattern to a digital code (see Figure 9.20). When you use the device, your pattern is read and compared to the one stored on the computer. Only users having an exact fingerprint or iris pattern match are allowed to access the computer.

Because no two people have the same biometric characteristics (fingerprints and iris patterns are unique), these devices provide a high level of security. They also eliminate the human error that can occur in password protection. You might forget your password, but you won't forget to bring your fingerprints when you're working on your computer! Some smartphones, such as the iPhone 5s, now include fingerprint readers. But since Touch ID (the Apple software for fingerprint identification) has already been hacked, you might be safer using a regular password. Other biometric devices, including voice authentication and facial recognition systems, are now widely offered in notebooks, tablets, and smartphones (such as the Samsung Galaxy phones).

Make sure to use some (or all) of these methods to keep your activities from prying eyes and to restrict access to your digital information. ∎

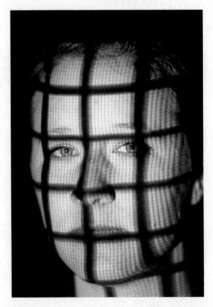

FIGURE 9.20 Face recognition software is now available on laptops. You might forget your password, but you won't forget to bring your face! *(© Jochen Tack/Alamy)*.

> **Before moving on to Part 2:**
> • **Watch Replay Video 9.1** ▶ .
> • **Then check your understanding of what you've learned so far.**

check your understanding// review & practice

For a quick review to see what you've learned so far, answer the following questions. Visit **pearsonhighered.com /techinaction** to check your answers.

multiple choice

1. When a hacker steals personal information with the intent of impersonating another individual to commit fraud, it is known as

   a. impersonation theft. **c.** identity theft.

   b. scareware theft. **d.** malware theft.

2. Viruses that are often launched from infected USB drives left in a computer are known as

   a. boot-sector viruses. **c.** time bombs.

   b. script viruses. **d.** encryption viruses.

3. Firewalls work by closing _____ in your computer.

   a. logical ports **c.** logical doors

   b. software gaps **d.** backdoors

4. An attack that renders a computer unable to respond to legitimate users because it is being bombarded with data requests is known as a _____ attack.

   a. stealth

   b. backdoor

   c. scareware

   d. denial-of-service

5. A large group of software programs used to launch coordinated DoS attacks is known as a _____.

   a. rootkit

   b. botnet

   c. Trojan horse

   d. zombienet

To take an autograded version of this review, please go to the companion website at **pearsonhighered.com/techinaction**, or go your MyITLab course.

Continue

TRY THIS ▶ Testing Your Network Security

A properly installed firewall should keep you relatively safe from wily hackers. But how do you know if your computer system is safe? Many websites help test your security. In this exercise, we'll use tools provided by Gibson Research Corporation (**grc.com**) to test the strength of your protection.

Step 1   Open a web browser and navigate to **grc.com**. From the pull-down Services menu at the top of the screen, select **ShieldsUP!** On the ShieldsUP! welcome screen, click the Proceed button. *(Courtesy of the Gibson Research Corporation)*

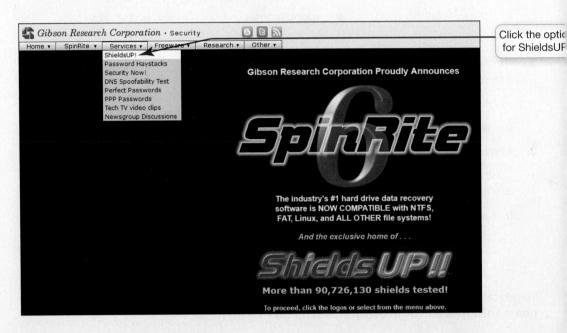

Click the option for ShieldsUP!

Step 2   Click the **Common Ports** link to begin the security test. It will take a few moments for the results to appear, depending on the speed of your Internet connection. *(Courtesy of the Gibson Research Corporation)*

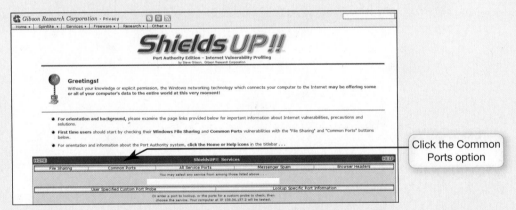

Click the Common Ports option

Step 3   Hopefully, you'll see a report indicating that your computer has passed the TruStealth analysis test. This means that your computer is very safe from attack. However, don't panic if your results say **failed for true stealth analysis**. Consider these common issues:

- Ports that only report as being closed will result in a TruStealth analysis failure. As long as all common ports are reporting as stealth or closed, you are well protected. However, if any ports report as being open, this means your computer could be exposed to hackers. Consult your firewall documentation to resolve the problem.
- Another common failure on the TruStealth test is ping reply. This means GRC attempted to contact your computer using a method called ping and it replied to the GRC computer. This is not a serious problem. It

just means it's a little easier for a hacker to tell your computer network is there, but that doesn't mean that a hacker can break in. Often your ISP has your home modem configured to reply to ping requests to facilitate remote diagnostics if there is ever a problem with your modem. As long as your ports are closed (or stealthed), your system should still be secure. *(Courtesy of the Gibson Research Corporation)*

Make This

The android icon image.

TOOL: AI TinyDB

MAKE: A Password Generator

Want to make sure your passwords are randomly selected so they are more secure, but afraid you'll forget what you chose?

In this exercise, you'll continue your mobile app development by using the TinyDB component in **App Inventor** to store information on your phone so it can be recalled by your application the next time it runs. This is called data persistence and as you'll see, it is very easy to do!

The TinyDB component allows you to store data on your device to use the next time the app opens.

For the instructions for this exercise, please go to pearsonhighered.com/techinaction or MyITLab.

Protecting Your Digital Property from Yourself

Often, we can be our own worst enemies when using computing devices. If you're not careful, you might be taken in by thieves or scam artists who want to steal your digital and physical assets. Being aware of the tricks and traps that criminals use allows you to take steps to avoid being scammed.

 managing online
ANNOYANCES

Surfing the web, using social networks, and sending and receiving e-mail have become common parts of most of our lives. Unfortunately, the web has become fertile ground for people who want to advertise their products, track our browsing behaviors, or even con people into revealing personal information. In this section, we'll look at ways in which you can manage, if not avoid, these and other online headaches.

Malware: Adware and Spyware

What is malware? Malware is software that has a malicious intent (hence the prefix *mal*). There are three primary forms of malware: adware, spyware, and viruses. Adware and spyware are not physically destructive like viruses and worms, which can destroy data. Known collectively as *grayware*, most malware are intrusive, annoying, or objectionable online programs that are downloaded to your computer when you install or use other online content such as a free program, game, or utility.

What is adware? Adware is software that displays sponsored advertisements in a section of your browser window or as a pop-up box. It's considered a legitimate, though sometimes annoying, means of generating revenue for those developers who do not charge for their software or information. Fortunately, because web browsers

such as Firefox, Safari, and Internet Explorer have built-in pop-up blockers, the occurrence of annoying pop-ups has been greatly reduced.

Some pop-ups, however, are legitimate and increase the functionality of the originating site. For example, your account balance may pop up on your bank's website. To control which sites to allow pop-ups on, you can access the pop-up blocker settings in your browser (see Figure 9.21) and add websites for which you allow pop-ups. Whenever a pop-up is blocked, the browser displays an information bar

FIGURE 9.21 Firefox's Allowed Sites - Pop-ups dialog box lets you control which sites you'll allow to display pop-ups. *(Courtesy of the Mozilla Foundation)*

>*To display the pop-up blocker in Firefox, from the Tools menu, select* **Options**, *and then click the* **Content** *tab.*

or plays a sound to alert you. If you feel the pop-up is legitimate, you can choose to accept it.

What is spyware? Spyware is an unwanted piggyback program that usually downloads with other software you install from the Internet and that runs in the background of your system. Without your knowledge, spyware transmits information about you, such as your Internet-surfing habits, to the owner of the program so that the information can be used for marketing purposes. Many spyware programs use tracking cookies (small text files stored on your computer) to collect information. One type of spyware program known as a **keystroke logger (key logger)** monitors keystrokes with the intent of stealing passwords, login IDs, or credit card information.

Can I prevent spyware from spying on me?
Anti-spyware software detects unwanted programs and allows you to delete the offending software easily. Most Internet security suites now include anti-spyware software. You can also obtain stand-alone anti-spyware software and run it on your computer to delete unwanted spyware. Because so many variants of spyware exist, your Internet security software may not detect all types that attempt to install themselves on your computer. Therefore, it's a good idea to install one or two additional stand-alone anti-spyware programs on your computer.

Because new spyware is created all the time, you should update and run your anti-spyware software regularly. Windows comes with a program called Windows Defender, which scans your system for spyware and other potentially unwanted software. Malwarebytes Anti-Malware, Ad-Aware, and Spybot–Search & Destroy (all available from **download.com**) are other anti-spyware programs that are easy to install and update. Figure 9.22 shows an example of Malwarebytes in action.

Spam

How can I best avoid spam? Companies that send out **spam**—unwanted or junk e-mail—find your e-mail address either from a list they purchase or with software that looks for e-mail addresses on the Internet. Unsolicited instant messages are also a form of spam, called *spim*. If you've used your e-mail address to purchase anything online, open an online account, or participate in a social network such as Facebook, your e-mail address eventually will appear on one of the lists that spammers get.

One way to avoid spam in your primary account is to create a free e-mail address that you use only when you fill out forms or buy items on the web. For example, both Outlook.com and Yahoo! let you set up free e-mail accounts. If your free e-mail account is saturated with spam, you can abandon that account with little inconvenience. It's much less convenient to abandon your primary e-mail address.

Another way to avoid spam is to filter it. A **spam filter** is an option you can select in your e-mail account that places known or suspected spam messages into a special folder (called "Spam" or "Junk Mail"). Most web-based e-mail

FIGURE 9.22 After performing a routine scan of a computer, Malwarebytes returns a log of problems found on the system. *(Courtesy of Malwarebytes)*

On law enforcement TV shows, you often see computer technicians working on suspects' computers to assist detectives in solving crimes. It may look simple, but the science of computer forensics is a complex step-by-step process that ensures evidence is collected within the confines of the law.

Forensic means that something is suitable for use in a court of law. There are many branches of forensic science. For example, forensic pathologists provide evidence about the nature and manner of death in court cases involving deceased individuals. **Computer forensics** involves identifying, extracting, preserving, and documenting computer evidence. Computer forensics is performed by individuals known as *computer forensic scientists*, who rely primarily on specialized software to collect their evidence.

Phase 1: Obtaining and Securing Computer Devices

The first step in a computer forensics investigation is to seize the computer equipment that law enforcement officials believe contains pertinent evidence. Police are required to obtain a warrant to search an individual's home or place of business. Warrants must be very specific by spelling out exactly where detectives can search for evidence and exactly what type of evidence they're seeking. If a warrant indicates that the police may search an individual's home for his laptop computer, they can't then confiscate a tablet computer they notice in his car. It is important to specify in the warrant all types of storage devices where potential evidence might be stored, such as external hard drives, flash drives, and servers.

Once permission to collect the computers and devices containing possible evidence has been obtained, law enforcement officials must exercise great care when collecting the equipment. They need to

ensure that no unauthorized persons are able to access or alter the computers or storage devices. The police must make sure the data and equipment are safe; if the equipment is connected to the Internet, the connection must be severed without data loss or damage. It's also important for law enforcement officials to understand that they may not want to power off equipment because potential evidence contained in RAM may be lost. After the devices are collected and secured, the computer forensic scientists take over the next phase of the investigation.

Phase 2: Cataloging and Analyzing the Data

It's critical to preserve the data exactly as it was found, or attorneys may argue that the computer evidence was subject to tampering or altering. Because just opening a file can alter it, the first task is to make a copy of all computer systems and storage devices collected (see Figure 9.23). The investigators then work from the copies to ensure that the original data always remains preserved exactly as it was when it was collected.

After obtaining a copy to work from, forensics professionals attempt to find every file on the system, including deleted files. Files on a computer aren't actually deleted, even if you empty the Recycle Bin, until the section of the hard disk they're stored on is overwritten with new data. Therefore, using special forensic software tools such as SIFT, EnCase, and FTK, the forensic scientists catalog all files found on the system or storage medium and recover as much information from deleted files as they can. Forensic software like FTK can readily detect hidden files and perform procedures to crack encrypted files or access protected files and reveal their contents.

The most important part of the process is documenting every step. Forensic scientists must clearly

FIGURE 9.23 Portable computer forensic devices make it easy to copy storage devices at crime scenes. *(Intelligent Computer Solutions)*

log every procedure performed because they may be required to provide proof in court that their investigations did not alter or damage information contained on the systems they examined. Detailed reports should list all files found, how the files were laid out on the system, which files were protected or encrypted, and the contents of each file. Finally, computer forensic professionals are often called on to present testimony in court during a trial.

Criminals are getting more sophisticated and are now employing anti-forensics techniques to foil computer forensic investigators. Although techniques for hiding or encrypting data are popular, the most insidious anti-forensics techniques are programs designed to erase data if unauthorized persons (i.e., not the criminal) access a computer system or if the system detects forensics software in use. When computer forensic investigators detect these countermeasures, they must often use creative methods and custom-designed software programs to retrieve and preserve the data.

Computer forensics is an invaluable tool to law enforcement in many criminal investigations, but only if the correct procedures are followed and the appropriate documentation is prepared.

---

services, such as Gmail and Yahoo!, offer spam filters (see Figure 9.25). Microsoft Outlook also features a spam filter.

You can also buy third-party programs that provide some control over spam, including SPAMfighter, which you can download at **download.com**.

How do spam filters work? Spam filters and filtering software can catch as much as 95% of spam by checking incoming e-mail subject headers and senders' addresses against databases of known spam. Spam filters also check your e-mail for frequently used spam patterns and keywords, such as "for free" and "over 21." Spam filters aren't perfect, and you should check the spam folder before deleting its contents because legitimate e-mail might end up there by mistake. Most programs let you reclassify e-mails that have been misidentified as spam (see Figure 9.24).

How else can I prevent spam? Here are a few other ways you can prevent spam:

1. Before registering on a website, read its privacy policy to see how it uses your e-mail address. Don't give the site permission to pass on your e-mail address to third parties.

2. Don't reply to spam to remove yourself from the spam list. By replying, you're confirming that your e-mail address is active. Instead of stopping spam, you may receive more.

3. Subscribe to an e-mail forwarding service such as VersaForward (**versaforward.com**) or Sneakemail (**sneakemail.com**). These services screen your e-mail messages, forwarding only those messages you designate as being okay to accept.

Cookies

What are cookies? Cookies are small text files that some websites automatically store on your hard drive when you visit them. When you log on to a website that uses cookies, a cookie file assigns an ID number to your computer. The unique ID is intended to make your return visit to a website more

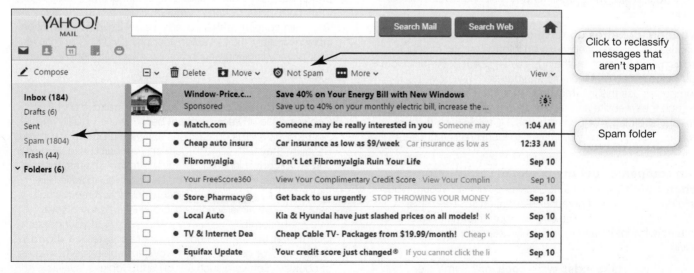

FIGURE 9.24 In Yahoo! Mail, messages identified as spam are directed into a folder called "Spam" for review and deletion. *(Courtesy of Yahoo, Inc.)*

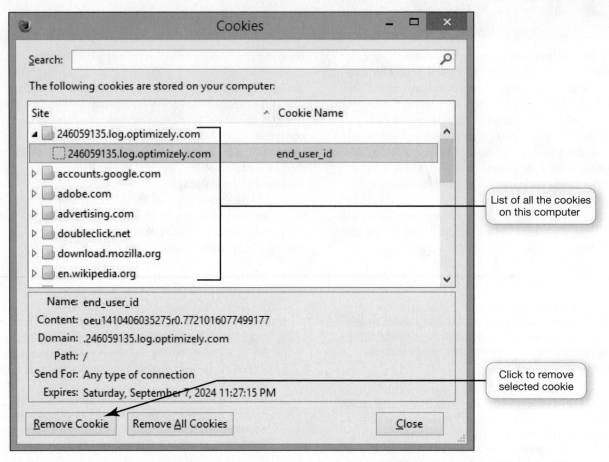

FIGURE 9.25 Tools are available, either through your browser (Firefox is shown here) or as separate programs, to distinguish between cookies you want to keep and cookies you don't want on your system. *(Courtesy of the Mozilla Foundation)*

>*On the Firefox menu toolbar, click* **Tools***, click* **Options***, choose the* **Privacy tab***, choose* **Use custom settings for history***, and then click the* **Show Cookies** *button to display the Cookies dialog box.*

efficient and better geared to your interests. The next time you log on to that site, the site marks your visit and keeps track of it in its database.

What do websites do with cookie information?
Cookies can provide websites with information about your browsing habits, such as the ads you've opened, the products you've looked at, and the time and duration of your visits. Companies use this information to determine the traffic flowing through their website and the effectiveness of their marketing strategy and placement on websites. By tracking such information, cookies enable companies to identify different users' preferences.

Can companies get my personal information when I visit their sites? Cookies do not go through your hard drive in search of personal information such as passwords or financial data. The only personal information a cookie obtains is the information you supply when you fill out forms online.

Do privacy risks exist with cookies? Some sites sell the personal information their cookies collect to web advertisers who are building huge databases of consumer preferences and habits, collecting personal and business information such as phone numbers, credit reports, and the like. The main concern is that advertisers will use this information indiscriminately, thus invading your privacy. And you may feel your privacy is being violated by cookies that monitor where you go on a website.

Should I delete cookies from my hard drive?
Cookies pose no *security* threat because it is virtually impossible to hide a virus or malicious software program in a cookie. Because they take up little room on your hard drive, and offer you small conveniences on return visits to websites, there is no great reason to delete them. Deleting your cookie files could actually cause you the inconvenience of reentering data you have already entered into website forms. However, if you're uncomfortable with the accessibility of your personal information, you can periodically delete cookies (as shown in Figure 9.25) or configure your browser to block certain types of cookies. Software such as Powerful Cookies (available at download.com) also can help you monitor cookies. ■

ethics in IT

You're Being Watched … But Are You Aware You're Being Watched?

Think you aren't being closely watched by your employer? Think again! A recent survey of employers by the American Management Association and the ePolicy Institute revealed that, of the employers surveyed:

- 73% monitored e-mail messages
- 66% monitored web surfing
- 48% monitored activities using video surveillance
- 45% monitored keystrokes and keyboard time
- 43% monitored computer files in some other fashion

As you can see, there is a high probability that you're being monitored while you work and when you access the Internet via your employer's Internet connection.

The two most frequently cited reasons for employee monitoring are to prevent theft and to measure productivity. Monitoring for theft isn't new—monitoring cameras have been around for years, and productivity monitoring has been used for assembly line workers for decades. However, the Internet has led to a new type of productivity drain of concern to employers. **Cyberloafing**, or cyberslacking, means using your computer for nonwork activities while you're being paid to do your job. Examples of cyberloafing activities include playing games and using social networks. Some employees even do multiple nonwork tasks at the same time, which is known as *multishirking*.

Estimates of business productivity losses due to cyberloafing top $50 billion annually.

Do you have a right to privacy in the workplace? Laws such as the 1986 Electronic Communications Privacy Act (ECPA), which prohibits unauthorized monitoring of electronic communications, have been interpreted by the courts in favor of employers. The bottom line is that employers who pay for equipment and software have the *legal* right to monitor their usage (see Figure 9.26).

So, is it *ethical* for employers to monitor their employees? Certainly, it seems fair that employers ensure they're not the victims of theft and that they're getting a fair day's work from their employees, just as employees have an obligation to provide a fair effort for a fair wage. The ethical issue is whether employees are adequately informed of monitoring policies. Employers have an ethical responsibility (and a legal one as well, depending on the jurisdiction) not to place monitoring devices in sensitive locations such as bathrooms and dressing areas. However, in many states, the employer does not legally need to inform employees in advance that they're being monitored. Conscientious employers include monitoring disclosures in published employee policies to avoid confusion and conflict.

The bottom line? Because employers may have a legal right to monitor you in the workplace, operate under the assumption that everything you do on your work computer is subject to scrutiny and behave accordingly. Do your online shopping at home!

BIG BROTHER IS WATCHING YOU

FIGURE 9.26 George Orwell was right—at least when you're at work! It's legal for employers to monitor your computer usage. *(RedDaxLuma/Shutterstock)*

keeping your
DATA SAFE

People are often too trusting or just plain careless when it comes to protecting private information about themselves or their digital data. In this section, we discuss ways to keep your data safe from damage, either accidental or intentional, and to keep unscrupulous individuals from tricking you into revealing sensitive information.

Protecting Your Personal Information

If a complete stranger walked up to you on the street and asked you for your address and phone number, would you give it to him or her? Of course you wouldn't! But many people are much less careful when it comes to sharing sensitive information online. And often people inadvertently share information that they really only intended to share with their friends. With cybercrimes like identify theft rampant, you need to take steps to protect your personal information.

What information should I never share on websites? A good rule of thumb is to reveal as little information as possible, especially if the information would be available to everyone. Figure 9.27 gives you some good guidelines.

Your Social Security number, phone number, date of birth, and street address are four key pieces of information that identity thieves need to steal an identity. This information should never be shared in a public area on any website.

How can I tell who can see my information on a social network? Social networking sites like Facebook make privacy settings available in your profile settings. If you've never changed your default privacy settings in Facebook,

you're probably sharing information more widely than you should.

How can I protect my information on Facebook? To begin, you need to change your privacy settings in your profile from some of the default options. In general, it's a bad idea to make personal information available to the public, although this is a default setting for some items in Facebook (see Figure 9.28). It's a good idea to set most of the options in your profile's Basic Information section to Friends or to Only Me because, presumably, these are personal details you should wish to share only with friends.

In the Contact Information section, restricting this information only to friends or to yourself is imperative. You don't want scammers contacting you via e-mail or snail mail and trying to trick you into revealing sensitive information.

Backing Up Your Data

How might I damage the data on my computer? The data on your computer faces three major threats:

1. Unauthorized access
2. Tampering
3. Destruction

As noted earlier, a hacker can gain access to your computer and steal or alter your data. However, a more likely scenario is that you'll lose your data unintentionally. You may accidentally delete files. You may drop your laptop on the ground, causing the hard drive to break and resulting in complete data loss. A virus from an e-mail attachment you opened

FIGURE 9.27

(Mograph/Fotolia; Kevin Largent/Fotolia)

Internet Information-Sharing Precautions

Information Identity Thieves Crave

STOP

- Social Security Number
- Full Date of Birth
- Phone Number
- Street Address

Never make this information visible on websites!

Other Sensitive Information

CAUTION

- Full Legal Name
- E-mail Address
- Zip Code
- Gender
- School or Workplace

Only reveal this information to people you know—don't make it visible to everyone!

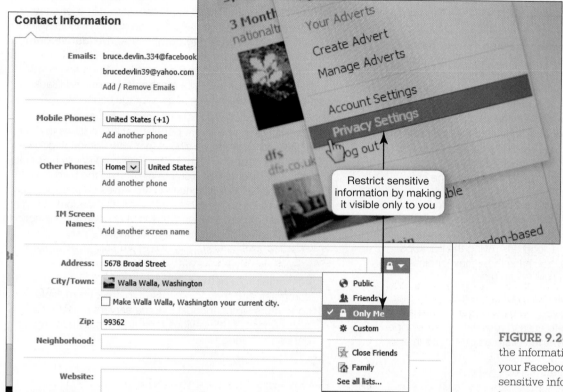

FIGURE 9.28 You should review the information privacy settings in your Facebook profile to ensure your sensitive information can only be seen by you. (© David Lee / Alamy)

may destroy your original file. Your house may catch fire and destroy your computer. Because many of these possibilities are beyond your control, you should have a strategy for backing up your files (see Figure 9.29). **Backups** are copies of files that you can use to replace the originals if they're lost or damaged.

What types of files do I need to back up? Two types of files need backups:

1. **Program files** include files used to install software, usually found on DVDs or downloaded from the Internet. As long as you have the DVDs in a safe place, you shouldn't need to back up these program files. If you've downloaded a program file from the Internet, however, you should make a copy of the program installation files on a removable storage device as a backup.
2. **Data files** include files you've created or purchased, such as research papers, spreadsheets, music and photo files, contact lists, address books, e-mail archives, and your Favorites list from your browser.

What types of backups can I perform? There are two main options for backing up files:

1. An **incremental backup** (or **partial backup**) involves backing up only files that have changed or have been created since the last backup was performed. Using backup

FIGURE 9.29

An Effective Backup Strategy

Files to Back Up

- **Program files:** Installation files for productivity software (i.e., Microsoft Office)
- **Data files:** Files you create (term papers, spreadsheets, etc.)

Types of Backups

- **Incremental (partial):** Only backs up files that have changed
- **Image (system):** Snapshot of your entire computer, including system software

Where to Store Backup Files

- Online (in the cloud)
- External hard drives
- Network-attached storage devices or home servers

software that has an option for incremental backups will save time because backing up files that haven't changed is redundant.

2. An **image backup** (or **system backup**) means that all system, application, and data files are backed up, not just the files that changed. Although incremental backups are more efficient, an image backup ensures you capture changes to application files, such as automatic software updates, that an incremental backup might not capture. The idea of imaging is to make an exact copy of the setup of your computer so that in the event of a total hard drive failure you could copy the image to a new hard drive and have your computer configured exactly the way it was before the crash.

Where should I store my backups? To be truly secure, backups must be stored away from where your computer is located and should be stored in at least two different places. You wouldn't want a fire or a flood destroying the backups along with the original data. You have three main choices for where to back up your files (see Figure 9.30):

1. *Online (in the cloud):* The beauty of online storage is that you don't need to be at your home computer or lug around your external hard drive to access your data. More importantly, because the information is stored online, it's in a

secure, remote location, so data is much less vulnerable to the disasters that could harm data stored in your computer or external hard drive. Free storage options include Microsoft OneDrive (**onedrive.com**) and ADrive (**adrive.com**). However, image backups probably won't fit within the storage limits offered by free providers. For a fee, companies such as Carbonite (**carbonite.com**) and IBackup (**ibackup.com**) provide larger storage capacity.

2. *External hard drives:* External hard drives, or even large-capacity flash drives, are popular backup options that are usually connected to a single computer. Although convenient and inexpensive, using external hard drives for backups still presents the dilemma of keeping the hard drive in a safe location. Also, external hard drives can fail, possibly leading to loss of your backed-up data. Therefore, using an external hard drive for backups is best done in conjunction with an online backup strategy for added safety.

3. *Network-attached storage (NAS) devices and home servers:* NAS devices are essentially large hard drives connected to a network of computers instead of one computer, and they can be used to back up multiple computers simultaneously. Home servers also act as high-capacity NAS devices for automatically backing up data and sharing files.

FIGURE 9.30

A Comparison of Typical Data Backup Locations

BACKUP LOCATION	PROS	CONS
Online (in the Cloud)	• Files stored at a secure, remote location • Files/backups accessible anywhere through a browser	• Most free storage sites don't provide enough space for image backups
External Hard Drive	• Inexpensive, one-time cost • Fast backups with USB 3.0 devices connected directly to your computer	• Could be destroyed in one event (fire/flood) with your computer • Can be stolen • Slightly more difficult to back up multiple computers with one device
Network-Attached Storage (NAS) Device and Home Server	• Makes backups much easier for multiple computing devices	• More expensive than a stand-alone external hard drive • Could be destroyed in one event (fire/flood) with your computer • Can be stolen

(mipan/Fotolia; © Prapass Wannapinij/Fotolia; © darkdesigns/Fotolia)

How often should I back up my data files? You should back up your data files every time you make changes to them, which can be difficult to remember to do. Fortunately, most backup software can be configured to do backups automatically so you don't forget to perform them. For example, with the Windows 8 File History utility, you can have Windows automatically save your data files from your libraries, desktop, contacts, and favorites to an external hard drive or NAS device. The default setting for File History saves files you changed every hour to the backup location you specify. File History even keeps previous versions of the file on the backup drive so you can revert to a previous version of the file if you need to do so.

To set up File History, you first need to connect an external hard drive to your computer or a NAS device to your network. You can then access File History through the Control Panel (in the System and Security group) and set it up (see Figure 9.31). Once configured, your data files will be backed up as often as you indicate. You can also restore files that you've backed up from the File History utility.

How often should I create an image backup? Because your program and OS files don't change as often as your data files, you can perform image backups on a less frequent basis. You might consider scheduling an image backup of your entire system on a weekly basis, but you should definitely perform one after installing new software.

How do I perform an image backup? Windows 8 includes the System Image Backup utility, which provides a quick and easy way to perform image backups. You can access this utility from the System Image Backup link on the File History screen (see Figure 9.31). Before starting this utility, make sure your external hard drive or NAS device is connected to your computer or network and is powered on. To set it up, follow these steps:

1. The first screen displayed (see Figure 9.32a) shows a list of available backup devices. Select a device (usually an external hard drive), and click Next to proceed.

FIGURE 9.31 You can use the Windows 8 File History utility to back up files and restore files from a previous backup.
>*Access the Control Panel, select* **System and Security**, *and then click the* **File History** *link.*

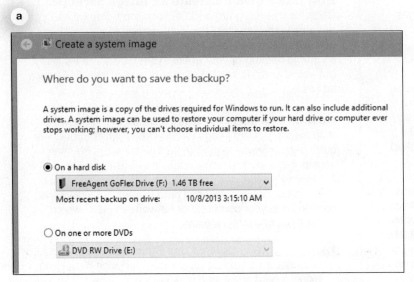

a

Create a system image

Where do you want to save the backup?

A system image is a copy of the drives required for Windows to run. It can also include additional drives. A system image can be used to restore your computer if your hard drive or computer ever stops working; however, you can't choose individual items to restore.

● On a hard disk

🖴 FreeAgent GoFlex Drive (F:) 1.46 TB free

Most recent backup on drive: 10/8/2013 3:15:10 AM

○ On one or more DVDs

💿 DVD RW Drive (E:)

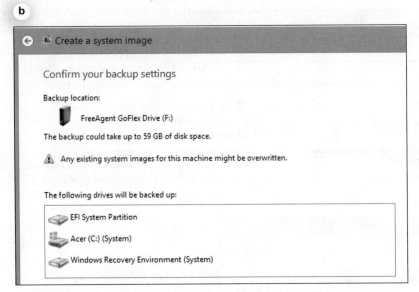

b

Create a system image

Confirm your backup settings

Backup location:

🖴   FreeAgent GoFlex Drive (F:)

The backup could take up to 59 GB of disk space.

⚠ Any existing system images for this machine might be overwritten.

The following drives will be backed up:

🖴 EFI System Partition

🖴 Acer (C:) (System)

🖴 Windows Recovery Environment (System)

FIGURE 9.32 The System Image Backup utility allows you to perform an image backup. (a) Select your backup destination. (b) Review options and start the backup.

2. You can review your settings on the following screen (see Figure 9.32b). Windows decides what to include in your system image backup: all data files and system files on all partitions on your hard drive. When you click the Start Backup button, your system image backup is created on the drive you selected.

From the File History screen, you can access advanced recovery tools (such as creating a system repair backup and System Restore) by clicking the Recovery link. A system repair backup is a copy of files that you can use to boot your computer in case of a serious Windows error.

What about backing up Apple computers? For OS X users, backups are very easy to configure. The Time Machine feature in OS X detects when an external hard drive is connected to the computer or a NAS device is connected to your network. You're then asked if you want this to be your backup drive. If you answer yes, all of your files (including OS files) are automatically backed up to the external drive or NAS device.

Should I back up my files that are stored on my school's network? Most likely, if you're allowed to store files on your school's network, these files are backed up regularly. You should check with your school's network administrators to determine how often they're backed up and how you would request that files be restored from the backup if they're damaged or deleted. But don't rely on these network backups to bail you out if your data files are lost or damaged. It may take days for the network administrators to restore your files. It's better to keep backups of your data files yourself, especially homework and project files, so that you can immediately restore them. ■

 SOUND BYTE
Managing Computer Security with Windows Tools

In this Sound Byte, you'll learn how to monitor and control your computer security using features built into the Windows OS.

social ENGINEERING

Social engineering is any technique that uses social skills to generate human interaction that entices individuals to reveal sensitive information. Social engineering often doesn't involve the use of a computer or face-to-face interaction. For example, telephone scams are a common form of social engineering because it is often easier to manipulate someone when you don't have to look at them.

How does social engineering work? Most social engineering schemes use a pretext to lure their victims. **Pretexting** involves creating a scenario that sounds legitimate enough that someone will trust you. For example, you might receive a phone call during which the caller says he is from your bank and that someone tried to use your account without authorization. The caller then tells you he needs to confirm a few

personal details such as your birth date, Social Security number, bank account number, and whatever other information he can get out of you. The information he obtains can then be used to empty your bank account or commit some other form of fraud. The most common form of pretexting in cyberspace is *phishing*.

Phishing and Pharming

How are phishing schemes conducted? Phishing (pronounced "fishing") lures Internet users to reveal personal information such as credit card numbers, Social Security numbers, or other sensitive information that could lead to identity theft. The scammers send e-mail messages that look like they're from a legitimate business such as an online bank. The e-mail usually states that the recipient needs to update or confirm his or her account information. When the recipient clicks on the provided link, he or she goes to a website. The site looks like a legitimate site but is really a fraudulent copy that the scammer has created. Once the e-mail recipient enters his or her personal information, the scammers capture it and can begin using it.

Is pharming a type of phishing scam? Pharming is much more insidious than phishing. Phishing requires a positive action by the person being scammed, such as going to a website mentioned in an e-mail and typing in personal information. **Pharming** occurs when malicious code is planted on your computer, either by viruses or by your visiting malicious websites, which then alters your browser's ability to find web addresses. Users are directed to bogus websites even when they enter the correct address of the real website. You end up at a fake website that looks legitimate but is expressly set up for the purpose of gathering information.

How can I avoid being caught by phishing and pharming scams? Follow these guidelines to avoid falling prey to such schemes:

- Never reply directly to any e-mail asking you for personal information.
- Don't click on a link in an e-mail to go to a website. Instead, type the website address in the browser.
- Check with the company asking for the information and only give the information if you're certain it's needed.
- Never give personal information over the Internet unless you know the site is secure. Look for the closed padlock, *https*, or a certification seal such as Norton Secured to help reassure you that the site is secure.
- Use phishing filters. The latest versions of Firefox, Chrome, and Internet Explorer have phishing filters built in, so each time you access a website, the phishing filter checks for the site's legitimacy and warns you of possible web forgeries.
- Use Internet security software on your computer that's constantly being updated.

BITS&BYTES

I Received a Data Breach Letter ... Now What?

Data breaches are becoming more common, and companies that are the subject of data breaches now routinely notify customers of data breaches…usually by physical letter, but sometimes via e-mail. Here's what you should do if you receive such a letter:

1. Take it seriously. 22.5% of recipients of these letters become the victim of identity theft per a study by Javelin Strategy and Research.

2. Contact one of the three big credit bureaus (Equifax, Experian, and TransUnion) and have a fraud alert put on your credit report. This alerts people accessing your credit report that your identity information has been stolen and that the person who is applying for credit in your name might be an imposter.

3. For even better security, contact all three credit bureaus and have a credit freeze put on your credit reports. This prevents anyone (even you) from getting credit in your name. You can always unfreeze your accounts later if you need to apply for credit yourself.

4. Review your credit reports regularly. You are entitled to one free credit report per year from each of the three big agencies. Go to **annualcreditreport.com** and request a report from one of the agencies. Repeat the process every 4 months from a different agency. Review the reports for any suspicious activity.

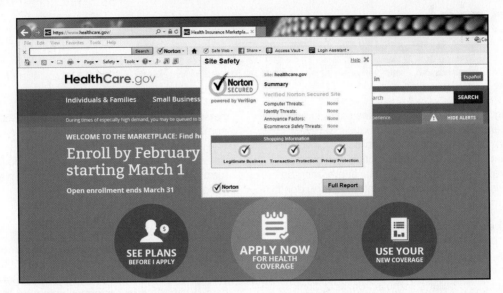

FIGURE 9.33 Not sure whether you're on the Healthcare.gov website or a cleverly disguised phishing site? Norton Site Safety reassures you that all is well. *(Courtesy of HealthCare.gov; Courtesy of the Symantec Corporation)*

Most Internet security packages can detect and prevent pharming attacks. The major Internet security packages—for example, McAfee and Norton (see Figure 9.33)—also offer phishing-protection tools. When you have the Norton Toolbar displayed in your browser, you're constantly informed about the legitimacy of the site you are visiting.

Scareware

What is scareware? Scareware is a type of malware that downloads onto your computer and tries to convince you that your computer is infected with a virus (see Figure 9.34) or other type of malware. Pop-ups, banners, or other annoying types of messages will flash on your screen saying frightening things like, "Your computer is infected with a virus . . . immediate removal is required." You're then directed to a website where you can buy fake removal or antivirus tools that provide little or no value. Panda Security estimates that scareware scams generate in excess of $34 million a month for cybercriminals. Some scareware even goes so far as to encrypt your files and then demand that you pay to have them unencrypted, which is essentially extortion.

Scareware is a social engineering technique because it uses people's fear of computer viruses to convince them to part with their money. Scareware is often designed to be extremely difficult to remove from your computer and to interfere with the operation of legitimate security software. Scareware is usually downloaded onto your computer from infected websites or Trojan horse files.

How do I protect myself against scareware? Most Internet security suites, antivirus, and anti-malware software packages now detect and prevent the installation of scareware. But make sure you never click on website banners or pop-up boxes that say "Your computer might be infected, click here to scan your files" because these are often the starting points for installing malicious scareware files on your computer. ■

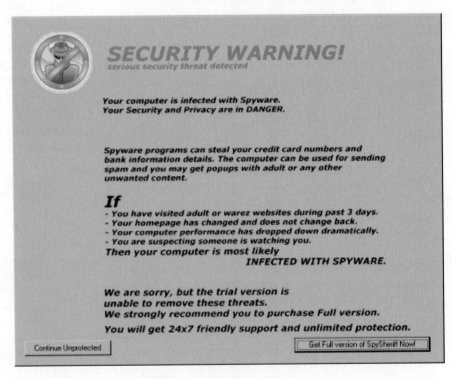

FIGURE 9.34 Preying on people's fears, scareware attempts to convince you that your computer is infected with a virus and you need to purchase a "solution." *(Courtesy of McAfee, Inc.)*

Most people have vast amounts of personal data residing in the databases of the various companies with which they conduct business. Amazon.com has your credit card and address information. Your bank has your Social Security number, birth date, and financial records. Your local supermarket probably has your e-mail address from when you joined its loyalty club to receive grocery discounts. All this data in various places puts you at risk when companies responsible for keeping your data confidential suffer a data breach.

A **data breach** occurs when sensitive or confidential information is copied, transmitted, or viewed by an individual who isn't authorized to handle the data. Data breaches can be intentional or unintentional. Intentional data breaches occur when hackers break into digital systems to steal sensitive data. Unintentional data breaches occur when companies controlling data inadvertently allow it to be seen by unauthorized parties, usually due to some breakdown in security procedures or precautions.

Unfortunately, data breaches appear to be quite common, as there always seems to be another one in the news. The Identity Theft Resource Center, a nonprofit organization that monitors data breaches, reported 533 data breaches for U.S. companies in the first eight months of 2014. At least 18.7 million records were exposed, although this data is not available for all the breaches. These breaches pose serious risks to the individuals whose data has been compromised, even if financial data is not involved. The data thieves now have the basis with which to launch targeted social engineering attacks even if they just have contact information, such as e-mail addresses.

With regular phishing techniques, cybercriminals just send out e-mails to a wide list of e-mail addresses, whether they have a relationship with the company or not. For example, a criminal might send out a general phishing e-mail claiming that a person's Citibank checking account had been breached. People who receive this e-mail that don't have any accounts at Citibank should immediately realize this is a phishing attack and ignore the instructions to divulge sensitive data.

But when cybercriminals obtain data on individuals that includes information about which companies those individuals have a relationship with, they can engage in much more targeted attacks known as **spear phishing**. Spear phishing e-mails are sent to people known to be customers of a company and have a much greater chance of successfully getting individuals to reveal sensitive data. If cybercriminals obtain a list of e-mail addresses of customers from Barclays Bank, for example, they can ensure that the spear phishing e-mails purport to come from Barclays and will include the customer's full name. This type of attack is much more likely to succeed in fooling people than just random e-mails sent out to thousands of people who might not have a relationship with the company mentioned in the phishing letter.

So how can you protect yourself after a data breach? You need to be extra suspicious of any e-mail correspondence from companies involved in the data breach. Companies usually never contact you by e-mail or phone asking you to reveal sensitive information or reactivate your online account by entering confidential information. Usually, these requests come via regular snail mail.

So, if you receive any e-mails or phone calls from companies you deal with purporting to have problems with your accounts, your best course of action is to delete the e-mail or hang up the phone. Then contact the company that supposedly has the problem by a phone number that you look up yourself either in legitimate correspondence from the company (say, the toll-free number on your credit card statement) or in the phone book. The representatives from your company can quickly tell if a real problem exists or if you were about to be the victim of a scam.

protecting your physical
COMPUTING ASSETS

Your computer, tablet, and phone aren't useful to you if they're damaged. Therefore, it's essential to select and ensure a safe environment for these devices. This includes protecting them from environmental factors, power surges, power outages, and theft.

Environmental Factors

Why is the environment critical to the operation of my computer equipment? Computers are delicate devices and can be damaged by the adverse effects of abuse or a poor environment. Sudden movements, such as a fall, can damage your computing device's internal components. You should make sure that your computer sits on a flat, level surface, and if it's a laptop or a tablet, you should carry it in a protective case.

Electronic components don't like excessive heat or excessive cold. Don't leave computing devices and phones in a car during especially hot or cold weather because components can be damaged by extreme temperatures. Unfortunately, computers generate a lot of heat, which is why they have fans to cool their internal components. Chill mats that contain cooling fans and sit underneath laptop computers are useful accessories for dissipating heat. Make sure that you place your desktop computer where the fan's intake vents, usually found on the rear of the system unit, are unblocked so air can flow inside.

Naturally, a fan drawing air into a computer also draws in dust and other particles, which can wreak havoc on your system. Therefore, keep the room in which your computer is located as clean as possible. Finally, because food crumbs and liquid can damage keyboards and other computer

components, consume food and beverages away from your computer.

Power Surges

What is a power surge? Power surges occur when electrical current is supplied in excess of normal voltage. Old or faulty wiring, downed power lines, malfunctions at electric company substations, and lightning strikes can all cause power surges. A **surge protector** is a device that protects your computer against power surges (see Figure 9.35).

Note that you should replace your surge protectors every two to three years. Also, after a major surge, the surge protector will no longer function and must be replaced. And it's wise to buy a surge protector that includes indicator lights, which illuminate when the surge protector is no longer functioning properly. Don't be fooled by old surge protectors—although they can still function as multiple-outlet power strips, they deliver power to your equipment without protecting it.

Besides my computer, what other devices need to be connected to a surge protector? All electronic devices in the home that have solid-state components, such as TVs, stereos, printers, and smartphones (when charging), should be connected to a surge protector. However, it can be inconvenient to use individual surge protectors on everything. A more practical method is to install a **whole-house surge protector** (see Figure 9.36). Whole-house surge protectors function like other surge protectors, but they protect *all* electrical devices in the house. Typically, you'll need an electrician to install a whole-house surge protector, which will cost $300 to $500 (installed).

Is my equipment 100% safe when plugged into a surge protector? Lightning strikes can generate such high voltages that they can overwhelm a surge

FIGURE 9.35 Surge protectors such as this one are critical for protecting your electronic devices.
(Aberenyi/Fotolia)

 SOUND BYTE
Surge Protectors

In this Sound Byte, you'll learn about the major features of surge protectors and how they work. You'll also learn about the key factors you need to consider before buying a surge protector, and you'll see how easy it is to install one.

Surge protector

FIGURE 9.36 A whole-house surge protector is usually installed at the breaker panel or near the electric meter.

protector. As tedious as it sounds, unplugging electronic devices during an electrical storm is the only way to achieve absolute protection.

Deterring Theft

What do I need to worry about if my computing device is stolen? Because they're portable, laptops, tablets, and phones are easy targets for thieves. You have four main security concerns with mobile devices:

1. Keeping them from being stolen
2. Keeping data secure in case they are stolen
3. Finding a device if it is stolen
4. Remotely recovering and wiping data off a stolen device

Keep Them Safe: Alarms

What type of alarm can I install on my mobile device? Motion alarm software is a good, inexpensive theft deterrent. Free software such as LAlarm (**lalarm.com**) is effective for laptops. Apps such as Motion Alarm and Alarmomatic help secure your iPad or iPhone. Alarm software either detects motion, like your device being picked up, or sounds near your device and then sets off an ear-piercing alarm until you enter the disable code. Thieves normally don't like it when attention is drawn to their activities, so alarms can be a very effective theft deterrent.

Keeping Mobile Device Data Secure

How can I secure the data on my mobile devices? Encrypting the data on your mobile device can make it extremely difficult, if not impossible, for thieves to obtain sensitive data from your stolen equipment. *Encryption* involves transforming your data using an algorithm that can only be unlocked by a secure code (or key). Encrypted data is impossible to read unless it's decrypted, which requires a secure password, hopefully known only to you.

Safe is an app that provides 256-bit encryption, which is very hard to crack, for data and images on your iPhone and iPad. If your password is not entered, no one can access the data and images on your iPhone or iPad. Mobile StrongBox is a similar app for Android devices. SensiGuard and SafeHouse are available for laptop computers to provide encryption for files or even entire hard drives.

Software Alerts and Data Wipes

How can my computer help me recover it when it is stolen? You've probably heard of LoJack, the theft-tracking device used in cars. Similar systems now exist for computers. Tracking software such as LoJack for Laptops (**absolute.com**), PC PhoneHome, and Mac PhoneHome (**brigadoonsoftware.com**) enables your computer to alert authorities to the computer's location if it is stolen. A similar tracking app for Android and iOS devices is iHound.

To enable your mobile device to help with its own recovery, you install the tracking software on your device. The software contacts a server at the software manufacturer's website each time the device connects to the Internet. If your device is stolen, you notify the software manufacturer. The software manufacturer instructs your device to transmit tracking information, such as an IP address, WiFi hotspot, or cell tower location, that will assist authorities in locating and retrieving the mobile device.

What if the thieves find the tracking software and delete it? The files and directories holding the software aren't visible to thieves looking for such software, so they probably won't know the software is there. Furthermore, the tracking software is written in such a way that even if the thieves tried to reformat the hard drive, it would detect the reformat and hide the software code in a safe place in memory or on the hard drive. This works because some sectors of a hard drive are not rewritten during most reformatting. That way, the tracking software can reinstall itself after the reformatting is complete.

What if my device can't be recovered by the authorities? In the event that your laptop can't be recovered, software packages are available that provide for remote recovery and deletion of files. LoJack for Laptops has these features and allows you to lock your device to keep the thieves from accessing it or to remotely wipe its contents by deleting all your data from your laptop.

FIGURE 9.37 The Find My iPhone app can really help if your iOS device goes astray. You can play a sound to help you find it (if it's misplaced where you are), display a message on the device (Lost Mode), or erase all data on the device. *(LearningStockImages/Alamy)*

FIGURE 9.38

Computer Security Checklist

Virus and Spyware Protection

- Is antivirus and anti-spyware software installed on all your devices?
- Is the antivirus and anti-spyware software configured to update itself automatically and regularly?
- Is the software set to scan your device on a regular basis (at least weekly) for viruses and spyware?

Firewall

- Do all your computers and tablets have firewall software installed and activated before connecting to the Internet?
- Is your router also able to function as a hardware firewall?
- Have you tested your firewall security by using the free software available at grc.com?

Software Updates

- Have you configured your operating systems (Windows, OS X, iOS) to install new software patches and updates automatically?
- Is other software installed on your device, such as Microsoft Office or productivity apps, configured for automatic updates?
- Is the web browser you're using the latest version?

Protecting Your Devices

- Are all computing devices protected from electrical surges?
- Do your mobile devices have alarms or tracking software installed on them?

For all iOS devices, Apple offers the Find My iPhone service, which is now part of iCloud. Enabling this service on your device provides you with numerous tools that can assist you in recovering and protecting your mobile devices. Did you forget where you left your iPad? Just sign in with your Apple ID at the iCloud website to see a map showing the location of your iPad (see Figure 9.37). You can send a message to your device, remotely password lock the device, or wipe all data from the device to completely protect your privacy. For Android devices, Where is My Droid? offers similar features, such as texting your device and having it reply with its location. You can even capture images with the front and rear cameras to see what your device is looking at (such as the thief)!

How can I ensure that I've covered all aspects of protecting my digital devices? Figure 9.38 provides a guide to ensure you haven't missed critical aspects of security. If you've addressed all of these issues, you can feel reasonably confident that your data and devices are secure. ■

Before moving on to the Chapter Review:
- **Watch Replay Video 9.2** ▶ .
- **Then check your understanding of what you've learned so far.**

check your understanding // review & practice

For a quick review to see what you've learned so far, answer the following questions. Visit **pearsonhighered.com /techinaction** to check your answers.

multiple choice

1. A technique that uses illegally obtained information about individuals to perform targeted attacks in the hopes of getting them to reveal sensitive information is known as
   a. spear phishing.
   b. pretexting.
   c. keystroke logging.
   d. logic bombing.

2. A backup of only the files on your computing device that have been created (or changed) since the last backup is known as a(n)
   a. total backup.
   b. incremental backup.
   c. image backup.
   d. global backup.

3. Software that pretends your computer is infected with a virus to entice you into spending money on a solution is known as
   a. scareware.
   c. adware.
   b. spyware.
   d. trackingware.

4. Small text files that some websites automatically store on your computer's hard drive are known as
   a. greyware.
   c. adware.
   b. spam.
   d. cookies.

5. A social engineering technique in which you send people an e-mail for the purpose of inducing them into revealing sensitive information is known as
   a. spyware.
   c. pharming.
   b. phishing.
   d. key logging.

To take an autograded version of this review, please go to the companion website at **pearsonhighered.com/techinaction**, or go your MyITLab course.

Continue

9 Chapter Review

summary //

Cybercrime and Identity Theft

1. What is cybercrime, and who perpetrates it?

- Cybercrime is any type of crime perpetrated via a computer or a website.
- Major types of cybercrime are identity theft, credit card fraud, computer viruses, illegal access of computer systems, and auction fraud.
- Cybercriminals use computers, the Internet, and computer networks to commit their crimes.

Protecting Yourself from Computer Viruses

2. What are the types of viruses from which I need to protect my computer?

- A computer virus is a program that attaches itself to another program and attempts to spread to other computers when files are exchanged.
- Computer viruses can be grouped into six categories: (1) boot-sector viruses, (2) logic bombs and time bombs, (3) worms, (4) scripts and macro viruses, (5) e-mail viruses, and (6) encryption viruses. Once run, viruses perform their malicious duties in the background and are often invisible to the user.

3. What can I do to protect my computer from viruses?

- The best defense against viruses is to install antivirus software. You should update the software on a regular basis and configure it to examine all e-mail attachments for viruses. You should periodically run a complete virus scan on your computer to ensure that no viruses have made it onto your hard drive.

Protecting Digital Assets from Hackers

4. How can hackers attack my computing devices, and what harm can they cause?

- A hacker is defined as anyone who breaks into a computer system unlawfully. Hackers can use software to break into almost any computer connected to the Internet, unless proper precautions are taken.

- Once hackers gain access to a computer, they can potentially (1) steal personal or other important information, (2) damage and destroy data, or (3) use the computer to attack other computers.

5. What is a firewall, and how does it keep my computer safe from hackers?

- Firewalls are software programs or hardware devices designed to keep computers safe from hackers. By using a personal firewall, you can close to invaders open logical ports and potentially make your computer invisible to other computers on the Internet.

6. How do I create secure passwords and manage all of my passwords?

- Secure passwords contain a mixture of upper- and lowercase letters, numbers, and symbols and are at least 14 characters long. Passwords should not contain words that are in the dictionary or easy-to-guess personal information, like your pet's name.
- Online password checkers can be used to evaluate the strength of your passwords.
- Utilities built into web browsers and Internet security software can be used to manage your passwords and alleviate the need to remember numerous complex passwords.

7. How can I surf the Internet anonymously and use biometric authentication devices to protect my data?

- The current versions of popular browsers include tools, such as Google Chrome's Incognito feature, that hide your surfing activities by not recording websites that you visit or files that you download in your browser's history files.
- Biometric authentication devices use a physical attribute that is not easily duplicated to control access to data files or computing devices. Some laptops and smartphones today feature fingerprint readers and facial-recognition software to control access.

Managing Online Annoyances

8. How do I manage online annoyances such as spyware and spam?

- The web is filled with annoyances such as spam, pop-ups, cookies, spyware, and scams such as phishing that make surfing the web frustrating and sometimes dangerous.
- Installing anti-malware software tools helps to prevent, detect, and/or reduce spam, adware, and spyware.

Keeping Your Data Safe

9. What data do I need to back up, and what are the best methods for doing so?

- Data files created by you, such as Word and Excel files, or purchased by you, such as music files, need to be backed up in case they're inadvertently deleted or damaged. Application software, such as Microsoft Office, may need to be reinstalled if files are damaged, so backups, such as the DVDs the application came on, must be maintained.
- An incremental backup means only files that have been changed or created since the last backup was performed will be backed up. Image backups copy all system, application, and data files regardless of whether they changed since the last backup.
- Websites such as ADrive and OneDrive are great for backing up individual files. External hard drives are popular choices for holding image backups of your entire system, as are online (cloud) storage sites. Windows and OS X contain solid backup tools that help automate backup tasks.

10. What is social engineering, and how do I avoid falling prey to phishing?

- Social engineering schemes use human interaction, deception, and trickery to fool people into revealing sensitive information such as credit card numbers and passwords.

- Phishing schemes usually involve e-mails that direct the unwary to a website that appears to be legitimate, such as a bank site, but that is specifically designed to capture personal information for committing fraud. To avoid phishing scams, you should never reply directly to any e-mail asking you for personal information and never click on a link in an e-mail to go to a website.
- Don't fall for scareware scams that attempt to frighten you by pretending there is something wrong with your computer.

Protecting Your Physical Computing Assets

11. How do I protect my physical computing assets from environmental hazards, power surges, and theft?

- Computing devices should be kept in clean environments free from dust and other particulates and should not be exposed to extreme temperatures (either hot or cold).
- You should protect all electronic devices from power surges by hooking them up through surge protectors, which will protect them from most electrical surges that could damage the devices.
- Mobile devices can be protected from theft by installing software that will (1) set off an alarm if the computer is moved; (2) help recover the computer, if stolen, by reporting the computer's whereabouts when it is connected to the Internet; and/or (3) allow you to lock or wipe the contents of the digital device remotely.

> Be sure to check out the companion website for additional materials to help you review and learn, including a Tech Bytes Weekly newsletter—**pearsonhighered.com/techinaction**. And don't forget the Replay Videos ⊙ .

key terms//

chapter quiz// assessment

For a quick review to see what you've learned, answer the following questions. Submit the quiz as requested by your instructor. If you are using MyITLab, the quiz is also available there.

multiple choice

1. Which of the following is NOT a major type of cybercrime reported to the IC3?

   a. FBI-related scams

   b. identity theft

   c. malware fraud

   d. advance fee fraud

2. Viruses that compress files and then demand money to restore them are known as

   a. boot-sector viruses.

   b. script viruses.

   c. polymorphic viruses.

   d. encryption viruses.

3. Software designed to close logical ports in your computer is known as a(n)

   a. firewall.

   b. packet filter.

   c. anti-malware blocker.

   d. network address translator.

4. Which tool do hackers use to gain access to and take control of your computer?

   a. stealth viruses

   b. backdoor programs

   c. scareware

   d. phishing software

5. A computer that a hacker has gained control of in order to launch DoS attacks is known as a _____ computer.

   a. rootkit

   b. compromised

   c. zombie

   d. breached

6. A backup of all the files on your computer, which essentially creates a "snapshot" of what your computer looks like at that point in time, is known as a(n)

   a. total backup.

   b. incremental backup.

   c. image backup.

   d. modification backup.

true–false

_____ **1.** Password strength is only partially determined by the length of the password.

_____ **2.** One of the best and simplest ways to keep hackers out of your computer is to use a firewall.

_____ **3.** Sending e-mails to lure people into revealing personal information is a technique known as pharming.

_____ **4.** Encrypting data is not an appropriate measure for protecting mobile devices such as tablets.

critical thinking

1. Protecting Your Data from Data Breaches

You most likely have provided personal information to many websites and companies. What information have you provided to companies that you wish you had never disclosed? What types of information have companies asked you to provide that you believe was unnecessary? List specific companies and examples of the extraneous information.

2. Phishing

Have you or anyone you know ever been a victim of a phishing scam? What sorts of scams have you heard about?

Protecting a Network

Problem

Along with easy access to the web comes the danger of theft of digital assets.

Task

A school alumnus is in charge of the county government computer department. The network contains computers running Windows 8, Windows 7, and OS X. He asked your instructor for help in ensuring that his computers and network are protected from viruses, malware, and hackers. He is hoping that there may be free software available that can protect his employees' computers.

Process

1. Break the class into three teams. Each team will be responsible for investigating one of the following issues:

   a. **Antivirus software:** Research alternatives that protect computers from viruses. Find three alternatives and support your recommendations with reviews that evaluate free packages.

   b. **Anti-malware software:** Research three free malware alternatives and determine whether the software can be updated automatically. You may want to recommend that the county purchase software to ensure that a minimum of employee intervention is needed to keep it up to date.

   c. **Firewalls:** Determine if the firewall software provided with Windows 8, Windows 7, and OS X is reliable. If it is, prepare documentation (for all three OSs) for county employees to determine if their firewalls are properly configured. If additional firewall software is needed, research free firewall software and locate three options that can be deployed by the county.

2. Present your findings to the class and provide your instructor with a report suitable for eventual presentation to the manager of the county office network.

Conclusion

With the proliferation of viruses and malware, it is essential to protect computers and networks. Free alternatives might work, but you should research the best protection solution for your situation.

Content Control: Censorship to Protect Children

In this exercise, you'll research and then role-play a complicated ethical situation. The role you play might or might not match your own personal beliefs; in either case, your research and use of logic will enable you to represent the view assigned. An arbitrator will watch and comment on both sides of the arguments, and together, the team will agree on an ethical solution.

Problem

Many parents use web-filtering software (content-control software) to protect their children from objectionable Internet content. In 2000, the U.S. federal government began requiring libraries to use content-control software as a condition to receiving federal funds under the provisions of the Children's Internet Protection Act (CIPA). Some states, such as Virgina, have passed laws requiring libraries to install filtering software even if they did not receive federal funds. Upon installation of the software, it's up to the library administrators to decide what content is restricted. Therefore, content restriction can vary widely from library to library.

Research Areas to Consider

- U.S. Supreme Court case *United States v. American Library Association* (2003)
- Content-control software and First Amendment rights
- Violation of children's free speech rights
- Children's Internet Protection Act (CIPA)

Process

1. Divide the class into teams. Research the areas above and devise a scenario in which someone has complained about innocuous content that was blocked.

2. Team members should write a summary that provides background information for their character—for example, library patron, library administrator, or arbitrator—and that details their character's behaviors to set the stage for the role-playing event. Then, team members should create an outline to use during the role-playing event.

3. Team members should present their case to the class or submit a PowerPoint presentation for review by the class, along with the summary and resolution they developed.

Conclusion

As technology becomes ever more prevalent and integrated into our lives, more and more ethical dilemmas will present themselves. Being able to understand and evaluate both sides of the argument, while responding in a personally or socially ethical manner, will be an important skill.

Computer Security

You have been asked to prepare a report on computer security using Word 2013. You have written the majority of the report, but you have to make some final modifications and refinements such as adding the results of some research of good antivirus software, adding a cover page and generating a table of contents.

You will use the following skills as you complete this activity:	
• Create and Modify Tables	• Create and Update Table of Contents
• Insert Tab Stops	• Add Footnote
• Add Watermark	• Use Find and Replace
• Insert Cover Page	

Instructions:

1. Open the TIA_Ch9_Start file, and save as TIA_Ch9_LastFirst.

2. Find all instances of email and replace with e-mail.

3. Open the Navigation pane, find the first instance of malware. Place the cursor after the word *malware* (before the period) and insert the footnote: **Malware is defined as software that is intended to gain access to, or damage or disable computer systems, for the purposes of theft or fraud.** Close the Navigation pane.

4. In the section, Types of Viruses, highlight the six lines of text that outline the categories of computer viruses and variants. Add a right align tab stop at 1 ½" and a left align tab stop at 2".

5. Place cursor at the end of the paragraph in the Antivirus Software section. Press Enter, then insert a 3×4 table. Type **Product Name, Description/Review**, and **Cost** in the top three cells. Adjust the width of the Description/Review column to 3.5" and the width of the Cost column to 1". Add a row at the top of the table, merge the cells and type **Antivirus Software Reviews**, and Align Center the contents. Format the table with Grid Table 4 - Accent 1 style.

6. Go to www.pcmag.com/reviews/antivirus. Research four antivirus software programs and place the software name, review, and cost of the software in the respective columns in the table.

    a. **Hint:** You will need to add an additional line to the table.

7. Press CTRL+Home, then insert the Banded Cover Page. Type Computer Security for the title, and add your name as the Author, if necessary. Delete the Company Name and Company address placeholders.

8. Insert Page Numbers at the bottom of the page using the Plain Number 3 format. Make sure "Different First Page" is checked. Close Header and Footer.

9. On the second page of the document, place the cursor before the report title, Computer Security, add a Page break, then place the cursor at the top of the new blank page.

10. Insert a Table of Contents using the Contents format.

11. Scroll to page 5 of the document, select the Firewalls heading, and modify the Heading style to Heading 2, modify the Software Firewalls and Hardware Firewalls heading style to Heading 3.

12. Update the Table of Contents to reflect the changes in headings, making sure you update the entire table.

13. Remove the Draft Watermark from the first page of the report.

14. Save and submit for grading based on your instructor's directions.

Technology in Focus

Careers in IT

It's hard to imagine an occupation in which computers aren't used in some fashion. Even such previously low-tech industries as waste disposal and fast food use computers to manage inventories and order commodities. In this Technology in Focus feature, we explore various information technology (IT) career paths open to you.

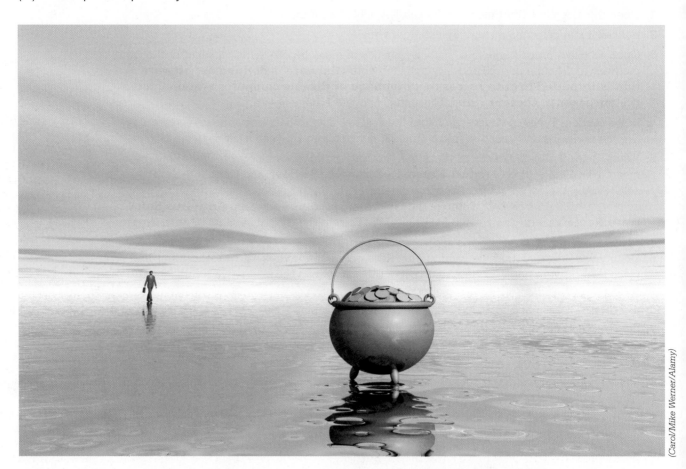

(Carol/Mike Werner/Alamy)

Rewards of Working in Information Technology

There are many great reasons to work in the exciting, ever-changing field of IT. In this section, we'll explore some reasons why IT fields are so attractive to graduates looking for entry-level positions.

IT Workers Are in Demand

If you're investigating a career with computers, the first question you may have is, "Will I be able to get a job?" Consider the following:

- According to projections by the U.S. Department of Labor's Bureau of Labor Statistics, computer-related jobs

FIGURE 1

High-Growth IT Jobs*

OCCUPATION	MEDIAN PAY ($)	10-YEAR GROWTH RATE (%)	TOTAL NEW JOBS
Software developers	93,350	22	222,600
Computer systems analysts	79,680	25	127,700
Computer support specialists	48,900	17	123,000
Network and computer systems administrators	72,560	12	42,900
Web developers	62,500	20	28,500
Computer programmers	74,280	8	28,400
Information security analysts	86,170	37	27,400
Computer network architects	91,000	15	20,900
Database administrators	77,080	15	17,900

*Excerpted from Occupational Outlook Handbook, 2014 Edition, Bureau of Labor Statistics

are expected to be among the fastest-growing occupations through 2022 (see Figure 1).

- In 2014, *US News and World Report* published a list of the best careers to consider based on employment opportunity, good salary, work–life balance, and job security. Computer systems analyst, software developer, and web developer were included among the top 10 careers. Three other IT careers—information security analyst, IT manager, and database administrator—were in the top 25.

- According to the National Association of Colleges and Employers (NACE) April 2014 Starting Salaries for New College Graduates Survey, the average starting salary for computer science majors is $61,741 and was the second highest average salary on the list, trailing only engineering majors.

The number of students pursuing computer science degrees also has been increasing over the past several years. Fields of specialization such as game development, information security, and mobile app development are very popular. Yet, shortages of computing professionals in the United States are still projected over the next 5 to 10 years. What does all this mean? In terms of job outlook, now is a perfect time to consider an IT career.

IT Jobs Pay Well

As you can see from Figure 1, median salaries in IT careers are robust. But what exactly affects your salary in an IT position? Your skill set and your experience level are obvious answers, but the size of an employer and its geographic location are also factors. Large companies tend to pay more, so if you're pursuing a high salary, set your sights on a large corporation. But remember that making a lot of money isn't everything— be sure to consider other quality-of-life issues such as job satisfaction. Of course, choosing a computer career isn't a guarantee you'll get a high-paying job. Just as in any other profession, you'll need appropriate training and on-the-job experience to earn a high salary.

So how much can you expect to start out earning? Although starting salaries for some IT positions (computer desktop support and helpdesk analysts) are in the modest range ($42,500 to $46,500), starting salaries for students with bachelor's degrees in IT are fairly robust. But IT salaries vary widely, depending on experience level, the geographic location of the job, and the size of the employer.

To obtain the most accurate information, you should research salaries yourself in the geographic area where you expect to work. **Salary.com** provides a free salary wizard to help you determine what IT professionals in your area are making compared with national averages. You can add information such as your degree and the size of the company to your search selection to fine-tune the figures further.

Figure 2 shows that for an entry-level programming position in Chicago, you could expect to earn a salary of between $47,434 and $74,879 with a bachelor's degree. Hundreds of IT job titles are listed in **Salary.com**, so you can tailor your search to the specific job, location, and industry in which you're interested.

IT Jobs Are Not Going "Offshore"

In the global economy in which we now operate, job outlook includes the risk of jobs being outsourced, possibly to other countries. **Outsourcing** is a process whereby a business hires a third-party firm to provide business services (such as customer-support call centers) that were previously handled by in-house employees. **Offshoring** occurs when the outsourcing firm is located (or uses employees) outside the United States.

India, China, and Romania and other former Eastern Bloc countries are major players in providing outsourcing services for U.S. companies. The big lure of outsourcing and offshoring is cost savings: Considering that the standard of living and salaries are much lower in many countries than they are in the United States, offshoring is an attractive option for many U.S. employers.

However, outsourcing and offshoring don't always deliver the cost savings that CEOs envision. Demand for personnel overseas has led to increased costs (primarily due to wage

FIGURE 2 The salary wizard at **Salary.com** is easy to tailor to your location. *(Courtesy of Kenexa)*

increases) for service providers in foreign markets. Furthermore, other, less-tangible factors can outweigh the cost savings from outsourcing. Communications problems can arise between internal and external employees, for example, and cultural differences between the home country and the country doing the offshoring can result in software code that needs extensive rework by in-house employees. Data also can be less secure in an external environment or during the transfer between the company and an external vendor. Although outsourcing and offshoring won't be going away, companies are approaching these staffing alternatives with more caution and are looking more to U.S. companies to provide resources.

So, many IT jobs are staying in the United States. According to *InformationWeek* magazine, most jobs in the following three categories (see Figure 3) will stay put:

1. *Customer interaction:* Jobs that require direct input from customers or that involve systems with which customers interface daily
2. *Enablers:* Jobs that involve getting key business projects accomplished, often requiring technical skills beyond the realm of IT and good people skills
3. *Infrastructure jobs:* Jobs that are fundamental to moving and storing the information that U.S.-based employees need to do their jobs

In addition, jobs that require specific knowledge of the U.S. marketplace and culture, such as social media managers, are also very likely not to be offshored.

Women Are in High Demand in IT Departments

Currently, women make up about 25% of the IT workforce (per the National Center for Women and Information Technology). This presents a huge opportunity for women who have IT skills, because many IT departments are actively seeking to diversify their workforces. In addition, although a salary gender gap (the difference between what men and women earn for performing the same job) exists in IT careers, it's smaller than in most other professions.

You Have a Choice of Working Location

In this case, location refers to the setting in which you work. IT jobs can be office-based, field-based, project-based, or home-based. Because not every situation is perfect for every individual, you can look for a job that suits your tastes and requirements. Figure 4 summarizes the major job types and their locations.

You Constantly Meet New Challenges

In IT, the playing field is always changing. New software and hardware are constantly being developed. You'll need to work hard to keep your skills up to date. You'll spend a lot of time in training and self-study trying to learn new systems and

FIGURE 3

Jobs That Will Likely Remain Onshore		
CUSTOMER INTERACTION	**ENABLERS**	**INFRASTRUCTURE JOBS**
Web application developers	Business process analysts	Network security
Web interface designers	Application developers (when customer interaction is critical)	Network installation technicians
Database and data warehouse designers/developers	Project managers (for systems with users who are located predominantly in the United States)	Network administrators (engineers)
Customer relationship management (CRM) analysts		Wireless infrastructure managers and technicians
Enterprise resource planning (ERP) implementation specialists		Disaster recovery planners and responders

FIGURE 4

Where Do You Want to Work?

TYPE OF JOB	LOCATION AND HOURS	SPECIAL CONSIDERATIONS
Office-based	Report for work to the same location each day and interact with the same people on a regular basis; requires regular hours of attendance (such as 9 a.m. to 5 p.m.)	May require working beyond "normal" working hours; may also require workers to be on call 24/7
Field-based	Travel from place to place as needed and perform short-term jobs at each location	Involves a great deal of travel and the ability to work independently
Project-based	Work at client sites on specific projects for extended periods of time (weeks or months)	Can be especially attractive to individuals who like workplace situations that vary on a regular basis
Home-based (telecommuting)	Work from home	Involves very little day-to-day supervision and requires an individual who is self-disciplined

(Mardis Coers/Fotolia; Harvepino/Shutterstock; Nestor Costa/Fotolia; Paul Maguire/Fotolia)

techniques. Many individuals thrive in this type of environment because it keeps their jobs from becoming dull or routine.

You Work in Teams

When students are asked to describe their ideal jobs, many describe jobs that involve working in teams. Despite what some people think, IT professionals are not locked in lightless cubicles, basking in the glow of their monitors and working alone on projects. Most IT jobs require constant interaction with other workers, usually in team settings. People skills are highly prized by IT departments. If you have good leadership and team-building skills, you'll have the opportunity to exercise them in an IT job.

You Don't Need to Be a Mathematical Genius

Certain IT careers such as programming involve a fair bit of math. But even if you're not mathematically inclined, you can explore many other IT careers. IT employers also value such attributes as creativity, marketing, and artistic style, especially in jobs that involve working on the Internet or with social media.

IT Skills Are Transferable

Most computing skills are transferable from industry to industry. A networking job in the clothing manufacturing industry uses the same primary skill set as a networking job for a supermarket chain. Therefore, if something disastrous happens to the industry you're in, you should be able to switch to another industry without having to learn an entirely new skill set. Combining business courses with IT courses will also make you more marketable when changing jobs. For example, as an accounting major, if you minor in IT, employers may be more willing to hire you because working in accounting today means constantly interfacing with management information systems and manipulating data.

Challenges of IT Careers

Although there are many positive aspects of IT careers, there can be some challenges. The discussions that follow aren't meant to discourage you from pursuing an IT career but merely to make you aware of exactly what challenges you might face in an IT department.

Stress

Most IT jobs are hectic (see Figure 5). Whereas the average American works 42 hours a week, a survey by *InformationWeek* revealed that the average IT staff person works 45 hours a week and is on call for another 24 hours. On-call time (hours an employee must be available to work in the event of a problem) has been increasing because most IT systems require 24/7 availability.

Women Are in the Minority

A majority of IT jobs are filled by men, so some women view IT departments as *Dilbert*-like microcosms of antisocial geeks and don't feel like they would fit in. Unfortunately, it is true that in most IT departments, women are underrepresented. As companies begin to push to address this imbalance, new opportunities are emerging for women with technical skill sets.

Lifelong Learning Is Required

Although the constantly changing nature of IT can alleviate boredom, keeping up with the changes can also cause some stress. You'll need to take training courses, do self-study, and perhaps take additional college courses, such as getting a graduate degree, to keep up with the vast shifts in technology.

Choosing Your Realm of IT

Figure 6 shows an organizational chart for a modern IT department at a large corporation that should help you understand the variety of careers available and how they interrelate. The chief information officer (CIO) has overall responsibility for the development, implementation, and maintenance of information systems and its infrastructure. Usually, the CIO reports to the chief operating officer (COO).

The responsibilities below the CIO are generally grouped into two units:

1. Development and integration (responsible for the development of systems and websites)
2. Technical services (responsible for the day-to-day operations of the company's information infrastructure and network, including all hardware and software deployed)

In large organizations, responsibilities are distinct and jobs are defined more narrowly. In medium-sized organizations, there can be overlap between position responsibilities. At a small company, you might be the network administrator, database administrator, computer support technician, and social media manager all at the same time. Let's look at the typical jobs found in each department.

Working in Development and Integration

Two distinct paths exist in this division:

1. Web development
2. Systems development

Because everything involves the web today, there's often a great deal of overlap between these paths.

(Jenn Mackenzie/Shutterstock; Stephen Coburn/Shutterstock; LWPhotography/Shutterstock; Wavebreakmedia/Shutterstock; Johan Larson/Shutterstock)

FIGURE 5 Stress comes from multiple directions in IT jobs.

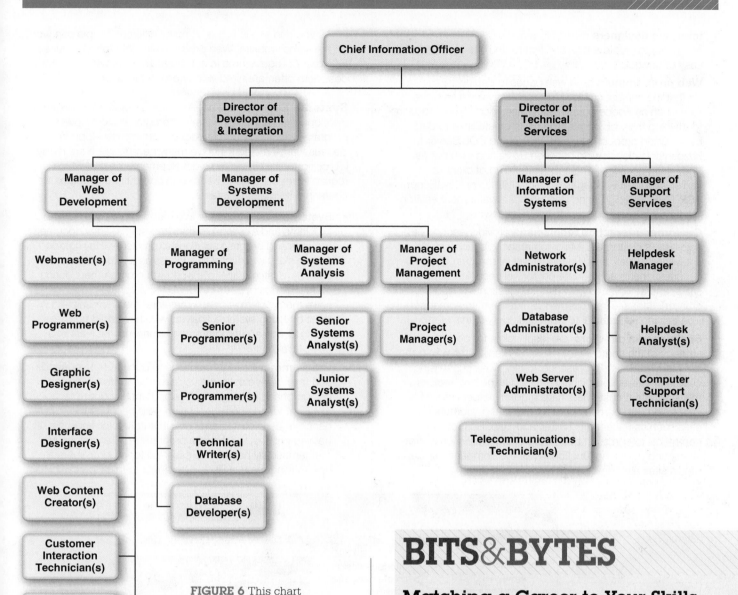

FIGURE 6 This chart represents a typical structure for an IT department at a large corporation.

Web Development. When most people think of web development careers, they usually equate them with being a webmaster. Webmasters used to be individuals who were solely responsible for all aspects of a company's website. However, today's webmasters usually are supervisors with responsibility for certain aspects of web development. At smaller companies, they may also be responsible for tasks that other individuals in a web development group usually do, such as the following:

- **Web content creators** generate the words and images that appear on the web. Journalists, other writers, editors, and marketing personnel prepare an enormous amount of web content, whereas **video producers**, **graphic designers**, and **animators** create web-based multimedia. Web content creators have a thorough understanding of their own fields as well as HTML, PHP, and JavaScript.

BITS&BYTES

Matching a Career to Your Skills

Trends in technology and business often give clues to up-and-coming IT jobs. Consider these trends when considering your educational choices:

Drone aircraft: Drones are making their way from the military to businesses and households. Companies that make or use drones will need drone programmers.

Cyber spying: Recent revelations of widespread cyber spying and espionage point to a continued demand for IT security professionals.

Google Glass: The release of virtual technology products and the ongoing development of heads-up displays and transparent screens is signaling that virtual reality developers will be needed in the future.

Driverless cars: As vehicles become ever more sophisticated, so do their IT systems. Developers of artificial intelligence systems for vehicles and business equipment will be highly sought after.

- **Interface designers** work with graphic designers and animators to create a look and feel for the site and make it easy to navigate.
- **Web programmers** build web pages to deploy the materials that the content creators develop. They wield software tools such as Adobe Dreamweaver and Microsoft Expression to develop the web pages. They also create links to databases using products such as Oracle and SQL Server to keep information flowing between users and web pages. They must possess a solid understanding of client- and server-side web languages (HTML, XML, Java, JavaScript, ASP, PHP, Silverlight, and Perl) and of development environments such as the Microsoft .NET Framework.
- **Customer interaction technicians** provide feedback to a website's customers. Major job responsibilities include answering e-mail, sending requested information, funneling questions to appropriate personnel (technical support, sales, and so on), and providing suggestions to web programmers for site improvements. Extensive customer service training is essential to work effectively in this area.
- **Social media directors** are responsible for directing the strategy of the company on all social media sites where the company maintains a presence. Often, while supervising customer interaction technicians, social media directors make sure that customers have a quality experience while interacting with company employees and customers on sites such as Facebook, Twitter, and Yelp. Responding to comments left on such sites, developing promotional strategies, and designing functionality of the company's social media sites are common job responsibilities.

As you can see in Figure 7, many different people can work on the same website. Web programming jobs often require a four-year college degree in computer science, whereas graphic designers often are hired with two-year art degrees.

Systems Development. Ask most people what systems developers do and they'll answer "programming." However, programming is only one aspect of systems development. Because large projects involve many people, there are many job opportunities in systems development, most of which require four-year college degrees in computer science or management information systems:

- **Systems analysts** gather information from end users about problems and existing information systems. They document systems and propose solutions to problems. Having good people skills is essential to success as a systems analyst. In addition, systems analysts work with programmers during the development phase to design appropriate programs to solve the problem at hand. Therefore, many organizations insist on hiring systems analysts who have solid business backgrounds and programming experience (at least at a basic level).
- **Programmers** attend meetings to document user needs, and they work closely with systems analysts during the design phase of program development. Programmers need excellent written communication skills because they often generate detailed systems documentation for end-user training purposes. Because programming languages are mathematically based, it is essential for programmers to have strong math skills and an ability to think logically.

FIGURE 7 It takes a team to create and maintain a website. *(Courtesy of the United States Department of Agriculture)*

- Programmers build the software that solves problems

- Systems analysts document systems and propose solutions

- Project managers supervise, organize, and coach team members

- Database developers ensure data is accessible when it's needed

FIGURE 8 There are many important team members in systems development. *(Bah69/Fotolia; Rob/Fotolia; Fotoluminate LLC/Fotolia; HaywireMedia/Fotolia)*

- **Project managers** manage the overall systems development process: assigning staff, budgeting, reporting to management, coaching team members, and ensuring deadlines are met. Project managers need excellent time management skills because they're often pulled in several directions at once. They usually have prior experience as programmers or systems analysts. Many project managers obtain master's degrees to supplement their undergraduate degrees.

In addition to these key players, the following people are also involved in the systems development process:

- **Technical writers** generate systems documentation for end users and for programmers who may make modifications to the system in the future.
- **Network administrators** help the programmers and analysts design compatible systems, because many systems are required to run in certain environments (UNIX or Windows, for instance) and must work in conjunction with other programs.
- **Database developers** design and build databases to support the software systems being developed.

Large development projects may have all of these team members on the project. Smaller projects may require an overlap of positions, such as a programmer also acting as a systems analyst. As shown in Figure 8, team members work together to build a system.

Working in Technical Services

Technical services jobs are vital to keeping IT systems running. The people in these jobs install and maintain the infrastructure behind the IT systems and work with end users to make sure they can interact with the systems effectively. There are two major categories of technical services careers:

1. Information systems
2. Support services

Note that these also are the *least likely* IT jobs to be outsourced because hands-on work with equipment and users is required on a regular basis.

Information Systems. The information systems department keeps the networks and telecommunications up and running at all times. Within the department, you'll find a variety of positions.

- **Network administrators** (sometimes called *network engineers*) are involved in every stage of network planning and deployment (see Figure 9). They decide what equipment to buy and what media to use, they determine the network's topology, and they help install the network (by supervising contractors or doing it themselves). Network administrators plan disaster-recovery strategies (such as what to do if a fire destroys the server room). When equipment and cables break, network administrators must fix the problem. They also obtain and install updates to network software and evaluate new equipment to determine whether the network should be upgraded. In addition, they monitor the network's performance and often develop policies regarding network usage, security measures, and hardware and software standards.

FIGURE 9 At smaller companies, network administrators may be fixing a user's computer in the morning, installing and configuring a new network operating system in the afternoon, and troubleshooting a wiring problem (shown here) in the evening. *(ArtPix/Alamy)*

The video gaming industry in the United States has surpassed the earning power of the Hollywood movie industry. In 2013, U.S. consumers bought $15.39 billion worth of video games and accessories, whereas Hollywood took in just over $10.9 billion. Although some aspects of game development, such as scenery design and certain aspects of programming, are being sent offshore, the majority of game development requires a creative team whose members need to work in close proximity. Therefore, it's anticipated that most game development jobs will stay in the United States.

Consoles such as the Xbox One and the PlayStation 4 generate demand for large-scale games. The popularity of mobile devices such as smartphones and tablets is driving demand for lower-end, casual game applications. Casual games are games that can be played relatively quickly, such as puzzle games (see Figure 10). Demand for family-friendly games without violence, sex, and profanity is on the rise. With all this demand, there are many opportunities for careers in game development.

Game development jobs usually are split along two paths: designers and programmers.

- **Game designers** tend to be artistic and are responsible for creating 2-D and 3-D art, game interfaces, video sequences, special effects, game levels, and scenarios. Game designers must master software packages such as Autodesk 3ds Max, Autodesk Maya, NewTek LightWave 3D, Adobe Photoshop, and Adobe Flash.

- **Game programmers** are responsible for coding the scenarios developed by the designers. Using languages and toolsets such as Objective-C, Unity, Apple Xcode, C, C++, Assembly, and Java, programmers build the game and ensure that it plays accurately.

Aside from programmers and designers, play testers and quality-assurance professionals play the games with the intent of breaking them or discovering bugs within the game interfaces or worlds. **Play testing** is an essential part of the game development process because it assists designers in determining which aspects of the game are most intriguing to players and which parts of the game need to be repaired or enhanced.

No matter what job you may pursue in the realm of gaming, you'll need to have a two- or four-year college degree. If you're interested in gaming, look for a school with a solid animation or 3-D art program or a computer game–programming curriculum. Programming requires a strong background in math and physics to enable you to realistically program environments that mimic the real world. Proficiency with math (especially geometry) also helps with design careers.

For more information on gaming careers, check out the International Game Developers Association site (**igda.org**) and the Game Career Guide (**gamecareerguide.com**).

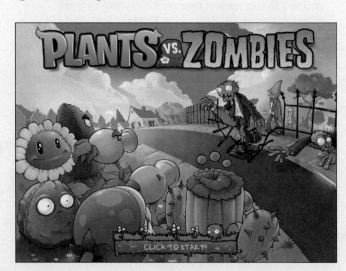

FIGURE 10 Plants vs. Zombies, which has you grow plants to fend off encroaching zombie hordes, is an example of a popular casual game available for many different platforms. *(Vinod Kurien/Alamy)*

- **Database administrators (DBAs)** install and configure database servers and ensure that the servers provide an adequate level of access to all users.

- **Web server administrators** install, configure, and maintain web servers and ensure that the company maintains Internet connectivity at all times.

- **Telecommunications technicians** oversee the communications infrastructure, including training employees to use telecommunications equipment. They are often on call 24 hours a day.

Support Services. As a member of the support services team, you interface with users (external customers or employees) and troubleshoot their computer problems. Support service positions include the following:

- **Helpdesk analysts** staff the phones, respond to Internet live chats, or respond to e-mails and solve problems for customers or employees, either remotely or in person. Often, helpdesk personnel are called on to train users on the latest software and hardware.

- **Computer support technicians** go to a user's location and fix software and hardware problems. They also often have to chase down and repair faults in the network infrastructure.

As important as these people are, they may receive a great deal of abuse by angry users whose computers are not working. When working in support services, you need to be patient and not be overly sensitive to insults!

Technical services jobs often require a two-year college degree or training at a trade school or technical institute. At smaller companies, job duties tend to overlap between the helpdesk and technician jobs. These jobs are in demand and require staffing in local markets, so they are staying onshore. You can't repair a computer's power supply if you are located in another country!

Preparing for a Job in IT

A job in IT requires a robust skill set and formal training and preparation. Most employers today have an entry-level requirement of a college degree, a technical institute diploma, appropriate professional certifications, experience in the field, or a combination of these. How can you prepare for a job in IT?

1. **Get educated.** Two- and four-year colleges and universities normally offer three degrees to prepare students for IT careers: computer science, management information systems, and information technology (although titles vary). Alternatives to colleges and universities are privately licensed technical (or trade) schools. Generally, these programs focus on building skill sets rapidly and qualifying for a job in a specific field. The main advantage of technical schools is that their programs usually take less time to complete than college degrees. However, to have a realistic chance of employment in IT fields other than networking or web development, you should attend a degree-granting college or university.

2. **Investigate professional certifications.** Certifications attempt to provide a consistent method of measuring skill levels in specific areas of IT. Hundreds of IT certifications are available, most of which you get by passing a written exam.

Software and hardware vendors (such as Microsoft and Cisco) and professional organizations (such as the Computing Technology Industry Association) often establish certification standards. Visit **microsoft.com**, **cisco.com**, **comptia .org**, and **sun.com** for more information on certifications.

3. **Get experience.** In addition to education, employers want you to have experience, even for entry-level jobs. While you're still completing your education, consider getting an internship or part-time job in your field of study. Many schools will help you find internships and allow you to earn credit toward your degree through internships.

4. **Do research.** Find out as much as you can about the company and the industry it's in before going on an interview. Start with the company's website, and then expand your search to business and trade publications such as *BusinessWeek* and *Inc.* magazines.

Getting Started in an IT Career

Training for a career is not useful unless you can find a job at the end of your training. Here are some tips on getting a job:

1. **Use the career resources at your school.** Many employers recruit at schools, and most schools maintain a placement office to help students find jobs. Employees in the placement office can help you with résumé preparation and interviewing skills and can provide you with leads for internships and jobs.

2. **Develop relationships with your instructors.** Many college instructors still work in or previously worked in the IT industry. They can often provide you with valuable advice and industry contacts.

3. **Start networking.** Many jobs are never advertised but instead are filled by word of mouth. Seek out contacts in your field and discuss job prospects with them. Find out what skills you need, and ask them to recommend others in the industry with whom you can speak. Professional organizations such as the Association for Computing Machinery (ACM) offer one way to network. These organizations often have chapters on college campuses and offer reduced membership rates for students. Figure 11

FIGURE 11

Professional Organizations		
ORGANIZATION NAME	**PURPOSE**	**WEBSITE**
Association for Computing Machinery (ACM)	Oldest scientific computing society; maintains a strong focus on programming and systems development	**acm.org**
Association for Information Systems (AIS)	Organization of professionals who work in academia and specialize in information systems	**aisnet.org**
Association of Information Technology Professionals (AITP)	Heavy focus on IT education and development of seminars and learning materials	**aitp.org**
Institute of Electrical and Electronics Engineers (IEEE)	Provides leadership and sets engineering standards for all types of network computing devices and protocols	**ieee.org**
Information Systems Security Association (ISSA)	Not-for-profit, international organization of information security professionals and practitioners	**issa.org**

FIGURE 12

Resources for Women in IT

ORGANIZATION NAME	PURPOSE	WEBSITE
Anita Borg Institute for Women and Technology	Organization whose aim is to "increase the impact of women on all aspects of technology"	**anitaborg.org**
Association for Women in Computing (AWC)	A not-for-profit organization dedicated to promoting the advancement of women in computing professions	**awc-hq.org**
The Center for Women in Technology (CWIT)	An organization dedicated to providing global leadership in achieving women's full participation in all aspects of IT	**cwit.umbc.edu**
Diversity/Careers in Engineering & Information Technology	An online magazine whose articles cover career issues of technical professionals who are members of minority groups, women, or people with disabilities	**diversitycareers .com**
Women in Technology International (WITI)	A global trade association for tech-savvy, professional women	**witi.com**

lists major professional organizations you should consider investigating.

If you're a woman and are thinking about pursuing an IT career, many resources and groups cater to female IT professionals and students (see Figure 12). The oldest and best-known organization is the Association for Women in Computing, founded in 1978.

4. **Check corporate websites for jobs.** Many corporate websites list current job opportunities. For example, Google provides searchable job listings by geographic location. Check the sites of companies in which you are interested and then do a search on the sites for job openings or, if provided, click their employment links.

5. **Visit online employment sites.** Most of these sites allow you to store your résumé online, and many sites allow employers to browse résumés to find qualified employees. Begin looking at job postings on these sites early in your education because these job postings detail the skill sets employers require. Focusing on coursework that will provide you with desirable skill sets will make you more marketable. Figure 13 lists employment sites as well as sites that offer other career resources.

The outlook for IT jobs should continue to be positive in the future. We wish you luck with your education and job search.

BITS&BYTES

Certifications: How Important Are They?

Employees with certifications generally earn more than employees who aren't certified. However, most employers don't view a certification as a substitute for a college degree or a trade school program. You should think of certifications as an extra edge beyond your formal education that will make you more attractive to employers. To ensure you're pursuing the right certifications, ask employers which certifications they respect, or explore online job sites to see which certifications are listed as desirable or required.

FIGURE 13

Resources for IT Employment

SITE NAME	URL
CareerBuilder	**careerbuilder.com**
ComputerJobs.com	**computerjobs.com**
ComputerWork.com	**computerwork.com**
Dice	**dice.com**
Gamasutra	**gamasutra.com**
JustTechJobs	**justtechjobs.com**
LinkedIn	**linkedin.com**
Monster	**monster.com**
TechCareers	**techcareers.com**

check your understanding// review & practice

For a quick review of what you've learned, answer the following questions. Visit **pearsonhighered.com /techinaction** to check your answers.

multiple choice

1. The individuals responsible for generating images for websites are referred to as
   a. network administrators.
   b. graphic designers.
   c. web programmers.
   d. interface designers.

2. What type of job involves working at client locations and the ability to work with little direct supervision?
   a. field-based
   b. project-based
   c. office-based
   d. home-based

3. Which position is *not* typically a part of the information systems department?
   a. helpdesk analyst
   b. telecommunications technician
   c. network administrator
   d. web server administrator

4. Outsourcing is thought to be an attractive option for many companies because of
   a. the emphasis on employee training.
   b. the cost savings that can be realized.
   c. increased data security.
   d. decreased travel and entertainment costs.

5. Which of the following IT positions is responsible for directing a company's strategy on sites such as Facebook, Twitter, and Yelp?
   a. project manager
   b. customer interaction technician
   c. social media director
   d. social web analyst

6. Which of the following statements about IT careers is *false*?
   a. IT employers typically prefer experience over certification.
   b. Women who have IT skills have ample opportunities for securing IT employment.
   c. Many IT jobs are staying in the United States.
   d. Most IT jobs require little interaction with other people.

7. Which task is *not* typically performed by a network administrator?
   a. developing network usage policies
   b. installing networks
   c. planning for disaster recovery
   d. web programming

8. The oldest scientific computing organization is
   a. Institute of Electrical and Electronics Engineers.
   b. Association for Computing Machinery.
   c. Information Systems Security Association.
   d. Association for Women in Computing.

9. If you are artistic and have mastered software packages such as Adobe Photoshop, Autodesk 3ds Max, and Autodesk Maya, you might consider a career as which of the following?
   a. game programmer   c. game tester
   b. game designer   d. web designer

10. Which position is a part of the systems development department?
    a. webmaster   c. programmer
    b. interface designer   d. database administrator

Glossary

3-D sound card An expansion card that enables a computer to produce omnidirectional or three-dimensional sounds.

4G The latest mobile communication standard with faster data transfer rates than 3G.

A

access time The time it takes a storage device to locate its stored data.

accounting software An application program that helps business owners manage their finances more efficiently by providing tools for tracking accounting transactions such as sales, accounts receivable, inventory purchases, and accounts payable.

adware A program that downloads on your computer when a user installs a freeware program, game, or utility. Generally, adware enables sponsored advertisements to appear in a section of a browser window or as a pop-up ad.

affective computing A type of computing that relates to emotion or that deliberately tries to influence emotion.

aggregator A software program that finds and retrieves the latest update of web material (usually podcasts) according to your specifications.

all-in-one computer A desktop system unit that houses the computer's processor, memory, and monitor in a single unit.

all-in-one printer Combines the functions of a printer, scanner, copier, and fax into one machine.

analog Waves that illustrate the loudness of a sound or the brightness of the colors in an image at a given moment in time.

analog-to-digital converter chip Converts analog signals into digital signals.

antivirus software Software specifically designed to detect viruses and protect a computer and files from harm.

app bars Bars that float above the screen and that contain applications such as the Tabs bar and the Address bar; a new feature of Internet Explorer 10.

application programming interface (API) A set of software routines that allows one software system to work with another.

application software The set of programs on a computer that helps a user carry out tasks such as word processing, sending e-mail, balancing a budget, creating presentations, editing photos, taking an online course, and playing games.

aspect ratio The width-to-height proportion of a monitor.

assembly language See *second-generation language (2GL)*.

audio-editing software Programs that perform basic editing tasks on audio files such as cutting dead air space from the beginning or end of a song or cutting a portion from the middle.

audio MIDI interface Interface technology that allows a user to connect guitars and microphones to their computer.

authentication The process of identifying a computer user, based on a login or username and password. The computer system determines whether the computer user is authorized and what level of access is to be granted on the network.

augmented reality A combination of our normal sense of the objects around us with an overlay of information displayed.

B

backdoor program Program that enables a hacker to take complete control of a computer without the legitimate user's knowledge or permission.

backup A copy of a computer file that can be used to replace the original if it's lost or damaged.

backward compatibility The accommodation of current devices being able to use previously issued software standards in addition to the current standards.

bandwidth The maximum speed at which data can be transmitted between two nodes on a network; usually measured in megabits per second (Mbps). See also *data transfer rate*.

base transceiver station A large communications tower with antennas, amplifiers, and receivers/transmitters.

basic input/output system (BIOS) A program that manages the data between a computer's operating system and all the input and output devices attached to the computer; also responsible for loading the operating system (OS) from its permanent location on the hard drive to random access memory (RAM).

beta version A version of the software that's still under development. Many beta versions are available for a limited trial period and are used to help the developers correct any errors before they launch the software on the market.

binary digit (bit) A digit that corresponds to the on and off states of a computer's switches. A bit contains a value of either 0 or 1.

binary language The language computers use to process data into information, consisting of only the values 0 and 1.

biometric authentication device A device that uses some unique characteristic of human biology to identify authorized users.

black-hat hacker A hacker who uses his or her knowledge to destroy information or for illegal gain.

blog (weblog) A personal log or journal posted on the web; short for *web log*.

Bluetooth (technology) A type of wireless technology that uses radio waves to transmit data over short distances (approximately 3–300 feet depending on power); often used to connect peripherals such as printers and keyboards to computers or headsets to cell phones.

Blu-ray disc (BD) A method of optical storage for digital data, developed for storing high-definition media. It has the largest storage capacity of all optical storage options.

bookmarks Features in some browsers that place markers of websites' Uniform Resource Locators (URLs) in an easily retrievable list.

Boolean operator A word used to refine logical searches. For Internet searches, the words AND, NOT, and OR describe the relationships between keywords in the search.

boot process The process for loading the operating system (OS) into random access memory (RAM) when the computer is turned on.

boot-sector virus A virus that replicates itself into the master boot record of a flash drive or hard drive.

botnet A large group of software applications (called *robots* or *bots*) that run without user intervention on a large number of computers.

breadcrumb trail A navigation aid that shows users the path they have taken to get to a web page or where the page is located within the website; it usually appears at the top of a page.

broadband A high-speed Internet connection such as cable, satellite, or digital subscriber line (DSL).

business-to-business (B2B) E-commerce transactions between businesses.

business-to-consumer (B2C) E-commerce transactions between businesses and consumers.

byte Eight binary digits (bits).

C

cable Internet A broadband service that transmits data over coaxial cables.

cache memory Small blocks of memory, located directly on and next to the central processing unit (CPU) chip, that act as holding places for recently or frequently used instructions or data that the CPU accesses the most. When these instructions or data are stored in cache memory, the CPU can more quickly retrieve them than if it had to access the instructions or data from random access memory (RAM).

Cat 6 cable A UTP cable type that provides more than 1 Gb/s of throughput.

cellular (cell) phone A telephone that operates over a mobile network. Cell phones can also offer Internet access, text messaging, personal information management (PIM) features, and more.

central processing unit (CPU, or processor) The part of the system unit of a computer that is responsible for data processing; it is the largest and most important chip in the computer. The CPU controls all the functions performed by the computer's other components and processes all the commands issued to it by software instructions.

charms Special shortcuts for performing common tasks, such as searching or sharing information, created for Windows 8.

client A computer that requests information from a server in a client/server network (such as your computer when you are connected to the Internet).

client/server network (server-based network) A type of network that uses servers to deliver services to computers that are requesting them (clients).

clock speed The steady and constant pace at which a computer goes through machine cycles, measured in hertz (Hz).

cloud computing The process of storing data, files, and applications on the web, which allows access to and manipulation of these files and applications from any Internet-connected device.

cloud storage Refers to a service that keeps files on the Internet (in the "cloud") rather than storing files solely on a local device.

cluster The smallest increment in which data is stored on hard disks; hard disks are divided into *tracks*, then *wedges*, then *sectors*, then clusters.

coaxial cable A single copper wire surrounded by layers of plastic insulation, metal sheathing, and a plastic jacket; used mainly in cable television and cable Internet service.

codec A rule, implemented in either software or hardware, which squeezes a given amount of audio and video information into less space.

cognitive surplus The combination of leisure time and the tools needed to be creative.

cold boot The process of starting a computer from a powered-down or off state.

collaborative consumption Joining together as a group to use a specific product more efficiently.

command-driven interface Interface between user and computer in which the user enters commands to communicate with the computer system.

compact disc (CD) A method of optical storage for digital data; originally developed for storing digital audio.

computer A data-processing device that gathers, processes, outputs, and stores data and information.

computer-aided design (CAD) A 3-D modeling program used to create automated designs, technical drawings, and model visualizations.

computer forensics The application of computer systems and techniques to gather potential legal evidence; a law enforcement specialty used to fight high-tech crime.

computer literate Being familiar enough with computers that a user knows how to use them and understands their capabilities and limitations.

connectivity port A port that enables a computing device to be connected to other devices or systems such as networks, modems, and the Internet.

consumer-to-consumer (C2C) E-commerce transactions between consumers through online sites such as eBay.

cookie A small text file that some websites automatically store on a client computer's hard drive when a user visits the site.

copyleft A simplified licensing scheme that enables copyright holders to grant certain rights to a work while retaining other rights.

core A complete processing section from a central processing unit, embedded into one physical chip.

course management software A program that provides traditional classroom tools, such as calendars and grade books, over the Internet, as well as areas for students to exchange ideas and information in chat rooms, discussion forums, and e-mail.

CPU benchmarks Measurements used to compare performance between processors.

CPU usage The percentage of time the central processing unit (CPU) is working.

CPU usage graph Records your central processing unit (CPU) usage for the past several seconds.

crisis-mapping tool A tool that collects information from e-mails, text messages, blog posts, and Twitter tweets and maps them, making the information instantly publicly available.

crowdfunding Asking for small donations from a large number of people, often using the Internet; a style of generating capital to start a business through social media.

crowdsourcing The phenomenon of consumers checking in with the voice of the crowd before making purchases.

custom installation The process of installing only those features of a software program that a user wants on the hard drive.

cybercrime Any criminal action perpetrated primarily through the use of a computer.

cybercriminal An individual who uses computers, networks, and the Internet to perpetrate crime.

cyberloafing Doing anything with a computer that's unrelated to a job (such as playing video games) while one's supposed to be working. Also called *cyberslacking*.

D

data Numbers, words, pictures, or sounds that represent facts, figures, or ideas; the raw input that users have at the start of a job.

data breach When sensitive or confidential information is copied, transmitted, or viewed by an individual who is not authorized to handle the data.

data file A file that contains stored data.

data mining The process by which great amounts of data are analyzed and investigated. The objective is to spot significant patterns or trends within the data that would otherwise not be obvious.

data plan A connectivity plan or text messaging plan in which data charges are separate from cell phone calling charges and are provided at rates different from those for voice calls.

data transfer rate The maximum speed at which data can be transmitted between two nodes on a network; measured in megabits per second (Mbps) or gigabits per second (Gbps).

database software An electronic filing system best used for larger and more complicated groups of data that require more than one table and the ability to group, sort, and retrieve data and generate reports.

denial-of-service (DoS) attack An attack that occurs when legitimate users are denied access to a computer system because a hacker is repeatedly making requests of that computer system that tie up its resources and deny legitimate users access.

desktop computer A computer that's intended for use at a single location. A desktop computer consists of a case that houses the main components of the computer, plus peripheral devices.

desktop publishing (DTP) software Programs for incorporating and arranging graphics and text to produce creative documents.

device driver Software that facilitates the communication between a device and its operating system or between a network adapter and a server's operating system and the operating system of the computer in which the adapter is installed.

digital convergence The use of a single unifying device to handle media, Internet, entertainment, and telephony needs; expressed in the range of devices now on the market.

digital divide The discrepancy between those who have access to the opportunities and knowledge that computers and the Internet offer and those who do not.

digital rights management (DRM) A system of access control that allows only limited use of material that has been legally purchased.

digital signal processor A specialized chip that processes digital information and transmits signals very quickly.

digital subscriber line (DSL) A type of connection that uses telephone lines to connect to the Internet and that allows both phone and data transmissions to share the same line.

digital video (or versatile) disc (DVD) A method of optical storage for digital data that has greater storage capacity than compact discs.

digital video–editing software A program for editing digital video.

digital video interface (DVI) port Video interface technology that newer LCD monitors, as well as other multimedia devices such as televisions, DVD players, and projectors, use to connect to a PC.

directory A hierarchical structure that include files, folders, and drives used to create a more organized and efficient computer.

Disk Cleanup A Windows utility that removes unnecessary files from the hard drive.

disk defragmenting A utility that regroups related pieces of files on the hard drive, enabling faster retrieval of the data.

distributed denial-of-service (DDoS) attack An automated attack that's launched from more than one zombie computer at the same time.

distributions (distros) Linux download packages.

domain name A part of a Uniform Resource Locator (URL). Domain names consist of two parts: the site's host and a suffix that indicates the type of organization (example: popsci.com, where *popsci* is the domain name and *com* is the suffix).

drawing software (illustration software) Programs for creating or editing two-dimensional line-based drawings.

drive bay A special shelf inside a computer that is designed to hold storage devices.

drive-by download The use of malicious software to attack a computer by downloading harmful programs onto a computer, without the user's knowledge, while they are surfing a website.

E

e-commerce (electronic commerce) The process of conducting business online for purposes ranging from fund-raising to advertising to selling products.

electronic ink (E ink) A very crisp, sharp grayscale representation of text achieved by using millions of microcapsules with white and black particles in a clear fluid.

electronic text (e-text) Textual information stored as digital information so that it can be stored, manipulated, and transmitted by electronic devices.

e-mail (electronic mail) Internet-based communication in which senders and recipients correspond.

e-mail client A software program that runs on a computer and is used to send and receive e-mail through an Internet service provider's server.

e-mail virus A virus transmitted by e-mail that often uses the address book in the victim's e-mail system to distribute itself.

embedded computer A specially designed computer chip that resides inside another device, such as a car. These self-contained computer devices have their own programming and typically neither receive input from users nor interact with other systems.

encryption virus A malicious program that searches for common data files and compresses them into a file using a complex encryption key, thereby rendering the files unusable.

End User License Agreement (EULA) See *software license*.

e-reader A device that can display e-text and that has supporting tools, like note taking, bookmarks, and integrated dictionaries.

ergonomics How a user sets up his or her computer and other equipment to minimize risk of injury or discomfort.

error-checking A Windows utility that checks for lost files and fragments as well as physical errors on a hard drive.

Ethernet network A network that uses the Ethernet protocol as the means (or standard) by which the nodes on the network communicate.

Ethernet port A port that's slightly larger than a standard phone jack and that transfers data at speeds of up to 10,000 Mbps; used to connect a computer to a DSL or cable modem or to a network.

event The result of an action, such as a keystroke, mouse click, or signal to the printer, in the respective device (keyboard, mouse, or printer) to which the operating system responds.

expansion card (adapter card) A circuit board with specific functions that augment the computer's basic functions and provide connections to other devices; examples include the sound card and the video card.

extension (file type) In a file name, the three letters that follow the user-supplied file name after the dot (.); the extension identifies what kind of family of files the file belongs to, or which application should be used to read the file.

external hard drive A hard drive that is enclosed in a protective case to make it portable; the drive is connected to the computer with a data transfer cable and is often used to back up data.

F

Favorites A feature in Microsoft Internet Explorer that places a marker of a website's Uniform Resource Locator (URL) in an easily retrievable list in the browser's toolbar. (Called Bookmarks in some browsers.)

feature phones Inexpensive cell phones with modest processors, simple interfaces, and, often, no touch screens.

fiber-optic cable A cable that transmits data at close to the speed of light along glass or plastic fibers.

fiber-optic service Internet access that is enabled by transmitting data at the speed of light through glass or plastic fibers.

file A collection of related pieces of information stored together for easy reference.

file allocation table (FAT) An index of all sector numbers that the hard drive stores in a table to keep track of which sectors hold which files.

file compression utility A program that takes out redundancies in a file in order to reduce the file size.

File Explorer The main tool for finding, viewing, and managing the contents of your computer by showing the location and contents of every drive, folder, and file; called Windows Explorer prior to Windows 8.

File History A Windows utility that automatically creates a duplicate of your libraries, desktop, contacts, and favorites and copies it to another storage device, such as an external hard drive.

file management The process by which humans or computer software provide organizational structure to a computer's contents.

file name The first part of the label applied to a file; generally the name a user assigns to the file when saving it.

file path The exact location of a file, starting with the drive in which the file is located and including all folders, subfolders (if any), the file name, and the extension (example: C:\Users\username\Documents\Illustrations\EBronte.jpg).

File Transfer Protocol (FTP) A protocol used to upload and download files from one computer to another over the Internet.

financial planning software Programs for managing finances, such as Intuit's Quicken, which include electronic checkbook registers and automatic bill-payment tools.

firewall A software program or hardware device designed to prevent unauthorized access to computers or networks.

FireWire 800 An interface port that transfers data at 800 Mbps.

firmware System software that controls hardware devices.

flash drive A drive that plugs into a universal serial bus (USB) port on a computer and that stores data digitally. Also called a USB drive, jump drive, or thumb drive.

flash memory card A form of portable storage; this removable memory card is often used in digital cameras, smartphones, video cameras, and printers.

folder A collection of files stored on a computer.

freeware Any copyrighted software that can be used for free.

full installation The process of installing all the files and programs from the distribution media to the computer's hard drive.

G

geotag Data attached to a photograph that indicates the latitude and longitude where you were standing when you took the photo.

gigabit Ethernet The most commonly used wired Ethernet standard deployed in devices designed for home networks; provides bandwidth of up to 1 Gbps.

gigabyte (GB) About a billion bytes.

gigahertz (GHz) One billion hertz.

global positioning system (GPS) A system of 21 satellites (plus 3 working spares), built and operated by the U.S. military, that constantly orbit the earth. The satellites provide information to GPS–capable devices to pinpoint locations on the earth.

graphical user interface (GUI) Unlike the command- and menu-driven interfaces used in earlier software, GUIs display graphics and use the point-and-click technology of the mouse and cursor, making them much more user friendly.

graphics double data rate 5 (GDDR5) A standard of video memory.

graphics processing unit (GPU) A specialized logic chip that's dedicated to quickly displaying and calculating visual data such as shadows, textures, and luminosity.

green computing A movement that encourages environmentally sustainable computing (or IT).

grey-hat hacker A cross between black and white—a hacker who will often illegally break into systems merely to flaunt his or her expertise to the administrator of the system he or she penetrated or to attempt to sell his or her services in repairing security breaches.

H

hacker Anyone who unlawfully breaks into a computer system (whether an individual computer or a network).

hard disk drive (HDD) The computer's nonvolatile, primary storage device for permanent storage of software and documents.

hardware Any part of a computer or computer system you can physically touch.

head crash Impact of the read/write head against the magnetic platter of the hard drive; often results in data loss.

hibernate A power-management mode that saves the current state of the current system to the computer's hard drive.

high definition A standard of digital TV signal that guarantees a specific level of resolution and a specific *aspect ratio*, which is the rectangular shape of the image.

high-definition multimedia interface (HDMI) A compact audio–video interface standard that carries both high-definition video and uncompressed digital audio.

home area network (HAN) A network located in a home that's used to connect all of its digital devices.

home network server A device designed to store media, share media across the network, and back up files on computers connected to a home network.

host The portion of a domain name that identifies who maintains a given website. For example, berkeley.edu is the domain name

for the University of California at Berkeley, which maintains that site.

hyperlink A type of specially coded text that, when clicked, enables a user to jump from one location, or web page, to another within a website or to another website altogether.

Hypertext Transfer Protocol (HTTP) The protocol that allows files to be transferred from a web server so that you can see them on your computer by using a browser.

hyperthreading A technology that permits quicker processing of information by enabling a new set of instructions to start executing before the previous set has finished.

I

identity theft The process by which someone uses personal information about someone else (such as the victim's name, address, and Social Security number) to assume the victim's identity for the purpose of defrauding another.

image backup (system backup) A copy of an entire computer system, created for restoration purposes.

image-editing software Programs for editing photographs and other images.

impact printer A printer that has tiny hammer-like keys that strike the paper through an inked ribbon, thus making a mark on the paper. The most common impact printer is the dot-matrix printer.

incremental backup (partial backup) A type of backup that only backs up files that have changed since the last time files were backed up.

information Data that has been organized or presented in a meaningful fashion; the result or output that users require at the end of a job.

information technology (IT) The set of techniques used in processing and retrieving information.

inkjet printer A nonimpact printer that sprays tiny drops of ink onto paper.

inoculation A process used by antivirus software; compares old and current qualities of files to detect viral activity.

input device A hardware device used to enter, or input, data (text, images, and

sounds) and instructions (user responses and commands) into a computer. Some input devices are keyboards and mice.

instant messaging (IM) A program that enables users to communicate online in real time with others who are also online.

internal hard drive A hard drive that resides within the computer's system unit and that usually holds all permanently stored programs and data.

Internet A network of networks that's the largest network in the world, connecting billions of computers globally.

Internet backbone The main pathway of high-speed communications lines over which all Internet traffic flows.

Internet of Things (IoT) Interconnection of uniquely identifiable embedded computing devices that transfer data over a network without requiring human-to-human or human-to-computer interaction.

Internet Protocol (IP) address The means by which all computers connected to the Internet identify each other. It consists of a unique set of four numbers separated by dots, such as 123.45.178.91.

Internet service provider (ISP) A company that specializes in providing Internet access. ISPs may be specialized providers, like Juno, or companies that provide other services in addition to Internet access (such as phone and cable television).

interrupt A signal that tells the operating system that it's in need of immediate attention.

interrupt handler A special numerical code that prioritizes requests from various devices. These requests then are placed in the interrupt table in the computer's primary memory.

J–K

kernel (supervisor program) The essential component of the operating system that's responsible for managing the processor and all other components of the computer system. Because it stays in random access memory (RAM) the entire time the computer is powered on, the kernel is called memory resident.

keyboard A hardware device used to enter typed data and commands into a computer.

keystroke logger (keylogger) A type of spyware program that monitors keystrokes with the intent of stealing passwords, login IDs, or credit card information.

keyword (1) A specific word a user wishes to query (or look for) in an Internet search. (2) A specific word that has a predefined meaning in a particular programming language.

kilobyte (KB) A unit of computer storage equal to approximately 1,000 bytes.

L

laptop (or notebook) computer A portable computer with a keyboard, a monitor, and other devices integrated into a single compact case.

laser printer A nonimpact printer known for quick and quiet production and high-quality printouts.

latency (rotational delay) The process that occurs after the read/write head of the hard drive locates the correct track and then waits for the correct sector to spin to the read/write head.

legacy technology Comprises computing devices, software, or peripherals that use techniques, parts, and methods from an earlier time that are no longer popular.

library Introduced with Windows 7, a folder that's used to display files from different locations as if they were all saved in a single folder, regardless of where they are actually stored in the file hierarchy.

light-emitting diode (LED) A newer, more energy-efficient technology used in monitors. It may result in better color accuracy and thinner panels than traditional LCD monitors.

Linux An open-source operating system based on UNIX. Because of the stable nature of this operating system, it's often used on web servers.

liquid crystal display (LCD) The technology used in flat-panel computer monitors.

live bookmark A bookmark that delivers updates as soon as they become available, using Really Simple Syndication (RSS).

local area network (LAN) A network in which the nodes are located within a small geographic area.

logic bomb A computer virus that runs when a certain set of conditions is met, such as when a program is launched a specific number of times.

logical port A virtual communications gateway or path that enables a computer to organize requests for information (such as web page downloads and e-mail routing) from other networks or computers.

logical port blocking A condition in which a firewall is configured to ignore all incoming packets that request access to a certain port so that no unwanted requests will get through to the computer.

M

Mac OS The first commercially available operating system to incorporate a graphical user interface (GUI) with user-friendly point-and-click technology.

machine cycle The series of steps a central processing unit goes through when it performs a program instruction.

macro A small program that groups a series of commands to run as a single command.

macro virus A virus that's distributed by hiding it inside a macro.

mainframe A large, expensive computer that supports hundreds or thousands of users simultaneously and executes many different programs at the same time.

malware Software that's intended to render a system temporarily or permanently useless or to penetrate a computer system completely for purposes of information gathering. Examples include spyware, viruses, worms, and Trojan horses.

management software Software applications tailored to the specific needs of a particular company or industry.

master boot record A small program that runs whenever a computer boots up.

megabyte (MB) A unit of computer storage equal to approximately 1 million bytes.

memory module (memory card) A small circuit board that holds a series of random access memory (RAM) chips.

menu-driven interface A user interface in which the user chooses a command from menus displayed on the screen.

metasearch engine A search engine, such as Dogpile, that searches other search engines rather than individual websites.

metropolitan area network (MAN) A wide area network (WAN) that links users in a specific geographic area (such as within a city or county).

microphone (mic) A device that allows you to capture sound waves, such as those created by your voice, and to transfer them to digital format on your computer.

Microsoft Account Registered user profile with specific user id and password to log into Windows account from any machine and access familiar desktop and applications.

mobile broadband Connection to the Internet through the same cellular network that cell phones use to get 3G or 4G Internet access.

mobile switching center A central location that receives cell phone requests for service from a base station.

monitor (display screen) A common output device that displays text, graphics, and video as soft copies (copies that can be seen only on screen).

Moore's Law A prediction, named after Gordon Moore, the co-founder of Intel; states that the number of transistors on a central processing unit chip will double every two years.

motherboard A special circuit board in the system unit that contains the central processing unit, the memory (RAM) chips, and the slots available for expansion cards; all of the other boards (video cards, sound cards, and so on) connect to it to receive power and to communicate.

mouse A hardware device used to enter user responses and commands into a computer.

multi-factor authentication A process that requires two of the three assigned factors be demonstrated before authentication is granted.

multimedia Anything that involves one or more forms of media plus text.

multimedia message service (MMS) A service that allows users to send messages that include text, sound, images, and video clips to other phones or e-mail addresses.

multimedia software Programs that include image-, video-, and audio-editing software, animation software, and other specialty software required to produce computer games, animations, and movies.

multipartite virus Literally meaning "multipart" virus; a type of computer virus that attempts to infect computers using more than one method.

multitask The ability of an operating system to perform more than one process at a time.

multiuser operating system (network operating system) An operating system that enables more than one user to access the computer system at one time by efficiently juggling all the requests from multiple users.

N

netbook A computing device that runs a full-featured operating system but that weighs two pounds or less.

network A group of two or more computers (or nodes) that are configured to share information and resources such as printers, files, and databases.

network adapter A device that enables the computer (or peripheral) to communicate with the network using a common data communication language, or protocol.

network address translation (NAT) A process that firewalls use to assign internal Internet protocol addresses on a network.

network administration Involves tasks such as (1) installing new computers and devices, (2) monitoring the network to ensure it's performing efficiently, (3) updating and installing new software on the network, and (4) configuring, or setting up, proper security for a network.

network architecture The design of a computer network; includes both physical and logical design.

network-attached storage (NAS) device A specialized computing device designed to store and manage network data.

network interface card (NIC) An expansion card that enables a computer to connect to other computers or to a cable modem to facilitate a high-speed Internet connection.

network navigation device A device on a network such as a router or switch that moves data signals around the network.

network operating system (NOS) Software that handles requests for information, Internet access, and the use of peripherals for the rest of the network node, providing the services necessary for the computers on the network to communicate.

network-ready device A device (such as a printer or an external hard drive) that can be attached directly to a network instead of needing to attach to a computer on the network.

node A device connected to a network such as a computer, a peripheral (such as a printer), or a communications device (such as a modem).

nonimpact printer A printer that sprays ink or uses laser beams to make marks on the paper. The most common nonimpact printers are inkjet and laser printers.

nonvolatile storage Permanent storage, as in read-only memory (ROM).

O

open source software Program code made publicly available for free; it can be copied, distributed, or changed without the stringent copyright protections of proprietary software products.

operating system (OS) The system software that controls the way in which a computer system functions, including the management of hardware, peripherals, and software.

optical drive A hardware device that uses lasers or light to read from, and even write to, CDs, DVDs, or Blu-ray discs.

optical media Portable storage devices, such as CDs, DVDs, and Blu-ray discs, that use a laser to read and write data.

optical mouse A mouse that uses an internal sensor or laser to control the mouse's movement. The sensor sends signals to the computer, telling it where to move the pointer on the screen.

organic light-emitting diode (OLED) displays Displays that use organic compounds to produce light when exposed to an electric current. Unlike LCDs, OLEDs do not require a backlight to function and therefore draw less power and have a much thinner display, sometimes as thin as 3 mm.

output device A device that sends processed data and information out of a computer in the form of text, pictures (graphics), sounds (audio), or video.

overclocking Running the central processing unit at a speed faster than the manufacturer recommends.

P

packet (data packet) A small segment of data that's bundled for sending over transmission media. Each packet contains the address of the computer or peripheral device to which it's being sent.

packet analyzer (sniffer) A computer hardware device or software program designed to detect and record digital information being transmitted over a network.

packet filtering A process in which firewalls are configured so that they filter out packets sent to specific logical ports.

paging The process of swapping data or instructions that have been placed in the swap file for later use back into active random access memory (RAM). The contents of the hard drive's swap file then become less active data or instructions.

path (subdirectory) The information after the slash that indicates a particular file or path (or subdirectory) within the website.

path separator The backslash mark (\) used by Microsoft Windows and DOS in file names. Mac files use a colon (:), and UNIX and Linux use the forward slash (/) as the path separator.

peer-to-peer (P2P) network A network in which each node connected to the network can communicate directly with every other node on the network.

peer-to-peer (P2P) sharing The process of users transferring files between computers.

peripheral device A device such as a monitor, printer, or keyboard that connects to the system unit through a data port.

personal area network (PAN) A network used for communication among devices close to one person, such as smartphones, laptops, and tablets, using wireless technologies such as Bluetooth.

personal firewall A firewall specifically designed for home networks.

personal information manager (PIM) software Programs such as Microsoft Outlook or Lotus Organizer that strive to replace the various management tools found on a traditional desk such as a calendar, address book, notepad, and to-do lists.

petabyte (PB) 10^{15} bytes of digital information.

pharming Planting malicious code on a computer that alters the browser's ability to find web addresses and that directs users to bogus websites.

phishing The process of sending e-mail messages to lure Internet users into revealing personal information such as credit card or Social Security numbers or other sensitive information that could lead to identity theft.

physical memory The amount of random access memory (RAM) that's installed in a computer.

piggybacking The process of connecting to a wireless network without the permission of the owner of the network.

pinning The process through which you choose which applications are visible on the Windows Start screen.

pixel A single point that creates the images on a computer monitor. Pixels are illuminated by an electron beam that passes rapidly back and forth across the back of the screen so that the pixels appear to glow continuously.

platform The combination of a computer's operating system and processor. The two most common platform types are the PC and the Apple.

platter A thin, round, metallic storage plate stacked onto the hard drive spindle.

plotter A large printer that uses a computer-controlled pen to produce oversize pictures that require precise continuous lines to be drawn, such as maps and architectural plans.

Plug and Play (PnP) The technology that enables the operating system, once it is booted up, to recognize automatically any new peripherals and to configure them to work with the system.

plug-in (player) A small software program that "plugs in" to a web browser to enable

a specific function—for example, to view and hear certain multimedia files on the web.

podcast A clip of audio or video content that's broadcast over the Internet using compressed audio or video files in formats such as MP3.

polymorphic virus A virus that changes its virus signature (the binary pattern that makes the virus identifiable) every time it infects a new file. This makes it more difficult for antivirus programs to detect the virus.

port An interface through which external devices are connected to the computer.

power-on self-test (POST) The first job the basic input/output system (BIOS) performs, ensuring that essential peripheral devices are attached and operational. This process consists of a test on the video card and video memory, a BIOS identification process (during which the BIOS version, manufacturer, and data are displayed on the monitor), and a memory test to ensure memory chips are working properly.

power supply A power supply regulates the wall voltage to the voltages required by computer chips; it's housed inside the system unit.

preemptive multitasking When the operating system processes the task assigned a higher priority before processing a task that has been assigned a lower priority.

presentation software An application program for creating dynamic slide shows, such as Microsoft PowerPoint or Apple Keynote.

pretexting The act of creating an invented scenario (the pretext) to convince someone to divulge information.

printer A common output device that creates tangible or hard copies of text and graphics.

processing Manipulating or organizing data into information.

productivity software Programs that enable a user to perform various tasks generally required in home, school, and business. Examples include word processing, spreadsheet, presentation, personal information management, and database programs.

program A series of instructions to be followed by a computer to accomplish a task.

program files Files that are used in the running of software programs and that do not store data.

projector A device that can project images from your computer onto a wall or viewing screen.

proprietary (commercial) software Custom software application that's owned and controlled by the company that created it.

Q

quarantining The placement (by antivirus software) of a computer virus in a secure area on the hard drive so that it won't spread infection to other files.

QR (quick response) codes Technology that lets any piece of print in the real world host a live link to online information and video content.

QWERTY keyboard A keyboard that gets its name from the first six letters on the top-left row of alphabetic keys on the keyboard.

R

RAID 0 The strategy of running two hard drives in one system, cutting in half the time it takes to write a file.

RAID 1 The strategy of mirroring all the data written on one hard drive to a second hard drive, providing an instant backup of all data.

random access memory (RAM) The computer's temporary storage space or short-term memory. It's located in a set of chips on the system unit's motherboard, and its capacity is measured in megabytes or gigabytes.

read-only memory (ROM) A set of memory chips, located on the motherboard, which stores data and instructions that cannot be changed or erased; it holds all the instructions the computer needs to start up.

read/write head The mechanism that retrieves (reads) and records (writes) the magnetic data to and from a data disk.

real-time operating system (RTOS) A program with a specific purpose that must guarantee certain response times for particular computing tasks or else the machine's application is useless. Real-time operating systems are found in many types of robotic equipment.

Really Simple Syndication (RSS) An XML–based format that allows frequent updates of content on the World Wide Web.

Recycle Bin A folder on a Windows desktop in which deleted files from the hard drive are held until permanently purged from the system.

redundant array of independent disks (RAID) A set of strategies for using more than one drive in a system.

Refresh your PC A new utility program in Windows 8 that attempts to diagnose and fix errors in your Windows system files that are causing your computer to behave improperly.

registry A portion of the hard drive containing all the different configurations (settings) used by the Windows operating system as well as by other applications.

resolution The clearness or sharpness of an image, which is controlled by the number of pixels displayed on the screen.

root directory The top level of the filing structure in a computer system. In Windows computers, the root directory of the hard drive is represented as C:\.

rootkits Programs that allow hackers to gain access to your computer and take almost complete control of it without your knowledge. These programs are designed to subvert normal login procedures to a computer and to hide their operations from normal detection methods.

router A device that routes packets of data between two or more networks.

S

sampling rate The number of times per second a signal is measured and converted to a digital value. Sampling rates are measured in kilobits per second.

satellite Internet A way to connect to the Internet using a small satellite dish, which is placed outside the home and is connected to a computer with coaxial cable. The satellite company then sends the data to a satellite orbiting the Earth. The satellite, in turn, sends the data back to the satellite dish and to the computer.

scanner A type of input device that inputs images into computers.

scareware A type of malware that's downloaded onto your computer and that tries to convince you that your computer is infected with a virus or other type of malware.

script A list of commands (mini-programs or macros) that can be executed on a computer without user interaction.

search engine A set of programs that searches the web for specific words (or keywords) you wish to query (or look for) and that then returns a list of the websites on which those keywords are found.

sector A section of a hard drive platter, wedge-shaped from the center of the platter to the edge.

Secure Sockets Layer (SSL) A network security protocol that provides for the encryption of data transmitted using the Internet. The current versions of all major web browsers support SSL.

seek time The time it takes for the hard drive's read/write heads to move over the surface of the disk to the correct track.

semantic web (Web 3.0) An evolving extension of the World Wide Web in which information is defined in such a way as to make it more easily readable by computers.

server A computer that provides resources to other computers on a network.

service set identifier (SSID) A network name that wireless routers use to identify themselves.

short message service (SMS) Technology that enables short text messages (up to 160 characters) to be sent over mobile networks.

simulation program Software, often used for training purposes, which allows the user to experience or control an event as if it's reality.

sleep mode A low-power mode for electronic devices such as computers that saves electric power consumption and saves the last-used settings. When the device is "woken up," work is resumed more quickly than when cold booting the computer.

smartphone A device with features of a computer including a wide assortment of apps, media players, high-quality cameras, and web connectivity.

social bookmark (tagging) A keyword or term that Internet users assign to a web resource such as a web page, digital image, or video.

social commerce A subset of e-commerce that uses social networks to assist in marketing and purchasing products.

social engineering Any technique that uses social skills to generate human interaction for the purpose of enticing individuals to reveal sensitive information.

social networking A means by which people use the Internet to communicate and share information among their immediate friends and to meet and connect with others through common interests, experiences, and friends.

software The set of computer programs or instructions that tells the computer what to do and that enables it to perform different tasks.

Software as a Service (SaaS) Software that's delivered on demand over the Internet.

software license An agreement between the user and the software developer that must be accepted before installing the software on a computer.

software piracy Violating a software license agreement by copying an application onto more computers than the license agreement permits.

software suite A collection of software programs that have been bundled together as a package.

solid-state drive (SSD) A storage device that uses the same kind of memory that flash drives use but that can reach data in only a tenth of the time a flash drive requires.

sound card An expansion card that attaches to the motherboard inside the system unit and that enables the computer to produce sounds by providing a connection for the speakers and microphone.

source code The instructions programmers write in a higher-level language.

spam Unwanted or junk e-mail.

spam filter An option you can select in your e-mail account that places known or suspected spam messages into a folder other than your inbox.

speakers Output devices for sound.

spear phishing A targeted phishing attack that sends e-mails to people known to be customers of a company. Such attacks have a much greater chance of successfully getting individuals to reveal sensitive data.

spooler A program that helps coordinate all print jobs being sent to the printer at the same time.

spreadsheet software An application program such as Microsoft Excel or Lotus 1-2-3 that enables a user to do calculations and numerical analyses easily.

spyware An unwanted piggyback program that downloads with the software you want to install from the Internet and then runs in the background of your system.

Start screen The first interaction you have with the Windows operating system and the pace where you begin your computing activities.

stealth virus A virus that temporarily erases its code from the files where it resides and hides in the active memory of the computer.

streaming audio Technology that enables audio files to be fed to a browser continuously. This lets users avoid having to download an entire file before listening.

streaming media Multimedia (audio and video) that is fed continuously fed to the browser to avoid waiting for the entire file to download completely before listening to or watching it.

streaming video Technology that enables video files to be fed to a browser continuously. This lets users avoid having to download the entire file before viewing.

stylus A pen-shaped device used to tap or write on touch-sensitive screens.

subject directory A structured outline of websites organized by topics and subtopics.

supercomputer A specially designed computer that can perform complex calculations extremely rapidly; used in situations in which complex models requiring intensive mathematical calculations are needed (such as weather forecasting or atomic energy research).

SuperFetch A memory-management technique used by Windows 7. Monitors the applications you use the most and preloads them into your system memory so that they'll be ready to go.

surge protector A device that protects computers and other electronic devices from power surges.

surround sound A type of audio processing that makes the listener experience sound as if it were coming from all directions.

surround-sound speaker A system of speakers set up in such a way that it surrounds an entire area (and the people in it) with sound.

swap file (page file) A temporary storage area on the hard drive where the operating system "swaps out" or moves the data or instructions from random access memory (RAM) that haven't recently been used. This process takes place when more RAM space is needed.

switch A device for transmitting data on a network. A switch makes decisions, based on the media access control address of the data, as to where the data is to be sent.

synchronizing (or syncing) The process of updating data on portable devices (such as a cell phone or iPod) and a computer so that they contain the same data.

system evaluation The process of looking at a computer's subsystems, what they do, and how they perform to determine whether the computer system has the right hardware components to do what the user ultimately wants it to do.

system files The main files of an operating system.

system requirements The set of minimum storage, memory capacity, and processing standards recommended by the software manufacturer to ensure proper operation of a software application.

System Restore A utility in Windows that restores system settings to a specific previous date when everything was working properly.

system restore point In Windows, a snapshot of your entire system's settings used for restoring your system to a prior point in time.

system software The set of programs that enables a computer's hardware devices and application software to work together;

it includes the operating system and utility programs.

system unit The metal or plastic case that holds all the physical parts of the computer together, including the computer's processor (its brains), its memory, and the many circuit boards that help the computer function.

T

tablet computer A mobile computer, such as the Apple iPad or Samsung Galaxy Tab, integrated into a flat multitouch-sensitive screen. It uses an onscreen virtual keyboard, but separate keyboards can be connected via Bluetooth or wires.

tablet (or convertible) PC A laptop computer designed specifically to work with handwriting-recognition technology.

tagging (social bookmarking) A bookmark that saves a favorite website to a social bookmarking site so that it can be shared with others.

taskbar In later versions of Windows operating systems, a feature that displays open and favorite applications for easy access.

Task Manager A Windows utility that shows programs currently running and permits you to exit nonresponsive programs when you click End Task.

tax preparation software An application program, such as Intuit's TurboTax or H&R Block's At Home, for preparing state and federal taxes. Each program offers a complete set of tax forms and instructions as well as expert advice on how to complete each form.

telephony The use of equipment to provide voice communications over a distance.

template A form included in many productivity applications that provides the basic structure for a particular kind of document, spreadsheet, or presentation.

terabyte (TB) 1,099,511,627,776 bytes or 2^{40} bytes.

tethering Approach which makes sure that as long as you have a 3G signal, your computer can access the Internet even when it tells you there are no available wireless networks. Several smartphones offer this capability.

thermal printer A printer that works either by melting wax-based ink onto ordinary paper (in a process called *thermal wax transfer printing*) or by burning dots onto specially coated paper (in a process called *direct thermal printing*).

thrashing A condition of excessive paging in which the operating system becomes sluggish.

throughput The actual speed of data transfer that's achieved. It's usually less than the data transfer rate and is measured in megabits per second (Mbps).

Thunderbolt port A high speed input/output port; Thunderbolt 2 provides two channels of 20 Gbps capacity on one port.

time bomb A virus that's triggered by the passage of time or on a certain date.

top-level domain The suffix, often of three letters (such as .com or .edu), in the domain name that indicates the kind of organization the host is.

touch pad (trackpad) A small, touch-sensitive screen at the base of a laptop keyboard that's used to direct the cursor.

touch screen A type of monitor (or display in a smartphone or tablet computer) that accepts input from a user touching the screen.

track A concentric circle that serves as a storage area on a hard drive platter.

transmission media The radio waves or the physical system (cable) that transports data on a network.

Trojan horse A computer program that appears to be something useful or desirable (such as a game or a screen saver), but at the same time does something malicious in the background without the user's knowledge.

twisted-pair cable Cables made of copper wires that are twisted around each other and are surrounded by a plastic jacket (such as traditional home phone wire).

U

ultrabook A full-featured but lightweight laptop computer that features a low-power processor and a solid-state drive; it tries to reduce its size and weight to extend battery life without sacrificing performance.

Uniform Resource Locator (URL) A website's unique address; an example is microsoft.com.

uninterruptible power supply (UPS) A device designed to power a computer from large batteries for a brief period during a loss of electrical power.

universal serial bus (USB) port A port that can connect a wide variety of peripheral devices to the computer, including keyboards, printers, mice, smartphones, external hard drives, flash drives, and digital cameras.

UNIX An operating system originally conceived in 1969 by Ken Thompson and Dennis Ritchie of AT&T's Bell Labs. In 1974, the UNIX code was rewritten in the standard programming language C. Today there are various commercial versions of UNIX.

unshielded twisted-pair (UTP) cable The most popular transmission media option for Ethernet networks. UTP cable is composed of four pairs of wires that are twisted around each other to reduce electrical interference.

user interface Part of the operating system that enables individuals to interact with the computer.

utility program A small program that performs many of the general housekeeping tasks for the computer, such as system maintenance and file compression.

V

vertical market software Software that's developed for and customized to a specific industry's needs (such as a wood inventory system for a sawmill) as opposed to software that's useful across a range of industries (such as word processing software).

video card (video adapter) An expansion card that's installed inside a system unit to translate binary data (the *1*s and *0*s the computer uses) into the images viewed on the monitor.

video graphics array (VGA) port A port to which a cathode ray tube monitor connects.

video log (vlog or video blog) A personal online journal that uses video as the primary content in addition to text, images, and audio.

video memory Random access memory that's included as part of a video card.

virtual memory The space on the hard drive where the operating system stores data if there isn't enough random access memory to hold all of the programs you're currently trying to run.

virus A computer program that attaches itself to another computer program (known as the host program) and attempts to spread itself to other computers when files are exchanged.

virus signature A portion of the virus code that's unique to a particular computer virus and that makes it identifiable by antivirus software.

Voice over Internet Protocol (VoIP) A technology that facilitates making telephone calls across the Internet instead of using conventional telephone lines.

volatile storage Temporary storage, such as in random access memory. When the power is off, the data in volatile storage is cleared out.

W

warm boot The process of restarting the system while it's powered on.

Web 2.0 Tools and web-based services that emphasize online collaboration and sharing among users.

web authoring software Programs you can use to design interactive web pages without knowing any HyperText Markup Language (HTML) code.

web-based application A program that's hosted on a website and that doesn't require installation on the computer.

web-based e-mail A type of e-mail system that's managed by a web browser and that allows access to e-mail from the web.

web browser (browser) Software installed on a computer system that allows individuals to locate, view, and navigate the web.

webcam A small camera that sits on top of a computer monitor (connected to the computer by a cable) or that's built into a laptop computer and is usually used to transfer live video.

webcast The broadcast of audio or video content over the Internet. Unlike a podcast, a webcast is not updated automatically.

web server A computer running a specialized operating system that enables it to host web pages (and other information) and to provide requested web pages to clients.

website A location on the web.

white-hat hacker (ethical hacker) A hacker who breaks into systems just for the challenge of it (and who doesn't wish to steal or wreak havoc on the systems). Such hackers tout themselves as experts who are performing a needed service for society by helping companies realize the vulnerabilities that exist in their systems.

whole-house surge protector A surge protector that's installed on (or near) the breaker panel of a home and that protects all electronic devices in the home from power surges.

wide area network (WAN) A network made up of local area networks (LANs) connected over long distances.

wiki A type of website that allows anyone visiting the site to change its content by adding, removing, or editing the content.

Windows An operating system by Microsoft that incorporates a user-friendly graphical interface.

Windows 8 Newest release of Microsoft's operating system that provides, a new interface optimized for touch-screen devices.

Windows 8 apps Applications specifically designed to run in the Windows 8 interface; these apps are displayed full screen, without borders or controls.

Windows 8 interface New interface designed for Windows 8; features large type with clean, readable block images inspired by metropolitan service signs such as those found on bus stations and subways.

Windows account A tool for allowing multiple people to share a Windows 8 computer while maintaining individual settings and preferences.

wireless fidelity (WiFi) The 802.11 standard for wireless data transmissions established by the Institute of Electrical and Electronics Engineers (IEEE).

wireless Internet service provider (wireless ISP) An ISP that provides service to wireless devices such as smartphones.

wireless range extender A device that amplifies your wireless signal to get it out to parts of your home that are experiencing poor connectivity.

wizard A step-by-step guide that walks a user through the necessary steps to complete a complicated task.

word processing software Programs used to create and edit written documents such as papers, letters, and résumés.

World Wide Web (WWW or the web) The part of the Internet used the most. What distinguishes the web from the rest of the Internet are (1) its use of common communication protocols (such as Transmission Control Protocol/Internet Protocol, or TCP/IP) and special languages (such as the HyperText Markup Language, or HTML) that enable different computers to talk to each other and display information in compatible formats and (2) its use of special links (called hyperlinks) that enable users to jump from one place to another in the web.

worm A program that attempts to travel between systems through network connections to spread infections. Worms can run independently of host file execution and are active in spreading themselves.

Z

zombie A computer that's controlled by a hacker who uses it to launch attacks on other computer systems.

Index

EDITION 12 twelfth

JPEG (Joint Photographic Experts Group) files, 335
Julliard School of Music, dance/music programs at, 17
Jump drives, 55. *See also* Flash drives
Justin.tv, 244, 337

K

Kahn, Robert, 77
Karma WiFi, 259
Kaspersky, 319
KB (kilobyte), 31, 32
Kernel (supervisor program), 173
Keyboards, 35–37
    defined, 35
    Dvorak, 36
    flexible, 37
    QWERTY, 35
    touchscreen, 35
    virtual laser, 35, 37
Keylogger, 356, 372
Keystroke logger, 372
Keystroke shortcuts, 38
Keywords, 98, 100
Khan, Salman, 18
Khan Academy, computerized education and, 18
Kickstarter, 9
Kilby, Jack, 120
Kildall, Gary, 115
Kilobyte (KB), defined, 31, 32
Known viruses, 354

L

LaCie, 245
LAlarm, 385
LAN (local area networks), 262–263
Lands, 235
Laptop computers
    defined, 31
    speakers of, 247
    ultrabooks *vs.*, 321–322
Laser printers, 46
Latency, 234
Law enforcement, computer uses, 19
LCD (liquid crystal display) monitors
    defined, 43
    factors affecting quality of, 43–44
LED (light-emitting diode) monitors, 43
Legacy technology, 43
Level 1 cache, 304
Level 2 cache, 304
Level 3cache, 304
Light-emitting diode (LED) monitors, 43
Linux, 161, 162, 163
    advantages of using, on shared computers, 365–366
    availability of, 163
    computers that use, 163
    Mac OS X and, 181–182
    Windows 8 and, 181–182

Liquid crystal display (LCD) monitors
    defined, 43
    factors affecting quality of, 43–44
Liquid plastic resin, 311
Lisa personal computer, 116
Live bookmarks, 98
Live Icons, 185
Local area networks (LAN), 262–263
Logical port blocking, 361
Logical ports, 359
    common, 362
Logic bombs, 350
LoJack for Laptops, 385
Lotus 1-2-3, 115
Lovelace, Ada, 117
Low-level formatting, 234
Lumosity site, 144

M

MAAWG (Messaging Anti-Abuse Working Group), 349
MACH (My Automated Conversation Coach), 21–22
Machine cycle, 227
    decode stage, 303, 305–306
    execute stage, 303, 306
    fetch stage, 303, 304
    store stage, 303, 306–307
Machine language, 305
Macintosh personal computer, 116
Mac OS X, 160, 161, 162–163
    Linux and, 182
    Windows and, 170, 181–182, 183
Mac PhoneHome, 385
Macros, 133
Macro viruses, 351
MAGIX Music Maker, 143
Mainframe computers, 33
MajorGeeks, 146
MakeTechEasier site, 133
Malware, 370
MAN (metropolitan area networks), 263
Mann, Stephen, 21
Master boot record, 350
Mastery, defined, 8
Mauchly, John W., 119
Maxthon, 95
MB (megabyte), 31, 32
Mbps (megabits per second), 261
McAfee, 319
Mechanical hard drives. *See* Hard disk drives (HDDs)
MediaFire, 280
MediaWiki, 82
Medicine, computer technology and, 19–21
Megabits per second (Mbps), 261
Megabyte (MB), 31, 32
Memory
    RAM, 53
    ROM, 53
Memory cards, 53, 230

Memory management, 167–168, 170
Memory modules, 230
Memory resident, 173
Menu-driven interface, 166
Mesh network, 279
Messaging Anti-Abuse Working Group (MAAWG), 349
Metasearch engines, 100
Metro apps, 178
    downloading, 189
Metropolitan area networks (MAN), 263
Mice, 35, 37–39
    with touch screen, 37–38
Microphones, types of, 40, 41
Microprocessors, 120, 299
Micro SD flash cards, 314
Microsoft, 113, 114
    in China, 216–217
Microsoft account, 173
Microsoft Disk Operating System (MS-DOS), 166
Microsoft Excel, 115, 128
Microsoft Expression Web, 135
Microsoft Knowledge Base, 249
Microsoft Office, 126
Microsoft OneNote, 131
Microsoft Outlook, 132
Microsoft PowerPoint, 129
    alternatives to, 130
Microsoft SkyDrive, 55
Microsoft Windows, 162
    vs. Mac OS X, 170
Microsoft Windows 8. *See* Windows 8
Microsoft Word, 115, 127
Mint, 133, 135
MIT Media Lab, 21
MMS (multimedia message service), 317
mobicoupons, 9
Mobile barcodes, 125
Mobile broadband, 271
    vs. wired Internet networks, 271
Mobile commerce, 125
Mobile coupons, 9, 125
Mobile devices
    alarms, installation of, 385
    keeping data secure on, 385
    operating systems for, 162
Mobile hotspot, 271
Mobile Internet, 317–319
Mobile payments, 125
Mobile switching center, 315
MobileVoice, 9
MoMA (Museum of Modern Art), New York, 17
Monitors
    factors affecting quality of LCD, 43–44
    features to consider when shopping for, 44–45
    internal processes of, 43
    size of, 44
    types of, 43